Architecture Solutions for E–Learning Systems

Claus Pahl
Dublin City University, Ireland

INFORMATION SCIENCE REFERENCE

Hershey · New York

Acquisitions Editor:	Kristin Klinger
Development Editor:	Kristin M. Roth
Assistant Development Editor:	Meg Stocking
Editorial Assistant:	Deborah Yahnke
Senior Managing Editor:	Jennifer Neidig
Managing Editor:	Sara Reed
Assistant Managing Editor:	Carole Coulson
Copy Editor:	Ashley Fails
Typesetter:	Lindsay Bergman
Cover Design:	Lisa Tosheff
Printed at:	Yurchak Printing Inc.

Published in the United States of America by
Information Science Reference (an imprint of IGI Global)
701 E. Chocolate Avenue, Suite 200
Hershey PA 17033
Tel: 717-533-8845
Fax: 717-533-8661
E-mail: cust@igi-global.com
Web site: http://www.igi-global.com/reference

and in the United Kingdom by
Information Science Reference (an imprint of IGI Global)
3 Henrietta Street
Covent Garden
London WC2E 8LU
Tel: 44 20 7240 0856
Fax: 44 20 7379 0609
Web site: http://www.eurospanonline.com

Library of Congress Cataloging-in-Publication Data

Architecture solutions for E-learning systems / Claus Pahl, editor.
       p. cm.
  Summary: "This book provides fundamental research on the architecture of learning technology systems, discussing such issues as the common structures in LTS and solutions for specific forms such as knowledge-based, distributed, or adaptive applications of e-learning. Researchers, and scholars in the fields of learning content software development, computing and educational technologies, and e-learning will find it an invaluable resource"--Provided by publisher.
  Includes bibliographical references and index.
  ISBN 978-1-59904-633-4 (hardcover) -- ISBN 978-1-59904-635-8 (ebook)
 1. Educational technology. 2. Instructional systems--Design. 3. Computer-assisted instruction. I. Pahl, Claus.
  LB1028.3.A73 2007
  371.33'4--dc22
                              2007023536

British Cataloguing in Publication Data
A Cataloguing in Publication record for this book is available from the British Library.

All work contributed to this book set is original material. The views expressed in this book are those of the authors, but not necessarily of the publisher.

Table of Contents

Foreword xiii

Preface xv

Acknowledgment xxiii

Section I:
Architectural Types

Chapter I
Moving Towards a Generic, Service-Based Architecture for Flexible Teaching and
Learning Activities / *Christian Gütl* 1

Chapter II
Collaborative E-Learning System and E-Pedagogy: Learning Resource Infrastructure
for Distributed Knowledge Sharing / *Toshio Okamoto, Toshie Ninomiya,*
Mizue Kayama, and Naomi Nagata 25

Chapter III
Service-Based Grid Architectures to Support the Virtualization of Learning
Technology Systems / *Gerard Gleeson and Claus Pahl* 44

Chapter IV
From E-Learning to M-Learning: Architectures to Support University Teaching /
Philip Grew, Elena Pagani, and Francesco Giudici 62

Chapter V
Architectures of Existing and Conceptual Applications of Podcasting in
E-Learning Systems / *Stephen R. Chastain and Jason Caudill* 80

Section II:
Software Architecture and Software Engineering

Chapter VI
A Step Towards a Pattern Language for E-Learning Systems / *Andreas Harrer and Alke Martens* 98

Chapter VII
Model-Driven Engineering (MDE) and Model-Driven Architecture (MDA) Applied
to the Modeling and Deployment of Technology Enhanced Learning (TEL) Systems:
Promises, Challenges, and Issues / *Pierre Laforcade, Thierry Nodenot,*
Christophe Choquet, and Pierre-André Caron 116

Chapter VIII
Accessibility, Digital Libraries, and Semantic Web Standards in an E-Learning
Architecture / *Sean W. M. Siqueira, Maria Helena L. B. Braz,*
and Rubens N. Melo 137

Chapter IX
End-User Quality of Experience-Aware Personalized E-Learning / *Cristina Hava Muntean*
and Gabriel-Miro Muntean 154

Chapter X
E-Learning Systems Re-Engineering: Functional Specifications and
Component-Based Architecture / *Lahcen Oubahssi and Monique Grandbastien* 175

Section III:
Applications and Educational Perspectives

Section III.a:
Specific Application Contexts

Chapter XI
An Integrated Architecture for Supporting Vocational Training / *C. Bouras, E. Giannaka,*
and Th. Tsiatsos 197

Chapter XII
A Generic Platform for the Systematic Construction of Knowledge-Based Collaborative
Learning Applications / *Santi Caballé, Thanasis Daradoumis, and Fatos Xhafa* 219

Section III.b:
Adaptivity

Chapter XIII

From Learning Objects to Adaptive Content Services for E-Learning / *Peter Brusilovsky,*
Vincent P. Wade, and Owen Conlan 243

Chapter XIV

An Adaptive E-Learning Platform for Personalized Course Generation / *Enver Sangineto* 262

Section III.c:
Education and Content Perspective

Chapter XV

Pedagogical Scenario Modeling, Deployment, Execution, and Evolution / *Yvan Peter,*
Xavier Le Pallec, and Thomas Vantroys 283

Chapter XVI

Impact of Context-Awareness on the Architecture of Learning Support Systems /
Andreas Schmidt 306

Chapter XVII

Design and Evaluation of Web-Based Learning Environments using Information
Foraging Models / *Nikolaos Tselios, Christos Katsanos, Georgios Kahrimanis,*
and Nikolaos Avouris 320

Compilation of References 340

About the Contributors 374

Index 383

Detailed Table of Contents

Foreword xiii

Preface xv

Acknowledgment xxiii

Section I:
Architectural Types

Chapter I
Moving Towards a Generic, Service-Based Architecture for Flexible Teaching and
Learning Activities / *Christian Gütl* 1

Modern, computer-supported learning must go far beyond simply delivering learning content in a one-fit-for-all approach to students. It instead should include a variety of didactic aspects and cognitive characteristics. Furthermore, diverse systems and information must be taken into account for individualized learning processes. In light of this information, the objective of this chapter is to delineate an open, distributed, and service-based architecture for flexible teaching and learning activities. Backed by relevant research strands in this context, an architecture for an enhanced e-learning system developed within the AdeLE research project shall be depicted and experiences gained so far will be discussed. Based on this, a proposal is given for a generic and flexible architecture for adaptive e-learning towards the end of this chapter.

Chapter II
Collaborative E-Learning System and E-Pedagogy: Learning Resource Infrastructure
for Distributed Knowledge Sharing / *Toshio Okamoto, Toshie Ninomiya,*
Mizue Kayama, and Naomi Nagata 25

This chapter describes collaborative e-learning system and e-pedagogy with Learning Resource Infrastructure for distributed knowledge sharing. In the background section, we start to discuss the design of e-learning environment, collaborative learning and pedagogical framework, and pedagogical considerations of collaborative learning. Next, we introduce RAPSODY-EX that is a collaborative learning and knowledge management system, with meaning of RAPSODY-EX in learning resource infrastructure system, and knowledge market. Then the schema of RAPSODY-EX is described with these topics, agent's roles in Learning Resource Infrastructure, schema and functions of learning resource, collaborative memory, and function of RAPSODY-EX. In addition, we give examples of knowledge management in RAPSODY-EX. Finally, the standardization of collaborative technology in WG2, ISO/IEC-JTC/SC36, as a future trend, is portrayed.

Chapter III

Service-Based Grid Architectures to Support the Virtualization of Learning
Technology Systems / *Gerard Gleeson and Claus Pahl*.. 44

E-Learning has been a topic of increasing interest in recent years, due mainly to the fact that content and tool support can now be offered at a widely affordable level. As a result, many e-learning platforms and systems have been developed. Client-server, peer-to-peer and recently Web services architectures often form the basis. Drawbacks of these architectures are often their limitations in terms of scalability and the availability and distribution of resources. This chapter investigates grid architectures in the context of e-learning as a proposed answer for this problem. The principles and technologies of grid architectures are discussed and illustrated using learning technology scenarios and systems.

Chapter IV

From E-Learning to M-Learning: Architectures to Support University Teaching /
Philip Grew, Elena Pagani, and Francesco Giudici... 62

The term e-learning indicates products that differ very much both in services supplied and in design. E-learning platforms do not necessarily involve networking as a fundamental component. However, networking is important both to ease access to course material and to support interaction among users. Networking should be exploited to allow remote access to students who cannot be present at lessons, to allow asynchronous learning whenever students have time, and to supply users with tools for cooperative learning regardless of their physical location. The spread of wireless networking technologies and their standardization will lead to innovations in all three of these aspects. This chapter focuses on the services whose deployment computer networks make possible in order to boost interactivity, cooperation and involvement in learning, with specific attention to ubiquitous learning and for the impact of wireless technologies on the general framework.

Chapter V

Architectures of Existing and Conceptual Applications of Podcasting in
E-Learning Systems / *Stephen R. Chastain and Jason Caudill*... 80

Podcasting has quickly emerged as a leading technology in the new field of mobile learning. Tracing this new technology's history over the past two years reveals just how broadly the use of digital audio files may become in the fields of education and training. The ease of use, low cost of creation and hosting, and most importantly pervasiveness of user access to compatible hardware combine to make podcasting a major force in both traditional and distance education. This chapter explores the history, technology, and application of podcasting as an instructional tool.

Section II:
Software Architecture and Software Engineering

Chapter VI
A Step Towards a Pattern Language for E-Learning Systems / *Andreas Harrer and Alke Martens* 98

Computer-based teaching and training systems in general, and intelligent tutoring systems (ITSs) in particular, are usually based on similar fundamental structures. In contrast to this, analyses of the state of the art of teaching and training system development have revealed that software engineering techniques are seldom used for realizing those systems. In the last years, some approaches tried to change this: pattern mining took place; methods covering the specifics of ITS project development have been deployed. These approaches usually focus on a specific system type or on a certain application domain, thus re-usability is often not possible. What is missing is a combination of different approaches in a pattern language or a pattern catalogue for ITS. The purpose of such a pattern catalogue is to provide pattern for different types of software and to support the software development starting from design and ending with the implementation. A step towards a pattern language for ITS is described in this paper.

Chapter VII
Model-Driven Engineering (MDE) and Model-Driven Architecture (MDA) Applied
to the Modeling and Deployment of Technology Enhanced Learning (TEL) Systems:
Promises, Challenges, and Issues / *Pierre Laforcade, Thierry Nodenot,*
Christophe Choquet, and Pierre-André Caron 116

This chapter deals with the application of model-driven engineering and model-driven architecture approaches in a technology enhanced learning (TEL) context. Such Software Engineering approaches provide concrete benefits (productivity, interoperability, adaptability) by means of intensive uses of models, meta-models and transformations. Such benefits can also be met in a TEL context. Because computer scientists or engineers cannot currently find well-defined frameworks about this new trend, we have chosen to report recent results of our working group (initiated in 2003) in order to provide readers with a survival kit. Our results, illustrated in this chapter, argue that model-driven engineering can help designers to reduce the gap between specific instructional requirements (domain point of view) and the software architectures that practically support the implementation, the run-time and the regulation of this instruction.

Chapter VIII
Accessibility, Digital Libraries, and Semantic Web Standards in an E-Learning
Architecture / *Sean W. M. Siqueira, Maria Helena L. B. Braz,*
and Rubens N. Melo 137

As people have come to realize that the use of technology can improve the learning process, e-learning has began to increase in importance. However, e-learning tools are not usually developed to interoperate with each other, making the creation of a fully functional environment a difficult task. Organizations such as IMS Global Learning Consortium, Advanced Distributed Learning and IEEE Learning Technology Standards Committee are aware of this problem and are working to develop technical standards, recommended best practices and guides for learning technology. There are also proposals for e-learning architectures which try to structure and describe the fundamental components to be included in this kind of environment. The main aim of this chapter is to provide an overview of existing standards and e-learning architectures, discussing their evolution and presenting the most significant results and initiatives. In addition, accessibility, digital libraries and semantic Web technologies are discussed within this context.

Chapter IX

End-User Quality of Experience-Aware Personalized E-Learning / *Cristina Hava Muntean and Gabriel-Miro Muntean* 154

Lately, user quality of experience (QoE) during their interaction with a system is a significant factor in the assessment of most systems. However, user QoE is dependent not only on the content served to the users, but also on the performance of the service provided. This chapter describes a novel QoE layer that extends the features of classic adaptive e-learning systems in order to consider delivery performance in the adaptation process and help in providing good user perceived QoE during the learning process. An experimental study compared a classic adaptive e-learning system with one enhanced with the proposed QoE layer. The result analysis compares learner outcome, learning performance, visual quality and usability of the two systems and shows how the QoE layer brings significant benefits to user satisfaction improving the overall learning process.

Chapter X

E-Learning Systems Re-Engineering: Functional Specifications and Component-Based Architecture / *Lahcen Oubahssi and Monique Grandbastien* 175

In this chapter, we propose functional specifications and a component-based architecture for designing e-learning platforms. An important feature is that the proposed specifications and architecture are based on the experience gained in an e-learning company and result from a re-engineering process. To guide the re-engineering process, we used two reference models, which are the e-learning global process and the e-learning global cycle. The functional specifications are described according to the e-learning global cycle phases and they are used to propose a software component-based architecture. The proposed kernel of components was completed with services to allow interoperability and standard compliance between several e-learning platforms. We hope that this case study exemplifies e-learning platform suppliers' needs and available pragmatic solutions. We conclude on foreseeable evolutions of e-learning actors' needs and practices and on new platform features for fulfilling such needs.

Section III
Applicatons and Educational Perspectives

Section III.a:
Specific Application Contexts

Chapter XI

An Integrated Architecture for Supporting Vocational Training / *C. Bouras, E. Giannaka,
and Th. Tsiatsos*.. 197

E-learning and Web-based training have evolved over time from a newborn trend for complementing the learning process to a major form of education and training for supporting mainly geographically scattered users. The basic aim of this chapter is the description of a platform for open and distance training, which is mainly focused at supporting the needs of vocational training centers as well as of institutions providing life-long adult training and learning. In particular, the issues that this chapter focuses on are vocational education and training characteristics and requirements, the current situation and technological trends in ICT-supported VET, the development framework and processes while it also proposes basic vocational training services and the system architecture of the integrated platform. The presented platform aims to provide services of both synchronous and asynchronous and collaborative distance learning.

Chapter XII

A Generic Platform for the Systematic Construction of Knowledge-Based Collaborative
Learning Applications / *Santi Caballé, Thanasis Daradoumis, and Fatos Xhafa*.............................. 219

This study aims to explore the importance of efficient management of event information generated from group activity in collaborative learning practices for its further use in extracting and providing knowledge on interaction behavior. The essential issue here is how to design a platform that can be used for real, long-term, complex collaborative problem-solving situations and which enables the instructor to both analyze group interaction effectively and provide an adequate support when needed. The achievement of this task first involves the design of a conceptual model that structures and classifies the information generated in a collaborative learning application at several levels of description. This conceptual model is then translated into a computational model that not only allows the efficient management of the knowledge produced by the individual and group activity but also the possibility of exploiting this knowledge further as a meta-cognitive tool for real-time coaching and regulating the collaborative learning process. The computational model becomes the central issue in this contribution while the conceptual model is briefly introduced.

Section III.b:
Adaptivity

Chapter XIII

From Learning Objects to Adaptive Content Services for E-Learning / *Peter Brusilovsky,*
Vincent P. Wade, and Owen Conlan 243

This chapter argues that a new generation of powerful e-learning systems could start on the crossroads of two emerging fields: courseware reuse and adaptive educational systems. We argue for a new distributed architecture for e-learning systems based on the idea of adaptive reusable content services. This chapter discusses problems that have to be solved on the way to the new organization of e-learning and reviews existing approaches and tools that are paving the way to next-generation e-learning systems. It also presents two pioneer systems—APeLS and KnowledgeTree that have attempted to develop a new service-based architecture for adaptive e-learning.

Chapter XIV

An Adaptive E-Learning Platform for Personalized Course Generation / *Enver Sangineto* 262

In this chapter we show the technical and methodological aspects of an e-learning platform for automatic course personalization built during the European funded project Diogene. The system we propose is composed of different knowledge modules and some inference tools. The knowledge modules represent the system's information about both the domain-specific didactic material and the student model. By exploiting such information, the system automatically builds courses whose didactic material is customized to meet the current student's degree of knowledge and her/his learning preferences. Concerning the latter, we have adopted the Felder and Silverman pedagogical approach in order to match the student's learning styles with the system learning objects' types. Finally, we take care to describe the system's didactic material by means of some present standards for e-learning in order to allow knowledge sharing with other e-learning platforms and knowledge searching by means of possible Semantic Web information retrieval facilities.

Section III.c:
Education and Content Perspective

Chapter XV

Pedagogical Scenario Modeling, Deployment, Execution, and Evolution / *Yvan Peter,*
Xavier Le Pallec, and Thomas Vantroys 283

The rise of the pedagogical scenario approach supported by the standardization of IMS learning design is changing the focus from the pedagogical objects to the activities that support learning. With the standardization, comes the promise of the reuse of successful designs for the pedagogical scenarios. However, the uptake of this approach relies on a sound support of the users both at the design phase and at the execution phase and the level to which successful design can be adapted for reuse in both phases. This chapter covers the whole lifecycle of pedagogical scenarios and shows the current level of support one can find in existing learning management systems and tools. It presents, also, the way to enhance this support through the use of model-driven engineering for the design and deployment phase and implementation techniques to provide execution engines that allow flexible runtime execution.

Chapter XVI
Impact of Context-Awareness on the Architecture of Learning Support Systems /
Andreas Schmidt 306

Recently, the situatedness of learning has come to the center of attention in both research and practice, also a result of the insight that traditional learning methods in the form of large de-contextualized courses lead to inert knowledge; that is, knowledge that can be reproduced, but not applied to real-world problem solving. In order to avoid the inertness, pedagogy tries to set up authentic learning settings, an approach increasingly shared in e-learning domain. If we consider professional training, it is the immediacy of purpose and context that makes it largely different to learning in schools or academic education. This immediacy has the benefit that we actually have an authentic context that we need to preserve. The majority of current e-learning approaches, however, ignores this context and provides de-contextualized forms of learning as a multimedia copy of traditional presence seminars. We show how making learning solutions aware of the context actually affects their architecture and present a showcase solution in the form of the Learning in Process service-oriented architecture.

Chapter XVII
Design and Evaluation of Web-Based Learning Environments using Information
Foraging Models / *Nikolaos Tselios, Christos Katsanos, Georgios Kahrimanis,
and Nikolaos Avouris* 320

In this chapter, methods and tools for effective design and evaluation of Web-based learning environments are presented. The main aspect addressed by this proposal is that of increasing findability of information in large Web sites of learning information content by applying methods and tools based on the information foraging model. It is argued that through this approach, issues of learning content structure and usability may be also addressed. In particular, we propose four different ways to have information foraging theory informing the design. Directives, to ensure proper learning content structuring and cues with strong scent, tools based on LSA to automate the design and evaluation process, methods to construct archetypal learner's profiles from user data and added functions to realize collaborative information filtering and personal information patch creation, thus allowing learners to organize their reference materials in a meaningful and constructive way.

Compilation of References 340

About the Contributors 374

Index 383

Foreword

Several times, I have wondered about the priorities that we as academics and humans of modern societies set for our individual and collective contributions. I respect the episteme of absolute specialization, but I would love to see scientists dealing with the real issues of our society, and I would love to see people dedicating their scientific endeavors to the guidance of humanistic visions. The authors and the editor of this edition made an excellent work in this direction. It is not only the fact that it discusses an up-to-date theme, but it is mostly because in the work promoted the vision for Technology Enhanced Learning as a core component of the knowledge society. In most cases, humanistic or social sensitive visions require a rigorous engineering part. Visions require hard work in terms of technology support and it is often painful to realize that no technology is a panacea for the central issues. From this perspective, *Architecture Solutions for E-Learning Systems* goes beyond the typical verbalism. The adoption of e-learning is discussed with a holistic point of view; the edition covers the central issues of the current e-learning research agenda and provides key answers to e-learning engineering and pedagogical themes.

Everybody talks about the knowledge society. And everybody talks about the importance of developing flexible learning infrastructures that will disseminate learning content through personalized and adaptive methods to learners of different learning styles and needs. But on the other hand, societies require e-learning solutions, functional architectures, and systems that work and provide meaningful learning. In the last years, billions of dollars have been spent on technology enhanced learning systems. A sad finding is that often funded e-learning projects stop to offer their services after the completion of the project. In this situation, community can provide a solution. Web 2.0 and social software, collaborative authoring techniques and learning communities show the way for the evolution of e-learning field. Community is involved in content authoring and knowledge distribution and through collaborative filtering and community annotation, quality standards are met.

A couple of years ago, I had an interview with Professor Robert Zmud, and Chair Michael F. Price in MIS, University of Oklahoma. Given his legendary work in the adoption of technologies in business and organizational contexts, I asked him in a way how can we promote emerging technologies to the business world. His answer has influenced all of my research activities since.

As with all adoption situations, this is an information and communication problem. One needs to segment the base of potential adopters (both in the IT community and in the business community) and then develop communication programs to inform each distinct segment of, first, the existence of the innovation (know-what), then the nature of the innovation (know-how), and finally why this innovation would be useful to them (know-why). These adopter segments are likely to be very different from each other. Each will have a different likelihood of adoption and will likely require that a somewhat unique communication strategy be devised and directed toward the segment.

This is why this edition gives an excellent answer to the needs and questions of many people. E-learning is discussed here in the triptych know-what, know-how and know-why and the editing strategy of the book boosts the excellent quality of contributors. Many excellent academics and practitioners collaboratively worked for this edition. E-learning is and will continue to be one of the most significant pillars of the knowledge society. In this sense, *Architecture Solutions for E-Learning Systems* provides a critical step forward in the understanding of the state of the art in e-learning solutions. I am convinced that the future Web 2.0, social software, Semantic Web and other emerging technologies will drive a new era of e-learning solutions. With its transparent capacity of e-learning to support every business domain, a milestone of the knowledge society will be for sure an e-learning primer. A lot of effort must be paid to the introduction of e-learning into modern curricula. *Architecture Solutions for E-Learning Systems* can be used as an excellent text book for the relevant themes.

As a concluding remark, I would like to share with you some thoughts. There is always the question of the pace of change and the current stage of the maturity or contribution of e-learning. At this stage, we need strategy and hard work. Educating people in e-learning in for instance computer science or business departments means making them realize that knowledge and learning exploitation are our mankind characteristics that we must bring to the electronic world. If we do not support them, then our virtual world will remain unexploited. We must exploit the collective knowledge of humanity for learning and educating people.

I like the engineering approach of this edition. We must be able to address the e-learning challenge with concrete computer engineering in order to make sustainable solutions for real world problems. The fine grain of strategy, pedagogy and computer science will lead e-learning to a maturity level for unforeseen value diffusion. My invitation is to be part of this exciting, just started journey in the world of learning and knowledge and to keep in mind that the people who dedicate their lives in the promotion of disciplines for the common wealth from time to time need encouragement and support because their intellectual work is not valued in financial terms. This is why I would like to express my deepest appreciation and respect for the authors' and editor's contributions. The authors and editor have done a great job. And dear readers, from all over the world, you made a good choice. Let us explore together e-learning architectures for the society. And why not let us put together the new milestones towards a better world through the adoption of leading edge technologies in humanistic visions. Knowledge and learning for all can be a nice motto for the new century in our turbulent times.

Miltiadis D. Lytras
Athens, Greece
June 2007

Preface

INTRODUCTION

E-learning has become a major form of education, not limited to the classical forms of education provided by schools, colleges, and universities. E-learning can overcome time and space constraints and can create tailored solutions for specific learner styles and requirements in different situations. E-learning is facilitated through e-learning systems (ELS) comprising what is usually called managed learning environment, virtual learning environment, or learner/content management system, and also learning objects and resource infrastructures. The ELS notion includes learning content, but also the infrastructure that allows content to be created, stored, accessed, and delivered and the learners and the learning process to be managed. The architecture of these ELS is a crucial aspect in this context. Architectures define structural and behavioral characteristics of a system. Architectures define structures that connect an ELS as a software and information system with its instructional and educational context (Bouras & Tsiatsos, 2005).

Architecture is a widely used term that is applied in different situations with different scope. The notion shall be deployed here in a broad, integrative sense covering a range of facets of ELSs:

- Software architecture refers to components and their connection and interaction.
- The information architecture refers to the structure and organization of data and content.
- The information technology architecture puts both software and information architecture in a common framework and relates them to the application context.

Information technology is only one of the aspects that need to be considered from a broad architectural point of view. The notion of a conceptual architecture links aspects of the application context with information technology, e.g. instruction design and software design in the e-learning context. The learning architecture is another notion that aims to connect the educational layer with its underlying software infrastructure.

Although architectures aim to separate different concerns and e-learning infrastructure is often pedagogy-neutral, these types of architectures are inextricably linked. The software architectures need to enable instruction and need to facilitate the learning experience for the aforementioned learning situations, styles, and requirements (Capuano et al., 2005). Interaction is notion that is central in both instruction and the implementation of software architectures. Architecture is, in addition to its meaning as a structural organization of components, also a notion that is used by software engineers to denote a framework in a wider sense with its tools, techniques, and methods for development.

THE CHALLENGES

The architecture of an ELS needs to provide a conceptual framework for content and software infrastructure in order to implement instruction and sound education, i.e. needs to realize the successful and effective learning experience. Challenges for ELS architecture as a research and development focus arise therefore in relation to the following aspects:

- The introduction of suitable principles and components of the IT architectures of modern and anticipated future ELS.
- The demonstration of how instruction is reflected in IT architectures of ELS, for example, how interaction design is implemented in and enabled by software component interaction.
- The creation of an understanding of how ELS are architecturally designed, implemented, and operated in terms of the instructional and content aspects involved.
- An investigation into the platform technologies that can actually facilitate and implement ELS architectures.

Specifically, common structures in ELS architectures, but also solutions for specific forms such as knowledge-based, distributed, or adaptive applications of e-learning are sought. In another dimension, aspects from foundations to deployment experience to standards need to be investigated. The integrating element of all individual challenges is the architecture notion with its different facets. An overall architectural perspective in a broad sense will ensure a coherent direction of research, but also a broad enough spectrum that will benefit different types of ELS stakeholders such as learners, instructors, administrators, providers, and developers due to the different architectural facets. The aim for researchers and technology developers in this area needs to be to enhance the conceptual understanding, but also to provide practical guidelines that would allow system developers to design their own ELS infrastructure based on advanced techniques and concepts.

Investigations are needed that reflect current practice and advances in the technology and that lay out a path towards advanced solutions that meet the requirements of modern and future e-learning systems and their users.

SEARCHING FOR SOLUTIONS

Architectures of e-learning system have received some attention over the past years—reflected in standardization efforts such as the IEEE Learning Technology System Architecture LTSA (a high-level reference architecture) and SCORM RunTime Environment RTE (an architectural interface specification that defines interactions between learning objects and their deployment infrastructure). However, both are lowest common denominators of technologies in use. Advanced applications require advanced architectural solutions. Some of these are reflected in current activities such as CORDRA (content object repository discovery and registration/resolution architecture), which is an open, standards-based model for how to design and implement software systems for the purposes of discovery, sharing and reuse of learning content. These developments and trends are some of the aspects that will influence architecture solutions for e-learning systems in the future.

Advanced technical solutions and research efforts are needed, based on a reflection of current trends and developments. Advances in learning technology need to be linked with recent software technology, in particular Web and architecture technology as an enabler of the learning experience.

- Technological advances in software architecture (SOA), see e.g. (Avgeriou et al., 2003), and knowledge technologies (ontologies and intelligent agents), see e.g. (Okamoto et al., 2000), can contribute to adequate solutions if these are connected to recent trends in learning technology (personalized, active, and collaborative learning and also synchronous, asynchronous, and blended forms of delivery), see e.g. (De Bra et al., 1999) or (Bote-Lorenzo et al., 2002).
- Activity in terms of standards (e.g., ADL SCORM and IEEE LTSC), which are a reflection of the most common concepts, are another factor influencing future architecture solutions.

ELS and e-learning architectures have been discussed recently in some academic and professional communities, which is reflected in conference and journal contributions, but also by multinational consultancy companies such as IDC and Forrester Research. This book aims to bring together advanced and novel aspects of architectural issues in a comprehensive account, targeting a wide audience of e-learning technology users, developers, and providers.

In order to provide a comprehensive solution of architectural issues in e-learning systems, the following aspects need to be addressed:

- Basic architecture building blocks such as content and infrastructure services, learning objects, and infrastructure components (Pankratius & Vossen, 2003).
- Developer activities that enable the educationally sound assembly and reuse of services, content, and components (Devedzic & Harrer, 2005; Murray, 1999).
- deployment and evaluation to provide quality educational content and services to learners and support for instructors (Tattersall et al., 2005; Weibelzahl & Weber, 2002).
- Knowledge and content solutions based on knowledge architectures and infrastructures based on Semantic Web, intelligent, adaptive, ontology-based, and annotation techniques (Dolog et al., 2004; Woelk & Agarwal, 2002).
- Content and infrastructure aspects focusing on learning objects in their (learner or learning content) management infrastructure (Vossen & Westerkamp, 2004).
- The application and limitations of standards.
- Current trends towards mobile and ubiquitous platforms and devices (Weiser, 1998; Warlick, 2005).

The general theme which guides these solutions is how instructional aspects are reflected by architectural issues. Instruction and learning content—and of course ultimately the learner—always need to be the focus and the drivers of ELS architecture.

Architecture is a notion that is interpreted in many ways in the e-learning context. A systematic organization of the different architectures facets, but also the foundations to applications and standards dimension, results in the following aspects.

- General software architecture frameworks for ELS need to identify the common building blocks of ELS architectures. A comprehensive account of architectural styles can enable the quality-driven development of ELS architectures and systems. Architectural styles are the first step that provides a framework for the definition of functional models and activities. Learning objects as identifiable units of content play a special role as learning content determines and drives the design of architectures. With the recent advent of service architectures, the provision of content as services is a specific aspect.

- Conceptual and learning architectures capture instruction and content development in the context of architecture modeling. In addition to infrastructure-oriented approaches, a development framework and processes also need to be supported for instruction and content. The development of instruction and content needs to be integrated with the software architecture perspective. Content and learning object architectures shift the focus even more towards architectures constructed from learning objects. The reusability is a central aim of learning object developments, which is a consequence of the often complex and costly development of media-rich and interactive learning objects. In particular, active learning objects that provide knowledge-level interactions require adequate support from the infrastructure architecture.
- Another dimension is the management architecture. E-learning systems are often used in a distributed context. Educational offerings can be provides across institutions. The organizational requirements arising from this situation needs to be reflected on the architectural level.
- Architectures for e-learning systems are often characterized by the use of specific techniques or the focus on specific types of learning support. Specific implementation technologies are knowledge-based, intelligent, adaptive, or multimedia techniques. Specific application types are personalized, distributed or collaborative learning.
- Standards and interoperability are central factors that determine the architecture of an e-learning system. Standards often describe reference architectures or standard interfaces that standards-compliant systems are expected to implement. Some example in the educational technology context are the SCORM Runtime Environment (RTE) standard, which defines infrastructure interfaces that enable packaged learning objects to be launched and controlled during their lifecycle. The IEEE Learning Technology System Architecture (LTSA) defines a reference architecture based on common components and their functionality and interaction. CORDRA is a reference architecture for content object repositories that highlights the importance of content objects in e-learning architectures. These domain-specific standards are complemented by a range of platform-specific standards such as Web services and the Semantic Web for the Web platform. This range of standards, in particular those mentioned in the context of educational technology, clearly highlight the importance of architectural aspects for e-learning systems.

A perspective that complements the previous categorization of architectural perspectives is architecture quality and evaluation. Evaluation itself is often the starting point of a cycle of formative evaluations resulting in re-engineered, re-factored evolving systems.

ORGANIZATION OF THE BOOK

The book is organized into three parts:

- **Section I:** "Architectural Types" discusses the impact of a number of architectural platforms that have recently emerged, such as services, Grids, mobile systems and podcasting, on e-learning.
- **Section II:** "Software Architecture and Software Engineering" consists of a number of different perspectives on the different stages of software engineering and architecture techniques applied to e-learning systems.
- **Section III:** "Applications and Educational Perspectives" discusses specific educational contexts, the issue of adaptivity and some pedagogical perspectives on e-learning systems and architectures.

Section I. Architectural Types

Chapter I (Moving Towards a Generic, Service-Based Architecture for Flexible Teaching and Learning Activities) discusses service-based architectures to support teaching and learning activities. Based on research on aspects of adaptivity, multi-paradigm support and distribution in the AdeLE project, suggestions for a generic architecture are made.

Chapter II (Collaborative E-Learning System and E-Pedagogy: Learning Resource Infrastructure for Distributed Knowledge Sharing) focuses on the important aspect of collaboration in e-learning systems. A Grid architecture is utilized to implement knowledge sharing. It demonstrates how the pedagogical principle of collaboration can be realized using such an architecture.

Chapter III (Service-Based Grid Architectures to Support the Virtualization of Learning Technology Systems) discusses principles of Grid architecture and how these can be used to support learning content management and learner management systems. The principles of service-based Grid architectures are introduced and it is demonstrated how this infrastructure can be deployed to implement a broker that mediates between common components of an e-learning system.

Chapter IV (From E-Learning to M-Learning: Architectures to Support University Teaching) looks at the recently emerging mobile devices and platforms to support third-level education. Architectures based on wireless technologies are explored in order to provide solutions for asynchronous and collaborative virtual teaching and learning. A case study is used to discuss challenges and possible solutions.

Chapter V (Architectures of Existing and Conceptual Applications of Podcasting in E-Learning Systems) investigates podcasting, which has recently received much attention in the entertainment context, as a specific form of mobile learning. Audio podcasting is reviewed in its impact on pedagogical principles and architectural and infrastructure requirements.

Section II. Software Architecture and Software Engineering

Chapter VI (A Step Towards a Pattern Language for E-Learning Systems) looks at the development of e-learning systems. Focusing particularly on intelligent tutoring systems, a pattern-based development technique, which is widely used in software engineering, is deployed. Common structures at the architecture level can be identified through patterns, for which a pattern language is discussed and a catalogue of patterns is suggested.

Chapter VII (Model-Driven Engineering (MDE) and Model-Driven Architecture (MDA) Applied to the Modeling and Deployment of Technology Enhanced Learning (TEL) Systems: Promises, Challenges, and Issues) provides another perspective on the development of e-learning systems. Model-driven architecture is presented in its principles and related to well-known development approaches for teaching and learning content and systems.

Chapter VIII (Accessibility, Digital Libraries, and Semantic Web Standards in an E-Learning Architecture) looks at the issue of standardization in the context of e-learning systems development and deployment. An overview of learning technology standards is given. Their impact on interoperability and architectures for e-learning systems is discussed using a learning object repository architecture for illustration.

Chapter IX (End-User Quality-of-Experience Aware Personalized E-Learning) addresses the evaluation of e-learning systems. In addition to pedagogical qualities, technical aspects such as performance are gaining importance in particular in distributed and mobile environments. A quality-of-experience architectural layer to monitor and evaluate quality is proposed and illustrated in the context of adaptive learning content delivery.

Chapter X (E-Learning Systems Reengineering: Functional Specifications and Component-Based Architecture) focuses on re-engineering of existing e-learning systems. A re-engineering method based on two reference models—a functional and a component-based view—is introduced. A staged development, resulting in a layered architecture of interoperable services, is presented.

Section III. Applications and Educational Perspectives

III.a Specific Application Contexts

Chapter XI (An Integrated Architecture for Supporting Vocational Training) investigates the needs and architectural requirements of vocational and adult learning and training. A development framework and an architecture based on specific vocational training services that enables both synchronous and asynchronous forms of collaborative learning and training is proposed.

Chapter XII (A Generic Platform for the Systematic Construction of Knowledge-Based Collaborative Learning Applications) looks at group activities and interactions in the context of collaborative learning. The requirements of an infrastructure for the management of knowledge to support these group activities are discussed. An information architecture in the form of a computational model that structures required information and knowledge.

III.b Adaptivity

Chapter XIII (From Learning Objects to Adaptive Content Services for E-Learning) presents a discussion of the important principle of adaptivity for e-learning. Adaptive content services are proposed. Two widely known systems, APeLS and Knowledge Tree, are used to elicit the specific challenges of adaptivity and possible solutions in service-based architectures.

Chapter XIV (An Adaptive E-Learning Platform for Personalized Course Generation) addresses adaptivity from the perspective of the information architecture. The different information models, their ontological support and their integration are discussed. The Diogene architecture is used to discuss information integration and access in this context.

III.c Education and Content Perspective

Chapter XV (Pedagogical Scenario Modeling, Deployment, Execution, and Evolution) presents an investigation into the development of e-learning systems driven by pedagogical scenarios as a specific form of learning design. Based on the IMS Learning Design and embedded into model-driven engineering this realizes a development method for e-learning systems.

Chapter XVI (Impact of Context-Awareness on the Architecture of Learning Support Systems) aims to draw attention to the notion of situatedness in the context of learning. An ontology-based formalized notion of context and context-awareness, which is introduced to denote the link between content and its context, are looked at in order discuss the impact on architectures of learning support systems.

Chapter XVII (Design and Evaluation of Web-Based Learning Environments Using Information Foraging Models) investigates information foraging as a specific aspect of the information architecture of e-learning systems. Information foraging is an information seeking and retrieval technique that is applied to learning content. A tool is presented to support the development and evaluation of e-learning environments.

REFERENCES

Avgeriou, P., Retalis, S., & Skordalakis, M. (2003). An architecture for open learning management systems. In Y. Manolopoulos et al. (Eds.), *Advances in Informatics*, (LNCS 2563, pp. 183-200). Berlin Heidelberg: Springer-Verlag.

Bote-Lorenzo, M.L., Hernández-Leo, D., Dimitriadis, Y. A., Asensio-Pérez, J. I., Gómez-Sánchez, E., Vega-Gorgojo, G. & Vaquero-González, L.M. (2002). Towards reusability and tailorability in collaborative learning systems using IMS-LD and grid services. *International Journal on Advanced Technology for Learning*, *1*(3), 129-138.

Bouras, C. & Tsiatsos, T. (2005). Educational virtual environments: Design rationale and architecture. *Multimedia Tools and Applications Journal*. Kluwer Academic Publishers.

Capuano, N., Carrolagi, P., Combas, J., Crestani, F., Gaeta, M., Herber, E., Sangineto, E., Stefanov, K., & Vergara, M. (2005). Learning design and run-time resource binding in a distributed e-learning environment. *Proceedings of 1st International Kaleidoscope Learning GRID Special Interest Group Workshop on Distributed e-Learning Environments*.

De Bra, P., Brusilovsky, P. & Houben, G.J. (1999). Adaptive hypermedia: From systems to framework. *ACM Computing Surveys 31*(4), Article No.12.

Devedzic, V., & Harrer, A. (2005). Software patterns in ITS architecture. *International Journal of Artificial Intelligence in Education*, *15*(2), 63-94.

Dolog, P., Henze, N., Nejdl, W., & Sintek, M. (2004). The personal reader: Personalizing and enriching learning resources using semantic web technologies. *Lecture Notes in Computer Science, Adaptive Hypermedia and Adaptive Web-Based Systems*, Volume 3137 (pp. 85-94). Berlin / Heidelberg: Springer.

Murray, T. (1999). Authoring intelligent tutoring systems. *International Journal of Artificial Intelligence in Education*, *10*(3/4), 98-129.

Okamoto, T., Cristea, A.I. & Kayama, M. (2000). Towards intelligent media-oriented distance learning and education environments. *Proceedings of the International Conference of Computer on Education 2000* (pp. 61-72).

Pankratius, V. & Vossen, G. (2003). Towards e-Learning grids: Using grid computing in electronic learning. *Proc. IEEE Workshop on Knowledge Grid and Grid Intelligence* (pp. 4-15). IEEE.

Tattersall, C., Vogten, H., Brouns, F., Koper, R., van Rosmalen, P., Sloep, P., and van Bruggen, J. (2005). How to create flexible runtime delivery of distance learning courses. *Educational Technology and Society*, *8*(3), 226-236.

Vossen, G. & Westerkamp, P. (2004). Maintenance and exchange of learning objects in a web services based e-Learning System. *Electronic Journal of E-Learning*, *2*(2), 292-304.

Warlick, D. (2005). Podcasting. *Technology & Learning*, *26*(2), 70.

Weibelzahl, S., & Weber, G. (2002). Advantages, opportunities, and limits of empirical evaluations: Evaluating adaptive systems. *Künstliche Intelligenz Journal*, *3*, 17-20.

Weiser, M. (1998). The future of ubiquitous computing on campus. *Communications of the ACM, 41*(1), 41-42.

Woelk, D., Agarwal, S. (2002). Integration of e-learning and knowledge management. *Proceedings of the World Conference on E-Learning in Corporate, Government, Health Institutions, and Higher Education*, Volume 1 (pp. 1035-1042).

Acknowledgment

The editor would like to acknowledge the help of all involved in the preparation and review process of the book, without whose support this project could not have been satisfactorily completed.

I am grateful to and deeply appreciate the contributions of my colleagues and research students at Dublin City University for their support of our activities in e-learning and software engineering research. In particular, Claire Kenny, Edmond Holohan, Declan McMullen, and Mark Melia have, with their efforts, made a project like this book possible.

Special thanks go to the School of Computing at Dublin City University for providing the resources for the early stages of this book project. I would also like to thank the Software Engineering group at the Department of Computing Science at the University of Oldenburg, where I spent my sabbatical during the last stages of the book preparation, for their support.

Most of the authors of chapters included in this book also served as referees for articles written by other authors. Thanks go to all those authors who provided constructive and comprehensive reviews. Special thanks go to Edmond Holohan and Mark Melia from Dublin City University, to Francois Magnan from the University of Quebec in Montreal, and to Ivan Ganchev and Stanimir Stojanov from the University of Limerick who helped to provide additional reviews.

Special thanks also go to all the staff at IGI Global, whose contributions throughout the whole process from inception of the initial idea to final publication have been invaluable. In particular, I am grateful to Lynley Lapp, Meg Stocking, and Deborah Yahnke, who continuously helped to keep the project on schedule and provided support and answers for my queries, and to Kristin Roth, who motivated me to initially accept her invitation for taking on this project.

In closing, I wish to thank all of the authors for their insights and excellent contributions to this book. I am also grateful to all the people who assisted me in the reviewing process. Finally, I want to thank my wife and daughter for their love and support throughout this project.

Claus Pahl
Dublin, Ireland
June 2007

Section I
Architectural Types

1

Chapter I
Moving Towards a Generic, Service–Based Architecture for Flexible Teaching and Learning Activities

Christian Gütl
Graz University of Technology, Austria

ABSTRACT

Modern, computer-supported learning must go far beyond simply delivering learning content in a one-fit-for-all approach to students. It instead should include a variety of didactic aspects and cognitive characteristics. Furthermore, diverse systems and information must be taken into account for individualized learning processes. In light of this information, the objective of this chapter is to delineate an open, distributed, and service-based architecture for flexible teaching and learning activities. Backed by relevant research strands in this context, an architecture for an enhanced e-learning system developed within the AdeLE research project shall be depicted and experiences gained so far will be discussed. Based on this, a proposal is given for a generic and flexible architecture for adaptive e-learning towards the end of this chapter.

INTRODUCTION

The increasing amount of knowledge and its dynamic requires efficient and improved learning activities in all educational settings, such as in general school, university and vocational education. e-learning can be very useful for various learning activities in these educational settings. There is no doubt, however, that modern, computer-based learning support must go far beyond simply delivering learning content in a one-fit-for-all approach to students. From

Copyright © 2008, IGI Global, distributing in print or electronic forms without written permission of IGI Global is prohibited.

the teacher's perspective, didactic aspects must be considered by flexible sequences of learning assets or more generalized by a flexible chain of learning activities. From the student's viewpoint, pre-knowledge, preferred learning styles, and learning media must be adequately considered for personalization purposes built on context-sensitive and fine-grained user profiles.

From the perspective of information and communications technology (ICT), various systems and applications must be taken into account in order to access the required information, process it and deliver individually-tailored learning activities to students based on their learning situation and environmental context.

In light of the situation stated so far, the AdeLE research project was began in 2003 for the purpose of developing an enhanced and flexible computer-based learning solution. The AdeLE project addresses the following research and development objectives:

1. The support of various learning and teaching paradigms.
2. The personalized retrieval, management and presentation of relevant and topical information for learning activities.
3. The improvement of knowledge about user behavior in the field of human-computer interaction and, in particular, of computer-based learning activities for the purpose to gain new insights and input for (1) and (2) as well.

Based on the goals stated above, AdeLE's research results include (1) a solution approach for a student-centered environment, (2) a personalized knowledge transfer process by utilizing static and dynamic e-learning knowledge repositories, and (3) the application of fine-grained information about the students, which is gained from user input (such as user record data and summative assessments) and user observation (such as real-time gaze movement tracking and content tracking).

It results in the development and implementation of an enhanced adaptive e-learning system by applying a service-based approach.

The objective of this chapter is to delineate the architecture of AdeLE's enhanced e-learning system, discuss experiences gained so far and—backed by that—propose a generic architecture for a multi-purpose e-learning system for flexible teaching and learning activities.

BACKGROUND

As clearly pointed out in Bransford, Brown and Cocking (2000), educational goals have significantly changed in recent decades. The modern, knowledge-based society expects much more from students and teachers than ever before. Consequently, the consideration of various learning and teaching styles (Ramsay & Ransley, 1986; Felder, 1993; Riding, 1997; Bransford, Brown, & Cocking 2000) becomes increasingly important. Information and communication technologies (ICT) can foster learning activities in many ways (Bransford, Brown, & Cocking, 2000; Oblinger & Oblinger, 2005), such as technical presentation support in traditional learning or e-learning. Financial aspects relating to the creation and maintenance of learning material, especially in the context of various teaching and learning styles, are also becoming increasingly important. Thus, the reuse of learning material, as well as interchangeability of content and organizational information, such as user information, is a key requirement. Consequently, various e-learning standards for content description and exchange as well as for didactical goals and student information have emerged, such as IMS and ADL SCORM (Paramythis & Loidl-Reisinger, 2004). By narrowing down to future-oriented e-learning systems, based on the situation stated so far, it is obvious that such systems must be flexible and adaptable in order to consider diverse didactic goals and student's learning needs.

Although the concept of adaptation of instructions can be traced to the fourth century B.C., it was not until the twentieth century that actual systematic efforts were taken for the development of an adaptive instructional design system (Park & Lee, 2003). Three different approaches can be identified: the macro-adaptive approach (MaA), the aptitude-treatment interaction approach (ATI), and the micro-adaptive approach (MiA). In recent decades, diverse types of adaptation systems for various application scenarios have emerged such as computer aided instruction (CAI), computer managed instruction (CMI), recommender systems, personalized systems of instruction (PSI) and intelligent tutoring system (ITS); see also Gütl, García-Barrios and Mödritscher (2004) and García-Barrios (2006b). In order for ITS to be enhanced, it was combined with the provision of learning material organized as hypertext. This was the starting point of adaptive hypermedia systems for education. Research on adaptive hypermedia can be traced back to the beginning of the 1990s. Web-based adaptive educational hypermedia systems have emerged with the increasing popularity of the WWW. In 1996, a period of rapid growth of activities in adaptive hypertext research began (Brusilovsky, 2000; Brusilovsky, 2001). Since that time, numerous Web-based adaptive systems have been developed. An overview about early systems, as well as more recent approaches, can be found in Brusilovsky (2000), Brusilovsky and Peylo (2003), and Sadat and Ghorbani (2004)

At the end of the 1990s, AHAM, a reference model for adaptive hypermedia based on the Dexter Model was developed. The model took into account most existing functions supported by adaptive systems developed by that time (De Bra, Houben, & Wu, 1999). Roughly speaking, AHAM distinguishes link and content adaptation based on information provided by appropriate models. Due to its main focus on learning systems, it encompasses a domain model, a user model and a teaching model. Furthermore, Koch and Rossi (2002) describe patterns for adaptive

Web applications and they supplement link and content adaptation by adaptive presentation, for example using different layouts or user control elements.

By focusing on the architectural viewpoint, various interesting types of adaptive systems can be identified: (1) the classical client-server concept, such as SmexWeb (Albrecht, Koch, & Tiller, 2000) and the AHA! system (De Bra & Calvi, 1998; De Bra, Smits, & Stash, 2006), (2) the multi-agent architecture, such as the system described by Boticario and Gaudioso, (2000), (3) a distributed architecture, such as KnowledgeTree (Brusilovsky, 2004), and (4) a Web-service-based architecture, such as the concept of the HyperService Composition System (Conlan, Lewis, Higel, O'Sullivan, & Wade, 2003) and the Personal Reader (Dolog, Henze, Nejdl, & Sintek, 2004b).

Considering the findings stated so far, we can identify three of the most important landmarks along the course towards an open and modern adaptive e-learning architecture: (1) flexibility in terms of the support of various teaching and learning activities as well as the support of different e-learning standards, (2) openness for utilization and inclusion of existing systems, and (3) interchangeability of learning resources and organizational information as well. Furthermore, we mean by interchangeability that a given learning management system should be easily replaced by another one based on concrete needs. These abstract requirements also must be complemented with aspects of security, reliability and scalability. In light of this, we advocate a distributed e-learning platform, built on a service-oriented architecture; see also Gütl et al. (2004).

In order to back our architectural decision, a more general viewpoint in this context is given in the remainder of this section. IT developers and IT executives have increasingly been facing problems of budget cuts and the utilization of existing and partly out-of-date technologies over various platforms. At the same time, they must continuously remain competitive, follow fast changing business decisions, and serve customer needs in a personalized way. (Kapur, 2004; Endrei et al., 2004; Sommerville, 2006) Software engineering models, methods and processes have been strongly influenced by the situation stated above. This is also reflected in the evolution of architecture paradigms. In recent years, the service-oriented architecture (SOA) has become increasingly popular to overcome the problems stated so far (Endrei et al., 2004; Wang & Fung, 2004; Nickull, 2005). In short, in the SOA paradigm, a distributed system can be built by a composition of interacting services. Services map business functions and might be fine- or coarse-grained depending on the corresponding business processes, and they are implemented by one or more software components. Well-defined interfaces provide a mechanism to access functionality and define contracts between the service provider and service consumer (other services or end-consumer). The interface for services is platform-independent, and services can be located and invoked dynamically. Additionally, the service-oriented approach must deal with further functional aspects (such as service registry and runtime environment, service description, service transport and communication protocols) and quality of service aspects (such as security, reliability, scalability and policy). In contrast to theses challenges of the SOA, there are interesting and important benefits, such as providing existing functionalities as services, simplifying the integration of new services, offering faster time-to-market and reduced costs, increasing reuse, and allowing for more flexibility for future changes (Papazoglou, 2003; Turner, Budgen, & Brereton, 2003; Wang & Fung, 2004; Endrei et al., 2004; Fröschl, 2005). Finally, it is important to mention that the service-oriented idea has been conceptualized in diverse technology initiatives, such as .NET, Web services and Openwings (Bieber & Carpenter; Papazoglou, 2003; Nickull, 2005).

THE FIRST VERSION OF THE ADELE ARCHITECTURE

Based on the main objectives, findings and requirements stated so far, this section will outline the initial version of the AdeLE architecture, its important aspects, and first experiences gained with the system. In accordance with our institute's main research activities within the AdeLE research project, however, the main focus is on the server-side system.

The Overall Architecture of the System

The first version of the AdeLE architecture is shown in Figure 1. It is built up of strong separated client-side and server-side systems, briefly outlined in the following paragraphs (Gütl & García-Barrios, 2005b; Gütl & Mödritscher, 2005; Gütl et al., 2005; Pivec, Pripfl, & Trummer, 2005; Mödritscher, García-Barrios, Gütl, & Helic, 2006).

At the client-side of AdeLE's e-learning environment, the Web Client—a simple web browser—renders the learning content delivered from the server-side. It also provides control and navigation elements for interacting with the server-side located Learning Management System and the Information Retrieval System. In order to extend the observation of the student's behavior, the Eye-Tracking System (ETS) reads and analyzes the gaze movements of the rendered content within the area of the Web browser. ETS is composed of the 'Tobii 1750' hardware eye-tracker and the gaze-tracking analysis software module written in Java. We want to emphasize that detecting students' behavior from eye-gaze movements is very challenging. Thus in the first version of our implementation, characteristics of interest for the user behavior analysis include scan path, reading and memorizing patterns, areas of attention and disorientation, as well as frequency and time spent on such activities. This requires a

Figure 1. Overview of the AdeLE architecture

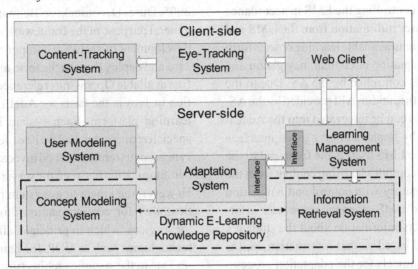

high temporal and spatial resolution for the gaze movement tracking, and consequently a large amount of measure values must be processed. The challenging task of the analysis software is to compute these characteristics without appreciable delays. Furthermore, the spatial information of the gaze activities must be mapped with the logical partition of information rendered in the browser, such as headings, sections, graphics, and tables. This is performed by the content-tracking system (CTS). It reads tag information describing the segments of interest from the source of content pages based on the document object model (W3C 2006a). Tag information may include a unique identifier and more descriptive labels, such as media type, learning style and didactic goals. In addition, the spatial areas of the segments of interest rendered by the browser are determined. Our first implementation supports the Microsoft Internet Explorer 6.x by applying the plug-in library JExplorer from TeamDev (2006). Finally, the CTS maps the segments of interest rendered by the browser with spatial-based gaze pattern information from the ETS. At the end of the client-side's processing chain, the analyzed student behavior characteristics for each specified page segment

of interest together with the information of corresponding segment are sent to the server-side and feed the user modeling system. To illustrate this, let us consider an example how the AdeLE system can handle simple didactic information. The teacher can define didactic goals (scan, read and learn) for segments in the content by tagging them. The CTS gets this tagged information and performs, together with the ETS, a gaze pattern analysis of the student for this spatial area in order to determine scanning, reading or learning activities. At the end of the process chain, the intended didactical goal for each segment, together with the analyzed activity is sent to the server-side. The communication between the Web client and the server-side located systems is handled by HTTP requests, synchronous RMI is applied for information exchange between the client-side located CTS and the server-side located user modeling system.

To follow the course towards a flexible adaptive learning environment, AdeLE's server-side architecture is divided into three main systems: the learning management system (LMS), the adaptation system (AS), and the user modeling system (UMS). The AS is located in the center of the server-side architecture. It governs the adaptation steps for controlling the LMS in accordance with proper user information from the UMS and information about available learning objects form the LMS. Adaptation of content, navigation and presentation is controlled by the AS. Due to the open architecture and an API provided by the AS, existing LMSs can be integrated into the AdeLE environment by implementing a given interface definition. The LMS itself is the front-end to the client-side. It compiles learning content from the learning repository with control and navigation elements. The UMS manages static user information, collects information about the student's behaviors and based on that information, builds specific user models for the adaptation process. Student information is obtained by two different sources and information paths. Firstly, the content-tracking system directly feeds the UMS with gaze tracking related information. Secondly, information about the student's interaction with the LMS is transmitted through and augmented with adaptation-relevant information by the AS. In addition to the three core systems of AdeLE's adaptive learning environment, a dynamic e-learning knowledge repository is provided by applying a context-sensitive concept modeling system (CMS) and a specialized information retrieval system (IRS). The latter one builds an index of selected Web resources and keeps them up-to-date. Pre-defined concepts and corresponding queries composed for specific learning contexts are managed by the CMS. The AS requests concepts for particular learning tasks (for a specific learning context) in order to provide additional information as part of the learning content delivered by the LMS.

For the purpose of developing a platform-independent and flexible e-learning system, the design of the main systems at the server-side follows the service-oriented approach, which was briefly described in the previous section. The implementation is based on Openwings, a framework for service-oriented software development (Carpenter & Bieber, 2003; Fröschl, 2005, Dusa, Deconinck, & Belmans, 2005). The general purpose of the framework is to enable the development of software components written in Java and deploy them in the form of services. The free available Openwings reference implementation in Java is the basis for AdeLE's server-side learning platform. Each system is built up of specialized services, and we have decided to apply synchronous remote method invocation (RMI) for communication between the server-side systems. However, the Openwings system provides great flexibility for communication through connector services, which in principle, allows applying technologies such as IIOP, JSM and SOAP.

Due to the specific architecture of the AdeLE learning platform and the application of the service-oriented approach, security and privacy issues are of particular importance. Openwings addresses these issues by providing appropriate security mechanisms which include: (1) code security: a policy describes grant clauses for specific components regarding platform features, such as accessing the file system, (2) transport security: communication between components can be secured by specific connectors, and (3) service security: role concepts with access rights and context specification allow a fine-grained security management. In our first implementation we depended on these mechanisms for managing platform security and utilized LMS's user management for student identification as well as for managing the access to the learning environment and content.

User Modeling System

This section is based on research activities partially documented in Gütl and García-Barrios (2005b) and García-Barrios (2006a). From a general viewpoint, AdeLE's user modeling system (UMS) performs tasks such as receiving, logging and processing personal user information from other systems, managing user data and delivering it to other systems on request. Focusing on the input tasks, user interaction data, (such as actively filled form data and passively traced user behavior) as well as adaptation process data must be captured. Concentrating on processing tasks, the UMS handles assumptions, reasoning and model building based on captured user data. Finally, focusing on the output tasks, specific facts or model information must be delivered for further processing by other systems.

From a logical perspective, we distinguish between user profiling and user modeling based on the abstraction level of data and functions. The profiling unit subsumes simple functions (such as user trait representation and user behavior logging) and it manages simple data values as well. In contrast, the modeler unit includes enhanced functionalities (such as statistic computations, interpretations, and reasoning) and it manages information on a higher semantic level as well. To illustrate this, let us consider the WAVI model, which describes the cognitive characteristics in terms of the wholist (W) and analyst (A) dimension. The model also addresses the preferred media type by the verbalizer (V) and imager (I) dimension. (Graff, 2003) For example, to cope with the preferred media type, the profiler captures, logs, and delivers relevant user behavior data such as consumed learning objects and gaze pattern on rendered learning content. The modeler applies specific procedures in order to interpret the logged user data and computes the verbalizer and imager value. This information can be requested by other systems, such as the AS for content selection.

From an abstract requirement's perspective, a flexible UMS must deal with various input streams and data formats from other systems. It also must cope with various models and metadata sets. In light of the previous paragraph, a logical separation of profiler and modeler task can support these requirements. Furthermore, security and privacy issues are key for sensitive data, such as user behavior data or summative analysis of them. To be more concrete, the requirements for

the first AdeLE UMS include basic functions such as the logging of user behavior (data from gaze-tracking and interacting with LMS), recording of adaptation steps (adaptation rules and underlying facts), and managing user information records. Enhanced functions, logically grouped in the modeler unit, focus on the support of the WAVI model and on the observation of the states modeler for tracking the didactic goals. In our first implementation, the state modeler compares predefined, simple didactic goals (scan, read, learn) with analyzed user behavior for sections of interest in the learning content as described before. It dynamically manages the user state by applying comparison rules, for further details see Garcia (2006a). Finally, the UMS must provide single facts and groups of such facts based on profiler and modeler data structures.

Following the service-oriented approach at the design phase, specialized services must be identified, which provides logically clustered functions derived from the requirements stated so far. At this time, however, we have yet to hypothesize about how much functionality should be implemented to such a specialized service. In order to gain experience, we have decided to implement two approaches, what we have decided to name the 'micro' and the 'macro' approach; they are an alternative to each other and perform the same function but with different specifications. The micro approach is composed of a high number of very specialized services rather than the macro approach, which encapsulates more functionality for each of the services.

At the micro approach design (see left side of Figure 2), a flexible communication between other systems and the UMS is assured by the communicator (CO) through the application of data structures encapsulated in a specific communication object instance (COI). The CO delegates the COI for further processing to the communication interpreter (CI), which parses the particular data structure by applying a corresponding auxiliary service. To illustrate this,

Figure 2. Micro approach architecture and macro approach architecture (adapted from Fröschl, 2005) of the user modeling system.

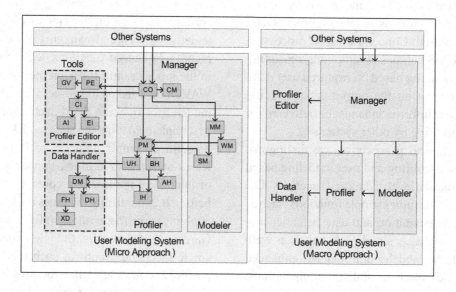

the COI of the eye-tracking system is handled by the eye-tracking communication interpreter (EI) and adaptive system communication is handled by the adaptive system communication interpreter (AI). The parsed data structure is returned in an internal standardized representation to CO and sent to a context manager (CM). The CM analyzes the given data structure and determines the corresponding context, that is, it selects either the profiler or the modeler context. In the next step, the CM delegates the data structure for further processing either to the profile manager (PM) or to the modeler manager (MM). The result is returned to the external system that initiated the request. In addition, further specialized services, logically grouped as tool services, may prepare particular result representations for other systems, e.g. the profiler editor (PE) prepares a particular visualization by means of the auxiliary service GUI visualization (GV) for the external Test Client System.

Tasks in the profiler context are controlled by the PM, which delegates data structures for fur-

ther processing to more specialized services. To illustrate this with one example, 'user information records' are handled by the user information handler (UH) by means of tools services specialized in data management. Thus, data manager (DM), file handler (FH) and XML file handler (XH) manage corresponding XML file structures. To give another example, 'user behavior information' is handled by the behavior handler (BH), and then delegated either to the instruction handler (IH) or to the action handler (AH). This information is managed in a database by means of DM and the database handler (DH). Tasks in the modeler context are handled in the same way. It is important to mention that more advanced functionalities are addressed in the modeler context by the modeler manager (MM), which is also reflected by the topology of the systems' architecture. Thus, the PM is used as an auxiliary service by the modeler services like the states modeler (SM) and WAVI modeler (WM).

The macro approach design (see right side of Figure 2) is derived by a logical grouping of specialized services from the micro approach architecture. It is composed of five services, namely the manager, the profiler editor, the modeler, the profiler and the data handler. The macro approach implementation provides the same functionality as the above described micro approach. Further detail can be found in Fröschl (2005).

Adaptation System and Learning Management System

This section is based on research activities documented in Mödritscher, García-Barrios and Gütl (2004a), Mödritscher, García-Barrios and Gütl (2004b), and Gütl and Mödritscher (2005). From a general point of view, AdeLE's Adaptation System performs adaptation steps in accordance to some influencing factors, such as didactical objectives, cognitive styles, available content alternatives, and capabilities of the LMS. Furthermore, AS communicates with UMS, CM and LMS in order to send or receive information, and it also controls the LMS for the purpose of adapting towards the user. The LMS provides basic functionality for user and content management, control and navigation elements for user interaction, and content representation and delivery to the students as well.

From the logical perspective of the adaptation process for e-learning, we distinguish three adaptation types: (1) 'sequencing' is the adaptation process to estimate the most appropriate learning activity, (2) 'aggregation' encompasses adaptation tasks either to select the best content page from page alternatives or to compile a tailored content page from a set of content assets, and (3) 'representation' comprises adaptation tasks to present the learning environment and the learning content in accordance to users' needs and device capabilities. Each adaptation process of any adaptation type is based on a particular learning context, determined by several influencing factors. These can be clustered in user-independent factors (such as didactic goals), and user-dependent factors

(such as cognitive style). To provide the AS with proper information about the learning context, we propose to apply the following models: (1) 'domain knowledge' for modeling the subjects, concepts and its relations, (2) 'course model' for describing the course structure and linked content objects, including media alternatives and knowledge level alternatives, (3) 'didactic model' for describing didactic goals, and (4) 'user model' for representing the user's information records, preferences and behaviors. Furthermore, we claim that in the case of insufficient information or disputable adaptation steps, students must be involved to acquire the necessary information.

From the requirement's perspective on an abstract level, a flexible AS in the e-learning domain must cope with various cognitive styles and didactic objectives. In order to support a wide range of LMSs, the AS must deal with different functionalities, types of learning object repositories, and e-learning standards. Furthermore, the AS must also handle communication tasks and information flow with different systems. In light of these abstract requirements, it is obvious that movement towards a generic and flexible AS is very challenging. To focus on the more concrete requirements for the first version of AdeLE's AS, we have decided to concentrate on SCORM-based content and to apply the SCORM runtime environment as an example for an external LMS, see ADL (2006). To interact with the LMS, students can use control elements (such as next and previous learning activity) and navigation elements (such as the learning activity tree). In order to follow background information related to specific learning activities, an additional sidebar, similar to the activity treeview, is added to the SCORM runtime environment, (see also the following section). Finally, the LMS must render and deliver dynamically composed content pages initiated by the AS. This is given by the need to involve the student in case of disputable adaptation steps, or to acquire and update user record data stored in the UMS.

Adaptation tasks are performed according to the learning context composed of the course model and the didactic model (derived from the SCORM manifest file), as well as the user model (given by the WAVI model). These adaptation tasks manipulate navigation elements based on the preferred cognitive style and didactical goals. To be concrete, as a first approach, we have decided to minimize the learning activity tree and the background sidebar for preferred analytic learning style and to render both elements in normal size for the wholist group of students. Further, the adaptation tasks also address the selection of suitable learning content and the management of control and navigation elements based on preferred learning media and didactic goals. It is also worth mentioning in this context that our system follows two important principles. Students should be assisted at their learning processes by the AdeLE system through guidance and the pre-selection of learning activities and content alternatives. It is also important, however, that students also have the freedom to overrule the system and make their own decisions. The second principle addresses an important usability principle that students should always receive the same content if they revisit learning activities or follow a particular learning activity path. To guarantee that system behavior,

adaptation decisions and underlying facts are sent to the UMS for logging purposes in order to be reused in comparable learning situations. Generally speaking, on the one hand the AS sends adaptation information for each adaptation step to the UMS. On the other hand, it requests necessary information for adaptation decisions from UMS, such as facts from the WAVI model or adaptation decisions. Concerning the information flow, students' behavior, in terms of interacting with the LMS must be taken into account for profiling and modeling purposes at the UMS. Thus, any students' interactions with the LMS must be sent through the AS to the UMS.

An overview of AdeLE's architecture and its interaction with other systems is depicted in Figure 3. Unlike the micro and macro approach design of the UMS, the AS is implemented as one single service in the Openwings framework and synchronous RMI is applied for communication with other services of the AdeLE system. This decision is given by the fact that a comparison of different design approaches in our service-based architecture is important for our further research activities in this context.

Any task of the adaptation system is started by a request from the LMS initiated through students' interaction with the platform. In order to

Figure 3. *Architecture overview of the adaptation system*

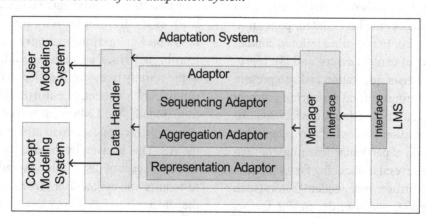

be flexible in terms of supporting a wide range of LMSs, a controlling and communication interface has been specified and implemented in the AS and the SCORM runtime environment. This is based on a service request and a response object. In light of the requirements stated above, the interface must support the following functions: (1) transmitting information about the course and learning content to the AS, such as didactic rules and course structure, (2) notifying the AS of any user action, (3) controlling the LMS for the purpose of adapting instructional sequencing, aggregation and representation, (4) sending content to LMS in order to be displayed for the user, and (5) gaining feedback from the student via LMS using content generated by the AS or UMS, such as forms and selection boxes. AdeLEs' interface definition includes an error recovery strategy. The LMS performs a silent catch and continues with a 'default behavior' if for any reason a request fails, for example because of a network connection error or a timeout. The manager receives requests from the LMS and delegates them based on the type of method call and the content of the communication object either to the adaptor or to the data handler. At the end of the process chain, the manager embeds the result into the communication object and returns it to the LMS.

By focusing on the core adaptation activities, the adaptor performs requests for certain adaptation aspects of the LMS. Within the adaptor module, the request is internally handled by one of three specialized adaptor components, namely the sequencing adaptor, the aggregation adaptor and the representation adaptor. This specialization in the architectural design is in accordance with the adaptation types and their responsibilities for specific tasks as stated above. Each of the specialized adaptors implements five necessary methods, always executed in the same order: (1) The 'get course model' method tries to retrieve the course model from the LMS, which is the DOM representation of the SCORM-based course's manifest file.

The course model is cached by the AS for further use, modifications of the course content and manifest file are observed by any further method call. (2) The 'adapt by course rules' method computes the adaptation step for the depicted aspect of the LMS with respect to didactical rules. Thus, this adaptation task is achieved solely through user-independent factors. If this operation results in a certain decision, it is saved in the model repository to be reused independent of users for the same adaptation decisions. (3) The 'adapt by student rules' method performs the personalization process itself, where the adaptor tries to adapt the chosen aspect of the LMS for the student on the basis of the user model given by the modeling system. If the previously described method call results in a disputable adaptation step, the following method call is performed. (4) The 'adapt by user feedback information' method generates a feedback form to ask the user to complete the adaptation step. Finally, (5) 'create LMS response' generates a response object to control the LMS. Focusing on the data handler, this module manages internal data repositories such as the course model cache and the AS logger. It also handles the data exchange with the UMS and the CMS. The data handler itself receives requests from the specialized adaptors to write the information about the course model in the internal cache, or to store the adaptation decisions and underlying facts in the UMS. Continuing on, the specialized adaptors request WAVI information and stored adaptation decisions by means of the data handler from the UMS to perform their adaptation steps. The data handler also receives requests directly from the manager for the purpose of connecting through the data flow to the UMS and the CMS. To give one example, information about the student's interaction with the LMS is received by the manager and delegated to the data handler in order to send this information to the UMS for logging purposes.

Dynamic E-Learning Knowledge Repository

This section is based on research activities documented in García-Barrios, Gütl and Mödritscher (2004), Gütl and García-Barrios (2005a), Safran (2006) and Safran, García-Barrios and Gütl (2006). From a general point of view, the dynamic e-learning knowledge repository (DEKOR) aims at the provision of a set of dynamically compiled information, which we also call dynamic information for short; whereby each such set of information is linked to a concept and a set of concepts is coupled to a certain context. Unlike static background knowledge repositories, DEKOR complements AdeLE's static course content by dynamically delivering topical information from various information systems.

In light of the proposed dynamic e-learning knowledge repository, the application of concepts is key for the provision of dynamic information. Concepts denote abstract ideas and thoughts. They can capture teachers' and students' internal views of a learning subject. On an abstract level, a set of concepts can reflect the content of a lecture, an entire course or even a curriculum. Moreover, concepts can classify and link similar objects or entities. Consequently, they can also be linked to descriptions and information about themselves. A concept is distinctively defined in a specific domain (such as the knowledge domain) and in a particular context (such as a specific viewpoint) by a symbol or a term. Thus, concepts represent a powerful tool, which allow humans to symbolize ideas, and link concepts to exemplary instances and descriptive information. For a specific learning context such as a learning task, a set of concepts could be used to draw attention to important related background information. For the purpose of topical information accessibility, these concepts should not be linked directly to documents in a static manner, but instead linked in order to query information systems and to dynamically retrieve relevant documents. The

following example is given to illustrate the idea stated so far. A teacher defines learning contexts in an e-learning course and assigns them to the learning tasks of a course. The context, 'basics on topic,' for example is assigned to the introduction page and as a next step, the teacher identifies important concepts for each context, such as related topics or methods to be applied. Finally, the teacher selects appropriate information systems for each concept for the purpose of dynamically linking different types of content, such as news and definition. Students can use the concepts given in this specific learning context to follow up on particular background information, such as news or a definition about a related topic.

From an abstract requirement's perspective, a dynamic e-learning knowledge repository must model various contexts and related sets of concepts. Thus, contexts, concepts, and their relationships must be managed. Furthermore, contexts must be linked to learning activities and concepts to content of different information systems. The AdeLE project's tangible requirements demand that DEKOR manages the access to content of arbitrary Web information systems at the same time. DEKOR, therefore, must deal with proper information about how to access and query such systems. The logical connection to AdeLE's core learning system must be realized by means of the learning context. Consequently, DEKOR must cope with different learning contexts, linking them to learning assets and assigning them to groups of concepts. For each concept in a context, a concept name, description, supported information systems and proper queries must be managed. To be applicable for various e-learning systems and functionalities, DEKOR must be flexible in terms of communication and information delivery. In order to guarantee the autonomy of the selection and quality of Web resources applicable as background knowledge, the decision was made to add an information retrieval system to AdeLE's server-side architecture.

In light of the requirements stated so far, the architectural overview of involved systems and their information flow is depicted on the left side of Figure 4. We have decided to split DEKOR in two logical parts, the context-sensitive concept modeling system (CMS), and loosely coupled information systems. One of them, a tailored version of the Web information retrieval system xFIND (Andrews, Gütl, Moser, Sabol, & Lackner, 2001) is part of AdeLE's server-side system. The information flow starts with the student's Web client interaction which controls the LMS to deliver personalized learning assets in form of selected content pages. The information about the delivered content page, together with the expected extent and format of the result for background information, is passed through the AS to the CMS, which determines the learning context and type of response. In principle, the AS can perform adaptation steps on the result before sending it back to the LMS, but in the first ver-

sion we do not implement such functionality. The LMS handles the representation of the results as part of the navigation frame. For each concept, a group of hyperlinks allows students to follow up dynamically compiled information from different information systems, such as the IR system.

The right side of Figure 4 depicts the Architecture of the context-sensitive concept modeling system. Backed by our first experiences gained on the user modeling system, we have decided to implement the logical part for managing contexts and concepts also as a modeling system by applying the macro-based service approach (see also section "User Modeling System"). The manager takes requests and delegates them either to the profiler or the modeler. The profiler manages the raw information about contexts and concepts and also enables the access to this basic information. The modeler accesses the profiler component in order to fetch the basic information about the context and performs specific processing steps

Figure 4. Logical information flow (left side) and overview of the concept modeling system architecture (right side, adapted from safran, 2006)

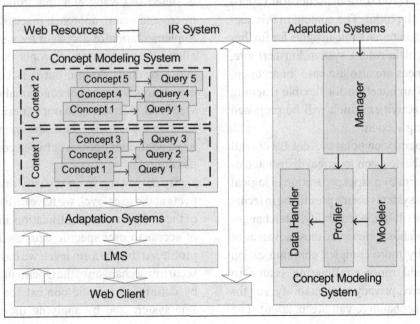

to infer semantically richer information. It enables the access of more advanced information by means of assumptions and inferences. Thus, either models of whole contexts or of an individual context and related information can be retrieved. Furthermore, the Data Handler is responsible for storage and retrieval of the data managed by the Profiler. In the current version, the profiles are stored in XML files.

Lessons Learned

The aim of this section is to discuss experiences so far concerning development, implementation and the application of the AdeLE e-learning system outlined in the previous sections. Practical insights are gained by laboratory experiments and studies of running prototype implementations of AdeLE's subsystems and their integration. Additionally, real-life experiences were gained by the application of the server-side part of the AdeLE platform in an e-learning experiment performed with 60 students within the course "Distributed Systems" at Graz University of Technology. Some of these experiences are also outlined in Gütl and García-Barrios (2005), Gütl and Mödritscher (2005), Mödritscher et al. (2006) and Safran et al. (2006). The content in this section is focused on remarkable insights for further improvements of the AdeLE system. Furthermore, these experiences are also the base for an open, service-based architecture for flexible teaching and learning activities which will be proposed in the following section.

From a general viewpoint of AdeLE's overall architecture, the decision for a real distributed e-learning platform by a strict separation in logical and functional systems seems promising in terms of openness, flexibility, extensibility, interchangeability, and scalability. However, these advantages are opposed by more complex communication procedures and more challenging issues in terms of security, privacy and reliability; see for example (Tannenbaum & van Steen, 2006). The

application of a service-based approach causes additional effort in terms of managing, discovering and invoking services; see for example (Wang & Fung, 2004). Nevertheless, our experiences with the AdeLE project have shown that the SOA can offer a solution for a flexible and open e-learning environment, and SOA technologies are available to support an efficient development process.

From our point of view, the application of a service-based approach is an important cornerstone in the movement towards generic e-learning system for flexible teaching and learning activities. This concept enables to easily select, combine, and replace specific functions of such services for the purpose of creating specialized e-learning applications.

With respect to the appropriate size of services in our specific context, based on our experience with the "micro approach," we can report that the application of small and specialized services is very complex. It causes a communication overload due to its higher number of service intercommunication, yet it may provide high flexibility and reuse of services. Detailed evaluation results in the context of the AdeLE system can be found in (Fröschl, 2005) and a more general discussion is stated in (Wang & Fung, 2004). Unlike the micro and macro approach discussed above, the implementation of a system by a single service allows the application of proper design patterns and a compact design, but it is very inflexible concerning the reuse of functionality on the service level. According to our experiences, a good solution appears to be the macro approach because it is a good compromise between complexity and flexibility.

By narrowing in on security and privacy aspects at the user level, we have utilized functions of the LMS for user identification and the control of access to user specific data, such as the user profile. At the platform level, we have built on the security mechanism of the Openwings framework by defining a specific context for each server-side system and by applying the identification mechanism for the usage of service interaction. We have faced problems, however, that the current version of Openwings only allows identification by an interactive process using a login window. We are currently working on an adapted connector service solution to overcome this problem by applying a ticketing system.

By addressing the decision for synchronous communication between the systems, we can report on the advantage of its easy implementation. Among others, however, there is the following major drawback: AdeLE's Communication processes are triggered by the LMS or CTS, while other systems can only reply to the requests and are not able to actively start the communication. Asynchronous communication can solve this problem, but it causes a complex communication management and more implementation efforts.

As a concluding remark according to our experiences, the Openwings specification and reference implementation offers a convenient framework for our service-based implementation in terms of efficient development of services, flexibility of communication aspects and scalability aspects. Two drawbacks exist, however. A long training period is required to become familiar with Openwings and learn how to productively build applications on its system. Security mechanisms must be adapted as well.

The integration of the SCORM runtime environment in the AdeLE platform has required less effort. The implementation of the specified adaptation control interface and the enhancement of adaptation functionality were mainly encapsulated into a separate package, requiring minor adaptation to the original LMS. We believe that this proposed approach might be applicable for a variety of information systems (for e-learning systems and others) and that it points in the right direction to a more generic solution. Information system vendors can therefore concentrate on the implementation of adaptation and functions for personalization, thereby making them more useable by the specified interface. The advantage of

this flexibility, in terms of supporting various LMSs, is that it is opposed by a more complex interface design. The AdeLE system must also deal in this context with a variety of functions for different LMSs. To overcome these problems, we intend to improve our first approach. A model about supported functions and features of systems can keep the AS more flexible. Furthermore, the adaptation control interface and the response mechanism for synchronous communication must be designed in a more generalized way to provide adaptation of general aspects applicable for a variety of LMSs. As a next step towards our flexible solution, we will integrate the Moodle System (Moodle, 2006) and the Hyperwave e-Learning Suite (Hyperwave, 2006).

The first implementation of the AS is specifically tailored to support functions of the SCORM runtime environment and to deal with the SCORM content packaging format. This was achieved by a product factory of adaptors for sequencing, aggregation and representation. For the purpose of supporting another LMS or learning standard, the application of the abstract factory pattern allows the exchange of the whole product family (adaptor for sequencing, aggregation, representation) accordingly. A set of adaptors, however, must be implemented for any new system or standard. To overcome this problem and to be prepared for supporting other information systems, ongoing research is being conducted in two different approaches. Firstly, specific adaptation functionality is composed by a chain of small and specialized adaptation functions, linked by a set of adaptation rules. Secondly, generic services provided by the AS are tied together with tailored services provided by the information system. These specific services implement adaptation functions for a concrete information system. In order to focus specifically on adaptation tasks at the AS, we intend to externalize repositories (such as information about course structure, content alternatives and didactic objectives) to specialized modeling systems.

Findings at the dynamic e-learning knowledge repository are concentrated on the concept modeler system. From the functional viewpoint, we want to enhance the system in order to enable a personalized management of contexts, concepts and linked resources to create individualized background information. Furthermore, the sharing of such entities between users is a goal for further implementation. Another emerging research activity addresses the application of contexts and concepts for describing course content and its application for a fine-grained profile of the users' knowledge as well.

The architecture of the user modeling system is promising because it enables an easy adjustment of the functionality for supporting a variety of information systems and their models and standards. We can report that the logical separation into profiler, modeler, and tool services supports an efficient implementation of required functions by simply replacing or adding some services. For example, the effort of extending a system with a further model only requires developing the new modeling service. Profiling and tools services do not need to be enhanced or exchanged because of their generic data processing and storage features. Furthermore, the implementation of the CMS as a specific modeling system has caused minimal effort due to the reuse of software and the application of UMS generic services. In light of these findings, one of the current research activities is to develop a multi-purpose modeling system which will enable various modeling systems to be built with minimal effort, for example, modeling for course structure and didactic objectives.

In order to supplement the findings stated so far and to give an idea about the applicability of the AdeLE system, we want to outline briefly the possible application domains and scenarios. We want to emphasize that at present, the application is restricted because of the high costs of eye-tracking hardware. In light of this, interesting scenarios include (1) efficient and observed group training in sensible subjects, such as subjects in military, aviation and nuclear power plant topics, (2) efficient and cost-effective survey of course material in laboratory conditions, and (3) support for studies on e-learning issues based on fine-grained, multi-modal information about students' behavior. In the foreseeable future, it is very likely that eye-tracking hardware will become cheaper, thus enabling a broader application of the AdeLE environment. E-learning environments without eye-gaze information utilization and subsystems such as user modeling systems or dynamic e-learning knowledge repository systems, however, are already applicable in a variety of learning situations.

FUTURE TRENDS

The aim of this section is to propose a future-oriented open architecture for flexible teaching and learning activities. It is based on experiences gained so far and backed with emerging and possible future trends in the context of a distributed and adaptive e-learning environment.

Wireless Internet-based communication, its wide-spread usage and a variety of wireless devices has been the base for the ubiquitous e-learning paradigm and ubiquitous e-learning applications (Beuschel, 2003; Grew & Pagani, 2005; Loidl, 2006). A flexible learning platform, therefore, must support different clients for computer workplaces and mobile devices as well. Consequently, learning activities and the extent of content and representation must be personalized and adapted to different devices. In light of this, context aware systems (Henricksen & Indulska, 2006; Celentano & Gaggi, 2006) and activities of the W3C on device independence, addressing *"access to a unified Web from any device in any context by anyone"* (W3C, 2006b), provide valuable findings for enhanced e-learning systems as well. Substantial information about the physical learning environmental conditions and user behaviors is important for effective adaptation to the device and the user. Physical environmental conditions, such as ambient noise and lighting, must be used to adjust device settings for situation-based use, since they impact learning behavior and motivation (Oblinger, 2006). For the purpose of gaining a more comprehensive picture about users' behavior, we also propose various client-side sensors applicable for specific devices such as gaze pattern tracking, facial expression, gesture and other physiology information (Loh, Wong, & Wong, 2005; Pivec, Pripfl, & Trummer, 2005; Wang, Chignell, & Ishizuka, 2006; Prendinger & Ishizuka, 2005). By observing research activities over the last few years, we assert that the application of client-side sensors will supplement the server-side user behavior tracking in many ways.

Similar to the support of various devices mentioned above, we also propose the support of different types of information systems applicable for a variety of learning activities. This may be backed by Helic (2006) and Kolbitsch & Maurer (2006), and the emerging research topic of e-learning 2.0 (Feldstein & Masson, 2006; Pitner & Drasil, 2006; Alexander, 2006). For the purpose of adding adaptation functionality, we propose the control by external adaptation systems and the application of a generic adaptation and communication interface. This is in accordance with the fact that distributed adaptive e-learning architectures (Brusilovsky, 2004; Dolog, Henze, Nejdl, & Sintek, 2004a; Türker, Görgün, & Conlan, 2006) and the approach to control adaptation functionality of e-learning management systems by external systems (Türker et al., 2006) are becoming increasingly popular design decisions. Consequently, the support of a variety of devices and information systems, as well as various learning and teaching activities, requires a number of diverse information structures which can be managed by specific modeling systems. This can be handled either by the multi-model approach (Conlan, 2005), or by the newly emerged approach of a multi-purpose modeling system

(García-Barrios, 2006b). By focusing on user modeling systems, we believe that more attention will be given to security issues (Kobsa, 2001; Brar & Kay, 2005; Wang & Kopsa, 2005) and to scrutability aspects (Kay, 2000) for the purpose of managing access to external systems on a fine-grained level and for enabling the user to access and browse collected user data. The increasing dispersion of personal information management (Teevan, Jones, & Bederson, 2006) is becoming an interesting source for comprehensive information about the user. Based on this, we assert that both the comprehensive user model and the access to virtually any accessible personal information can support highly personalized and contextualized learning experiences. Learning activities can not only be built on pre-existing knowledge, but additionally, specific learning context and examples can also be linked with personal information repositories.

In light of some emerging and possible future trends relevant for adaptive learning stated so far and supplemented with former experiences, we propose a future-oriented open architecture for flexible teaching and learning activities. Figure 5 shows the generic overall architecture, which is composed of client-side and server-side systems.

At the client-side of the learning platform, the user client system (UCS) provides the interface to the user for information delivery and interaction with the system. In order to support context-dependent and situation-dependent learning, various end devices and appropriate clients must be supported, for example, PCs and handhelds. On the upper left side in Figure 5, the sensory system (SS) tracks user behavior (such as mouse & keyboard interaction and gaze movements) and the environmental situation (such as noise level and lighting). Data is pre-processed and delivered to the server-side for the purpose of providing the basis for adaptation and personalization procedures.

The server-side of the learning platform is split into three systems: the modeling system (MS),

Figure 5. A generic architecture for flexible teaching and learning activities

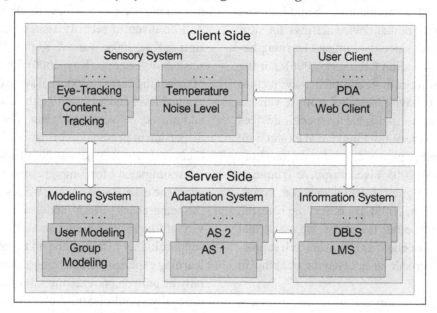

the adaptation system (AS) and the information system (IS). In order to provide flexibility in terms of didactic approaches and to support various learning styles, different systems must be managed along the lines of a proper chain of learning activities. Units—such as learning management system, dynamic knowledge repository, discussion forum and wiki system—form the IS block, as depicted in the lower right of Figure 5. In the middle of the platform's server-side, different instances of adaptive systems control corresponding functionality of various information systems. Adaptation is based on several modeling instances, such as user modeling, group modeling, system modeling, and concept modeling.

Our ongoing research is mainly focused on both a multi-purpose modeling system and a multi-purpose adaptation system, both built on a service-based design. In order to gain the highest flexibility, we are currently investigating several approaches. For example, the rule-based combination of very specific functions provided by a pool of tiny services, or what we call functionlets, similar

to portlets or plugins and provided by external systems. Generally speaking, we believe that service-based approaches in e-learning are becoming increasingly popular. Furthermore, semantic Web and Web 2.0 technologies will influence and also increasingly form e-learning architectures. Interesting and contemporary research strands in this context include the application of e-learning in digital business ecosystems (Peltoniemi &Vuori, 2004; Lavrin & Zelko, 2005) and the application of business process modeling for controlling the learning activities (Helic, 2006; Cesarini, Monga, & Tedesco, 2004).

CONCLUSION

In this chapter we have argued that ICT-supported flexible teaching and learning requires adaptation to various devices and the individual needs of the users. Our first experiences of a flexible adaptive learning platform built on a distributed architecture and a service-based approach are promising.

Experiences gained within the AdeLE research project over the last three years led us to propose a more flexible and open, service-based architecture for flexible teaching and learning activities. Our current and future work is concentrated on multi-purpose modeling and adaptation systems for an improved and modern knowledge transfer. As a final note, however, we want to emphasize that ICT-based learning should not become an end in itself. Humans and their needs should always be the focus of attention. This should be the overarching goal for research conducted on enhanced adaptive systems for knowledge transfer processes.

ACKNOWLEDGMENT

The AdeLE project is partially funded by the Austrian ministries BMVIT and BMBWK, through the FHplus impulse program. The support of the Department of Information Design, Graz University of Applied Sciences (FH JOANNEUM) and Institute for Information Systems and Computer Media (IICM), Faculty of Computer Science at Graz University of Technology as well as individuals involved in the AdeLE project are gratefully acknowledged.

REFERENCES

ADL (2006). *SCORM*. Advanced Distributed Learning. Retrieved September 23, 2006, from http://www.adlnet.gov/scorm/index.cfm

Albrecht F., Koch N., & Tiller T. (2000). SmexWeb: An adaptive Web-based hypermedia teaching system. *Journal of Interactive Learning Research, Special Issue on Intelligent Systems/Tools in Training and Lifelong Learning*, 367-388.

Alexander, B. (2006). A new wave of innovation for teaching and learning? *EDUCAUSE Review, 40*(March/April), 32-44.

Andrews, K., Guetl, C., Moser, J., Vedran Sabol, V., & Lackner, W. (2001). Search result visualization with xFIND. In E. Kapetanios & H. Hinterberger (Eds.), *Proceedings of the Second International Workshop on User Interfaces to Data Intensive Systems (UIDIS 2001)* (pp. 50-58). Zurich, Switzerland: IEEE Computer Society Press.

Beuschel, W. (2003). Ubiquitous e-learning: Are we there yet? In P. Walsh & J. Meade (Eds.), *Proceedings of the 3rd IEEE International Conference on Advanced Learning Technologies (ICALT'03)* (pp. 414-415). Los Alamitos, USA: IEEE Computer Society.

Bieber, G., & Carpenter, J. *Introduction to service-oriented programming (Rev 2.1)*. Retrieved February 6, 2007, from http://www.openwings. org/download/specs/ServiceOrientedIntroduction.pdf

Biström, J. (2005). *Peer-to-peer networks as collaborative learning environments*. Paper presented at HUT T-110.551 Seminar on Internetworking. Retrieved October 13, 2006 from http://www.sit.fi/~johnny/collp2p.pdf

Boticario, J., & Gaudioso, E. (2000). A multi-agent architecture for a Web-based adaptive educational system. *Tech. Rep. TR SS-00-01*. Retrieved October 10, 2006 from http://citeseer.ist.psu.edu/390570.html

Bransford, J.D., Brown, A.L., & Cocking; R.R. (Eds.). (2000). *How people learn: Brain, mind, experience, and school. Expanded Edition*. Washington, DC: National Academies Press.

Brar, A., & Kay, J. (2005). Privacy and security in ubiquitous personalized applications. In *Proceedings of the UM 2005 Workshop on*

Privacy-Enhanced Personalization (pp 47-54). Retrieved October 6, 2006 from http://www.isr. uci.edu/pep05/papers/w9-proceedings.pdf

Brusilovsky, P. (2000). Adaptive hypermedia: From intelligent tutoring systems to Web-based education (LNCS 1839, pp. 1-7). Berlin/Heidelberg: Springer.

Brusilovsky, P. (2001). Adaptive hypermedia. In A. Kobsa (Ed.) *User Modeling and User Adapted Interaction, Ten Year Anniversary Issue, 11*(1/2), 87-110.

Brusilovsky, P., & Peylo, C. (2003). Adaptive and intelligent Web-based educational systems. In P. Brusilovsky & C. Peylo (Eds.), *International Journal of Artificial Intelligence in Education 13* (2-4), 159-172.

Brusilovsky, P. (2004). KnowledgeTree: A distributed architecture for adaptive e-learning. In *Proceedings of the 13th International World Wide Web Conference* (pp. 104-113).

Carpenter, J., & Bieber, G. (2003). *Openwings component service specification Ver 1.0 Final, 2003*. Retrieved September 19, 2006, from http:// www.openwings.org/download/specs/Openwings_Component_Services.pdf

Celentano, A., & Gaggi, O. (2006). Context-aware design of adaptable multimodal documents. *Multimedia Tools and Applications, 29*(1), 7-28.

Cesarini, M., Monga, M., & Tedesco; R. (2004). Carrying on the e-learning process with a workflow management engine. In *Proceedings of the 2004 ACM Symposium on Applied Computing* (pp. 940-945). New York: ACM Press.

Conlan, O., Lewis, D., Higel, S., O'Sullivan, D., & Wade, V. (2003). Applying adaptive hypermedia techniques to semantic Web service composition. In *Proceedings of the International Workshop on Adaptive Hypermedia and Adaptive Web-Based*

Systems (AH 2003). Retrieved October 13, 2006 from http://wwwis.win.tue.nl/ah2003/proceedings/paper5.pdf

Conlan, O. (2005). *The multi-model, metadata driven approach to personalized e-Learning services.* Unpublished doctoral dissertation University of Dublin, Trinity College, Dublin. Retrieved October 10, 2006 from https://www. cs.tcd.ie/Owen.Conlan/publications/Conlan_Thesis.pdf

De Bra, P., & Calvi, L. (1998). AHA! An open adaptive hypermedia architecture. *The New Review of Hypertext and Multimedia, 4*, 115-139.

De Bra, P., Houben, G.-J., & Wu, H. (1999). AHAM: A Dexter-based reference model for adaptive hypermedia. In J. Westbomke, U.K. Wiil, J.J. Leggett, K. Tochtermann, & J.M. Haake (Eds.), *Proceedings of the Tenth ACM Conference on Hypertext and Hypermedia* (pp. 147-156). New York, USA: ACM Press.

De Bra, P., Smits, D., & Stash, N. (2006). The Design of AHA! In U.K. Wiil, P.J. Nürnberg, & J. Rubart (Eds.), *HYPERTEXT 2006, Proceedings of the 17th ACM Conference on Hypertext and Hypermedia* (pp. 171-195). Retrieved October 11, 2006 from http://portal.acm.org/citation. cfm?id=1149941.1149942

Dolog, P., Henze, N., Nejdl, W., & Sintek, M. (2004a). Personalization in distributed e-learning environments. In *Proceedings of the 13th International World Wide Web Conference* (pp. 170-179).

Dolog, P., Henze, N., Nejdl, W., & Sintek, M. (2004b). The personal reader: Personalizing and enriching learning resources using semantic Web technologies. *Lecture Notes in Computer Science, Adaptive Hypermedia and Adaptive Web-Based Systems, Volume 3137/2004* (pp. 85-94). Berlin / Heidelberg: Springer.

Dusa, A., Deconinck, G., & Belmans, R. (2005). On dependable embedded services and Openwings. In *Proceedings of the International Conference on Next Generation Web Services Practices (NWeSP 2005)*. Retrieved February 6, 2007, from http://ieeexplore.ieee.org/iel5/10610/33519/01592440.pdf?arnumber=1592440

Endrei, M., Ang, J., Arsanjani, A., Chua, S., Comte, P., Krogdahl, P., et al. (2004). Patterns: Service-oriented architecture and Web services. *IBM Redbook*. Retrieved February 9, 2007, from http://www.redbooks.ibm.com/redbooks/SG246303/

Felder, R. (1993). Reaching the second tier: Learning and teaching styles in college science education. *Journal of College Science Teaching, 23*(5), 286-290.

Feldstein, M., & Masson, P. (2006). Unbolting the chairs: Making learning management systems more flexible. *eLearn Magazine, 1*(2).

Fröschl, C. (2005). *User modeling and user profiling in adaptive e-learning systems.* Unpublished master's thesis, Graz University of Technology, Graz, Austria. Retrieved September 19, 2006, from http://www.iicm.tu-graz.ac.at/thesis/cfroeschl.pdf

García-Barrios, V. M., Gütl, C., & Mödritscher, F. (2004). EHELP—Enhanced E-Learning Repository: The use of a dynamic background library for a better knowledge transfer process. In M. Auer & U. Auer (Eds.), *Proceedings of the International Conference on Interactive Computer Aided Learning (ICL 2004).*

García-Barrios, V. M. (2006a). Real-time learner modeling: Using gaze-tracking in distributed adaptive e-Learning environments. In M. Cicin-Sain, I.T. Prstacic & I. Sluganovic (Eds.), *Proceedings of the international Convention MIPRO 2006 (CE)* (pp. 185-190).

García-Barrios, V. M. (2006b). Adaptive e-Learning systems: Retrospection, opportunities and challenges. In *Proceedings of the International Conference on Information Technology Interfaces (ITI 2006).*

Graff, M. (2003). Cognitive style and attitudes towards using online learning and assessment methods. *Electronic Journal of e-Learning, 1*(1), 21-28.

Grew, P., & E. Pagani, E. (2005). Towards a wireless architecture for mobile ubiquitous e-Learning. In *Proceedings of the International Workshop on Learning Communities in the Era of Ubiquitous Computing* (pp. 20-29).

Gütl, C., García-Barrios, V. M., & Mödritscher, F. (2004). Adaptation in e-Learning environments through the service-based framework and its application for AdeLE. In J. Nall & R. Robson (Eds.), *Proceedings of the World Conference on E-Learning in Corporate, Government, Healthcare, and Higher Education (E-Learn 2004)* (pp. 1891-1898).

Gütl, C., & García-Barrios, V.M. (2005a). The application of concepts for learning and teaching. In M. Auer & U. Auer (Eds.), *Proceedings of the International Conference on Interactive Computer Aided Learning (ICL 2005).*

Gütl, C., & García-Barrios, V.M. (2005b). Towards an advanced modeling system applying a service-based approach. In P. Goodyear, D. Sampson, D.J. Yang, Kinshuk, T. Okamoto, R. Hartley, & N. Chen (Eds.), *Proceedings of the IEEE International Conference on Advanced Learning Technologies (ICALT 2005)* (pp. 860-862). IEEE Computer Society Press.

Gütl, C., & Mödritscher, F. (2005). Towards a generic adaptive system applicable for Web-based learning management environments. In A. Jedlitschka & B. Brandherm (Eds.), *Proceedings of the Annual Workshop of the SIG Adaptivity and User Modeling Interactive Systems (ABIS 2005)* (pp. 26-31).

Gütl, C., Pivec, M., Trummer, C., García-Barrios. V. M., Mödritscher, M., Pripfl, J., et al. (2005). AdeLE (Adaptive e-Learning with Eye-Tracking): Theoretical background, system architecture and application scenarios. *European Journal of Open, Distance and E-Learning (EURODL), 2005, 2*. Retrieved October 13, 2006, from http://www.eurodl.org/materials/briefs/2005/Christian_Gutl_GBA.htm

Helic, D. (2006). Technology-supported management of collaborative learning processes. *International Journal of Learning and Change, 1*(3), 285-298.

Henricksen, K., & Indulska, J. (2006). Developing context-aware pervasive computing applications: Models and approach. *Pervasive and Mobile Computing, 2*(1), 37-64.

Hyperwave. (2006). E-Learning Suite (eLS). Learning Management System (LMS). Retrieved February 6, 2007, from http://www.hyperwave.com/e/products/elearning_suite

Kapur, G. (2004). *Project management for information, technology, business and certification.* Upper Saddle River, NJ: Prentice Hall.

Kay, J. (2000). Stereotypes, student models and scrutability. *Lecture Notes in Computer Science, Intelligent Tutoring Systems, Volume 1839/2000* (pp. 19-30). Berlin / Heidelberg: Springer.

Kobsa, A. (2001). Generic user modeling systems. *Journal of User Modeling and User-Adapted Interaction, 11*(1-2), 49-63.

Koch, N., & Rossi, G. (2002). Patterns for adaptive Web applications. In *Proceedings of the Seventh European Conference on Pattern Languages of Programs* (pp. 179-194). Universitätsverlag Konstanz.

Kolbitsch, J., & Maurer, H. (2006). The transformation of the Web: How emerging communities shape the information we consume. *Journal of Universal Computer Science, 12*(2), 187-213.

Lavrin, A., & Zelko, M. (2005). Knowledge sharing in digital ecosystems for small and medium enterprises. In *Proceedings of the 13th Interdisciplinary Information Management Talks (IDIMT-2005)*. Retrieved October 7, 2006, from http://www.sea.uni-linz.ac.at/conferences/idimt2005/session_f.pdf

Loh, M.-P., Wong, Y.-P., & Wong, C.-O. (2005). Facial expression analysis in e-Learning systems— The problems and feasibility. In P. Goodyear, D. Sampson, D.J. Yang, Kinshuk, T. Okamoto, R. Hartley, & N. Chen (Eds.), *Proceedings of the IEEE International Conference on Advanced Learning Technologies (ICALT 2005)* (pp. 442-446). IEEE Computer Society Press.

Loidl, S. (2006). Towards pervasive learning: WeLearn.Mobile. A CPS package viewer for handhelds. *Journal of Network and Computer Applications archive, 29*(4), 277 -293.

TeamDev (2006). JExplorer Features. *TeamDev Ltd.* Retrieved September 20, 2006, from http://www.jniwrapper.com/pages/jexplorer/overview

Mödritscher, F., García-Barrios, V. M., & Gütl, C. (2004a). Enhancement of SCORM to support adaptive e-Learning within the Scope of the Research Project AdeLE. In J. Nall and R. Robson (Eds.), *Proceedings of the World Conference on E-Learning in Corporate, Government, Healthcare, and Higher Education (E-Learn 2004)* (pp. 2499-2505).

Mödritscher, F., García-Barrios, V. M., & Gütl, C. (2004b). The past, the present and the future of adaptive e-Learning: An approach within the scope of the research project AdeLE. In M. Auer & U. Auer (Eds.), *Proceedings of the International Conference on Interactive Computer Aided Learning (ICL 2004)*.

Mödritscher, F., García-Barrios, V.M., Gütl, C., & Helic, D. (2006). The first AdeLE Prototype at a Glance. In E. Pearson & P. Bohman (Eds.), *Proceedings of the World Conference on Educational Multimedia, Hypermedia and Telecommunications (ED-MEDIA 2006)* (pp. 791-798).

Moodle (2006). *About Moodle*. Retrieved February 8, 2007, from http://docs.moodle.org/en/About_Moodle

Nickull, D. (2005). Service-oriented architecture. Whitepaper. *Adobe Systems, Inc.* 2005, Retrieved February 9, 2007, from http://www.adobe.com/enterprise/pdfs/Services_Oriented_Architecture_from_Adobe.pdf

Oblinger, D.G., & Oblinger, J.L. (Eds.). (2005). *Educating the Net Generation*. Washington, D.C.: EDUCAUSE. Retrieved October 8, 2006, from http://www.educause.edu/ir/library/pdf/pub7101.pdf

Oblinger, D.G. (2006). *Learning Spaces*. Washington, D.C.: EDUCAUSE. Retrieved October 6, 2006, from http://www.educause.edu/books/learningspaces/10569

Papazoglou, M.P. (2003). Service-oriented computing: Concepts, characteristics and directions. *Proceedings of the Fourth International Conference on Web Information Systems Engineering (WISE'03)*. Retrieved February 9, 2007, from http://csdl.computer.org/dl/proceedings/wise/2003/1999/00/19990003.pdf

Paramythis, A., & Loidl-Reisinger, S. (2004). Adaptive learning environments and e-Learning standards. *Electronic Journal on E-Learning, 2*(1), 181-194.

Park, O., & Lee, J. (2003). Adaptive instructional systems. *Educational Technology Research and Development, 2003*(25), 651-684.

Peltoniemi, M., & Vuori, E. (2004). Business ecosystem as the new approach to complex adaptive business environments. In *Proceedings of eBusiness Research Forum (eBRF 2004)*. Retrieved October 7, 2006, from http://www.tut.fi/units/tuta/tita/tip/Peltoniemi_Vuori_eBRF2004.pdf

Pitner, T.; Drasil, P. (2006). An e-Learning 2.0 Environment—Principle, technology and prototype. In K. Tochtermann, & H. Maurer (Eds.), *Proceedings of I-KNOW '06, 6th International Conference on Knowledge Management* (pp. 543-550).

Pivec, M., Pripfl, J. & Trummer, C. (2005). Adaptable e-learning by means of real-time eye-tracking. In P. Kommers & G. Richards (Eds.), *Proceedings of World Conference on Educational Multimedia, Hypermedia and Telecommunications 2005* (pp. 4037-4041). Chesapeake, VA: AACE.

Prendinger, H., & Ishizuka, M. (2005). Human physiology as a basis for designing and evaluating affective communication with life-like characters. *IEICE Transactions on Information and Systems, Special Section on Life-like Agent and its communication, E88-D*(11), 2453-2460.

Ramsay, W. & Ransley, W. (1986). A method of analysis for determining dimensions of teaching style. *Teaching and Teacher Education, 2*(1), 69-79.

Riding, R.J. (1997). On the Nature of Cognitive Style. *Educational Psychology, 17*(1-2), 29-49.

Sadat, H., & Ghorbani, A.A. (2004). On the evaluation of adaptive Web systems. In *Proceedings of Workshop on Web-based Support Systems 2004* (pp. 127-136).

Safran, C. (2006). *A concept-based information retrieval approach for user-oriented knowledge transfer*. Unpublished master's thesis, Graz University of Technology, Graz, Austria. Retrieved October 7, 2006, from http://www2.iicm.edu/cguetl/education/thesis/csafran

Safran, C., García-Barrios, V. M., & Gütl, C. (2006). A Concept-based context modelling system for the support of teaching and learning activities. In C. M. Crawford, R. Carlsen, K. McFerrin, J. Price, R. Weber, & D. A. Willis (Eds.), *Proceedings of the International Conference on Society for Information Technology and Teacher Education (SITE 2006)* (pp. 2395-2402). Chesapeake, VA: AACE.

Sommerville, I. (2006). *Software Engineering* (8th ed.). Upper Saddle River, NJ: Pearson Education.

Tannenbaum, A. & van Steen, M. (2006). *Distributed systems: Principles and paradigms* (2nd ed). Upper Saddle River, NJ: Pearson Prentice-Hall.

Teevan, J., Jones, W., & Bederson, B.B. (2006). Personal information management. *Communications of the ACM, SPECIAL ISSUE: Personal information management, 49*(1), 40-43.

Turner, M., Budgen, D., & Brereton, P. (2003). Turning software into a service. *Computer, 36*(10), 38-44.

Türker, A., Görgün, I., & Conlan, O. (2006). The challenge of content creation to facilitate personalized e-Learning experiences. *International Journal on E-Learning, 5*(1), 11-17.

W3C (2006a). Document Object Model (DOM). *World Wide Web Consortium.* Retrieved September 18, 2006, from http://www.w3.org/DOM/

W3C (2006b). Device Independence. Access to a Unified Web from Any Device in Any Context by Anyone. World Wide Web Consortium. Retrieved October 5, 2006, from http://www.w3.org/2001/di/

Wang, H., Chignell, M., & Ishizuka, M. (2006). Empathic tutoring software agents using real-time eye tracking. *Proceedings of the 2006 Symposium on Eye Tracking Research & Applications* (pp. 73-78).

Wang, G., & Fung, C.K. (2004). Architecture paradigms and their influences and impacts on component-based software systems. In *Proceedings of the 37th Annual Hawaii International Conference on System Sciences.* Retrieved February 9, 2007, from http://csdl.computer.org/comp/proceedings/hicss/2004/2056/09/205690272a.pdf

Wang, Y., & Kopsa, A. (2005). A software product line approach for handling privacy constraints in Web personalization. In *Proceedings of the UM 2005 Workshop on Privacy-Enhanced Personalization* (pp. 35-46).

Chapter II
Collaborative E-Learning System and E-Pedagogy:
Learning Resource Infrastructure for Distributed Knowledge Sharing

Toshio Okamoto
University of Electro-Communications, Japan

Toshie Ninomiya
University of Electro-Communications, Japan

Mizue Kayama
Shinshu University, Japan

Naomi Nagata
University of Electro-Communications, Japan

ABSTRACT

This chapter describes collaborative e-learning system and e-pedagogy with Learning Resource Infrastructure for distributed knowledge sharing. In the background section, we start to discuss the design of e-learning environment, collaborative learning and pedagogical framework, and pedagogical considerations of collaborative learning. Next, we introduce RAPSODY-EX that is a collaborative learning and knowledge management system, with meaning of RAPSODY-EX in learning resource infrastructure system, and knowledge market. Then the schema of RAPSODY-EX is described with these topics, agent's roles in Learning Resource Infrastructure, schema and functions of learning resource, collaborative memory, and function of RAPSODY-EX. In addition, we give examples of knowledge management in RAPSODY-EX. Finally, the standardization of collaborative technology in WG2, ISO/IEC-JTC/SC36, as a future trend, is portrayed.

INTRODUCTION

As a response to the society advance, it is necessary to construct a new learning ecology such as learning organization and learning community. To date, the need for an understanding of e-learning issues has not been met by a coherent set of principles for examining past work and plotting fruitful directions. Obviously, it would be difficult to document the many seeds sown now.

The e-learning environment is catalogued as follows (Okamoto, 2000):

- Individual learning environment with learning materials.
- Group learning/collaborative learning environment with some shared tools/applications.
- Classroom learning (lecturing).

This learning ecology has the mixed mode of either synchronous or asynchronous by using any teaching and learning contents, audio-visual devices such as video-conference and communications tools.

E-Learning is a learning, education style using information technologies. In past days, this type of learning, education was called in varied names, such as "distance learning," "distance education," "cyber learning," "virtual learning," "Web-based training (WBT)," "Web-based learning (WBL)," "online learning" and so on. Nowadays, e-learning is innovated by using the latest information technologies. For instance, WWW technology for e-learning course delivery, movie and speech compression technology for e-learning contents production and the learning technology standards (SC36, 2004), like as learning object metadata (LOM), sharable content object reference model (SCORM) and collaborative technology, for keeping interoperability of e-learning systems.

The main advantages of e-learning are, as is well known, from and to any place, at any time attributes. Often, the free education aspect also appears, although much of the offered educational software today is not free, and many educational institutions offer e-learning programs at a price. Plain, text-based course materials are not enough anymore. The very recent increases in bandwidth made more expression ways possible, images on the Internet are commonplace, sound tracks and videos are used with growing frequency, other (multi or mixed) media types evolved (animation, simulation, collaboration etc.).

Before now, based on learner modeling, adapting teaching strategies and intelligent user adaptation in intelligent tutoring system (ITS) were developed. More recently, the field of adaptive hypermedia (De Bra et al., 1999) emerged, at the crossroads of hypertext/hypermedia and user modeling. Adaptive presentation of the educational material can mean one or more of the following: providing prerequisite, additional or comparative explanations, conditional inclusion of fragments, stretch-text, providing explanation variants, reordering information, etc. Adaptive navigation support can mean one or more of the following: direct guidance, sorting of links, links annotation, link hiding, link disabling, link removal and map adaptation. Another main advantage of the Internet is that it favors collaborative work, which in turn favors learning (Dillenboug, 1999).

Moreover, e-learning finds a justification in the life-long learning concept. The recent technological changes are influencing our society, and each member of this society must acquire new knowledge all the time. Education has to be provided for all sorts of people. People who have different backgrounds, different knowledge levels and various cognitive styles are equally entitled to receive their education. An e-learning is one answer to the rigidity of the present Web-based courses and courseware.

The educational environment is changing from traditional classroom teaching ecology to the adaptive individual and collaborative learning one by development of Internet, mobile and wireless technology. Therefore, we need to develop the new pedagogy in consideration of such new technologies. Especially, our knowledge and wisdom are cultivated by interactive learning, problem solving, or building something through collaborative activities (R. Kaye, 1994). In this chapter, we would like to examine the meanings and ecology of "collaborative learning" again and explore the new technologies of communications, which evokes and enhances it.

In the advanced network society, Varieties of knowledge will be taking a form of multi-modal in education, medicine, industry and so on (Dillenbourg, 1999; Roschelle & Teasley, 1995, pp.69-97). The wide usage of educational applications and teaching or learning systems will be seemed in many educational and training institutions. However, the problem is that we need ability to grasp the essence of that knowledge. Also this knowledge should not be enclosed just in a human understanding of the world. An ability to create a new knowledge out of that understanding is sought now. The knowledge in a closed textbook will be transferred to this real world. It is important to form a live knowledge. So, this kind of learning requires collaborative and creative activities in its process, therefore we need to exploit a new learning ecology and explore e-pedagogy.

In the post-modern age, our new learning viewpoint is as follows:

1. Group modeling and collaboration for social activities.
2. Exploration-minded experimental learning.
3. Learning (urged) by asking, explaining and teaching to make a new insight.
4. Interactive diagnosis and open learning model.

BACKGROUND

The Design of E-Learning Environment

When we think modality of computerization on education, it is generally categorized as follows:

1. Self-study entity through electronic information media-based materials/courseware.
2. Learning entity with the electronic information media (e.g., computer) as learning/problem-solving/representing/knowledge-transmitting tools.
3. Learning entity about information and communication technology/social problems/others.
4. Computerizing entity of the education itself.

The relationships among those entities should be compensated mutually and an e-learning cycle is developed. The ideas here are in line with building the environment for "anybody" to learn something from "anywhere" and at "anytime" in the e-society. There are two purposes of these expansions: on one hand to enlarge the study opportunity and on another to develop people's new competence.

When people build their e-learning environment, at least three issues should be considered (Okamoto, 2000). The first one is the pedagogical goal representing the ability/knowledge as learning objectives, the second one is the subject contents and the third one is the learning modes. Among them, the learning modes are defined by seven learning environments:

1. Distance individual learning environment for the mastery learning provides courseware for knowledge/skills acquisition,

i.e., the typical e-learning course such as WBT/VOD (video on demand) systems (Hui, 2000).

2. Distance individual learning environment for the discovery learning using various search engines (VOD search and navigation mechanism).

3. Distance individual learning environment for the problem-solving learning using simulations, interactive learning environment (ILE), and so on.

4. Video conference system in the classroom environment for discussion, instructional presentation, questions-answers and tele-communications (Chen & Shin, 2001; Nieminen, 2001).

5. Collaborative learning environment for a small group/pairs using video conference, some kinds of communication tools, various applications accompanied with screen shared viewer and learning log tracking mechanism.

6. Collaborative simulation learning environment for different learners perform, different functions in team-work learning pattern, and as such to form a special skill in the learner's own domain (e.g., a collaborative activity within the jet plane's cockpit).

7. Linkage/coordination among different organizations and/or areas (e.g., access online school's library, online museum, etc.).

In the establishment of e-learning environments, the most important idea is to start by defining the instructional goal, and then classifying of learning contents which is best equipped to build the learning environment. Moreover, the research on the method is required to build the asynchronous collaborative learning contents (Dryden &Vos, 2001). Further research directions should be put on the study of the learning environment with the virtues of individualized learning and collaborative learning as well. In this case, the transmission of the real images and voice data is required. The fundamental environment components for e-learning systems include the whole information system related to e-learning environments. It consists of several management functions such as curriculum/learning-materials management, learners' profile/log-data management, learning supporting as the core framework, learning management system (LMS) and learning contents management system (LCMS). In order to construct those educational management systems, we need, technologically. several data/file-processing modules such as distributed file system, synchronous data communications and so on. If any applications and tools related to e-learning can be plugged in the core framework, we would build an integrated e-learning environment where learners can share/operate these software/data in real time. In addition, the total management system of e-learning is required for executing a real educational project/practice, which means research project management, learning schedule management, courseware developing and so on.

Collaborative Learning and Pedagogical Framework

In this chapter, we examine the GRID technology (Pankratius & Vossen, 2003a; Pankratius & Vossen, 2003b; The United Kingdom Government, 1993) as the knowledge management for supporting collaborative learning. RAPSODY-EX, we have developed, is a network-based distributed learning environment organized as a self/group learning platform. This system can effectively support collaborative learning activities in asynchronous/synchronous learning mode. The mixed distributed learning environment is utilized as a new learning ecology, where individual learning, collaborative learning and video conference are performed on the multimedia communication network. In this mixed distributed learning environment, people can arrange, modify and integrate educational information for the purpose of investigating, decision making, planning, problem solving, building knowledge and so on. Various information in the educational context is referred and reused as knowledge which oneself and others can practically utilize. We aim at constructing the growing digital portfolio database for collaborative learning knowledge management in Internet environment. In addition, we explore the grid technology of activating human-interactivity for knowledge mining/discovering.

Furthermore, this concept is being extended toward knowledge grid, grid intelligence, distributed artificial intelligence for effective knowledge communication, knowledge building and management. We investigate the mechanism of transmission and management of knowledge for the development of the knowledge community in the learning space, within the educational context. There are some trials to collect collaborative learning designs and reuse them in the context of knowledge grid (M.L Bote-Lorenza et al., 2004).

In this chapter, we also discuss the technologies for the knowledge representation/management to support collaborative learning in consideration of GRID technology under the context of e-learning. Here, the concept of distributed learning means ecological situation with the various usages of information technologies from remote sites in any time in order to provide learning opportunities widely. Some examples of distributed learning technologies include the World Wide Web, e-mail, video conferencing, groupware, simulations and instructional software. A distributed learning environment facilitates a learner-centered educational paradigm and promotes active learning. Distributed learning is a learning type where individual learning and collaborative learning are conducted through the multimedia communication network. In this environment, learners and teachers can arrange and integrate the learning information in order to improve their learning/teaching activities. The significant information in this educational context should be referred and reused as knowledge utilized by all of participants. We aim at constructing the incremental digital portfolio based on the agent technology.

Pedagogical Considerations of Collaborative Learning

In consideration of the past researches, Okamoto et al. (2000) pointed out that collaborative learning should emphasize:

1. Process/situated context.
2. Individual learning achievement such as knowledge acquisition, skill formation and concept formation, learning set.
3. Versatile cognition for both of holistic and serialistic thinking schema.
4. Understandings of objective relationship among self/you/he or she.
5. Effects of observation learning (reflection/self-monitoring).

This is further illustrated in Table 1.

Table 1. Emphases of collaborative learning

Activity-cognitive level	Activity-social level
+ Discussing	+ Observing/Suggesting
+ Planning/Designing	+ Role-taking/Cooperating
+ Data/Idea sharing	+ Coordinating/Controlling
+ Evaluating/Finding solution	+ Social interacting
+ Building knowledge	+ Facilitating/Supervising

Table 2. The dimensions on features of collaborative learning

Learning Structure	Highly structured	⇔	Non structured
Teacher Control	Highly	⇔	Low
Moderation	External	⇔	Internal
Motivation	External	⇔	Internal
Learning Content	Curriculum based	⇔	Learner based
Assessment	By teacher	⇔	By learner

Individual learning mode may be sometime embedded in the process of collaborative learning under some pedagogical reason in schools and vice versa. Table 2 shows the dimensions on features of collaborative learning. In general, we can divide the activities on collaborative learning into two classes.

Collaborative learning is a participant's initiative learning form that has been more and more stressed out with the paradigm shift from the teaching side to the learning side in the current learning ecology. The objectives of collaborative learning are the effective/efficient group activity and the collaborative mutual interdependence-relations within the group(s). In collaborative learning, each learner is submitted a sub-task and s/he is expected to accomplish it. As the result, the group goal and each learner's learning goal would be achieved.

Distributed collaborative learning is a type of collaborative learning that can take place in the Internet environment (e.g., e-learning environment) with multiple learners geographically far from one another (O'Malley, 1994). Geographically a distanced situation can mean remote or far physically, but this also covers cases where direct interaction and dialogue is not possible among participants due to other reasons. Distributed collaborative learning support is a research domain that explores how to support the collaboration of multiple learners in cooperative curriculum activities. This type of learning is called computer supported collaborative learning (CSCL). CSCL focuses not on efficient groups working but deep and comprehensive understanding with self reflecting/monitoring (Dillenboug, 1999). The ordinary CSCL-management software provides two types of activity space: a private working space and a collaborative working space, where the learners can exchange information in synchronous/asynchronous manners. Many researches are discussing these two types of activity space, the information exchange types that exist and those that are necessary (Synnes et al., 1999).

Based on these activities, the resources required in collaborative learning environment are as follows:

1. Technologically mediated dialogue channel.
2. Shared workplace for a group.
3. Personal workplace.
4. Learning materials/ learning tools.
5. Analyzing tools of data/information.
6. Repository/Memory for data/information revealed in collaborative learning.
7. Reference channel for the collaborative repository.
8. Modeling tools for monitoring the process of collaborative learning, and so forth.

This system can store all learning activities log in the digital portfolio holder and participants can review those data in order to diagnose/evalu-

Figure 1. The model of collaborative learning

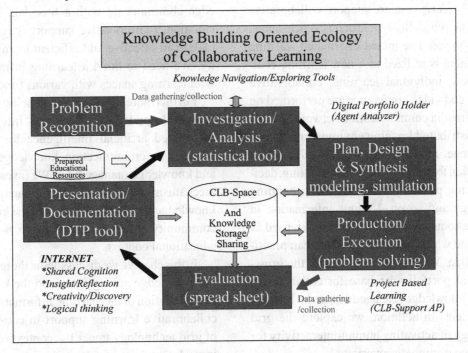

ate their achievements. Also, the participants can refer to the flow/stock of knowledge for an arbitrary situation of collaborative learning. Figure 1 shows the e-pedagogical model as for knowledge building through net-based collaborative learning. There are six stages which are: (1) problem recognition, (2) investigating & analysis, (3) plan & design, (4) production & execution, (5) evaluation, and (6) presentation documentation through collaborative working with the shared digital resources. In some sense, this model reveals knowledge building oriented ecology for evolution of participants and their knowledge. The repository-module at the center of Figure 1 can work to analyze and manage knowledge that each of participants revealed/found in the process of collaborative learning. We discuss the details about this function in the following chapters with RAPSODY-EX as collaborative learning and knowledge management system.

RAPSODY-EX: COLLABORATIVE LEANING AND KNOWLEDGE MANAGEMENT SYSTEM

Meanings of RAPSODY-EX in Learning Resource Infrastructure System

Here, the processing described in the previous section is considered as a process of the knowledge management in the learning context. Knowledge management is defined as follows (Davenport, 1997). The knowledge management is "the systematic process of finding, selecting, organizing, distilling and presenting information in a way that improves an employee's comprehension in a specific area of interest."

In this chapter, we examine the grid technology as the knowledge management for supporting collaborative learning. RAPSODY-EX is a distributed learning support environment organized as a learning infrastructure. RAPSODY-EX can effectively carry out to support collaborative learning activities in asynchronous/synchronous learning mode. The mixed distributed learning environment is utilized as a new learning ecology, where individual learning, collaborative learning and video conference are performed on the multimedia communication network. In this mixed distributed learning environment, people can arrange, modify and integrate educational information for the purpose of investigating, decision making, planning, problem solving, building knowledge and so on. Various information in the educational context is referred and reused as knowledge which oneself and others can practically utilize. We aim at constructing the growing digital portfolio database for collaborative learning knowledge management in the Internet environment. In addition, we explore the grid technology of activating human-interactivity for knowledge mining/discovering.

The development of the recent information communication technology is remarkable. As an effect of this, the education environment is being modified to a new environment that differs qualitatively from the previous one (Kuhn, 1962). The new education environment contains not only computer but also communication infrastructures such as the information communication network represented by the Internet (Cumming et al., 1998; Elliot, 1993). We call this learning environment the Internet learning space. Information is transmitted for the learner in this learning space from the external space. The information quantity that is available to the learner is enormous. However, there is a limit to the information quantity, which the learner can process. The imbalance of this information processing quantity is a peculiar phenomenon in postmodern ages. Secondary phenomena are also triggered by this problem. These phenomena become factors which inhibit the sound transmission of knowledge and the progress of learning (McNeil et al., 1998; Chan et al., 1997). In asynchronous learning, the trans-

former of knowledge and the transferee of knowledge communicate with a time lag. In such a situation, more positive support is required to realize an effective and efficient learning activity. We need to build a learning infrastructure with learning spaces with various functions.

Furthermore, this concept is being extended toward knowledge grid, grid intelligence, distributed artificial intelligence for effective knowledge communication, knowledge building and knowledge management. We investigate the mechanism of transmission and management of knowledge for the development of the knowledge community in the learning space, within the educational context.

In this chapter, we discuss about the technology the knowledge management and the knowledge representation of the learning information for the collaborative learning support in consideration of grid technology under the context of e-learning. The purpose of this study is to support the learning activity in the Internet learning space. RAPSODY-EX is a distributed learning support environment organized as a learning infrastructure (Okamoto et al., 2000). RAPSODY-EX can effectively carry out collaborative learning support in asynchronous/synchronous learning mode. Distributed learning means using a wide range of information technologies to provide learning opportunities beyond the bounds of the traditional classroom. Some examples of distributed learning technologies include the World Wide Web, e-mail, video conferencing, groupware, simulations and instructional software. A distributed learning environment facilitates a learner-centered educational paradigm and promotes active learning. Distributed learning is a learning style where individual learning and collaborative learning are carried out on the multimedia communication network. In this environment, arrangement and integration of the learning information are attempted to support the decision making of learners and mediators. Various information in the educational context is referred and reused as knowledge which oneself and others can practically utilize. We aim at the construction of a growing digital portfolio based on the agent technology. In addition, the architecture of the learning environment including such a database is researched.

Knowledge Market

Here, we propose the functions of learning resource infrastructure as knowledge management between RAPSODY-EX and collaborative learning environment. It guarantees the mutual interactivity among learners and activates knowledge building. In some sense, grid means the role of exchanging knowledge or artifacts in a marketplace that can stock the various kind of information. At the same time, learners need the value of sense with sharing and re-using manners. We have developed grid technology as knowledge mining in collaborative learning process. Figure 2 shows the meaning of learning resource infrastructure which plays roles of the marketplace for knowledge transmission,

transformation and exchange. Moreover, the function of learning resource infrastructure is in charge of bringing about building and discovering knowledge through assimilation/accommodation, differentiating/integrating occurred in collaborative learning.

The knowledge management in educational context is defined as follows: "the systematic process of finding, selecting, organizing, distilling and presenting information in a way that improves a learner's comprehension and/or ability to fulfill his/her current learning objectives." Our system aims to support participants' activities in the C (combination of knowledge) phase (Nonoka, 1995).

Moreover, it affects not only the process of knowledge conversion from the C phase to the I (internalization of knowledge) phase, but also from the E (externalization of knowledge) phase to the C phase. The information of learning entity contains the expressed knowledge by learners. This overt knowledge can be represented by

Figure 2. The scheme and function of learning resource infrastructure

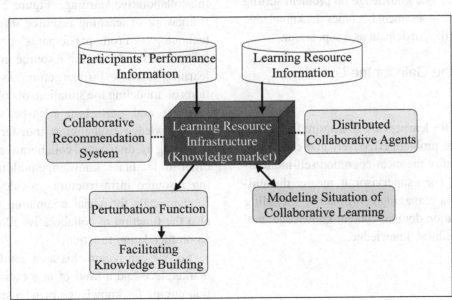

natural language as verbal information. So, we can regard this knowledge as one that would be elicited from the learner's tacit knowledge.

In this situation, we have to consider the following questions.

Who Engages in Knowledge Management?

We focus on the persons who play a role of supervising each learner in the group learning process, including "turn taking roles". Each learner's task is to acquire the ability/skill for problem solving. On the other hand, the supervisor's tasks are to support acquisition of ability/skill for each learner and support learners' problem solving activities. A supervisor means a facilitator/tutor/coach/organizer etc.

What are the Knowledge Resources in the Learning Group?

Learners themselves become the knowledge resources for the effective and efficient problem solving in collaborative learning world. Moreover, every learner has the opportunity to become a supervisor. The knowledge on problem setting and activity assessment becomes the knowledge source for the participant as a supervisor.

What is the Gain for the Learning Group?

The gains for learners are to acquire the ability to solve the problem effectively and efficiently, and to acquire the meta-cognition/self-monitoring ability. For a supervisor, it means the ability of meta-managing/coordinating including the acquisition domain content-knowledge and meta-procedural knowledge.

How are the Knowledge Resources Utilized to Guarantee the Expected Gain for the Learning Group?

By eliciting/mining the common and valuable knowledge in the collaborative memory along with learning context, we try to manage the knowledge in this memory. By creating the collaborative portfolio between individual and group learning, we have developed the relational knowledge space based on the knowledge acquired by each learner. This method means knowledge extraction (summarizing the process of problem solving) from learning history and dialogue-log by applying text/data mining technology. We measure the distance between the expected goal and the present status.

Learning Recourse Infrastructure

Agent's Roles in Learning Resource Infrastructure

Our concept of learning resource grid means the knowledge market with exchanging, re-organizing and sharing knowledge generated during e-learning/collaborative learning. Figure 2 shows the framework of learning resource infrastructure technology. From participants' performance information and learning resource information, learning resource infrastructure has the functions of modeling the situation of collaborative learning and perturbing a learner's behavior for knowledge exchanging, transforming and acquiring by distributed collaborative agents in order to facilitate knowledge building. Learning resource infrastructure provides adhesive fundamentals for social computing which has also the function of collaborative filtering with recommendation function.

So, we can regard this as a conductor in a marketplace and a kind of negotiation-circulation engine for knowledge management. Every agent is embedded in every learning resource infrastructure in Internet space. Each agent tries to communicate, exchange need-information among learning resource infrastructure. In some cases, plural agents behave collaboratively or competitively for taking well knowledge negotiation along with participants' requirement. Therefore, the agent's roles become to be quite important within/among learning resource infrastructures in our system .We set up two kinds of agent who are (1) learning resource grid agent, (2) knowledge -messenger agent for investigation, collaboration and whole-watching in RAPSODY-EX.

Schema and Functions of Learning Resource

Learning resource plays roles of encouraging collaborative learning. Figure 2 shows the framework of learning resource technology. From participants' performance information and learning resource information, learning resource has the functions of modeling the situation of collaborative learning and perturbing a learner's behavior for knowledge exchanging, transforming and acquiring by distributed collaborative agents in order to facilitate knowledge building. Learning resource provides adhesive fundamentals for social computing which has also been the function of collaborative filtering with recommendation function.

So, we can regard this as a conductor in a marketplace and a kind of negotiation-circulation engine for knowledge management. Every agent is embedded in every learning resource in Internet space, each agent tries to communicate, exchange need-information among learning resource. In some cases, plural agents behave collaboratively or competitively for taking well knowledge negotiation along with participants' requirement. Therefore, the agent's roles become to be quite important within/among learning resources in our system. We set up two kinds of agent who are 1) learning resource agent, 2) knowledge-messenger

agent for investigation, collaboration and whole-watching in RAPSODY-EX.

Collaborative Memory

In the collaborative memory (CM), information generation/arrangement/housing/reference/visualization are the management processes of expressive knowledge in the learning space. RAPSODY-EX is a learning environment, which possesses a knowledge management mechanism. In this environment, (1) the review of the learning process, (2) the summarization of the problem solving process and (3) the reference of other learners' problem solving method are realized in the learning space. Learning information is expressed by a unified format. Then, that information is accumulated in the CM. This information becomes the reference object of the learner. The generation and the management of the information on the learning performance and the portfolio of the learner and group are main objects of the knowledge management. In this study, learning information is obtained from the application tools for the CL. It is necessary to control the learning record, the reference log of the others' learning information and the log of problem solving and learning progress. To realize this control not only techniques based on symbolic knowledge processing approach, but also techniques based on sub-symbolic knowledge processing approach are used.

The CM consists of two layers. One is the information storage layer and the other one is the management layer of the stored information. At the information storage layer, four kinds of information are mainly processes:

1.   Learning information.
2.   Information on the learner.
3.   Information on the setting of the learning environment.
4.   Information on the learning result.

Figure 3. Communication scheme in the RAPSODY-EX

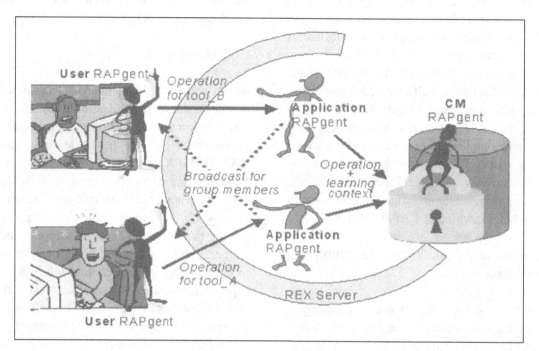

At the information management layer, the reference, arrangement, and integration of learning information are processed. The individual learner profile information is composed of information following the IEEE Profile information guidelines (IEEE, 2000). The group information is expressed by the expansion of the individual learner profile information. The conversion from the learning log data to learning information is necessary to develop this profile database. The information, which should apply in learning information, is as follows:

1. Information and/or data on its learning context and/or learning situation.
2. Information about the sender and the sender of the information.
3. Significance and/or outline in the educational context.
4. Information on the relation structure of the learning information.

5. Reference pointer to individual learner and group who proposed or produced the information.
6. Relation with other material.

By adding above information, the learning information is arranged into a unique form. If a learner requires some information related to his/her current learning, RAPSODY-EX shows the (estimated) desired information to the learner. Figure 3 shows a communication scheme in the RAPSODY-EX. Three types of agents exists in the RAPSODY-EX. These agents perform each mission with user (user-RAPgent), each CL tool (application-RAPgent) and the CM in RAPSO-DY-EX server (CM-RAPgent). Communication protocol between RAPgents is defined based on the FIPA ACL communicative act. The missions of each RAPgent are to transform information adaptively to create group portfolio, to maintain learning contexts in the group member and to let refer information in CM. To realize the knowledge management in RAPSODY-EX, application-RAPgents develop some learning contexts by using learning information in the CM. Then they refer the suitable learning information for the collaborative tool/application.

Functions of RAPSODY-EX

In order to maintain group activities, the smooth transmission of knowledge among group members should be guaranteed in the learning community. By sharing and reusing valuable knowledge, we can suppose that group activities would become productive and cooperative much more.

RAPSODY-EX can support to transmit knowledge in the learner group and promote the learning activities. It is indispensable that this system has the following functions:

1.   Function which maintains learning information for the individual learner and the group.
2.   Function which manages learning information of the learner for mediation.

The learner and group information are produced from the learning space. This information will be stored in the collaborative memory. This information is defined as learning information. We also define the method of information management in the collaborative memory and mention its structure.

Figure 4 shows the simple mechanism to manage learning information developed in this study. RAPSODY-EX has three layers, (1) learning environment producing layer, (2) learning information management layer and (3) storage layer. Learning environment producing layer is

Figure 4. The mechanism of the RAPSODY-EX

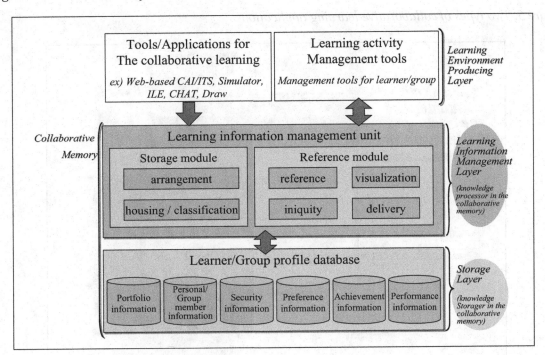

a module that offers the learning environment. Learning information management layer and storage layer work as collaborative memory that manages various information/data produced in the learning environment. In learning environment producing layer, there are two types of function. One is learning activity management tools, which has a function for monitoring the process of learning progress. Another is tools/applications for the collaborative learning which has a function for incorporating tools/applications into collaborative learning platform. The former function works to control the learning history/record of individual learner and progress of the collaborative group learning. The latter function works to prepare the environment of the space/workplace for collaborative synchronous/asynchronous learning. Collaborative memory has two modules. One is reference module, which is knowledge processing function, and another is storage module, which is

knowledge storage function. In the former, after inputting learning information, it is reformed to the defined form. In the latter, it adds the formatted information to some attributes related to the content. In collaborative memory, the above all information processing is done.

Examples of Knowledge Management

Figure 5 shows the window images of the collaborative applications on RAPSODY-EX. Two types of applications are loaded. One is a chat tool for the text communication among the group member. Another application is a collaborative simulator. Each application has each application-RAPgent. By the functions of these RAPgents, learning history data at this session is stored in the CM and formulates a set of the group portfolio.

Figure 5. Two types of collaborative learning applications

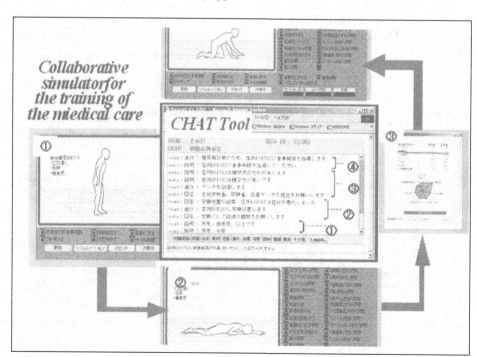

Figure 6. Examples of knowledge management in RAPSODY-EXfuture Trend

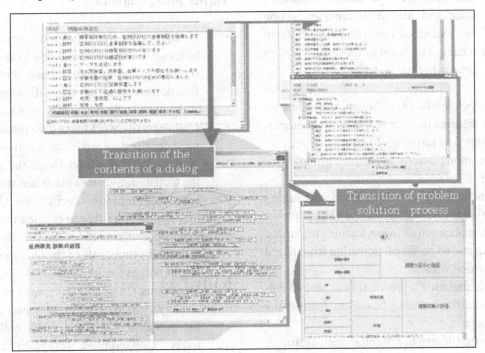

The examples of knowledge management at this session are shown in the Figure 6. A log data of this dialog is visualized by three kinds of methods. These results are produced by three application RAPgents.

The first method is visualization of the dialog structure. The dialog layers are reasoned based on the dialog proceeding model (Inaba & Okamoto, 1997) and the utterance intention information that were given to the dialog log. The result is shown as tree structure.

The second method is visualization of transition of the contents of a dialog. An appearance of the important term that is in a dialog is searched for using the term dictionary about the current discussion/learning domain (Chiku et al., 2001). This result and the timing connection of each utterance are considered to detect a transition of the contents of a dialog. The result is shown as a graph structure.

The third method is visualization of transition of problem solution process. One utterance can

be unified as meaningless unit for the problem solving process from the first and the second processing result and an educational mentor's expertise/educational intentions. The result re-constituted as problem solution process is shown with the structure that imitated the dendrogram.

As one future trend, we would like to introduce the systematic framework of collaborative technologies and e-pedagogical issues in reference to WG2 (collaborative technology) activities in SC36 (learning technology), ISO/IEC-JTC1 (ISO/IEC JTC1 SC36 WG2, http://collab-tech.jtc1sc36.org/)

In WG2, the following three items have been discussed:

- Collaborative workplace.
- Learner to learner interaction scheme.
- Agent to agent architecture.

At the moment, the two projects of "collaborative workplace" and "learner to learner interaction scheme" are examined under the experts from many countries. The goals of those activities in order to standardize are as follows:

1. Independent on any pedagogical/psychological theories in order to warranty interoperability and re-using of learning objects.
2. Common platform to enhance group learning.
3. Functions of plug-in & data model of learning log-data in order to share and use/operate any application software, learning resources/data and so on for participating from plural learning sites.
4. Accumulating a practical case base of collaborative learning based on instructor's rationale.
5. General description of collaborative learning entity as meta-data.

Collaborative Workplace

The purpose of this standard is to contribute the promotion of collaborative learning with e-learning. This standard defines:

1. The collaborative workplace data model for grouping of the learners, and for defining the using resources shared by group.
2. The collaborative workplace log data model for interoperates between one collaborative workplace and another collaborative workplace.

There is a risk of improper access and misuse of personal and private data facilitated by use of the collaborative workplace log data model. It is the responsibility of the implementer to ensure proper use of a participant identifier.

Terms and Definitions

- **Collaborative workplace:** Abstract concept to group with participants and to define resources shared by a group, and to offer the function to record the information regarding event in the collaborative workplace.
- **Collaborative workplace data model:** This provides the data model for a collaborative workplace. This model forms the core of the Collaborative workplace and should be taken as a minimum specification. Users of this standard are free to provide their own extensions. This defines the function, data type, and syntax rule of the data model for a collaborative workplace.
- **Functions:** "Collaborative workplace" is used by a group of two or more participants for processing multiple tasks collaboratively. "Collaborative workplace" may be implemented by a management system, for example a learning management system (LMS). The management system is one that supports collaboration, and also tools, and collaboration tools that enables collaborative work.

Syntax Rules

- The content of "collaborative_workplace_id" identifies each "collaborative workplace" implemented in a management system.
- The content of "collaborative_workplace_name" is the alias for "collaborative_workplace_id." It is optional.
- The content of "group_id" identifies the corresponding group of participants in a management system.
- The content of "shared_resource_id" identifies the shared resource in a management system.

- The content of "location" identifies the resource location. For example, URL.
- The content of "application" identifies the type of application tool that will execute the shared resource. For example, chat, Word, SCORM.
- The content of "collaborative_workplace_log_set_id" identifies the set of collaborative workplace log in a management system.

Learner to Learner Interaction Scheme

This international standard provides a data model for the information that will be given to a learning support system for a collaborative learning to setup the learning space where learners interact with one another. The whole information consists of information on what resources the learners can use in that learning space and how they interact with those resources and/or other learners. The information also contains characteristics about the collaborative learning itself, such as, objectives, results learners required, learning activities, evaluation methods as additional information, for the sake of attaching a rationale to the setup information, providing a search clue, and etc. We call such information "learner to learner interaction scheme" since it expresses the characteristics about the learning space where learners interact. This international standard is applicable to on-line learning, education, and training involving multiple learners learning in groups.

Collaborative Learning Support System

The standard "learner to learner interaction scheme" assumes a collaborative learning support system that accepts data for the specification of learning environment. There are several relationships between a collaborative learning support system and a learning management system. In some cases, a collaborative learning support system may be an application launched by a learning management system and in other cases it may be embedded into a learning management system.

Group Characteristic Data and Roles

Any data, which characterize a group for the purpose of informing a collaborative learning support system with the way the participants, are managed. The example of group characteristic data may be a list of roles with the information about their privilege to learning resources, a set of possible relations among participants, the group organization method such as 'jigsaw group' which ensures the group is composed of different skill participants, and so forth.

There may be several methods to express such a group characteristic data, for example, classification of several group kinds, or some analytic methods that declares "what roles are in the group?" An example of the group kind in a classification is "jigsaw group" which is a group of participants of different skills. In this standard, we provide a representation method called "interaction graph" as a one of analytic methods. It represents the group characteristic data as a pair of roles in the group and the relations between the roles. A signature to participants expresses their character in the learning. Sometimes, it holds information about the privilege to learning resources. Examples are "learner," "teacher," "helper," and so forth.

Target Collaborative Learning Systems

We concentrate on IT-based collaborative learning shown in Figure 1. In the figure, two or more participants in a group learn collaboratively communicating through their computers connected to a network. On the network, a "collaborative learning environment," that is, virtual shared area where learners can cooperate, is provided. In the learning, usually, some assignments such as "to solve a certain problem collaboratively" are given to the group. The participants may have roles. Sometimes, participants are assigned different roles perform individual goals, for example, "presenter" and "audience," "salesman" and "customer" in a learning that uses role-playing technique. Sometimes the roles are used to control the participants' access right to resources.

CONCLUSION

In this chapter, we discussed collaborative e-learning system and e-pedagogy, especially about the design of e-learning environment, and pedagogical framework and considerations. Based on these discussions, we developed a collaborative learning and knowledge management system. The purpose of our research is to support the learning activity in the Internet learning space. We examine the knowledge management and the knowledge representation of the learning information for the collaborative learning support.

RAPSODY-EX is an integrated distributed learning environment and has various functions for supporting tools/applications for the collaborative learning.

In learning resource infrastructure, it is important to connect various information among learners' profiles, log-data in learning process and learning resources for the purpose of sharing with interoperability of applications/tools used in collaborative learning process. As one of current big issues in e-learning world, the concept and technology of learning resource is proposed in order to build the learning environment for the mutual and sharable utilization of learning resources.

We would like to clear its framework and discuss the relationship between new e-pedagogy and learning resource infrastructure from collaborative learning point of view. We suppose that learning resource infrastructure is to drive distributed computing and seamless accessibility for learning resources and communication activities with interoperability and knowledge sharing.

Under this environment, we need to establish new e-pedagogy in order to create the effective and significant systems for the future education.

Finally, we expect standardization of the infrastructure for collaborative learning environment in order to share data, materials, tools and applications related to the events of collaborative learning. The standardization of e-learning technologies is indispensable to diffuse the contents, platforms, collaborative tools and applications and so on to users in conditions of easy usage and low cost. Then, we introduced the systematic framework of collaborative technologies and e-pedagogical issues in reference to WG2 (collaborative technology) activities in SC36 (learning technology), ISO/IEC-JTC1 as a future trend. It would be useful to have these points of view when discussing and developing a collaborative learning system and new e-pedagogy.

REFERENCES

Bote-Lorenzo, M. L., et al. (2004). Towards reusability and tailorability in collaborative learning systems using IMS-LD and grid services. *International Journal on Advanced Technology for Learning, 1*(3), 129-138.

Chan, T. et al. (1997). *Global Education ON the Net*. Berlin: Springer-Verlag.

Chen, N. & Shin, Y. (2001). Stream-based lecturing system and its instructional design. In *Proceedings of International Conference of Advanced Learning Technologies* (pp. 94-95).

Chiku, M. et al. (2001). A dialog visualization tool Gijiroku, *Proceedings of the 62nd Annual Conference of the Information Processing Society of Japan* (pp. 241-244).

Cumming, G., Okamoto T. & Gomes, L. (1998). *Advanced research in computers in education*. Amsterdam: IOS Press.

Davenport, T. (1997). *Working knowledge.* Boston: Harvard Business School Press.

De Bra, P., Brusilovsky, P. & Houben, G.J. (1999). Adaptive hypermedia: From systems to framework. *ACM Computing Surveys, 31*(4).

Dillenboug, P. (1999). *Collaborative learning, cognitive and computational approaches.* Amsterdam: Pergamon Press.

Dryden, G. & Vos, J. (2001). *The learning revolution.* London: Network Educational Press Ltd.

Elliott, J. (1993). What have we learned from action research in school-based evaluation. *Educational Action Research, 1*(1), 175-186.

Hui, S. (2000). *Video-On-Demand in Education.* Retrieved from http://www.cityu.edu.hk/~ccncom/net14/vod2.htm

IEEE, (2000). Draft Standard for Learning Technology—Public and Private Information (PAPI) for Learner. *IEEE P1484.2/D6.* Retrieved from http://ltsc.ieee.org/

Inaba, A. & Okamoto, T. (1997). Negotiation process model for intelligent discussion coordinating system on CSCL environment. In *Proceedings of the AIED 97* (pp. 175-182).

ISO-IEC JTC1 SC36. (2004). *SC36 HomePage.* Retrieved from http://jtc1sc36.org/

Kaye, R. (1994). Computer supported collaborative learning in a multi-media distance education environment. In C.E. O'Malley (Ed.), *Computer Supported Collaborative Learning* (pp. 125-143). Berlin: Springer-Verlag.

Kuhn, T. (1962). *The structure of scientific revolutions.* University of Chicago Press.

McNeil, S., Price, J.D., Boger-Mehall, S., Robin, B. & Willis, J. (Eds.), *Technology and Teacher Education Annual 1998.* Charlottesville, VA: Association for the Advancement of Computing in Education.

Nieminen, P. (2001). Video lecturing for international students. In *Proceedings of International PEG Conference* (pp. 162-168).

Nonoka, I. (1995). *The knowledge-creating company.* Oxford University Press.

Okamoto, T. (2000). A distance ecological model to support self/collaborative-learning via Internet. In *Proceedings of the International Conference of Computer on Education 2000* (pp. 795-799).

Okamoto, T., Cristea, A.I. & Kayama, M. (2000). Towards intelligent media-oriented distance learning and education environments. In *Proceedings of the International Conference of Computer on Education 2000* (pp. 61-72).

O'Malley, C. (Ed.). (1994). Computer supported collaborative learning. *NATO ASI series.* F-128. Berlin: Springer-Verlag.

Pankratius, V. & Vossen, G. (2003a). Towards e-learning resource infrastructures: Using grid computing in electronic learning. *Technical Report* 98. Dept. of Information Systems, University of Muenster.

Pankratius, V. & Vossen, G. (2003b). Towards the utilization of grid computing in e-learning. In J. C. Cunha & O. F. Rana (Eds.), *Grid computing: Software environments and Tools.* Springer Verlag.

Roschelle, J. & Teasley, S.D. (1995). The construction of shared knowledge in collaborative problem solving, In C.E. O'Malley (Ed.), *Computer-Supported Collaborative Learning* (pp. 69-97). Berlin: Springer-Verlag.

Synnes, K., Parnes, P., Widen, J. & Schefstroem, D. (1999). Student 2000: Net-based learning for the next millennium. In *Proceedings of the World Conference on the WWW and Internet 1999* (pp. 1031-1036).

The United Kingdom Government (1993). *Connecting the learning society.* The United Kingdom Government's consultation paper.

Chapter III
Service–Based Grid Architectures to Support the Virtualization of Learning Technology Systems

Gerard Gleeson
Dublin City University, Ireland

Claus Pahl
Dublin City University, Ireland

ABSTRACT

E-Learning has been a topic of increasing interest in recent years, due mainly to the fact that content and tool support can now be offered at a widely affordable level. As a result, many e-learning platforms and systems have been developed. Client-server, peer-to-peer and recently Web services architectures often form the basis. Drawbacks of these architectures are often their limitations in terms of scalability and the availability and distribution of resources. This chapter investigates grid architectures in the context of e-learning as a proposed answer for this problem. The principles and technologies of grid architectures are discussed and illustrated using learning technology scenarios and systems.

INTRODUCTION

Many organizations have embraced e-learning as the answer to the need to constantly educate and train students and employees. E-learning offers a solution to this dilemma by making courses and content available when and where needed. These organizations attempt to find solutions in order to implement e-learning services by using e-learning portals, virtual classrooms, Web applications and many others technologies. Globalization is one factor that requires organizations to address learning and training in heterogeneous environments, crossing language, culture, and technology boundaries. Education providers such as universities are recently also under pressure to collaborate on an international level. The types of e-learning solutions that meet these needs arising from these trends require flexible architectural platforms.

Current e-learning solutions for distributed learning and training are often based on client-server or peer-to-peer architectures, recently more and more involving the Web services platform. Drawbacks of these architectures are often their limitations in terms of scalability of the system architecture and the availability and distribution of shared resources in federated, heterogeneous systems (Pankratius & Vossen, 2003). This chapter investigates grid architectures in the context of e-learning as a proposed answer for this problem. In grid computing, computing becomes pervasive and individual users and applications access resources with little or no knowledge of where those resources are located or what the underlying platform is. Its key values lie in the underlying distributed computing infrastructure technologies in support of cross-organizational application and resource sharing. Virtualization across technologies, platforms, and organizations is the central idea behind grid computing (Foster, Kesselman, & Tuecke, 2001). Grid architectures and grid computing provide benefits addressing the shortcoming of current architectural solutions in this context.

This chapter investigates the use of grid computing and grid architectures in the context of e-learning. It focuses on the implementation of grids from using platform-specific architectures, in particular the adaptation of grids to service-oriented architectures based on Web services. The objectives are:

- To address the developers of infrastructure technologies, who need an understanding

of the underlying platform of e-learning applications, ranging from Web services at the bottom to grid toolkits at the highest platform layer.

- To address developers of learning solutions, who need an understanding of how e-learning scenarios are mapped onto supporting architectures (i.e., implementing these scenarios within the capabilities and constraints of the platform).

We discuss the specific benefits, but also difficulties, of using Web services as the underlying distribution platform technology for e-learning grids, having in particular the non-experts in mind as an audience. Understanding the platform infrastructure on which grid applications run is essential for anyone attempting to implement such a system. A number of learning and training scenarios, stemming from the outlined needs of globalized learning and training, are discussed in terms of their implementation using grid technology.

We present three scenarios illustrating the benefits of grid-based learning technology systems:

- We present the grid-based learning object repository infrastructure (GLORIS) system prototype in our first scenario on distributed resource sharing to illustrate the grid architecture implications for learning technology systems. GLORIS is a broker component that connects content management, learning object repository and delivery components of a learning technology system.

- The second scenario illustrates distributed execution of learning activities using a virtual lab system for illustration. The grid architecture allows the lab resources to be used interactively by geographically distributed learners.

- The third scenario addresses distributed collaboration and analyses. Grid architectures can also provide support for collaborating distributed teams of learners that compile results, which are processed remotely.

The organization of the chapter is as follows. The next section provides a first overview of learning technology systems and their architectures, addressing classical and grid architectures. We give a detailed explanation of grid architectures and underlying service technologies in the following section. We then review three learning scenarios and suitable grid architectures for their implementation. We also evaluate e-learning grid applications overall, summarizing their benefits, but also shortcomings, and discuss some related work there. Finally, we end with some conclusions.

ARCHITECTURES FOR LEARNING TECHNOLOGY SYSTEMS

Learning and training in globally distributed and collaborative heterogeneous environments requires adequate architectures. Current solutions and the potential of grid architecture shall briefly be discussed.

Figure 1. Overall LTS architecture

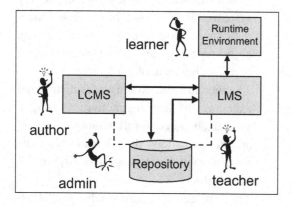

Architectures and Learning Objects for Learning Technology Systems

A general consensus exists regarding the roles played by participants in a learning environment as well as the core functionality of modern e-learning systems, see Figure 1. The main players in learning technology systems are the learners and authors; others include teachers and administrators. Authors create content which is stored under the control of a learning content management system (LCMS), typically in a database. Existing content can be exchanged with other systems. A learner management system (LMS) is under the control of an administrator; it interacts with a runtime management environment which is used by learners. These three components—LCMS, content repository, LMS—can be logically and physically distributed, i.e. installed on distinct machines and provided by different vendors or content suppliers. In order to make such a distribution feasible, standards try to ensure plug and play compatibility (IMS, 2001). SCORM (ADL, 2004), for instance, standardizes content packages and runtime environment functionality. The Web services standards (Alonso et al., 2004) such as WSDL and SOAP provide a service invocation platform for the distributed environment that would allow LCMS, repository and LMS to interact.

Content consumed by learners and created by authors is commonly handled, stored and exchanged in units of learning objects (LOs). Basically, LOs are units of study that can be authored independently of the delivery medium and be accessed dynamically using platforms such as the Web (Vossen & Westerkamp, 2004). Ideally, LOs can be reused by different LMS and plugged together to build courses that are intended to serve a particular purpose or goal. Therefore, LOs need to be context-free, i.e. they have to carry useful information on the type and context in which they may be used. Learning objects can be stored in learning object repositories.

Learning objects in distributed environments such as grid architectures pose a number of challenges. Learning objects in the grid context are often composite objects that use grid functionality internally in addition to classical learning content to incorporate other content resources. Pankratius and Vossen (2003) propose to wrap up grid learning objects as Web services that would provide metadata, the required communications abilities and the exposure of classical learning content.

Grid Architectures for Learning Technology Systems

With the rapid development in Internet and Web technology, along with the gradual improvements found in network bandwidth and quality, real-time transmission of high-quality video and audio and other media-based interactions has become a reality. These platform technologies can leverage educational activities for example as follows:

- Creating virtual classrooms by interconnecting lecturers to geographically scattered students. This requires a distributed infrastructure with substantial requirements in terms of multimedia transmission and allowing an ongoing interaction between learners, content and instructors.
- Making educational material, such as tutorials and recorded lectures, available worldwide through high-storage infrastructures, which requires a high-performance learning object and resources repository that can be searched in terms of educational needs.
- Digitalizing and making textbooks available through high-storage infrastructures, which requires the automation of resource generation and annotation for the storage repositories.
- Integrating library search engines and digital content, requiring an adequate publication, search and retrieval functionality.

More than other distributed computing platforms, grids can provide the required level of stateful connections, interoperability, and support of required levels of sharing of computational and content resources (Ritrovato et al., 2005). Virtualization is the term that captures these characteristics. The learning scenarios, which are discussed later, focus on aspects of the first, second and fourth item of this list.

Virtualization needs arise for e-learning organizations from, firstly, reuse and sharing aims and, secondly, the distributed nature of the learning and training activities. Many e-learning platforms and systems that have been developed are based on client-server, on peer-to-peer and on Web service architectures (Neijdl et al., 2001; Vossen & Westerkamp, 2004). A grid architecture, compared with these architectures, allows computation and data resource sharing across different distributed e-learning applications in a transparent, seamless and secure way, providing increased scalability and availability. With the use of grid-enabled e-learning, students can obtain great advantage through a constantly available access to instructional material, lecture notes, and multimedia content, such as video recordings of classes, made available by instructors or even by other students.

Grid computing can mean different things to different individuals. The grand vision is often presented as an analogy to power grids where users (or electrical appliances) get access to electricity through wall sockets with no care or consideration of where or how the electricity is actually generated (Foster, 2002). In this view of grid computing, computing becomes pervasive and individual users (or client applications) gain access to computing resources (processors, storage, data, applications, and so on) as needed with little or no knowledge of where those resources are located or what the underlying technologies, hardware, operating system, and so on are. Its key values are in the underlying distributed computing infrastructure technologies that are evolving in support of cross-organizational application and resource sharing—in a word, virtualization across technologies, platforms, and organizations (Foster et al., 2002).

Virtualization in the context of e-learning systems means the creation of virtual classrooms and transparent creation, provision and availability of learning resources in digital form as part of virtual educational organizations—as outlined in the four educational activities outlined above. A grid architecture for learning technology systems, where sharing and reuse of educational resources in form of learning objects between a number of educational organizations and a group of distributed learners is paramount, is the central objective here.

WEB SERVICES AND GRID ARCHITECTURE

Understanding the principles of the Web service-based grid platform is essential, if a grid-enabled e-learning solution has to be implemented. A more detailed look at the grid platform is also necessary to justify the platform decision and to understand how the chosen platform can help developers to achieve the desired characteristics of virtual e-learning systems that overcome limitations of traditional architectural solutions.

Web Services

By moving off-line activities online, Web services (Alonso et al., 2004) enable partners to (re)use easily applications via the Internet. A Web service is essentially a stand-alone software component that has a unique address (a unique uniform resource identifier URI) and that operates over the Internet and particularly the World Wide Web. The basic premise is that Web services have a provider and users or subscribers. Web services can be combined to build new ones with a more

comprehensive functionality. Clearly, Web services need to be interoperable. Moreover, they have to be independent of the operating systems; they should work on every Web service engine regardless of their implementation language; and they should be able to interact with each other. To achieve these goals, Web services are based on standards. Currently, the most common ones are the XML-based specifications simple object access protocol (SOAP) as the message-based invocation protocol, universal description, discovery and integration (UDDI) as a marketplace for publication and search, and Web services description language (WSDL) as the abstract service interface and invocation description notation.

In Figure 2, the typical steps of an invocation of a Web service are shown. In a first step, suppose that a client needs to find a Web service which provides a specific functionality. This is done by contacting a UDDI registry (step 1), which returns the name of a server where an appropriate service is located (step 2). Since the client still does not know how to invoke the desired service, a WSDL description is requested which contains the name and parameters of the operation(s) of the service

Figure 2. Web service infrastructure

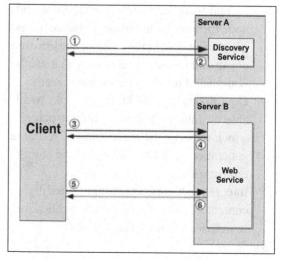

(steps 3 and 4). The client is now able to invoke the service using the SOAP protocol, which essentially puts the data in a message envelope and sends it over the Web. The service provider receives the request and executes the desired operation(s) on behalf of that client (step 5). The results are sent back to the client by using SOAP again (step 6).

The idea of utilizing this service architecture by making e-learning offerings available as Web services has been developed in (Vossen & Westerkamp, 2004). As described there, the various functionalities of an e-learning system can be decomposed and made available individually as Web services. Learning objects, as discussed earlier, can be made available through services in the same way as infrastructure functions.

Open Grid Services Architecture

Until recently, network-based education and grid technologies were two distinct areas. But e-learning increasingly addresses learning resources sharing and reuse, interoperability and various modes of interactions. Grid technology can provide solutions for virtual e-learning solutions.

The kind of virtualization aimed at by grid technology is only achievable through the use of open standards. Open standards help ensure that applications can transparently take advantage of whatever appropriate resources can be made available to them. An environment that provides the ability to share and transparently access resources across a distributed and heterogeneous environment not only requires the technology to virtualize certain resources, but also technologies and standards in the areas of scheduling, security, accounting, systems management, and so on. The goal is to create the illusion of a simple yet large and powerful virtual computing and data storage facility. Grid architectures provide the platform for grid computing.

The open grid services architecture (OGSA), developed by the global grid forum (GGF), aims to define a common standard and open architecture for grid-based applications. The goal of the OGSA (Foster et al., 2001; Foster et al., 2002) is to standardize the services commonly found in a grid application—such as job management services, resource management services, and security services—by specifying a set of standard interfaces for these services, and also a set of requirements that must be met by the interface implementations.

In implementing this architecture, a choice of a distributed middleware platform on which to base the architecture had to be made. In principle, any distributed middleware, for instance CORBA, DCOM or Java-RMI, can be used. The Web Services framework, however, is a distributed middleware platform that provides a standardized and interoperable way to transfer data from one system to another without having to resort to platform- or language-specific methods. Early grid applications actually used other, less portable methods than Web services. The central reason was an architectural one. Although a grid application may be implemented on a number of machines, it is still a single stateful application—which can be difficult to reconcile with an architecture that is essentially stateless such as Web services.

Statefulness is an important element of virtual e-learning systems, where often in learning interactions between learner and content or between learner and instructor the history (i.e., the state) of communication is needed. Interactive learning objects that enable complex learning activities retain state, thus capturing and tracking the learner's input in the system. Web services are, however, based on a single request (e.g., submitting a request) and response (e.g., a successful response) communication. There is no ongoing session management. Like for the HTTP protocol—which is usually used by Web services for the layer below SOAP—each request is independent of the previous request. Web services have no access to or use of information that is not part of the current input message. The Web Services Resource Framework (WSRF) aims to solve that problem by creating the notion of state and a way to manipulate state for Web services.

Stateful Web Services Resources

The Web services resource framework (WSRF) specifies how Web services can be made stateful (Czajkovski et al., 2005). WSRF was developed by OASIS—an industrial standardization body—and is a joint effort by the grid and Web service communities. A stateful resource is something that exists beyond interactions. State also includes the idea of properties and how we interact with state in terms of these properties. A Web service resource, WS-Resource, is the combination of a Web service and a stateful resource on which the service acts (Czajkowski et al., 2005). The WSRF is a series of specifications that define standard message patterns for service interactions, enabling to request the value of a property or to request that those properties should be altered. This can for instance be used to track learner input in an interactive exercise or retain assessment levels to adapt learning resources to individual learner capabilities. The WSRF defines standard formats of interaction with WS-Resources, from working with their properties to grouping them together for purposes such as authentication to lifecycle management. The WSRF defines these interaction operations in terms of WSDL. A WSDL specification defines the messages that pass between the two sides of a Web services conversation.

The WSRF comprises several different specifications. At the core is WS-ResourceProperties, which specifies the form in which ResourceProperties are defined in WSDL. It also specifies the form of messages that request and receive the values of these properties, and explains how to change, add, and remove properties from a WS-Resource. Other specifications include WS-ResourceLifetime, which defines lifecycle manage-

ment functionality, and WS-ServiceGroup, which defines a way to create a collection of Web services, such as a registry of available services.

The central resources in the e-learning technology context are learning objects. These learning objects enable possibly interactive, stateful learning activities. These can be managed by the WRSF as stateful resource, made available in form of services, within an e-learning grid architecture. In addition to the interaction-related information, also learning object metadata can be represented in form of these properties.

The WSRF utilizes two further techniques—WS-Addressing and WS-Notification—which shall be briefly introduced:

- WS-Addressing is the location and addressing framework used by the WSRF for Web resources. WS-Addressing (W3C, 2006) provides a way to specify information about a location other than a Universal Resource Identifier (URI) or URL. WS-Addressing introduces the concept of an EndpointReference to capture this information. An EndpointReference is used to specify the location of a WS-Resource.
- WS-Notification (WSN) is a family of related specifications that define a standard Web services approach to notification using a topic-based publish/subscribe pattern (OASIS, 2006). WS-Topics are used to present a set of items of interest for subscription. A service can publish a set of topics that clients can subscribe to, and receive a notification whenever the topic changes. WS-BaseNotification and WS-BrokeredNotifications define the standard interfaces of notification. Notification producers have to expose a subscribe operation that notification consumers can use to request a subscription. Consumers, in turn, have to expose a notify operation that producers can use to deliver the notification. In brokered notifications, notifications are

delivered from the producer to the consumer through an intermediate entity called the broker.

Notification is central in managing the life-cycle of learning resources, for example, to notify user of any changes. The hierarchical nature of topic trees can be utilized to handle changes in equally hierarchically structured units of study. An instructor can use the notification mechanisms to request notifications on behalf of learners. An LMS can act as a notification broker.

The Globus Grid Application Development Toolkit

The Globus Toolkit is a software toolkit, developed by the Globus Alliance, which is used to program grid-based applications (Globus, 2006a). The toolkit includes a number of high-level services that can be used to build grid applications. These services implement the OGSA requirements, that is, the Globus Toolkit includes a resource monitoring and discovery service, a job submission infrastructure, a security infrastructure, and data management services. Most of the Globus services are implemented on top of WSRF. The summary of all technologies and their interdependencies can be seen in Figure 3.

The resource monitoring and discovery services (MDS) shall be introduced in more detail (Globus, 2006b). The other three components are less central for our given context. Globus' version of MDS serves to satisfy the following requirements and motivations for information services in a grid environment: to provide service discovery to identify and characterize components in a virtual organization (VO), to provide Web resource status information, and to enable application execution supervision for adaptive resource usage. MDS addresses these issues and allows us to gather, manage, index, and respond to queries regarding resources and computation status. MDS enables us to define properties for

which we can provide monitoring and discovery. MDS is made up of resource- and client-side tools for grid information services.

Grid resources are part of a virtual organization from which a user wants to obtain information about a resource such as a file, program, Web service, or another network-enabled service such as a learning object. Information sources contain details about a grid resource to be monitored. Information services collect and format the required information compatible with MDS. Information sources can be executables, or they can be Java classes, as in the case of WSRF-compliant Web services. Such services need simply to make status and state information available as WSRF-resource properties. Globus is configured to use MDS components for discovery and monitoring of services. As MDS is based on WSRF, it employs Web service interfaces to simplify the registration of information sources and also locating and accessing the desired information. MDS provides a polling service that actively requests resource properties from WSRF services and a subscrip-

Figure 3. System implementation view: Technology platform

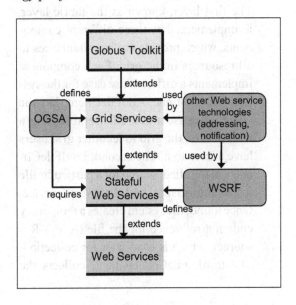

tion service that receives resource properties from WSRF services using the subscription/notification model. The next section discusses the application of these technologies in more detail.

GRID-BASED E-LEARNING SCENARIOS AND SYSTEMS

The architectural principles of grids and the grid platform technologies shall now be applied in the e-learning domain. The aims of this section are to demonstrate the technical feasibility and the benefits of e-learning grid architectures over more traditional approaches. Basic grid middleware architectures shall be outlined, before three different learning scenarios and their implementation through e-learning grids are described.

Grid Middleware and E-Learning Grid Applications

The OGSA suggests a layered architecture, which we apply as our middleware platform for the e-learning grid applications that will be described. We outline the layers and principles of this architecture (Figure 4):

- The first layer, known as the fabric layer, is implemented as three different components, which provide uniform interfaces to all resources in the grid. Each component implements a different use case for the system. The first one, AddFileClient, lets the client advertise a new file (representing a resource) on the grid to let other grid users have access to it. The second, FindFileClient, lets the client search for a particular file in the information and discovery service. Once found, the system creates a temporary endpoint reference for the file (A WS-Resource), which is used later for collection. The third, FileCollectClient, collects the

file found by the FindFileClient using the endpoint reference.

- The resource layer contains an information service which is aware of the properties of each file on the grid. By accessing a client registry, the information service is able to determine whether and where files are available.

- The collective layer essentially provides a broker. The broker is responsible for distributing files across the grid and also for receiving requests of files and invoking the file transfer operation in the file sharing service.

Three learning scenarios shall be introduced to discuss the benefits of this layered grid architecture for e-learning applications. We will explain in the first scenario in detail how the GLORIS system is built from the services of the individual layers, using the file sharing services to reuse and share learning objects. The aim is to illustrate how the grid platform is actually used to support e-learning applications. The two other scenarios will be less detailed in terms of the technology, but will still outline the required

Figure 4. System conceptual view: Layered architecture

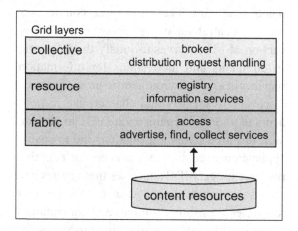

grid services and features. These two scenarios aim to illustrate further benefits of grid-based e-learning systems.

Scenario 1: Distributed Learning Content Resources

The first e-learning grid scenario shall be described using a grid infrastructure to access distributed learning resources. A collaboration between two or more universities, for instance, could share multimedia resources for particular courses. Since this type of material is expensive to produce, providers are, however, inclined to keep control over these resources by providing them through their local content repositories to a possibly distributed group of students across several institutions.

The GLORIS system shall be used to illustrate an architecture for an e-learning grid solution for scenario 1 (Gleeson, 2006). GLORIS, the Grid-based learning object repository infrastructure, is a broker component. The wider aim of GLORIS is to provide an engine in the wider context of an ontology-based authoring and delivery system—an issue that will be addressed later on. GLORIS is implemented using the widely used Globus toolkit for grid-based applications. This broker component connects a

learning content management system, a range of possibly distributed learning object repositories, and a learner management system with runtime delivery environment. GLORIS brokers requests from the runtime environment and dispatches them across the other components. The GLORIS system is a broker component that connects a learner management system (LMS) with content management and repository infrastructure—all based on OGSA-compliant Web service-based grid middleware. The LMS interacts transparently with the grid middleware so that a learner is not aware of the grid.

Three learning-specific GLORIS functions shall be discussed, which are mapped onto the standard grid use cases und functions supported by the OGSA (Figure 5):

- **ADV:** Publishing and advertising a learning object is the first use case. The learning object author is in grid terminology the sharer who provides reusable content. The AddFileClient function provides the core support (Figure 6).
- **FND:** Searching and finding suitable learning objects is the second use case. A learner or instructor, called the collector in grid terminology, might try to find a learning resource that matches certain requirements. The FindFileClient function provides the core support (Figure 7).
- **CLT:** Retrieving and collecting a learning object is the third use case. A collector (learner or teacher) retrieves a resource that has previously been located (found). The FileCollectClient function provides the core support (Figure 8).

GLORIS is a generic e-learning grid infrastructure component, which is not specific to any subject or field. GLORIS is only limited by the types of objects the repositories and learner management systems can handle.

Figure 5. GLORIS context

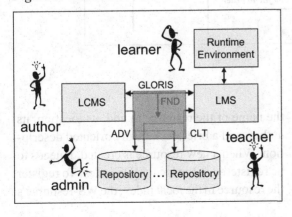

Figure 6. ADV – Advertising a File/Resource

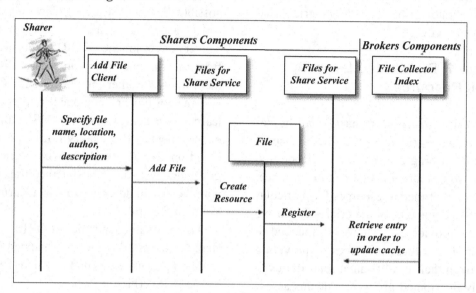

Figure 7. FND – Finding a File/Resource

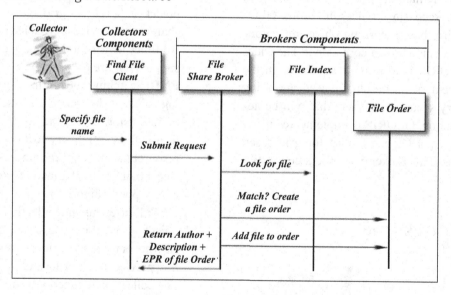

The AddFileClient service is composed of a factory service and an instance service. The addFile operation is in the instance service, which can be used to create stateful learning resources. The addFile operation expects four parameters: the name of the resource to add, its location, its author, and a brief, technically oriented description. When a new resource is created, it needs to be registered in the local MDS index. To register the resource in the local index, the WS-resource's

Figure 8. CLT – Collecting a File/Resource

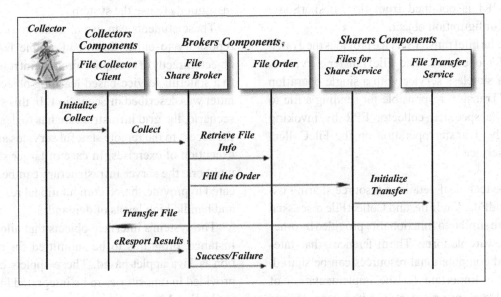

endpoint reference (EPR) needs to be supplied. Parameters from the configuration file are read first, then the EPR is created and registered.

The Find operation of the FindFileClient component expects one parameter, the file's name. The client then submits the request to the GLORIS broker. The broker class queries the index service (MDS) to see if there are any files with the specified name. This is done using a WSRF service provided by Globus that allows resource properties to be queried. From this file, a FileOrder resource is created and its EPR returned.

The endpoint references can denote learning resources from simple static Web pages to interactive and stateful applet-based learning objects. The GLORIS broker allows instructors and learners across the virtual learning organization to locate learning objects. This technique could be improved by adding semantical, ontology-based properties about learning objects—which shall be briefly discussed in the discussion section below.

The FileCollectClient component provides three individual services of importance for the implementation of the retrieval of learning objects in the GLORIS system:

- The FileCollectionService is a collection operation. The acquisition of a resource begins in the FileCollect client, which is responsible for initiating the process in the FileBroker, but is also responsible for receiving the file from the FileTransfer service. The file EPR is retrieved from the FileOrder resource. The EPR is used to invoke the fileOrder operation on the sharer's FilesForShare service. In this call we relay the collector's EPR, which the sharer will then pass on to the FileTransfer service.

- The FilesForSale service provides the fileOrder operation. The fileOrder operation retrieves the name and location of the file to transfer from the file resource, which are sent to the FileTransfer service, along with the collector's EPR. The transfer service's URI is obtained from the FilesForShare configuration object.

- The FileTransferService provides the Transfer operation. The FileTransfer service is a stateless service with a single operation (Transfer) responsible for sending a file to the specified collector EPR by invoking the Transfer operation on the FileCollect service.

The technical details of resource sharing using AddFile, FindFile, and CollectFile discussed here are similar to functionality provided by other middleware platforms. The difference is that stateful and computational resources can be shared, which is important for the implementation of virtual learning organization with heterogeneous resources and access and delivery mechanisms. The detailed discussion here shall emphasize the fact that grids actually satisfy the infrastructure needs of learning resource sharing in virtual learning organizations.

Scenario 2: Distributed Lab Exercise Execution

The second scenario shall be illustrated by a concrete system that is in use for undergraduate teaching at our university for several years and that has recently been re-engineered to allow its features to be used in a distributed form beyond the previous campus-based access. The aim of the system is to provide a virtual laboratory that can be used by students at any time and from any location.

This system is an active learning environment that allows learners to execute programming exercises remotely in the system and to work on projects within the learning environment (Murray et al., 2003). While these features are in use in an on-campus version for a long time, the scenario also illustrates the use of grid technology to al-

low a larger number of students from different institutions to use the system.

These students can use a broker to access a repository to either download simple learning objects directly or to acquire an endpoint reference to a stateful, service-based learning object. The latter was described in Scenario 1. In this second scenario, the grid infrastructure has to deal with the access to the remote stateful services and the execution of exercises. In case of larger student numbers, the server infrastructure can be replicated to provide shared computational resources and handle high levels of demand.

The system's interface objects that allow, for instance, programs to be submitted for execution is Java applet-based. These applets can be provided in repositories to be integrated into the student's LMS. Once active, the applet can use grid networking features to remotely execute the programs. The active learning and training system is an adaptive system that provides personalized feedback based on user activities in stateful learning sessions. Stateful services in a grid architecture are therefore a necessity.

Scenario 3: Collaborative Teams and Result Processing

Collaboration and team work are important contributors to successful learning approaches. Collaborating teams of learners might even be distributed. The infrastructure needs to facilitate sharing of resources and a joint workspace, such as access to storage facilities. The Globus data management services can be deployed in this case. The layered grid architecture broker, registry, and resource access layers coordinate the collaboration between learners.

An example for advanced result processing is a feature, which we have not mentioned in the previous scenario. The system presented earlier on analyses submissions for execution, i.e. it analyzes the correctness of submissions, classifies the errors, and gives learners a detailed feedback.

These analyses, correction and feedback features are often computationally demanding. The possibility of spreading the workload in case of high numbers of submissions is of essential importance to guarantee the availability and reliability of these services.

DISCUSSION

The previously introduced technologies and scenarios shall now be discussed in terms of their limitations, related work, and expected future directions and trends. Virtual learning organizations are currently the focus of various research initiatives. These range from the investigation of problems arising from educational collaborations beyond country, language, and cultural boundaries to new paradigms for collaborative and experimental learning to grid platform technologies for learning support. Comprehensive implementations are, however, not likely to be successfully implemented in the near future. The system implementations that have been described here—such as GLORIS and the programming learning and training courseware environment—have demonstrated the benefits of grid technology. GLORIS is an experimental prototype that we have used to explore the feasibility of implementing a Web service-based learning grid using the Globus toolkit. GLORIS implements core broker and communications features. Extended versions might also take over functionality from the LCMS and LMS components. The programming learning and training system is an environment that, although only supporting a single subject, demonstrates the scale of the difficulty of the problem.

Three scenarios have been discussed here. A wide range of scenarios—some similar to the ones here—have been presented in the literature in order to illustrate benefits and applications of grid technology for learning technology systems. Two other scenarios (Laria, 2005) shall briefly be introduced:

- **Immersive virtual reality:** Some learning applications are computationally intensive. Medical training or flight simulators are examples that require extensive computational resources. Grid computing can help here to improve the availability of the learning feature.
- **Field trips:** A group of students on a field trip might use mobile devices such as PDAs to send collected information to a dedicated grid service. This service will authenticate the students and collate and analyze their results. The grid infrastructure can provide the communications platform and the result processing services.

In order to illustrate grid applications in e-learning further beyond the examples here, other widely discussed approaches to learning resource sharing—related to the first scenario—shall be discussed:

- Vossen et al. (Pankratius & Vossen, 2003; Vossen & Westerkamp, 2004) discuss the service-based implementation of e-learning offerings. The authors propose to provide a uniform, service-based realization of both learner and content management and the context itself.
- Edutella is, although not grid-based, similar to the aims of the first scenario. Edutella adds another perspective to the grid infrastructure. Semantics is important in distributed, cross-organizational applications. Content and functionality needs to be adequately described and understood by all participants. The semantic grid initiative captures this endeavor in the grid context—which will be briefly addressed below.
- Yang and Ho (2005) have presented another approach to sharing learning resources using a data grid infrastructure. Similar to (Pankratius & Vossen, 2003) packageable learning objects—here based on SCORM-

compliant content objects—form the basis. Like GLORIS, it is based on distributed learning object repositories.

Furthermore, three other, larger research initiatives shall be mentioned to outline the state-of-the-art in learning grid technology:

- ELeGI is the European Learning Grid Initiative (ELeGI, 2006), which aims at a pedagogy-driven, service-oriented software architecture based on grid technologies. The support of knowledge construction and collaboration as new paradigms for the e-learning technology area aim at a more contextualized, personalized and ubiquitous learning. The grid-based architecture is the enabler of these aims.
- Kaleidoscope (Kaleidoscope, 2006) is another EU-funded initiative that, among other aspects, addresses grid-based learning. The Learning Grid addresses the benefits of Grid computing for processing-intensive learning applications.
- Diogene (Capuano et al., 2005) aims at the realization of a distributed virtual organization for the provision of learning services. Again, the services notion and semantics play central roles.

In addition to these research initiatives, two specific systems in the context of grid technologies, which illustrate the potential of the architecture platform and the current state-of-the-art in e-learning grid tool support, shall be mentioned:

- The GridCole system (Bote-Lorenzo, 2004) combines grid service technologies with IMS learning design (LD) specifications to provide an improved, learning flow-based collaborative learning system. A Web portal and clients interact with a learning flow engine that implements and executes the learning designs. The clients and the portal use a service-based grid to access individual learning resources.
- GRASP is a grid-based application service provider (ASP) infrastructure (Dimitrakos et al., 2004). A layered architecture enables, for example, federated and many-to-many ASP business models. In an e-learning context, the architecture can provide access to different learning portals and can handle SLA (service-level agreement) management and security issues between learner and provider.

The presentation of the grid architecture and technology platform here as well as most of the related work discussed have focused on aspects of service-orientation for the support of specific scenarios. Based on these scenarios, some directions for research and technology development that address some of the limitations of the system implementations discussed here shall be discussed:

- The semantic grid is an endeavor of adding a knowledge layer to service-based grid infrastructures. In heterogeneous environments, the abstract annotation of services is necessary to facilitate the automated discovery and composition of services. The scenarios we discussed assumed technically oriented service and resource-level descriptions. In an area like learning, where knowledge is paramount, a comprehensive knowledge infrastructure is needed that integrates content- and service-level knowledge in a sharable format. Ontologies provide a suitable formal framework for description and reasoning.
- Virtualization is an aim that can be achieved using grid technologies. The aim is to create a virtual organization (VO), in which a number of different distributed organization share data and computational resources. The

sharing approach is defined through sharing rules, i.e. these sharing rules actually define the VO. While this is an area of intensive research in the business community, the increasing trend towards global collaboration of educational institutions makes virtualization also an e-learning issue. In particular frameworks to capture the rules that govern the sharing of resources are under investigation.

Crucial factors that determine the success of grid architectures for e-learning applications are the cost of migrating to this architecture and adapting to its standards and the complexity of the resulting infrastructure. With the OGSA framework, a platform is available that makes e-learning grids feasible and that is itself based on widely accepted standards such as Web services and XML. In order to reliably migrate existing systems, more experience with e-learning-specific solutions such as GRASP or GridCole.

CONCLUSION

An e-learning platform requires a learning management system (LMS) to store and manage the learning content. The LMS plays two important roles which are to provide access to and deliver the courseware when and as needed and also to track the learner's reactions and responses. Educational technology standards aims to establish a mechanism for repeated use and sharing of courseware as a way to reduce time and cost in developing courseware and make courseware reusable and interoperable with different LMS. Using these concepts, grid technologies can be used to set up a courseware-sharing platform.

Grid technology is not a new concept. In fact, the collaboration and sharing of resources in a geographically distributed environment is an idea that has arisen since networked computer systems are available. The more recent World Wide Web

is, however, not enough to enable a global collaboration of resources, but in the meanwhile other platform technologies such as services and grids have emerged, which will enable users to easily access and share resources connected through the Internet.

In this chapter, the main technological concepts of implementing e-learning systems using grid computing based on different learning scenarios have been presented. What has been discussed is intended to give an insight to how grid computing can be exploited in e-learning. It has become clear that e-learning grids and virtual learning organizations are still far from been fully investigated. The focus has been on the administrative side of resources sharing, but not on how grids can directly enhance the learning experience. Yet, current research and technology development demonstrate the feasibility and also the significant potential that encourages researchers and developers to pursue work in this area, as there is considerable hope for being able to extend the achievements of e-learning beyond the limits of individual computers and learners.

REFERENCES

Advanced Distributed Learning ADL (2004). SCORM Sharable Content Object Reference Model. Retrieved February 2, 2006, from http://www.adlnet.org/index.cfm?fuseaction= scormabt

Alonso, G., Casati, F., Kuno H. & Machiraju, V. (2004). *Web services: Concepts, architectures and applications.* Berlin, Germany: Springer Verlag.

Bote-Lorenzo, M.L., Hernández-Leo, D., Dimitriadis, Y. A., Asensio-Pérez, J. I., Gómez-Sánchez, E., Vega-Gorgojo, G. & Vaquero-González, L.M. (2002). Towards reusability and tailorability in collaborative learning systems using IMS-LD and grid services. *International Journal on Advanced Technology for Learning, 1*(3), 129-138.

Capuano, N., Carrolagi, P., Combas, J., Crestani, F., Gaeta, M., Herber, E., Sangineto, E., Stefanov, K., & Vergara, M. (2005). Learning design and run-time resource binding in a distributed e-learning environment. In *Proceedings of 1ˢᵗ International Kaleidoscope Learning GRID Special Interest Group Workshop on Distributed e-Learning Environments*.

Czajkowski , K., Ferguson, D.F., Foster, I., Frey, J., Graham, S., Sedukhin, I., Snelling, D., Tuecke, S. & Vambenepe, W. (2005). *The Web services resource framework (WSRF)*.

Dimitrakos, T., Mac Randal, D., Wesner, S., Serhan, B., Ritrovato, P. & Laria, G. (2004). Overview of an architecture enabling grid-based application service provision. In *Proceedings of European Across Grids Conference AxGrid 2004*. Berlin: Springer Verlag (LNCS 3165).

ELeGI (2006). *European Learning Grid Infrastructure*. EU IST Research Project. Retrieved from http://www.elegi.org/

Fosster, I., Kesselman, C., Nick, J.M. & Tuecke, S. (2002). The Physiology of the Grid: An Open Grid Services Architecture for Distributed Systems Integration. In *Proceedings of 4ᵗʰ Global Grid Forum Workshop*.

Foster, I., Kesselman, C. & Tuecke, S. (2001). The anatomy of the grid: Enabling scalable virtual organizations. *International Journal of Supercomputer Applications and High Performance Computing*, 200-222.

Foster, I. (2002). What is the Grid? A Three Point Checklist. *GRID Today*, July.

Gleeson, G. (2006). *The Investigation of Grid Architectures in the Context of E-Learning*. Project Report.

Globus (2006a). *Globus Toolkit GT4*. Retrieved from http://www.globus.org/toolkit/

Globus (2006b). *Information Services (MDS): Key Concepts*. Retrieved from http://www-unix.globus.org/toolkit/docs/4.0/info/keyindex.html

IMS Global Learning Consortium (2001). *IMS Content Packaging Best Practice Guide Version 1.1.2*. IMS.

Kaleidoscope (2006). *Kaleidoscope*. EU IST Research Project. Retrieved from http://www.noe-kaleidoscope.org/

Laria, G. (2005). Learning GRID Scenarios. *Kaleidoscope Learning GRID newsletter, 3*. Kaleidoscope.

Murray, S., Ryan, J., & Pahl, C. (2003). A tool-mediated cognitive apprenticeship approach for a computer engineering course. In *Proceedings of International Conference on Advanced Learning Technologies ICALT'03* (pp. 2-6). IEEE.

Nejdl, W., Wolf, B., Qu, C., Decker, S., Sintek, M., Naeve, A., Nilsson, M., Palmer, M. & Risch, T. (2002). EDUTELLA: A P2P Networking Infrastructure Based on RDF. In *Proceedings of World-Wide Web Conference WWW'2002*. ACM.

OASIS (2006). *Web Services Notification 1.3*. Retrieved from http://docs.oasis-open.org/wsn/wsn-ws_base_notification-1.3-speccs-01.pdf

Pankratius, V. & Vossen, G. (2003). Towards e-Learning grids: Using grid computing in electronic learning. In *Proceedings of IEEE Workshop on Knowledge Grid and Grid Intelligence* (pp. 4-15). IEEE.

Ritrovato, P., Allison, C., Cerri, S.A., Dimitrakos, T., Gaeta, M. & Salerno, S. (2005). *Towards the Learning Grid*. Amsterdam: IOS Press.

Sotomayor, B. (2006). *The Globus Toolkit 4 Programmer's Tutorial*. University of Chicago Department of Computer Science.

Vossen, G., & Westerkamp, P. (2004). Maintenance and exchange of learning objects in a Web service- based e-Learning system. *Electronic Journal of e-Learning, 2*(2), 292-304.

W3C (2006). *Web Services Addressing 1.0.* Retrieved from http://www.w3.org/Submission/ws-addressing/

Yang, C.-T. & Ho, H.-C. (2005). A sharable e-Learning platform using data Grid technology. In *Proceedings of IEEE International Conference on e-Technology, e-Commerce and e-Service EEE'2005* (pp. 592- 595). New York: IEEE.

Chapter IV
From E–Learning to M–Learning:
Architectures to Support University Teaching

Philip Grew
Università degli Studi di Milano, Italy

Elena Pagani
Università degli Studi di Milano, Italy

Francesco Giudici
Università degli Studi di Milano, Italy

ABSTRACT

The term e-learning indicates products that differ very much both in services supplied and in design. E-learning platforms do not necessarily involve networking as a fundamental component. However, networking is important both to ease access to course material and to support interaction among users. Networking should be exploited to allow remote access to students who cannot be present at lessons, to allow asynchronous learning whenever students have time, and to supply users with tools for coopera- tive learning regardless of their physical location. The spread of wireless networking technologies and their standardization will lead to innovations in all three of these aspects. This chapter focuses on the services whose deployment computer networks make possible in order to boost interactivity, cooperation and involvement in learning, with specific attention to ubiquitous learning and for the impact of wireless technologies on the general framework.

DEFINING THE PROBLEM

Our focus is on the services whose deployment is enabled by computer networks, services that boost interactivity, cooperation, and involvement in learning activities, with specific interest for *ubiquitous* and *pervasive* learning. Ubiquitous learning involves interaction during which tools provide new learning opportunities by bridging space and time gaps and curtailing the relevance of the user's location. Such interaction may combine with *pervasive* learning systems, which adjust themselves to the needs and interests of each specific learner so as to continue the learning process as the user changes location while engaging in a variety of other activities.

Mobile devices are poised to bring major changes to learning systems. Although wireless technologies may provide the same services as wired networks with fewer constraints on time and location, they can also be used to supply additional services that are otherwise difficult or impossible to deploy. For example, university campuses bring together parties that cooperate with each other. In addition to students, teachers, and staff, other segments of the university community like concessions or bookstores may exchange reservations, orders, and various information. While traditional Web pages and bulletin-boards allow such exchange, mobile devices enable notices to be *pushed* to potentially interested users as soon

as available, with no user effort (asynchronous and remote). Wireless can offer supplementary functions to students actually in class at a given moment, such as automated testing, gathering feedback, and immediate content sharing. Without systems, these services are extremely time-consuming and almost impossible to manage. In a classroom with computers and wired network, the results of such cooperation stay on university equipment, limiting subsequent availability. Wireless networking also brings traditional e-learning functions within ubiquitous reach.

Figure 1 represents schematically the main interactions among on-campus roles, reflecting both information type and exchange direction.

Some of the interactions shown in Figure 1 are unicast, e.g. questions transmitted from student to teacher (B), while others, like the dissemination of urgent notices, are multicast to all users interested (I).

Interactions may follow three different models:

Figure 1. Scheme of interactions among different roles

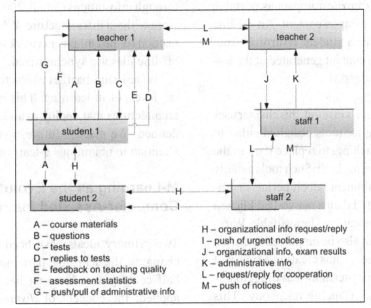

A – course materials
B – questions
C – tests
D – replies to tests
E – feedback on teaching quality
F – assessment statistics
G – push/pull of administrative info

H – organizational info request/reply
I – push of urgent notices
J – organizational info, exam results
K – administrative info
L – request/reply for cooperation
M – push of notices

1. **Physical co-presence:** The people involved are in the same place at the same time. Here, the impact of electronic tools lies in the ability of computer-mediated communication to foster cooperative work and interactivity distinct from what a traditional chalkboard offers. However, with the introduction of mobile devices, there is a gray area spanning the formerly stark distinction between blended and remote e-learning.

2. **Remote synchronous:** The people involved are in different places but take part in the learning activities at the same time. The major changes that mobile devices bring to remote synchronous interaction, as compared to wired e-learning applications, involve allowing user mobility during the interaction.

3. **Asynchronous:** The people involved participate in the learning activities at different times. Although user location rarely factors into wired asynchronous interaction, mobile devices can authenticate user location even when the presence occurs at a different time from the group meeting. In the more immediate term—and with less investment in dedicated infrastructure—mobile devices may have their greatest impact as portable containers for campus content. An off-line device can give a student returning from class access to content generated at the lesson s/he just attended.

Bearing these models in mind, this chapter uses the term **e-learning** for tools designed either to enhance in-class teaching, to replace it or, in the case of blended learning, both. Such tools usually require specific equipment (albeit perhaps nothing more sophisticated than a networked kitchen computer) that may not always be available. Wireless technologies can also be employed to enrich the learning experience, thus creating a subset of e-learning that we may term **m-learning**, that is "mobile" in the sense of "mobile telephony." This really implies two different functions of mobility: members of the learning community can be recognized from anywhere (mobile connectivity and authentication) and/or they can work on the go (portability). An initial improvement allows students access to learning tools via their own devices, coordinated by a server, the model adopted by ActiveCampus (activecampus.ucsd.edu), for example. Students' devices store work performed and can continue off-line. Allowing participants to congregate spontaneously anywhere, regardless of equipment, aside from their own devices (e.g., servers), emphasizes geographic ubiquity, though without supporting remote learning. This model can be deployed through wireless technologies that ease automated setup of *ad hoc* networks. Fully ubiquitous, remote, asynchronous learning is obtained when the environment involves broad wireless-network coverage—or an infrastructured network—so participants can be in various locations or even on the move.

This chapter's reference scenario involves users owning thin devices like laptops, palmtops or 3G cell phones. Devices enable using locally held material while disconnected from the campus network. They also allow interaction among users, e.g. data sharing, and with the environment, e.g. through infostations (Small, 2003) or cooperative work without infrastructure. When wireless connection to the campus network is re-established, off-line files are synchronized.

Table 1 summarizes characteristics of different levels of m-learning. This chapter analyzes architectures that deploy e- and m-learning thus defined. We discuss future trends with special attention to ubiquitous e-learning.

M-Learning as the Evolution of Computer-Assisted Instruction

Two primary ideals have been instrumental in changing the learning paradigm over the last half century as e-learning has become widely applied: the concept of *distance learning* (on

Table 1. Scheme of different classes of platforms for e-learning and m-learning

Approach	Interaction	Equipment	Pros & Cons
E-Learning	In-presence (in classroom)	Wired network; equipped classroom.	Enhancement of in-class activities. NO ubiquity.
	Remote synchronous	Wired network; access via Web. Independent of access point.	Supports students unable to attend class. Available anywhere Internet is accessible.
	Remote asynchronous	Wired network; access via Web. Independent of access point.	As above. Also supports anytime learning.
M-Learning	In-presence (in classroom)	Participants' devices with wireless networking communicate through server.	Work remains on student's device; offline work possible.
	In-presence (wherever)	Ad hoc network of participants' wireless devices.	As above. No equipment needed. Geographic ubiquity supported.
	Remote synchronous	Access through ad hoc or infrastructure network.	As above. Supports students unable to attend class.
	Remote asynchronous	Access through ad hoc or infrastructure network.	As above. Also supports anytime learning. Fully ubiquitous.

electronic remote systems) and the concept of *computer-mediated communication*. Early classroom experimentation with *computer-assisted instruction*, what is now called *blended learning* or "hybrid e-learning," eventually grew into *distributed systems* that spawned communities based on forum and chat functionalities. The quality of being distributed exemplifies how architectural and social features go hand-in-hand. System architectures also reflect social relations through sophisticated sets of differentiated access permissions for managing document databases.

When a *learning-management system* (LMS) is designed from the outset to integrate remote learning with computer-mediated communication among participants physically present in the same place at the same time, a new mode of thought envisioned by J.C.R. Licklider under the rubric

"cooperative thinking" is enabled. However, because overcoming the prepared-slide paradigm depends on being able to "thumb through a speaker's primary data without interrupting him to substantiate or explain" (Licklider, 1968), the envisioned interactivity actually outstrips that so far achieved in synchronous, non-remote contexts. M-learning is uniquely poised to bring to fruition an ideal of classroom interactivity older than the term "e-learning" itself. Wireless devices finally blend computer-mediated communication into in-class learning.

The move toward m-learning is thus a further example of social factors marching hand-in-hand with system architecture. Today's college student may arrive on campus with experience in text messaging as the medium that enabled peers to live a continuously shared existence in a parallel reality created by mobile technologies for networked communication within a social group (Rheingold, 2002). The integration of such 'informal' classroom discourse into institutional e-learning efforts has begun (Nagaoka, 2005; Grew, 2006b). Initial experience points toward future e-learning systems no longer able to ignore the mobile devices already populating student's knapsacks and clothing.

Mobile devices yield various opportunities for classroom application. One of the most compelling is support for cooperative work. This requires services that enable human interaction like that in the real world but is not usually considered part of the learning environment *per se*—termed *informal learning* (Collier, 2002). Such services are thus often disregarded in designing e-learning infrastructures. Furthermore, wired networking technologies impose time, space, and equipment constraints. Informal interactions, not scheduled in advance, may occur anywhere, anytime. Wire-less technologies entail exactly this flexibility. This is one functionality m-learning might clearly support that distinguishes it from traditional e-learning. Infrastructure designed for m-learning will thus need to support such services.

Other changes brought on by wireless include: ad hoc networking, immediate or asynchronous use of downloaded material on portable devices, and the growth of e-learning systems into a variety of new roles. Especially at the outset, m-learning will tend to be interdisciplinary. Its systems will be used even in real time and among those physically present. Many existing m-learning setups make no attempt to integrate into wired e-learning legacy architecture. However, integration is likely to set the trend, especially where a given functionality already exists and need not be duplicated. Hence, a look at the functionalities provided by wired e-learning architectures helps envision m-learning situations. Table 2 compares functionalities provided by some wired e-learning

Table 2. Comparison of e-learning platforms

Platform (LMS name)	Offline synchronization	Open-source	Content management	Assessment	Synchronous cooperation	Asynchronous cooperation	Security	Modular customizable
Lotus Virtual Classroom	yes	no	yes	yes	yes	yes	yes	no
FirstClass	yes	no	some	no	yes	yes	yes	no
Moodle	no	yes	yes	yes	yes	yes	yes	yes
JLI!	no	yes	yes	yes	yes	yes	yes	yes
eduCommons	no	yes	some	no	no	no	yes	yes
Blackboard	no	no	yes	yes	yes	yes	yes	some
Open Courseware	no	N/A	some	no	no	no	N/A	N/A
WebCT	no	no	yes	yes	yes	yes	yes	some

platforms (see Figure 3). The JLI! platform in use at the University of Milano is briefly overviewed in a subsequent subsection.

Platforms generally have an LMS server that provides content according to user profile and implements the "intelligence" to support learning. The client side is typically a Web browser. In most of these wired systems, no activity can take place if the server is not accessible. This limitation, preventing full application to portable devices, is emblematic of the challenges faced in adapting wired systems to m-learning. Our small sample of platforms includes two notable exceptions, systems that synchronize off-line content, FirstClass and Lotus Virtual Classroom. Each other system has at least one feature ripe for adaption to m-learning. However, no single platform has all the functionalities warranted by m-learning needs.

Traditional e-learning platforms focus primarily on publishing course content and on assessment. They manage the remote asynchronous interaction of Table 1. Proprietary platforms usually limit customization to configuring working parameters upon installation. None of these systems provides for collaborative group work among directly networked user devices. None, therefore, yield complete ubiquity or fully exploit networking potential.

Given the desirability of a single-system to optimize both, authentication and information management platforms (especially proprietary ones) tend to aggregate functions onto the LMS. While achieving sought-after integration, single-solution systems pave the way to vendor lock-in (Davis, 2004), especially when the licensed institution has invested heavily in course creation. As a result, integration with existing e-learning platforms is a tactical but not strategic aspect of m-learning design. Significantly, a modular customizable platform will allow the integration of m-learning requirements. For this reason, the following section focuses definitions on the set

of functionalities required and the set of services available to provide them.

Case Study: E-Learning Support at the University of Milan

At the Information Science departments of the Università degli Studi di Milano, an integrated platform supports teacher, staff, and student activities, partially automated assessment, monitoring of teaching quality, and interactivity. The system had to be *scalable*, adaptable to teachers' differing skills, and easily extensible with tools teachers were used to before adopting the platform. Its distributed infrastructure can be easily expanded with additional tools, either proprietary or open-source. The infrastructure aims not to become the container for content and data but rather to run diverse tools collaboratively, offering a uniform interface for accessing them. Access is via Web browser.

Figure 2 sketches overall system architecture. Its functionalities aim to provide students a uniform work environment for all teaching resources supplied by teachers, gathering their work for different courses and interacting with teachers. The environment also includes facilities for teacher cooperation and interaction with staff. The three main components of the infrastructure are *WebCen*, the information portal, *JLI!*, and *SILab*, the students' computer center. These three independent components interface with one another. Both *WebCen* and *JLI!* allow teachers and staff to publish course materials, downloadable content, and notices, the latter with tracking mechanisms. *JLI!* uses *SILab* resources for authentication even during electronic testing.

JLI!–Just Learn It! (JLI, 2005a; Grew, 2004; Grew, 2005a) is an open-source, SCORM-compliant e-learning platform initially developed in the framework of a European project to support training in small-to-medium enterprises. *JLI!* allows teachers to manage course content. It in-

Figure 2. Architecture of e-learning platform used at University of Milano

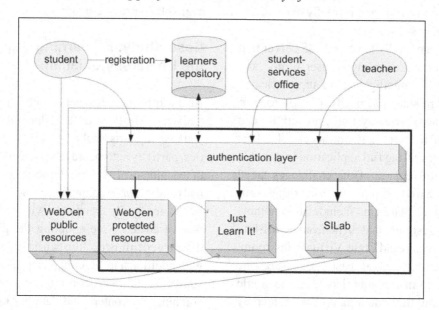

cludes facilities for broadcast e-mail, interfaces with external forum and wiki applications, and furnishes an extensive set of testing modules for exams and exercises that partially automate correction and collect statistics on test results. A *JLI!* course supports the *community* of users involved with both individual workspace and group coursework functions. Full documentation and source code can be found on the project Web site (JLI, 2005b).

Our multi-platform setup has evolved over the last several years to meet the common needs of various university courses. Some 20 courses currently use *JLI!*; more than 16,000 assessments have been performed on it, and 7,000 students have/had a workspace in the system. The large number of users testifies to the soundness and scalability of the architecture. Many of the platform's improvements were suggested by teachers (Grew, 2004; Grew, 2005a) and it is instructive to observe the resulting emphasis on security and authentication.

Security initially became a concern because students may earn course credit for work done online while physically present, that is, in a blended situation. The architecture thus reflects the primacy of a concern bound to play a pivotal role in many m-learning deployments. Security considerations were also called into play when importing from administration databases, not all of whose fields teachers are permitted to see.

A common *authentication layer* was therefore designed into the system to support various user roles (students, faculty, staff). In addition to controlling access to protected content, the shared layer prevents data duplication, inconsistencies, and outdated information. It checks identifiers (login name, password) stored in a database accessed by various system components through LDAP (Sermersheim, 2006) so the system can serve different views according to user role. The architectural lesson implies a system-wide task for security services that will have to embrace wireless authentication, no longer simply user-specific but now also device-dependent.

FUNCTIONAL MODEL

Figure 3 shows the main functionalities of e-learning architectures. These functionalities are a superset of those needed to supporting e-learning and m-learning. This model partially overlaps with service models proposed in (Collier, 2002; Grew, 2005a; Grew, 2005b).

The functionalities fall into four classes. **Learning** functionalities (e-learning platform, learning engine, materials creation, and content maintenance) allow teachers to create learning materials and configure policies that determine what material is shown to the learner based on profile information, such as courses s/he is enrolled in or feedback on previously presented topics. They allow all the *roles* shown in Figure 1 to access data depending on user identity and preferences. **Assessment** functionalities include mechanisms that serve students tests, (partially) automate grading, and gather statistics from test results, e.g. as feedback on teaching quality or to determine a student's subsequent learning schedule. **Security** functionalities are used by all other

modules to authenticate users, check authorization to perform actions, guarantee non-reputability of data, and protect user privacy. **Communication** functionalities comprise services starting with applications for cooperative work (chats, forums, wikis, etc.) and extending to network protocols for message exchange, push/pull of information to/from interested users, and upload/download of contents to/from servers. While wired-network protocols are stable and standardized, things are different for wireless technologies. In theory, wireless gives users greater flexibility in accessing all other functionalities.

As shown in Figure 4, users can access services from their own devices through either Internet access points (APs) or the provider's infrastructure, curtailing constraints on when and where services are used. Access to servers and repositories of learning material is filtered through firewalls and security managers. Although wireless allows deploying additional services that are difficult or impossible to implement otherwise, such as detaching part of the infrastructure from the whole campus system while still guaranteeing

Figure 3. Functional model for e-learning and m-learning

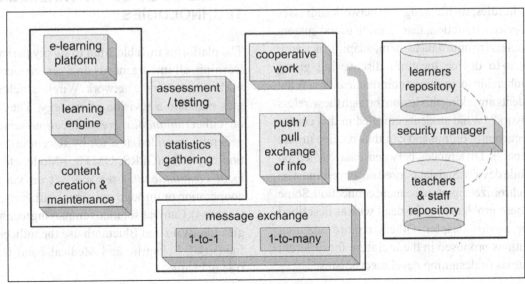

Figure 4. Overview of the communication infrastructure

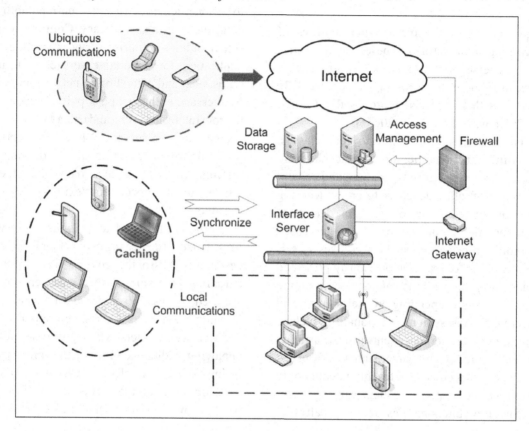

the availability of most services, it also creates new hurdles, such as assigning network addresses to devices in motion, determining users' current locations to route data to them, adapting network routes to device location, discovering group membership for multicast communications (What students are taking this lesson through the wireless network? What students enrolled in this course are currently online and can thus receive urgent notices?). Differences between data cached on mobile devices and data stored on servers must be synchronized upon subsequent connection. Some of these problems can be dealt with as described later in this chapter. Others require adapting solutions proposed in the literature for different contexts or designing novel mechanisms.

ISSUES RELATED TO WIRELESS TECHNOLOGIES

The platforms in Table 2 fail to supply pervasive learning: all intelligence is on a server accessed via browser over the network. Wireless technologies mandate a revision of strategy. They rely on either *ubiquitous communication services*, generally provided at a fee by telecommunication operators (GPRS, UMTS, i-Mode, etc.), or *local communication services* set up via user cooperation or through university infrastructure (Figure 4). Campus solutions employing technologies like WiFi and Bluetooth use the unlicensed Industrial, Scientific and Medical band (ISM) free of charge.

Ubiquitous communication services allow information access from anywhere: GPRS and UMTS offer access to multimedia content; SMS text messages convey notices. These services are only slightly better than requiring a fixed-infrastructure Internet connection. Even if every student had a flat-rate always-on wireless connection, security management, which is wholly up to the provider, would be of no use for authenticating campus users. In many places such services are costly, which discourages students from using them. Moreover, there is a strong commitment to university independence. For this reason we focus on local communication services.

Two different kinds of wireless environment, **infrastructured** and **ad hoc**, require different strategies and solutions. The latter entails more setup problems. Both require careful security management.

In an **infrastructured environment** devices connect through APs that coordinate clients. Clients are not allowed to connect to one another directly. Authentication is needed to control access to resources. Confidentiality, required to preserve user privacy, can be obtained through data encryption. These two goals are achieved in one shot by deploying a central authority that authenticates users. Once a user has been recognized, his/her profile adapts learning content and authorizes access. A user's profile may also include his/her cryptographic key.

Two possible strategies are WiFi Protected Access (WPA) and virtual private network (VPN). *WPA enterprise* needs an authentication server on the network: user name and password establish connection to the AP. These are sent to the authentication server, which validates the user, provides access to resources, and allows association with the AP. The connection is encrypted to ensure user privacy.

VPN-based solutions provide open connection to the network through APs. Once connection is established, the user must be separately authenticated over the VPN. If authentication is successful, an encrypted tunnel to the VPN server is established. Critical resources are accessed through the VPN server, which forwards only messages from authorized tunnels. Legacy devices support authentication through Wired Equivalent Privacy (WEP), which has flawed security and does not scale. Such devices cannot adopt WPA, which requires firmware support from APs. However, they could use VPN, after software installation on the client device. VPN is more secure, because traffic is encrypted along the whole route from source to destination, rather than only up to the first AP as with WPA. VPN software is user upgradable. WPA requires manufacturers to implement upgrades but is easier to deploy.

To guarantee service, APs must cover the entire area. These systems are more prone to denial-of-service attacks than wired systems because of their shared radio channel.

In **ad hoc networks**, all nodes are hosts and routers simultaneously. Hosts move around and topology changes quickly. Though still difficult to achieve, ad hoc networking is included in the specifications of major wireless technologies. For WiFi, different manufacturers implement specifications in different—not completely compliant—ways, which sometimes causes inconsistent behavior. For Bluetooth, network cards have yet to implement the whole specification, which—for its part—does not standardize mechanisms for setting up ad hoc networks. Novel strategies have been designed to route data through the resulting topology (AODV (Perkins, 1999)), look up resources and services available on the network, and create connections with hosts beyond radio range. Research into these not-yet-standardized mechanisms is still underway. Security is also a hot topic in wireless networking, because radio communication is more prone to attacks and eavesdropping than wired networks. User authentication can be performed in two ways: a central server is reached using ad hoc connectivity or a distributed strategy is employed, requiring a message-authentication primitive. Different cryptographic primitives are possible, including HMAC (Message Authentication Codes) and DS (Digital Signature). HMAC uses symmetric keys, which can be deployed on thin devices, but requires a secret key for every pair of hosts and is not suitable for broadcast transmissions. DS relies on asymmetric key cryptography; only N pairs of private/public keys are needed in a network of N nodes, but computation cost is too high for thin devices and the approach is less resilient to denial-of-service attacks. DS is suitable for signed broadcast messages.

The following sections analyze existing proposals that support m-learning with wireless technologies. A novel wireless infrastructure designed by the authors is also described.

ARCHITECTURES FOR M-LEARNING

Existing Architectures and Solutions

M-learning solutions proposed in the literature emphasize anywhere, anytime learning. Georgiev (2004) surveys devices and wireless technologies suited to m-learning, while Zhang (2005) discusses social aspects in ubiquitous learning through wireless devices.

One important experience, the *Leonardo da Vinci* European Project (Landers, 2002a), designed a wireless virtual learning environment for distance education based on PDAs, wireless palmtops, and WAP cell-phone technologies. Teaching is primarily supported by desktop or laptop hosts. When the primary host is unavailable (e.g., as user travels), handheld devices are used to download content, participate in forums or exchange e-mail. Network connection is achieved through WAP-enabled cell phones; hence, using the platform requires payment. Devices do not communicate among themselves directly: all communication is server-mediated.

The existing infrastructure that comes closest to having the features identified above, *Active-Campus* (activecampus.ucsd.edu), consists of two parts: *ActiveClass* to support in-class activities and *ActiveCampus Explorer* to support cooperative work. AC Explorer implements a set of services to support the learning community. Users' PDAs enable interaction with the environment, leave 'graffiti,' send messages to other users, discover possible buddies or relevant places nearby, use navigation based on the campus map, and receive general-interest announcements. This augments the physical environment with information from the virtual world comprising user interactions and relationships. ActiveClass supports classroom activities by managing questions and answers, gathering feedback, and polling via PDA. Both modules employ client-server structure, with lightest possible client-side processing load. Griswold (2002) discusses details for implementing AC Explorer and scalability limits due to the centralized approach.

MOBIlearn (www.mobilearn.org) applies m-learning to MBAs. It focuses on defining an open framework for m-learning, context/location awareness, content for mobile devices, and collaborative learning, while emphasizing ambient intelligence. Its infrastructure offers point-to-point and multicast communication using both wireless LAN technology and GPRS supplied by providers, although the Project Final Report stresses the former.

Nagaoka (2005) uses cell phones with i-Mode technology for in-class assessment. However, since i-Mode technology is not available worldwide, this solution is not universally suitable. And it is expensive.

Among the many other experiments, several target children (Yatani, 2004; Curtis, 2002). Landers (2002b) surveys a numerous m-learning projects. These projects' university-level learning activities consist of porting existing applications for note-taking, collaboration, and assessment to mobile devices, as well as supplying courses and content. The wireless technology used—when networking is needed—is WAP or 3G mobile telephony; hence, these solutions do not come free to users.

The next section describes our architecture designed to support ubiquitous m-learning. A comparison of m-learning architectures follows.

ARISTOTLE Architecture

Our proposed ARISTOTLE architecture (*A*d hoc wi*R*eless *I*nfra*S*tructure for ubiqui*TO*us *T*eaching and *LE*arning, named for the philosopher's peripatetic teaching) uses wireless technologies to support fully ubiquitous, remote asynchronous m-learning and graceful cooperation among students, faculty, and staff (Grew, 2006a; Grew, 2005b). The two main characteristics of ARISTOTLE are:

1. Its wireless technologies use unlicensed ISM spectrum (WiFi, Bluetooth), making services available free.
2. Its modular architecture does not implement all modules on all devices, depending on device type and user requirements.

ARISTOTLE services rely only on users' devices, making the platform usable even when no other equipment is available. Figure 5 shows ARISTOTLE's architecture. Four classes of service correspond to different platform-usage scenarios:

- **In-class activities** are supported both in the classroom (whether equipped or not) and outside (e.g. during field work). ARISTOTLE's learning and communication functionalities (Figure 3) belong to this service class. Communication functionalities support user cooperation. Students can send the teacher questions, which may be made anonymous and re-multicast to all students, and show

interest in another student's question or reply to a question. The e-learning platform ranks questions so the teacher can adjust lesson pace dynamically and skew content according to feedback. The teacher can generate content dynamically, sending it immediately to students, allowing annotation. Students may exchange content (e.g., late arrivals could download missed lesson segments from classmates).

- **Group-learning** functionalities are much like those for in-class activities. The main difference lies in organization: in work-groups, any student may assume the role of resource provider. In both cases, a peer-to-peer approach seems most appropriate, with a flat peer-to-peer group for cooperative learning or a teacher as super-peer for in-class activities. Internetworking can support cooperative work among participants in different locations.

- The **announcement subsystem**, along with the ambient-intelligence subsystem described below, implements some cooperative-work services, though "cooperation" has much broader meaning than usual in the proposed framework. The announcement system implements a *push* service to ease retrieval of pertinent information. When faculty or staff need to publish announcements, in addition to posting on the Web, they directly message affected subscribers.

- The **ambient-intelligence** subsystem enables users around campus to interact in two ways: retrieving information and annotating the environment. Users locate themselves and their campus destinations. They find out whether a given study hall has seats, whether the bookshop has a title in stock, what thesis projects a teacher offers, and so forth. They can announce a study session being organized, post comments on cafeteria offerings, and so on. This is achieved by equipping relevant points around campus with wireless devices, *intelligent tags* or infostations that communicate with users' thin devices. Locations for such devices might include faculty and student-services offices, common areas (cafeterias, study halls, bookstores), and possible 'totems' scattered around.

To illustrate the tasks assigned to each module and how the modules interoperate, we consider each class of services separately and then discuss implementation.

In-Class Activities

The following steps are executed:

1. Teacher *T* authenticates at the *security manager* and obtains authorization, through the *data access filter*, to download the list of his/her students' identifiers to his/her own device. Student IDs and profiles are retrieved from the *user profile database* and contain: ‹student name, student number, preferences for service fruition, record for this course›. The optional last field might also come from the teacher's personal database.

2. Once at lesson venue, wireless devices set up an *ad hoc* network *N*. *T* gives students a network name and initializes the network with his/her own device. To guarantee network connectivity among "clouds" of devices with different wireless technologies, *ad hoc gateways* may be created by equipping some devices with additional wireless network interface cards. The *resource discovery* service detects any available Internet APs. APs and gateways automatically reformat data packets for various technologies. Every link, whether wired or wireless, is considered for *routing*.

3. The *e-learning platform* is run. Students configure *T*'s device as lesson server. Students, authenticated by the e-learning platform, log onto *T*'s device. This allows students' network addresses to be sent to *T*'s device along with authentication information, populating *T*'s *name server* tables for future unicast communications. At the end of this step, both unicast and multicast routing tables are computed. *Multicast* groups are typically the group *S* of students and the group *P* of all participants ($P = S \cup \{T\}$).

Figure 5. ARISTOTLE architecture

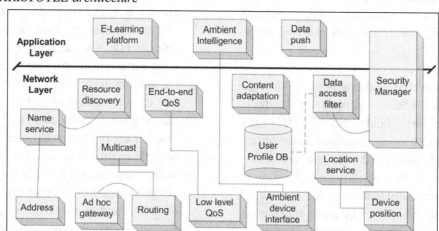

4. During class, routing tables are continuously updated despite device movement (e.g. lessons held outside the classroom). An AP within range also allows content download from the Internet. Multimedia may require quality of service (*QoS*) guarantees of the network. Content retrieval is assured by equipping the e-learning platform with search criteria, which are handled by the *resource discovery* module. Searches may include hardware resources, such as "the nearest color printer." Assuming heterogeneous devices will be connected to the network, complex content needs adaptation to device characteristics.

Group Learning

The following steps are executed:

1. Students set up a study group using local ad hoc networking. They configure content-adaptation and resource-sharing preferences for the particular session.

2. If another group somewhere on campus is studying the same subject, the two may merge. To this end, the *resource discovery* module should be able to detect the existence of similar interest groups. Metadata maintained by the *resource discovery* service associates each device with information about user interests published for cooperation purposes. If like-minded groups exist, the *location service* module locates them on the campus network in one of two ways: if connection is through an AP, then the user ID or MAC address is used as a search key to discover that AP; otherwise, the geographic location is looked up, using GPS or triangulation techniques or the positions of the APs in range. Geographic position is determined by the *device position* module. The network and MAC-layer modules use location information to build the communication infrastructure that connects groups. This network may be either ad hoc, if wireless coverage suffices for all interested devices, or infrastructured, if portions of the fixed campus network are used. Users in motion can participate if in wireless range.

3. The network is used for cooperative work and content exchange as with in-class activities.

Announcement System

The following steps are executed:

1. The *user profile DB* shows how users wish to receive urgent notices, whether by e-mail, instant message, or cell-phone text message. The profile includes e-mail address, IM address, or cell-phone number, respectively. For instant messages, users must be online when the notice is published. Users may also specify alternatives: "send me an instant message if online, otherwise an SMS." They must specify information type, e.g. notices about certain courses, grants for undergraduates, etc.

2. The presence of online campus-network users is recorded by both the *resource discovery* and the *location* services—as for group learning. When an announcement is generated, the *data push* module retrieves a list of interested users, with delivery preferences, from the *data access filter*. The *data push* module discovers whether and where each user who prefers instant messages is online from the *resource discovery* and *location* services. For those online, the announcement is properly reformatted by the *content adaptation* module and sent through the routing infrastructure built by the *multicast* module. The *QoS* modules guarantee reliable and low-latency message delivery.

For all other users, the announcement is formatted as either e-mail or a 160-byte SMS and sent.

Ambient Intelligence

The steps for interaction between a thin device and the environment are:

1. The user discovers wireless resources within range. This is performed at the MAC layer, by the *ambient device interface*. Ambient devices can then be queried for metadata describing their role (e.g., "tag on Prof. W's office door") through the *ambient intelligence* module at the application layer. The information exchanged is application- and technology-dependent, as in experiments with Bluetooth technology (Pagani, 2004). The user chooses an ambient device and establishes a session through the *ambient intelligence* application.

2. Information uploaded by the user is held in the device's memory for access by other users. If the user asks about resource avail-

ability, available resources matching desired characteristics are retrieved through interaction between the *ambient intelligence* and the *resource discovery* modules.

3. Location-dependent information—such as the route to a certain point or identity of the nearest resource of a given kind—can be retrieved by determining the current user's position. As discussed above, the *device position* and *location service* modules accomplish this. The location service tracks users so they are reachable for buddy seeking and announcements.

Table 3 compares ARISTOTLE and other m-learning solutions discussed above.

In terms of equipment, ARISTOTLE is the only solution involving ad hoc networking. Even without infrastructure, ARISTOTLE provides services for in-class activities and group learning (though without Internet). All one-to-one interactions between a thin device and an ambient device are possible but no information except that on the two devices can be retrieved. The announcement system could deploy only when wireless devices

Table 3. Comparison of m-learning solutions

	ARISTOTLE	Active-Campus	Leonardo	MOBIlearn
Education	Blended	In presence	Distance	Blended
Wireless technology	Free (WiFi, Bluetooth)	Free (WiFi)	Paid (WAP, GPRS, UMTS)	Mixed (WiFi, GPRS)
Classroom support	Yes (distributed)	Yes (centralized)	No	Yes
Equipment	No (but support for services may be partial)	Server in class, APs around campus	Server	Portal
Groupwork	Yes	No	Limited (forum, e-mail)	Yes
Announcments	Yes (personalized)	Yes (generalized)	Yes (personalized)	No
Ambient intelligence	Yes	Yes	No	Yes

are dense enough to cover the campus area, perhaps employing opportunistic networking (but this is still open research).

Implementation

While implementing an ARISTOTLE prototype, we discuss some of the solutions adopted. Our solution uses an infrastructured network with potential ad hoc connectivity. WiFi APs around campus deny outside access by using VPN authentication. A novel localization protocol discovers whether and where a user is connected to infrastructure through wireless links. Multicast group membership is preset and entered in user repositories. We are experimenting with routing protocols proposed in the literature (AODV for ad hoc networks, epidemic algorithms for data diffusion) and developing open-source code for notebooks and palmtops. The software, to be freely available to run on users' mobile devices, includes ad hoc networking protocols, allowing access the platform even when off the campus wireless LAN. Our prototype implementation tested two methods for connecting wireless clouds to the Internet (Step 2 for In-Class Activities), once an ad hoc network is up. Though performed with Bluetooth devices, the same considerations apply to WiFi technology. The teacher can assign IP addresses manually, from lists of enrolled students. RIP (Malkin, 1998) runs on routers. The second method, which proved more flexible and scalable, can be implemented when Internet access is through a LAN with a DHCP server: the teacher's device is configured as a bridge to the LAN, DHCP assigns IP addresses, and routing is performed by routers on the LAN. QoS comes from appropriate protocols at the application layer, RTP (Schulzrinne, 1996) or RTSP (Schulzrinne, 1998), and below, M-CAMP (Pagani, 2001). Our prototype adapts content accessed through the Web by employing Cocoon (cocoon.apache.org) to extract client-device and browser information from HTTP requests. With this information,

documents stored in XML are translated into the appropriate format by XSLT transformation rules. More sophisticated personalization is possible through CCPP (W3C, 2006) and DELI (DElivery context LIbrary). Besides device characteristics, CCPP profiles contain users' preferences (e.g. sound volume, cookies on/off, etc.), which can be modified during the session. DELI enables Cocoon to manage CCPP profiles. Profiles may be contained either in HTTP requests or in student records stored on a teacher's device. A student's profile may also be configured on his/her e-learning client and sent to the teacher during network setup. Content is adapted through XSLT according to preferences.

OUTLOOK

Learning platforms began with a server-client approach, the client merely a terminal for Web-based content on the same LAN. Technology improvements and the Internet brought users access to content via portal from any connected computer. This raised new security issues but also opened new access opportunities.

Wireless technologies make learning ubiquitous: infrastructured local communication services (deployed APs) and ubiquitous communication services (commercial wireless) offer access anywhere. Local services on ad hoc networks provide connectivity anywhere, even without infrastructure. The platform itself becomes ubiquitous: teachers can proactively download part of the e-learning infrastructure for later access over the ad hoc network. Hence, m-learning reaches beyond the client-server paradigm that has dominated e-learning.

Moreover, ad hoc networking adds real-time tools to the process, enabling cooperation through devices to enrich collaborative learning. This completes the transition from e-learning to m-learning systems, where ubiquity is brought first to clients, then learning applications. Applied (pp. 20-29).

Pervasive Learning.

Conference on Web-Based Education.

pervasively or synchronously, the transition takes us beyond the bulletin-board paradigm of pulled information and the prepared-slide paradigm of the lecture.

Wireless technologies over unlicensed radio spectrum—without special networking equipment, providers or APs—offer unique flexibility: interaction whenever devices come into contact. As public APs spread and device costs fall, new opportunities for computer-mediated communication abound. Asynchronous content will remain important with data portability on thin devices. As pervasive technologies profoundly affect social interaction, learning infrastructures will change apace. Some interesting campus scenarios for mobile devices are described in Weiser (1998).

Distinctions between remote and in-presence interaction or between synchronous and asynchronous communication will grow more nuanced, establishing parallel reality both as part of real-time, physical campus life and apart from it. Mediating relations via computer will prove advantageous in some circumstances. One drawback of the information society, overload, will be met by networked systems that combine preferences stored on mobile devices with location- and context-awareness to select information of interest and adjust application behavior to location and activity. ActiveCampus Explorer employs such principles to find nearby buddies. Similarly, content-adaptation applications will interface with devices optimized for users' specific different physical abilities.

Portable devices thus promise to create an *extended campus* with two interwoven facets: the real and the *virtual*. Virtual users—personified by avatars with preference and profile data—collaborate by sharing content and distributed applications. Mobility not only extends learning opportunities across time and space barriers but enriches learning experiences with added dimensions.

REFERENCES

Collier, G. (2002). E-*Learning Application Infrastructure*. Sun Microsystems White Paper.

Curtis, M., Luchini, K., Bobrowsky, W., Quintana, C., & Soloway, E. (2002). Handheld use in K-12: A descriptive account. In *Proceedings IEEE International Workshop WMTE*.

Davis, A. (2004). Developing an infrastructure for online learning. In T. Anderson and F. Elloumi (Eds.), *Theory and Practice of Online Learning*. Athabasca University, Athabasca, AB.

Georgiev, T., Georgieva, E., & Smrikarov, A. (2004). M-learning—A new stage of e-learning. In *Proceedings CompSysTech 2004*.

Grew, P., Longhi, I., Pagani, E., De Cindio, F., & Ripamonti, L. (2004). An open-source LMS evolves as learning/teaching/testing environment. In *Proceedings of the International Conference on Technology-Enhanced Learning (TEL'04)*.

Grew, P., Longhi, I., & Pagani, E. (2005a). Functional architecture of a Web-based distributed system for University Curricula Support. In *Proceedings of the IASTED International Conference on Web-Based Education* (pp. 332-337).

Grew, P., & Pagani, E. (2005b). Towards a wireless architecture for mobile ubiquitous e-Learning. In *Proceedings of the International Workshop on Learning Communities in the Era of Ubiquitous Computing* (pp. 20-29).

Grew, P., Giudici, F., & Pagani, E. (2006a). Specification of a functional architecture for e-Learning supported by wireless technologies. In *Proceedings of the 2nd IEEE International Workshop on Pervasive Learning*.

Grew, P., & Pagani, E. (2006b). Channeling the bricks-and-mortar lesson onto students' devices. In *Proceedings of the IASTED International Conference on Web-Based Education*.

Griswold, W., Boyer, R., & Brown, S. et al. (2002). *ActiveCampus—Sustaining educational communities through mobile technology.* UCSD CSE Technical Report #CS2002-0714, University of California, San Diego.

JLI! Development Group (2005a). *JLI!—Just Learn It! Home Page.* Retrieved from http://jli.retecivica.milano.it/index.php

JLI! Development Group (2005b). JLI!—Just Learn It! *SourceForge Project.* Retrieved from http://sourceforge.net/projects/jli/

Landers, P. (2002a). *Leonardo da Vinci Project—Home Page.* Retrieved from http://learning.ericsson.net/mlearning2/project_one/index.html

Landers, P. (2002b). *M-learning Initiatives in 2001.* Retrieved from http://learning.ericsson.net/mlearning2/project_one/thebook/chapter4.html

Licklider, J.C.R. (1968). The computer as a communication device. *Science and Technology.*

Malkin, G. (1998). Routing Information Protocol (RIP)—Version 2. *RFC 2453.* Work in progress.

Nagaoka K. (2005). A response analyzer system utilizing mobile phones. In *Proceedings of the IASTED International Conference on Web-Based Education* (pp. 579-584).

Pagani, E., & Rossi, G.P. (2001). A framework for the admission control of QoS multicast traffic in mobile ad hoc networks. In *Proceedings of the ACM International Workshop WoWMoM* (pp. 3-12).

Pagani, E., Tebaldi, S., & Rossi, G.P. (2004). A service discovery infrastructure for heterogeneous wired/bluetooth networks. In *Proceedings of the International Workshop on Ubiquitous Computing (IWUC 2004).*

Perkins, C., & Royer, E. (1999). Ad hoc on-demand distance vector routing. In *Proceedings of the 2ⁿᵈ IEEE Workshop Mobile Computing Systems and Applications.*

Rheingold, H. (2002). *Smart mobs.* New York: Perseus Books.

Schulzrinne, H., Casner, S., Frederick, R., & Jacobson, V. (1996). RTP: A transport protocol for real-time applications. *RFC 1889.* Work in progress.

Schulzrinne, H., Rao, A., & Lanphier, R. (1998). Real time streaming protocol. *RFC 2326.* Work in progress.

Sermersheim, J. (2006). Lightweight directory access protocol. *RFC 4511.* Work in progress.

Small, T. & Haas, Z. (2003). The shared wireless infostation model—A new ad hoc networking paradigm (or Where there is a Whale, there is a Way). In *Proceedings of the ACM International Symposium MobiHoc* (pp. 233-44).

W3C—World Wide Web Consortium. (2006). *Composite Capabilities/Preferences Profile Public Home Page.* Retrieved from http://www.w3.oorg/Mobile/CCPP/

Weiser, M. (1998). The future of ubiquitous computing on campus. *Communications of the ACM, 41*(1), 41-42.

Yatani, K., Onuma, M., Sugimoto, M., & Kusunoki, F. (2004). Musex: A system for supporting children's collaborative learning in a museum with PDAs. *Journal of Systems and Computers in Japan, 35*(14), 54-63.

Zhang, G., Jin, Q., & Lin, M. (2005). A framework of social interaction support for ubiquitous learning. In *Proceedings of the 19ᵗʰ IEEE International Conference AINA.*

Chapter V
Architectures of Existing and Conceptual Applications of Podcasting in E–Learning Systems

Stephen R. Chastain
The University of Tennessee, USA

Jason Caudill
The University of Tennessee, USA

ABSTRACT

Podcasting has quickly emerged as a leading technology in the new field of mobile learning. Tracing this new technology's history over the past two years reveals just how broadly the use of digital audio files may become in the fields of education and training. The ease of use, low cost of creation and hosting, and most importantly pervasiveness of user access to compatible hardware combine to make podcasting a major force in both traditional and distance education. This chapter explores the history, technology, and application of podcasting as an instructional tool.

INTRODUCTION

This chapter will explore audio podcasting from both the theoretical and practical perspectives. Through a combination of research findings and professional experience, the authors will relate what is involved in the use of podcasting in instructional environments, including pedagogy, design, technical specifications, implementation, and operation. Given the relatively new emergence of podcasting as an e-learning technology, there is very little literature about the architecture of podcasting applications specifically. Therefore, to address the implementation of this new technology, it is necessary to utilize architectures of other e-learning applications that are similarly distributed with similar purposes. In doing this, the reader will gain an understanding of how podcasts are created and distributed as well as how learners benefit from having access to podcasts.

Podcasts are architecturally unique in their relationship to e-learning, in large part because of the many different ways they can be employed. Because a podcast can be a recording of a live event or a specially prepared recorded message it is more than just another media format for course documentation; it can serve as a record of learning activities for use in the future. In order to capitalize on this capacity it is necessary to consider the full range of podcasting implementation, from initial creation to access by the learners.

The objective of the chapter is to provide the learner with definitions of what podcasting is and also an understanding of how podcasting works. After reading this chapter, the learner should be prepared to move towards the implementation of a podcasting program in their own organization.

BACKGROUND

Defining Podcasting

To begin the discussion of podcasting, it is first necessary to build an understanding of what podcasting is and just how prevalent its use has become in a very short period of time. In examining the lifespan of podcasting to the time of this writing in 2006, there has really only been about two years since its public inception. Despite this short time in the public eye, podcasting has already expanded beyond the expectations of even its most zealous advocates.

In a blog entry dated September 28, 2004, Doc Searls, a co-author of the book *The Cluetrain Manifesto* discussed podcasting in some detail

and noted that a Google search on "podcasts" brought up 24 hits. Searls went on to predict that in another year, the same search would "pull up hundreds of thousands, or perhaps even millions" of hits. That estimate probably seemed liberal to Searls, but in reality it was far too conservative. On May 25, just eight months later, a commenter on Searls's blog entry clicked on the search link and found 4,460,000 Google hits for "podcasts." On June 23, that same Google search link returned well over 6,000,000 hits. On August 28, it returned over 21,000,000 hits. On September 18, the number had exceeded 60,000,000. Clearly, this medium has caught the imagination of a large and growing audience (Cambell, 2005). On August 4, 2006, the same search produced 390,000,000 hits in .05 seconds. These numbers are evidence of the fact that podcasting's popularity continues to grow exponentially.

In March 2005 a survey was conducted by Pew Internet and American Life Project that discovered 29% of adult owners of MP3 players have listened to a podcast—amounting to a current podcast audience estimated to exceed six million people (Rainie & Madden, 2005). Another recent Pew Internet survey reveals some very interesting facts about this new phenomenon called podcasting:

- More than six million American adults have listened to a podcast, 29% of those own MP3 players.
- Some 11% of American adults surveyed said they own an iPod or other type of MP3 player. That amounts to over 22 million people.
- Almost one in five (19%) of people ages 18-28 have iPods/MP3 players. Fully 14% of those ages 29-40; and 11% of younger Baby Boomers (ages 41-50) are all owners of MP3/iPod players. That compares to 6% of older Baby Boomers (ages 51-59), 6% of those 60-69 and 1% of those 70 and older.
- Nearly half of those between the ages of 18-28 who own iPods/MP3 players have downloaded a podcast as compared to about

20% age 29 or older have downloaded a podcast (Rainie & Madden, 2005).

What exactly is a podcast? It is perhaps best defined as: "(1) Podcasting is an audio content delivery based on Web syndication protocols such as RSS and/or Atom. (2) Podcasting aims to distribute content to be used with mobile and digital audio/video players such as iPods including all other MP3 players, cell phones, and PDAs" (Cebeci & Tekdal, 2006). The word podcasting[1] came about in 2004 through the combination of the words iPod and broadcasting. Even though the name of this new technology is derived from the iPod, it is not necessary to have an iPod to listen to a podcast. A podcast can be played back on any MP3 player or computer with a sound card and speakers. The editors of the New Oxford American Dictionary chose podcasting as the 2005 word of the year, defining it as "a digital recording of a radio broadcast or similar program, made available on the Internet for downloading to a personal audio player" (Eash, 2006). Erin McKean, editor-in-chief of the New Oxford American dictionary, said the term podcast was considered for inclusion last year but it was viewed as a technology that not enough people were using or even understood its meaning. "This year it's a completely different story," she said. "The word has finally caught up with the rest of the iPod phenomenon" (Training et al., 2005).

In simple terms, a podcast is an audio blog with one exception. This difference is that a podcast is presented in audio form instead of text. The audio files are created in MP3 format to make them small enough to be stored on a server and allow for quick download to the listener. The audio content can be anything including: a person's feelings about an issue, a lecture from a prominent educator, an interview, or music; content is at the producer's discretion. If it is audio it can be produced into a podcast. The recording can be created on a handheld digital recorder or from a microphone attached to a computer sound card.

Once the recording is created, the audio file is uploaded to a Web site or blog where it can be downloaded by listeners.

By using a technology called RSS (Really Simple Syndication) listeners can subscribe to podcasts and have them automatically downloaded to their computer and/or mp3 player. This RSS allows the listener to stop focusing on constantly looking for new podcast content they want to listen to from a particular producer. The listener subscribes to the podcast, and the aggregator (RSS) finds the data and downloads it to the computer. The easiest way to think about this is to imagine a podcast as a digital magazine subscription; a person subscribes to the podcast through an RSS feed, and when a new issue is produced it is delivered to you. Programs like iTunes, iPodder and Podcast Alley have provided a simple method of downloading and listening. From the e-learning architecture perspective, these feeds are similar to learning portals, which work to deliver appropriate media to learners and provide a distribution conduit for instructors (Brusilovsky, 2004).

The distribution channels of podcasting are just one half of the equation in their popularity, the other is the ubiquity of mobile technology. There appears to be a universal shift towards mobile devices with an increasing number of people now owning digital gadgets such as iPods, Smart phones, PDAs and WiFi digital cameras. This technological ownership will, in the future, have the potential to provide a new method of learning. To survive in the market, educational institutions "have to give clients—whether they are individuals or large corporations—what they want, when they want it, and where they want it" (Wright, 2005).

Uses of Podcasting

According to a survey by Kineo, over 50% of respondents use audio learning at least occasionally and 50% of people stated that an MP3 player was their preferred method of using audio learning.

Matt Fox, a partner with Kineo, issued a challenge to the educational community:

We've reached the point where audio learning must be part of what we consider in our learning solutions. It's easy to create, gives experts a real voice, and is informal and disposable. But we have to do two things: design it properly—short, modular clips, not 30 minute monologues. And, make access easier—nearly 40% of survey respondents believe they don't have the right technology to access audio. (Kineo.co.uk, 2005)

Research conducted by Cebeci and Tekdal of Cukurova University, in Adana, Turkey, found that podcasting can be considered a complimentary tool for e-learning. "Therefore, podcasting should be taken into account as a means to utilize and evaluate the growing prevalence of mobile players in e-learning" (Cebeci & Tekdal, 2006). They found that podcasting serves the student by allowing students to retrieve information on a needs basis, not only relying on time in the classroom for learning to take place. Because thousands of students already use MP3 players for entertainment, it seems that providing educational information via podcast is an effective way to pass information on to students. "Perhaps, one of the most important pedagogic characteristics offered by podcasting is learning through listening" (Cebeci & Tekdal, 2006). They state that for many people "listening may be more attractive and less tedious than reading" (Cebeci & Tekdal, 2006). They also say that many students learn better from listening than they do from reading, and that podcasting can provide a means of learning to students who do not enjoy reading.

In addition to serving learners who do not enjoy reading, podcasts can provide access to materials for individuals who have visual challenges (Cebeci & Tekdal, 2006). Podcasting can be integrated into Web-based learning management systems (LMSs), such as Blackboard, where audio

recordings (podcasts) could be posted to be used by students with learning problems. The recording of lectures has taken place for many years and with the advent of digital recording, the cost of recording has been reduced drastically. Caryl Oliver (2005) from the William Angliss Institute states, "There's so much technology out there but most is developed for business purposes. For education, we must explore, change and alter everything to see if it can work." We have passed over the threshold where it is clear that these tools will be definitive shapers of both economies and educational institutions (Oliver, 2005).

Reasons for Podcasting Growth

In a March 2003 interview with Jon Udell, lead analyst and blogger-in-chief at the InfoWorld Test Center, five major factors behind the fast pace growth of podcasting were identified:

- Internet activity is pervasive.
- Broadband has grown very rapidly, which makes it far easier to "consume large media objects."
- The multimedia personal computer can "more or less be taken for granted."
- The "distinction between streaming and downloading of media content has begun to blur.... People can now have the experience of streaming while enjoying the simplicity of downloading."
- Finally, there is the iPod phenomenon and "the rapid adoption of portable MP3 playback devices"—up to eleven million devices in the United States alone. Udell calls the portable audio device "the new transistor radio" and points to the beginnings of a "renaissance of creative stuff happening." Because this renaissance coincides with the Creative Commons phenomenon, traditional business models need not constrain the artist's work (Cambell, 2005).

Many educational podcasts focus on lectures and other instructional content. Yet some researchers think that another value of podcasting is that of building community and giving learners the ability to create. In support of this idea, there are models of system architecture such as the RAED (Role-based Access Control for the Evolution of Distributed Courseware) project "...based on the fact that higher education involves inducting the student into a community of learners in which learning results from not only student-student and student-tutor interaction, but also via vicarious learning from observed interactions amongst other community members" (Neely, Lowe, Eyers, Bacon, Newman, & Gong, 2004). This podcasting function would integrate into what is referred to as a student model server, an accessible network location where student materials are stored, accessed, and reviewed, as well as a place where students can create and upload their own original content (Brusilovsky, 2004). In a pilot study at Charles Stuart University, researchers looked at how three to five minute student-produced podcasts can be used to help new students with class anxiety. "The preconceptions and anxiety that students bring into the classroom act as barriers that must be overcome before effective learning can take place" (Chan & Lee, 2005). Chan and Lee conducted a study about these barriers and how podcasting could help alleviate some of the anxieties students face. Ramsden states that any anxiety students have about a subject will affect the learning styles they exhibit (Ramsden, 1992). Together they looked at ways that podcasting could help students in preparation for classes. Chan and Lee concluded that the affective and cognitive benefits associated with audio, along with its cost-effectiveness, make podcasting an ideal medium for producing materials to address students' preconceptions about a subject and its content, and to alleviate the anxiety that students bring into the classroom (Chan & Lee, 2005).

Podcasting is obviously a diverse and rapidly growing component of the technology-enhanced communication field. Given the broad range of technical components that go into producing and distributing podcasts, an in-depth examination of how podcasts can be created and how, once created, they can be applied to an instructional purpose will contribute to an overall understanding of podcasting as a discipline.

PODCASTING ARCHITECTURE

Introduction

To effectively use podcasting as an instructional tool it is necessary to understand the technical aspects of the media. By understanding how podcasts are created, how they can be distributed, and what kinds of devices can be used by a learner to access podcasts, it is possible for an instructor to construct a picture of the architecture associated with podcasts. This architecture includes not only creating and distributing media, but accounting for factors such as user access to technology, intended learning outcomes of the implementation, and the different categories of people involved in the process. All of these categories and more are a part of the architecture of podcasting in an instructional environment, and by knowing what is involved in the architectural structure of podcasts a practitioner can begin to establish their own design.

The Technology of Podcasting

The technology behind podcasting comprises four basic categories: media, software, networking, and hardware. An interesting point to begin with is that neither the media nor the software behind podcasting are really new developments. The mobile networking and mobile hardware that really support the portability and mobile learning applications of podcasting, however, are much more recent developments. One point that it is important to repeat in this introduction is that while the term podcast was derived from Apple Computer's popular MP3 device, the iPod, it is not necessary to have an iPod to play a podcast. The hardware section will cover options in detail, but there are a wide variety of devices capable of playing podcasts; they are not limited to just MP3 players.

In its initial form, the podcast was a recorded audio file distributed to mobile devices, most often as an MPEG-1 Audio Layer 3 file, commonly referred to as an MP3. In this form, the podcast basically works as an on-demand radio stream. Users can access the file when and where they want to listen, at which point they listen to a recorded audio stream via headphones or speakers, as much as they would listen to a radio broadcast. As the technology of podcasts advanced, they progressed from being just audio files to audio accompanied by still digital images. Most often, these images work as presentation slides to accompany the audio with bullet points of the major topics or printed details of information that can be accessed separate from the audio stream. At this stage, the podcast is much more like a lecture or presentation than a radio broadcast because the audience gets both the audio information and images to support the audio.

The next, and so far final, step of podcasting evolution is that of full video files. Depending on use these presentations are usually referred to as either video podcasts or vodcasts. These files may be distributed in a variety of formats, although the most common are variations of the Moving Picture Experts Group (MPEG), Audio Video Interleave (AVI), or QuickTime. In this instance, a podcast can give the viewer the experience of attending the lecture as they can hear the audio of the presentation, see the slides that are used, and also see the presenter as the information is delivered.

In the chapter's discussion of podcasting, the focus is on audio only and audio plus still image podcasts, as the vodcast is in many ways a different means of sharing information. In large part,

this difference lies in the fact that without a video component an individual can listen to the broadcast without watching the screen at all times. Even for podcasts with digital still images, it may only be necessary for someone to occasionally look at the screen to see supporting information; they do not have to devote their attention to it.

The software applications being utilized for podcasting are not new or unique applications. For audio only podcasts, all that is necessary is to have a quality audio recording package. On Windows and Linux computers one of the popular applications currently available is the open source program Audacity. This application allows users to record live audio, convert audio files to other formats, and perform advanced audio editing functions such as working with multiple tracks and adjusting the speed or pitch of a recording. With these recording and editing features it is possible to prepare an audio podcast for distribution. Also, being an open source product, it is readily available to users regardless of budget or platform. On the Mac operating system, Audacity is also an option, but the most popular application currently is the Apple software package Garage Band, which is included with Mac's OS X.x releases. In addition to the audio recording and editing features that are included in Audacity, Garage Band features preloaded sound clips and features that make it easy for users to create introductions and other effects with a recording. Also, Garage Band is equipped to create podcasts that combine audio and still digital images, with the capability for users to insert images at specific points in the recording and also to hold images in place for a given period of time.

Following the requirements for media and software are the necessities of having the appropriate hardware and networking to make podcast information available to the intended audience. Fortunately, there are a wide variety of options that all successfully meet the requirements of podcasting distribution.

Any electronic device capable of playing MP3 files can be used to play a podcast. The only exception to this is that devices that are capable of audio playback only can obviously not be used to display images embedded in podcasts, but the audio file in MP3 format will work. This means that basically any computer can be used to listen to a podcast, as well as MP3 players, and, additionally, most new personal digital assistants (PDAs) and mobile phones are equipped to play back MP3 files for users. This plethora of available hardware choices is important to the use of podcasting in an educational setting. As said by Petrova (2004), "…in the near future mobile communication devices will exceed the number of personal computers." What this means is that the technology will saturate the target population, a critical factor in its successful implementation (Viteli, 2000). Having defined the hardware that is available, and the importance of hardware availability, what is meant by the term mobile device?

While podcasts can be played on a wide variety of hardware, the mobile use of a podcast requires mobile technology. Generally, any device that can fit in a pocket, an MP3 player, mobile phone, or PDA, qualifies as being mobile (Mellow, 2005; Andronico, Carbonaro, Casadei, Colazzo, Molinari, & Ronchetti, 2003). Under this definition, laptop computers are not truly mobile. While they do have independent power sources and wireless networking capability, they are not small enough for someone to drop in their pocket or purse and carry all the time every day. In this chapter, mobile will be defined as small enough to fit in a shirt pocket. As stated by Mellow (2005), "This would include such devices as mobile phones, portable digital assistants (PDAs) and iPods. It would not include laptops, as while they are portable, they are not mobile.…Mobile devices should fit in your pocket." With such a wide variety of devices capable of playing podcasts, the remaining question is how podcasts are transmitted to users.

One way to look at podcasts is as on-demand radio broadcasts. A user does not have to listen to the podcast when the file is downloaded, but at some point the file does have to move from a server location to a user's playing device. This is where mobile networking technologies merge with podcasting to vastly improve accessibility. With the IEEE 802.11 wireless standard, commonly referred to as Wi-Fi, users with a wide variety of notebook computers or PDAs can access the Internet from many public locations. These public locations where free Wi-Fi access is provided by businesses are often referred to as hotspots, and have quickly expanded from being just educational locations to include many retail businesses and in some areas entire downtown districts (Balachandran, Voelker, & Bahl, 2003). Utilizing Wi-Fi and a portable electronic device a user can quickly and easily download podcast files at a hotspot and then listen to them at their convenience. The same holds true for using traditional wired network connections, the primary difference being that wireless technology allows a user to be much more location-independent in accessing the podcast files. What the use of wireless delivers to the overall architecture of e-learning is a unique community where learners are at anytime and any place connected to the learning environment, with components of that immersion including interactivity with colleagues and instructors, support for learners, better distribution of information, and access to campus resources from remote locations (Grew & Pagani, 2005). As an overall focus, the architecture of e-learning using mobile devices, particularly enhanced by wireless connectivity, is referred to as mobile ubiquitous computing.

Having established that podcasts can, and likely will be distributed via the Internet and accessed via mobile devices, there is a question of how to construct an appropriate architecture to support e-learning in the mobile environment, in this case through the use of podcasts. The first priority of such architecture is to provide flexibility to the end user. As seen in the discussion of mobile devices, there is a broad, and ever-increasing, range of devices available for learners to use to access podcasts. For podcasting to be successful it is necessary for the delivery system to be accessible to a variety of devices so that learners will not be restricted due to the type of device they are using to access the network. Also, in the interest of building an e-learning system that is of value to the organization, there needs to be a focus on creating modular architecture that will allow media objects to be reused in multiple sessions or scenarios as appropriate (Sharma, &Kitchens, 2004).

When podcasting's four major components are all in place and working, a listener has the ability to access, transport, and use the informational file that makes up a podcast. With the end user's process defined, it is necessary to look at what is involved in creating and deploying podcasts for these users.

Podcasting Implementation

Implementing a podcasting program can be a relatively simple and low-cost proposition for an individual or institution having an interest in distributing information in this manner. The process consists of selecting material, recording and editing the media files, and uploading the completed files to a user-accessible location.

What kind of information is good material for a podcast? Anything that can be delivered verbally, without the need for physical demonstrations or video, is a potential candidate for a podcast. As just one example, the authors attended a keynote session at a national technology conference where the speaker had his laptop computer on the podium with Audacity running to record the presentation. When the presentation ended, the speaker had a complete audio file of his lecture that could then be uploaded for conference attendees to access

later or for people who were not in attendance at the session to hear. This technique can be used in similar situations such as classroom lectures or important meetings where information presented needs to be recorded and disseminated to people who were not able to attend.

The other side of podcasting information is the recording and distribution of files that people may want to access on their own time. There are a wide variety of specialty podcasts on the Internet that cover many different topics. These podcasts are much more like on-demand radio than recordings of events available for playback. In these podcasts, the creators have a set of information that they wish to convey and through a planned presentation they deliver that set of information over the course of a podcast. While the medium is the same, the preparation of these two different kinds of podcasts is different. One is simply a recording of a live event, while the other is a recorded presentation that is planned, recorded, and edited with the intent of distribution as a professional learning tool.

The actual recording and editing process has been discussed in regards to software, and the only remaining aspect of implementation is uploading the files. For many podcasters, this may be the most involved and most expensive part of the process, but that fortunately is changing. In order to distribute podcasts to users, it is necessary for a podcaster to have access to an online location, most often a Web site, with sufficient storage space and bandwidth to support the uploading and downloading of audio files. Traditionally, this has meant that a podcaster would have to have access to a Web server, create Web pages, upload and manage files, and maintain links for users to access the podcasts on the site. Currently, however, it is possible to do a certain amount of podcasting for free using in-place, third-party managed resources available on the Internet. A quick search through one of the major search engines for "free podcast hosting" will bring up many services where it is possible to just upload a podcast and then distribute the link to interested listeners.

In order to produce a podcast there are four roles, very similar to those described as a part of context aware delivery. Coordinators manage the content and delivery, authors create the media, learners access and use the media, and administrators manage the systems that are in use (Schmidt &Winterhalter, 2004). Behind these functional areas of responsibility is a framework of design for instructional media, again similar to Schmidt and Winterhalter's (2004) work, consisting of organizational ontology, process ontology, task ontology, and knowledge area ontology. By focusing on these four areas, a podcaster can tailor the media product to best fit the operating environment, the learner, and the goal of the podcast.

Podcasting Operation

Podcasting operations are much like any other distributed information system. The primary consideration is to maintain and update the files in order to keep them relevant and useful to the user population. Also, regular testing will ensure that links are working and files are functional when downloaded. It is important to remember that no matter how good or how proven a technology is, it is worth very little if it does not work when deployed, so testing and maintenance are critical to keep the system running and the listeners happy.

From an architectural perspective, the operation of a successful podcast works just as the creation of other electronically distributed learning objects. The process begins with a learning coordinator making decisions about what is required of the learning object, an author then creates the learning object, the object is delivered through the delivery system available to the learner, and then the users' access of the materials is assessed (Schmidt & Winterhalter, 2004). Borrowing from

the architecture of educational virtual environments (EVEs), these podcasts can be distributed in a manner that facilitates the creation of virtual collaborative environments. Most importantly, podcasts deployed via an EVE would provide access to students and give those students not only access to the media itself, but opportunities for multiple forms of communication and collaboration in an environment that as closely as possible resembles a physical classroom setting (Bouras & Tsiatsos, 2006). For communication, technologies to provide students with podcasting creation tools could be included, as could more traditional features such as message boards, text chat areas, and links to e-mail.

Podcasting Pedagogy

Podcasting will never replace reading, listening to lectures or other ways learners take in information, but it will add to the many tools educators use on a regular basis. At its base, podcasting is a constructivist learning media in that learners must take independent action to access and listen to the materials that are distributed by the instructor, placing the instructor in the role of a facilitator, in this case facilitating the distribution of information via podcast to learners. As described in Neely et al. (2004), the learner acquires knowledge in the constructivist environment through their own exploration and actions which are followed by assessment from the instructor. In the realm of podcasting the learner's actions could range from coming to the next physical discussion meeting with points prepared to offer based on a podcast's information to using information gained from a podcast in a virtual discussion environment or in the execution of an assigned task.

With this framework for podcasting as an instructional tool in mind, what are the uses for podcasting in this constructivist environment? According to Eva Kaplin-Leiserson, associate editor of *Learning Circuits*, there are seven ways podcasting can contribute to the learning process:

assist auditory learners, provide a channel for review of materials, assist non-native speakers, provide feedback to learners, enable educators to review training or lectures, present full lectures and/or guest speakers, and provide supplementary content (Kaplan, 2006).

Schools must be involved in the process of "preparing students for life, but also preparing them for the world of work" (Fryer, 2005). The work world is increasingly influenced, shaped, and defined by digital information and computer technologies. Schools which fail to adequately prepare students for vocational success in this environment belong in the 20th century, not the 21st (Fryer, 2005). Steve Sloan of epodder.com has offered the following uses for podcasting for educators (Sloan, 2005):

- Distance learning
- Facilitation of self-paced learning
- Re-mediation of slower learners
- Allow faculty to offer advanced and or highly motivated learners extra content
- Help for students with reading and/or other disabilities
- Multilingual education
- Provide the ability for educators to feature guest speakers from remote locations
- Allow guest speakers the ability to present once to many sections and classes
- Allow educators to escape the tedium of lecturing
- Offer a richer learning environment

"Podcasting can promise a unique approach to improving foundational pedagogical approaches to information processing and conceptual learning. Conceptual learning is contextual, relevant, holistic and at times requires intentional gaps" (Hargis & Wilson). Research has found that greater conceptual learning is fostered when teachers use interactive-based teaching strategies (to train students to link everyday experiences in the real physical world) rather than formal school

concepts (Ibrahim, 2001). Muller indicated that students identified three factors that led to their conceptual learning: (1) they were able to actively explore and construct their own understanding; (2) the social interaction in small groups; and (3) real-life learning tasks provided a meaningful way of learning (Muller, 1998). A podcast allows learners to listen to the ideas of others which will capture their attention and cause them to learn. Second, learners can publish their own podcast which allows them to hear their own thoughts; this can sometimes produce self- correction when the listener hears his/her own thoughts (Hargis & Wilson).

Academic podcasting gives students the opportunity to take part in research collaboration. "Innovative and exciting pedagogy such as class discussion, conference announcement and on-campus activities can be recorded and distributed as podcasts" (Carlson, 2004). Podcasting can provide a new way for people to improve communication, collaboration and social networking.

"All over the country, college faculty and administrators are plugging themselves into one of the newest—and hottest—technologies in an effort to better connect with students" (Lum, 2006). Gardner Campbell, assistant vice president for Teaching and Learning Technologies and professor of English at the University of Mary Washington, speculated about the possibilities of a learning environment where podcasting was an integral part of the institutional culture. He envisions an educational setting where podcasting supplements the traditional modes of learning and students are engaged and excited about the learning process as a result (Campbell, 2005).

For some time, educators have used collaborative software such as wikis, blogs and learning management systems to post lecture notes and other important information dealing with the class and subject. Though this style of distribution has worked for many years, it is still old technology and presents problems. "For example, an instructor may not be able to update her website promptly, which leads her students to continuously check on the non-updated website: a student who misses her class can retrieve the lecture PowerPoint slides, but miss out on important topics that came up during class discussion" (Ractham & Zhang, 2006).

The problem of students having to search learning management systems to find updated information can be lessened by using a content management software such as iTunes. Students subscribe to an educator's lecture in iTunes and when new information is made available, that information is sent to the student's computer, saving the student time and providing the student with the assurance that he has the most current class information.

Students can use iTunes and other podcatchers as management systems to help them listen, read, and view distributed materials. They can also transfer these materials to an MP3 player, making this information available when needed. A good example of this is the iPod project conducted at Duke University in 2004 (Carlson, 2004).

Cambell states that people in higher education owe it to the students to bring podcasting and other rich media into courses, by doing so learning and understanding is lifted to a whole new level (Cambell, 2005). The number of academics turning to technology to record lectures and distribute them to students is quickly growing, and the new term *coursecasting* is rising to the top of teaching methods. "The portability of coursecasting, its proponents say, makes the technology ideal for students who fall behind in class or those for whom English is a second language. Some advocates say that coursecasting can be more than just a review tool, that it can also liven up classroom interaction and help lecturers critique themselves" (Read, 2005). Through coursecasting (podcasting) an educator enters into the student's culture. Students are more likely to show up for class when they feel that the teacher is attempting to communicate on their level. "Students already have this stuff. Why not let them use the things?" (Read, 2005) says Patrick Thaddeus Jackson,

assistant professor of International Relations at American University.

Purdue's podcasting project arose from a desire to let students study without being tethered to their computers, according to Michael Gay, the university's manager of broadcast networks and services for information technology. "We're trying to give people as many options as possible if they miss a course and need to catch up—or if they just want to review," he says (Read, 2005).

At the University of Michigan, Ann Arbor's School of Dentistry has used podcasting for most of its lectures since January 2005. Like Purdue, the university has tried to make it as easy as possible for professors to participate. But instead of giving that work to technology staff members, the university has recruited students to do it. The students tap into the lecture hall sound system to record class sessions, and then they digitize the recordings and put them online (Read, 2005).

Duke University's faculties are podcasting shows weekly. In 2004, Duke passed out 1,650 iPods to all the incoming freshmen. These iPods were loaded with orientation information, academic calendars, introductions from Duke Administrators, advise from current Duke students, athletics schedules, lyrics to the school fight song, and more (Flanagan & Calandra, 2005). The iPods were used by the freshmen for sixteen courses during the fall semester and thirty-three courses in the spring. Faculties at Duke are using the devices for lectures but also to allow students to record critiques of each others work.

Arizona State University President Michael M. Crow is podcasting a few times a month, in addition to blogging, in an effort to stay connected with the students. ASU students have responded well to Dr. Crow's efforts to stay in touch with them.

At Mansfield University, administrators are using the reality TV method and producing podcasts looking at student life, especially for freshmen. The administrators interview students on topics including their favorite Saturday night pastimes and what they believe is the most important lesson they have learned while a student at Mansfield University.

Dr. M. Ann Bock, a New Mexico State University nutritional professor has provided online classes for a long time, but just recently she has started producing podcasts for her students who want flexibility in their learning experience. Brock also requires students in her Diet Therapy class to podcast a case study on a medical condition, like pregnancy (Lum, 2006).

Linda Herkenhoff, adjunct assistant professor in the graduate business program at St. Mary's College in California, produces two different types of podcasts both containing highlights of the lecture. One goes over the tricky concepts that were covered in class and another gives additional material aimed at the more advanced students who want to go deeper into the different topics.

The Duke University iPod First Year Experience Final Report placed the academic use of podcasting into five categories: (Flanagan & Calandra, 2005):

- Course content dissemination
- Classroom recording
- Field recording
- Study support
- File storage and transfer

The Duke University team also found benefits for both faculty and students in using podcasts. Some of these benefits include: portable course content, added flexibility to student learning, podcasts are easy to use, produced greater class involvement, and they enhanced support for individual learning (Flanagan & Calandra, 2005).

Mark Gura, educational technology author and a former director of instructional technology for the New York City Department of Education, and Dr. Kathy King, director of the RETC and professor of adult education, have used Podcasting to establish a popular mobile learning professional development vehicle (King & Gura, 2006). "In

effect, we are offering and modeling Professional Development on Demand. Indeed, we at Fordham University's RETC understand that podcasting, the simple technology with the power to truly transform professional development, will figure strongly in our efforts as we continue to explore promising technologies and their applications" (King & Gura, 2006).

The Techpod: Podcast for Teachers offers interviews with educators, authors, and "ed techies." This podcast offers curriculum ideas, news resources, technology tips, and research that educators can use in the classroom. It is available any time and any place: on the beach, in the supermarket, or while commuting to work. Teachers who want to be "in the know" can fit professional development into their schedules rather than having to make their schedules fit someone else's (King & Gura, 2006).

Despite the fact that it is still a relatively new trend, librarians from all types of libraries have already begun to experiment with podcasting. Library podcasts have been developed to promote and market library services, to share recordings of library events and lectures, and to teach students about the library. Many libraries have started using podcasting to distribute news and information, to provide audio tours of the library, and to make the audio portions of library programming available to the world. At Dowling College, Chris Kretz started producing the Dowling Library Omnibus podcast in October 2005. His podcast has been very successful due to his careful attention to details and making sure that he understood the audience he was trying to reach.

Sarah Chauncey is the media specialist at Grandview Elementary School in Monsey, New York. She spent 29 years writing financial software for Morgan Guaranty and several other top-tier corporations before taking her position at Grandview. In September 2005, she started a picture book podcast for k-3 students at her school, and posted them to the library's Web page (www.grandviewlibrary.org). Chancy did most of the narrations herself, but students can also have books read to them by their peers. "The nice thing about podcasting is that kids can feel they are being heard, but you don't raise privacy issues by showing their faces or names" (Ishizuka, 2005). At the end of each book podcast there are questions to help the child talk about the book with their parents.

The growing popularity of MP3 players has led many colleges and universities to slowly begin to experiment with podcasts in many different ways. Presently the majority of podcasting is dealing with the academic side of education; however, it is slowly moving into other areas of student life.

Using the RAED project as an example, podcasting distribution can be assigned roles that in the RAED project are titled atoms. The atoms of a podcasting program would mirror those identified by the RAED project:

1. **Atom-core:** The background material (prerequisites, links to supporting material, reading list—whatever the subject-expert chooses;

2. **Atom-ex (n):** The exercise, set by the subject-expert; in general there is a choice of exercises and it is this which leads to there being different instances (or versions) n of an atom. Usually it will be local organizers who choose which instance their students will do.

3. **Trail(atom-ex (n)):** The trail; this will consist of all tertiary material except that belonging to the current exercise.

4. **Atom-local (d):** The local arrangements for submitting an atom, written by each local organizer at domain d for their own students.

5. **Atom-notes (n):** Teaching notes for the atom (or a particular instance of it), which could include a variety of materials such as tutor guidance notes and model answers. All roles except that of student have read access to

this: it is a matter of local policy as to what access students have (none; access subject to constraints such as the submission deadline having passed, etc.)." (Neely, Lowe, Eyers, Bacon, Newman, & Gong, 2004).

FUTURE TRENDS

Based on the incredibly rapid rise of podcasting as an educational tool over the past two years, it is reasonable to project that this growth will continue and podcasting will find a place as a regular tool in the instructional environment. One likely possibility is that the growth of podcasting will slow. Very often new technology sees a considerable spike between inception and large-scale adoption, jumping from a relatively unknown quantity to something that many users are taking advantage of. This spike has probably already occurred for podcasting, and the technology's growth from now through the next several years will likely be a matter of converting individuals a few at a time rather than capturing entire groups of people in a short period of time.

In the educational arena, podcasting is likely to become a regular component of many classes, just as learning management systems have risen to an almost universal presence across higher education institutions. Complimenting the ease of access to the technology to create and distribute podcasts is the prevalence of individually-owned hardware, whether MP3 players, PDAs, or just a regular home computer, capable of taking advantage of the podcast format. This makes podcasting different from the opening days of other educational technologies where the average user only had access to a computer, or, later, the Internet, while on campus. The wide array of commonly owned devices capable of playing back podcasts makes it possible for new users to quickly and easily begin listening to the media.

There are some considerations in the implementation of podcasting components that will require different planning than other educational media. Because so many learners may be accessing networked resources via wireless mobile device, it will be necessary to focus on design and implementation of podcasting systems that are compatible with these devices. It may be necessary to either modify existing platforms or create new ones that are compatible with wireless e-learning platforms (Grew & Pagani, 2005). Also, to address the issue of having users distributed both geographically and across multiple operating systems, it will be necessary to address user access in order for podcasting to reach its full potential as an integrative, collaborative learning tool. The emerging technology best suited to answer this need is the use of Web services. Web services not only provide networked access to learning resources, they also allow users on multiple computing platforms to communicate and collaborate (Sharma & Kitchens, 2004).

Having addressed the need for distribution and access, it will also be important to plan for users to be able to make use of the information that podcasts provide. One of the biggest challenges of learning management systems in the future is going to be organization; with more and more media being incorporated into the system it is critical that learners are provided with appropriate tools to classify, link, share, recommend, and distribute learning objects (Vuorikari, 2005).

The future is, of course, unknown, and in technology the rate of change can very quickly move beyond the best of projections. That said, if a radically new technology does not surface in the near future to supplant podcasting as a media delivery method, its future is very bright.

CONCLUSION

Given the increasing demands and all too often decreasing resources available to educators at every level, the application of technology as not only an educational resource but also as a device to improve productivity and efficiency of resources is more important now than it ever has been before. It has been shown through multiple studies that students and student performance respond positively to podcasts, so the use of the technology as an educational resource is already well established.

Because of the ease of creation, the open source software alternatives, and the ability to use existing hardware podcasting also addresses the issue of generating productive, efficient educational products for a minimal expenditure. What this means to the practitioner is that the underlying architecture of podcasting, including such diverse factors as participant roles, hardware and networking technology, and distribution channels, building a working podcasting system can be accomplished at little or no financial cost. What is critical to the implementation, far more than money, is a knowledgeable group of individuals who are prepared to invest the time and focus to properly create and deploy this unique learning resource. By understanding and applying the theories behind this technology, today's educator has the opportunity to enhance not only their students' experiences, but also their own working life and the overall effectiveness of their institution.

REFERENCES

Andronico, A., Carbonaro, A., Casadei, G., Colazzo, L., Molinari, A., & Ronchetti, M. (2003). Integrating a multi-agent recommendation system into a Mobile Learning Management System. *Artificial Intelligence in Mobile System 2003*.

Audio learning is back. (2005, March 12, 2005). from http://www.kineo.co.uk/kineo-press-releases/audio-learning-survey.html

Baird, D. E., & Fisher, M. (2005). Neomillennial user experience design strategies: Utilizing social networking media to support "Always on" Learning styles. *Journal of Educational Technology Systems, 34*(1), 5-32.

Balachandran, A., Voelker, G., & Bahl, P. (2003). Wireless hotspots: Current challenges and future directions. In *Proceedings for WMASH'03.*

Balas, J. L. (2005). Blogging is so last year—now podcasting is hot. *Online treasures. Computers in Libraries, 25*(10), 29-32.

Barack, L. (2006). American library association sponsors tech boot camp. *School Library Journal, 52*(7), 20-20.

Borja, R. R. (2005). Podcasting craze comes to k-12 schools. *Education Week, 25*(14), 8.

Bouras, C. & Tsiatsos, T. (2005). Educational virtual environments: Design rationale and architecture. *Multimedia Tools and Applications Journal.* New York: Kluwer Academic Publishers.

Briggs, L. L. (2006). Born-again technologies. *T H E Journal, 33*(9), 18-19.

Brusilovsky, P. (2004). Knowledge Tree: A Distributed Architecture for Adaptive E-Learning. *Proceedings of the 13th International World Wide Web Conference* (pp. 104-113). New York.

Bull, G. (2005). Podcasting and the long tail. *Learning and Leading with Technology, 33*(3), 24-25.

Cambell, G. (2005). There's something in the air: Podcasting in education. *EDUCAUSE Review, 40*(6), 32-47.

Carlson, S. (2004). Duke university will give ipod music players to all freshmen (Duke university). *Chronicle of Higher Education, 50*(47), 1.

Carnevale, D. (2005). To size up colleges, students now shop online. *The Chronicle of Higher Education, 51*(40), A25-26.

Carr, N. (2006). Keys to effective communications. *American School Board Journal, 193*(8), 40-41.

Cebeci, Z. & Tekdal, M. (2006). Using podcasts as audio learning objects. *Interdisciplinary Journal of Knowledge and Learning Objects, 2,* 47-57.

Chan, A., & Lee, M. J. W. (2005). *An mp3 a day keeps the worries away: Exploring the used of podcasting to address preconceptions and alleviate pre-class anxiety amongst undergraduate information technology students.* Paper presented at the Good practice in practice: Proceedings of the Student Experience Conference, Charles Stuart University.

Clyde, L. (2005). Some new internet applications coming now to a computer near you. *Teacher Librarian, 33*(1), 54-55.

Crawford, C., Smith, R. A., & Smith, M. S. (2006). *Podcasting in the learning environment: From podcasts for the learning community, towards the integration of podcasts within the elementary learning environment.* Paper presented at the Society for Information Technology and Teacher Education International Conference 2006, Orlando, Florida, USA.

Descy, D. (2005). Podcasting: Online media delivery—with a twist. *TechTrends, 49*(5), 4-6.

Dewey, J. (1897). My pedagogic creed. *The School Journal, LIV*(3), 77-80.

Eash, E. K. (2006). Podcasting 101. *Computers in Libraries, 26*(4), 16-20.

Flanagan, B., & Calandra, B. (2005). Podcasting in the classroom. *Learning and Leading with Technology, 33*(3), 20-22, 25.

Fryer, W. A. (2005). *Digital definers of the new teacher education.* Texas Tech University.

Gordon-Murnane, L. (2005). Saying "I do" To podcasting. *Searcher, 13*(6), 44-51.

Grew, P. & Pagani, E. (2005). Towards a Wireless Architecture for Mobile Ubiquitous E-Learning. In *Proceedings of the International Workshop on Learning Communities in the Era of Ubiquitous Computing*, Milan, 2005, pp. 20-29.

Growth in virtual learning, data management, blogging and podcasting expected in 2006. (2006). *Electronic Education Report* Retrieved 2, 13.

Hargis, J., & Wilson, D. Fishing for learning with a podcast net.

Heppell, S. (2006). Pushing podcasts. *The Times Educational Supplement*, 82.

Ibrahim, H. (2001). *Examining the impact of the guided constructivist teaching method on students' misconceptions about concepts of Newtonian physics.* University of Central Florida, Orlando, Florida.

I.P.O.C. ('ipods on campus'). (2006). *BizEd, 5*(2), 46, 48.

Isakson, C. (2006). Podcasts in education. *The Education Digest, 71*(8), 79-80.

Ishizuka, K. (2005). Tell me a story. *School Library Journal, 51*(9), 24-25.

Kadel, R. (2006). Coursecasting: The wave of the future? *Learning and Leading with Technology, 33*(5), 48-49.

Kaplan, E. (2006). Trend: Podcasting in academic and corporate learning. *Learning Circuits*.

Lim, K. Y. T. (2005). *Now hear this—exploring podcasting as a tool in geography education.*

Lum, L. (2006). The power of podcasting. *Diverse Issues in Higher Education, 23*(2), 32-35.

Mellow, P. (2005). The media generation: Maximize learning by getting mobile. *Proceedings*

for ASCILITE 2005: Balance, Fidelity, Mobility: Maintaining the momentum? (pp. 469-476).

Muller, T. (1998). *A sound study of conceptual understanding during constructivist teaching.* University of North Dokota, Grand Forks.

Neely, S., Lowe, H., Eyers, D., Bacon, J., Newman, J., & Gong, X. (2004). An architecture for supporting vicarious learning in a distributed environment. In *Proceedings of the 2004 ACM symposium on applied computing* (pp. 963-970). ACM Press.

Naj. (2005). Ask naj. *Distance Education Report, 9*(19), 3-4.

Oliver, B. (2005). *Mobile blogging, 'skyping' and podcasting: Targetting undergraduates' communication skills in transnational learning contexts.*

Oliver, C. (2005, September 13). College's course material soon to be all in hand. *Sydney Morning Herald*, p. 38.

Pethokoukis, J. M. (2005). Podcasting: Grab your mike and go. *U.S. News & World Report, 139*(11), 58-58.

Petrova, K. (2005). Mobile Learning Using SMS: A Mobile Business Application. In *Proceedings for the 18th Annual Conference of the National Advisory Committee on Computing Qualifications* (pp. 412-417).

Production, R. E. C. a. (2006). *Exploiting the educational potential of podcasting.* Retrieved from http://recap.ltd.uk/articles/podguide4.html

Ractham, P., & Zhang, X. (2006). Podcasting in academia: A new knowledge management paradigm within academic settings. *SIGMIS-CPR*, 314-317.

Rainie, L., & Madden, M. (2005). Online *activities and pursuits: Podcasting catches on*. Pew

Internet and American Life Project, April 3, 2005, pp. 1-5.

Ramsden, P. (1992). *Learning to teach in higher education.* New York: Routledge.

Read, B. (2005). Abandoning cassette tapes, Purdue University will podcast lectures in almost 50 courses. *The Chronicle of Higher Education, 52*(3), A32.

Read, B. (2005). Lectures on the go. The *Chronicle of Higher Education, 52*(10), A39-42.

Read, B. (2006). Berkeley offers free podcasts of courses through iTunes. *The Chronicle of Higher Education, 52*(35), A44.

Read, B. (2006). Turning campus radio on its head. *The Chronicle of Higher Education, 52*(30), A35-37.

Schmidt, A. & Winterhalter, C. (2004). User context aware delivery of e-learning material: Approach and architecture. *Journal of Universal Computer Science (JUCS), 10*, 28-36.

Sharma, S. & Kitchens, F. (2004). Web services architecture for m-Learning. *Electronic Journal on e-learning, 2*(1), 203-216.

Sloan, S. (2005). Podcasting: *An exciting new technology for higher education.* Paper presented at the Emerging Technology in Education, San Jose State University.

Sprankle, B. (2006). Podcasting with purpose. *Principal, 85*(4), 62-63.

Swain, H. (2006). Let them tune in to the degree dj. *The Times Higher Education Supplement(1728),* 58-59.

Training, C. (2005). *Podcasting in academic and corporate learning.* eCornell Research Blog, www.ecornell.com

Viteli, J. (2000). Finnish future: From e-learning to m-Learning? In *Proceedings for the ASCILITE Conference.*

Warlick, D. (2005). Podcasting. *Technology & Learning, 26*(2), 70.

Weiss, A. (2005). The power of collective intelligence. *netWorker, 9*(3), 16-23.

Wiley, D. L. (2006). Secrets of podcasting: Audio blogging for the masses. *Online, 30*(1), 62-62.

Williams, P. E., & Nsw, O. *Tools of the trade: Learning technologies for distance learners.*

Wright, R. (2005). Tafe gets the e-learning formula right. *Business Strategy Australasia,* (4).

Young, J. R. (2005). New princeton web service offers recordings of public-policy lectures. *The Chronicle of Higher Education, 51*(49), A34.

Young, J. R. (2005). Stanford university makes podcasts of lectures available through Apple's iTunes. *The Chronicle of Higher Education, 52*(11), A44.

ENDNOTE

[1] Due to the possibility of infringement on the word "pod" that is tightly related to Apple Corporation, the term podcast is transitioning to the term "netcast."

Section II
Software Architecture and Software Engineering

Chapter VI
A Step towards a Pattern Language for E–Learning Systems

Andreas Harrer
University of Duisburg-Essen, Germany

Alke Martens
University of Rostock, Germany

ABSTRACT

Computer-based teaching and training systems in general, and Intelligent Tutoring Systems (ITSs) in particular, are usually based on similar fundamental structures. In contrast to this, analyses of the state of the art of teaching and training system development have revealed that software engineering techniques are seldom used for realizing those systems. In the last years, some approaches tried to change this: pattern mining took place; methods covering the specifics of ITS project development have been deployed. These approaches usually focus on a specific system type or on a certain application domain, thus re-usability is often not possible. What is missing is a combination of different approaches in a pattern language or a pattern catalogue for ITS. The purpose of such a pattern catalogue is to provide pattern for different types of software and to support the software development starting from design and ending with the implementation. A step towards a pattern language for ITS is described in this paper.

INTRODUCTION

The term e-learning covers a set of quite heterogeneous types of systems, for example, tele-teaching, CD-Rom, and various computer-based teaching and training systems (Kaplan-Leiserson, 2002). The type of e-learning system, with which the analysis described in this chapter is started, is the intelligent teaching and training system (ITTS), which is also often called intelligent tutoring system (ITS).

Intelligent tutoring systems can look back on a comparably long history. They are usually based on similar fundamental structures, which are called the ITS architecture. This architecture consists of the following components: expert module (encapsulating expert and pedagogical knowledge), learner module, user interface module, and steering module. This architecture has been described by several researchers, for exmple, by Clancey (1984), Lelouche (1999), and Martens (2003). The ITS architecture can be seen as a pattern in the broad sense (Devedzic, 2001). But whereas a pattern should support comparable and similar realizations of software, the pure architecture description does not provide guidance in software development. Thus, in ITS design a situation has developed, where the component of different systems provide a quite homogeneous naming (with only slight variations, e.g., user model instead of learner model) but are in most cases based on a completely heterogeneous and non-interchangeable realization. Moreover, the interpretation of each component's role and functionality varies a lot (Johnson et al., 2000; Martens, 2003). What makes the situation even more confused is the insight, the term 'component' is seldom used in the software engineering sense (Szyperski, 2002), but more often in the common language sense as equivalent of 'part of' or 'constituent.' One result of this situation is that—from the perspective of computer science—ITSs are hardly comparable.

In recent years, several approaches have been made toward establishing uniformity in the development of teaching and training systems. Two main directions of research can be distinguished:

- Development of standards (or similar approaches, which intent to predefine terms,

e.g., nomenclatures or metadata description).
- Development of software engineering methods.

Examples for standards and similar approaches are standardized architectures like the learning technology system architecture (LTSA) (see http://www.edutool.com/ltsa; Farance & Tonkel, 2001), approaches for learning project management like Essen learning model (ELM) (Pawlowski, 2000), and Extensible Markup Language (XML) descriptions for teaching and training content like the Dublin core metadata (see http://dublincore.org; DCMI, 2002). The main advantage of these approaches is the predefinition of terms, which is a step towards exchangeability. Main drawback is that the contribution remains on the level of terms. Standards and similar approaches usually lack a specific description of how to realize and implement the system parts.

Examples for an explicit focus on software engineering methods in ITS development are not so widespread (e.g., Illmann et al., 2000) and systematic theoretical approaches can rarely be found (e.g., Devedzic, 1999; Devedizc & Harrer, 2002; Harrer, 2003). Using methods of software engineering in teaching and training systems is based upon the idea that software development is mainly an engineering science, not an art—although the latter perspective usually describes how software development is done in several different branches of computer science, and also in the area of ITS. To organize work according to the engineering perspective has some consequences: the development of software is based on techniques, which are clear, definite, and traceable, and which explicate different aspects of the development process and of the result (i.e., the software).

Taking up methods of software engineering and clear definition of concepts, this chapter describes a stepwise approach to develop a pattern language for e-learning systems of the ITS type. The chapter is organized as follows: after giving an extended introduction to the field, the applied methods and the used terminology, the following section will also be about related work, comparing software development in general and software engineering in e-learning in particular. The subsequent section is used to suggest a terminology for describing an ITS pattern language and to sketch the patterns. Afterwards two examples of ITSs are given, which are developed based on software engineering approaches. The paper closes with a summary and a discussion that also refers to a wider scope of e-learning systems beyond the ITS type.

METHODS AND TERMINOLOGY

Currently, the situation in e-learning research and development is the following: systems for learning support that do not rely on methods of artificial intelligence (AI), like Web-portals (e.g., Post-nuke, http://www.post-nuke.net) and platforms for structured discussion forums (e.g., Future Learning Environment FLE3, see Muukkonen et al., 1999), are usually developed according to established software engineering principles (e.g., modularization, extensibility). Functional extensions by other developers can frequently be found (e.g., Pinkwart et al., 2005; Dolonen et al., 2003). By contrast, complex AI-based systems, like ITSs, are usually not developed according to software engineering criteria.

ITSs and AIED Systems (artificial intelligence for education) are in most cases developed specifically for a certain application domain. Usually, they are based on a cognitive or pedagogical theory and are focused on research and evaluation on these issues, while the engineering aspects are not considered as an important issue. Details of architecture descriptions, explication of interfaces or background information about implementation details cannot be found in most cases. Most of the systems are not extensible and not re-usable. These symptoms are not only related to scientific traditions in a field of research—utterances like "AI kept fighting and losing against software engineering" (Rohmer, 2004) reveal a lot about the atmosphere of rivalry between these fields.

From the engineering perspective, ITSs are complex software systems, which should be conceptualized and developed based on software engineering. Advantage of this perspective is a reduction of complexity in modules and components of the system. Based on a good design it should be easy to integrate application domain experts into the development process of the ITS. Usually experts of the application domain should not need to know implementation details but should have insight in the specific design of parts, for example, the expert knowledge module. An appropriate software design would separate between an application domain oriented specification (e.g., domain knowledge) and technical aspects of implementation. Thus, integrating methods and techniques of software engineering into ITS research can support the development of new ideas and insights.

In software engineering there are several approaches which can support the development of teaching and training systems:

- *Reference architectures* and *architectural patterns* are used to specify the basic structure and relationships between the main components of a software system. There are some examples for ITS reference architectures, some of which are formal, like LTSA, and some of which are verbal descriptions (Clancey, 1984). Both mentioned approaches are system oriented. Other perspectives are possible, for example, the student oriented perspective (Brusilovsky, 1995). Architectural patterns, which are on a more abstract level than reference architectures, have been described in (Devedzic, 2001) for layered decomposition of ITS systems, and have been realized concretely, for example, in (Illmann et al., 2001).

- *Design patterns* are used to describe typical solutions for recurring design problems of smaller scale. They help to refine and complete system structures. Devedzic (2001) has introduced design patterns in ITS research and educational systems. Compared to the classic design patterns a la Gamma et al. (1995), ITS-specific patterns have either a clear focus on ITS topics, such as management of learner models, or are adaptions of classic patterns in the ITS domain. Discussion and examples (e.g., the knowledge Model-View architecture as an adoption of Model-View-Controller) for this can be found in Devedzic and Harrer (2005).

- *Process patterns* and *learning design* follow the idea to explicitly model process oriented aspects and to make them re-usable. In ITSs, they help to transform implicit principles (e.g., related to pedagogical principles) to explicit declarations. This supports and facilitates the work of domain experts; resulting concepts and designs can be re-used. Examples are an exchangeable catalogue of tutoring rules (Harrer, 1997), the formal description of instructional design patterns (Inaba et al., 2001), and the sequencing of learning activities in the IMS Learning Design (IMS, 2003).

- *Component-based design* aims at a flexible combination of different components. Each component must be developed based on predefined interfaces and exchange formats (see Szyperski, 2002). Components can have different backgrounds, for example, simulation components, concept mapping components, components supporting hypotheses generation, and annotation components. Examples for specialized approaches are the graph-based modeling of different exchangeable and extensible visual languages (Pinkwart,

2005), scalable architecture for interactive learning (SAIL) (2005), which focuses on the flexible combination of components, and an approach to extend the component-based simulation system JAMES II with ITS components (Martens & Himmelspach, 2005).

- *Ontologies* are used to structure concepts and relations in a certain application domain. They are developed to predefine terms, which are used e.g., for communication between components and for interface descriptions. Ontologies are necessary for re-usability and interoperability. An example for the usage of Ontologies for teaching and training systems is the work started in Mizoguchi, Ikeda and Sinitsa (1997) and that has continuously evolved to a full-fledged ontology on educational design supported by intelligent system (Omnibus ontology at URL: http://edont.qee.jp/omnibus). Another application area for ontologies in educational field is the usage with semantic Web approaches for e-learning, widely discussed at the respective conferences, e.g., in the SW-EL (semantic Web for e-learning) workshop series.

- *Refactoring* is used to extend existing software systems. It supports an optimization of the software structure, for example, at the level of modularity, flexibility and extensibility, without changing the system's functionality (e.g., Fowler, et al. 1999). In combination with the component based approach, refactoring can be used to transform existing system interfaces, so that they meet the requirements of the component based architecture. This allows to embed existing components in new architectures, like for example, in the SAIL project (SAIL, 2005). Refactoring has also been discussed in the context of teaching and training systems (Harrer, 2003).

- *Frameworks* are used to specify a software system at program level. Parts of the framework can be used and re-used unchanged, other parts have to be adapted. Frameworks, which are based on object oriented programming, are used via instantiation of existing entities, implementation of pre-defined interfaces, or specialization of classes. Examples are FITS—the framework for ITS (Ikeda & Mizoguchi, 1994), and the framework for open distributed learning environments (e.g., Müllenbrock, Tewissen & Hoppe, 1998).

Besides these mentioned methods, other aspects, such as unified data formats and re-usability of learning content also support the design and usage of e-learning systems. Especially the topic of learning objects, their re-use in different contexts and the retrieval of appropriate learning material are discussed widely in the field and manifest itself in research and development projects: Among these are standardization initiatives as sharable content object reference model (SCORM) and initiatives for flexible retrieval of material from content repositories, such as simple query interface (SQI, Website http://ariadne. cs.kuleuven.be/lomi/index.php/LorInteroperability) and content object repository discovery and registration/resolution architecture (CORDRA, Website at http://cordra.net/introduction/).

Our specific focus in this chapter will be the development of e-learning systems of the ITS type and how this can be supported by a mix of several of the presented methods. Because of their similar orientation of capturing design knowledge, not so much concrete implementations, a combination of the pattern-oriented methods is a very promising direction to provide guidelines for ITS development not only on an implementation level. The combination of all these concepts in one pattern language or a pattern catalogue is a complex task. Thus, in the following section, a stepwise approach is described.

PATTERN LANGUAGES

The knowledge of different patterns helps to solve typical recurring problems. Moreover, by using a combination of different patterns, complete systems can be designed and developed. The advantage is that systems and subsystems are based on a clear and explicit description.

A necessary step towards designing and implementing systems and subsystems with a pattern oriented approach is to make the implicit relations between different patterns explicit. These implicit relations are:

- Patterns can be used to realize patterns.
- Patterns complement patterns.
- Patterns can be used alternatively.
- Patterns have similarities and differences.

A collection of patterns which explicitly describes these relations is called a *pattern language* (Schmidt et al., 2000). Pattern-oriented software development proceeds stepwise. Based on the requirements of a system to develop, a certain entry point is selected, usually an architectural pattern. This first pattern provides a structure but no details. Thus, a refining pattern is used, which meets the requirements. Step by step, the system design will be refined by selecting subsequent patterns. This procedure continues until all requirements are met or if no refining patterns are available.

To combine the software engineering concepts mentioned in the former section in a pattern language is a complex task. Thus, in the following, a stepwise approach is described. A pattern language, which can be used in the described way to develop a complete system from scratch, is called a *generative* or *complete* pattern language. Usually, generative or complete pattern languages are available for only a few classes of applications with limited scope. In the broader context of e-Learning systems there are some initiatives and projects, such as the e-LEN project (http://www2.

tisip.no/E-LEN/) or the TELL project (http://cosy. ted.unipi.gr/tell/) for collaborative networked learning. For ITS currently only few approaches towards pattern language development can be found: for example, a pattern language for tutoring systems, based on the layer decomposition (Devedzic, 2001), and the blended learning process patterns (Derntl & Motschnig-Pitrik, 2004). Both are specialized on a certain ITS aspect and use a homogeneous set of patterns.

TOWARDS A PATTERN LANGUAGE FOR ITS

When developing a pattern language, the first step is to look for entry points. The basic pattern underlying most ITSs is the ITS architecture (e.g., Clancey, 1984; Martens, 2003,2004). The elements of the architecture are described as models, modules or as components (see Martens, 2004). In the following the term module is used to name the parts of an ITS. A module is not necessarily a well defined and clearly structured model—the term module is used to characterize one entity of a complete system. Accordingly, an ITS consists of expert module, learner module, user interface module, and process regulation module. In Figure 1, which describes the entry point pattern for this architecture, the aggregation

Figure 1. Entry point pattern: Modules of an ITS

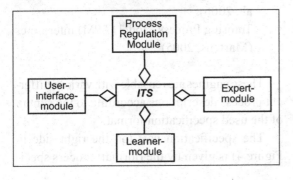

without label is used—usually only one instance of each module exists.

Another approach found in the literature (Ritter & Koedinger, 1996) is the architectural proposal of "Tool and Tutor," that conceptualizes an ITS as consisting of a *tool*, that provides the user interface with which the learner solves specific tasks in the learning domain, and one or more (Ritter, 1997) *tutors*, that analyze the user input, make a diagnosis and give adaptive feedback according to these user actions. This architectural approach has been used in several other contexts (Murray, 2005; Harrer et al., 2006) and is thus considered as an alternative entry point pattern for ITS development. According to its competencies the tool can be associated with a specific form of user interface module, while the tutor might be considered monolithical or decomposed optionally into an expert module, learner module, and pedagogical process regulation module. This is sketched in Figure 2.

The extension of the pattern will be pursued on basis of the entry point pattern in Figure 1. Each module can be concretized by a refining pattern. This is exemplarily shown in Figure 3. The expert module can be realized, for example, as pedagogical agent, as case-based expert knowledge module, and as expert knowledge model based on production rules. The learner module can, for example, be specialized as CSCL (Computer Supported Collaborative Learning) learner module (Harrer, 2000), as cognitive tutor (Anderson et al., 1995), which uses model tracing for evaluation of learner behavior (Anderson et al. 1990), as the simple learner profile, which has no further information for correction or evaluation (Martens, 2004), as classical bug library (Brown & Burton, 1978), and as overlay module (Goldstein, 1970).

The specialization of the process regulation module is closer to the implementation level. This refinement is added in the next step and can be seen in Figure 4. The specification of the process itself, which differs depending on the process description, is separated from the specification

Figure 2. Alternative entry point pattern: Tool and Tutor with first extension

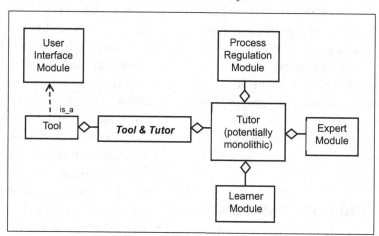

Figure 3. Exemplary extension of some modules of the ITS

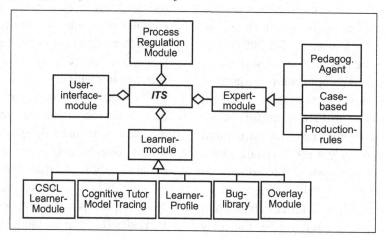

of the execution semantics, which should be the same for different processes. The result is a clear distinction between engine part and specification part.

The engine part (on the left side in Figure 4) describes the semantics of the process regulation module, i.e. how the regulation process is realized and executed. Examples are:

- Learning design (LD) engines (for example Coppercore http://www.coppercore.org).

- Intelligent Distributed Learning Environment (IDLE) Agent (Harrer, 2000).
- Learning Design Infrastructure (Martel et al., 2006).
- Tutoring Process Model (TPM) interpreter (Martens, 2005).

These engines are reusable with various different process descriptions according to the syntax of the used specification format.

The specification part (on the right side in Figure 4) is given by the (formal) process speci-

Figure 4. Extension of the process regulation module: Separation of engine and specification

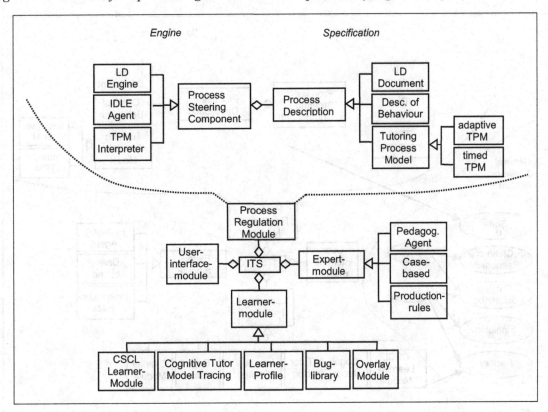

fication. Examples, which are corresponding to the engines listed above, are the following:

- LD-Documents (IMS, 2003), which describe a learning scenario together with activities, services and learning resources, to be used in the LD-Engine.
- The behavior of the IDLE Agent according to the intended role of the agent in a learning community.
- The description of collaborative learning activities using the Learning Design Language (LDL) (Martel et al., 2006).
- A formally described Tutoring Process Model (TPM), which can be refined, for example, as an adaptive TPM (Martens, 2005) or timed TPM (Martens, 2006).

Given interoperability between different engines or the usage of one engine within different learning applications, it is possible to re-use the process specifications in varying contexts. An example are different collaborative applications using the Coppercore engine for LD specifications, such as the GRIDCOLE approach (Bote-Lorenzo et al., 2004) or the Remote Control approach for the FreeStyler application (Harrer, Malzahn & Roth, 2006), where the same basic learning designs could be applied within different learning environments. The best practices of learning design are currently compiled in repositories and can be seen as separate homogenous pattern languages, similar to the one proposed by Inaba et al. (2001) or Derntl and Motschnig-Pitrik (2004).

Figure 5. Extension with general software patterns

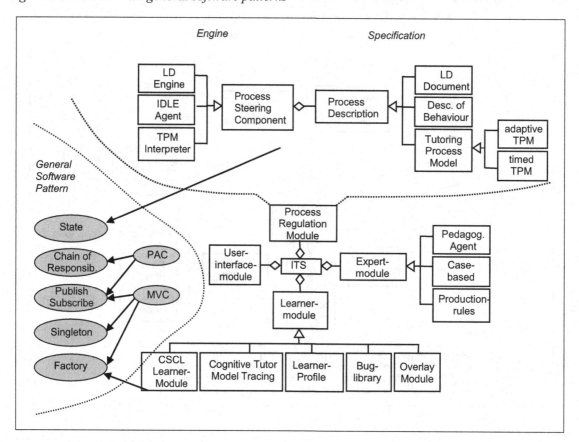

On the next level of refinement, which is shown in Figure 5, general software patterns are integrated in the language. The figure shows exemplarily only a few general patterns. These general patterns are not closely related to the ITTS, thus another graphical notation, i.e. ovals instead of boxes) are used to highlight the difference. The general patterns can be used for the design of the user interface module, but also for the design of other modules. Examples for both variations are shown in the subsequent section. As examples for general patterns have been used the presentation abstraction control (PAC) pattern and the model view controller (MVC) pattern (both in Buschmann et al., 1996).

PAC uses for example the pattern chain of responsibility (Gamma et al., 1995) and the publisher-subscriber pattern (Buschmann et al., 1996) for the notification and distribution of events between system components. The publisher-subscriber pattern can also be used by the alternative MVC oriented implementation. MVC would use the Singleton and the Factory pattern (both in Gamma et al., 1995) to guarantee uniqueness of critical system components and the controlled creation of other system components. The Factory pattern also lends itself for the realization of the CSCL learner module, where matching pairs of learner data and models have to be instantiated. For the realization of the process steering component, a state pattern (Gamma et al., 1995) can be used to implement the state dependencies in the tutoring process execution in an elegant way. For the interoperability of components and the re-usability of components in different contexts, the general design patterns Facade and Adapter (both in Gamma et al., 1995) can be used frequently for definition and use of the interfaces of the components.

A unique feature of our pattern language proposal is the combination of different types of patterns and even other pattern languages into an unified approach: Architectural patterns are used as entry point patterns and are then incrementally refined by smaller scale design patterns, both ITS-specific (as in Figures 1-4) or general patterns (as in Figure 5). The separation of the process regulation module into an engine and specification part (in Figure 3) allows the collection of diverse best practice specifications for different pedagogical scenarios or tutoring strategies into own libraries/pattern catalogues; the specifications can be used interchangeably and with the same engine, thus facilitating the flexible change of the system's tutoring style by using another specification. The creation of libraries of instructional designs is currently a topic of several research initiatives as UNFOLD (Project website at URL: http://www.unfold-project.net/) or LORNET (Project website at URL: http://www.lornet.org/).

APPLICATIONS OF THE PATTERN LANGUAGE

To show the practical usefulness of our proposed pattern language, two extended examples are given. The first one is an analytical usage of the pattern language to explore the structure of the medical ITS Docs 'n Drugs, whereas the other one is a pattern-oriented extension of a pre-existing system towards an ITS.

Docs 'n Drugs: Case- and Web-Based ITS for Clinical Medicine

"Docs 'n Drugs—the virtual hospital" is a Web-based ITS for training of clinical medicine in a case-based way (Illmann et al., 2001; Martens et al., 2001). The learner acts as physician and has to decide about diagnoses and treatment of a given patient. In a case-based scenario, where each training case reflects a different patient with a different history, the learner's activities range from acquisition of different anamneses, execution of body examinations, technical, and laboratory examinations, and to decide on a final therapy or treatment. Thus, on an abstract level, the learner has to decide about how to proceed in a given situation: he/shehas to act and react to the patient's utterances and to potential changes in the patient's health state. Moreover, he/she has to record and continually actualize a list of differential diagnoses. Since 2000, the system is part of the medical education at the University of Ulm, Germany (http://www.docs-n-drugs.de). Docs 'n Drugs has been implemented based on the classical ITS architecture (Martens, 2005). The implementation of the system was based on the PAC pattern (presentation-abstraction-control) (Illmann et al., 2000). PAC describes a system based on a set of interacting agents, each of which has presentation, abstraction and control parts. In Docs 'n Drugs, ten agents have been found and described. These modules reflect the entry point pattern shown in Figure 1: expert module, learner module, process regulation module, and user interface module. These core agents have been refined during the design phase (see Figure 6—dotted lines denote unused part). The *expert module* is realized consisting of two sub-modules: the medical knowledge agent for the expert knowledge module, and the case-based knowledge agent for the pedagogical knowledge module. The *learner module* is part of the tele-collaboration agent, which is also responsible for the tele-collaboration between case authors. The *process regulation module* is described by the tutoring process agent. The *user interface module* is part of the execution coordinator agent.

As PAC is not directly related to the realization of one of the entry point modules, but to all of them, Figure 6 lacks a connection between the general software patterns, that is, the used PAC pattern, and any of the entry point modules or another component. Thus, the general software pattern should be seen on a meta-level in Figure 6.

Additionally, a repository access agent and an intelligent tutor agent have been identified—both of which are not directly depicted in the entry point pattern in Figure 1, but can be seen as extensions of the patterns given in Figure 3. Alternatively, both parts can also be located in the tool and tutor pattern shown in Figure 2. The repository access

agent provides an interface between external repositories and system. Given the first entry point pattern, this can be seen as an extension of the case-based realization of the expert module in Figure 3. In Figure 2, it would be part of the tool. The intelligent tutor agent is comparable to a pedagogical agent for guiding and supporting the learner in Figure 3. Alternatively and more directly connected it is a variant of the tutor in the tool and tutor pattern in Figure 2.

Using the PAC pattern as basic description for ITS development had the advantage of a clear and explicit structure. Docs 'n Drugs had been a project of mid size, consisting of experts, for example, artificial intelligence, media computer science, computer graphics, and several medical experts. Separating the system in several sub-

Figure 6. Parts of the pattern catalogue used by Docs 'n Drugs

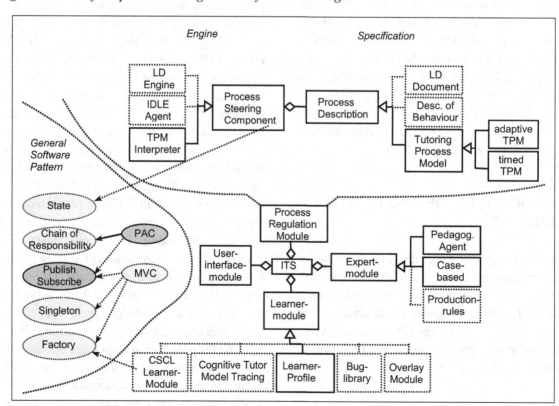

parts, which communicate via interfaces, facilitated not only the system design, but also the interaction of the different experts. The approach showed one drawback: several levels of granularity regarding the module design have been mixed in one approach. For example, the tutoring process agent has a completely different functionality and structure than the medical knowledge agent. This has led to the effect that most of the agents had to be refined in a complex way (see Illmann et al., 2000). Moreover, the PAC-based approach has been quite difficult to communicate to the non-computer scientists of the project. A better structured approach, like the direct usage of a pattern language, would shift parts, which are in computer terminology, for example, agents, in the responsibility of computer scientists, whereas inter-project communication can take place at a level which is easier to grasp independent of the developer's expertise.

FreeStyler/Cool Modes: Towards an ITS for Collaborative Modeling

FreeStyler and Cool Modes (Pinkwart, 2005) have been conceived as collaborative synchronous applications for graphical modeling in different domains, for example, concept mapping, mathematical modeling, or for the development of computational models like Petrinets and finite automata. The focus was on graphical representational issues and collaborative processes conducted by students in co-located classroom or distance scenarios. Tutoring functionality was initially not available. Thus, the user interface module was well developed, yet learner module, expert module, and process control module were lacking in early versions.

The user interface component of Cool Modes can be analyzed by using the suggested pattern language: The graphical model created by students is separated into visual representation (view), internal data model (model) and the components

handling the user input (control) according to the *model-view-controller* architecture pattern (Buschmann et al., 1996). For the synchronization of the students' multiple instances of the application an event propagation mechanism (MatchMaker based on Java RMI) is used—an example for the *publisher-subscriber* design pattern. To guarantee controlled instantiation of graphical objects and uniqueness of a student's identification, the *Factory* and *Singleton* design patterns have been used (Gamma et al., 1995). The parts of the pattern catalogue, which are used, can be seen in Figure 7 (dotted lines denote unused parts).

After successful use of the application in teacher-supervised classroom scenarios (Lingnau et al., 2003), the support of remote and unsupervised scenarios became a topic of interest. Possible modes of desired support are the sequencing of specific collaborative and/or individual work phases and direct feedback with respect to the quality and completeness of the created models. The proposed pattern language has been used to extend the application towards an ITS for graphical modeling—for example, by adding modules for student information, expert knowledge, and process regulation (see Figure 7).

The models are realized as follows: For the *student model* a logging mechanism (Jansen, 2003) is used that captures all the raw information of the collaborative user actions, for example, time stamp, user id, type of action, targeted object, and associated parameters. The student model has been realized as a combination of CSCL learner module and cognitive tutor model tracing (Harrer, McLaren, et al., 2005), two possible continuation patterns of the student module pattern. In the realization of the cognitive tutor model tracing we used an adapter component bridging between the existing interface of the cognitive tutor and the collaboration architecture. The joint use of two pre-existing applications from very different fields decreased implementation efforts drastically (cf. Harrer et al., 2006 for details).

Figure 7. Parts of the pattern catalogue used by Freestyler/Cool Modes

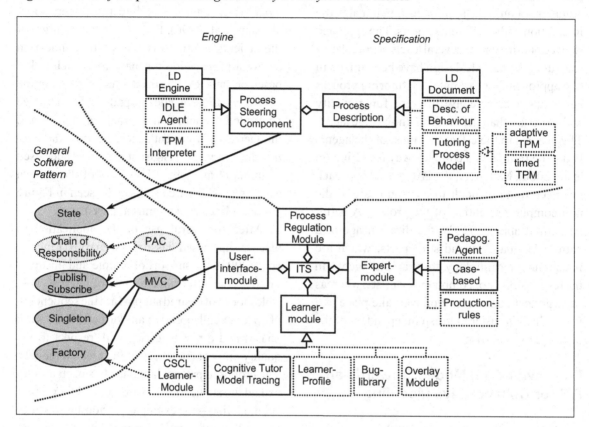

The *expert module* is case-based. Teachers and/or experts of a specific graphical domain can specify relevant situations and configurations of graphical objects and their relations (Herrmann et al., 2003). Cases are situations directly targeted at specific tasks/problems, but can be also more conceptual entities, for example, a conflicting argumentative structure in a typed graphical discussion.

In complex collaborative learning scenarios, such as in scientific inquiry learning (van Joolingen et al., 2005), students often need some scaffold, for example, what to do in a specific phase, which tools to use, and which phases might follow each other. This is similar to pedagogical control in an ITS with interventions, yet more specifically

tailored to the needs of collaborative learning. The IMS/LD specification (IMS, 2003) provides a standardized vocabulary for the definition of (collaborative) learning processes and implementations. Based on the pattern language a *process regulation module* for FreeStyler/Cool Modes has been conceptualized. The used refining patterns are *LD engine* and *LD document* in Figure 7. The pattern approach has then been combined with a componentbased approach, using the existing Coppercore IMS/LD engine as a loosely coupled process regulation module (see Harrer, Malzahn, et al., 2005).

After the integration of an expert module, user module, and process regulation module, the collaborative application can be considered an intelligent tutoring system for collaborative scenarios.

The FreeStyler/Cool Modes example shows that the pattern language is useful for analytical purposes (as discussed for the UI module) as well as for the pattern-oriented development and incremental extension and refinement towards an ITS (expert, user, and process regulation modules).

SUMMARY AND DISCUSSION

The investigation of different teaching and training systems, for example, ITS, AIED, and CSCL systems, has revealed that methods of software engineering are seldom used. This can be the reason for the following three problems:

1. Re-use of existing systems in different teaching and training domains and also re-use of system components is, in most, cases not possible.
2. System requirements have to be communicated. Communication is difficult between different ITS research groups, and even more between different researchers, for example, software developers, experts of the application domain, and pedagogical researchers.
3. Comparison of teaching and training systems often takes place by evaluation of the learner's satisfaction and the learner's success. Aspects like re-usability of components, performance, or way of implementation, all of which could be used to compare systems in the same application domain and based on similar didactical approaches, are not taken into account.

Promising regarding all three mentioned problem areas is the idea to combine different software engineering approaches. Example architectures (e.g., reference architectures, architectural patterns, and frameworks), implementation oriented approaches from the field of software engineering

(e.g., patterns, component-based design, and refactoring), and formal tutoring process descriptions can be combined and related to each other. Together, all of these different descriptions can constitute a pattern language. An approach following this direction has been described in this chapter. Starting with the classical ITS architecture as an entry point pattern, examples of refining patterns are given for the expert module, learner module, and for the process regulation module. By separating engine and specification part, the possibility to re-use the semantics of process execution arises. The combination of specific ITS patterns with general software patterns makes the pattern language more flexible and richer for a pattern-oriented development of ITS.

Two examples for the practical application of this pattern-based approach with ITS systems have been sketched. In Docs 'n Drugs a pattern-based approach has been used for system design. In Freestyler/CoolModes a non-ITS system has been evolved towards an ITS based on the pattern language.

The current conceptual character of the proposed pattern language can be complemented by a more practical support in developing ITS. The potential of the suggested approach for providing tool support by associating patterns with instantiable framework classes and ready-to-use components for specific system parts has been shown in recent work (Harrer et al., 2006) and will be explored further by us. For example the integration of the Coppercore LD engine as specific implementation of a process engine can be facilitated by providing standardized adapter components linking the engine to a learning environment. This can be supported by a pattern browser where a developer navigates through the pattern language choosing patterns and partially instantiating components and classes during this process. This operational perspective of a pattern language comes close to authoring systems for ITS, such as surveyed in Murray (1999). Formal models of the required patterns, for example, specified using ontologies or models used with model-driven approaches, are a first step towards moving from conceptual also to operational and implementational support for development of ITSs.

Other challenges for our approach in future work will be which aspects and patterns of ITS-specific nature can be transferred to more general usage in the design and development of e-learning systems. For example, the integration of patterns for management of learning objects and other content is an interesting strand for the synergies of task-supporting e-learning (ITS) with content-delivering e-learning (learning management systems).

REFERENCES

Anderson, J., Corbett, A., Koedinger, K., & Pelletier, R. (1995). Cognitive tutors: Lessons learned. *The Journal of Learning Sciences, 4*, 167-207.

Anderson, J. R., Boyle, C. F., Corbett, A. T., & Lewis, M. W. (1990). Cognitive modeling and intelligent tutoring. *Artificial Intelligence, 42*, 7-49.

Bote Lorenzo, M., Hernandez Leo, D., Dimitriadis, Y., Asensio Perez, J., et al. (2004). Towards reusability and tailorability in collaborative learning systems using IMS-LD and Grid services. *Advanced Technology for Learning, 1*(3), 129-138.

Brown, J. S., & Burton, R. R. (1978). Diagnostic models for procedural bugs in basic mathematical dkills. *Cognitive Science, 2*, 155-192.

Brusilovsky, P. (1995). Intelligent learning environments for programming: The case for integration and adaptation. In *Proceedings of the International Conference on Artificial Intelligence in Education, AIED* (pp. 1-7). Washington, US.

Buschmann, F., Meunier, R., Rohnert, H., Sommerlad, P., & Stahl, M. (1996). *A system of patterns.* Chichester, UK: John Wiley & Sons.

Clancey, W. J. (1984). Methodology for building an intelligent tutoring system. In W. Kintsch, J. R. Miller, & P. G. Polson (Eds.), *Methods and Tactics in Cognitive Science* (pp. 51-84). Hillsdale, NJ: Lawrence Erlbaum Associates.

DCMI. (2002). *Dublin Core Metadata Initiative.* http://dublincore.org.

Derntl, M., & Motschnig-Pitrik, R. (2003). *Patterns for Blended, Person Centred Learning: Strategy, Concepts, Experiences, and Evaluation* (Tech. Rep.). University of Vienna.

Devedzic, V. (1999). Using design patterns in ITS development. In S. Lajoie & M. Vivet (Eds.), *Proceedings of the International Conference on Artificial Intelligence in Education, AIED* (pp. 657-659). Amsterdam, Netherlands.

Devedzic, V. (2001). A pattern language for architectures of intelligent tutors. In J. Moore, C. Redfield, & W. Johnson (Eds.), *Proceedings of the International Conference on Artificial Intelligence in Education AIED* (pp. 542-544). San Antonio, TX.

Devedzic, V., & Harrer, A. (2002). Architecural patterns in pedagogical agents. In S. Cerri, G. Gouarderes, & F. Paraguacu (Eds.), *Proceedings of the 6th International. Conference on Intelligent Ttutoring Systems ITS* (pp. 81-90). Biarritz, France: Springer.

Devedzic, V., & Harrer, A. (2005). Software patterns in ITS architectures. *International Journal of Artificial Intelligence in Education, 15*(2), 63-94.

Dolonen, J., Chen, W., & Morch, A. (2003). Integrating software agents with FLE3. In B. Wasson, S. Ludvigsen, & U. Hoppe (Eds.), *Proceeding of* the International Conference on Computer Supported Collaborative Learning CSCL (pp. 157-161). New York: Kluwer Academic Publishers.

Farance, F., & Tonkel, J. (2001). *LTSA Specification—Learning Technology Systems Architecture, Draft 8*. Retrieved from http://www.edutool.com/ltsa

Fowler, M., Beck, K., Brant, J., Opdyke, W., & Roberts, D. (1999). *Refactoring: Improving the design of existing code*. Boston: Addison-Wesley.

Gamma, E., Helm, R., Johnson, R., & Vlissides, J. (1995). *Design patterns: Elements of reusable object-oriented software*. Boston: Addison-Wesley.

Goldstein, I. P. (1970). *Overlays: A theory of modelling for computer aided instruction* (Tech. Rep. No. AI Memo 406). Cambridge, MA: MIT.

Harrer, A. (1997). Both sides of the coin—Blending cognitive and motivational aspects into a tutoring strategy. In T. Ottmann, Z. Halim, & Z. Razak (Eds.), *Proceedings of the International Conference on Computers in Education, ICCE* (pp. 188-195). Kuching, Malaysia.

Harrer, A. (2000). *Unterstützung von Lerngemeinschaften in verteilten intelligenten Lernsystemen*. Doctoral dissertation, Universität München, München, Germany.

Harrer, A. (2003). Software engineering methods for re-use of components and eesign in educational systems. *International Journal on Computers and Applications, Special Issue on Intelligence and Technology in Educational Applications, 25*(1).

Harrer, A., Malzahn, N., Hoeksema, K., & Hoppe, U. (2005). Learning design engines as remote control to learning support environments. *Journal of Interactive Media in Education, Special Issue on Advances in Learning Design*.

Harrer, A., Malzahn, N., & Roth, B. (2006). The Remote Control Approach—How to Apply Scaffolds to Existing Collaborative Learning Environments. In Y. Dimitriadis, I. Zigurs, & E. Gomez-Sanchez (Eds.), *Proceeding of CRIWG* (Vol. LNCS 4154, pp. 118-131). Berlin: Springer.

Harrer, A., McLaren, B., Walker, E., Bollen, L., & Sewell, J. (2005). Collaboration and cognitive tutoring: Integration, empirical results, and future directions. In C.-K. Looi, G. McCalla, B. Bredeweg, & J. Breuker (Eds.), *Proceedings of the International Conference on Artificial Intelligence in Education AIED* (Vol. 125, pp. 266-273). Amsterdam: IOS Press.

Harrer A., McLaren, B.M., Walker, E., Bollen, L., Sewall, J. (2006) Creating cognitive tutors for collaborative learning: Steps toward realization. User modeling and user-adapted interaction. *The Journal of Personalization Research, 16*, 175-209.

Herrmann, K., Hoppe, U., & Pinkwart, N. (2003). A checking mechanism for visual language environments. In U. Hoppe, F. Verdejo, & J. Kay (Eds.), *Proceedings of the 11th International Conference on Artificial Intelligence in Education, AIED* (pp. 97-104). Amsterdam: IOS Press.

Ikeda, M., & Mizoguchi, R. (1994). FITS—A framework for an ITS—A computational model of tutoring. *Journal of Artificial Intelligence in Education, 5*(3), 319-348.

Illmann, T., Martens, A., Seitz, A., & Weber, M. (2000). A pattern-oriented design of a Web-based and case-oriented multimedia training system in medicine. *In Proceedings of the 4th World Conference on Integrated Design & Process Technology*. Dallas, USA.

Illmann, T., Martens, A., Seitz, A., & Weber, M. (2001). Structure of training cases in Web-based case-oriented training systems. In K. Okamoto T. Hartley R. & K. J. (Eds.), *ICALT 2001—IEEE International Conference on Advanced Learning Technologies*. IEEE Computer Society.

IMS. (2003). *IMS—Instructional Management Systems—Global Learning Consortium—Version 1.0*, Final Specification, Draft 2003. Retrieved from http://www.imsproject.org/profiles/index.html

Inaba, A., Ohkubo, R., Ikeda, M., Mizoguchi, R. & Toyoda, J. (2001). An instructional design support environment for CSCL, artificial intelligence in education—AI-ED in the wired and wireless future. In J.D. Moore, C. Redfield & W.L. Johnson (Eds.), *Frontiers in Artificial Intelligence and Applications, 68* (pp. 130-141).

Jansen, M. (2003). Matchmaker—A framework to support collaborative Java applications. In U. Hoppe, F. Verdejo, & J. Kay (Eds.), *Proceedings of the 11th International Conference on Artificial Intelligence in Education AIED* (pp. 529-530). Amsterdam: IOS Press.

Johnson, W. L., Rickel, J., & Lester, J. (2000). Animated pedagogical agents: Face-to-face interaction in interactive learning environments. *International Journal of Artificial Intelligence in Education, 11*.

Kaplan-Leiserson, E. (2002). Glossary. American society for training & development (ASTD) *Online Magazine All About E-Learning*. Retrieved from http://www.learningcircuits.org/glossary.html

Lelouche, R. (1999). Intelligent tutoring systems from birth to now. *KI -Künstliche Intelligenz, 4*, 5-11.

Lingnau, A., Kuhn, M., Harrer, A., Hofmann, D., Fendrich, M., & Hoppe, U. (2003). Enriching traditional classroom scenarios by seamless integration of interactive media. In V. Devedzic, J. Spector, D. Sampson, & Kinshuk (Eds.), *Proceedings of the International Conference on Advanced Learning Technologies ICALT* (pp. 135-139). Los Alamitos, CA.

Martel, C., Vignollet, L., Ferraris, C., David, J.-P., & Lejeune, A. (2006). Modelling collaborative learning activities in e-learning platforms. In Kinshuk, R. Koper, P. Kommers, P. Kirschner, D. Sampson, & W. Didderen (Eds.), *Proceedings of the International Conference. on Advanced Learning Technologies ICALT* (pp. 707-709). Los Alamitos, CA: IEEE Computer Society.

Martens, A. (2003). Centralize the tutoring process in intelligent tutoring systems. In Ch. Jutz, F. Flückiger, K. Waefler (Ed.), *Proceedings of the 5th International Confernece on New Educational Environments ICNEE* (pp. 209-214). Lucerne, Switzerland: net4net.

Martens, A. (2004). *Ein Tutoring Prozess Modell für fallbasierte Intelligente Tutoring Systeme*. AKA Verlag infix.

Martens, A. (2005). Modeling of Adaptive Tutoring Processes. In Z. Ma (Ed.), *Web-based intelligent e-learning systems: Technologies and applications* (pp. 193-215). Hershey, PA: Information Science Publishing, Idea Group Inc.

Martens, A. (2006). Time in the adaptive tutoring process model. In T.-W. C. Mitsuru Ikeda Kevin D. Ashley (Ed.), *Proceedings of the 8th International Conference on Intelligent Tutoring Systems ITS* (pp. 134-143). New York: Springer.

Martens, A., Bernauer, J., Illmann, T., & Seitz, A. (2001). "Docs 'n drugs—the virtual polyclinic" An intelligent tutoring system for Web-based and case-oriented training in medicine. In *Proeedings of the American Medical Informatics Conference AMIA* (pp. 433-437). Washington, US.

Martens, A., & Himmelspach, J. (2005). Combining intelligent tutoring and simulation systems. *In Proceedings of the International Conference on Simulation in Human Computer Interfaces, SIMCHI, Part of the Western Multi Conference WMC* (pp. 65-70), New Orleans, USA.

Mizoguchi, R., Ikeda, M., & Sinitsa, K. (1997). Roles of Shared Ontology in AI-ED Research. In B. du Boulay & R. Mizoguchi (Eds.), *Proceedings of the International Conference on Artificial Intelligence in Education, AIED.*

Mühlenbrock, M., Tewissen, F., & Hoppe, U. (1998). A framework system for intelligent support in open distributed learning environments. *Journal of Artificial Intelligence in Education, 9*, 256-274.

Murray, T. (1999). Authoring intelligent tutoring systems. *International Journal of Artificial Intelligence in Education, 10*(3/4), 98-129.

Murray, W. (2005). Breaking the ITS monolith: A hybrid simulation and tutoring architecture for ITS. In C.-K. Looi, G. McCalla, B. Bredeweg, & J. Breuker (Eds.), *Proceedings of the International Conference on Artificial intelligence in education AIED* (Vol. 125, pp. 890-892). Amsterdam: IOS Press.

Muukkonen, H., Hakkarainen, K., & Lakkala, M. (1999). Collaborative technology for facilitating progressive inquiry: Future learning environment tools. In C. Hoadly & J. Roschelle (Eds.), *Proceedings of the International Conference on Computer Supported Collaborative Learning CSCL.*

Pawlowski, J. M. (2000). The Essen Learning Model—A multi-level development model. In *Proceedings of the International Conference. on Educational Multimedia, Hypermedia & Telecommunications ED-MEDIA.* Montreal, Quebec, Canada.

Pinkwart, N. (2005). *Collaborative Modelling in Graph Based Environments.* Unpublished doctoral dissertation, Gerhard-Mercator-Universität Duisburg.

Pinkwart, N., Harrer, A., Lohmann, S. & Vetter, S. (2005). Integrating portal based support tools to foster learning communities in university courses. In V. Uskov, (Ed.), *Proceedings of International Conference on Web-Based Education WBE* (pp. 201-206). Anaheim, CA: ACTA Press.

Ritter, S. (1997). Communication, cooperation and competition among multiple tutor agents. In B. du Boulay & R. Mizoguchi (Eds.), *Proceedings of the International Conference on Artificial Intelligence in Education AIED* (pp. 31-38). Kobe.

Ritter, S., & Koedinger, K. (1996). An architecture for plug-in tutor agents. *International Journal of Artificial Intelligence in Education, 7*(3/4), 315-347.

Rohmer, J. (2004). *Yesterday, Today, and Tomorrow of AI Applications.* Invited Talk at IFIP World Congress.

SAIL project (2005). *Scalable Architecture for Interactive Learning.* Retrieved from http://docs.telcenter.org/display/SAIL/Home

Schmidt, S., Stal, M., Rohnert, H., & Buschmann, F. (2000). *Pattern-oriented software architecture-patterns for concurrent and networked objects.* Chichester, UK: John Wiley & Sons.

Szyperski, C. (2002). *Component Software.* 2nd edition. Component Software Series. ACM Press, New York: Addison Wesley.

van Joolingen, W., Lazonder, A., de Jong, T., Savelsbergh, E., & Manlove, S. (2005). Co-lab: Research and development of an online learning environment for collaborative scientific discovery learning. *Computers in Human Behavior, 21*, 671-688.

Chapter VII
Model–Driven Engineering (MDE) and Model–Driven Architecture (MDA) Applied to the Modeling and Deployment of Technology Enhanced Learning (TEL) Systems:
Promises, Challenges, and Issues.

Pierre Laforcade
Université du Maine, France

Christophe Choquet
Université du Maine, France

Thierry Nodenot
Université de Pau, France

Pierre-André Caron
*Université des Sciences et
Technologies de Lille, France*

ABSTRACT

This chapter deals with the application of model-driven engineering and model-driven architecture approaches in a technology enhanced learning (TEL) context. Such Software Engineering approaches provide concrete benefits (productivity, interoperability, adaptability) by means of intensive uses of models, meta-models and transformations. Such benefits can also be met in a TEL context. Because computer scientists or engineers cannot currently find well-defined frameworks about this new trend, we have chosen to report recent results of our working group (initiated in 2003) in order to provide readers with a survival kit. Our results, illustrated in this chapter, argue that model-driven engineering can help designers to reduce the gap between specific instructional requirements (domain point of view) and the software architectures that practically support the implementation, the run-time and the regulation of this instruction.

INTRODUCTION

Historically, e-learning is considered as a specific information-systems domain among others (see e-business, e-health, and so on) and it is interesting to notice that e-learning draws on research conducted in information technologies and also in the *software engineering* domain: service oriented architectures, component-based development, engineering methods and tools, ontology development, design patterns approaches, etc. are now well-known topics of interest for the e-learning domain.

In a same way, this chapter discusses the application of *model-driven engineering* and *model-driven architecture* approaches in a *technology enhanced learning* (TEL) context. Such *software engineering* approaches can provide tangible and varied benefits (theories or principles but also techniques and concrete tools). Because computer scientists or engineers cannot currently find well-defined frameworks about this new trend, we have chosen to report recent results of our working group (initiated in 2003) in order to provide readers with a survival kit. Our results showed that model-drien engineering can help designers to reduce the gap between specific instructional requirements (domain point of view) and the software architectures that actively support the implementation, the run-time and the regulation of this instruction.

To this end, this chapter is divided into four parts. Firstly, we present (cf. part 1):

1. Current difficulties encountered by designers and developers of TEL systems. They result from the gap between the educational intents and the expression of these intents in the hundreds of lines (XML code, java code, PHP code, SQL queries, etc.) required to correctly tune a given learning management system.

2. Some recent technological and methodological initiatives to counter this lack of an integrated view.

From this background, we present (cf. part 2) the aims and principles of MDE-MDA (such as the three distinct kinds of models: Computer-Independent-Models -CIM, Platform-Independent-Models -PIM, and Platform Specific Models -PSM), and their promises within our context, particularly to facilitate the mapping between the learning activities imagined by designers and the requirements of the infrastructures chosen to deploy these activities.

From various experiments conducted in our laboratories, four challenges are then covered (cf. part 3):

*   From CIM to PIM models: development, use of Domain Specific Modeling languages.
*   From PIM to PSM models: transformation of Domain Specific Models into code that can be exploited by learning management systems (Moodle, ATutor, etc.).
*   From PSM to PIM models: re-engineering of learning activities from execution track exploitation (structured logs, …).
*   From PIM to CIM models: mapping, binding and visualization of formal models in order to be human-readable by designers and adapted to their Domain Specific Modeling languages.

In the last part of the chapter (cf. part 4), we discuss current research results and obstacles encountered in deploying educational applications from a model-drien engineering perspective. Finally, from our experiences and the analysis of this growing trend, we propose a list of MDE issues for practitioners.

BACKGROUND

Various open source and commercial e-learning platforms are available to practitioners and developers. Often, they offer quite similar functionalities including support for collaborative work (chat tools, discussion forums, etc.) but they differ because, on one hand, they are based on different terminologies and, on the other, they rely on different technological implementations (php, Java, Enterprise Java Beans, XML, MySql, etc.) (Dewanto, 2005). As a consequence, it is difficult to compare such e-learning platforms or to handle the migration of a course/functionality from one e-learning platform to another. In other respects, although these e-learning platforms have raised the level of abstraction, they still have a "computing-oriented" focus. In particular, they provide abstractions of the solution space, (that is the domain of computing technologies themselves) (Schmidt, 2006) rather than abstractions of the educational space that express designs in terms of learning goals, learning outcomes, educational events used to regulate learners' activities, etc.

As a consequence, there is no direct relationship between the design documents and models produced by the educational designers and the (technical) information required by e-learning platforms to achieve such design intents: technical development does not rely on the design documents and platform code is written and maintained manually. Since current e-learning platforms often rely on complex middleware, the gap between educational designers and e-learning developers is difficult to bridge.

To address such difficulties, different standards were recently proposed : (a) the *Sharable Content Object Reference Model* (SCORM) (ADL, 2004) suited to e-learning developers and (b) the IEEE *Learning Object MetaData* (LOM) (LTSC, 2003) and the IMS *Learning Design* specification (IMS-LD) (IMS, 2003) suited to educational designers. Yet, at the time, such standards did not radically change the situation. If we consider, for example,

the case of the IMS-LD specification, one can observe that:

1. This specification is often accepted as a language to encode the final result of an educational design process. Such language can be interpreted by IMS-LD compliant e-learning platforms such as *dotLRN* (Santos et al., 2005), *LAMS* (Dalziel, 2006), and *Moodle* (Berggren et al., 2005). But there are still so many powerful e-learning platforms that do not comply with this evolving standard, that we consider it will be necessary to continue transforming IMS-LD encoded specifications into code for IMS-LD non compliant platforms (such as Ganesha (Anéma, 2007), Claroline (Claroline, 2007), OpenUss, etc.) for a long time.

2. Many tools have been recently developed to enable educational designers to benefit from all IMS-LD expressive capabilities without using a XML editor. Yet, different studies have shown that most educational designers need dedicated visual tools and languages to support their creativity while exploring their problem-spaces and solutions (Botturi, 2006a), (Derntl, 2007). IMS-LD was not designed to play this role (Allert 2005), (Botturi, 2006b), (Pawlowski et al., 2006). Moreover, the mapping between the available *domain specific languages—DSL*—(Wile, 2001) used by designers and IMS-LD is neither automatic nor really thought through.

Considering these recurrent problems faced by researchers and by most Instructional Design Teams, the French TEL Research Community decided to work together in order to strengthen common understanding in 2003. The three considerations were the design languages and the middleware chosen in different labs (JavaEE, Web Services, Open Source Learning Content Management Systems), the way some partners specified and plugged in educational components to such middleware, and the way researchers can find, specify and specialize these components according to a given learning scenario (focus on *educational modeling languages* like IMS-LD, and on transformation techniques). The final report of this 2-year long project concluded that model-drien engineering Techniques and tools could impact positively on TEL system development and maintenance (ASPF, 2005).

MDE-MDA APPLIED: PROMISES

This section answers the questions: Why should researchers in the domain of TEL systems investigate the Software Engineering domains of model-drien engineering and model-driven architecture? What promises deserve this interest? This section first briefly presents a map overview of the theories and principles of these growing domains; then we apply these highlighted concepts to our common specific TEL context about instructional engineering processes and *educational modeling languages* (EML).

MDE-MDA Theories and Principles

The *model-driven architecture* approach (MDA) is a framework for software development, and the evolution of information systems adopted by Object Management Group (OMG) in 2001 (the MDA document Guide (OMG, 2006a) provides an overview and definitions of the used concepts). The goal of MDA is to provide a solution to the problem of software technologies continual emergence that forces companies to adapt their software systems every time a new "hot" technology appears (*adaptability* problem). MDA also wants to tackle the *productivity* problem (software development processes driven by low-level design and coding lead to difficult maintenance and understanding of the code), and the *interoperability*

problem (different modules built upon different technologies need to interoperate).

MDA aims to solve the adaptability problem. The first principle is to use *modeling* and *models* to develop software systems. The second principle is the *separation* of the enterprise functionalities of an information system from the implementation of those functionalities on specific technological platforms (EJB, CORBA, and so on). The abstract specification of the system becomes the main asset in software development: many implementations using concrete technologies may be derived from the abstract specification. It is *model-driven* because "it provides a means for using models to direct the course of understanding, design, construction, deployment, operation, maintenance and modification" (OMG, 2006a).

In an MDA software process, a system is developed by refining models, moving from higher towards lower levels of abstraction until the system's code is generated. These refinements are implemented by transformations to the models.

MDA comes with many key concepts and principles (Favre, 2004). In short, "a model is a simplification of a system built with an intended goal in mind" (Bézivin et al., 2001), and a *meta-model* is yet another abstraction, highlighting properties of the model itself. A model conforms to its meta-model in the same way a program conforms to the grammar of the programming language in which it is written. A meta-model is considered as the model of the *modeling language* used to specify models.

The MDA approach sorts models into three classes (see Figure 1). The *computation independent model* (CIM) view of a system is sometimes called the domain model or enterprise model: the modeling vocabulary used is the domain one. The CIM assumes an important role by bridging the gap between domain experts and their requirements on the one hand, and design experts of the artifacts that should satisfy the domain requirements, on the other. A CIM helps in specifying exactly what the system is expected to do. The CIM is useful, not only as a guide and a support to understanding a problem, but also as a reference of a shared vocabulary used in the other models. In an MDA specification of a system, CIM requirements should be traceable to the PIM and PSM constructs that implement them, and *vice versa* (see "mapping" in Figure 1).

The platform independent model (PIM) view of a system leads to independence from specific platforms but should be expressed in a computational way, so as to be suitable for use with a number of different platforms of similar type.

Finally, the platform specific model (PSM) view links the specifications in the PIM with the details that specify how this system will be implemented on a specific platform. Mappings between PIM and PSM can be accomplished by means of model transformations (the process of converting one model to another model of the same system). MDA aims at automating model transformations as much as possible. Finally, code can be generated from the PSM (Figure 1).

MDA also aims to integrate the existing technologies standardized by OMG. Models are expressed in unified modeling language (UML) (OMG, 2001) and UML profiles. If another modeling language (*domain-specific language*) is used, it should be defined using a specific meta-modeling language. For this reason, OMG defines the so-called OMG *meta-object facility* (MOF) (OMG, 2006c) which includes a four layer architecture (Alvarez et al., 2001): the meta-meta-model layer (M3), the meta-model layer (M2), the user model layer (M1) and the user object layer

(M0). UML is an example of M2 meta-models whereas the MOF is the unique, and self-defined, meta-meta-model. MDA also uses XML Metadata Interchange (XMI) (OMG, 2005a) for the serialization of MOF models in XML format. OMG proposes the *query/views/transformations* (QVT) language (OMG, 2005b) for the specification of transformations to MOF models.

Because MDA lacks the notion of a software development process, the *model-drien engineering* (MDE) is an enhancement of MDA in this direction and can be considered as a generalization of the MDA (Kurtev, 2005). (Kent, 2002) defines MDE on the base of MDA by adding the notion of software development processes and modeling space for organizing models. This modeling space is organized over several dimensions. MDA defines only one classification dimension for models based on the CIM-PIM-PSM categorization (separation of concerns based on the level of model abstraction). Therefore, one MDE dimension in the modeling space reflects the degree of *abstractness* or *concreteness* of models. Another dimension comes from the distinction of models based on the subject area they belong to. Different users of a system may have different views over the system focusing on a subset of the system's features. These views are reflected in different models of the same system. Concerns of interest (and separations based on them) are enumerated in another dimension in the modeling space. This dimension is nominal. No order is assumed among the concerns (examples of concerns: concurrency control, security, distribution, etc.). Kent defines other dimensions (the number of

Figure 1. Overview of the CIM-to-PIM-to-PSM process from the MDA framework

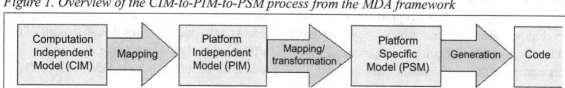

dimensions is not limited and depends on the specific needs in a development project). Favre (2004) proposes another vision on MDE where MDA is just one possible instance of the MDE implemented in the set of technologies defined by OMG. Because the concepts of model, meta-model and transformations are found in other technologies as well (Kurtev et al., 2002), Favre thinks that their meaning should be analyzed in a broader perspective and MDE should be able to accommodate various technological domains in a uniform way.

Many techniques (pattern, logic, contracts, etc.), approaches (direct manipulation, structure-driven, graph-transformation-based, relational approaches, etc.), standards (UML, XMI, QVT, etc.) and dedicated tools (see http://www.planet-mde.org/) can perform operations on models in MDE (Czarnecki, 2003; Kurtev, 2005; Mens et al., 2005).

MDE-MDA Promises in a Mixed Engineering and Re-Engineering TEL Context

Previous MDE and MDA theories and techniques are already applied to various related domains of the TEL context: ontology development (Gašević et al., 2006), generation of adaptable learning materials (Dodero et al., 2006), co-operative work (David et al., 2005), user-modeling (Marinilli, 2005), and so on.

Because the MDA framework proposes a separation of concerns between functional models (which could be vast in a TEL context) and various platform/architecture specific models (which correspond in a TEL context to the various *learning management systems* (LMS), e-learning platforms or other TEL environments delivering an educational support), the MDE/MDA application could bring benefits to productivity (focusing on instructional design independently from architecture choices), adaptability and interoperability

(one PIM model could be transformed into multiple PSMs for different TEL environments).

It is also important to notice that the MDE/MDA framework is process-independent and, in this way, is adapted for use in mixed engineering (CIM-to-PIM-to-PSM) and re-engineering (PSM-to-PIM-to-CIM) situations. The re-engineering (Chikofsky, 1990; Gowthaman et al., 2005) could be seen as an iterative design process in which instructional information is also extracted from the run-time phase of the TEL system and brought back to the designers. This situation can also benefit from this new framework: understanding of how instructional and content aspects are implemented and regulated in a specific TEL architecture, abstraction of educational concerns from the analysis of users' real activity tracks within a specific architecture, mapping and visualization transformations towards a designer-understandable format, and so forth.

In concrete terms, the MDE/MDA framework applied to the design and implementation of TEL systems seems a very promising and powerful approach to reduce the gap between instruction and the architecture supporting it. Many research works are conducted in this way but with some specific applications of the general MDE-MDA framework. Some of these works focus mainly on PIM-PSM aspects and are very architecture-centered, for example, the AndroMDA proposition for the component-based OpenUSS platform (Grob et al., 2006). Other works (Dodero et al., 2006) envisage following a model-driven development approach that provides different levels of automation to generate learning material adapted to a specific instructional purpose.

The next sections will deal with our current research studies about this MDE/MDA application. Considering that our research context involves the design and implementation of learning scenarios on specific TEL systems (the *learning management systems*—LMS), we propose now to stress our analogy of the previous MDE/MDA framework when applied to this learning design context.

The analogy of the CIM, PIM and PSM models for the learning scenarios is straightforward; to start, let us define CIM, PIM and PSM concepts:

- PIMs are learning scenarios that are independent from LMS aspects; IMS-LD scenarios are examples of such PIM and IMS-LD (IMS, 2003a) is an example of PIM languages. PIMs aim to describe any design of a teaching-learning process in a formal way while promoting the exchange and interoperability of e-learning material. So, PIMs like IMS-LD scenarios are learning-theory independent because of their pedagogical flexibility objective (IMS, 2003b). PIM editors are authoring-tools for expert end-users. PIMs address machines and, because they have to be interpreted by them, PIM languages usually have XML mappings.

- PSMs represent LMS-dependent scenarios, that is, scenarios "conformed" or "constrained" by the explicit meta-model, or the implicit internal format, of a chosen platform. For instance, a learning scenario could be described as a model for the Ganesha platform if we explicit the meta-model of this LMS (roles, groups, activities, etc.). From these specific scenarios, the next step of an instructional design process concerns the configuration of the chosen LMS. PSMs are used in this way as a guide, when they cannot be directly interpreted, or are executed on the appropriate platform.

- CIMs could be considered as pedagogical scenario models from the teacher-designer point of view; they focus on domain aspects and can be specific to some learning situations (problem-based learning, project-based learning, collaborative learning, and so on). The objectives of CIMs are to

act as a guide for the design and the reuse of learning scenarios; they also ease the exchange of different learning scenarios within a learning design "community of practice" that shares the same pedagogical approach. Of course, there can be textual or graphical kinds of CIMs, and also various supports for them. Because it is not one of their intrinsic properties, some CIMs are not machine-understandable whereas others can potentially be interpreted in an automatic way. In our context we focus on computerized CIMs because we also want to handle them with different kinds of transformations to capitalize their content. For example, CPM (Laforcade, 2005) is a visual language producing CIM diagrams for humans but whose models elements are embedded in a machine-interpretable model. Currently, CIMs editors have succeeded in providing models that are understandable by teacher-designers but target users of these tools still require experts or trained teachers.

With the application of the MDE/MDA framework, our general problematic can move from "give me a fixed learning scenario and I will set up a convenient TEL environment" to "how can I set up an adapted TEL environment when learning scenario specifications often vary?" Indeed, the core-system becomes the learning scenario. The instructional design process is composed of several activities (initial pedagogical requirements/needs, instructional analysis, etc.), depending on the embedded actors of the process, each of them producing various chunks or views of the learning scenario in-design (texts/documentations, diagrams, tables, formal specifications like XML documents, etc.). These learning 'artifacts' give different points of view or deal with different aspects of the same learning scenario under study.

So, the problem focuses on the ability to guarantee the coherence of these views, or, as a *minima*, to trace and identify the elements across the different views. The MDE/MDA application promises this unification thanks to the important use of the models (that can be specified with various formalisms) and the automatic transformations (or semi-automatic by the means of users' interactions) between these models. In addition, the separation of concerns, applied to the various activities and roles involved in the instructional design process, necessitates a better focus on requirements, objectives and public skills (knowledge and know-how) when dealing with learning scenarios. If we only consider the previous three CIM/PIM/PSM models of a learning scenario, we could easily stress different publics, objectives and requirements. The intensive use of models will enable us to adapt easily and integrate various aspects (didactic, pedagogical, structural, etc.) into the learning scenario by means of interactive and iterative transformations (in order to refine or enrich the scenario as well as to enable technological space changes depending on the underlying formalism used).

Because current propositions about the educational modeling languages (Koper et al., 2005; Kinshuk et al., 2006) are still abstract-EML-centered (PIM-centered), and in this way limited or constrained to the expressiveness of a unique language, the MDE/MDA framework proposes to capitalize the knowledge and know-how of teacher-designers at the start of CIM languages, insuring that CIM scenarios serve as a guide for the design. Another important point concerns the capitalization of these CIM scenarios in order to change them from contemplative to productive scenarios (PIM and PSM ones). In addition, learning scenario capitalization by progressive formalizations insures their reusability for other pedagogical contexts (other domains, other student levels, etc.) as well as for other TEL environments. Scenario transformations are part of this capitalization; they reify a know-how that is generally only located in the minds of the designers/experts.

The production of learning scenarios can be automated by capturing these transformations in another dedicated transformation model.

MDE-MDA APPLIED: CHALLENGES

In this section, we outline various research works engaged by our French research community. These works illustrate the application of the MDE/MDA framework to the general learning design process of pedagogical situations for TEL platforms. Each part of the following sub-sections will define the specific context in which such works occurred, then, challenges and results will be given. Each sub-section is entitled according to the models of the MDA classification that are tackled.

Focus on the CIM

Our research works, from one laboratory of our Special Interest Group, focus on the modeling of cooperative learning scenarios and the provisioning of dedicated languages and tools to designers dealing with such learning situations (CIM level). Considering that teachers and pedagogues often promote instructional scenarios relying on the constructivist and socio-constructivist theories at school, we put forward a language from which they can draw models of the learning scenarios that they favor. We provide them with the CPM (Cooperative PBL Meta-model) language (Nodenot et al., 2003) that enables a team of designers to describe what should be learnt from a scenario, the characteristics of students who will use the scenario (learner models), how the learners will acquire this knowledge (teaching and available learning strategies), etc. CPM models act as a support for thinking and communicating within a multidisciplinary design team. CPM does not try to encompass any type of educational situation but focuses on the study of Problem-Based Learning (PBL) situations during which groups of learners are involved in cooperative activities. To this end, CPM can be considered as a valuable CIM language for the design of learning scenarios.

In practice, CPM is based on the visual UML language (version 1.5 from (OMG, 2001)). CPM copes with PBL models from two distinct angles:

- **Horizontally:** Models differ in terms of objectives, abstraction, contents and potential uses.
- **Vertically:** Models capture different points of view about the same learning logics.

In CPM, a strong point is the differentiation of two target people categories. First of all, the CPM language addresses pedagogic engineers: this is a new job in distance learning. A pedagogic engineer's activity consists of coordinating all the actors involved in learning situations (teachers, pedagogues, didactics specialists, sociologists, etc). As a pre-requisite, pedagogic engineers have to know UML modeling principles. Next, the second category covers the multidisciplinary designer team including software engineers. The CPM models have to favor exchanges, the understanding and involvement of eclectic actors. This important difficulty generates the need for a simplified UML, namely a syntax (terminology and notation) and semantics that are tailored for education in general. Technically, the CPM abstract syntax is a meta-model while its concrete syntax is represented through the CPM profile (Laforcade et al., 2003). Preferred CPM diagrams are class diagrams, use case diagrams, state diagrams and activity diagrams. The semantics of the different CPM concepts and relations are written in object constraint language (OCL) (OMG, 2006b), with additional explanations in natural language.

In Figure 2, we show a screenshot from the CPM environment-tool as an add-on of the Objecteering CASE tool; the figure also shows a view (activity diagram) of the CPM model dedicated to the SMASH case study (one of the different case-studies that serve as validation experiments). The achievement of this case study (further details appear in (Laforcade, 2005)) especially proves that PBL situations may be easily and straightforwardly implemented by means of CPM.

In domain-oriented modeling languages, many barriers come from the fact that domain experts have problems when handling computer-based concepts (those of class or inheritance for instance). The difficulty for pedagogic engineers to adopt and put into practice UML is overridden here thanks to a stereotyped formalism (see icons for instance in Figure 2), but this does not preclude the need for good UML skills. In addition, the CPM language is now available within a module that can be integrated in and used with the free-of-charge version of the Objecteering/ UML Modeler.

From CIM to PIM

We also initiated an experimental study (Laforcade, 2005) about model transformation to allow new uses (e.g., to be played) for CPM models and not to restrict them to simple visual elements. Within this context, we tried to transform CPM models into IMS-LD-compliant ones by proposing a mapping between our language and the formal models generally used for detailed design (CIM to PIM transformation). For our experiments, the transformation consisted of mapping CPM activity diagrams with level-A IMS-LD models only (the IMS-LD information model is decomposed into three levels). The transformation of CPM models into the IMS-LD canonical format required a mapping that we built on the results of a study aimed at comparing these two languages.

Specifically, to operate such a transformation, we could have exported our selected CPM models into an external XMI format and then have operated a XSLT-based transformation towards an IMS-LD conform model (IMS-LD models are encoded with the XML language). We chose to apply another technique based on the interpreta-

Figure 2. Screenshot of the CPM tool

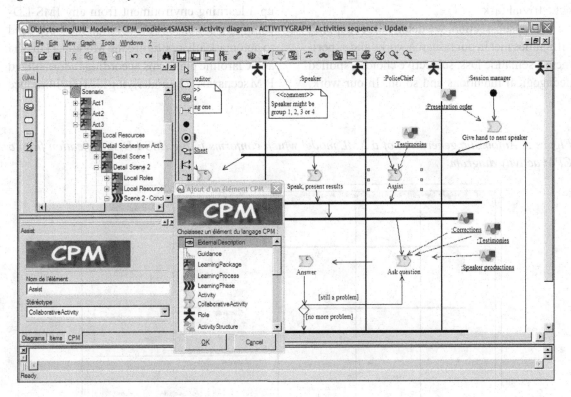

tion of UML models by the CASE tools, in our case, the Objecteering tool. Such a model processing is achievable thanks to specific extensible elements defined in UML profiles: stereotypes and tagged-values. These elements inform and guide the collection of information embedded in UML models. We applied this technique to some learning scenario specifications and in this way, demonstrated that it is possible to transform CPM activity diagrams into IMS-LD models.

Figure 3 illustrates the two-step process of the transformation: first, the designer asks for the creation of a *work product* (specific concept of Objecteering that manages the generation of external files) from a specific CPM activity diagram (the source model for the transformation); then, the generation of the IMS-LD target file is carried out by asking the corresponding service from the previous work product (the last XML extract we can see on the figure is what the user can expect to find after opening the generated file with a XML editor).

From PIM to PSM

Within this context, we consider it important that abstract scenarios (PIM) can not be reduced to the learning-flow approach claimed by some languages (e.g., IMS-LD). They may be related to collaborative activities (LDL) (Martel et al., 2006), to PCAB (Personal and Collective Actions Browser) (Caron et al., 2006), etc. Because existing TEL platforms do not support any kind of PIM scenario, we deduce that mapping an abstract scenario to a technological platform is not a trivial task.

In this sub-section, we detail some mapping difficulties met in our research works and experiments: semantic loss, subjective choices, spoiled pedagogical intentions and so on. In our work,

we propose a solution to construct and/or set up a learning environment from any IMS-LD-compliant scenario. This solution has been used to automatically configure the Moodle, Ganesha and Claroline platforms according to formalized PIM scenarios. The underlying idea is to introduce

Figure 3. Automatic generation of a XML model which conforms to the IMS-LD specification from a CPM activity diagram

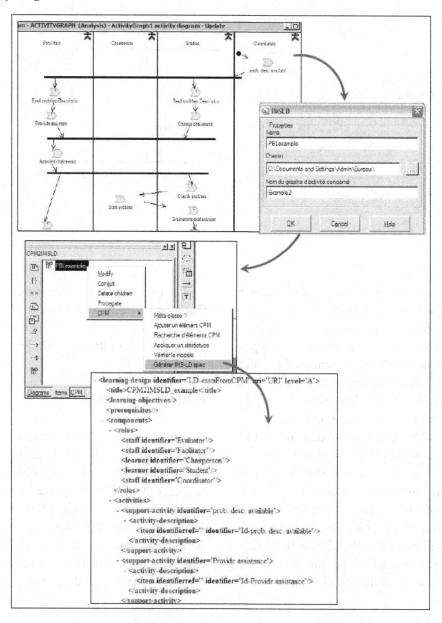

a new kind of learning scenario (a PSM one) as an intermediary model which takes into account architecture details from a specific TEL system chosen for the deployment and run-time of the learning situation. Such a solution requires three conditions. First, PSM scenarios are really practical and useful if they are automatically generated and if the generation can be driven by pedagogical intentions or other underlying aspects. Second, we need to provide tools allowing "users" to refine generated models according to their own intentions. Third, PSM scenarios have to be "productive": we need a piece of software that generates a concrete system from a PSM. This sub-section discusses the reasons for these three conditions and also describes possible mechanisms to fill these conditions.

The benefits of intermediary PSM models may be illustrated when considering situations where they are missing. The automatic construction of the learning environment directly from a PI model (i.e., PIM→Platform) raises some critical questions:

- Will technological adaptation choices satisfy designers?
- Will designers have a clear (over)view of the constructed environment when they access it?
- Interactions with designers would be required during the construction process to adapt the construction to their wishes. Will these choices be saved in order to be analyzed and to improve future construction?

These questions refer in fact to the weakness of the approach where PSM models missing. Using platform specific models (i.e., PIM→PSM→ Platform) significantly improves the situation. An intermediary PSM model clearly represents definitive technological choices that have been made concerning the corresponding environment creation. It also provides the designer with a more comfortable support with which to analyze such choices and to directly change them. There are two other benefits and they concern teachers. The first one is related to platforms a teacher is familiar with: s/he may participate more in the design process when addressing platform models (where underlying concepts are familiar) rather than addressing PIM models (where concepts may be more complex). The second one is that a PSM model may provide the teacher with a clear documentation of what has been constructed.

These are the reasons we use PSM models in our Bricoles project: to conscientiously respect pedagogical intentions when automatically constructing learning environment from pedagogical specifications. We have defined meta-models for Claroline, Ganesha and Moodle platforms (nearly a million users around the world) and we use these meta-models to define PSM models when constructing environments on such platforms from PIM models. To provide a current productive cycle, we have developed a complete infrastructure which consists of two tools: ModX and GenDep (Trigone, 2007). The infrastructure is illustrated on Figure 4 with the underlying example of *IMS-LD* (PIM) *towards Moodle* (PSM and platform).

ModX concerns the PIM, PIM→PSM, PSM steps. It is a graphic meta-editor and an MOF-compliant tool which allows the creation/edition of meta-models and their use to create/edit corresponding models. It also provides a framework to define transformation model rules and to execute them. Designers use ModX to create a PS model, to transform it into the platform technological context and to refine the resulting PSM model. Addressing a platform implies three starting tasks which have to be done by a software/pedagogical engineer due to their difficulty. The first task is to create the meta-model corresponding to the platform (abstract and concrete syntax). The second one is to create model transformation rules between PIM meta-model(s) and the new PSM one. The

Figure 4. Bricoles infrastructure for projection from IMS-LD to Moodle

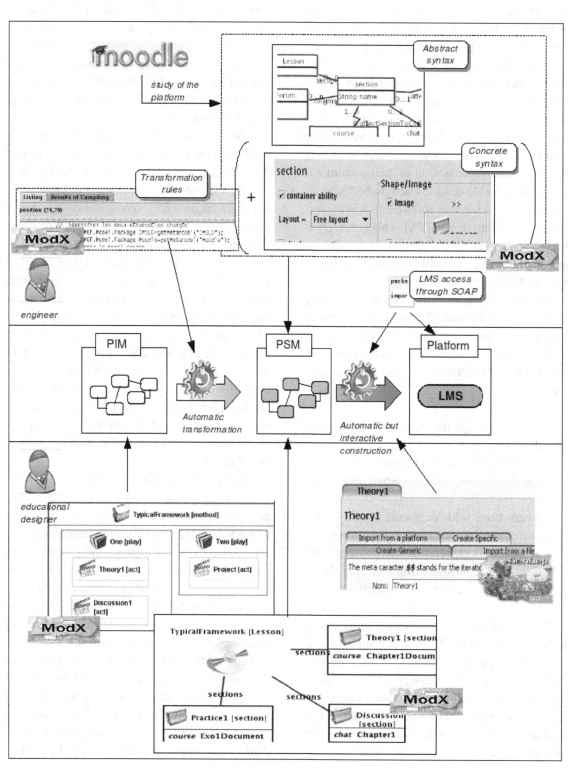

final task is to implement a SOAP plug-in for the platform, if it does not already exist, so that it may be accessed through the SOAP protocol.

GenDep concerns the PSM→Platform step. Traditional MDE code generators cannot be used in the e-learning context, because building learning environments on an e-learning platform involves interactions with it: during construction time, the platform is running and already contains other environments. Interactions are requests to create elements and to gain knowledge about the existing ones. GenDep interacts with a platform via SOAP and automatically generates the SOAP communication layer to a platform thanks to its associated meta-model. When someone uses GenDep to create an environment, s/he first selects the corresponding meta-model, s/he further selects the PSM model and finally refers it to the targeted instance of platform thanks to its URL. During construction, GenDep asks users questions through forms, to personalize its environment; for example "How many students?"; "How many wiki pages for each student?"

From PSM to PIM

In a model-driven reengineering framework, tracks or trails—what actors of a TEL system session leave behind (TRAILS, 2004)—have to be represented at a PIM level in such a way they could be compared with the predictive scenario—what designers have planned for the learning session (Corbière, & Choquet, 2004). This allows designers (1) to have a view of tracks collected in a model they can understand and then (2) to identify and qualify the differences between the predicted and the observed scenarios for re-engineering purposes.

Usage tracking language (UTL) is a meta-language which can be instantiated according to the PIM used to express the pedagogical scenario, and to the specific format log files, in which tracks are collected. At present, UTL is composed of two parts and is implemented in a XML-Schema.

Firstly, we propose to extract those representation language concepts for which we could have (log) tracks. In a second part, we associate these traceable concepts with the specific description of tracks—description given by the track format.

The connection with the representation model (e.g., PIM used for expressing a pedagogical scenario, IMS-LD for example) can be considered as an extension of the representation model. It is used to classify all concepts of the representation model that are traceable. We will use this information in the second part of UTL to link the model and the tracks. This section has been designed to be as generic as possible, because we want it to be compatible with the majority of designer models. In a representation model, we have a number of concepts used to describe the pedagogical scenario; for instance in IMS-LD, we can have *activity, learning object, role, etc.* A *traceable-concept* is a concept from which it is possible to track something, for instance, a resource and an activity are traceable concepts from which we can track the beginning, the end, the duration, etc. Figure 5 (left part) presents the information model of this part of UTL.

The description of the *traceable-concept* is composed of all relationships with other *traceable-concepts*, for instance: an *activity* is realized by a *resource*. The *title* of the relationship brings more semantics to the interpretation of the track context. This concept is typically an activity or an environment in the context of an *abstract-scenario* modeled with Learning Design. The other information consists of the *observed use*, which allows the description of the relationship between tracks and the traceable concept.

In order to work on the track itself, we need to identify it or a part of it. Thus, we have defined another section in UTL: the track representation presented in Figure 5 (right part). The model is also generic, and we propose an implementation that should work with the majority of log formats. We have tested it on typical log files (for instance, with OPEN-USS platform log files, see (Choquet, & Iksal, 2007)), and we have validated the use

Figure 5. Usage tracking language information model

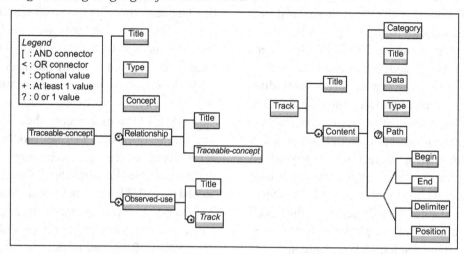

of XML log files and logs stored in databases. To manage each log format, we used two fields in our model, the *type* which refers to "text," "XML," "database," and perhaps others, and the *Path* which is optional and contains the path to the specific data to be described. A path can be expressed in XPath or SQL; it is not used for standard log formats. To describe the location of data inside a string, we propose to use character positions and/or tokens. This section of UTL is useful for retrieving specific tracks, extracting values and bringing meaning to each of them. We consider two categories of content in tracks: *keyword* is used to retrieve the track; it is a word (or a sentence) which is always present in the same kind of track. And *value* depends on the learner; it may be the time spent to read, the name of the page read or the score of an evaluation exercise.

The content locations are used to specify the position of the keyword or the value within the track. The specific attributes for the specification of the content locations are the following:

- **Title:** Is used to name the content—to associate semantics (for instance: Date or Task).

- **Begin:** Gives the first character position of the content.
- **End:** Gives the last character position of the content (-1 for the end of the line).
- **Delimiter:** Sets the delimiter used to break down the track into tokens.
- **Position:** Gives the position of the token.

The *data* field is used to store the value or to indicate the keyword. In an XML syntax, it is the textual content of the tag *content*.

From PIM to CIM

Recently, we have initiated a study about the automatic generation of graphical representations from abstract scenarios specified with EMLs (CIM representation of PIM scenarios) (Laforcade, 2007). Such research aims at providing teacher-designers with human-understandable scenario representations when these scenarios are only machine-readable. These model transformations facilitate the reuse and exchange of formal scenarios by a community of neophyte teacher-designers. In practical terms, our experiments

Figure 6. Vizualization of an IMS-LD compliant model (PIM) via an automatic transformation toward a UML activity diagram (CIM-equivalent model)—provided by the UML4LD tool

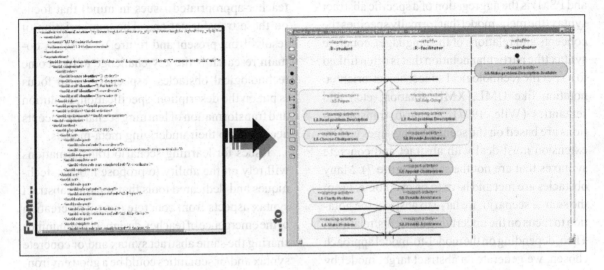

Figure 7. Highlighting abstract and concrete syntax aspects of CIM/PIM languages; scenario transformations have to deal with different obstacles: Abstraction from specific notation, meta-models mapping, binding and/or visualization towards concrete notation.

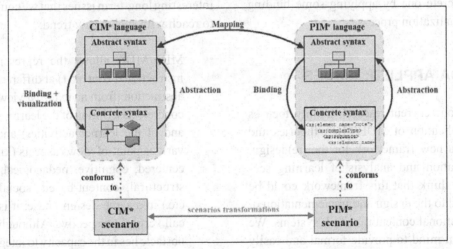

are based on a dedicated CASE-tool plug-in that automatically generates UML activity diagrams from the XML-based specification of an IMS-LD-compliant scenario (see Figure 6). Within a re-engineering research context of TEL systems, we envisage to generalize these experimental

works towards model transformations from PIM indicators to CIM ones at a "knowledge level" (Newell, 1982).

Such works are not easy to put into practice because of the numerous scientific and technological obstacles that come with the transformations when dealing with PIM and CIM scenarios. Each pedagogical language (CIM language as well as PIM and PSM) is the aggregation of a specific abstract syntax (the meta-model that formally specifies the concepts and relations of the language), concrete syntax (the particular notation that is often linked to a specific technological space: object-oriented notation like UML, XML notation, etc.) and semantics (Wile, 1997). Scenario transformations are based on the scenario languages and by extension must deal with abstract and concrete syntaxes that are not the same (Figure 7). Many obstacles are met and have to be overcome. From the source scenario, we have to abstract the notation to focus on the underlying concepts/relations. Then, depending on the model-to-model approach chosen, we generate an abstract target model by focusing on the mapping between the source meta-model (abstract syntax) and the target one. Finally, we still have to transform this abstract model (for example, an internal representation) into a concrete one by applying some binding and/or visualization processes.

MDE-MDA APPLIED: ISSUES

Although our current research mainly focuses on the application of MDE/MDA theories and results as a new framework for the (re)design, implementation and analysis of learning scenarios, we think that this framework could be generalized to the design and implementation of any instructional content into TEL systems. We also have in mind to provide formal and easily capitalized results.

Our current results already succeed in highlighting various obstacles (scientific, technological, etc.) that stakeholders have to encompass when following such a model-directed framework. Because this approach relies on the different transformations between domain-specific learning scenarios, platform-independent ones, platform-specific ones and *vice-versa*, success

will depend on the ability to provide designers and developers with techniques and tools (with teacher-appropriated issues in mind) that focus on these transformations. The appropriation of results from present and future MDE/MDA domain research is the key challenge to overcome technological obstacles, especially when focus is put on the description, specification, evolution and transformation of learning scenario concepts according to their underlying meta-models.

Issues for learning scenario transformations will rely on the ability to propose models, techniques and dedicated tools that separate abstract syntax aspects from concrete ones. The creation or the emergence of teacher-designer communities sharing the same abstract syntax and/or concrete syntax and/or semantics could be a good environmental factor to study and would put transformations between different but well-known practical models and languages into practice.

In addition, we can already outline some very interesting long-term issues that we could attempt to reach with such a new trend:

- MDE/MDA allows the representation of instructional content 1) at different levels of abstraction (from an external view to a very concrete description of the learning scenario and of the learner activities) and 2) from various point-of-views/aspects (knowledge-centered, cognitive, pedagogical, didactic, structural, content-based, social aspects, etc.) in a same design phase: it is what we call vertical perspective. Although the main obstacle lies in the capacity to integrate these various heterogeneous models (and their specific meta-models), current research is already tackling it using model composition and weaving.
- MDE/MDA enables us to split a learning specification into different focused models according to the underlying design process and moment: it is the horizontal view. Each model has its own objectives, public, terminol-

ogy, semantics and concrete notation (based on various technological spaces). All of them are conformed either to e-learning meta-models (see EMLs like IMS-LD or CPM) or of other well-known software engineering meta-models (SPEM, EDOC, ODP-RM, etc.). From this perspective, the key challenge lies in the ability to overcome model transformation obstacles and thus to enlarge the model's "abilities" to productive ones.

These two perspectives or axis are complementary and do not have to be considered separately.

This chapter has drawn an overview of the promises, challenges, obstacles and issues that the reader can expect to encompass or encounter when applying principles and theories from the MDE/MDA domains to the modeling and deployment of technology enhanced learning (TEL) systems. Since this chapter deals with these various points within a historical perspective and since it is based on pragmatical results obtained from our last three years' research, works presented in this chapter must be considered as an emerging part of the exciting issues the reader can expect to confront when applying the MDE/MDA framework. The future will tell us if current MDA/MDE promises will, in the long run, deeply affect the development of TEL systems.

REFERENCES

ADL—Advanced Distributed Learning (2004), *Sharable Content Object Reference Model (SCORM)* (2nd ed.). Retrieved from http://www.adlnet.org

Allert, H. (2005). *Modeling Coherent Social Systems for Learning*. Thesis Dissertation. Hannover University, Germany.

Álvarez, J.-M., Evans, A., & Sammut, P. (2001, October 1-5). Mapping between levels in the metamodel architecture. In *The Proceedings of the 4th International Conference UML* (pp. 34-46). Toronto, Canada.

Anéma (2007).The Ganesha plateform website. Retrieved March, 2007, from http://www.anemalab.org/ganesha/

ASPF (2005). Contribution de l'AS "Conception d'une plateforme pour la recherche en EIAH" à "l'ingénierie des EIAH." *Special issue "Conceptions et usages des plates-formes de formation" de la revue STICEF (Sciences et Technologies de l'Information et de la Communication pour l'Education et la Formation)*, (12).

Berggren, A., Burgos, D., Fontana, J.-M., Hinkelman, D., Hung, V., & Hursh, A., et al. (2005). Practical and pedagogical issues for teacher adoption of IMS learning design standards in Moodle LMS. *Journal of Interactive Media*.

Bézivin, J., & Gerbe, O. (2001). Towards a precise definition of the OMG/MDA framework. In *Proceedings of Automated Software Engineering*. USA.

Botturi, L., Cantoni, L., Lepori, B., & Tardini, S. (2007). Fast Prototyping as a Communication Catalyst for E-Learing Design. In M. Bullen & D. Janes (Eds.) *Making the transition to e-learning: strategies and issues* (pp. 266-283). Hershey, PA: Information Science Publishing.

Botturi, L., Derntl, M., Boot, E., & Gigl, K. (2006). A Classification Framework for Educational Modeling Languages in Instructional Design. In *Proceedings of the 6th IEEE International Conference on Advanced Learning Technologies (ICALT 2006)*. Kerkrade, The Netherlands.

Caron, P.-A., Derycke, A., & Le Pallec, X. (2005). The Bricoles project: Support socially informed design of learning environment. In *The Proceedings of the International Conference on Artificial Intelligence in Education (AIED 2005)* (pp. 759-761). Amsterdam: IOS Press.

Caron, P.-A., Le Pallec, X., & Sockeel, S. (2006). Configuring a web-based tool through pedagogical scenarios. In *IADIS Virtual Multi Conference on Computer Science and Information Systems* (MCCSIS 2006).

Chikofsky, E. J. & Cross, II J. H. (1990). Reverse engineering and design recovery: A taxonomy. *IEEE Software, 7*(1), 13-17.

Choquet, C. & Iksal, S. (2007). Modeling tracks for the model-driven re-engineering of a TEL system. *Journal of Interactive Learning Research (JILR), 18*(2), 161-184.

Claroline (2007). *The Claroline official website.* Retrieved March, 2007, from http://www.claroline.net/en

Corbiere, A. & Choquet, C. (2004). A model-driven analysis approach for the re-engineering of e-learning systems. In *ICICTE'04* (pp. 242-247). Samos, Greece.

Czarnecki, K. & Helsen, S. (2003). Classification of Model Transformation Approaches. In *Proceedings of the OOPSLA'03 Workshop on the Generative Techniques in the Context Of Model-Driven Architecture.* Anaheim, CA.

Dalziel, J. (2003). *Implementing learning design: The learning activity management system (LAMS).* Retrieved October 27, 2005, from http://www.lamsinternational.com/documents/ASCI-LITE2003.Dalziel.Final.pdf

David, B.T., & Chalon, R., & Delotte, O. (2005). Model-driven engineering of cooperative systems. In *The Proceedings of the 11th International Conference on Human-Computer Interaction (HCII 2005).* Las Vegas, NV.

Derntl, M. (in press). coUML: A visual language for modeling cooperative environments. In L. Botturi & T. Stubbs (Eds.), *Handbook of visual languages.*

Dewanto, B.-L. (2005). Model-driven architecture (MDA): Integration and model reuse for open source e-learning platforms. *Eleed Journal (E-learning and Education), 1.*

Dodero, J.M. & Diaz D. (2006). Model-driven instructional engineering to generate adaptable learning materials. *In IEEE International Conference on Advanced Learning Technologies (ICALT'2006)* (pp. 1188-1189). Kerkrade, The Netherlands.

Favre, J.M. (2004). Towards a basic theory to model driven engineering. In *3rd Workshop in Software Model Engineering (WiSME 2004).*

Gašević, D., Djurić, D., & Devedžić, V. (2006). *Model-driven architecture and ontology development.* New York: Springer.

Gowthaman, K., Mustafa, K., & Khan, R. A. (2005). Re-engineering legacy source code to model-driven architecture. In *Proceedings of the 4th Annual ACIS International Conference on Computer and Information Science (ICIS).*

Grob, H. L., Bensberg, F, & Lofi Dewanto, B. (2006). Model-driven architecture (MDA): Integration and model reuse for open source e-learning platforms. *Eleed. Digital peer publishing.* Retrieved from http://eleed.campussource.de/archive/1/81/

Kent, S. (2002). Model-Driven Engineering. *In Proceedings of IFM 2002* (LNCS 2335, pp. 286-298). Berlin Heidelberg: Springer-Verlag.

Kleppe, A., Warmer, J., & Bast, W. (2003). *MDA explained.* Boston: Addison-Wesley.

Kinshuk, Sampson, D.G., Patel, A., & Oppermann, R. (Eds). (2006). Special issue: Current research in learning design. *Journal of Educational Technology & Society, 9*(1).

Koper, R. & Tattersall, C. (2005). *Learning design—A handbook on modelling and delivering networked education and training,* Berlin Heidelberg: Springer-Verlag.

Kurtev, I., Bézivin, J., & Aksit, M. (2002). Technological spaces: An initial appraisal. *CoopIS, DOA'2002 Federated Conferences*. Irvine, CA: Industrial track.

Kurtev, I. (2005). *Adaptability of model transformations*. PhD Thesis. University of Twente, The Netherlands.

IMS (2003a). *IMS learning design information model—version 1.0*. IMS Global Learning Consortium, Inc. Retrieved from http://www.imsglobal.org/learningdesign/index.html

IMS (2003b). *IMS learning design version 1.0 final specification*. Technical report.

Laforcade, P., Barbier, F., Nodenot, T., & Sallaberry, C. (2003). Profiling co-operative problem-based learning situations. In *Proceedings of the 2nd IEEE International Conference on Cognitive Informatics (ICCI'2003)*. London: IEEE Computer Society Press.

Laforcade, P. (2005). Towards a UML-based educational modeling language. In *Proceedings of the IEEE International Conference on Advanced Learning Technologies ICALT'05* (pp. 855-859). Kaohsiung, Taiwan.

Laforcade, P. (2007). Graphical representation of abstract learning scenarios: The UML4LD experimentation. In *Proceedings of the IEEE International Conference on Advanced Learning Technologies ICALT'07*, Niigata, Japan.

Le Pallec, X., Renaux, E., & Moura, C. O. (2005). ModX. In *Tools Exhibition in European Conference on Model Driven Architecture—Foundations and Applications*. Nuremberg, Germany.

LTSC—Learning technology standards committee (2002). *IEEE standard for learning object metadata specification*.

Marinilli, M. (2005). *Model-driven user adapted systems and applications*. PhD Thesis.

Mens, T. & Van Gorp, P. (2005). A taxonomy of model transformation. In *Proceedings of the International Workshop on Graph and Model Transformation (GraMoT)*. Tallinn, Estonia.

Newell, A. (1982). *The knowledge level*. Artificial intelligence, *18*(1).

Nodenot, T., Laforcade, P., Marquesuzaà, C., & Sallaberry, C. (2003). Knowledge modeling of co-operative learning situations: Towards a UML profile. In *Proceedings of the 11th International Conference on Artificial Intelligence in Education (AIED'2003)*. Sydney, Australia. International AI-ED Society.

OMG (2001). *UML 1.4 specification formal/01-09-67*.

OMG (2005a). *MOF 2.0 / XMI Mapping Specification—v2.1, formal/03-05-01*.

OMG (2005b). *Meta Object Facility (MOF) 2.0 Query/View/Transformation Specification Final Adopted Specification ptc/05-11-01*.

OMG (2006a). *MDA specification guide*. Version 1.0.1. Report—omg/03-06-01.

OMG (2006b). *Object Constraint Language Specification version 2.0*. formal/2006-05-01 (full specification).

OMG (2006c). Meta Object Facility (MOF) Specification version 2.0. OMG document formal/06-01-01.

OpenUSS (2007). Open Source University Support System. Retrieved March, 2007, from http://openuss.sourceforge.net/openuss/

Pawlowski, J. & Bick, M. (2006). Managing and re-using didactical expertise: The didactical object model. *Educational technology and society, 9*(1), 84-96.

PlanetMDE (2006). *Planet MDE model driven engineering: Official website*. Retrieved March, 2007, from http://planetmde.org/

Santos, O. C., Boticario, J. G. & Barrera, C. (2005). aLFanet: An adaptive and standard-based learning environment built upon dotLRN and other open source developments. In *The 2005 dotLRN conference*. Madrid, Spain.

Schmidt, D. C. (2006). Model-driven engineering. *IEEE Computer, 39*(2).

TRAILS (2004). *Personalised and collaborative trails of digital and non-digital learning objects.* Retrieved May, 2006, from http://www.noe-kaleidoscope.org

Trigone (2007). *ModX, the Trigone MOF modelling tool*. Retrieved March, 2007, from http://noce.univ-lille1.fr/projets/ModX/

Wile, D. S. (1997). Abstract Syntax from Concrete Syntax. In *Proceedings of the 19th International Conference on Software Engineering* (pp. 472-480). Boston.

Wile, D. S. (2001). Supporting the DSL spectrum. *Journal of computing and information technology, 9*(4), 263-287.

Chapter VIII
Accessibility, Digital Libraries, and Semantic Web Standards in an E-Learning Architecture

Sean W. M. Siqueira
Federal University of the State of Rio de Janeiro, Brazil

Maria Helena L. B. Braz
Technical University of Lisbon, Portugal

Rubens N. Melo
Pontifical Catholic University of Rio de Janeiro, Brazil

ABSTRACT

As people have come to realize that the use of technology can improve the learning process, e-learning has began to increase in importance. However, e-learning tools are not usually developed to interoperate with each other, making the creation of a fully functional environment a difficult task. Organizations such as IMS Global Learning Consortium, Advanced Distributed Learning and IEEE Learning Technology Standards Committee are aware of this problem and are working to develop technical standards, recommended best practices and guides for learning technology. There are also proposals for e-learning architectures which try to structure and describe the fundamental components to be included in this kind of environment. The main aim of this chapter is to provide an overview of existing standards and e-learning architectures, discussing their evolution and presenting the most significant results and initiatives. In addition, accessibility, digital libraries and semantic Web technologies are discussed within this context.

INTRODUCTION

Education can be seen as a combination of three main elements: administration, pedagogy and technology, which through a variety of combinations result in different educational and training systems with different approaches. Whenever there is a new strategy, method or technique in one of these areas, then that innovation will soon be found in educational and training systems.

Nowadays, there is a growing consciousness of the importance of education in coping with the rapid changes in human society. Since time and space restrictions could prevent the access to education, and since the use of technology can circumvent these barriers and enhance the learning process, there is a great interest in the development of e-learning both in the business world and in academic forums. In addition, there is a movement towards cooperation and partnership, which has led to the development of communication tools important in the support of collaborative learning. The groupware approach complements this scenario as it also includes coordination and cooperation mechanisms for collaborative learning.

Several educational environments have been implemented and used, and a variety of e-learning courses have been offered. Thus, there are numerous different educational environments which have different approaches for e-learning and which provide diverse combinations of services. The existence of so many environments brings about many interoperability problems. This "world of differences" makes the cooperation between educational and training partners difficult as far as the reuse of e-learning content and services are concerned.

Some organizations are aware of these problems and have been working to develop technical standards, specifications, recommended best practices and guides for learning technology. Nevertheless, the main focus of their work has been on enabling content reuse, especially through the description of learning content (e.g., IMS Learning Resource Meta-Data Information Model, ("IMS Learning Resource", 2001), ADL SCORM ("SCORM," 2006) and IEEE Learning Object Metadata (LOM) ("Draft Standard," 2002)).

These standards and specifications are becoming increasingly important, but, although they are advancing the goals of learning content interoperability, they do not provide a general architecture that would guide the development of flexible and configurable e-learning systems.

In terms of e-learning architecture, IEEE LTSC (Learning Technology Standards Committee) presented in 2001 a proposal—the IEEE Learning Technology Systems Architecture (LTSA) ("Draft Standard," 2001), which specifies a high level architecture for information technology-supported learning, education, and training systems.

This draft standard identifies the objectives of human activities and computer processes and the categories of knowledge involved. Therefore the architecture is human-computer oriented and does not provide a general overview of software components and available technologies for building an e-learning environment.

In the literature, it is possible to find some proposals for general e-learning architectures; those we consider more interesting are presented and discussed in the next section, where we also present an overview of existing standards for e-learning, followed by a discussion of a generic architecture and its software components. We also consider the data and metadata components, and describe LORIS architecture. Learning objects repositories' integration system (LORIS) aims at providing an integrated view of Learning Objects for an entire e-learning community while maintaining the local autonomy of each member. The chapter concludes with some future trends and final conclusions about e-learning architectures.

The main aim of this chapter is to provide an overview of e-learning architectures, discussing their evolution and the efforts towards standardization. Accessibility, digital library and semantic

Web are important topics discussed in this context, as well as proposed e-learning standards, specifications and related works.

E-LEARNING STANDARDS AND ARCHITECTURES: AN OVERVIEW

With the increasing interest in e-learning systems, many organizations understood the usefulness of having standards and, then, addressed this problem. IEEE LTSC (Learning Technology Standards Committee) (http://ieeeltsc.org/), IMS Global Learning Consortium (http://www.imsglobal.org/), Advanced Distributed Learning (ADL) Initiative (http://www.adlnet.gov/index.cfm), Aviation Industry CBT Committee (AICC) (http://www.aicc.org/) and Association of Remote Instructional Authoring and Distribution Networks for Europe (ARIADNE) (http://www.ariadne-eu.org) were the most significant entities within this standardization process and now, instead of working separately, they have joined efforts and are committed to collaborating on the establishment of learning technology interoperability standards. More information about organizations involved in e-learning standards and specifications can be found in ("Who's involved," 2005). The main results of these efforts are IEEE learning object metadata (LOM) and Sharable Content Object Reference Model (SCORM), which are broadly accepted and have been adopted by many e-learning developers.

IEEE LOM specifies a conceptual data schema that defines the structure of a metadata instance for a learning object. This metadata instance describes relevant characteristics of the learning object to which it applies. Such characteristics are organized in a hierarchy of elements that are grouped in nine classification categories: general, life cycle, meta-metadata, educational, technical, rights, relation, annotation, and classification. The purpose of this standard is to facilitate the search for, and the evaluation, acquisition, and

use of learning objects. IEEE LOM was approved as a standard by IEEE in 2002 and this work has been extended by other standards through the specification of bindings of LOM data model in XML and RDF.

SCORM, now in its third (2004) edition, is a set of specifications concerning the development, packaging and delivery of learning objects. This edition is a collection of specifications and standards that defines the interrelationship of content objects, data models and protocols in such a way that objects are sharable across systems that conform to the model. In fact, the documentation for this edition includes four books: *The SCORM Overview*; *The SCORM Content Aggregation Model (CAM)*; *The Scorm Run-time Environment (RTE)*, and *The SCORM Sequencing and Navigation (SN)* ("SCORM," 2006).

It is interesting to notice that SCORM specifications are built on other standards and specifications proposed by other organizations. For instance, SCORM 2004 metadata is defined using IEEE 1484.12.1-2002 LOM Standard and IEEE 1484.12.3 Standard for Extensible Markup Language (XML) Binding for LOM Data Model. Other standards and specifications that are also used in SCORM specifications are: IMS Content Packaging Specification V.1.1.4; IEEE 1484.11.2 Standard for Learning Technology - ECMAScript Application Programming Interface (API) for Content to Runtime Services Communication; IEEE 1484.11.1 Standard for Learning Technology—Data Model for Content Object Communication; IMS Simple Sequencing Behavior and Information Model V.1.0.

Other important specifications related to content are:

- IMS learning design, which is a specification used to describe learning scenarios. It allows these scenarios to be presented to learners online, and enables them to be shared between systems. "It aims to represent the 'learning design' of 'units of Learning' in a semantic, formal and machine-interpretable way" (Koper & Oliver, 2004).

- IMS question and test interoperability, which is designed to make it easier to transfer information such as questions, tests and results between different software applications ("IMS Question," 2005).

Besides considering learning objects/content, it is also important to model user profiles in order to provide effective learning. From this point of view, there are three main results:

IMS learner information package (LIP) ("IMS Learner," 2005), IMS accessibility for LIP (ACCLIP) ("IMS AccessForAll," 2004), IEEE public and private information (PAPI) for Learners (PAPI Learner) ("PAPI Learner," 2002).

IMS LIP is based on a data model that describes those characteristics of a learner that are needed for the general purposes of:

- Recording and managing learning-related history, goals, and accomplishments.
- Engaging a learner in a learning experience.
- Discovering learning opportunities for learners.

It is designed to allow information about learners (including their progress and awards received) to be shared between different applications and is divided into 11 categories. There is an interesting category for describing hobbies and recreational activities, and also an accessibility category for describing physical issues (e.g. large print) and/or technical preferences (such as the computer platform).

IMS ACCLIP provides a means to describe how learners can interact with an online learning environment based on their preferences and needs. These preferences will influence the user interface of the learning delivery tools and how content is selected.

In this model, accessibility extends beyond disability to benefit users in learning situations which require alternative modes of use, such as in an extremely noisy environment where captions are needed for a video or a "hands-busy, eyes-busy" application as in just-in-time training while repairing an aircraft engine. The user preferences that have been defined will aid the user in displaying learning material in the style best suited to their particular needs.

The PAPI learner standard is a data interchange specification that describes learner information for communication among cooperating systems. It is a multi-part standard that specifies the semantics and syntax of learner information. Learner information is information associated to learners and used by learning technology systems which may be created, stored, retrieved, used, etc., by learning technology systems, individuals (e.g., teachers, learners, etc.), and other entities.

The PAPI learner standard defines and/or references elements for recording descriptive information about: knowledge acquisition, skills, abilities, personal contact information, learner relationships, security parameters, learner preferences and styles, learner performance, learner-created portfolios, and similar types of information. This standard permits different views of the learner information (from the perspectives of: learner, teacher, parent, school, employer, etc.) and substantially addresses issues of privacy and security.

In order to provide a better understanding of the whole e-learning context, it is important to consider architectures. From this point of view, there are many proposals in the existing literature. Besides IEEE LTSA, mentioned above, there are two other initiatives that, considering the participant entities and the goals established, must be mentioned and which are connected to the standardization efforts.

One of these which considers a service-oriented architecture, is the e-learning framework (ELF) project (http://www.elframework.org/).

ELF is endorsed by important institutions in the e-learning arena such as the Australian Department of Education (DEST), the United Kingdom's Joint Information Systems Committee (JICS) and the US Advanced Learning Initiative (ADL). It aims at providing both a common vocabulary and a roadmap for the development of the component services in an e-learning infrastructure. In this work, the services needed to support an e-learning environment are identified and classified as specific e-learning services or common services that can be used by other domain applications. Examples of the former services are course management and assessment and of the latter are authentication and chat.

Besides the identification of necessary services, ELF also indicates if there are standards and specifications that already support, at least partially, each of these services, and promotes the development of open source implementation toolkits to assist developers in implementing instances of the services.

This e-learning framework has been developed with the intention of being used as a guide to identify potential areas for collaboration, prioritize investment in standardization efforts and provide an instrument for the development of services and tools based upon open standards that will address requirements of e-learning environments.

Although ELF provides a good big picture of e-learning services, the interchange of educational content between different repositories is still a problem. The content object repository discovery and registration/resolution architecture (CORDRA) project intends to contribute to the solution of this problem. CORDRA has been developed since 2003 by the Learning Systems Architecture Lab at Carnegie Mellon University (http://lsal.org/). The initial aim of this project was the creation of a single instance of a federation of content repositories for the US Department of Defense. The main activity is the definition of the CORDRA reference model (Rehak, Dodds, & Lannom, 2005).

As it is stated in literature, "CORDRA is an open, standards-based model for how to design and implement software systems for the purpose of discovery, sharing and reuse of learning content through the establishment of interoperable federations of learning content repositories" (Rehak, Dodds, & Lannom, 2005). CORDRA is designed to be an enabling model to bridge the worlds of learning content management and delivery, and content repositories and digital libraries by defining how existing standards and specifications can be used and eventually customized in order to meet the stated goals ("CORDRA," 2004).

The advantage of having such a reference model is that it will establish guidelines and standards on how to design and implement a federation of content repositories allowing the use of existing technologies and with no restrictions on local polices and business rules. This project also aims at creating an operational infrastructure that will include a master federation of federations, built according to CORDRA, which will be a single point of discovery and access to content spread between the participating federations. Although this initiative seems very promising, it is still in an initial state and there are many open issues that must be solved before it can be used worldwide. Anyway, having these standards and guidelines will be very important and can provide a widespread contribution to the area of search for, retrieval and reuse of content.

Although ELF and CORDRA have different goals (ELF does not aim to deliver specifications itself but to determine where they are needed), they share some of their collaborators and can benefit from each other's work.

Finally, it is important to mention W3C (World Wide Web Consortium) (http://www.w3.org). This Consortium develops relevant technical standards referenced and used within learning technologies such as: HTTP, URL, HTML, XML and simple object access protocol (SOAP), to name but a few. Within W3C there is also an important initiative called Semantic Web Activity, which may bring many benefits to the e-learning area and vice-versa. Within this group, resource description framework (RDF), RDF Schema, Query Language for RDF (SPARQL) and Web Ontology Language (OWL) are the core standards to support the development of Semantic Web.

Ontology is usually defined as the explicit specification of a concept (Gruber, 2001). The use of ontologies to describe the implicit knowledge of data sources is an interesting solution for problems of semantic heterogeneity. The construction of common ontologies has been proposed as a promising approach to the interoperability of systems which means that they may also have an important role in e-learning.

Within W3C there is also the Semantic Web Services Interest Group (http://www.w3.org/2002/ws/swsig/), devoted to merging Web Services and Semantic Web technology. The aim of this group is to provide an open forum for W3C Members and non-Members to discuss Web Service topics essentially oriented towards the integration of Semantic Web technology into the ongoing Web Services work at W3C.

Web-Services are defined by the W3C as a software application or component that is identified by a universal resource identifier (URI), whose interfaces and connections are capable of being defined, described and discovered in XML and which supports interactions directly with other software applications using XML coded messages via Internet-based protocols. They provide interoperability among software components because they are based on standard mechanisms and protocols; they constitute, therefore, a possible technology to support the development of e-learning applications.

A GENERIC ARCHITECTURE FOR E-LEARNING

The development of e-learning initiatives should consider an e-learning infrastructure, which

should be based on an e-learning architecture, which, in turn, should be based on a generic approach. According to this principle, in 2003 we presented a proposal for an architecture for e-learning (Siqueira, Braz, &Melo, 2003a) in which we enumerated educational and training scenarios, which provided the requirements for the components of a generic architecture for educational and training systems according to courseware needs. This approach was important because it enabled an understanding of what components are necessary in an e-learning architecture. It led to a generic architecture that maps the most important components of educational and training systems, providing a clear overview of the whole field.

Even though other architectures for learning and training systems can be found, as previously mentioned, the architecture presented in our work (Siqueira, Braz, & Melo, 2003a, 2003b), and shown in Figure 1, is more generic and therefore lists more components. It is not oriented to a specific learning theory or approach but aims at providing the possible software components of an architecture for those systems.

The three reference models (administration, pedagogy and technology) support all the tasks of the architecture. They are intended to provide general policies, guidance and describe e-learning strategies that are the base for the organization. For instance, the technology reference model describes the programming environment, the network infrastructure, the development strategies (e.g., through Web services and ontologies), and the database management systems that are going to be used and so forth.

The users can perform needs assessment through the access to the database, finding information on those topics where students need more material or on what professional or academic goals need further, deeper support etc. Thus, after choosing a new educational/training goal, it is possible to identify the audience and insert data on learner database and on external factor database as well.

Figure 1. A generic architecture for educational and training systems

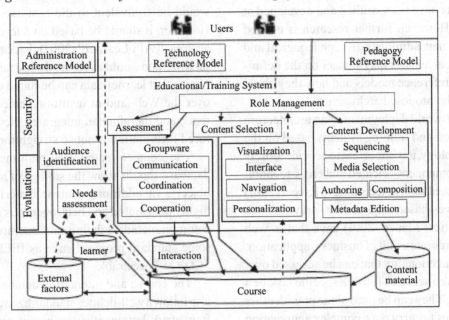

The learner database can (and should) be based on some standard such as IMS LIP.

For the execution of the other activities there is a role manager that is responsible for identifying the user and managing his/her interactions with the system from an educational/training point of view.

On content development it is possible to perform content sequencing, media selection, authoring and/or composition and respective metadata editing inserting data and metadata on the content material repositories as well as possibly on the course repository (when it is related to a specific course). Some work can be found about methodologies for developing learning objects such as those described in (Baruque, Porto, & Melo, 2003; Barritt & Lewis, 2000). Standards such as IEEE LOM, SCORM CAM, SCORM SN, IMS Content Packaging, IMS learning design and IMS Simple Sequencing Behavior and Information Model should be considered.

Before attending a course, the learner has to be enrolled in it. It is possible to visualize learn-ing content by accessing the course database. However, steps towards visualization must be followed before presenting the content.

On the other hand, groupware activities are insertions in the course and interaction databases, while assessment results are stored on the course database.

Finally, security tasks and overall evaluation are present in all the activities of the architecture.

This generic architecture should provide the necessary functionality to deal with educational and training requirements according to the courseware point of view. However, each environment is different in the sense that it can adopt different administrative, pedagogical and/or technological strategies, methods and techniques. Therefore, each instance of the generic architecture can use a different set of components that can, by themselves, incorporate different learning approaches.

From this architecture we were able to define components of a framework for e-learning systems

(Siqueira, Braz, & Melo, 2003c, 2004) whose components have been studied and developed at PUC-Rio. However, further research is needed on how the new administrative, pedagogical and technological aspects may impact on the definition of the reference models and how they could influence the proposed architecture.

In a real-world deployment of an architecture for education and training systems based on the Web technology, it is important to provide loosely coupled, component-oriented and cross-technology implementations. According to Kreger (2001) Web services-based applications provide such characteristics. Manes (2001) says that a Web service represents a unit of business, application, or system functionality that can be accessed over the Web. Web services fulfill a specific task or a set of tasks. They can be used alone or with other Web services to carry out a complex aggregation or a business transaction. With the maturing of Internet technology it is possible to explore the new technologies that can overcome some limitations of the previously mentioned approaches.

However, bringing semantics to Web services is an essential step. Therefore, in the development of Web-based education and training systems it would be interesting to consider architectures such as those proposed at (Bussler, Fensel & Maedche, 2002; Ankolenkar et al., 2001).

Considering (Bussler, Fensel, &Maedche, 2002) as an example, a Web service conceptual architecture is composed of data and applications (containing customer database, legacy database, application database, and ontology server with a repository and workflow engine), Web services components (centralized coordinator and manager, B2B protocol engine, discovery, negotiation, deployment, transport, security, audit/tracking, trading partner manager, semantic transformation, adaptors and Web service, goal, ontology and workflow manager), and front-end tools (modeling and deployment environment, simulation, and administration, management and configuration).

The learner database of the generic architecture would be equivalent to the customer database. However, it should be based on a learner model such as "PAPI Learner" (2002) that can be based on XML and would structure the learner database. Notice that learner data can be found distributed over the Web (and in institution/enterprise systems) and therefore an integrated view of structured information is not so straightforward.

The content material is multimedia so its database should allow the storage of multimedia objects. In addition, content material can be highly distributed and heterogeneous although a common metadata definition/structure based on some standard proposal such as IEEE LOM or SCORM is desirable.

The course and interaction databases should also follow a well-defined standardized conceptual framework, but since they are part of course implementation processes they are usually embedded in education and training systems according to proprietary solutions. The three reference models as well as the other database models could be implemented/managed through the use of the ontology technology.

Since we are considering Web-based education and training, besides authoring content, it is also necessary to publish it according to predefined access rights. If the content development is based on composition, it will be necessary to discover already published content, compose new content and then publish it. Notice that course definitions are also part of the services' functionality, as are defining a new course according to the available content, structuring and managing enrolling procedures, for example.

The course implementation focuses on content access and visualization, groupware activities and assessment. Content access is already considered in the Web-service architecture. In order to enable content visualization, several services such as those related to personalization and contextual navigation throughout the content should be provided.

Content hypermedia navigation could be based on guidelines or patterns such as those cited in (Lyardet, Rossi, & Schwabe, 1998). Therefore, it is important to define node units and navigational contexts, to provide background information to the participant without distracting his/her attention, to provide active reference in order to keep the reader informed as to which concept he/she is on, what concepts have been explored and those that are still missing.

Other services for enabling the real presentation of the content, such as video and sound plugging as well as video synchronization and simulation procedures must also be considered. Content visualization is tightly related to content development procedures and content characteristics, especially content media.

Communication tasks considered in the context of groupware functionality include asynchronous and synchronous events, such as e-mail, mail list, newsgroup, chat, instant message (peer contact), phone talk (voice over ip), teleconferencing, etc.

Coordination events include lesson plan, calendar, agenda, scheduling, workflow, contribution-track, follow-up reports etc. Cooperation events include co-authorship, group definition and related management accessibility, Web reference, bibliography, documentation, download, etc.

Assessment includes task assessment, multiple choice, true/false, fill in questions etc. According to Entwistle (2000), teachers who are content-oriented are likely to see assessment as designed to demonstrate detailed factual knowledge of the syllabus. They also tend to consider the outcomes of learning as being almost entirely the responsibility of the students themselves, depending on their ability and motivation. On the other hand, teachers who are student-oriented tend to use more varied methods of assessment and to be aware of their own responsibility for encouraging students to develop deep levels of understanding.

According to Scouller (1998), "Assessment which encourages students to think for themselves—such as essay question, applications to new contexts, and problem-based questions—shifts students in a class towards a deep approach. In contrast, procedures perceived by students as requiring no more than the accurate reproduction of information lead to a predominance of surface approaches." These different views about assessment must be considered and should be provided for.

Security is already considered in the Web-services architecture, although some issues such as authorship can be more complex. Needs assessment and audience identification can be seen as common marketing activities. Evaluation and role management are also general functions/services.

It is interesting to notice that many of the services identified in ELF framework are also included in the general architecture presented in Figure 1. However, as ELF lacks any detailed information about the services, a deeper analysis comparing both initiatives and discussing all the necessary mappings is not feasible at this moment.

As nowadays there is a shift towards using Web service architectures, and as our main background was in dealing with content, especially content integration, we refocused our work on this area. As a result, in 2005 we presented LORIS architecture (Moura et al., 2005a, 2005b, 2005c) covering the Content Selection service identified in the generic architecture (see Figure 1).

In the next section LORIS and its extensions will be presented.

LORIS ARCHITECTURE AND EXTENSIONS

LORIS architecture (Figure 2) aims at providing an integrated view of LOs throughout an e-learning community while each member keeps its local autonomy. Many components that were described in the generic architecture and/or ELF were not considered in the actual version of LORIS architecture because the main objective was sharing learning content. Therefore, the focus has been on content selection, development and visualization. Components such as security, evaluation, planning (audience identification, needs assessment), role management and the reference models were left to the next versions.

Since nowadays there is a big effort towards having an integrated view of learning content, which is distributed and highly heterogeneous, the architecture is based on a traditional approach on data integration, which is the use of mediators and wrappers. However, LORIS architecture extends this traditional approach through the definition of new layers called mappers and also provides a more flexible environment through the use of Web services (Booth et al., 2004). In addition, LORIS uses ontologies (Gruber, 2001) for providing better semantic information integration. The services-oriented architecture allows the sharing

and exchanging of content among heterogeneous repositories in a decentralized environment.

LORIS architecture provides access to autonomous, heterogeneous and distributed data sources, which can be anything ranging from database systems to collections of files. An important aspect of the architecture is related to the integrated view of the different content metadata structures that are used by the community members to describe their educational resources.

A user submits a query from the application to LORIS. The LORIS central mediator receives this query and subdivides it according to the different metadata structures/standards that are used by the data sources. As there can be different implementations of the same metadata structures/standards, these sub-queries are then mapped to a general schema of the metadata structure/standard and sent to the respective mediator. The intermediary

Figure 2. An Overview of LORIS architecture

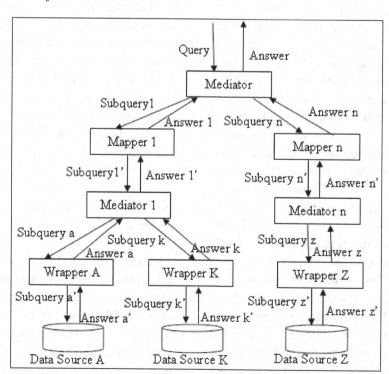

mediators break down the sub-queries according to the existing data sources of the e-learning community which conform to that specific metadata structure/standard. These (sub-)sub-queries are translated to the data source model and submitted to the source, which processes the sub-query and returns an answer. The answer is translated to the metadata structure/standard general schema. All the answers that are related to the same metadata structure/standard are integrated by the respective intermediary mediator that sends the integrated sub-answer to the mapper, which translates the answers to the global model. Finally, all the sub-answers (from all the metadata structures/standards) are integrated by the central mediator, which returns an integrated answer to the system that presents the result to the user.

Thus, the main components of the architecture are:

- **Data sources:** The autonomous and heterogeneous data sources, which were not usually designed with a focus on content sharing. Data sources can be databases, repositories of objects, knowledge bases, files, etc.
- **Wrappers:** Convert data from distributed and heterogeneous sources according to a common data scheme and convert the application queries into queries that are specific to the corresponding data sources.
- **Mediators:** Software modules that explore knowledge represented in a set or subset of data with the objective of generating information to applications that are in a higher layer. They can be seen as an intermediary layer between the application layer and the data source layer and their function is to apply specialized knowledge to a specific domain in order to aggregate value (Wiederhold, 1992).
- **Mappers:** Wrappers in the intermediary phase, which adjust a sub-query expressed according to the global model to the characteristics of a metadata structure.

LORIS Implementation

LORIS architecture has been implemented as Web-services, and therefore it uses open standard protocols such as Java, SOAP, WSDL and XML. Therefore, XML is used as a common language in description of the data sources' schema and in the queries and sub-queries that the mediators work with. We use XPath (Clark & DeRose, 1999) as the XML query language and SOAP (Gudgin et al., 2003a, 2003b) as communication protocol to send queries and get data from the wrappers.

Java was used for developing the system modules, except one of the considered wrappers that was developed on C#.

In order to provide communication among the data sources and the main mediator, a common query language is necessary. In LORIS a schema was created (in XML Schema) to represent the query language in an XML document.

Extending LORIS

Recently, with the growing acceptance of the concept of the Information Society, another problem has drawn attention: accessibility. This is not restricted to ensuring that disabled people can access information, although this is important and may be a legal requirement but it is about ensuring that a wide variety of users and devices can all gain access to information, thereby maximizing the potential audience and allowing users to experience the pages (or in our case, the learning content) in the way they choose. There is a real and growing need for accessibility; it brings benefits for both the information provider and the information consumer (http://www.acessibility.com/).

According to the Human Ability and Accessibility Center (http://www-306.ibm.com/able/), society has benefited in many ways from the information technology revolution. However, not everyone can reap the benefits of this technological change. People with disabilities cannot fully participate because much of the information is not designed for them; as designers and developers strive to meet deadlines and surpass competitive requirements the issue of their accessibility is overlooked.

Accessibility in e-learning takes several forms, from the creation of the LO, when it is important to consider accessibility questions (for instance, if the material is going to be Web pages, then the W3C provides some guidelines and techniques through the Web Accessibility Initiative—WAI (http://www.w3.org/WAI/), until its execution, when the LO selection can be personalized to better suit the user's needs and preferences according to the user profile.

Therefore, LORIS architecture was extended (AccessForAll-LORIS) with the capability to query LO repositories considering the user profile, needs and preferences by matching the received user profile with the received or generated LO accessibility metadata (Ghelman, Siqueira, & Melo, 2006). As far as users' needs and preferences are concerned, the aim is to improve the quality of learning and to include disabled people in the target audience.

AccessForAll-LORIS is also based on Web-services and ontologies. In order to search for LOs, the user can fill in his/her profile or alternatively it is possible to get the user profile through Web-services. From this moment on, all queries submitted by this user take into account his/her profile. If the user profile was obtained through the use of Web services, it can be in one of the known standards. It is also important to emphasize that the queries can still be executed without the user profile, and, in this case, AccessForAll-LORIS behave just as LORIS. As different metadata structures can be used for user profiles, it is necessary to deal with their heterogeneity. This was solved by using ontologies in a similar manner as to that explained below.

Another extension to LORIS was based on the fact that digital libraries represent a vast resource of good and reliable learning content.

In fact, it is widely accepted that digital libraries offer good support to learning and their content usually complements the learning resources that may be included in a learning management system (LMS). However, these two systems are usually independent and it is not possible to access information managed by one system when using the other one. As this is very limiting, it would be very interesting to see if they could be integrated. This integration with digital libraries was the motivation to extend LORIS, the original idea being to adapt LORIS in order to have one or more data sources as digital library's repositories.

For this reason, LORIS was extended to an architecture (LORDiLIS) (Gomes et al., 2005) for integrating distributed LO and digital library repositories (LORDiLIS stands for learning objects repositories and digital libraries integration system).

One of the main obstacles to the integration was the different metadata structures used by these repositories. Usually metadata standards are considered, for instance digital libraries can use MARC (Library of Congress, 2000) or Dublin Core (Dublin Core Metadata Initiative, 2004). When considering the metadata represented in the different standards (and other proprietary structures) for educational material and for digital bibliographic resources, it is important to have a "semantic understanding" among their concepts. LORDiLIS' global/common scheme takes into account concepts from bibliographic and e-learning metadata standards. In fact, to define the global/common scheme of LORDiLIS and to overcome the differences between possible metadata structures that can be used, it was decided to define an ontology including the most significant concepts from the point of view of their intended use and considering their definitions in the metadata standards. This ontology can be understood as a way to express the semantic meaning of the concepts included in the metadata structures. For this purpose, it is necessary to establish mappings between similar concepts of

Figure 3. Global/Common Schema Ontology classes in Protégé

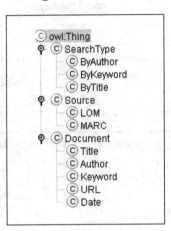

Figure 4. MARC Local Ontology in Protégé

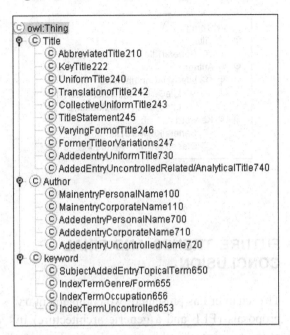

the common ontology and of the ontologies that represent the metadata structures considered in the data source applications.

The ontologies were represented in OWL—Web Ontology Language (http://www.w3.org/2004/OWL/) (McGuinness & Harmelen, 2004), which aims at providing a language that can be used to describe classes and relationships between them inherent in Web documents and applications. This language can be used to formalize a domain through the definition of classes and their properties, to define individuals and to assert properties about them and to provide logical reasoning about these classes and individuals to the degree allowed for the formal semantic of OWL.

In order to represent the semantic mappings, we explored the available OWL resources. The OWL properties that allow the inter-ontologies mapping are: equivalentClassm, equivalentProperty, sameAs, differentFrom, and AllDifferent (Smith, Welty, & McGuinness, 2004).

A case study was developed integrating LOs that were described on IEEE LOM (a LO repository available at the PUC-RIO) and digital docu-ments described on MARC (an extract of PUC-RIO's Library) (Gomes et al., 2006a, 2006b).

In this case study it was possible to search the repositories by author name, by keywords or by title. Three ontologies were defined to represent the necessary MARC fields, the relevant attributes of LOM and the global/common schema as well as respective mappings. These ontologies are presented in Figures 3, 4 and 5.

An example of mapping between existing concepts is shown in Figure 6.

This architecture provides the users with a transparent and integrated view of the learning objects and digital resources stored in the data sources. In fact, extracted LOs from the DL repository are seen as any other LO in the learning environment and can be used according to the learning approach that is used in the course/class. This integration is independent of data model, query language, operational system and localization.

Figure 5. LOM Local Ontology in Protégé

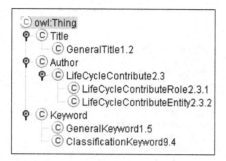

Figure 6. Concept Mapping

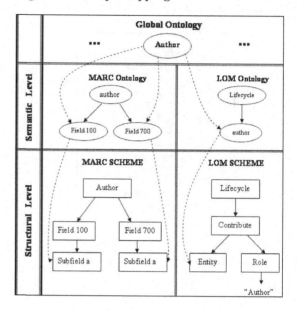

FUTURE TRENDS AND FINAL CONCLUSION

This chapter has presented two complementary proposals (ELF and a generic architecture) in order to give the 'big-picture' of e-learning services which should be the object of standardization so that initiatives in this area can easily be made interoperable. Because of the need to deal with distributed and heterogeneous content repositories, two proposals (CORDRA and LORIS) that deal with data integration in e-learning have also been presented. These four proposals can be considered the basis for e-learning initiatives. In addition, personalization matters are briefly discussed through the accessibility issues (AccessForAll-LORIS). As digital libraries and Web documents tend to greatly improve learning content availability, the integration of e-learning content and digital libraries (LORDiLIS) is explored. Finally, although e-learning and the semantic Web are evolving separately, they can be of mutual benefit, as shown in this chapter: e-learning can be implemented through semantic Web technology and semantic Web can get better results by using learning semantics. These three aspects (personalization/accessibility, e-learning integration with digital libraries and Web content, and use of semantic Web technology in e-learning) foster the development of next genera-

tion e-learning systems. Therefore, this chapter presents e-learning fundamentals in terms of architectures as well as important knowledge for future developments in this area.

From the point of view of implementation, there is a trend towards the use of Web services and software agents in the development of e-learning systems. These technologies allow better scalability and increased availability and they open the way for developing distributed e-learning systems that can easily adapt to user needs thus enabling personalization, here included in accessibility issues. Due to content processing by software agents, e-learning content tends to be more formally described, expressing the semantics in an unambiguous manner. The content amount that can be used in learning tends to be dramatically expanded with the re-organization/re-purposing of the documents of digital libraries (Web documents in general here included). Automatic composition of learning content according to user characteristics and learning objectives will, in the future, provide immediate access to the most suitable knowledge. The general architecture for e-learning systems, LORIS and its extensions, and the standards and specifications presented in this chapter contribute towards this scenario, but are only the beginning of Act One, Scene One.

REFERENCES

Ankolenkar, A., Burstein, M., Son, T.C., Hobbs, J., Lassila, O., Martin, D., McDermott, D., McIlraith, S., Narayanan, S., Paolucci, M., Payne, T., Sycara, K., & Zeng, H. (2001). *DAML-S: Semantic markup for Web services*. Retrieved October 14, 2006, from http://www.daml.org/services/daml-s/2001/05/daml-s.pdf

Barritt, C. & Lewis, D. (2000, April 22). Reusable learning object strategy—definition, creation process and guidelines for building. *Cisco Systems, Inc.* Retrieved October 14, 2006, from http://www.reusablelearning.org/Docs/Cisco_rlo_roi_v3-1.pdf

Baruque, L., Porto, F. A. M., & Melo, R. N. (2003). Towards an instructional design methodology based on learning objects. In *Proceedings of the IASTED International Conference on Computers and Technology in Education (CATE 2003)*, (pp. 259-264), Anaheim, Calgary, and Zurich: ACTA Press.

Booth, D., Haas, H., McCabe, F., Newcomer, E., Champion, M., Ferris , C., & Orchard, D. (Eds.). (2004). Web services architecture. *W3C Working Group Note 11 February 2004*. Retrieved October 14, 2006, from http://www.w3.org/TR/ws-arch/

Bussler, C., Fensel, D., & Maedche, A. (2002, December). A conceptual architecture for semantic Web enabled Web services. *SIGMOD Record, 31*(4), 24-49.

Clark, J., & DeRose, S. (Eds.). (1999). XML path language (XPath)—version 1.0. *W3C Recommen-dation 16 November 1999*. Retrieved October 14, 2006, from http://www.w3.org/TR/xpath

CORDRA: technical introduction and overview. (2004, May 2). *Learning Systems Architecture Lab at Carnegie Mellon University*. Retrieved October 14, 2006, from http://lsal.org/lsal/expertise/projects/cordra/intro/intro-v1p00.html

Draft standard for learning object metadata. (2002, July 15). *Learning technology standards committee of the IEEE*. Retrieved October 14, 2006, from http://ltsc.ieee.org/wg12/files/LOM_1484_12_1_v1_Final_Draft.pdf

Draft standard for learning technology—learning technology systems architecture (LTSA). (2001, November 30). *Learning Technology standards committee of the IEEE*. Retrieved October 14, 2006, from http://ltsc.ieee.org/wg1/files/IEEE_1484_01_D09_LTSA.pdf

Dublin Core Metadata Initiative. (2004, December 20). *Dublin core metadata element set, version 1.1: reference description*. Retrieved October 14, 2006, from http://dublincore.org/documents/dces/

Entwistle, N. (2000). Promoting deep learning through teaching and assessment: conceptual frameworks and educational contexts. In *Proceeding of the TLRP Conference*, Leicester. Retrieved October 14, 2006, from: http://www8.caret.cam.ac.uk/pub/ acadpub/Entwistle2000.pdf

Ghelman, R., Siqueira, S. W. M., & Melo, R. N. (2006). Providing accessibility to distributed and heterogeneous learning objects. In E. C. Zambrano & R. P. C. Nascimento (Eds.), *Euro-American Conference on Telematics and Information Systems (EATIS 2006)*. Accessibility and internationalization of Web-based information systems (pp. 150-156).

Gomes, G. R. R., Siqueira, S. W. M., Braz, M. H. L. B., & Melo, R. N. (2005). LORDiLIS: integrating learning objects repositories and digital libraries. In *PGL Conference: Vol. 3. Consolidat-*

ing eLearning Experiences. Sao Paulo: Getulio Vargas Foundation.

Gomes, G. R. R., Siqueira, S. W. M., Braz, M. H. L. B., & Melo, R. N. (2006a). Integrated searches over digital libraries and e-learning systems. *In WCCSETE 2006 Congresso Mundial de Educação em Engenharia, Tecnologia e Ciência da Computação.* Itanhaém / Santos.

Gomes, G. R. R., Siqueira, S. W. M., Braz, M. H. L. B., & Melo, R. N. (2006b). Integrated access to learning objects repositories and digital libraries. In *IRMA International Conference: Vol. 17. Emerging Trends and Challenges in Information Technology Management* (pp. 736-739). Hershey, PA: IRM Press.

Gruber, T.R. (2001, September 8). What is an ontology? *Knowledge systems, AI laboratory, Stanford University.* Retrieved October 14, 2006, from http://www-ksl.stanford.edu/kst/what-is-an-ontology.html

Gudgin, M., Hadley, M., Mendelsohn, N., Moreau, J. J., & Nielsen, H, F. (Eds.). (2003a). SOAP version 1.2 part 1: messaging framework. *W3C recommendation 24 June 2003.* Retrieved October 14, 2006, from http://www.w3.org/TR/soap12-part1/

Gudgin, M., Hadley, M., Mendelsohn, N., Moreau, J. J., & Nielsen, H, F. (Eds.). (2003b). SOAP version 1.2 part 2: adjuncts. *W3C Recommendation 24 June 2003.* Retrieved October 14, 2006, from http://www.w3.org/TR/soap12-part2/

IMS AccessForAll Meta-data Overview. (2004, July 12). *IMS Global Learning Consortium, Inc.* Retrieved October 14, 2006, from http://www.imsglobal.org/accessibility/accmdv1p0/imsac-cmd_oviewv1p0.html

IMS Learner Information Package Summary of Changes; (2005, January 4). *IMS Global Learning Consortium, Inc.* Retrieved October 14,

2006, from http://www.imsglobal.org/profiles/lipv1p0p1/imslip_sumcv1p0p1.html

IMS Learning Resource Meta-Data Information Model—Version 1.2.1 Final Specification; (2001,September 28). *IMS Global Learning Consortium.* Retrieved October 14, 2006, from http://www.imsglobal.org/metadata/imsmdv1p2p1/imsmd_infov1p2p1.html

IMS Question and Test Interoperability Overview. (2005, January 24). *IMS Global Learning Consortium, Inc.* Retrieved October 14, 2006, from http://www.imsglobal.org/question/qti_v2p0/imsqti_oviewv2p0.html

Koper, R. & Oliver, B. (2004). Representing learning design of units of learning. *Educational Technology & Society, 7*(3), 97-111.

Kreger, H.: Web Services—Conceptual Architecture (WSCA 1.0) (2001, May). *IBM Software Group.* Retrieved October 14, 2006, from http://www.ibm.com/software/solutions/webservices/pdf/WSCA.pdf

Library of Congress. (2000). Network Development and MARC Standards Office. MARC21 format for bibliographic data: including guidelines for content designation. 2000 ed.

Lyardet, F., Rossi, G., & Schwabe, D. (1998). Using design patterns in educational multimedia applications. In *Proceeding of ED-MEDIA'98*, Friburg, Germany. Retrieved October 14, 2006, from http://www.inf.puc-rio.br/~schwabe/papers/edmedia98.pdf

Manes, A.T. (2001, March 12). Enabling open, interoperable, and smart Web services—the need for shared context. *World Wide Web Consortium.* Retrieved October 14, 2006, from http://www.w3.org/2001/03/WSWS-popa/paper29

McGuinness, D. L., & van Harmelen, F. (Eds.). (2004). OWL Web ontology language—overview. *W3C Recommendation 10 February 2004*. Retrieved October 14, 2006, from http://www. w3.org/TR/owl-features/

Moura, S. L., Coutinho, F., Siqueira, S. W. M., & Melo, R. N (2005b). *Integrating repositories of learning objects using Web-services to implement mediators and wrappers*. Paper presented at The International Conference on Next Generation Web Services Practices 2005 (NWeSP'05), Seoul, South Korea.

Moura, S. L., Coutinho, F., Siqueira, S. W. M., & Melo, R.N (2005a). Integrating repositories of learning objects using Web-services and ontologies. *International Journal Of Web Services Practices, Seoul, 1*(1-2), 57-72.

Moura, S. L., Coutinho, F., Siqueira, S. W. M., & Melo, R.N (2005c). *LORIS: integrating distributed and heterogeneous metadata repositories of learning objects*. Paper presented at the 3rd PGL Conference: Consolidating eLearning Experiences, São Paulo, Brazil.

PAPI Learner, Draft 8 Specification. (2002, February 1). Retrieved October 14, 2006, from http://edutool.com/papi/

Rehak, D., Dodds, P. & Lannom, L. (2005). *A model and infrastructure for federated learning content repositories*. Paper presented at the 14th International World Wide Web Conference—WWW 2005, Chiba, Japan.

SCORM 2004 3rd Edition, Sharable Content Object Reference Model overview. (2006, August 18). *Advanced Distributed Learning Initiative*. Retrieved October 14, 2006, from http://www. adlnet.gov/downloads/290.cfm

Scouller, K. (1998) The influence of assessment method on students' learning approaches: Multiple choice question examination versus assignment essay. *Higher Education, 35*, 453-462.

Siqueira, S.W.M., Braz, M.H.L.B. & Melo, R.N. (2003a). From scenarios to a generic architecture

for education and training systems. In *Proceedings of the IASTED International Conference on Computers and Technology in Education (CATE 2003)* (pp. 103-108). Anaheim, Calgary, and Zurich: ACTA Press.

Siqueira, S.W.M., Braz, M.H.L.B. & Melo, R.N. (2003b). Web technology for education and training. In *4th International Workshop on Management of Information on the Web—Web-Based Teaching and Learning (MIW'2003)* (pp. 337-341). Prague, DEXA Workshops, IEEE Computer Society.

Siqueira, S. W. M., Braz, M. H. L. B., & Melo, R. N. (2003c). E-Learning environment based on framework composition. In *Proceedings of the 3rd IEEE International Conference on Advanced Learning Technologies (ICALT 2003)* (pp. 468-468). Athens, Piscataway: IEEE Computer Society.

Siqueira, S. W. M., Braz, M. H. L. B., & Melo, R.N. (2004). Composing frameworks to achieve an e-learning framework. In *Proceedings of the IASTED International Conference on Computers and Technology in Education (CATE 2004)* (pp. 118-123). Anaheim, Calgary, and Zurich: ACTA Press.

Smith, M. K., Welty, C., & McGuinness, D. L. (Eds.). (2004). OWL Web ontology language-guide. *W3C Recommendation 10 February 2004*. Retrieved October 14, 2006, from http://www. w3.org/TR/owl-guide/

Who's involved in standards? (2005, March 09). *CETIS—Centre for Educational Technology Interoperability Standards*. Retrieved October 14, 2006 from http://www.cetis.ac.uk/static/whos-involved.html

Wiederhold, G. (1992). Mediators in the architecture of future information systems. *IEEE Computer, 25*(3), pp. 38-49.

Chapter IX
End-User Quality of Experience-Aware Personalized E-Learning

Cristina Hava Muntean
National College of Ireland, Ireland

Gabriel-Miro Muntean
Dublin City University, Ireland

ABSTRACT

Lately, user quality of experience (QoE) during their interaction with a system is a significant factor in the assessment of most systems. However, user QoE is dependent not only on the content served to the users, but also on the performance of the service provided. This chapter describes a novel QoE layer that extends the features of classic adaptive e-learning systems in order to consider delivery performance in the adaptation process and help in providing good user perceived QoE during the learning process. An experimental study compared a classic adaptive e-learning system with one enhanced with the proposed QoE layer. The result analysis compares learner outcome, learning performance, visual quality and usability of the two systems and shows how the QoE layer brings significant benefits to user satisfaction improving the overall learning process.

INTRODUCTION

It is widely acknowledged that e-learners differ in skills, aptitudes and preferences, may have different perceptions of the same factors and some of them may have special needs due to disabilities. People also seek different information when accessing Web-based educational systems and may prefer certain learning styles. Therefore, various adaptive and personalized e-learning systems such as ApeLS (Conlan & Wade, 2004), WINDS (Specht et al., 2002), iClass (O'Keeffe, 2006), INSPIRE (Papanikolaou et al., 2003) and AES-CS (Triantafillou et al., 2002) were proposed in order to capture and analyze these user-related features, and personalize the educational material thus optimizing users' learning experience.

With the latest communication-oriented devices like smart phones, PDAs, laptops and network technologies such as 3G, WiFi, IEEE 802.11 family of standards (IEEE802.11, 1999), WiMax, IEEE 802.16 family (IEEE802.16, 2004), e-learners can access personalized information "anytime and anywhere." However, the network environments allowing this universal access have widely varying performance-related characteristics such as bandwidth, level of congestion, mobility support and cost of transmission.

It is unrealistic to expect that the personalized content delivery quality can be maintained at the same level in this variable environment. Rather an effort must be made to tailor the material served to each person to their operational environment including current network delivery conditions, ensuring high quality of experience (QoE) during the learning process.

QoE focuses on the learner and is considered in (Empirix, 2003) as a collection of all the perception elements of the network and performance relative to users' expectations. The QoE concept applies to any kind of network interaction such as Web navigation, multimedia streaming, voice over IP, etc. Different QoE metrics that assess user experience with the systems in term of responsiveness and availability have been proposed. QoE metrics may involve subjective elements and may be influenced by any sub-system between the service provider and the end-user.

It should be noted that some adaptive e-learning systems have already taken into consideration performance features such as device capabilities, the type of access to the network, download time, etc. in order to improve learning QoE (Chou et al., 2004; Brady et al., 2004; Smyth & Cotter, 2002;

Apostolopoulos & Kefala, 2003). However, these account for only a limited range of factors affecting QoE. Also, they were considered separately one from another, unlike the real life situation when there is a simultaneous influence on user interaction with the e-learning systems.

In order to address the effect the complex operational environment has on e-learning, a detailed analysis of the key factors that affect learner QoE was conducted. A *QoE adaptation layer* that extends the adaptation features of classic e-learning systems was proposed. It aims to provide high level QoE when users engage in a learning process via network environments with variable connectivity characteristics.

This chapter presents, in details, the proposed QoE layer in the context of a classic architecture for adaptive e-learning systems (AeLS). The most significant AeLS proposed to date are presented in the "Related Work" section that also includes a summarization of the methods most often used in AeLS evaluation. Results of a detailed experimental study that involved a well-known AeLS and a version of the same system enhanced with the proposed QoE layer are then presented. The consequent result analysis compares learner outcome, learning performance, usability and visual quality of the two systems and shows how the QoE layer brings significant benefits to the learning process. The chapter ends with conclusions.

RELATED WORKS

Adaptive E-Learning Systems (AeLS)

Most adaptive e-learning systems are adaptive hypermedia systems (AHS) with applicability in education. In general, AHS aim to help in any application area where the hyperspace is large enough and the system is used by heterogeneous groups of users that have different goals, knowledge, interests, preferences and tasks. Education is one of the major areas of AHS applicability that also includes: online information systems, online help systems, information retrieval, institutional information, and personalized views systems (Brusilovsky, 1996, 2001).

Adaptive e-learning systems (AeLS) in general and mainly Web-based AeLS have attracted considerable interest due to their potential to facilitate personalized learning. They are used by heterogeneous groups of students with different levels of knowledge on a particular subject. The goal of the students is to learn all the material or a reasonable part of it. These systems consider, as the most important feature of the user, the knowledge level of the subject being studied. In order to provide different content to different users and to the same user at different knowledge stages, the system "watches" the students during their learning process.

Before 1996, very few AeLS were developed and mainly in the form of lab systems built to explore some new methods that used adaptivity in an educational context (Brusilovsky, 2001). Examples include a hypertext-based system for teaching the C programming language (Kay & Kummerfeld, 1994), Anatom-Tutor, an intelligent anatomy tutoring system for use at university level (Beaumont, 1994) and ELM-PE, an on-site intelligent learning environment that supports learning of the LISP programming language through examples (Weber & Möllenberg, 1995).

After 1996, with the exponential increase in Internet popularity, the Web started to have an important effect on teaching and learning, mainly in higher education. Many online lecture notes or complex tutoring applications were distributed on the Web. The realization that there is a need to address heterogeneous audience of Web-based courses has led the development of a large number of Web-based AeLS, among which the most important are presented next.

ELM-ART

ELM-ART updated ELM-PE and provided live examples and intelligent diagnoses of problem solutions. Later on, new enhancements were added leading to the ELM-ART II (Weber & Specht, 1997). This system supports online exercises and tests, student-tutor communications via e-mail and student-student discussions via chat rooms. The exercises and tests results allowed the system to assess the student's knowledge more carefully and to infer user's knowledge state. In the next version of the ELM-ART, a multi-layered overlay model was introduced (Weber, 1999). Apart of the knowledge states, now users were able to declare knowledge units as already known. The users could change their associated student model whenever they wanted or switch back to the original state without any loss of information. The system was also extended with two new communication tools: discussion list and user group. The latest version of ELM-ART has been combined with NetCoach, an authoring tool for developing Web-based courses. With NetCoach (Weber et al., 2001), authors can create adaptive Web-based courses that are based on the multi-layered overlay model, that support different types of test items, and include all the communication tools mentioned.

InterBook

InterBook is a system for authoring and delivering adaptive electronic textbooks via the Web (Brusilovsky et al., 1996). It is an environment in which structured textbooks could be presented in a multiply navigable interface. All InterBook-served electronic textbooks have a generated table of content, a glossary, and a search interface. The system uses colored annotations to inform the user about the status of the node referred to by a link.

InterBook stores a domain model of concepts and their structure and an overlay model that helps the system to assess the user's knowledge on different topics and is built based on user-visited pages. These models are used by the system to provide adaptive guidance, adaptive navigation support, and adaptive help. The system also provides different options to the user in the form of direct guidance via the "teach me" button that links the most suitable nodes to be read in the current context. It also includes a glossary index of the concepts.

AHA!

AHA!, developed by the Database and Hypermedia group from Eindhoven University of Technology (De Bra & Calvi, 1998), does not offer support for developing and delivering adaptive courseware only, it is a general-purpose server-side Web-based adaptive system. However AHA! was exemplified and used in education for delivering adaptive university courses at Eindhoven. The first version was developed in 1998, based on the AHAM model (De Bra et al., 1999), and since then the system has undergone several revisions. AHA! includes a domain model, a user-model and an adaptation model. An adaptive engine both performs content and link adaptation and updates information in these models, based on level of user knowledge about concepts. User knowledge is accumulated while the users read pages and take tests. Content adaptation is performed based on the *fragment variants technique*. Unlike InterBook that uses link annotation only, *AHA! link adaptation is performed by using* both link hiding and *link annotation* techniques. The color scheme can be configured by the author and overridden by the user. The user is also allowed to choose between *link annotation* and *link hiding*.

More recently AHA! was enhanced with an authoring tool that implements the principles of

LAOS authoring model for adaptive hypermedia systems proposed in (Cristea & de Mooij, 2003).

Since AHA! system is open source, one of the latest introduced and well-known, it was used for the tests presented in his chapter.

INSPIRE

Many researchers are trying to integrate learning styles in the design of their AeLS, along with the classic learner's features such as goals/tasks, knowledge level, background, preferences and interests. INSPIRE is an AeLS that monitors learner's activity and dynamically adapts the generated lessons to accommodate diversity in learner's knowledge state and learning style (Grigoriadou et al., 2001). It emphasizes the fact that learners perceive and process information in very different ways, and integrates ideas from theories of instructional design and learning styles.

With regards to the adaptive dimension of INSPIRE, the selection of the lesson contents and the provided navigation support are both based on the domain model of the system which is represented in three hierarchical levels of knowledge abstraction: learning goals, concepts and educational material (Papanikolaou et al., 2003). The system makes, also, use of a learner model (user model) in order to exploit learners' knowledge level and individual traits (such as its dominant learning style) and to determine the appropriate instructional strategy. This strategy helps in the selection of lessons' contents, the presentation of the educational material, and the annotation of hyperlinks in the domain hyperspace. Several levels of adaptation are supported: from full system-control to full learner-control. It offers learners the option to decide on the level of adaptation of the system by intervening in different stages of the lesson generation process and formulating the lesson contents and presentation.

INSPIRE is used to support a course on Computer Architecture offered by the Informatics and Telecommunications Department, at Athens University, Greece.

JointZone

JointZone (Ng et al., 2002) is a Web-based learning application in Rheumatology for medical students. It combines user modeling, domain modeling and adaptive techniques in order to deliver personalized Web-based learning.

It uses keyword indexing and site layout structure information for domain modeling giving a conceptual and structural representation of the content. This reduces the involvement of a domain expert in organizing and labeling the content.

The content of JointZone exists in the form of an online electronic textbook, which is illustrated with photo images and videos taken on various forms of rheumatic diseases. In an additional section, there are a total of 30 interactive case studies that simulate a variety of rheumatic clinical scenarios where students can actively engage in problem solving rather than being passive recipients of information. The cases are subdivided into three groups designated "Beginner," "Intermediate" and "Advanced." The layout of these cases differs according to the degree of expertise of the user. In JointZone, the user model captures two aspects of the students' differences: individual browsing history and knowledge level in the Rheumatology domain. The model also involves the novel idea of using individual effective reading speed to better identify if a student has read a page. The user's knowledge level is initialized based on his/her first entry registration details. This knowledge value evolves through the user engagement with the application, based on student performance in the case study. The adaptation uses two adaptive techniques: link hiding and link annotation. Based on these techniques and the information from the user model, different personalized features are provided such as: personalized reading room, personalized site map, and personalized topic map.

AeLS Evaluation Methods

The method mostly used in the evaluation of adaptive educational systems adopts a "**with or without adaptation approach**" (Karagiannidis et al., 2001) and considers that the evaluated system can have adaptive and non-adaptive versions. The experiments are conducted between two groups of learners, one working with the adaptive version of the system and the other—with its non-adaptive version. This conventional method of comparing the adaptive and non-adaptive versions of an application is highly debatable as it depends on how the non-adaptive version was obtained. Possibilities may involve an original system to which enhancements were added to obtain the adaptive system, a system resulted from the adaptive system by switching off its enhancements and a system that maintains only some of all adaptive features.

Evaluation Strategy

Looking from **evaluation strategy** point of view, two main directions were taken.

A first approach targets system evaluation **"as a whole"** and is very often used in education (Brusilovsky et al., 2001). The evaluation process focuses mainly on overall learner performance and their satisfaction related to the use of the adaptive system. This user satisfaction can be quantified by selected and measurable criteria. The most used criteria in the evaluation process are: task completion time, learning performance assessed by comparing the results of a pre-test and post-test, number of navigation steps, number of times the subjects revisited "concepts" they were attempting to learn, and user's satisfaction reflected through questionnaires.

Recently, a novel **layered-based** evaluation of adaptive applications was recommended by a number of researchers such as Weibelzahl and Weber (2002) and Elissavet and Economides (2003). Unlike the previous approach, layered evaluation assesses the success of the adaptation by decomposing the system into different layers and evaluating them one by one. The different layers reflect various aspects and stages of the adaptation.

Although the proposed frameworks are described at different levels of granularity, the evaluation process was originally divided in two main phases: evaluation of the interaction assessment phase and evaluation of the adaptation decision-making phase (Karagiannidis et al., 2001):

- **Layer 1: Interaction Assessment Evaluation.** This layer tests if the system detected the learner's goals, knowledge, preferences, interests, and the user's experience with the respect of hyperspace. It also assesses whether the assumption drawn by the system concerning characteristics of the user-computer interaction is valid.
- **Layer 2: Adaptation Making Evaluation.** Layer 2 tests if the selected adaptive technique is appropriate, valid and meaningful for learner's goal or improves interaction for specific learner's interests, knowledge, etc.

The division of the evaluation process into the two layers that also reflect the main phases of the adaptation may help to determine where the fault (if any) of the adaptive system may be and to target the solutions accordingly. For example, it can be the case that adaptation decisions are reasonable but they are based on incorrect system assumptions, or that the system assumptions are correct but the adaptation decision is not meaningful.

A more detailed approach that consists of a four-layer framework for adaptive system evaluation was proposed in Weibelzahl and Weber (2002):

- **Layer 1: Evaluation of the Reliability and Input Data.** This evaluation prevents unreliable input data to result in miss-adaptation.
- **Layer 2: Evaluation of Inference.** This layer evaluation test the inference mechanism in different environments under real world conditions
- **Layer 3: Evaluation of Adaptation Decision.** The idea of the evaluation is that if some user properties have been inferred, several adaptation possibilities exist. (e.g., with/without adaptive guiding, with/without link annotations).
- **Layer 4: Evaluation of Interaction.** In this case human system interaction has to be evaluated to prevent confusion and dissatisfaction of the users. Different objective and subjective measures are taken into account such as: system usability, solution quality, frequency of tasks success, number of required hints, etc.

When assessing AeLS, most often application usability, learner achievement and learning performance are considered. Next, they are discussed in details.

Usability Evaluation Tests

One of the most important features of any software application is its usability. According to ISO 9241 standard, usability represents the effectiveness, efficiency and satisfaction that a software application offers to its users in a given context of use and task. In an educational environment the usability of software application is related to its pedagogical value. Although there is a large amount of knowledge related to educational software usability evaluation strategies, currently there are not well-defined techniques for usability evaluation of e-learning applications (Heines, 2000). This is mainly as e-learning is an area of relatively short history, users of e-learning tools can access them through various computer, network and social contexts and the characteristics of typical users of e-learning services can not be easily predicted.

Some of the most used methods proposed in the literature to be applied during the usability evaluation are: *query techniques* (interviews and questionnaires), *logging of user performance* in laboratory conditions, *timing and keystroke level measurements*, *subjects' observation* through adequate equipment, *heuristic evaluation*, etc. These methods are applied during or after the subjects have interacted with the system when performing one or multiple tasks. Usually the usability is analyzed through five major characteristics: usage efficiency, ease of remembrance, pleasant to use, easy to learn with and number of errors.

Questionnaires and interviews are the most widely used technique since they provide a quantitative measure of usability and they serve as an objective comparison of two systems. This technique offers a concise test of usability, it gets directly the users' viewpoint and attitude and it is suitable for wide range of end-users, especially students. A big advantage is that it does not require the presence of an evaluator. In this context, Preece (2000) suggested a list of guidelines for creating questions for the questionnaires, currently widely used for the usability evaluation of the Web-based systems.

Heuristic evaluation is also a widely accepted method for diagnosing the system's usability due to the fact that it can be completed in a relatively short period of time. This methodology involves an expert that evaluates the system using a set of recognized usability principles, called "heuristics" (Nielsen, 1994).

Learner Achievement Evaluation

Learning process evaluation should include assessment of quality and quantity of learning (learning outcome). Therefore, **learner achievement** (defined as the degree of knowledge accumulation by a person after studying a certain material) continues to be a widely used barometer for determining the utility and value of learning technologies. It is analyzed in the form of *course grades, pre/post-test scores, or standardized test scores*.

A course grade is a certification of competence that should reflect, as accurately as possible, a student's performance in a course. There are multiple methods for assigning grades, such as weighting, distribution gap method, curve, percent grading, relative grading, and absolute standard grading.

Pre/Post test scores are also a viable methodology to assess the extent to which an educational intervention has had an impact on student "learning." Pre-tests and post-tests are used to determine the subject's knowledge prior and after the study, respectively.

Standardized tests scores give a "standard" of measure of students' performance when a large number of students, often geographically distributed, take the same test.

Tests, quizzes or exams are methods used to evaluate students and assess whether they learned what is expected. Jacobs and Chase (1992) made a distinction between the three terms: tests, quizzes and exams, based on the scope of content covered. An examination is the most comprehensive form of testing. A test is more limited in scope, focusing on particular aspects of the course material. A quiz is very limited and usually is administered in fifteen minutes or less.

Among them, tests are most important in the evaluation of AeLS as they offer a feedback in the learning process, helping to optimise it and their results are the most reliable evidence that users have learned.

The evaluation based on tests, quizzes or exams may consist of five different types of test items:

- **Yes-No (True-False):** Users have to answer questions by selecting "Yes" or "No" only.

- **Forced-Choice:** Users have to answer by selecting only one of the alternative answers.
- **Multi-Choice:** Users have to answer by selecting all correct answers provided.
- **Essay (Free-Form)/Short Answer:** Users can type freely an answer to the question. Short answers are one to three paragraphs long.
- **Gap-Filling (Completion):** Users have to type in characters or numbers to complete a word or sentence.

Each type of test item has its relative strengths and weaknesses. Each has also a general value of difficulty and relevance for the tested concept.

Learning Performance Evaluation

Learning performance term refers to how fast a study task (e.g., learning task, searching for a piece of information or memorizing information displayed on the computer screen) takes place. The most used metric for measuring AeLS learning performance is *study session time*. The completion time for a study session is measured from the start of the session, when the subject logs into the system and starts to study, until the subject starts answering the questions from the evaluation test. Other metrics worth mentioning are: *number of navigation steps* performed during a study session, *number of pages re-visited, average time spent per page* for studying the information, and *average access time*.

QoE-AWARE ADAPTIVE E-LEARNING SYSTEM

Figure 1 illustrates the architecture of the proposed **quality of experience-aware adaptive e-learning system** (QoE-AeLS) resulted from the addition of the novel **QoE layer** to the classic AeLS. Apart from the QoE layer—represented in the figure with a different color and presented in more details in the following section, AeLS has four main components: domain model, user model, adaptation model and adaptation engine. These components provide adaptation functionality following the principles presented in the AHAM model (De Bra et al., 1999). Most adaptive e-learning systems based on AHAM include these components.

The **domain model (DM)** organizes the educational material in a hierarchical structure of concepts, among which logical relationships exist. At the lowest level, the concepts correspond to fragments of information. These fragments—stored in a Domain Database—are combined into composite concepts (also called pages) by defining relationships among them. Composite concepts may be further combined using relationships to eventually form more complex units of information. The content is selected from the DM and delivered to the learner based not only on these relationships, but also on learners' characteristics.

The **user model (UM)** maintains and stores in a user database various demographic information related to the learner (e.g., age, gender, learner's current goal and interest in the educational material), learner's navigational history, etc. Both explicit (via registration) and implicit (through normal navigation and content selection) information is used to generate and update the UM. In order to construct UM, to analyze the user profile and to derive new facts about the user, different user modeling methods have been proposed. The most common ones are the overlay method (De Bra & Calvi, 1998; Pilar da Silva et al., 1998) and the stereotype method (Boyle & Encarnacion, 1994; Murphy & McTear, 1997). Lately, Bayesian networks have become popular for modeling user knowledge and goals and to identify the best actions to be taken under uncertainty (Nejdl & Wolpers, 1999; Conati et al., 1997).

The **adaptation model (AM)** provides the adaptive functionality of the system. The main

Figure 1. Architecture of the quality of experience-aware adaptive e-learning system

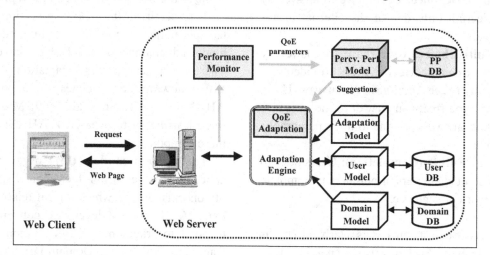

goal is to define how content adaptation, navigation support adaptation and updates of the UM are performed. Condition-action rules are used to express the adaptation mechanism. These rules combine information from the UM and DM and determine how UM is updated and which information will be delivered to the learner.

The **adaptation engine (AE)** interprets the condition-action rules described in the AM, performs the content selection from the DM, creates the navigational support (links), and delivers a personalized Web page to the learner according to its profile built by the UM.

QoE LAYER FOR QOE-AELS

The proposed *QoE layer* includes the following components: perceived performance model, performance monitor and QoE adaptation unit.

The **performance monitor (PM)** monitors different performance metrics (e.g., download time, round-trip time, throughput, user tolerance for delay) and learner behavior-related actions (e.g., abort and reload requests) in real-time during user navigation and delivers them to the Perceived Performance Model.

The **perceived performance model (PPM)** models this information using a stereotype-based technique, probability and distribution theory, in order to learn about the learner's operational environment characteristics, about changes in the network connectivity and the consequences of these changes on the learner's QoE. The PPM also considers the learner's subjective opinion about their QoE as explicitly expressed by the user. This introduces a degree of subjective assessment, specific to each user. Based on the gathered information, the PPM suggests optimal Web-based educational material characteristics (e.g., the number of embedded objects in the Web page, the dimension of the based-Web page without components and the total dimension of the embedded components) that will provide a satisfactory QoE. The PPM aims to ensure that the download time per delivered page, as perceived by the learner, respects the user tolerance for delay and stays within the user satisfaction zone (Sevcik, 2002; Bhatti et al., 2000; Bouch et al., 2000; Servidge, 1999, Ramsay et al., 1998).

The **QoE adaptation unit (QoEAU)** deploys a QoE adaptation algorithm (Muntean & McManis, 2006a) that uses PPM's content-related suggestions. Its objective is to determine and apply the correct transformations (e.g., modifications in the properties of the embedded images and/or elimination of some of them and placing a link to the image location) to the personalized Web page. This is performed in order to match the PPM suggestions on the Web page characteristics and thus to provide high QoE during learning process.

QoE-AWARE E-LEARNING PROCESS

The main goal of the QoE-AeLS is to provide personalized material that suits both learners' individual characteristics (e.g., goals, knowledge, learning style) and their operational environment in order to ensure high QoE during learning process. Therefore the process of adaptation and personalization of educational material allows for both *user-based* and *QoE-based* adaptations. *User-based* adaptation selects those pieces of information from the DM for inclusion in a learner-tailored document, based on the user profile from the UM. *QoE-based* adaptation is applied when the delivery of the personalized document in given environment characterized by certain connectivity would not provide a satisfactory QoE. Based on the result of PM communication monitoring, PPM makes suggestions and QoEAU applies them in order to increase user QoE.

More details about the proposed QoE-AeLS architecture and QoE-aware adaptation process can be found in Muntean and McManis, 2006a, 2006b, 2006c.

EVALUATION OF THE QoE LAYER

The proposed QoE layer has been assessed through both simulations and qualitative evaluation in the educational area (mainly distance learning), when learners interact with the system in a variable residential-like low bit rate operational environment. Simulation-based testing results that show

the benefit of using the QoE layer for delivering content in low-bitrate environments are presented in (Muntean & McManis, 2006a; Muntean et al., 2006). In order to perform qualitative evaluation, the proposed QoE layer was deployed on the open-source AHA! system (AHA, 2006), creating QoEAHA.

The experimental evaluation was performed in the Performance Engineering Laboratory, School of Electronic Engineering, Faculty of Engineering and Computing, at Dublin City University, Ireland. Two sets of task-based scenarios were developed and carried out in laboratory settings. The scenarios were created in order to provide real usage context for participants, as they would interact with the system in real study conditions.

The subjects involved in the tests were randomly divided into two groups. One group used the original AHA! system, whereas the second one used QoEAHA. The subjects were not aware of what version of the system they were using during the experiment. No time limitation was imposed on the execution of the required tasks. None of the students had previously used any of the two versions of the AHA! system and none of them had accessed the test material prior taking the tests. Therefore no previous practice with the environments was assumed for any of them. The material on which the students consisted of the original adaptive tutorial delivered with the AHA! system version 2.0.

Figure 2 graphically presents the network-based setup used for testing. It involved four PC Fujitsu Siemens desktops with single Pentium III (800MHz) processors and 128 MB memory each that acted as clients, an IBM NetFinity 6600 with dual Pentium III (800 MHz) processors and 1 GB memory as Web server and one Fujitsu Siemens desktop computer with Pentium III (800 MHz) processor and 512 MB RAM that acts as a router and has a NISTNET network emulator installed on it. NISTNET that allows for the emulation of various network conditions characterized by certain bandwidth, delay, loss rate and loss pat-

Figure 2. Laboratory testing setup

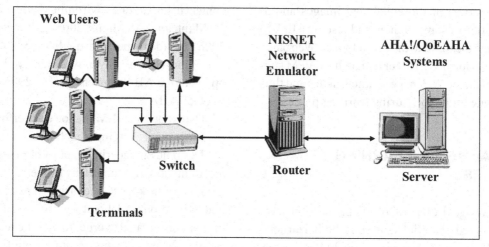

tern was used to create low bit rate residential-like operational environments with bandwidth in the 56 kbps to 128 kbps range. For both groups of subjects, same network conditions were emulated between their computers and the AeLS. These setup conditions offer similar connectivity to that experienced by residential users. These conditions determined performance-related adaptations when QoEAHA version was used.

The goal of the experimental study was to compare the learning outcome and learning performance, system usability, visual quality and user satisfaction when AHA! and QoEAHA systems were used respectively.

Scenario 1: Interactive Study Session

The first testing scenario covered an interactive study session of one chapter from the adaptive AHA! tutorial and delivered a network with emulated 56 kbps connectivity. This experimental test involved forty-two postgraduate students from the Faculty of Engineering and Computing, at Dublin City University, Ireland as subjects. Before and after the subjects completed the study task, they were asked to take online evaluation tests in order to assess their knowledge levels.

At the start of the study session, the subjects were given a short explanation about the AeLS usage and their required duties. They were asked to perform the following steps:

1. *Complete an online pre-test evaluation* in order to determine subjects' prior knowledge about the studied domain. It consisted of a questionnaire with six questions related to the learning topic.
2. *Log onto the system* and proceed to browse and *study the material*. Back and forward actions through the studied material were permitted.
3. *Complete an online post-test* at the end of the study period in order to determine the subjects' level of knowledge. The post-test consisted of a questionnaire with fifteen questions that tested recollection of facts, terms and concepts from the supplied material. The students were not allowed to return to the studied material.
4. *Answer a usability questionnaire* that assessed system usability and user QoE level.

It consisted of ten questions categorized into navigation, accessibility, presentation, perceived performance and subjective feedback.

In order to fully assess the subjects learning outcome, both pre-test and post-test were devised that consisted of a combination of four different types of test-items most commonly used in the educational area: "yes-no," "forced-choice," "multi-choice" and "gap-filling." For time-related reasons, 6 questions were included in the pre-test evaluation as follows: 3 "yes/no," 2 "forced choice" and 1 "multi-choice." The post-test evaluation consisted of 15 questions: 5 "yes/no," 6 "forced choice," 3 "multi choice" and 1 "gap filling." As the test-items have different degrees of difficulty, different corresponding weights in the final score have been assigned for a correct answer as follows: one point for "yes/no" questions, two points for "forced-choice" questions, three points for "multi-choice" questions and four points for "gap-filling" questions. For incorrect answers no points were given.

As the maximum scores were 10 and 30 points for pre-test and post-test respectively, the final scores of both the tests were normalized and were expressed in the 0-10 range.

Scenario 2: Search for Information

The second testing scenario focused on a search for information and involved subjective visual quality assessment in the case with the worse network connection—28kbps. Since the QoE-based adaptation mechanism involves modifications on the properties of the embedded images, the goal was to assess whether the quality of content is good enough to perform the required task. The subjects were asked to look up for two different terms and to answer two questions related to these terms. The terms were described in the embedded images. Objective and subjective visual quality assessments that involved the measurement of the time taken to complete the task and questionnaire-based evaluation techniques were used. The subjective assessment on a five-point quality scale (1-"bad," 2-"poor," 3-"fair," 4-"good," 5-"excellent") ascertained the impact of QoE-based content adaptation on subjects' learning experience.

Table 1. Scenario 1: Pre-test and post-test results

	Score	Mean	Min	Max	St.Dev
pre-test	AHA!	0.35	0.0	2.0	0.55
	QoEAHA	0.30	0.0	2.0	0.53
post-test	AHA!	6.70	4.30	9.30	1.401
	QoEAHA	7.05	4.60	9.00	1.395

Table 2. Scenario 2: Post-test results (answers found in embedded images)

	Score	Mean	Min	Max	St.Dev
post-test	AHA!	6.40	2.0	10.0	3.25
	QoEAHA	6.30	2.0	10.0	3.15

Scenario 2 involved twenty postgraduate students from the faculty of Engineering and Computing at Dublin City University, Ireland. The goal of these tests was to assess whether the resulted quality of images is good enough for the subjects to be able to perform the required task.

Learning Outcome

Learning outcome was analyzed in terms of pre-test/post-test scores of the two groups after a study session. Table 1 presents both pre-test and post-test scores resulted after the tests were performed according to scenario 1. Pre-test scores (AHA_{mean} = 0.35, $QoEAHA_{mean}$ = 0.30) showed that both groups of students had the same prior knowledge on the studied domain. The mean scores for the post-test were 7.05 for the subjects that used QoEAHA and 6.70 for the AHA! group. A two-sample t-test analysis on these values does not indicate a significant difference in the marks received by the two groups of subjects (α = 0.05, t = −0.79, t-critical = 1.68, p(t) = 0.21).

Since answers for three of questions from the post-test questionnaire have required the subjects to study the images embedded in the Web pages, an analysis of the students' learning outcome on these questions was also performed. After the scores related to these three questions were normalized in the 0 to 10 range, the mean value of the students' scores was 6.3 for the QoEAHA group and 6.4 for AHA! group. More details about these results are presented in Table 2. A two-sample t-test analysis, with equal variance assumed, performed on the two sets of results indicates with a 99% level of confidence that there is no significant difference

in the students' learning achievement (t = -0.08, t-critical = 2.71, p(t) = 0.93, α = 0.01). This result is very important as an adaptive degradation in the image quality (up to 34 % in size) was applied by the QoEAHA.

Therefore, it can be concluded that the addition of the QoE layer does not affect the learning outcome and that QoEAHA offers similar learning capabilities to the classic AHA! system, regardless of the characteristics of the operational environment.

Learning Performance

The impact of the QoE-based content adaptation on the **learning performance** was assessed through the following metrics: *study session time, study time per page* and *number of accesses to a page performed by a person*. These metrics were analyzed and compared for both groups of subjects.

Study Session Time

The distribution of the *study time* taken by the students in order to accumulate the information provided during the first scenario using the AHA! and QoEAHA systems respectively is presented in Figure 3. One can notice that on average students that made use of the QoEAHA system (Average Study Time = 17.77 min) have performed better than the ones that used the AHA! (Average Study Time = 21.23 min) (see Table 3). The very large majority of the students that used QoEAHA (71.43%) performed the task in up to 20 minutes with a large number of students (42.87 %) requir-

Table 3. Study time for the learning tasks when AHA! and QoEAHA were used

Study Time (min)	Mean	Min	Max	St.Dev
AHA!	21.23	12.95	31.84	5.90
QoEAHA	17.77	9.37	30.38	5.44

ing between 15 minutes and 20 minutes of study time. In comparison, when the AHA! system was used, only 42.85% of the students succeeded to finish the learning task in 20 min. The majority of them (71.42%) required up to 25 minutes with the largest number of students (28.57%) in the interval 20-25 minutes.

In Figure 3, one can also notice that 9.5% of the students from group 1 (using QoEAHA) succeeded to learn in less the 10 minutes while none of the students from group 2 (using AHA!) had this performance.

Study Time per Page

In order to assess the results of the comparison between the two AeLS, in terms of *study time per page*, two Web pages, out of those stud-

ied by the students as part of scenario 1, were considered. These pages—denoted page 1 and page 2—included a higher number of embedded images and a larger amount of data to be delivered to the learner. Consequently, the subjects perceived long waiting periods when the AHA! system was used. QoEAHA decreased the access time perceived by the students but has also performed some degradation into the quality of the content. Therefore the study time on those pages was analyzed when the two systems were used with the first scenario. *Study time per page* was measured from the moment when the system has received a request for the page until a request for a new page was sent.

The results presented in Table 4 show that on average the students from group 1 (using QoEAHA) spent less time on both page 1 and

Figure 3. Study time distributions for students involved in a learning task

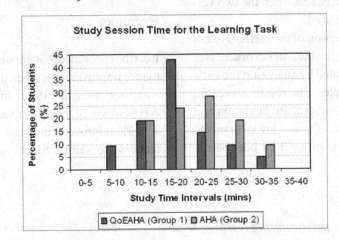

Table 4. Number of accesses per Web page per person during learning session

Number Accesses per Page	Page 1					Page 2				
	Avg	Min	Max	St.dev	σ^2	Avg	Min	Max	St.Dev	σ^2
QoEAHA (Group 1)	1.43	1.0	3.0	0.60	0.4	1.38	1.0	3.0	0.59	0.4
AHA! (Group 2)	1.76	1.0	4.0	0.83	0.7	1.71	1.0	4.0	0.90	0.8

page 2 for studying the information in these pages than the ones from group 2 (using AHA!). This observation was confirmed by statistical data analysis. By performing a two-sample t-test assuming unequal variances, for each of the two pages it can be said that there is a significant difference between the two groups' means with a confidence level of 95%.

Number of Accesses to a Page

Number of accesses to a page performed by subjects was also measured and analyzed for the same two pages. The average value of this parameter for page 1 was 1.43 when the QoEAHA system was used and 1.76 for the AHA! system, as presented in Table 5. Similar values were obtained for page 2: 1.38 and respectively 1.70. An unpaired two-tailed t-test analysis, with unequal variance assumed, has statistically confirmed with at least 92% confidence that there is a significant difference in the number of visits performed by a student to page 1 and page 2 when the two versions of the AHA! are used.

The effect of the version of the AHA! system used by the students had on the number of accesses to a page was investigated by analyzing the variability of the test samples. The results presented in Table 5 show that both standard deviation and variance of group 1 results are lower than the values corresponding to group 2 for both pages.

An f-test analysis was performed to determine if variance between the two groups is statistically significant. The results confirm that group 1 and group 2 results do not have the same variance and the difference between the two groups' variances is statistically significant.

It can be noticed that the group 2 results have a higher dispersion than those of group 1. Also a larger number of students (an average of 55%) that used the AHA! system (group 2) required more than one access to page 1 and page 2 for learning. At the same time, a large majority of students (an average of 65%) that used the QoEAHA (group 1) performed only one access to the same pages (See Figures 4 and 5). This shows that QoEAHA users have succeeded to focus better on the studied material. This is due to the fact that the material was delivered faster to the students and the students were constantly focused on their task. Long periods of waiting time for getting access to the material annoy the people and disturb their concentration on the learning task.

Remarks

It can be concluded that important learning performance improvements when the QoEAHA system was used were achieved in comparison when AHA! was used. For example, in tested conditions a 16.3% improvement in the Study Session Time alone was obtained. Since the download time per

Table 5. Study time per person during learning session

Study Time (min)	Page 1					Page 2				
	Avg	Min	Max	St.Dev	σ^2	Avg	Min	Max	St.Dev	σ^2
QoEAHA (Group 1)	4.28	2.09	7.91	1.48	2.2	4.23	2.15	7.7	1.44	2.1
AHA! (Group 2)	5.33	3.69	8.47	1.28	1.7	5.40	3.76	8.23	1.28	1.6

Figure 4. Distribution based on number of visits to Page 1

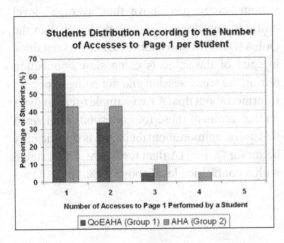

Figure 5. Distribution based on number of visits to Page 2

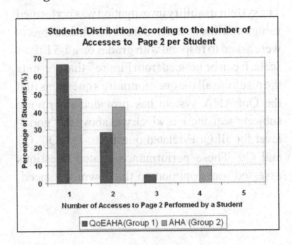

page provided by QoEAHA does not exceed the user tolerance for delay threshold (12-15 seconds is considered satisfactory for the Web users by the research community; the students were constantly focused on the required task and therefore study time per page decreased by 16.27%. It is noteworthy that most of the QoEAHA group students [71.43%] finished the study in up to 20 minutes whereas only 42.85% of the AHA! students finished in the same period of time. Therefore, the QoE-aware AeLS has ensured a smooth learning process. This observation is also confirmed when assessing Number of Accesses per page [on average 19% decrease with QoEAHA than the result obtained for AHA!]).

Visual Quality Assessment

Results on **visual quality assessment** confirmed that the controlled degradation of the quality of the content performed by the proposed QoE layer did not affect the functionality of the AeLS.

As seen in Figure 6, both groups of students succeeded to complete the "search for informa-

tion" task presented in scenario 2 in similar periods of time and they answered the questions correctly. The information targeted by the task was presented in the embedded images of two pages that have the biggest content size and QoEAHA imposed the highest level of image quality degradation as part of its adaptive process. For the worst operational environment case studied (28 kbps connectivity) QoEAHA applied a 57% size reduction to page 1 components and 18% for page 2 items. The subjective-based visual quality assessment investigated through a questionnaire shows that regardless of the high content reduction, the average quality grade given by the subjects to the QoSAHA system was 3.9, very close to "good" perceptual level, and only 4.4% lower than the average quality grade awarded to AHA! (4.3). This suggests that the cost of image quality reduction is not significant as far as user-perceived quality is concerned while at the same time yielding significant improvements in download time and learning performance.

System Usability

The **system usability** investigation was performed using an online questionnaire to which the subjects were asked to respond with grades on a 1-5 Likert scale. It can be noticed from Figure 7 that presents the results to all the questionnaire's questions that the QoEAHA system has provided improving subjects' satisfaction, which was above the "good" level for all QoE-related questions: Q5, Q6, Q7 and Q9. These performance related questions assessed users opinion on the download speed,

overall system responsiveness, and performance effect on learning and user satisfaction. The AHA! system scored just above the "average" level on these questions, significantly lower than the QoEAHA! This good performance was obtained in spite of the subjects using slow connection during the study session and not being explicitly informed about this. A two-sample t-test analysis on the results of these four questions confirmed that users' opinion about their QoE is significantly better for QoEAHA than for AHA!, a fact stated with a confidence level above 99%, ($p<0.01$).

Figure 6. Average completion time for search for a term task (term 1 was located in page 1, whereas term 2 was located in page 2)

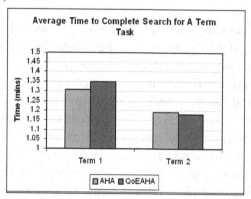

Figure 7. Average grade comparisons between AHA! and QOEAHA results on the usability questionare

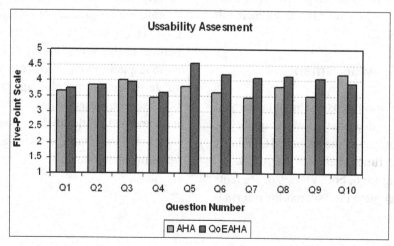

Overall, the mean value of QoE usability assessment, assuming that the questions were of equal importance, was 4.22 for QoEAHA and 3.58 for AHA. This leads to an improvement of 17.8% brought by QoEAHA system.

The usability assessment on the other questions related to the navigation and presentation features achieved an average score of 3.83 for AHA! and 3.89 for QoEAHA, demonstrating that these features were not affected by the addition of the QoE enhancements.

Finally, an overall assessment of the all questions from usability questionnaire when all ten questions were considered of equal importance shows that the students considered QoEAHA system (mean value=4.01) significantly more usable then the AHA! system (mean value=3.73). These results were also confirmed by the unpaired two-tailed t-test (t=2.44, p<0.03) with a 97% degree of confidence. This increase of 7.5% in the overall QoEAHA usability was mainly achieved due to the higher scores obtained in the questions related to end-user QoE.

By examining in details the provided answers (Figure 7), one can notice that only for the last question (Q10) AHA! has a slight advantage over QoEAHA while in most of the other questions QoEAHA received a higher score. Q10 is related to the user satisfaction with the quality of the provided images. The advantage of the AHA! system is justified by the fact that the QoEAHA system performs controlled image degradation in order to improve the end-user perceived performance. Yet, these image degradations did not disturb the users since they scored this question with an average of 3.9, very close to the "good" level.

CONCLUSION

This chapter describes a novel QoE adaptation layer for AeLS proposed as a solution for in-creasing end-user QoE. This QoE layer brings significant benefits when the personalized content is delivered to end-users that avail of Web services over various and changeable network conditions, by adapting the content to them.

The QoEAHA evaluation involved a comparison with the AHA! system in home-like low-bite rate operational environments. Different educational-based evaluation techniques such as learner outcome analysis, learning performance assessment, usability survey, and visual quality assessment were used in order to assess QoEAHA in comparison to AHA!. As the students received similar marks on the final evaluation test, regardless of the system used, it can be said that the QoE layer-enhanced system offers similar learning capabilities to the classic one. Results on visual quality assessment confirmed that the controlled degradation of the quality of the content performed by the QoE layer did not affect the functionality of the e-learning system.

At the same time, important learning performance improvements in terms of Study Session Time (16.27% decrease), Study Time per Page (13% decrease) and Number of Accesses to a Page (smaller) were obtained with the QoEAHA system. It is noteworthy that most of the QoEAHA group students (71.43%) finished the study in up to 20 minutes, while only 42.85% of the AHA! group students finished in the same period of time. In terms of system usability, the students thought the QoE layer enhanced system provided much higher user QoE than the classic one. Questions related to the other aspects of the system (e.g., navigation, presentation) achieved similar marks for both systems demonstrating that the QoE layer did not affect them.

In conclusion, the proposed QoE layer brings significant performance benefits to the users that access the adaptive Web content delivered in difficult network conditions.

REFERENCES

AHA! (2006). Retrieved from http://aha.win.tue.nl

Apostolopoulos, T. K. & Kefala, A. (2003). A configurable middleware architecture for deploying e-learning services over diverse communication networks. *IASTED CATE International Conference*. Rhodes, Greece.

Beaumont, I. (1994). User modeling in the Interactive Anatomy Tutoring System ANATOM-TUTOR. *User Models and User Adapted Interaction Journal*, *4*(1), 21-45.

Bhatti, N., Bouch, A., & Kuchinsky, A. (2000). Integrating user–perceived quality into Web server design. *Computer Networks Journal*, *33*(1-6), 1-16.

Bouch, A., Kuchinsky, A., & Bhatti, N. (2000). Quality is in the eye of the beholder: meeting users' requirements for Internet quality of service. *ACM Conference on Human Factors in Computing Systems* (pp. 297-304). Hague, The Netherlands.

Boyle, C. & Encarnacion, A. O. (1994). MetaDoc: An adaptive hypertext reading system. *User Models and User Adapted Interaction Journal*, *4*(1), 1-19.

Brady, A., Conlan, O., & Wade V. (2004). Dynamic composition and personalization of pda-based e-learning—personalized mlearning. *E-Learn'04 Conference* (pp. 234-242). Washington, USA.

Brusilovsky, P. (1996). Methods and techniques of adaptive hypermedia. *User Modeling And User-adapted Interaction Journal, Special Issue: Adaptive Hypertext & Hypermedia*, *6*(2-3), 87-129.

Brusilovsky, P., Schwarz, E., & Weber, G. (1996). *ELM-ART: An intelligent tutoring system on World Wide Web*. Intelligent tutoring systems, Berlin, Springer-Verlag, (LNCS 1086, pp. 261-269).

Brusilovsky, P., (2001). Adaptive hypermedia. *User Modeling and User-Adapted Interaction Journal*, *11*(1-2), 87-110.

Brusilovsky, P., Karagiannidis, C., & Sampson, D. (2001). The benefits of layered evaluation of adaptive applications and services. *International Conference on User Modeling, Workshop on Empirical Evaluations of Adaptive Systems* (pp. 1-8). Sonthofen, Germany.

Chou, L. D. Wu, C. H., & Lee, S. P. (2004). Position-aware multimedia mobile learning systems in museums. *Web-Based Education Conference* (pp. 416-229). Innsbruck, Austria.

Conati, C., Gertner, A., VanLehn, K., & Druzdzel, M. (1997). On-line student modeling for coached problem solving using Bayesian networks. *International Conference on User Modeling (UM97)* (pp. 231-242). Chia Laguna, Italy.

Conlan, O. & Wade, V. (2004). Evaluation of APeLS—an adaptive e-learning service based on the multi-model, metadata-driven approach. *International Conference on Adaptive Hypermedia & Adaptive Web-based Systems (AH2004)* (pp. 291-295). Eindhoven, Netherlands.

Cristea, A. I. & de Mooij, A. (2003). LAOS: Layered WWW AHS authoring model and their corresponding algebraic operators. *International World Wide Web Conference (WWW'03)*, Alternate Track on Education, Budapest, Hungary.

De Bra, P. & Calvi, L. (1998). AHA: A generic adaptive hypermedia system. *ACM HYPERTEXT'98 Conference, Workshop on Adaptive Hypertext and Hypermedia* (pp. 5-12). Pittsburgh, USA.

De Bra, P., Houben, G., & Wu, H. (1999). AHAM: A Dexter-based reference model for adaptive hypermedia. *ACM HYPERTEXT'99 Conference* (pp. 147-156). Germany.

Elissavet, G. & Economides, A. A., (2003). An evaluation instrument for hypermedia courseware. *Journal of International Forum of Educational Technology & Society and IEEE Learning Technology Task Force, 6*(2), 31-44.

Empirix (2003). *Assuring QoE on next generation networks.* White Paper, Retrieved from http://www.empirix.com/Empirix/Corporate/resources/resources+white+papers.html

Grigoriadou, M., Papanikolaou, K., Kornilakis, H., & Magoulas, G. (2001). INSPIRE: An intelligent system for personalized instruction in a remote environment. *Adaptive Hypertext and Hypermedia Workshop.* Sonthofen, Germany.

Heines, J. M. (2000). Evaluating the effect of a course Web site on student performance. *Journal of Computing in Higher Education, 12*(1), 57-83.

IEEE 802.11 (1999). Part 11: Wireless LAN Medium Access Control (MAC) & Physical Layer (PHY) Specifications, IEEE standard 802.11.

IEEE 802.16 (2004). Part 16: Air Interface for Fixed Broadband Wireless Access Systems, IEEE standard 802.16.

Jacobs, L. C. & Chase, C. I., (Eds.). (1992). *Developing and using tests effectively: A guide for faculty.* San Francisco: Jossey-Bass.

Karagiannidis, C., Sampson, D., & Brusilovsky, P. (2001). Layered evaluation of adaptive and personalized educational applications and services. *International Conference on Artificial Intelligence in Education, Workshop on Assessment Methods in Web-based Learning Environments and Adaptive Hypermedia* (pp. 21-29). San Antonio, TX.

Kay, J & Kummerfeld, R. J. (1994). An Individualised course for the C programming language. *International World Wide Web Conference.* Chicago.

Muntean, C. H. & McManis, J. (2006a). Fine grained content-based adaptation mechanism for providing high end-user quality of experience with adaptive hypermedia systems. *W3C International World Wide Web Conference (WWW'06), Hypermedia and Multimedia Track* (pp. 53-62). Edinburgh, UK. New York: ACM Press.

Muntean, C. H. & McManis, J. (2006b). *The value of QoE-based adaptation approach in educational hypermedia: Empirical evaluation.* Springer-Verlag, Berlin (LNCS 4018, pp.121-130).

Muntean, C. H. & McManis, J. (2006c). End-user quality of experience oriented adaptive e-learning system. *Journal of Digital Information, Special Issue on Adaptive Hypermedia, 7*(1). Retrieved from http://journals.tdl.org/jodi/issue/view/29

Muntean, C. H., McManis, J., & Muntean, G.-M. (2006). Improving the performance of content delivery in Web-based information systems. *China-Ireland International Conference on Information and Communications Technology* (pp. 430-435). Hangzhou, China.

Murphy, M. & McTear, M. (1997). Learner modeling for intelligent CALL. In Jameson A., Paris C. & Tasso C. (Eds.) *International Conference on User Modeling (UM97)* (pp. 301-312). Wien Austria: Springer-Verlag.

Nejdl, W. & Wolpers, M. (1999). KBS hyperbook—a data-driven information system on the Web. *W3C International World Wide Web Conference (WWW99).* Canada.

Ng, M. H., Hall, W., Maier, P., & Armstrong, R. (2002). The application and evaluation of adaptive hypermedia techniques in Web-based medical education. *Association for Learning Technology Journal, 10*(3), 19-40.

Nielsen J. (Ed.). (1994). *Heuristic evaluation. Usability inspection methods.* New York: Wiley.

O'Keeffe, I., Brady, A., Conlan, O., & Wade, V. (2006). Just-in-time generation of pedagogically sound, context sensitive personalized learning experiences. *International Journal on E-Learning (IJeL), Special Issue: Learning Objects in Context, 5*(1), 113-127.

Papanikolaou K. A., Grigoriadou M., Kornilakis H., & Magoulas G. D. (2003). Personalizing the interaction in a Web-based educational hypermedia system: The case of INSPIRE. *User Modeling and User-Adapted Interaction Journal, 13*(3), 213-267.

Pilar da Silva, D., Van Durm, R., Duval, E., & Olivié, H. (1998). Concepts and Documents for Adaptive Educational Hypermedia: A Model and a Prototype. *ACM HYPERTEXT'98 Conference, Workshop on Adaptive Hypertext and Hypermedia* (pp. 35-43). Pittsburgh, USA.

Preece, J. (Ed.). (2000). *Online communities: Designing usability, supporting sociability.* Chichester, UK: John Willey & Sons.

Ramsay, J., Barbasi, A., & Preece, J. (1998). A psychological investigation of long retrieval times on the World Wide Web. *Interacting with Computers Journal.* Elsevier Publishing House.

Servidge, P. (1999). How long is too long to wait for a Web site to load? *Usability News.*

Sevcik, P. J. (2002). Understanding how users view application performance. *Business Communications Review, 32*(7), 8-9.

Smyth, B. & Cotter, P. (2002). Personalized adaptive navigation for mobile portals. *European Conference on Artificial Intelligence* (pp. 608-612). Lyon, France.

Specht, M., Kravcik, M., Klemke, R., Pesin, L., & Huttenhain, R. (2002). Adaptive learning environ-ment in WINDS. *ED-MEDIA'02* (pp. 1846-1851), Denver, CO: AACE Press.

Triantafillou, E., Pomportsis. A, & Georgiadou, E. (2002). AESCS: adaptive educational system base on cognitive styles. *International Conference on Adaptive Hypermedia and Adaptive Web Based Systems (AH'2002), Workshop on Adaptive Systems for Web-Based Education* (pp. 10-20). Malaga, Spain.

Weber, G. & Möllenberg, A. (1995). ELM-Pro-gramming-Environment: A tutoring system for LISP beginners, cognition and computer pro-gramming. In Wender, K. F., Schmalhofer F. & Böcker, H. D. (Eds.) *Cognition and Computer Programming* (pp. 373-408). Toronto: Ablex Publishing Corporation.

Weber, G., Specht, M. (1997). User modelling and adaptive navigation supporting WWW-based tutoring systems. *International Conference on User Modeling (UM'97)* (pp. 289-300). Sardinia, Italy.

Weber, G. (1999). Adaptive learning systems in the World Wide Web. *International Conference on User Modeling (UM'99)* (pp. 371-378). Banff, Canada.

Weber, G., Kuhl, H. C., & Weibelzahl, S. (2001). Developing adaptive internet based courses with the authoring system NetCoach. *Workshop on Adaptive Hypertext and Hypermedia* (pp. 35-48). Sonthofen, Germany.

Weibelzahl, S. & Weber, G. (2002). Advantages, opportunities, and limits of empirical evalua-tions: Evaluating adaptive systems. *Künstliche Intelligenz Journal, 3*, 17-20.

Chapter X
E-Learning Systems Re-Engineering:
Functional Specifications and Component-Based Architecture

Lahcen Oubahssi
Université du Maine, France

Monique Grandbastien
Université Henri Poincaré, France

ABSTRACT

In this chapter, we propose functional specifications and a component-based architecture for designing e-learning platforms. An important feature is that the proposed specifications and architecture are based on the experience gained in an e-learning company and result from a re-engineering process. To guide the re-engineering process, we used two reference models, which are the e-learning global process and the e-learning global cycle. The functional specifications are described according to the e-learning global cycle phases and they are used to propose a software component-based architecture. The proposed kernel of components was completed with services to allow interoperability and standard compliance between several e-learning platforms. We hope that this case study exemplifies e-learning platform suppliers' needs and available pragmatic solutions. We conclude on foreseeable evolutions of e-learning actors' needs and practices and on new platform features for fulfilling such needs.

INTRODUCTION

The deployment of online training services generally relies on a software platform offering a variety of services. These platforms should be designed for fast, multiple evolutions because of new needs emergence for the actors and because of the advent of more powerful technological solutions.

Software engineering provides models, methods and tools for designing and implementing flexible software applications where requirements changes are systematically converted into code generation. The process works well for new applications. However, even if some free and open-source e-learning platforms are widely used, most systems are commercially developed. The platforms suppliers can make their offer evolve only from the existing one. In this context, general frameworks are missing for enabling designers to conceive new solutions from existing ones and to propose new services with an approach oriented towards interoperable and evolving components.

The proposals of this chapter are based on the experience gained when working within an e-learning company; they result from a re-engineering process and they aim at providing solutions that do not imply a design from scratch. We examined real users' needs as they were encountered in a company selling customized platforms and training solutions. Then, a re-engineering process conducted on the e-learning software provided by the company to its customers resulted in functional specification production according to a global formation view. Then, according to the identified functions, we organize existing components into a kernel of components, which implement the functions. Finally, based on the component kernel, we show how we implemented new services required by customers to allow interoperability between several platforms.

The chapter is structured as follows: In the next section, we briefly review some models which have been proposed in the e-learning domain and we present two models on which we have based our re-engineering work, which are the e-learning global process and the e-learning global cycle. In section three, we describe the functional specifications according to the e-learning global cycle phases. In section four, we detail a component-based kernel architecture elaborated from the functionalities specified in section three. Section five is devoted to describing the implementation of two services,

thus showing how it is possible to exploit the functional components defined in our kernel. We conclude by comparing these re-engineering achievements with other on-going approaches such as pattern languages, model-driven design, Web-services-based architectures and new needs emerging from new practices.

REFERENCE MODELS FOR E-LEARNING PLATFORMS DESIGN

As far as e-learning platforms architectures are concerned, we are interested in models that could act as a basis for design. Such models may belong either to software development models or to e-learning design models. In this paragraph we focus only on e-learning reference models. In this category, the processes that e-learning platforms should support are getting more and more complex, so this complex reality can only be represented through several viewpoints. Therefore, most of the existing models represent a partial view of the activity or are focused on a given category of actors. However, our goal is to rely on a model, which takes into account the whole life cycle of the production process from a small and medium enterprise (SME) perspective.

We first analyze as examples some proposed models, then we describe the two models on which we have based our re-engineering process.

Examples of Existing Models

Firstly, we briefly present one of the most complete sets of models that have been produced so far, the MISA Instructional Engineering Method for Learning Design by Paquette and his colleagues at LICEF (Paquette, 2004). Then, as increasing interoperability is crucial in the field, through agreement on standards, we describe the learning technology system architecture (LTSA) from (IEEE-LTSC, 2007) that has been discussed since the end of the 90s with a perspective of moving it to standardization bodies. Finally, we present the general ISO process production model that was refined into an open and distance learning (ODL) production process in our company. In addition to these partial models, there are also comparison studies, such as the e-learning platform benchmarks available from the Edutools Website (Edutools, 2007), based on a set of existing functions or roles or actors which could act as guidelines. Such approaches are useful, since partial models increase our understanding of a given actor or a given activity or a given sub-process, but they do not allow a global view of existing and forthcoming actors, roles and services. The ideal model should act as a framework for describing and comparing a wide range of existing and forthcoming systems.

The LICEF Model and the MISA Method

Paquette proposes a global view of the main processes in an e-learning system as well as the actors involved and the resources used (Paquette, 2004). MISA (Paquette et al., 1999) is an instructional engineering method supporting 35 main tasks and processes; it is strongly based on knowledge modeling and takes into account all the components of a learning system, relying on the solid experi-

ence gained by its authors in designing distance learning systems over time. The whole process is guided by general design principles. The method comes together with a myriad of various models representing different views at different abstraction levels, those models being provided to guide the learning system designer during the different steps of his activity. Progression into the method is through six phases and along four axes. MISA is supported by powerful tools such as MOT (for modeling using typed objects), its object-oriented knowledge model editor, allowing the construction of a graphic representation of knowledge as well as a formal one. It uses XML technologies, and is linked with the Explor@ platform.

Let us give an overview of the four axes. The first one is about content design; it allows modeling knowledge and skills. The second one is about pedagogical design, scenarios, activities and related issues. Support to new learning material production is brought through the third axis. Delivery planning is described through the last axis.

The proposed phases could fit our needs. However, MISA is very detailed, maybe too detailed, as many views have to be considered to guide platform architecture design. Moreover, other features as quality criteria, maintenance and updating, invoicing and other links for instance

Figure 1. MISA six phases and four axes adapted from Paquette (2004)

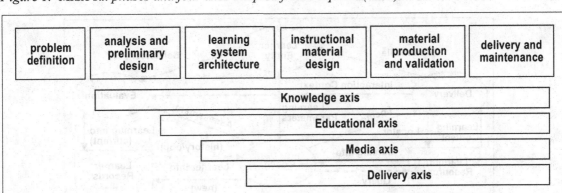

with accountancy services for day-to-day deployment in SMEs are less detailed or not taken into account.

LTSA: A Learning Technology System Architecture

The IEEE Learning Technology Standards Committee (IEEE LTSC) is made up of both people from industry and people from the academic area on an international level; it proposes an architecture (IEEE-LTSA draft 9, 2001) resulting from information technology and existing systems analysis and provides a framework for designing and comparing a range of learning systems over time.

This architecture takes into account different views of the learning activities and processes and of the associated software components:

- The context for the human actors.
- A component model of the organization.
- The software development cycle.

The architecture is first presented as a five-layer model. According to LTSA draft 9, these refinement layers are described as follows from highest to lowest levels:

- **Level 1:** This level is the most abstract and defines the tasks of acquisition, transfer, exchange and discovery for the learner as a result of the interactions with his environment. These environment and learner entities are seen as two systems exchanging information.
- **Level 2:** This layer, roughly detailed in the document, defines the learner's reaction to the environment.
- **Level 3:** A component system, defines an organization of a learning process seen from the data and control flow points of view.
- **Level 4:** This level exploits the component system directly in order to formalize the technological design constraints. It allows the identification of the system's activities during the learning process.
- **Level 5:** This level defines the abstract phases of the software development from a component-based approach.

They further develop layer 3 for the system components as shown in Figure 2. This central layer was the only mandatory one in the proposed standard specification.

The LTSA system components are:

Figure2. The LTSA system components

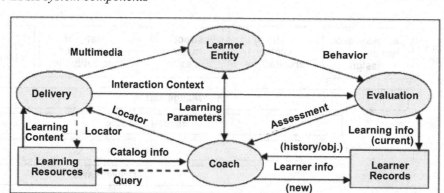

- **Processes:** Learner entity, evaluation, coach, and delivery.
- **Stores:** Learner records, learning resources.
- **Flows:** Learning preferences, behavior, assessment information, learner information (three times), query, catalogue info, locator (twice), learning content, multimedia and interaction context.

The architecture brings together contributions of several working groups from the educational technologies future standards. For example, take the group that defines metadata for a learning object. Its purpose is to respond to an interface requirement between the process controlling the learning process and the resources. This model was promoted as a standard within the IEEE committee and was submitted to the ISO/JTIC1/SC36 for standardization. The LTSA model did not receive the hoped-for success from the normalized educational technologies community. It is often criticized (O'Droma et al., 2003; Corbière & Choquet, 2004). Three principal limits of this model are highlighted: it is centered only on the technical aspects; it is limited to two storage units (learning resources & learner records); and it prohibits the creation or the update of a teaching resource.

Some of the categories (flows) encountered in the e-learning platform assessment exercise and considered for a future e-learning Virtual University Information System do not fit into the draft IEEE LTSA model. Therefore, this model (Layer 3 only) was modified to include additions and expansions of certain terms as shown in (O'Droma et al., 2003). For example, the locator flow was deemed to be too narrow in its focus. As such, it was expanded and ultimately replaced by the course materials development (CMD) flow. This flow not only covers the assigning of previously created material to a course, but also includes material creation, alteration, and removal functions. Any updating of the course learning material is dealt with through this flow. No options are included for the administration of the course by the instructor (coach). The LTSA model deals with learning content only. Therefore, the course configuration flow is included, which allows the course instructor to access the course's general configuration and set-up details.

The LTSA Layer 3 components only refer to an individual course. There is no allowance made for system administration functions in this model. These functions, along with the system administration flow are also included in the modified version.

Compared with our aims and needs, the LTSA also provides a rich set of models which focus on processes, stores and flows well adapted to our needs; however, the whole product life cycle is not well covered.

The ISO Production Process Model

To model a company's production process, we start from general models that reflect industrial production processes.

The general model recommended by ISO (International Organization for Standardization) for the production of any industrial activity can be considered as a commonly agreed synthesis of existing production process models. Therefore we take it as a starting reference. The general principles on which ISO9000 standards are based are the following:

Each industrial activity relies on a process. A process is defined as a set of interactive and interrelated activities, which transform input elements into output elements. So, each process is firstly described by its input data and its output data and the result of the process. Several processes may occur in a product life cycle; all together they describe the means and activities, which perform the transformation of input data into output data (ISO 8402). A process itself is composed of a set of transformations, which adds value to the input data. These transformations are dependent on external factors and resources, namely performances, material resources and human resources.

The Proposed Process-Oriented View

From these definitions we derive a process-oriented view of online learning production.

For open and distance learning production, input elements include knowledge, know-how, and curricula. Input elements suppliers are teachers, trainers, training resources designers, technicians, administrators and other domain specialists. Output elements include training sessions, evaluation and testing modules, scores and other learner information. The main customers for this data are the learners. The global process is enabled by external factors such as material resources (equipment, computer-based services) and human resources (teachers, tutors, training administrative staff). Other constraints or success criteria are described under the performance (financial cost, quality management, success criteria) and progress (duration, calendar constraints) items.

It is very important to start from a process-oriented approach, to facilitate the production of a training activity in the same framework as

any other production process in a company to be considered.

Moreover this model has been proposed and accepted during the ISO/JTC1/SC36 meeting in Seoul (2003). So, it is an internationally acknowledged model built in agreement with other general quality models.

However, we need complementary views to take into account the way in which sub-processes are scheduled over time and the support these sub-processes are given or are not given by existing services. Indeed we aim to design a "complete" distance learning platform; "complete" means that it follows the complete life cycle training production process. Thus in the next paragraph we present a life-cycle view of the process (Grandbastien et al., 2003).

The Proposed Life-Cycle View

As shown in Figure 4, we propose to describe the complete cycle of a course through five main phases: creation phase, orientation phase, training phase, evaluation phase, and administration phase. A presentation order has to be chosen, but it may be that these phases do not occur linearly as reality is more complex.

Figure 3. Open and distance learning production process

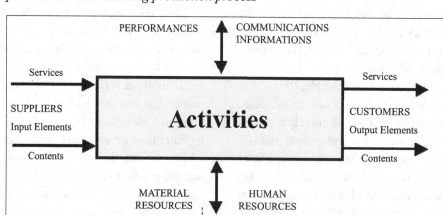

Creation Phase

In this phase the author creates educational material while using an authoring tool available on the platform. He can also import external modules and aggregate various formats.

Orientation Phase

This phase allows the adaptation of the available courses to the learner's or group of learners needs. The training adviser defines the sequence of training material that is going to be integrated in the learner's process. Every sequence takes into account, on one hand, users educational data (learners, groups, subgroup) such as the objectives and the levels, and on the other hand, information about the available educational elements (educational modules, training plans, degree course, booklet...).

Learning Phase

In this phase, the learner consults his/her electronic booklet and can follow his/her educational modules. He/she performs evaluation activities and he/she collaborates with the other actors on the platform (teachers and other learners). The communication tools used in this phase vary from a platform to another one (forum, chat, white board, etc.). According to the needs and the means, some feedback is provided to tutors for exploitation in the next sessions.

Follow-Up And Evaluation Phase

The follow-up of the learner and his/her evaluation are key elements in the training products cycle. Their use during a session is processed at the end of every session of training. Indeed, the educational follow-up allows the teachers to see

Figure 4. The life cycle of ODL products

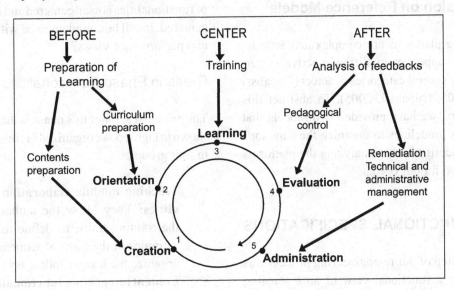

what activities are carried out by the learner during his/her training and to record data on these activities in order to analyze them.

The evaluation tests allow the teachers to measure the level reached by the learners and to compare it with the learning objectives. The tests can also be exploited for future training sessions. In addition to the learner follow up, there is also a need for product evaluation, experience feedback so as to further improve learning material and module sequencing.

Administration Phase

In this phase, the teachers (administrators of the course) manage the educational and administrative aspects of the course. The educational part includes learner management, group management, degree course management, certification delivery and experience feedback management.

The administrative aspects include: user management, access management, payment management, invoice issuing and links with other information systems.

Conclusion on Reference Models

E-learning platforms are complex artifacts designed to support many different activities performed by several categories of actors (Oubahssi et al., 2005; Oubahssi, 2005). To abstract this complexity, we have provided two models that we use as guidelines to organize the functions that we identified when analyzing the platforms customized for our clients.

THE FUNCTIONAL SPECIFICATIONS

The first step of our re-engineering process was to provide a functional view of an e-learning platform in order to design any new platform at a functional level (implementation independent level) before moving to a software-component architecture. A functional architecture (Pressman, 2005) is intended to provide a general framework, describing the expected functions of the system through several views.

The life-cycle viewpoint, together with the experience gained by working with e-learning customers, helps to list and organize the identified functions according to the five proposed phases. The result is described as a functionalities classification. The ODL production process model supports specifying the human and the material resources of an e-learning system as well as the system's expected performances. The corresponding functions are presented in the human and material resources specifications and in the system's performance specification subparagraphs. In the last section, we summarize the various functionalities, which cover the ODL life cycle and we observe the respective coverage degree for the different phases.

Functionalities Classification

In this section, we detail the functionalities according to the ODL cycle five phases. The resulting set of functionalities is user-centered and e-learning-centered. It will be complemented with technical and performance views.

Creation Phase Functionalities

The principal actor of this phase is the author. As shown in Figure 5, we organized his functionalities in four groups:

- **Teaching module elaboration functionalities:** They allow the author to define the training units, to define the teaching activities in the form of sequences, and to organize the learner follow-up.
- **Content integration functionalities:** They make it possible to integrate the contents (text and multimedia). To perform this task, the author is provided with dedicated func-

Figure 5. The creation phase functionalities

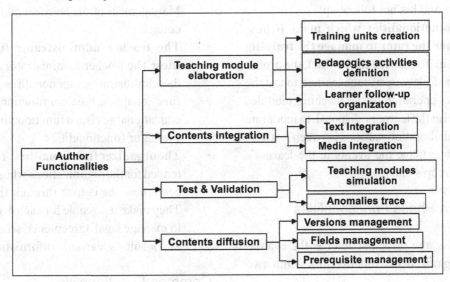

tions for hypertext creation and multimedia content production.

- **Test and validation functionalities:** They make it possible for the author to run the module, check its behavior and to trace anomalies.
- **Content diffusion functionalities:** They make it possible for the author to manage module versions and to publish them in the LMS by specifying their domain.

Orientation Phase Functionalities

The principal actor of this phase is the training adviser. We organized his/her functionalities in four groups:

- **Management of learner and groups functionalities:** They make it possible to create the educational path and the learner booklet and to integrate events in the calendar.
- **Sets of learning modules management functionalities:** Learning modules are packed together according to a given learn-

ing objective or organizational objective defined by the training adviser.

- **Contents definition and formation plans management functionalities:** A training plan is composed of a set of learning modules; it is characterized by a precise planning.
- **Planning management functionalities:** They are intended for commercial courses delivered during working hours (i.e., check and certify how much time the learner has spent).

Training Phase Functionalities

The principal actors of this phase are: the learner and the tutor. We organized their functionalities in two groups:

- **The functionalities which allow a learner to follow his/her training session:** to reach his/her booklet, to execute his/her teaching modules, to work in collaboration with the members of his/her groups, to carry out his/her evaluations and to consult his/her profile and his/her follow-up.

- **The functionalities which make it possible for the tutor to manage the training session:** To manage the booklet, the profile and the follow-up of each learner, to test the correct operation of the teaching modules placed at the learners' disposal, to moderate the collaboration sessions between learners and to manage the events in the learner's and group's diary.

Evaluation Phase Functionalities

In this phase, the principal actor is the evaluator. We organized his functionalities into two groups:

- **Elaboration tests functionalities:** They make it possible for the evaluator to create tests in the form of questions with single or multiple choices, association tests and open questions, using a built-in tool or any of the other existing tools.
- **Management functionalities:** They make it possible to manage the tests (attribution, modification and suppression). They allow also the management of learner follow-up.

Administration Phase Functionalities

In this phase, we distinguish four principal actors: general administrator, accounts manager, teacher administrator, and organizer. We have arranged the functionalities into four groups:

- **The general administrator functionalities:** to manage the training domains, the disciplines, the levels, the documents exchanged during the collaborative sessions, the teaching modules displayed in the platform, the user accounts, the schedules and the legal contracts for the paying formations.

- **The accounts manager functionalities:** Management of the learners and group accounts.
- **The teacher administrator functionalities:** The teacher administrator can access the administrative functionalities, the author functionalities, the tutor functionalities, the educational adviser's functionalities and the evaluator functionalities.
- **The organizer functionalities:** They are intended for the organizations whose employees follow the course through the system. They make it possible for each organization to manage legal agreements, schedules and to consult its learners' information.

Common Functionalities

In this part we grouped the common functionalities of the five-phase cycle such as the help functionalities, the diary functionalities, the documents management functionalities, etc.

Human And Material Resources Specifications

The functionalities relating to human and material resources, which support an e-learning system are essential ones for service quality, either at the material level (i.e., the components necessary for the system correct operation), or at the human level (i.e., the people who take care of the system maintenance).

The Human Resources Functionalities Specifications

The more complex e-learning systems become, the more functionalities they include and the more "technical"—either human or machine—support they need. That requires services and human resources, which maintain the correct system operation and which meet the user's needs if problems happen. The listed services are not specific to the e-learning sector, however, they are still often underestimated. This type of service is provided by private organizations that market this type of system. It has started to be taken into account in public organizations too. The principal tasks that should be provided by such a service include the following:

- System documentation and of documentation updates production when update evolutions are brought on the system. Let us note that documentation and online help represent major elements for the system users (administrators, teachers and learners).
- Training about the system functionalities. Most of the time these courses concern the teaching staff, they aim at making them familiar with this type of system, and to explain the role and the importance of each functionality to them. It can also be followed by technicians in charge of the system's technical maintenance.
- Personalization of the interfaces and the scenarios. The ergonomic aspects and the scenarios defined in this type of system, have a great impact on the users. Indeed, they offer a convivial environment for a better achievement of the training courses.
- Ensure the support and the maintenance of the system software and hardware. These functionalities are ensured by engineering departments deployed or by the organizations that market the system, or by the organizations' users. The role of these services is to even ensure the correct system operation by taking care on the system maintenance.

The Material Resources Functionalities Specifications

The material resources functionalities supplement those of human resources. The material resources

deployed for the e-learning system use have a great influence on the customers' choice. Indeed, the arrival of the open source solutions, and the proposal of adaptable kernel of functionalities such as free components for the production of this type of system have influenced the customers' choice. The principal material resources characteristics are:

- **Technology used:** We distinguish two particular cases, the first relates to the use of very advanced technologies. This case implies a high performance level for speed, system efficiency and the management of a large number of users. The second relates to the use of free technologies, in this case human resources must increase their efforts to solve problems resulting from this type of technology. Among the material resources used: the Web servers, data base systems, the customer specific software and user machine configurations (memory size, navigator version, etc.).
- **Configuration and installation of the system:** The technology used has a great influence on the configuration and the installation of the system and even on its maintenance. The configuration and installation functionalities of the system make it possible to define all elements necessary to start the system. Among these functionalities, we can note: the configurations of Web servers and the user station. The installation specifications thus allow us to define the procedure.

The security functionalities represent one of the major elements which define the performance of e-learning systems at the present time. We found four security points: system installation, system access, digital resources stored on the server and access to personal and administrative data within the system.

System Performances Specifications

The system performances are largely related to the material and human resources indicated above, they are also related to other external parameters with the system. We grouped the e-learning system performances under the following points:

- Access time, depending on the Internet connection type and of the network used.
- Server power, inducing performances in terms of storage of information and speed access to the data and the resources.
- Security, one of the most important criteria when choosing a system (already described in the previous paragraph).
- Management of multilingual versions, the simultaneous management of several languages, the possibility of an easy adaptation of a new terminology used by the new users.

Conclusion

In this part, we have described the functionalities of the system and organized them according to the five phases of the proposed ODL cycle. Let us remember that an important character of the work described here is that it is a bottom-up analysis based on the activities of the users as they appeared through the user requirements. Consequently, the described functions were implemented at least on one of the customized e-learning platforms sold by the company. As a first result of this organization, we observe the following features: the phases which are well covered by our platform functionalities are the creation, training and management phases. The phases which are less covered are the orientation and evaluation phases. This result led our company to develop new modules for a better coverage of the whole cycle (Oubahssi, 2005).

The two models have guided and supported the organization of the observed functionalities. We

could talk of a kind of "model aware" approach for organizing the listed functions. A real model-driven approach (Wang et al., 2003), would need a more formal functional model and then include steps and translation rules ensuring code generation, which is not compatible with a bottom-up approach. The next step of our re-engineering process aims at organizing software components in the same way as we organized functions. The adopted approach is again a very pragmatic one and should result into an operational set of reusable software components.

IMPLEMENTATION OF THE FUNCTIONALITIES IN A SET OF COMPONENTS

One of the present LMS characteristics is that they are neither adaptable to specific users needs or adapted to specified needs, nor implemented to be re-used in new contexts.

In this paragraph, we present the functional specifications implementation in the form of a components kernel. Component-based software design is now a current practice in software engineering. This approach aims at increasing production speed and at reusing existing code. Component- and service-oriented architectures help to build software that is more easily understood, changed and reused.

It is well adapted to the design or the adaptation of LMS. An important reason which prevents software engineers from reusing existing pieces of software is that the modularization principles applied at the functional level are not the same as those applied at the component level for organizing files into directory hierarchies (De Jonge, 2005). The proposed kernel represents an organization of the functionalities into reusable modules. The proposed components organization is derived from the functions described in the previous paragraph as well as from the constraints imposed by the existing pieces of code. We have tried to keep the same organization as described in the functional level. So there is no direct link with the ODL cycle phases; which function is implemented in which component is explained in the textual components description. Our approach can be seen as a compromise between a top-down approach (from functional specifications) and a bottom-up approach (from existing code).

A Multi-Layered Architecture

These components are organized in four levels, from a very high one to sets of more and more detailed parts.

Some components are not further subdivided because they are implemented as black boxes in the software we analyzed; they are also known as vertical components in software components categorization.

Figure 6 shows the various levels that constitute the kernel that we elaborated. Its first level comprises two large modules: A design module allowing the preparation of the e-learning resources, and a delivery module for the learning

management. Indeed some customers were only interested in the delivery functions and not in the authoring ones.

The Design Module

The components gathered under this label implement the functionalities specified in the creation phase. It is broken up into three modules: the elaboration module, the test module and the version management module. These three modules can be re-used independently. They are included in the category of the "pedagogic software components." They form reusable components devoted to the exploration of the teaching resources. They belong to the vertical components. They are not open; they are implemented in the form of a black box (Ambjörn et al., 2005; Grob et al., 2003, 2004).

The Elaboration Module

This module is made of two sub-modules, one for the conception of the learning modules, and

Figure 6. The kernel of components

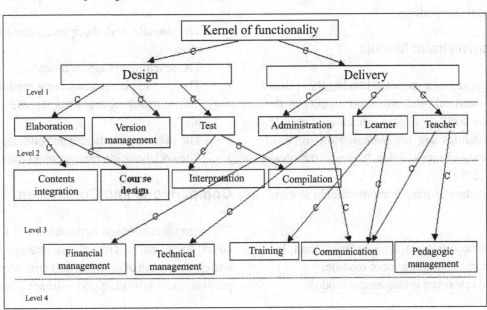

the other for the development and integration of the contents.

The Test Module

The test module makes it possible to test the operation of a teaching module. It allows us to find anomalies, and to correct them. It consists of two sub-modules: the interpreter who sequentially interprets the course sequence contents, and the compiler whose role is to translate the sources into the executable format.

The Version Management Module

The version management module allows the author, once he/she finalized his/her teaching module, to manage the module's version either for a media support (i.e., DVD), or for the Web.

The Delivery Module

Delivery is a composed component; it consists of three modules devoted to the administrator, learner and teacher activities. They also form reusable components devoted to the management of the formation. They belong to what is called the vertical components.

The Administrator Module

It is composed of a module allowing the technical and financial administration aspects of the course as well as a communication module. These modules are implemented as software components services (Allen & Frost, 1998; Najjar et al., 2003).

The technical management module is composed of:

- The accounts users management module.
- The rights management module.
- The resources management module.

The financial management module is composed of:

- The contracts management module.
- The payment management module.
- The conventions management module.

As for the communication module, it is composed of the following modules: forum, chat, diary, e-mail, NetMeeting, and resource sharing.

The Learner Module

The leader module is composed of a module allowing a learner to follow his training in the e-learning system and to communicate with his tutors and the members of his groups. The training module is composed of the following modules:

- The follow-up teaching module.
- The booklet module.
- The course module.

The Teacher Module

The teaching module is composed of the following modules:

- The domain and disciplines management module.
- The teaching resources module.
- The course plan management module.
- The learning courses management module.
- The planning management module.
- The collaboration management module.

Comparisons and Conclusion

The components-based approach takes into account requirements of reusability, interoperability and co-operation of systems, and aims to prevent programmers rewriting code already developed by others. It ensures that other programmers (and even the users) will be able to easily integrate these tools in a given environment. Such an approach generates a considerable saving of time and resources. In section 3, we followed a functional and downward approach. The one presented in this section is modular, technical and rather ascending, as we started from the existing code. We succeeded in providing a component-based architecture with maps corresponding to the proposed functional organization. Each component implements one or several of the identified functions. We hope that both models will allow the design and customization of new platforms including existing components and new developed components, allowing user centered design and interoperability of data and services.

This vision makes it possible to define a new engineering approach for ICT environments dedicated to education, according to which it is possible to build or adapt a given e-learning system starting from existing elements. It is opposed to the traditional approaches in which the construction of a new system starts from scratch and requires reinventing the wheel each time.

Lastly, we mentioned two important goals: to have a modular view, which will simplify adaptations to new customer requirements (to add or remove one component, to replace a given component by a more specific one), and in the second time, to identify the components sensitive to interoperability with external systems. In the next section, we present services implementation, which deals with interoperability issues.

SERVICE INTEROPERABILITY BETWEEN E-LEARNING SYSTEMS

In this paragraph, we show an example of services implementation, which exploits the kernel components to answer an LMS(s) interoperability request. Currently, e-learning actors are confronted with two main problems. On one

hand, a lack of open e-learning systems due to their closed vision of the services, on the other, a lack of consensus at an international level and, consequently, the absence of "standards," even if more and more commonly agreed specifications are becoming available. Consequently, today the problem of selecting a platform often arises in terms of choosing some existing standards to respect or to adopt, rather than in terms of suitable functionalities.

To illustrate this need, we describe two service-oriented components, which complement the previously described set of components. Our objective is to enable a given LMS to easily use the already existing services in another system, and to offer its own services to others.

The first one allows the management of standardized contents, in particular resources, which are AICC and SCORM compliant. The second service allows the management of learner data recorded during e-learning courses. To implement the needed exchanges, our solution is based on Web services, in particular on the following protocols: SOAP "Simple Object Access Protocol," WSDL "Web Services Language Description" and UDDI "Universal Description, Discovery and Integration" (WSDL) (Vossen & Westerkamp, 2003). Indeed new platform architectures are fully Web service-oriented such as TELOS from the LORNET project (Paquette et al., 2006).

Before describing each service, we will give a short overview of existing specifications for the e-learning standards field.

E-Learning Standards For Interoperability

Many key players in the field of Web-based learning content issues are joining their efforts under the leadership of ADL (advanced distributed learning, trademark) They aim to forge alliances in strategic technical areas in order to accelerate the speed of standard adoption and to allow Web-based contents to be widely reusable. One major result of their efforts is SCORM, a Sharable Content Object Reference Model (ADL). SCORM was built for vendors and toolmakers, not for designers. It deals with content aggregation and run-time environment, how to run content and to track learners, how to manage learner's data exchanges between the delivery place and the LMS. SCORM actors define a LMS as a server-based environment to control the delivery of learning content to the student. They intend to be LMS neutral.

As soon as this model was built, many educational designers pointed out that describing content was useless, without describing learning objectives, pedagogical scenarios in which learner and tutors activities and their interactions are organized. Several educational modeling languages (EML) (Rawlings et al., 2002; Koper, 2003) have been designed to fulfil this need. An EML is a semantic information model and binding, describing the content and process within a "unit of learning" from a pedagogical perspective in order to support reuse and interoperability of the given unit. EML from the NL Open University has been chosen as the basis for the IMS LD specification provided by the IMS consortium. Moreover, IMS LD features have recently been incorporated into SCORM. Similarly, the IMS Global Consortium develops open technical specifications to support distributed learning. Examples include Digital Repositories, Learner Information Package, Query Test Interoperability, etc.

SCORM and IMS actors are not yet providing standards for the whole learning delivery process. Specific services have yet to be developed to allow interoperability between e-learning platforms.

Content Management Service

The customer's request: The e-learning platform should be able to exchange learning contents with external providers and clients.

The content management service relates to the mechanisms of content declaration at the level of a provider system and the mechanisms of external access to these contents. To make sure that a customer system benefits from the services of a provider system, it must declare its resources at the level of this provider system. These resources can be hosted on any server and not necessarily the same one as the provider system. For each declared resource, the system provides the customer with the data allowing access to both resources and services for pedagogical follow-up data processing. The main ones are:

- A module code is a single access code to the module. According to the different cases, this module code will be able to be multi-user and will allow the launch of several sessions by different learners.
- An external access address for the pedagogical module.
- A return code is a code indicating the restitution method of the pedagogical follow-up data. According to the different cases, this data could be processed by the customer system or the provider system offering standard services.
- An access address to the pedagogical follow-up data processing services.

This information is provided to the customer system in the shape of a Web component in XML format which can be integrated directly at the level of the customer system. Corresponding files can be hosted anywhere. A provider system and its customer use open protocols such as SOAP, WSDL or a private data format. The external access to a pedagogical resource by a customer system requires the transmission of the following data: the access address to the pedagogical module, the pedagogical module code and the user code. With the launch of each pedagogical module, the provider system requests the pedagogical module code and an additional user code making it possible to distinguish the users. Depending on customer use, the user code can be generated in a dynamic way.

So a kind of packaging with key parameters transmission has been easily set up to fulfil the requirement and added to the existing components.

Learner Data Management Service

The customer's request: During a training session, learners should use a training module running on another e-learning platform.

The term "learner data" indicates here the follow-up (or feedback) of learner's activities and results of training. It includes the follow-up of pedagogical modules carried out, time spent, and the number of times that the learner required the tutor and tests results. Within the framework of a teaching solution, this course could be personalized according to the progress of the learner. In the learning course, the follow-up data are generated and managed by the provider system. Two cases are possible (Oubahssi & Grandbastien, 2006):

- **No assumption of responsibility of the follow-up data by the customer system.** If the customer system cannot deal with the management of the follow-up data, this data is recorded in a provider system data base which provides, in addition to the data, the access services to the follow-up data. The access to data and services is done according to the same protocol. When interested in a particular user, his/her user code can be specified.
- **Assumption of responsibility of the follow-up data by the customer system.** In this case, the customer system has his/her own data processing modules, this data is provided during the progress of the training and especially at the end of a learning session according to the protocol of data transmission desired by the customer: this data is exchanged through an XML format according to a predefined exploitable schema.

Again we have been able to design a service component to answer the customer's request. Confronted with the global solution of services offered by LMS and with the lack of consensus and the lack of a "standard" adopted by all, the objective of this study was to propose an interoperability solution for the contents and systems as well as a new framework oriented towards the opening of learning management. The application service provider (ASP) system model that we have just proposed is intended to facilitate the opening of the LMS. This approach should contribute to the opening of the learning management environments and provide more data exchanges and services between LMS. This opening allows standards to be used together within a heterogeneous environment. Likewise, provider systems provide companies with an economic model, which is both open and flexible, thus allowing them to be able to use pedagogical resources effectively internally or externally. A provider system has the economic advantage to resort only to services that are necessary and to give a good financial payoff.

CONCLUSION

There are many developments and papers dealing with e-learning platform architectures from different viewpoints. Some are based on the distribution of working tasks (content provider services, content discovery services, content brokering services, training services, etc.) (Capuano et al., 2003). Other architectures are based on the grid, for instance the "data grid" to integrate idle computer resources in enterprises into e-learning platforms, thus eliminating the need to purchase costly high-level servers and other equipment (Chao-Tung & Hsin-Chuan, 2005).

In this chapter, we have proposed two reference models, which are in line with production processes in companies and cover the application field properly. We have then proposed a functional specification and a component-based architecture for designing e-learning platforms. Both are the result of a re-engineering process conducted within a SME, customizing e-learning software to fulfill its clients' needs. Finally we have shown how to complement the proposed kernel of components with two services to allow interoperability and standard compliance between several e-learning platforms as requested by a client.

A next step should lead to a more visible standard compliance of requirements on the architecture, especially in the component decomposition. The platform producer is thus able to easily identify which components have to be updated or changed when a new standard is adopted and to schedule the updating process.

A promising approach in software engineering is to guide the design with a collection of software patterns. The same approach is mentioned by Avgeriou et al. (2003) and Koper and Tattersall (2005), for learning design where patterns are supposed to reflect the experts' experience in the field. At the crossroads of software engineering and learning design, e-learning platforms design should benefit from the same approach. In such a perspective, our proposed detailed function descriptions could act as a first set of pattern proposals. Another point that is worthwhile for further investigation is the possible relationship between architecture patterns and learning design patterns.

Another trend in software engineering is the model-driven approach (Avgeriou et al., 2003; Paquette et al., 2006). The models we have proposed have been used as informal guidelines and reference models. The question of deriving a complete e-learning platform design from an adequate set of models comes out of the present SME working context. It could also be a follow-up of the present work.

However, many challenges have to be considered for the future since existing platforms are more centralized on management tools than distributed learning enablers. There is a growing demand for blended learning and peer to peer communication support. In our view, the main points that future platforms should address evolution capacities and adaptability, completely distributed architectures and ubiquitous computing, which means dealing with context changes. Proposals in this direction have been made by the EDUTELLA project and are reported in Ambjörn et al. (2005).

REFERENCES

Allen, P. & Frost, S. (1998). *Component-based development for enterprise systems: Applying the SELECT perspective.* New York: Cambridge University Press.

Ambjörn, N., Mikael, N., Matthias, P., & Fredrik, P. (2005). Contributions to a public e-learning platform: Infrastructure; architecture; frameworks; tools. *International Journal of Learning Technology, 1*(3), 352-381.

Avgeriou, P., Papasalouros, P., Retails, S., & Skordalakis, E. (2003). Towards a pattern language for learning management systems. *Educational Technology & Society, 6*(2), 11-24. Retrieved from http://ifets.ieee.org/periodical/6-2/2.html

Avgeriou, P., Retalis, S., & Skordalakis, M. (2003). An architecture for open learning management systems. In Y. Manolopoulos et al. (Eds.), PCI 2001, Springer-Verlag, Berlin Heidelberg. (LNCS 2563, pp. 183-200).

Capuano, N., Gaeta, M., & Pappacena, L. (2003). An e-Learning platform for SME manager upgrade and its evolution toward a distributed training environment. In *2nd International LeGE-WG Workshop on e-Learning and Grid Technologies: A Fundamental Challenge for Europe.* Paris.

Chao-Tung, Y. & Hsin-Chuan, H. (2005). An e-Learning platform based on grid architecture. *Journal of Information Science and Engineering, 21*(5), 911-928.

Corbière, A. & Choquet, C. (2004). Designer integration in training cycles: IEEE LTSA model adaptation. *International Conference on Computer Aided Learning in Engineering Education (CALIE 2004)*, Grenoble (pp. 51-62).

De Jonge, M. (2005). Build level components. *IEEE Transactions on Software Engineering, 31*(7).

Edutools. (2007). Retrieved March, 2007, from http://www.edutools.info/index.jsp?pj=1

Grandbastien, M., Oubahssi, L., & Claës, G. (2003). A process-oriented approach for modelling online learning environments. In *Intelligent Management Systems, AIED2003 supplemental proceedings, volume 4* (pp. 140-152). University of Sydney pub., Retrieved March, 2007, from http://www.cs.usyd.edu.au/~aied/vol4/vol4_oubahssi.pdf

Grob, H L., Bensberg, F., & Dewanto, B L. (2003). Model-driven architecture (MDA): Integration and model reuse for open source e-learning platforms. *E-learning and education (eleed) Journal*. Retrieved from http://eleed.campussource.de/

Grob, H. L., Bensberg, F., & Dewanto, B. L. (2004). Developing, deploying, using and evaluating an open source learning management system. *Journal of Computing and Information Technology 12*(2), 127-134.

IEEE-LTSA draft 9. (2001). *Draft Standard for Learning Technology—Learning Technology System Architecture*. IEEE LTSC pub.

IEEE-LTSC. (2007). Retrieved March, 2007, from http://ieeeltsc.org

Koper, R. (2003). Combining re-usable learning, resources and services to pedagogical purposeful units of learning. In A. Littlejohn (Ed.), *Reusing online resources: A sustainable approach to eLearning* (pp. 46-59). London: Kogan Page.

Koper, R., & Tattersall, C. (2005). *Learning design: A handbook on modelling and delivering networked education and training*. Berlin: Springer-Verlag.

Najjar, J., Duval, E., Ternier, S., & Neven, F. (2003). Towards Interoperable Learning Object Repositories: the ARIADNE Experience. In *IADIS International Conference WWW/Internet 2003* (pp. 219-226). Algarve, Portugal.

O'Droma M.S., Ganchev, I., & McDonnell, F. (2003). Architectural and functional design and evaluation of e-learning VUIS based on the proposed IEEE LTSA reference model. *The Internet and Higher Education, 6*(3), 263-276.

Oubahssi, L. (2005). *Conception de plates-formes logicielles pour la formation à distance, présentant des propriétés d'adaptabilité à différentes catégories d'usagers et d'interopérabilité avec d'autres environnements logiciels*, PhD dissertation, University Paris5, René Descartes, France.

Oubahssi, L. & Grandbastien, M. (2006). From learner information packages to student models: Which continuum?. In M. Ikeda, K. Ashley & T.-W. Chan (Eds.), *The 8th International Conference on Intelligent Tutoring Systems Proceedings*. (LNCS 4053, pp. 604-614).

Oubahssi, L., Grandbastien, M., Ngomo, M., & Claës, G. (2005). The activity at the center of the global open and distance learning process. In *Proceedings of AIED (Artificial Intelligence in Education)* (pp. 386-394). Amsterdam: IOS Press.

Paquette, G. (2004). *Instructional engineering in networked environments*. San Francisco: Pfeiffer & Company, J. Wiley.

Paquette, G., Aubin, C., & Crevier, F. (1999). MISA: A knowledge-based method for the engineering of learning systems. *Journal of Courseware Engineering, 2.*

Paquette, G., Rosca, I., Mihaila, S., & Masmoudi, A. (2006). TELOS, a service-oriented framework to support learning and knowledge management. In S. Pierre (Ed.), *E-learning networked environments and architectures: A knowledge processing perspective.* Berlin: Springer-Verlag.

Pressman, R. S., (2005). *Software engineering—A practitioner's approach.* New York: McGraw-Hill Professional.

Rawlings, A., Van Rosmalen, P., Koper, R., Rodriguez-Artacho, M., & Lefrere, P. (2002). *Survey of Educational Modelling Languages (EMLs),* Version 1, CEN/ISSS WS/LT.

Vossen, G. & Westerkamp, P. (2003). E-Learning as a Web service, in *Proceedings of the Seventh International Database Engineering and Applications Symposium (IDEAS'03).*

Wang, H. & Zhang, D. (2003). MDA-based development of e-learning system. In *Proceedings of the 27th Annual International Computer Software and Applications Conference (COMPSAC'03).*

Section III
Applications and
Educational Perspectives

Section III.a
Specific Application Contexts

Chapter XI
An Integrated Architecture for Supporting Vocational Training

C. Bouras
Research Academic Computer Technology Institute and University of Patras, Greece

E. Giannaka
Research Academic Computer Technology Institute and University of Patras, Greece

Th. Tsiatsos
Research Academic Computer Technology Institute and Aristotle University of Thessaloniki, Greece

ABSTRACT

E-learning and Web-based training have evolved over time from a newborn trend for complementing the learning process to a major form of education and training for supporting mainly geographically scattered users. The basic aim of this chapter is the description of a platform for open and distance training, which is mainly focused at supporting the needs of Vocational Training Centers as well as of institutions providing life-long adult training and learning. In particular, the issues that this chapter focuses on are vocational education and training characteristics and requirements, the current situation and technological trends in ICT-supported VET, the development framework and processes while it also proposes basic vocational training services and the system architecture of the integrated platform. The presented platform aims to provide services of both synchronous and asynchronous and collaborative distance learning.

INTRODUCTION

Information and communication technologies (ICT) have been considered, from the early begin-

ing, a facilitator to education and knowledge. The evolution of these technologies in combination to the emerging of new technologies over time as well as the high degree of familiarization of individuals with their use offer advanced possibilities for learning and training. To this direction much research and work has been realized for defining the basic components an e-learning/training system should have as well as for extracting the basic needs of the users that these systems target. However, learning and training, can be applied to a wide variety of fields and areas, each of which is accompanied by some special characteristics related to the field of learning/training, the tools needed for the realization of the training process as well as the familiarization of the target audience to the selected technologies. Most of the technologies used for providing and supporting distance learning and training need to address a variety of challenges, which are related, among others, to the provision of education to an increasing number of users as well as the training with, and in fast, changing technologies, and improvement of the instructional systems (Herremans, 1995).

One of the cases where Web-based training can be effectively adopted is the vocational education and training (VET). At the beginning, the main goal of vocational education and training was to prepare trainees (workers or students) for entry-level jobs in occupations requiring less than a baccalaureate degree. However, as stated by Levesque et al. (2000), "The last decade, this purpose has shifted toward broader preparation that develops the academic, vocational, and technical skills of students in vocational education programs." The introduction and incorporation of ICT in vocation training for the development of new and advanced ways of training and learning emerges as a necessity in the rapidly changing technological society. Furthermore, advanced technologies for training (simulations, communication, collaboration and assessment tools) can increase the array of learning opportunities both for the trainees and the trainers (OVAE, 2006).

Currently, there is a great number of tools and systems developed for providing and supporting Web-based training processes. In their vast majority, these systems choose either a synchronous,

asynchronous or collaborative mode for achieving their goal with little or no integration and combination of these modes. The basic aim of this chapter is the description of a platform for open and distance training, which is mainly focused at supporting the needs of vocational training centers as well as of institutions providing life-long adult training and learning. The presented platform aims to provide services of synchronous, asynchronous and collaborative distance learning into one integrated system.

The chapter is structured as follows: Section 2 presents the background on vocational education and training, in terms of the current situation on ICT-supported VET as well as on the current trends in online VET technologies. Section 3 describes the basic vocational training features characteristics and requirements so as to define the differences and modification in regard to other types of education and for extracting the needs and motivation of the target users. The section that follows presents the framework for the support of vocational training, which is built upon the basic needs of the targeted users. Section 5 describes a set of proposed services that such a system should provide and support, based on the requirements, features and characteristics of a VET system, described in the previous section. Section 6 is engaged to the description of the system architecture, in terms of the logical view of the static structure of the architecture, the dynamic behavior of the system in terms of the specification of the system behavior, collaboration of components for achieving the system behavior and the physical view of the Web-based training system related to the deployment of the system. Section 7 summarizes and concludes the chapter, while section 8 presents the planned next steps.

BACKGROUND

There are many definitions for vocational education and training (VET). According to Wikipedia

(2006) VET, also called career and technical education (CTE), prepares learners for careers that are traditionally non-academic and directly related to a specific trade, occupation or vocation, hence the term, in which the learner participates. It is sometimes referred to as technical education, as the learner directly develops expertise in a particular techniques or technology.

Usually, VET is a term used to describe education and training arrangements designed to prepare people for work or to improve the knowledge and skills of people already working somewhere. It also describes one of the three major sectors of education and training, the other two being the school and higher education sectors. However, due to reforms in various countries, during the past decade we now see vocational education and training programs offered in secondary schools.

As the labor market becomes more specialized and economies are demanding more skills, governments and businesses are increasingly investing in the future of vocational education through publicly funded training organizations and subsidized apprenticeship or traineeship initiatives for businesses. At the post-secondary level vocational education is typically provided by an institute of technology, or by a local community college. It is indicative that over 94% of Australia's secondary schools now offer VET to their senior students. This means students can gain practical work skills and nationally recognized VET qualifications as part of their school education. This fact is very beneficial for the industry because the students already have some experience and possibly qualifications in the industry. Through their work experience placement they should have developed a realistic picture of the industry and be aware of such things as the expected level of grooming and required attitude to be successful.

According to the above we can definitely say that VET is very beneficial for a big portion of workers and/or students.

However, there are many people who can not participate in such a VET traditional program in a school or institute, due to time and/or distance limitations.

In such a case the usage of e-learning and ICT in VET process either exclusively (which means that the whole VET process will take place from distance using ICT) or partially (which means that ICT technology will support but not substitutes the traditional VET process) could be very useful. The next paragraphs investigates the current situation on ICT-supported VET as well as on the current trends in online VET technologies.

Current Situation on ICT-Supported VET

This paragraph presents an overview on the work done until now in the usage of e-learning and ICT in vocational training in order to support asynchronous, synchronous and collaborative learning services. The main goal of presenting the related work overview is to reply to the following question: Can e-learning technologies help the vocational education and training students and teachers?

Generally speaking, the usage of ICT for supporting vocational training is one of the highest priorities not only in Europe but also in other countries such as the U.S. and Australia. According to a study of Australian Flexible Learning Framework (2005), which presents the results of national surveys and demonstrate the level of uptake and use of e-learning in Australia's vocational education and training (VET) system, there is a modest but increasing level of uptake of e-learning. Furthermore, the surveys shown that e-learning would help the students by increasing their confidence and computer skill levels, by helping them to get a better job and by giving them flexibility in the place and time of their study.

In case of European countries, improving vocational education and training and a stronger cooperation throughout Europe in VET is increasingly being regarded as an important element for creating a European labor market, implementing the European employment strategy and meeting the Lisboan goals set for Europe's competitiveness, social cohesion and job creation. The final report to the EU Commission concerning the use of ICT for learning and teaching in initial vocational education and training (Ramboll Management, 2005), shows several clear patterns concerning the reasons for using e-learning in initial VET (motivations and objectives) and the expected results, outputs and impacts. These generally revolve around the following themes: the flexibility of e-learning, new learning methods, opportunities for furnishing students with real-life work skills, savings in time and money, the integration of theory and practice and attracting students. This study shows that the subjects/branches considered to be characterized by an intensive use of e-learning are: electricity, gas and water supply; financial intermediation and business activities; wholesale and retail trade, hotels, restaurants; manufacturing; transport; storage and communication. Furthermore, the study shows that the subjects/branches considered to be characterized by a moderate use of e-learning are: agriculture, fishing and quarrying; construction; public and personal services.

Concerning the extent to which e-learning is used in initial VET, the findings show that the EU as a whole is at an early stage of the process of integrating e-learning into its initial VET systems. In addition, the overall picture that emerges from the study shows that the use of e-learning in initial VET varies greatly among the Member States, as some are still at the beginning of their development in this area while others have been working to implement e-learning in initial VET for several years.

Concerning the impacts of the use of e-learning in initial VET in EU member states, the report of Ramboll Management (2005) refers that e-learning may: bring the practical and the theoretical

worlds closer together, enhance the level of knowledge, skills and competences of students and prepare students for working life. E-learning may also: increase flexibility, efficiency and quality of teaching, student motivation and parental involvement. Furthermore, the use of e-learning may: change the role of the teachers, make the students responsible for their own learning, prepare the students for the lifelong learning paradigm and generally lead to individualized learning.

According to the above it seems that we can answer our initial question and we can say that e-learning technologies can help the vocational education and training students and teachers.

Current Trends in Online VET Technologies

Distance learning and training has drawn increased research interest and a wide variety of architectures for supporting this type of learning and training have been proposed. In addition, to this direction many tools have been developed for supporting and assisting the realization of the Web-based training process and for increasing its benefits for the end users, which is the achievement of a higher degree of knowledge. Based on the above, the chapter will survey existing tools and platforms designed and developed. The technologies that could be used for vocational training could be divided into three major categories: (1) synchronous, (2) asynchronous and (3) collaborative. In the subsections that follow, an overview of the existing technologies in the above three categories is presented.

Technologies for Synchronous Communication

The technologies used for synchronous communication refer to the real time communication among the participating peers. To this direction there are mainly text messaging and voice chat technologies. In particular, the majority of the synchronous communication technologies include tools for conducting real time voice chatting, embed voice, set up threaded voice board and oral assessments into course materials. In addition, the majority of the existing platforms are accompanied by additional tools for facilitating the interaction among the users, such as file transfer, video communication and even mobile messaging. Some of the technologies of this category are Skype, MSN Messenger and ICQ, while similar tools can be built upon technologies that allow real time communication, such as Macromedia Communication Server.

Technologies for Asynchronous Learning and Training

Another category of systems that could allow collaboration are the systems that aim at providing a global platform for a whole educational program, such as WebCT, Learning Space, CENTRA, FirstClass, Claroline, CourseWork, Moodle, Eledge and Whiteboarb, CommunityZero. Most of the platforms mentioned above, provide tools which most of the early Web-mediated online courses were designed to complement conventional methodologies for dissemination of course content, connecting students to various online multimedia learning materials. Concerning the learners themselves, traditional platforms for distance education, dispose tools and functions that facilitate the exchange of information or materials (that is communication), without offering specific tools that could really allow collaboration among them.

Technologies for Collaboration

The technologies used for collaboration are mainly related to real time applications, which allow an advanced degree of interaction among the participating peers. Collaborative technologies could be considered as a superset of synchronous communication tools, which apart from the com-

munication feature extend the users' abilities by supporting advanced features which allow to a group of users to work together on a certain task. The most common characteristic of collaborative technologies is the real time sharing of applications among the participants along with a number of advanced features (whiteboard, co-Web browsing, brainstorming board, etc.), which facilitate the collaborative process. Some of the platforms available to this direction are the following: Centra Live, AcuConference, ScribeStudio, Netmeeting, Live Meeting, Live Classroom & Wimba Voice Tools.

Synopsis on Existing Technologies

The number of architectural models, platforms and tools developed for distance learning and training raises the question whether it is necessary to design and develop a new architecture so as to meet the needs of Web-based training. The review of the current trends in online VET technologies indicate that even though there is a majority of platforms and tools available that could be adopted for conducting and facilitating certain types of Web-based training processes, there is no integrated solution and architecture that combines all the necessary services into one platform. In particular, the majority of the existing platforms focus either on mainly synchronous collaborative tools or asynchronous learning tools for achieving the goals of the e-learning and training process. However, given the fact that both e-learning and Web-based training can be applied to a wide range of educational fields, it seems that a solution that could provide and support a set of synchronous, asynchronous and collaborative technologies would be more effective for the Web-based training process, as it could assist and facilitate both trainers and trainees as combinations of different types of tools could be adopted according to the topic of interest.

VOCATIONAL TRAINING CHARACTERISTICS AND REQUIREMENTS

The starting point when designing and developing an e-learning or Web-based training system is the identification of the special characteristics of the users it targets and the objectives it aims to achieve. In the case of vocational training the users of an e-learning vocational system are trainees (who are adults with some knowledge on the theme area that they will be trained on and they wish to enrich their knowledge), administrative staff and trainers. This section presents the special characteristics and particularities of life-long vocational training so as to define the differences and modification in regard to other types of education and for extracting the needs and motivation of the target users. Based on the needs and characteristics, this section outlines the different requirements that arise for vocational training and presents the pedagogical models that could be applied for assisting this type of training.

VET Features

According to the current situation concerning VET programs offered today world-wide, we can present the following general features of VET:

- VET covers education and training useful both before and during employment. It assumes that people will undertake VET throughout their working lives.
- VET includes both craft-based training (associated with traditional apprenticeships such as cabinet making and boiler making) and industry-wide training (for example, broad-based metals modules and office skills modules). It also includes general employment skills such as communication and occupational health and safety.

- VET is provided in institutes and in the workplace. Workplace training can be on-the-job, as with apprenticeships, or in the industry-based training programs and facilities (known as skills centers) found in some larger companies.
- VET programs could range from basic level and skill-specific courses to more advanced and broader courses awarding qualifications such as advanced diplomas.
- The VET programs should be accredited by the body responsible for accrediting training.

In general, the online VET technological systems do not seem to be characterized by a solid pedagogical framework in order to satisfy both learners' and VET organizations' requirements. This framework should be applied by using pedagogical methods suited to adults rather than to the young. This implies learning that is learner centered and contextualized to make it relevant to adults' experiences.

A social-constructivist learning approach through problem solving in both individual and collaborative framework seems to be an optimal solution. More specifically a socio-constructivist learning environment could be characterized by the following functionality (EduTechWiki, 2007): reflection and exchange, scaffolding and storyboarding, facilitation and content, monitoring and assessment, production, investigation psychological support and community.

Such an environment should be characterized by flexibility in provision to suit adults' circumstances and schedules. Furthermore, it should recognize the prior learning of the trainees (OECD, 2003). This could be done by assessing and giving credit for knowledge and skills acquired in work, home or community settings ensuring that adults do not waste time relearning what they already know.

In addition, Manninen et al. (2000) has presented criteria for pedagogical and technological innovations in vocational training environments.

The criteria for pedagogical innovations in vocational training environments are the following:

- **Constructiveness:** Teaching and learning are clearly based on the learner's active construction process and on the higher-level knowledge structures. In an ordinary VET environment teaching does not pay much attention to how the subject matter is integrated in the existing knowledge structures of the student.
- **Activeness:** Learning environment is based on the learner's active role and commitment. In an ordinary VET environment the learning environment does not support nor require the learner's own active role in the learning process.
- **Cooperativeness:** Learning is based on cooperative and collaborative principles and takes place in groups. In an ordinary VET environment learning takes place mainly alone.
- **Contextuality:** Learning takes place in a simulated or real-life situation, which equals the actual context where the knowledge will be applied. In an ordinary VET environment learning takes place in an institution and/or is separated from the concrete situation of application of the knowledge.
- **Problem-based:** Learning approach is problem-based and investigative. In an ordinary VET environment study objectives are based on study subjects in a traditional way, and cut into separate units in the curriculum.

The criteria for technological innovations in vocational training environments are the following:

- **Interactivity:** Tools are based on interactive technology (interactive video, interactive WWW-pages, learning programs). In an ordinary VET environment tools developed in the project are mainly based on passive receiving information (video, tv, WWW-pages).
- **Communicativeness:** Tools allow many-to-many-type communication. In an ordinary VET environment tools allow many-to-many-type communication.
- **Individuality:** The tools make it possible to create and follow individual study paths. In an ordinary VET environment, the learning process using the tools will be similar for all the users
- **Multimedia:** The product is an innovative combination of alternative tools supporting each other. In an ordinary VET environment, the product is based on a single tool.

According to the above we can extract the basic requirements and characteristics of an online VET system, which are described in the next paragraph.

Basic Requirements and Characteristics of an Online VET System

This section presents the basic requirements that should be taken into account by designers and developers when they are designing a virtual space for vocational training systems.

For extracting the basic design characteristics, we should first define the target groups that it involves. Thus, in the case of vocational training centers we should extract the design characteristics for the following entities (stakeholders):

- Vocational center administrative staff
- Trainers
- Trainees

From the perspective of the vocational center **administrative staff**, an online VET system should:

- Allow the vocational center to serve a greater number of trainers and trainees: the online substance of the Web-based training system overcomes the spatial limitation that a real class introduces and should therefore provide all the necessary means, in terms of resources, for the support of multiple trainers and trainees. In particular, the system should allow the assignment of more trainers for the conduction of a training course, as well as the ability to serve more trainees at the same course.

- Allow the vocational center to serve a greater number of training courses: the system should provide and support all the available online tools for the realization of different types of courses, which, based on the field of expertise, could demand different types of tools and services.

- Improve the administration and management of trainees' and trainers' performance: the online system should provide all the necessary tools for monitoring the trainees' profiles and performance as well as the effectiveness of the trainers' in the conduction of the Web-based training course. This information is of vital importance to the organization as it could create and maintain a unified view of the effectiveness and progress of the participating peers.

As far as it concerns the **trainers'** perspective, the system should:

- Facilitate content creation and manipulation and improve content availability: the content constitutes a critical factor for the learning and training success. Therefore, the system should provide all the necessary tools for the easy creation and manipulation of the content by the trainers, so that they will not be discouraged by spending time and efforts on how to complete these processes.

- Assist and improve the sharing and distribution of content within the course, among trainers and trainees: following the content creation is the content presentation and distribution. The system should assist the effective sharing of content within the course and among the participating trainees, as well as among the trainers of the system for increasing the reusability and training consistency.

- Improve communication both in and out of the training class with trainees and other trainers: the online VET system should effectively simulate the communication capabilities among trainers and trainees as well as among trainers themselves, in real-world vocational training situations. Therefore, the system should provide all the necessary communication tools and services for overcoming the boundaries that both time and spatial distribution of the participating entities introduce.

- Improve and facilitate assessment capabilities: the online VET system should provide to the trainers all the necessary tools for evaluating trainees' performance and understanding of the training material. The assessment options should not only efficiently "simulate" the real life assessment processes but additionally they should overcome the limitation of no physical presence of the participants and the lack of face-to-face contact.

Finally, from the **trainee's** perspective, a vocational training system should:

- **Improve overall training and facilitate the training process by decreasing the learning curve on IT technologies:** The online system should act not only as a facilitator to the training process but also as a coherent system that can meet the training needs of the trainees. In addition, the interface and the selection of the technologies should match the technological skills of the trainees for avoiding their discouragement by complex technological features, which in turn act as boundaries for gaining knowledge.

- **Provide effective Web-based training support:** Based on the fact that the online system refers mainly to scattered users, it should be able to provide all the necessary tools for the timely and efficient support on the Web-based training processes, which will facilitate trainees in completing these processes. The online system should also extend the support capabilities to the trainees by exploiting the advanced capabilities of existing technology.

- **Promote the personalized nature of the Web-based training process:** the online system should provide all the necessary tools for the creation of trainees' profiles, the extraction of the special needs that each of them introduces, their skills and possibly the areas that they need additional assistance and support. Based on this information, the trainee could have the opportunity to enter a training system with information, content and services that best match his/her interests and skills, which in turn could improve the effectiveness of the Web-based training process.

Another very significant issue is the content creation and its presentation to the users. An online VET system, which is a Web-based system, should definitely follow W3C's Web Content Accessibility Guidelines (W3C, 1999) concerning the representation of the content. Furthermore, the content should be relevant to the users' needs, learning topics and be able to be presented in various forms such as video, animation and/or text. Finally, the content should be created in

such a manner in order to support reusability of learning objects.

DEVELOPMENT FRAMEWORK AND PROCESSES

For an effective and flexible system for supporting vocational training, the investigation of a development framework is identified as a basic issue. This development framework will be used, among others, as a basis for the selection and/or the implementation of information and communication technologies in order to create an efficient VET technological system. In other words this framework could be considered as the skeletal support, which is used as the basis for the functional and technical development of the training system. The chapter presents a development framework for the support of vocational training, which is built upon the basic needs of the targeted users.

The framework consists of the following stages:

- **Stage 0:** Elaboration of requirements.
- **Stage 1:** Extraction of the basic technical characteristics of the system.
- **Stage 2:** Technology and standardization monitoring, Risk assessment and Selection of technologies and standards.
- **Stage 3:** Technical specifications and the system architecture.
- **Stage 4:** System development.
- **Stage 5:** User evaluation.

The correlation among these stages is depicted in Figure 1. It should be noted that the proposed framework includes four evaluation steps (three steps dedicated on formative evaluation and another step dedicated on summative evaluation). VET special characteristics necessitate all these steps. Some of these characteristics are the following:

Figure 1. Development framework and processes

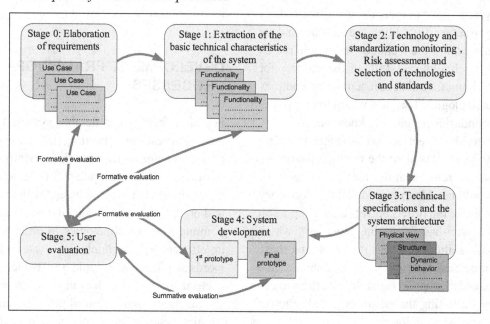

- Extremely different subject-matters.
- Various status of trainee's group (e.g., different age, different cognitive background, unemployed or not, etc.).
- Various dexterities on ICT technologies.
- Diverse learning curve on IT technologies of trainees' group as well as trainers' group.

These characteristics enforce the users' intervention in the system development process from an early step (i.e., use cases description) to the end of the development process (i.e., summative evaluation of the final prototype) design and evaluation.

Therefore, we can say that the proposed development framework can be characterized as a user-centered system development process. This fact will facilitate the users to use the system as a tool for their work or learning process. Furthermore, it will decrease the learning curve on the VET online system by avoiding problems reported in other system development processes (Seale, 2003). The next paragraphs are dedicated

on the description of the stages of the development framework.

Stage 0: Elaboration of Requirements

The proposed framework has the following basic inputs: (1) the VET characteristics (i.e., VET national system, VET regulation framework, VET special characteristics comparing with the other forms of education and training, etc.); (2) the end user requirements (i.e., the teachers, students and administrative stuff requirements, etc.); (3) the guidelines that stem from the application of pedagogical models in a distance learning environment; and (4) use case description. In essence, this stage is a pre-step during the system development process. More specifically it constitutes the collection of the whole set of requirements for the design and development of the system. The most significant step for the design of the system is the use case description. Use cases describes the context of the system and the problem(s) that it solves. The aim is to provide an introduction to the system that is accessible to non-domain experts. The problem description enumerates the key features of the system and how the system provides value to them. The focus of this step is on the features concerned with and communicating with the system, and on the roles of these features, not on the system itself. The results of this stage could be reported to the end users of the system in order to receive early feedback.

Stage 1: Extraction of the Basic Technical and Functional Characteristics of the System

This stage concerns a primary effort to extract some of the most basic technical characteristics of the system, based on the inputs and requirements collected on "Stage 0."

The main goal of this stage is to describe the system interface and system functionality (Section 3) as well as to document the services that the system provides in terms of responsibilities. Often the system interface may be organized into a set of sub-interfaces, each sub-interface corresponding to a distinct usage of the system, for example, there may be specific interfaces for system configuration, for normal system use, and for system management. This stage is mainly focused on the normal system use. Each system interface proposed to be presented as a wireframe. Along with the system interfaces the specific system functionality are described using the template presented in Table 1.

According to these characteristics the technological fields connected with the targeted system are detected.

This stage is mainly related to the list of services that need to be identified within the framework, which are based on the requirements, and for each of these, the definition of the scope and purpose of the service, a list of applicable standards and specifications are among others presented.

This step will help the project manager and the technical manager to anticipate the technical expertise needed for the successful development of the system.

Furthermore, the results of this stage could be reported to the end users of the system in order to receive early feedback.

Stage 2: Technology and Standardization Monitoring, Risk Assessment and Selection of Technologies and Standards

This stage concerns an extended monitoring of the technologies, platforms and/or standards available in each research field and from these explored there was a selection of the ones that met some basic criteria.

Table 1. Functionality template

Functionality Name	Name of the functionality
Relative Use Case(s)	Use Case(s) where the functionality could contribute
Relative Element	Feature that this functionality corresponds to (e.g. Forum)
Actors	Users or system components that will use this functionality
Input Data	Data needed for the implementation
Description	Process that will be followed for the achievement of the functionality
Output Data	Expected result

The main criteria for the selection of one technology in regard to another are the following:

- If and how this technology could contribute in the framework of a VET technological system.
- Compliance to the relative standards that Underlay in this research area.
- the functionalities that it provides.
- Its cost.
- The familiarization of the developers with this technology, and finally.
- The interoperability with operating systems and other technologies.

After that, an intermediate step concerns the risk assessment for each technologies, platforms and/or standards. More specifically, for each product an independent potential risks analysis should be carried out in the following categories: (1) Design/Planning; (2) Development; (3) Integration; (4) Implementation/Exploitation; (5) Ongoing Support; (6) Future Development.

Stage 3: Technical Specifications and System Architecture

The purpose of this stage is to define the technological basis for the system as well as to identify the relevant tools and protocols to be implemented. Furthermore, this document tries to define the system architecture in the form of functional blocks and their interrelations, including a description of hardware and software requirements on the server and client sides, providing as much detail as possible.

This stage has, as goals to describe the structure, the dynamic behavior and the physical view of the VET system

Stage 4: System Development

After describing the system architecture, the system development should start by implementing the system functionality. It should be noted that some parts of the system functionality should be released gradually to the end-users.

One of the main requirements that needs to be considered when launching such a system is that the introduction of additional technological features should proceed gradually and the added value of each feature must be clear to the user. This is why not all functionalities of the system will be launched at once so as not to overload users with too many unfamiliar features.

We propose two steps for launching the functionality:

- An intermediate prototype, including basic features and ready for formative evaluation.
- The final prototype, including the whole set of functionality and ready for summative evaluation.

Stage 5: User Evaluation

The main reasons for conducting evaluations are to discover the potential problems in advance as well as to contribute to our understanding of the application of new technologies to training and to be able to make generalizations from our work.

Two levels of evaluation were identified, the need for formative evaluation to identify problems at an early stage, and the need for summative evaluation to provide evidence to potential users:

- Formative evaluation is evaluation that includes a feedback loop leading to remedial actions. The results of the evaluation are used to modify the development process or output. Formative evaluation could be applied in three steps: (1) after the presentation of the use cases, (2) after the presentation of system functionality description, and (3) after the presentation of the intermediate prototype.

- Summative evaluation is evaluation that proposed to be carried out at the end of a project. Its purpose is not to improve the project outputs but to provide information, for example, to assist in decision making, to support claims, to assess achievement against goals.

PROPOSED VOCATIONAL TRAINING SERVICES

Besides from the architectural model, which is transparent to the end users, a basic issue of distance learning and training systems is the selection of the services that will be provided to the users for allowing and facilitating the corresponding processes. These services need to be selected, designed and implemented based on the special needs of the users they target. To this direction, this section presents the functional requirements of a Web-based training system, in the sense of the design characteristics and of the services that such a system should provide and support.

Based on the requirements of vocational Web-based training and the design characteristics, this section presents the services that the integrated architecture should combine for meeting the needs of vocational centers and of the trainers. The vocational training services are divided in the following basic categories: (1) synchronous communication services, (2) collaboration services, (3) asynchronous services and (4) content related services. These services should satisfy the criteria for pedagogical and technological innovations in vocational training environment. For satisfying these criteria the available services should be designed and implemented as modules that could support an adaptive learning environment not only to the VET organization needs but also to the users' needs.

Table 2 presents what services satisfies which requirement. These services are presented in detail in the following paragraphs.

Synchronous Communication Services

The main synchronous communication services are text and voice chat:

- **Text chat:** This feature allows two participants to communicate in a synchronous mode. In a vocational training system text chat can be used by trainees, which do not necessarily take the same classes or courses as a means of social communication and interaction. In the framework of a collaborative training environment, text chat can be proven to be extremely helpful for trainees who can meet out of classes and discuss issues that concern them, pose questions, and generally interact without being supervised and rated. In addition, a group, of people who share common interests, can create its own chat rooms. Also, this component. Text chat could be found in many forms, as public and private chat rooms or as public chat, where all participants can view the messages being exchanged and whisperings, where the communication is realized only between two peers. In a vocational training synchronous session, text chat could be integrated so as to allow participants to pose questions to the trainer or comment the content being presented.

- **Voice chat:** This service allows users to communicate through audio by using a microphone and speakers. Voice chat in a training system can be used for the delivery of a training course but mainly it is used as a supporting tool for the communication among the participating peers and in many cases floor control by the trainer should be available for a more effective coordination of the training and communication process.

Table 2. VET environment requirements and services

Requirements \ Services	Text Chat	Voice Chat	Shared whiteboard	Application sharing	Slides creation and presentation	Multimedia presentation	Video Conference	Intelligent agents	E-mail	Forums	Glossary of terms	Calendar of events	Access to learning content, Content creation, Content manipulation	Manage Trainees, Manage Trainers, Manage Courses, Manage Lessons, Manage system modules
Reflection, Exchange & Activeness	✓	✓	✓	✓	✓	✓	✓	✓	✓	✓				
Scaffolding, Storyboarding & Constructiveness			✓	✓										
Facilitation and Cooperativeness	✓	✓	✓	✓	✓	✓	✓	✓	✓	✓				✓
Content					✓	✓					✓		✓	
Monitoring and Assessment								✓						✓
Investigation & Problem based			✓					✓						✓
Community										✓		✓	✓	✓
Recognize the prior learning of the trainees				✓				✓						
Contextuality	✓	✓	✓	✓										✓
Interactivity	✓	✓	✓	✓	✓	✓	✓	✓	✓	✓				✓
Communicativeness	✓	✓	✓	✓	✓	✓	✓	✓	✓	✓				✓
Individuality								✓					✓	
Multimedia	✓	✓	✓	✓	✓		✓	✓	✓	✓				✓

Collaboration Services

The main collaboration services are shared whiteboard, application sharing, slides creation and presentation, multimedia presentation, video conference and intelligent agents:

- **Shared whiteboard:** The whiteboard supports line, circle and ellipsis drawing in a wide range of colors and text input in many sizes and colors. It can also offer "undo last action" capability as well the erasure of all previous actions on the whiteboard.

- **Application sharing:** This service allows a moderator (usually the trainer) or participant to share any application, a specific region on the desktop or the entire desktop with other attendees. The host of the application can grant remote control of his or her shared application(s). This allows for true hands-on training, demonstrations and support applications.

- **Slides creation and presentation:** This tool allows the creation of slides by participants of a session, where only one participant can add information on the slides table. However, the slides presentation is viewed by all participating peers.

- **Multimedia presentation:** This service is used for the presentation in various formats (text, video, flash files, etc.) of information relevant to the objectives of the vocational training course. For example, the multimedia presentation could be used for the projection of a video which shows in detail the functions and problems of a complex system or machine.

- **Video conference:** This service can be used for supporting not only communication (as text and audio chat) but also for the collaboration among the participating peers using open and private meeting rooms. This service, when used in a training system, either uses the video for the representation of

the trainer, who delivers the course, or with the video representation of all participants of the same session. In most cases, this type of service consists of additional tools, which are integrated so as to constitute a completely functional service to the end user. It should be mentioned that in particular, some of the tools integrated in video conferencing services are:

- **Intelligent agents** for assisting the users during the synchronous sessions: as mentioned above, the majority of the trainees in vocational training centers are adults with little or no knowledge on the subject in which they are trained. The introduction of the technology for providing courses can additionally burden the effort of the trainees and discourage them on using the system. For avoiding the discouragement of the users, intelligent agents can be adopted, which monitor the users' behavior in the synchronous collaborative session, in terms of the actions they perform and the degree of participation they present. When the users' performance in certain categories falls under a certain limit, which can be set according to the area of Web-based training, intelligent agents can produce messages that trigger the users to participate or even propose "action" paths that the user could follow for facilitating the training process.

Asynchronous Services

The main asynchronous services are e-mail, forums, glossary of terms, calendar of events, and intelligent agents:

- **E-mail:** This service is the most common and widely used among users. E-mail allows the asynchronous communication among peers, which have the ability to write their opinions, pose questions and attach files. In a vocational training system, e-mail can be used for the communication among trainees as well as a means for contacting the trainer in order to pose questions or for submitting reports and assessments.

- **Forums** (structured and unstructured): It is a tool, which aims to support asynchronous communication among the community members in order for them to exchange views and information. It supports open and closed moderated forums for the whole community as well as subgroups of members. In order to motivate the users' discussions in a more convenient way a notification for every post of the forum is sent to the forum members by e-mail.

- **Glossary of terms:** This service could be considered as an online dictionary with terms relevant to the topic of interest. Especially in vocational training, where the areas of training can significantly vary, this service can be proven very beneficial for trainees who need to obtain some basic knowledge on the basic terms used in the field they are trained on. The glossary of terms tool provides the name of the term and a short or more detailed description of the explanation of this term, the concept it aims to describe and the context it can be used.

- **Calendar of events:** The calendar of events is a timetable that stores a collection of events and lists them in chronological order. It is an asynchronous mean of communication, which can be used for the scheduling of events that take place in the Web-based training system. Each user can dispose a private calendar of events, which means that only this user can see the contents and posts in this calendar. The calendar can support three types of events: public, private and related to each training course. In the public calendar of events the users can post their announcements to the administrator, who

in turn, will decide if the announcement is "qualified" to be posted. Furthermore, there can be a course calendar that includes class schedules and venues, schedules assignments, examinations and topics to be covered. The calendar consists of three views. The day view, which is also time scheduled, the month view and the year view.

- **Intelligent agents** for matching users' profiles and encouraging the communication and collaboration between them: as the term indicates, a collaborative training environment should motivate the communication between its members. In particular, better communication can be achieved between members who share common ideas and interests. Therefore, every member of the system, at the time of his/her subscription to the system enters personal information, which includes his/her interests, hobbies, the research/work areas, which s/he prefers, etc. Thereby, a profile for each user is created which is constantly enriched with additional information, which arises from the selection of courses that s/he decides to attend. An intelligent collaborative Web-based training environment should be able to match users with common interests and encourage the communication among them. This functionality could be achieved with multiple queries in the users' profiles and selections of courses in order to track down areas of mutual interest, which will contribute to the distribution and extension of knowledge. In addition, a system should be able to compare the users' profiles, and especially the fields of research interests, with the available courses and suggest some possible alternatives. These functionalities could contribute to an interplay between the members and the system, which in turn could result in effective distribution of knowledge.

Content-Related Services

The main content-related services are: access to learning content, content creation, and content manipulation:

- **Access to learning content:** This service allows the trainees to view the provided learning content. However, the access to learning content may vary from system to system or among training courses in regard to the navigation paths that the user can follow. In particular, in certain courses the trainees could be able to follow a linear path for accessing the content while in other cases, where certain variables are used the trainers are sent to different directions based on training criteria or responses to specific questions. Courses created using variables are more complex to design, but they account for a range of knowledge and skill sets.

- **Content creation:** This service enables trainers to integrate an array of media to create professional, engaging, interactive training content relevant to the area of learning and training. Even though content used to consist of simple, independent files, as documents, videos and presentation, the current trend requests for content creation services, which are compatible with educational standards, as AICC, SCORM, IMS and LRN. This option makes possible the repurpose of digitized elements or learning objects from an existing training course for reuse in a new one (Harris, 2002). Furthermore, content creation services are not related only to the information that will be presented to the end user (trainer) but also to the creation of the necessary question types (fill-in-the-blank, matching, true or false, short or long essay) for evaluating the trainer's performance and understanding on the content being delivered to him/her.

- **Content manipulation:** A simulation of a training course presupposes that the trainer has the capability to add and manage learning content, which could be dynamically changed, and dispose knowledge to the trainees, providing them the capability to have and process this learning material. In addition, there could be no efficient simulation if the trainees did not have the capability to maintain their own notebook, which in terms of a Web-based training environment means a directory with files and folders for personal use. Such functionality can be supported with two basic operations, the uploading and downloading of files, in the framework of the vocational training environment.

Administrative Services

The main administrative services are the management of trainees, of trainers, of courses, of lessons and of the system modules:

- **Manage trainees:** This service allows to the organization (vocational center) to administer the registered trainees in terms of being able to view their profiles and create reports regarding the trainees' skills and performance in various assessments. Furthermore, the administration of the trainees is also related to their assignment to course cycles and lessons being offered by the online vocational training system.

- **Manage trainers:** The trainers constitute one of the most vital entities of the VET system, who, based on their skills and educational background undertake courses in the online system. This service enables the organization to keep a record of the trainers available as well as of the profile of these trainers and based on these data it enables the assignment of at least one trainer per lesson.

- **Manage courses:** As mentioned in the previous section, the vocational Web-based training system could be engaged to various fields of education and training. Each of these areas is comprised by a set of courses, which in turn can contain a number of lessons. This service allows the organization the creation of new courses, the deletion of outdated courses and the general administration of the information related to each course.
- **Manage lessons:** This service enables the organization to administer the lessons available within the provided courses. The administration, alike the case of the courses, is related to the ability of creation of new lessons, the modification of existing lessons as well as to the deletion of outdated or no longer relevant material.
- **Manage system modules:** This service provides to the organization full access to the system, in which it can add, remove and modify functionalities and fix possible feeblenesses of the system.

SYSTEM ARCHITECTURE

As mentioned in Molter (1998):

An architecture comprises a set of views on different characteristics of the system. Among these are structural views on different abstraction levels, describing, for example, the highest-level decomposition of the system into components, which collaborate by using connectors, object-oriented models of the system, and its module architecture. Each level of structural description defines a specific set of component and connector types, as well as rules and constraints describing specific constellations of instances of these types. The definition of component and connector types also comprises the description of their semantics and communication protocols.

The architecture of a VET online system should be based on the following principles:

- Ease of installation and usage concerning users' side: support of the most common Web browsers.
- Support of standardized Web services.
- Open standards, modular and extensible Web-architecture.

An n-tier application architecture could support the above principles by providing a model to create a flexible and reusable application. In this type of architecture each application is broken into tiers or layers. Therefore, when there is a need to change the presentation or scale of an application, the programmers have only to modify a specific layer, rather than have to rewrite the entire application. Thus, this solution is cost and time effective. Other benefits of such a solution are:

- Support of thin clients, which means that the users are able to run the user interface on less-powerful machines.
- Reduced maintenance, because the possible changes are applied only to the required components.
- Reusability by using existing components and tiers to provide services to new applications.

As mentioned in the previous section, the proposed system architecture combines synchronous, asynchronous and collaborative services into one unified, integrated platform for meeting the needs of vocational Web-based training. Thus, our proposal is an n-tier architecture based on several components, which communicate and interact for providing the desired and needed functionality. Our n-tier architecture has the following layers:

- Presentation layer (or client side), which is responsible for displaying user interface and "driving" that interface using business layer rules.

- Business layer (part of the server side including application and Web servers) which implements the logic of each application. More specifically, it manages the business rules, the data, custom and user controls, etc. It handles access to the data layer to retrieve, modify and delete data to and from that layer and sending the results to the presentation layer.
- Data layer, which is the database of the system.

Furthermore, the system should be based on a variety of communication protocols, be scalable, be platform independent and be based on open standards. Figure 2, presents the integrated architecture, which consists of various components/modules, each of which supports certain

types of functionality. These components are described in the paragraphs that follow.

As mentioned, the integrated platform comprises three basic modes of interaction: synchronous, asynchronous and collaborative, which are depicted in Figure 2 as the vertical dimension. In each of these modes, there are a number of provided services for providing, supporting and maintaining the tele-learning process which were described in the previous section. Apart from these services, there are additional tools, which are related to: (1) the creation, provision, access and distribution of the content, (2) intelligent agent support for facilitating the training process and promoting user participation and (3) administrative services for allowing the organization to manage the entities of the system as well as the provided services. These three types of tools can be based on services that run on all three types of interaction (synchronous, asynchronous and

Figure 2. Integrated system architecture

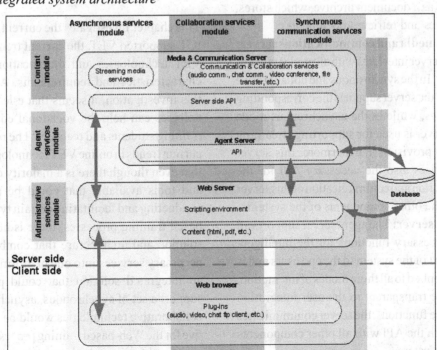

215

collaborative) and are therefore depicted in Figure 2 as the horizontal dimension.

From a more technical point of view the systems is comprised by the server side, which contains all the functionality and services and from the client side, which comprises the components needed for the user to access and interact with the system.

Server Side

The server side consists of all the necessary components for the provision and support of different types of services. In particular, the proposed system is comprised by the following components/servers:

- **Web server:** this server contains all the asynchronous system features and acts on server side as an integration platform through an extended API. This server supports the core of the scripting environment as well as a content repository, which allows managing several kinds of documents and works as a document archive, which stores, archives and retrieves documents.
- **Multimedia and communications server:** This server interferes with all modes of interaction. In the synchronous and collaborative mode, the server supports the corresponding services, while in the asynchronous mode the server is used for supporting streaming media provision. Furthermore, this server comprises also the necessary API for the interaction and communication of this server with the other components of the system.
- **Agent server:** The agent server supports all the necessary functions for the intelligent support of the system to the end users and is also applied to all three modes of interaction. For the transparent to the user integration of these functions, the server communicates through the API with all other components of the system.

- **Database:** The database constitutes the major information repository of the system, which manipulates user and content information as well as data for the intelligent agent support.

Client Side

The client side consists of all the necessary components, which allow the end user to access and interact with the system. For the proposed system, the user can access the system through a Web browser. However, given the fact that multiple modes of interaction are supported, the Web browser should be enabled with the necessary plug-ins. These plug-ins mainly concern the synchronous and collaborative part of the proposed system as well as the agent component. Thus, the Web browser should provide the necessary plug-ins for audio, video and chat communication as well as an ftp client.

CONCLUSION

This chapter investigates the current situation on ICT-supported VET, the current trends in online VET technologies and the vocational training characteristics and requirements. According to this investigation, it seems that e-learning technologies can help the vocational education and training students and teachers. The review of the current trends in online VET technologies indicate that even though there is a majority of platforms and tools available that could be adopted for conducting and facilitating certain types of Web-based training processes, there is no integrated solution and architecture that combines all the necessary services into one platform. Therefore, an integrated solution that could provide and support a set of synchronous, asynchronous and collaborative technologies would be more effective for the Web-based training process, as it could assist and facilitate both trainers and trainees as combinations of different types of tools could be adopted according to the topic of interest.

This chapter presents also a development framework that will be used as the basis for the functional and technical development of such an integrated online VET system.

According to that framework an integrated e-learning architecture for supporting vocational education and training has been described. This architecture aims to be the basis of an integrated vocational e-learning system, giving emphasis in pedagogical, administrative as well as the technological texture of such an e-learning place. Therefore, the platform is constituted by a number of interlinked components, each of which supports certain types of services for providing to the participating users an integrated learning environment. The variety of learning services that could be supported by this architecture, in the asynchronous, synchronous and collaborative mode will facilitate the students and participants of the e-learning environment to engage in VET programs.

FUTURE WORK

The next step after the description of the current architecture is the implementation of a working prototype based on this architecture. This prototype will include only basic features of the final system and will be used for formative evaluation by the end users. After that, the introduction of additional technological features and more advanced services will take place gradually in order to avoid the overload of the inexperienced users with new services whose added value is not clear to the users.

The final step is the launching of the final prototype, which will include the whole set of functionality and it will be ready for summative evaluation.

REFERENCES

Australian Flexible Learning Framework. (2005). *E-learning Benchmarking, Project—Report*, I & J Management Services, Australian Flexible Learning Framework (Framework), September 2005.

EduTechWiki. (2007). *Socio-Constructivism*. Retrieved October 20, 2006, from http://edutechwiki.unige.ch/en/Socio-constructivism

Harris, J. (2002). *An Introduction to Authoring Tools*. ASTD's Learning Circuits online magazine, Retrieved October 20, 2006, from http://www.learningcircuits.org/2002/mar2002/harris

Herremans, A. (1995). *Studies #02 New Training Technologies*. UNESCO Paris, ILO International Training Centre.

Levesque, K., Lauen, D., Teitelbaum, P., Alt, M., Librera, S., & Nelson, D. (2000). *Vocational education in the United States: Toward the Year 2000*. Washington, DC: U.S. Department of Education, Office of Educational Research and Improvement.

Manninen, J., Nevgi, A., Matikainen, J., Luukannel, S. & Porevuo, M. (2000). *Ohjelman tuottamat pedagogiset ja teknologiset innovaatiot*. Leonardo da Vinci Report.

Molter, G. (1998). *The notion of Software Architecture*. Retrieved October 20, 2006, from http://wwwagss.informatik.uni-kl.de/Projekte/GeneSys/

OVAE. (2006). *Technology and Distance Learning*. Office of Vocational and Adult Education, U.S Department of Education, Adult Education and Literacy. Retrieved October 20, 2006, from http://www.ed.gov/about/offices/list/ovae/pi/AdultEd/tdlearn.html

OECD. (2003). *Beyond rhetoric: Adult learning policies and practices*. Paris: OECD Publications, 2003.

Ramboll Management. (2005). *The use of ICT for learning and teaching in initial vocational education and training.* Final Report to the EU Commission, DG Education & Culture, November.

Seale, J. (2003). *E-learning accessibility practices within higher education: A review.* Paper presented at the British Educational Research Association Annual Conference, Heriot-Watt University, Edinburgh, 11-13 September 2003. Retrieved October 20, 2006, from http://www.leeds.ac.uk/educol/documents/00003152.htm

W3C. (1999). *Web Content Accessibility Guidelines 1.*0. W3C Recommendation. Retrieved October 20, 2006, from http://www.w3.org/TR/1999/WAI-WEBWEBCONTENT-19990505/

Wikipedia. (2006). *Vocational Education.* Retrieved October 20, 2006, from http://en.wikipedia.org/wiki/Vocational_education

Chapter XII
A Generic Platform for the Systematic Construction of Knowledge–Based Collaborative Learning Applications

Santi Caballé
Open University of Catalonia, Spain

Thanasis Daradoumis
Open University of Catalonia, Spain

Fatos Xhafa
Polytechnic University of Catalonia, Spain

ABSTRACT

This study aims to explore the importance of efficient management of event information generated from group activity in collaborative learning practices for its further use in extracting and providing knowledge on interaction behavior. The essential issue here is how to design a platform that can be used for real, long-term, complex collaborative problem-solving situations and which enables the instructor to both analyze group interaction effectively and provide an adequate support when needed. The achievement of this task first involves the design of a conceptual model that structures and classifies the information generated in a collaborative learning application at several levels of description. This conceptual model is then translated into a computational model that not only allows the efficient management of the knowledge produced by the individual and group activity but also the possibility of exploiting this knowledge further as a meta-cognitive tool for real-time coaching and regulating the collaborative learning process. The computational model becomes the central issue in this contribution while the conceptual model is briefly introduced.

INTRODUCTION

Computer supported collaborative learning (CSCL) is an emerging paradigm (Koschmann, 1996) for research in educational technology that focuses on the use of information and communications technology (ICT) as a mediation tool within collaborative methods of learning. When designing and implementing environments that support online collaborative learning, several issues must be taken into account in order to ensure full support to the online learning activity. One such issue is the representation and analysis of group activity interaction.

Interaction analysis is a core function for the support of coaching and evaluation in online collaborative learning environments. It relies on information captured from the actions performed by the participants during the collaborative process (Dillenbourg, 1999; Martínez, de la Fuente, & Dimitriadis, 2003). The efficient embedding of this information and of the extracted knowledge into applications sets the basis for enhancing monitoring, awareness (Gutwin, Stark, & Greenberg, 1995) and feedback (Zumbach, Hillers, & Reimann, 2003) to achieve a successful learning process in collaborative environments. Therefore, the success of CSCL applications depends to a great extent on the capability of such applications to embed information and knowledge of group activity and use it to achieve a more effective group monitoring (Gutwin, Stark, & Greenberg, 1995).

CSCL applications are characterized by a high degree of user-user and user-system interaction and hence are generating a huge amount of event information. This information can be conveniently collected and automatically processed by computers as a data source to extract relevant knowledge of the collaboration. Note that in this context information refers to the event data generated by the learning group and knowledge refers to the result of the treatment of this information. Knowledge is acquired by means of analysis techniques and interpretations that will be presented to the same group that generated it.

As a result, the event information management is the cornerstone in this context, aiming at achieving three main goals: (1) Provide an analysis of the group's information by obtaining and classifying the necessary information gathered from the collaborative activity into three essential types of categories (Daradoumis, Martínez, & Xhafa, 2006), namely the *outcome of collaboration* (the members' contributing behavior to the task), the *functioning of the group* (the management and organizational processes underlying the collaborative learning activities, such as participation behavior, role playing, etc.), and *individual and group scaffolding* (social support and task- or group functioning-oriented help); (2) Given that the large amount of information generated during online group activity may need much time to be processed, an effective way to collect, analyze and present this information is required; (3) Efficiently embed the information and knowledge obtained into CSCL applications so as to both facilitate tutors to monitor the learning activity and constantly provide group members with as much awareness and feedback as possible.

Achieving a clear and well-structured conceptual model constitutes a principled manner for the design of a computational model that implements the process of embedding information and knowledge into a CSCL application. Indeed, the structuring and classification of the event information into specific collaborative processes can contribute and facilitate the building of a portable, general and reusable collaborative learning ontology for the representation, learning and inference of knowledge about each collaborative process. This allows the design of effective computational models that reflect as accurately as possible task performance, individual and group behavior, interaction dynamics, members' relationships and group support.

To this end, a generic, robust, reusable platform is provided for the systematic construction of CSCL applications endowed with enriched capabilities for providing more efficient knowledge management and scaffolding. This platform, called the Collaborative Learning Purpose Library (CLPL) (Caballé et al., 2004), acts as a computational model of collaborative learning interaction and can be used to embed information and knowledge into collaborative learning applications in an efficient manner.

This chapter is organized as follows: We first present an overview of other existing collaborative learning platforms which leads us to identify and discuss the main problems to be faced in the construction of our generic platform. Then, we enter the description of design principles that conducted the development of the CLPL and its architecture, which will be described in detail. Finally, the construction of a real application, a structured discussion forum, is discussed to validate the possibilities offered by our platform as regards data analysis and management. We conclude highlighting the main points and remarks covering this chapter and pointing out ongoing and further work.

DISCUSSION ON EXISTING PLATFORMS FOR COLLABORATIVE LEARNING APPLICATIONS

Generic platforms, frameworks and components are normally developed for the construction of complex software systems through the reuse technique (Czarnecki, 2005). This approach has been successfully applied to different domains thus providing applications of increased quality reducing both cost and development time. For this reason, it has attracted the attention of developers from the collaborative learning domain, mainly from Web-based distributed development from which the most popular platforms have arisen.

With the increasing interest in the World Wide Web over the last decade, several proposals have been made for the development of Web-based

platforms for collaborative learning applications. These platforms are mainly focused on standardizing learning metadata schemes, course structures, and software interfaces to provide interoperability between applications and learning resources (Anido-Rifón et al., 2001).

We will now briefly review some of these proposals and point to several important considerations related to the collaborative learning domain. Particular attention will be paid to those aspects related to the information and knowledge embedding which have been, to the best of our knowledge, little investigated.

Bacelo et al. (2002), though focusing on collaborative learning environments in general, introduce an interesting approach to component-based architecture to support collaborative application designs. In this study, the authors concentrate on how reuse techniques (components and object-oriented framework) can be applied to collaborative learning domains and make some preliminary proposals for the component-based architecture. At the level of analysis there are some interesting ideas. However, they present certain limitations as only communication, cooperation, and information sharing aspects are considered. Aspects such as awareness and knowledge management need to be taken into account and analyzed at a deeper level.

Other approaches describe an initial attempt to remediate this deficiency. Thus, Anido-Rifón et al. (2001) propose a three-layered component-based framework focused on Web-based interactive and collaborative educational applications. In this approach, events produced by a given component are handled and delivered to remote components in the same application. Thus, an auditing tool registers the actions that each particular user executes (e.g., which application resources are used, when they are used, for how long, and by whom). Another component allows the sharing and distribution of events performed on the shared application's user interface, where users' actions will be forwarded to every other user in the group. Although the proposed framework supports most scenarios with their particularities, it again fails to focus neither on processing and analyzing the event information from the user actions nor on how to present this information so as to provide users' fundamental needs for groupware environments such as dynamic support to group awareness, specific components for awareness and feedback management.

At this point, one the one hand, we state the importance of the information management as a cornerstone of the collaborative learning environments. The aim is to model different aspects of interaction and thus at helping all the actors involved understand the outcomes of the synchronous and asynchronous collaborative learning process. Indeed, the specification of high-level collaborative learning processes constitutes the first step towards the classification of the many different variables that characterize collaborative interaction. In addition, this allows the identification and measurement of these variables in terms of the user and system specific events (or actions). This conceptualization enables the construction of a computational model to gather information in a structured manner and, consequently, to provide an easier and more efficient further processing and analysis of this information through different techniques (such as statistical and data mining, social network analysis etc.). The ultimate aim is to interpret the analysis results and extract, reveal and provide the actors with valuable knowledge for each of the three high-level collaborative learning processes.

On the other hand, in distributed systems, independence from any platform and interoperability between different technologies are crucial issues. In addition, in the domain of groupware applications, the interoperability between different applications to support collaborative work is fundamental. Many popular Web-based platforms have turned up in the market for the construction of distributed collaborative applications, such as

WebCT[1], PhpBB[2], and Moodle[3]. However, even though they support many aspects of collaborative applications, they do not fully support interoperability thus making the applications dependent from the programming language, underlying infrastructure, and so on. It is worth mentioning here some approaches such as Amin, Nijsure, and von Laszevski (2002), and Bote-Lorenzo, Dimitriadis, and Gómez-Sánchez (2003), which point to the use of great-scale, distributed computing environments in the development of components for collaborative learning domains. These approaches aim at meeting many important needs of collaborative learning applications, such as group activity data analysis and management, in a highly effective manner. In this context, interoperability becomes essential to meet these demanding requirements. For instance, Grid computing (Foster & Kesselman, 1998) offers high-throughput and data-intensive computing, which greatly facilitate the process of embedding information and knowledge into these applications making it possible to provide users with constant real-time awareness and feedback.

To sum up, the problems to be faced for knowledge-based collaborative learning applications are: (1) How to efficiently process the large amount of information collected during the group activity in order to facilitate its later analysis and make the extracted knowledge available to the participants even in real time; (2) How information should be analyzed and what kind of knowledge should be extracted to be fed back to the participants in order to provide the best possible support and monitoring of their learning and instructional processes. Finally, there is a need for providing an efficient and robust computational approach that enables the embedding of the collected information and the extracted knowledge into a CSCL application.

In the next section, we take these entire approaches one step further by incorporating a generic, interoperable, distributed point of view by means of our collaborative learning platform as a computational model focused on data analysis and management.

PRINCIPLES IN DESIGNING A COMPUTATIONAL MODEL FOR DATA ANALYSIS AND MANAGEMENT

CSCL applications are characterized by a high degree of user-system interaction thus generating a huge amount of action events. The management of action events is a key issue in these applications. On the one hand, the analysis of data gathered from real-life online collaborative learning situations would help one understand important issues in group functioning and collaborative learning process. On the other hand, the study of the action events can be used as a guide both in designing more functional workspaces and software components and in developing better facilities such as awareness, feedback, monitoring of the workspace, assessment and tracking of the group's work by a coordinator, tutor, etc. Indeed, by filtering out the data, an adequate event management makes it possible to establish a list of parameters that can be used for analyzing group space activities (e.g., tutor-to-group or member-to-member communication flow, asynchronism within the group space, etc.). These parameters would allow the efficiency of group activities to be improved and group behavior and individual attitudes of its members in the shared workspace to be predicted.

In addition, in designing CSCL applications it is necessary to correctly organize and administer both the resources offered by the system and the users accessing these resources. All of this user-resource and user-user interaction generates events or logs, which are collected in log files and represent the information basis for the performance of statistical processes aimed at obtaining

useful knowledge of the system. This knowledge will facilitate the collaborative learning process by keeping users aware of what is going on in the system (e.g., the contributions of others, the new documents created, etc.) and controlling users' behavior in order to provide them with support (e.g., helping students who are not able to accomplish a task on their own). Furthermore, user-user and user-resource interaction is crucial in any learning collaborative application to make it possible for groups of students to communicate with each other and to accomplish common objectives effectively (e.g., a collaborative classroom activity).

To achieve these goals, a generic, robust, interoperable, reusable, component-based and service-oriented Collaborative Learning Purpose Library (CLPL) [4] (Caballé et al., 2004) is proposed. The CLPL is based on the Generic Programming paradigm (Caballé & Xhafa, 2003) as a computational model to embed information and knowledge from group activity into CSCL applications. This platform constitutes the implementation of the above-mentioned high-level types of categories and the conceptual model of data analysis and management (see next section and Daradoumis, Martínez, & Xhafa, 2006 for a complete description of these three categories and a complete understanding of the conceptual model). The ultimate aim is to support an efficient embedding of the information collected from users and the later knowledge acquired into CSCL applications.

In developing the CLPL, we paid attention to distribution, reusability, flexibility and interoperability as key aspects to address the current strong needs for meeting more and more changing and demanding requirements in software development in general and specifically in the e-Learning domain. Indeed, over the last decade, e-Learning needs have been changing in accordance with ever more complex pedagogical models as well as with technological evolution resulting in e-Learning environments with very dynamic and changing teaching and learning requirements. These requirements represent a great challenge for the latest trends of software development to be completely satisfied.

In order to meet these requirements, we based the development of the CLPL on the model-driven development (MDD) paradigm and the framework supporting it, namely model-driven architecture (MDA). This new development paradigm has been recently attracting a lot of attention given that it allows software developers and organizations to capture every important aspect of a software system through appropriate models (Czarnecki, 2005). MDA provides great advantages in terms of complete support to the whole cycle development, cost reduction, software quality, reusability, independence from the technology, integration with existing systems, scalability and robustness, flexible evolution of software and standardization, as it is supported by the Object Management Group[5] (OMG).

In proposing MDA, two key ideas have had significant influence in OMG aiming at addressing the current challenges in software development: Service-oriented architectures (SOA) and product line architectures (PLA) (see OMG Web site). As to the former, SOA provides great flexibility to system architectures by organizing the system as a collection of encapsulated services. Hence, SOA relies on services which represent the behavior provided by a component to be met and used by any other components based only on the interface contract. As to the latter, PLA promotes developing large families of related software applications quickly and cheaply from reusable components. In PLA, a certain level of automation is provided in the form of generators (also known as component configuration tools) to realize solutions for large parts of the systems being developed (Czarnecki & Eisenecker, 2000). Taking these approaches into consideration, the CLPL is based on SOA and the Generic Programming paradigm (Czarnecki & Eisenecker, 2000; Caballe & Xhafa, 2003) as the central part of the development in MDD.

There are many views and opinions about what MDA is and is not. However, the OMG, as the most authoritative view, focuses MDA on a central vision (Czarnecki, 2005): Allow developers to express applications independently of specific implementation platforms (such as a given programming language or middleware). To this end, OMG proposes the following principles for MDA developments: First, the development of a UML-based platform independent model (PIM), second, one or several models which are platform specific models (PSM). Finally, a certain degree of automation by means of descriptions is necessary for mapping from PIM to PSM. The development of the CLPL fully followed the first and second principles while ongoing work is dealing with the last by introducing a certain level of automation by means of WSDL descriptions.

In particular, in developing the CLPL, we first created our PIM by applying the following Generic Programming ideas (Caballé & Xhafa, 2003): (1) Define the semantics of the properties and domain concepts, (2) extract and specify the common and variable properties and their dependencies in the form of abstractions found in the CSCL domain, and (3) isolate the fundamental parts in the form of abstractions from which the basic requirements were obtained, analyzed and designed as a traditional three-layer architecture (i.e., presentation, business and information). To this end, first, our PIM was expressed using UML as the standard modeling language promoted by the OMG. Second, two different PSM have been constructed so far from the PIM: A Java implementation in the form of a generic component-based library and a collection of WSDL files organized in directories that are automatically turned into generic Web-services implemented in the desired programming language and allowing developers to implement the services according to specific needs. On the one hand, the Java programming language provides great predisposition to the adaptation and correct transmission of generic software design, which make the software highly reusable. On the other hand, in order to increase flexibility and interoperability, our service-oriented PSM provides great predisposition to be involved in distributed environments supporting different middleware and programming languages. Finally, in order to automate as much as possible the transition from the PIM to the appropriate PSM, the latest research results are leading us to deal with XMI files (see OMG Web site for details), which are XML-tagged files as the result of coding UML diagrams. In combination with XSL style sheets, it is possible to turn the PIM's XMI files into WSDL files, which represent the input for a Web-service working environment to transform them into a specific-language architecture design (PSM). Lack of comply with standards of the existing UML case tools is the major problem to face next as well as how to provide a more complete and detailed realization of the desired PSM.

The design of the user interface in CSCL collaborative applications (e.g., multi-user editors) offers many more challenges than the design of interfaces for single user applications. The user interface must provide information about what others are doing to efficiently support collaborative tasks, and awareness information regarding the effects of other users' activities has to be communicated by visual or audio signals. The user interface is therefore the main way to support awareness in multi-user collaborative environments. Even though in collaborative learning environments the user interface will usually be in graphic mode, our approach considers a generic focus in order to make the logic part of the application independent from the specific design of the graphic user interface.

The design of the persistence in the CLPL is also generic and thus a disk manager abstraction has been considered. The disk manager acts as a bridge between the future application and its data to make the design of the persistence independent from the specific technology that will manage the data. This way, it is possible to treat both ordinary text files and different database system managers

during particularization. Furthermore, a complete technology-independent conceptual data model is provided as part of the PIM, which may be realized in different technologies managing generic persistence.

Finally, robustness is offered through a complete hierarchy of error treatment. As a result, a high degree of component quality and reliability is guaranteed without depending on the error treatment of the specific platform supporting the software.

The ultimate aim of the CLPL is to enable a complete and effective reutilization of its generic services and components as the skeleton for the construction of any collaborative learning application, and in particular CSCL applications. Thus, this platform implements the conceptualization of the fundamental needs existing in any collaborative learning experience. In addition, the CLPL is highly interoperable in distributed environments permitting complete flexibility of the services offered in terms of implementation languages and underlying software and hardware platforms.

THE CLPL ARCHITECTURE DESCRIPTION

The CLPL is made up of five components in all (see Figure 1) handling user management, security, administration, knowledge management and functionality. The aim is to map the essential elements involved in any CSCL collaborative learning application. The first three components are briefly described here. Due to its importance for the scope of this chapter, the last two components are explained in great detail later on.

CSCL user management: This component deals with the behavior related to user management encountered in any CSCL applications, that is, who can act as a group coordinator, group member, group-entity and system administrator. It tackles both the basic user management functions in a learning environment (namely registration,

Figure 1. Graphical representation of the CLPL components

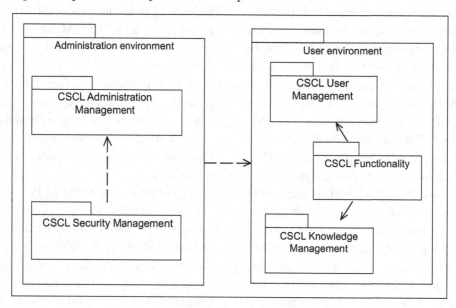

de-registration, modifications, joining a group, or meeting group members) and the user profile management. The latter implements the user and group models within a collaborative environment, thus this component provides a generic user profile entity which dynamically allows new user and group needs to be met.

CSCL Security Management: This component contains all the generic descriptions of the measures and rules decided upon to resolve authentication and authorization issues. The aim is to protect the system from both unknown users and the intentional or accidental ill use of its resources. This component's genericity lets programmers implement security issues ad hoc using the latest cryptographic security mechanisms.

CSCL Administration: This component is responsible for managing the specific data coming from log files and those analyses required to perform all the system control and maintenance for the correct administration of the system. The aim is to improve the system functioning in terms of performance and effectiveness. Although

user interaction is the most important point to be managed in CSCL applications, it is normally also important to be able to monitor and control the performance and general functioning of the system. This will enable the administrator to continuously track the critical parts of the system and act if necessary. Furthermore, this adds an implicit security layer by monitoring the system (e.g., controlling users' habits make it possible to detect fraudulent use of the system by unauthorized users). Moreover, this component manages the resources of the collaborative workspace, which can be managed by a group member acting as an administrator within the group.

Embedding Information and Knowledge into CSCL Applications

As mentioned previously, our platform represents a computational model that implements the conceptualization of the fundamental needs existing in collaborative learning applications especially for data analysis and management. This is performed by two specific components related to the knowledge management and functionality support. In the context of our research, the specific aim of this computational model is to entirely cover a process of embedding information and knowledge from group activity into CSCL applications in an efficient and effective manner. This process involves four separate, necessary steps: collection of information, processing, analysis and presentation (see Figure 2 and next subsection for details). The entire process fails if one of these steps is omitted. During the first step, a tight structuring and classification of the generated event information is needed, which is processed in an efficient way in the second step. This information is then analyzed and interpreted in order to extract the desired knowledge. The final step is to provide users with the essential awareness and feedback from the obtained knowledge.

In this section, we are therefore interested in explaining in more detail the last two components of the CLPL, namely CSCL knowledge management and CSCL Functionality. Given that these two components form the core of the computational model for data analysis and management, they are described in great detail.

CSCL Knowledge Component

The CSCL knowledge management component will manage and analyze all the specific and large user events in order to record user interaction data as information which is crucial for the correct control and administration of the collaborative learning applications. Therefore, this component completely specifies and implements the first two stages (collection of information and analysis) of the mentioned process of embedding information and knowledge into CSCL applications (Figure 2).

The final objective of this component is to extract valuable information from the events processed for later statistical analysis with the aim of revealing useful knowledge from the group

Figure 2. The process of embedding information and knowledge into applications

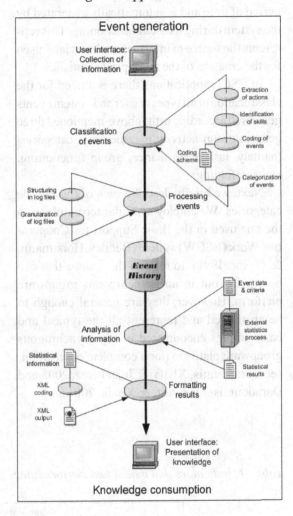

activity. This component is made up of the CSCL Activity Management and CSCL Knowledge Processing subsystems, which are explained here.

CSCL Activity Management Subsystem

This subsystem collects, classifies and structures the event information contained in the CSCL application log files so as to make it possible to facilitate its later statistical analysis.

The *log file* is a key entity made up of all the action events occurring in the system over a given period of time and is automatically generated by the system during its usual functioning. This represents the source of information that is later used for the creation of the appropriate statistics.

In CSCL applications there is a need for the classification of all types of user and system events generated according to the above-mentioned three generic group activity parameters o categories (namely, task performance, group functioning, and scaffolding).

Next, we briefly describe each of these three categories. We employ a similar terminology to the one used in the Basic Support for Cooperative Work (BSCW) system (Bentley, Horstmann, & Trevor, 1997) to refer to the actions that can be carried out in an asynchronous groupware platform. However, they are general enough to be abstracted and represent all the typical and basic actions encountered in any asynchronous groupware platform (for a complete description, see Daradoumis, Xhafa, & Juan Pérez, 2005 and Daradoumis, Martínez, & Xhafa, 2006):

Collaborative learning outcome (or task performance) measures those skills that characterize the students who participate in a learning collaborative situation in order to achieve effective group and individual performance of the task and thus obtain a successful learning outcome (see Table 1).

Group functioning indicates the skills that students should exhibit in order to enhance participation accomplish well-balanced contributions, promote better communication and coordination. Moreover, this parameter indicates adequate work load distribution, task management and workspace organization. The purpose of group functioning is to achieve an effective group interaction and functioning in a collaborative learning situation (see Table 2).

Scaffolding shows the different types of social support and help services (McGrath, 1991) that have been identified and accounted for in our model. The participants' actions and contributions aiming at getting or providing help are classified and measured according to whether they refer to the task or group functioning (see Table 3).

Table 1. Indicators that model task performance

Skills	Sub-skills (Learning outcome contribution)	Actions (&objects) involved
Basic active learning skills	Knowledge/info generation	Create doc/note
Supporting active learning skills	Knowledge/info refinement	Edit doc
	Knowledge/info elaboration	Version/Replace doc
	Knowledge/info revision	Revise/Branch doc
	Knowledge/info reinforcement	Create_Noteboard doc/URL /Notes (attach a note to a document, url or debate)
Information processing (perception) skills	Knowledge/info acknowledge	Read event

Table 2. Indicators that model group functioning

Skills	Sub-skills (Group functioning contribution)	Actions (&objects) involved
Active participation behavior and peer involve-ment skills	Participation in managing (generating, expanding and processing) info	Create Event, Change Event, Read Event
Social grounding skills	Well-balanced contributions, adequate reaction attitudes, and role playing	Create Event, Change Event, Read Event, Move Event
Task processing skills	Task planning	Create/Link Appointment Create/ChangeAccess WSCalendar
	Task (and knowledge) management	Create Folder Create Notes (create a debate space)
Workspace processing skills	Workspace organization and maintenance	Move event (cut, drop, copy, delete, forget)
Communication processing skills	Clarification	Change Description/ Change Event doc Change Description url
	Evaluation	Rate document/url
	Description (illustration)	Edit/Change Description Folder Change Description Notes
	Communication improvement	Edit Note Chvinfo/Chvno/Checkin/ Checkout doc Rename Folder/Notes/doc/url/ Appointment/WSCalendar
	Meeting accommodation	ChangeDesc/ChangeDate / ChangeLocation Appointment

Table 3. Indicators that model scaffolding

Social support
Members' commitment toward collaboration, joint learning and accomplishment of the common group goal
Level of peer involvement and their influential contribution to the involvement of the others
Members' contribution to the achievement of mutual trust
Members' motivational and emotional support to their peers
Participation and contribution to conflict resolution

Help Services
Help is timely
Help is relevant to the student's needs
Help is qualitative
Help is understood by the student
Help can readily be applied by the student

At this point, we start introducing and describing step-by-step the above-mentioned process of embedding information and knowledge into CSCL applications (see Figure 2). That will go through the rest of subsystems of the Knowledge Management component and also the Functionality component, which we will explain later.

During the first step of the process, collection and classification of the information, the aim is to correctly classify the users' interaction according to the three generic types of categories described. To this end, a complete and tight hierarchy of events (Figure 3) is provided in this subsystem. In this hierarchy, a certain degree of redundancy is allowed since both the same events to measure different elements are expected and desired. For instance, a group processing event can be simultaneously addressed as both a quantitative parameter to measure group functioning and a qualitative parameter to measure scaffolding.

Furthermore, in a collaborative learning experience, the group activity is driven by participants' actions on the generic collaborative learning resources and these actions are aggregated to

the user events to form another hierarchical tree (included in Figure 3). In this hierarchy, at a first level, we can differentiate between active and passive user actions depending on whether or not the student contributes directly to achieving the group objective. At this same level, the support action (i.e., help, motivation and encouragement) is also considered and constitutes another distinct category.

In order to correctly classify the user actions on the resources during group activity according to the event hierarchy, we propose a classification process and a coding scheme (see Table 4) for asynchronous environments based on our conceptual model. In this process, the event information collected from the log files is handled in sequential steps consisting of extraction, identification, coding, and categorization (see Figure 2).

Thus, firstly, we extract from the log files the specific action performed by a user on a resource (e.g., create a note). Secondly, this action is interpreted depending on the type of event that was involved, such as in response to a previous contribution. This represents the essential information

Figure 3. A hierarchy to collect and classify all events generated during the group activity

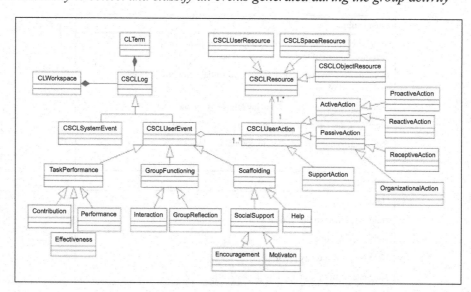

Table 4. Excerpt of a generic coding scheme for asynchronous environments

Code	Action	Event type	Skills	Category
cdc	Create document	Creation	Information generation	Contribution
cda	Create document	Activity	Active participation	Interaction
cdr	Create document	Reply	Information revision	Effectiveness
cde	Create document	Evaluation	Task contribution	Group Reflection
cnc	Create note	Creation	Information reinforcement	Performance
cns	Create note	Support	Members' involvement	Motivation
cnr	Create note	Reply	Information revision	Effectiveness
cna	Create note	Activity	Active participation	Interaction
rdp	Read document	Processing	Information acknowledge	Performance
rda	Read document	Activity	Passive participation	Interaction
mdr	Modify document	Revision	Information revision	Contribution
mda	Modify document	Activity	Active participation	Interaction
mde	Modify document	Evaluation	Task contribution	Group Reflection
rde	Replace document	Elaboration	Information elaboration	Effectiveness
rda	Replace document	Activity	Active participation	Interaction
rde	Replace document	Evaluation	Task contribution	Group Reflection

in the identification of the real intentions or skills shown by the user (e.g., creating a note during a debate can be interpreted as either revision or reinforcement of the information depending on whether the note was created in the context of a reply, an observation, agreement, etc.). Then, during the third step of the process, we uniquely codify the user event according to both the user action performed and the real user skill identified in the context of the action. Thus, for instance, creating a replying note is codified with a unique code. Finally, we categorize the user event into one of the above-mentioned group activity indicators (see Tables 1 through 3).

Given that this classification process is highly generic, we only provide the most abstract form of categorization based on the above-mentioned generic event hierarchy (see Figure 3). Thus, the specific applications using this process should categorize their event information according to their particularization of this categorization.

Note that although it is possible to use the same classification process for both synchronous and asynchronous environments, we will focus on the latter as this is still the most usual way to collaborate in online collaborative learning environments and permits the complete automation of the classification process. In contrast, in synchronous environments most of this process has to be performed manually and it needs a different coding scheme to codify the user actions.

Once the event information generated in the group activity is collected as log files and correctly classified, CSCL applications need to structure this information. The goal is to make it possible to both prepare information to facilitate its later processing and analysis and allow it to be efficiently addressed in a distributed environment where available (such as in a grid environment). Detailed information about how to structure and parallelize the processing of event log files can be found at Xhafa, Caballé, Daradoumis, and Zhou (2004) and Caballé, Paniagua, Xhafa, and Daradoumis (2005). This forms the second step of the process of embedding information and knowledge into collaborative learning applications (see Figure 2).

At this point in the process, we find the information has been collected, classified and well-structured so that it can easily and efficiently be processed and analyzed during the work of the CSCL Knowledge Processing subsystem.

CSCL Knowledge Processing Subsystem

After the event information from the structured files has been processed, the results of data processing are stored in a database manager system where all the information contained in the structured files should be correctly represented, even if they are distributed in different machines. The aim is to make it possible to consult both the desired data from the database directly (e.g., the number of connected users, the type of documents in a certain workspace) and the computed complex statistical results produced from processing these data as part of the analysis step in the process of information management (Figure 2).

The ultimate objective of this subsystem is to define a bottom-up analysis approach that processes and analyses the user events in order to decode the specific actions of the users describing their interaction during the collaboration activities. This analysis aims at identifying those sequences of actions that can be used to determine typical patterns of interactions (Inaba, Ikeda, & Mizoguchi, 2003).

Thus, at this point in our research our objective is to identify as many best collaborative learning practices as possible, which can then be translated into typical collaborative learning patterns. Based on a model of desired interaction, the system allows us to compare the learners' real interaction processes with the typical interaction patterns in order to infer whether or not the process is effective for the learner. Furthermore, the knowledge revealed by this analysis can enhance self and peer evaluation, which in turn improves the efficiency of group activities, monitoring group behavior and the individual attitudes of its members in the shared workspace. In addition, this knowledge is useful in assisting the tutor by providing the necessary means to support and assess individual and group learning outcomes.

CSCL Functionality Component

This component, which has five subsystems in all, defines the three elemental parts involved in any form of cooperation, namely coordination, communication and collaboration (Caballé et al., 2004). Coordination involves the organization of groups to accomplish the important objectives of members such as workspace organization and group structure and planning. Collaboration lets group members share any kind of resources while communication represents the basis of the whole component since it enables coordination and collaboration to be achieved by providing them with low-level communication support. Here we describe briefly three subsystems of this component that provide support to the mentioned areas.

CSCL coordination: This subsystem manages both members and resources within a collaborative group so as to both organize and coordinate the learning group and enable tutors to monitor and assess the learning process.

CSCL collaboration: The main purpose of this subsystem is to let participants share resources such as files and applications in a collaborative learning environment. Resource sharing may be in both synchronous and asynchronous modes.

CSCL communication: This subsystem manages all the low-level interactions between two or more participants within a collaborative learning group in both synchronous and asynchronous modes.

The final objective of this component is to provide functional support to CSCL applications in terms of group organization, resource sharing, user interaction, and so on. Moreover, this component implements the last stage of the process of embedding information and knowledge into CSCL applications (Figure 2) by presenting the knowledge generated to users in terms of immediate awareness and constant feedback of what is going on in the system. Due to the importance of this component, we describe here in more detail the specific subsystems of this component, namely *CSCL Awareness* and *CSCL Feedback* that explicitly provide support for awareness and feedback.

CSCL Awareness Subsystem

Awareness is essential for any of the three forms of cooperation seen. It allows implicit coordina-

tion of collaborative learning, opportunities for informal, spontaneous communication, and it keeps users informed as to what is happening in the system (Gutwin, Stark, & Greenberg, 1995). On the one hand, when awareness is synchronous, users know in real time what other co-participants are doing (e.g., during a multi-user editor session, who is editing and what is being shown) and which documents are being used by others. On the other hand, when awareness is asynchronous, users receive delayed knowledge of who, when, how and where shared resources have been created, changed or read by other users.

In order to provide the essential awareness information to support collaboration, communication and coordination effectively, this subsystem defines three generic entities respectively, namely *resource state, user status* and *group memory*. Each of these abstractions acts as a vehicle so that awareness information can be classified and presented to users in the correct form depending on the type of activity involved. Thus, first, in resource sharing (e.g., a multi-user editor session), participants are continuously modifying the state of the shared application (e.g., writing a new text comment, deleting somebody else's sketch, etc.). This way, the current application state has to be continuously propagated to the users as a news warning signal. Second, it is essential to show the current participants' status so as to be aware of the availability of them for communication (e.g., before sending a message to others it is crucial to know whether or not they are available). Finally, the persistent storage of awareness information is needed during coordination since it allows us to access documents and data, which are commonly stored for later retrieval, and also the context in which they were created. Thus, being aware of others' activities is essential for coordination (e.g., in decision-making, group organization, social engagement, etc.).

Furthermore, as regards the presentation format, this subsystem defines a *flag* as a single abstraction supporting the presentation of awareness information to users through the user interface by any means: Ranging from a visual and simple signal for warning purposes to complex visual and audio effects to keep participants aware of what is happening in the group activity.

The ultimate objective of this subsystem is to present awareness information to users in a correct, effective and immediate fashion as the presentation step in the process of embedding knowledge into CSCL applications we have been carrying out so far (Figure 2).

CSCL Feedback Subsystem

Feedback in Web-based collaborative learning environments is receiving a lot of attention due to its positive impact on the motivation, emotional state, and problem-solving abilities of groups in online collaborative learning (Zumbach, Hillers, & Reimann, 2003). It aims to influence group participants in a positive manner by means of a steady tracking of parameters outside the task itself (such as motivation and emotional state) and by giving a constant feedback of these parameters to the group. Therefore, when users participate in a CSCL application, they may enhance their abilities by increasing their knowledge about others in terms of motivation, interaction behavior and so on.

Feedback goes one step further than awareness by providing exhaustive information of what is going on in the group over a long period of time (e.g., constantly showing to each group member the absolute or relative amount of the contributions of others). Furthermore, feedback may be obtained about the emotions and motivation of participants through asking them about these states. In all cases, feedback implies receiving information simultaneously both synchronously and asynchronously since the history information shown is continuously updated.

During the feedback process, all new information communicated to the users will have been previously collected, classified and analyzed by the CSCL knowledge management component. As a consequence of the complex knowledge provided to participants in form of feedback (e.g., group's member relative and absolute amount of contributions, group's members variation in motivation and emotional state during last two hours, etc.) this subsystem makes a strong use of the statistical analysis and need to show the results obtained in complex graphical formats.

In this subsystem we define certain generic entities such as *history*, *pool* and *diagram* and functions such as *sorting*. Based on these abstractions it is possible to dynamically gather and store great amounts of history data and statistical results from the group activity in order to constantly update and present them to participants in the appropriate diagrammatic form (e.g., pie chart, histograms, etc.).

AN APPLICATION EXAMPLE: THE DEVELOPMENT OF A STRUCTURED DISCUSSION FORUM

To illustrate the approach, a prototype of a Web-based structured discussion forum was developed to validate the possibilities offered by our computational platform during data analysis and management.

We describe the main guidelines that conducted the design of this prototype that gives new opportunities to learning methodologies, such as learning by discussion, and is applied to new learning scenarios. To this end, a complete discussion and reasoning process is proposed. This application provides significant benefits for students in the context of project-based learning, and in education in general.

Pedagogical Background and Requirements

In collaborative learning environments, the discussion process forms an important social task where participants can think about the activity being performed, collaborate with each other through the exchange of ideas arising, propose new resolution mechanisms, and justify and refine their own contributions and thus acquire new knowledge (Caballé et al., 2004).

To this end, we propose a complete discussion and reasoning process based on three types of generic contributions, namely specification, elaboration and consensus. Specification occurs during the initial stage of the process carried out by the tutor or group coordinator who contributes by defining the group activity and its objectives (i.e., statement of the problem) and the way to structure it in sub-activities. Elaboration refers to the contributions of participants (mostly students) in which a proposal, idea or plan to reach a solution is presented. The other participants can elaborate on this proposal through different types of participation such as questions, comments, explanations and agree/disagree statements. Finally, when a correct proposal of solution is achieved, the consensus contributions take part in its approval (this includes different consensus models such as voting); when a solution is accepted the discussion terminates.

In a discussion process, participants perform a role according to their profile (e.g., coordinator, member, guest, etc.), have personal collaborative preferences (e.g., language) and must set up environment features (e.g., sound or visual effects, text or voice warnings, etc.) according to their personal characteristics. Participant needs are not static and they evolve as the discussion moves forward.

The Design of the Application

During the design of this application, the generic types of contributions mentioned above were supported by allowing the application to take advantage of the CLPL components. Certain correspondences are described here.

In designing the specification phase, coordination needs to be supported by essential elements such as an *agenda* and a *calendar* so as to perform all the typical tasks in this initial stage of the discussion process (such as group formation, definition of objectives, structuring the task in sub-activities and labor division). During this phase, the CSCL Coordination subsystem gave support through certain generic entities that were particularized into specific needs of this application and as a result the mentioned essential entities and processes were provided. In order to enable the tutor to both monitor and assess the discussion process, the application took advantage of the generic *report* system provided by this subsystem so as to keep track of the performance of participants and assess their contributions.

The application design includes certain thematic annotation cards (such as idea, evaluation, reply, etc.—see Figures 4 and 5) that structure the elaboration phase and can offer full help as well. All events generated are recorded as user actions, analyzed and presented as information to participants either in real time (to guide directly students during the learning activity) or after the task is over (in order to understand the collaborative process). To this end, the CSCL knowledge management component provided full support to the event management. In particular, during the elaboration phase, a complete treatment of the structured task performance events generated enables the system to keep participants aware of the contributing behavior of others, to check certain argumentative structures during discussion and also to open up the possibility to provide feedback based on the data produced. Equally, group analysis outcomes produced by the treatment of group functioning events constitute an important data source that can assist in achieving a more satisfactory solution to the problem during the consensus phase. Furthermore, the coordinator can use this same information to organize well-balanced groups during the specification phase.

Figure 4. The inclusion and setting up of parameters or indicators in the form of labels to classify the participants' interaction in a specific workspace

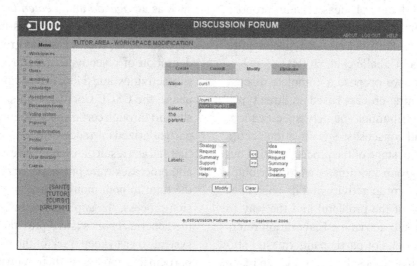

Figure 5. The discussion forum: A list of labels to categorize a contribution

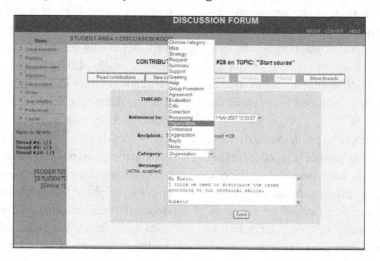

Personal features of the discussion group participants (their role, collaboration preferences and so on) were taken into account and a user and group model were designed so as to allow participants to add new services while their needs evolve as the discussion moves forward. All these user features were included by the CSCL user management component through the CSCL user profile management subsystem, providing a solid support for building and maintaining the user and group model.

Therefore, on the one hand, the structured discussion forum supports a complete discussion process through the realization of three generic contribution types and an open user and group model. On the other hand, this application constitutes a valuable resource that takes advantage of the computational platform to greatly improve essential features of a discussion process such as awareness of participant contributions and enhance the abilities of users by increasing their knowledge of each other in terms of motivation, interaction behavior and so on.

Implementation Issues

This prototype is currently working as a typical client-server Web-based application at the Open University of Catalonia and evolving rapidly to be completed. Taking advantage of the flexibility of the service-oriented approach, we used different languages for the development of the client and the server sides. Thus, on the one hand, PHP resulted in a very suitable programming language to implement the Web pages forming the user interface on the client side. Indeed, the ease of use and create forms and other graphical objects on the client side as well as being supported by most of existing Web servers, convinced us to use this popular programming language. On the other hand, the generic Web-services supporting the business and persistence layers on the server side were implemented in Java as a powerful and experienced language offering great characteristics with regard to robustness, portability, ease of use and extensibility, which create an ideal context for the implementation of the server side.

Experimental Results

From our experience at the Open University of Catalonia, the collection of structured information from an asynchronous discussion forum is highly desired for supporting the learning process. Indeed, the analysis results of this information provide the appropriate knowledge to be presented to participants in terms of awareness and feedback as well as for monitoring purposes. Our prototype allowed us to achieve these goals by supporting the following process: (1) participants are urged to label their contributions according to certain indicators (see Figure 5) based on the generic group activity parameters introduced in Section 1; (2) all information generated during the discussion is collected in log files and processed according to different criteria such as participants and time and type of contribution; (3) this information is then analyzed in order to extract desired statistics such as percentage of each participant's contributions and most active participants; (4) these analysis results are presented to participants in terms of flags showing new contributions that are pending to read, bar-charts with updated statistical information about the relative amount of contributions of each participant, etc. (see Figure 6).

In order to measure the impact of knowledge-based collaborative learning applications, such as our prototype, on the real learning experience at the Open University of Catalonia, a report is usually conducted on several groupware-based courses. Table 5 shows the results of a structured and qualitative report conducted at the end of each term in a course called "Management of Information Systems," which is formed by about 300 students distributed into 4 classrooms and 60 working groups. In this report, students are requested on evaluating the results of using the set of collaborative learning tools provided by our university to support both synchronous and asynchronous group activity.

CONCLUSION AND FUTURE WORK

This chapter describes an architecture solution that provides an efficient management of information that comes from online collaborative learning activity in order to enhance the collaborative learning process. To this end, a computational model of collaborative learning interaction in the form of a generic platform was described in detail that can be used for constructing collaborative learning applications that are enabled to manage information and knowledge in an efficient manner. This

Figure 6. Snapshot of the application showing the current list of discussion threads. Awareness of what is happening and where is presented by news and flags. Updated feedback is presented in the form of numeric and graphical quantitative statistics that allows participants to compare their performance to that of their group mates.

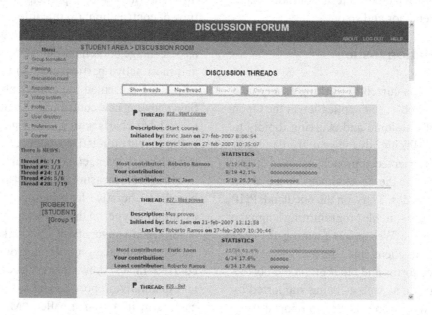

Table 5. Excerpt of a report of using knowledge-based collaborative learning applications

Selected questions	Average of structured responses (Strong positive, Positive, Neutral, Negative)	Excerpt of selected students' comments
Assess the collaborative learning tools (CLT) used.	Positive	"Apart from technical problems with the server, the CLT run smoothly and fulfilled my expectations" " Despite the distance, CLT achieved to support our work"
Did the CLT help you achieve the course goals?	Positive	"We failed not because of having problems with the CLT but the lack of engagement of certain members" "The CLT eased the group discussion, which enhanced our work."
Evaluate how the CLT fostered your active participation?	Strong positive	"It is always hard to work form the distance and keep in touch with the other group members. The CLT made this part easier by constantly providing information about what the other group mates are doing"
Describe problems and conflicts found in using the CLT.	Neutral	"I needed to make an effort to learn how to deal with the CLT but after a while I got used to it."

computational approach implements a conceptual model of data analysis and management that was briefly introduced. Finally, in order to validate the possibilities offered by this platform, a prototype of a structured forum was developed and used in experimental online collaborative learning activities. The experience gained gave us very useful insights and the confidence to use this application further in real collaborative learning situations in the Open University of Catalonia.

Currently, we are working on how to automatically describe WSDL files from our PIM model as part of the MDA-based development so that it is possible to generate PSM implementations of our collaborative learning platform in different programming languages and middleware. The next step for our prototype is to install the service-oriented PSM in the form of Web services in the nodes of a real distributed platform such as PlanetLab turned into a Grid environment. The aim is to greatly increase the application's performance by parallelizing the clients' requests and thus making it possible to provide costly functionality, such as the constant presentation of complex knowledge in real time. Our experience (Xhafa et al., 2004; Caballé et al., 2005) in dealing with distributed environments makes us confident of being successful.

Further work focuses on investigating how to integrate a portable, general and reusable collaborative learning ontology into our generic platform as a declarative representation of the knowledge embedded into collaborative learning applications with the aim of both describing how these systems are built and understanding how real groups work.

ACKNOWLEDGMENT

This work has been partially supported by the Spanish MCYT project TSI2005-08225-C07-05. We would also like to thank our colleagues at the Open University of Catalonia, the Polytechnic University of Catalonia, and the University of Valladolid in Spain for their human and scientific support as well as all the students who eagerly participated in this experience.

REFERENCES

Amin, K., Nijsure, S., & von Laszevski, G. (2002). Open Collaborative Grid Services Architecture (OCGSA), In *Euroweb 2002 Conference, The Web and the GRID: From e-Science to e-Business* (pp. 101-107). Oxford, UK: The British Computer Society.

Anido, L., Llamas, M., Fernández, M.J., Caeiro, M., Santos, J., & Rodríguez, J. (2001). A component model for standardized web-based education. *ACM Journal of Educational Resources in Computing, 1(2)*, 1-21.

Bacelo P.T.A., & Becker, K. (2002). A component-based architecture to support collaborative application design, In Haake & J. Pino (Eds.), *Groupware: Design, implementation and use.* (LNCS 2440, pp. 134-143). London: Springer-Verlag.

Bentley, R., Horstmann, T., & Trevor, J. (1997). The World Wide Web as enabling technology for CSCW: The case of BSCW. *Computer-Supported Cooperative Work: The Journal of Collaborative Computing, 6(2)*, 111-134.

Bote-Lorenzo, M. L., Dimitriadis, Y. A., & Gómez-Sánchez, E. (2003). Grid characteristics and uses: A grid definition. In F. Fernández et al. (Eds.), *European Across Grids Conference* (LNCS 2970, pp. 291-298). Berlin: Springer-Verlag.

Caballé, S., & Xhafa, F. (2003). A study into the feasibility of generic programming for the construction of complex software. In *Proceedings of the 5th Generative Programming and Component Engineering/Net.Objectsdays 2003* (pp. 441-446). Retrieved March 10, 2007, from http://www.old.netobjectdays.org/pdf/03/papers/ws-yrw/441.pdf

Caballé, S., Xhafa, F., Daradoumis, T., & Marquès, J.M. (2004). Towards a generic platform for developing CSCL applications using grid infrastructure. In *Proceedings of the First International Workshop on Collaborative Learning Applications of Grid Technology*. Chicago: IEEE Computer Society

Caballé, S., Paniagua, C., Xhafa, F., & Daradoumis, Th. (2005). A grid-aware implementation for providing effective feedback to on-line learning groups. In R. Meersman et al. (Eds.), *On the Move to Meaningful Internet Systems 2005* (LNCS 3762, pp. 274-285). Berlin: Springer-Verlag.

Czarnecki, K. (2005). Overview of Generative Software Development, In J.-P. Banâtre et al. (Ed.), *Unconventional Programming Paradigms (UPP) 2004* (LNCS 3566, pp. 313-328). Berlin: Springer-Verlag.

Czarnecki, K., & Eisenecker, U.W. (2000). *Generative programming: Methods, techniques, and applications*. Boston: Addison-Wesley.

Daradoumis, T., Xhafa, F., & Juan Pérez, A. (2005). A framework for assessing self peer and group performance in e-learning. In T.S. Roberts (Ed.), *Self, peer, and group assessment in e-learning* (pp. 279-294). Hershey, PA: Idea Group.

Daradoumis, T., Martínez, A. & Xhafa, F. (2006). A layered framework for evaluating online collaborative learning interactions. *International Journal of Human-Computer Studies. Special Issue on "Theoretical and Empirical Advances in Groupware Research,"* 64(7), 622-635.

Dillenbourg, P. (1999). Introduction; What do you mean by "Collaborative Learning?" In P. Dillenbourg (Ed.), *Collaborative learning. Cognitive and computational approaches* (pp. 1-19). Oxford: Elsevier Science.

Foster, I., & Kesselman, C. (1998). *The Grid: Blueprint for a future computing infrastructure.* San Francisco: Morgan Kaufmann.

Gutwin, C., Stark, G., & Greenberg, S. (1995). Support for workspace awareness in educational groupware. In J. L. Schnase & E. L. Cunnius (Eds.) *ACM Conference on Computer Supported Collaborative Learning* (pp. 147-156). Mahwah, NJ: Lawrence Erlbaum Associates.

Inaba, A., Ikeda, M., & Mizoguchi, R. (2003). What learning patterns are effective for a learner's growth?—An ontological support for designing collaborative learning. In *Proceedings of the International Conference on Artificial Intelligence in Education* (pp. 219-226). Sydney, Australia.

Koschmann, T. (1996). Paradigm shifts and instructional technology: An introduction. In T. Koschmann (Ed.), *CSCL: Theory and practice of an emerging paradigm* (pp. 1-23). Mahwah, NJ: Lawrence Erlbaum Associates.

Martínez, A., de la Fuente, P., & Dimitriadis, Y. (2003). Towards an XML-based representation of collaborative interaction. In B. Watson et al. (Eds.), *Proceedings of the International Conference on Computer Support for Collaborative Learning 2003*, Bergen (pp. 379-384). Dordrecht: Kluwer Academic Publishers.

McGrath, J.E. (1991). Time, interaction and performance: A theory of groups. *Small Group Research, 22*(2), 147-174.

Watson, P. (2003). Databases and the grid. In F. Berman et al. (Eds.), *Grid computing: Making the global infrastructure a reality* (pp. 363-384). Chichester, UK: John Wiley & Sons, Inc.

Xhafa, F., Caballé, S., Daradoumis, Th., & Zhou, N. (2004). A grid-based approach for processing group activity log files. In R. Meersman et al. (Eds.), *On the Move to Meaningful Internet Systems 2004* (LNCS 2392, pp. 175-186). Berlin: Springer.

Zumbach, J., Hillers, A., & Reimann, P. (2003). Supporting distributed problem-based learning: The use of feedback in online learning. In T. Roberts (Ed.), *Online collaborative learning: theory and practice* (pp. 86-103), Hershey, PA: Idea Group.

ENDNOTES

[1] WebCT Learning Systems is found at: http://www.webct.com (Web page as of March 2007).

[2] PhpBB Community Building Software is found at: http://www.phpbb.com/ (Web page as of March 2007).

[3] Moodle is found at: http://moodle.org/ (Web page as of March 2007).

[4] The Java API of the CLPL is found at: http://cv.uoc.edu/~scaballe/clpl/api/ (Web page as of March 2007).

[5] Object Management Group: Model-Driven Architecture is found at: http://www.omg.com/mda (Web page as of March 2007).

Section III.b
Adaptivity

Chapter XIII
From Learning Objects to Adaptive Content Services for E-Learning

Peter Brusilovsky
University of Pittsburgh, USA

Vincent P. Wade
Trinity College, Ireland

Owen Conlan
Trinity College, Ireland

ABSTRACT

This chapter argues that a new generation of powerful e-learning systems could start on the crossroads of two emerging fields: courseware reuse and adaptive educational systems. We argue for a new distributed architecture for e-learning systems based on the idea of adaptive reusable content services. This chapter discusses problems that have to be solved on the way to the new organization of e-learning and reviews existing approaches and tools that are paving the way to next-generation e-learning systems. It also presents two pioneer systems—APeLS and KnowledgeTree that have attempted to develop a new service-based architecture for adaptive e-learning.

INTRODUCTION

Adaptive Web-based educational systems and standard-based courseware reuse systems con-

stitute two significant streams of research and development in the field of e-learning. *Courseware reuse* systems have emerged as a reaction to the standard practice of "hardwiring" high-quality educational materials within course content. This practice made it impossible to reuse educational material and resulted in the wasted efforts of the educational community as a whole to the need to re-develop the same material again and again. The early answer to this problem was a database of educational resources and a courseware-reuse approach to authoring new courses (Olimpo, Persico, Sarti, & Tavella, 1990). The courseware reuse ideas have found a fertile ground in Web-enhanced education. Some early large projects in the field of Web-based education like ARIADNE (Forte, Forte, & Duval, 1996) and MTS (Graf & Schnaider, 1997), funded by the European Community, were centered on such a courseware reuse approach. ARIADNE provides a very good example of a courseware reuse architecture. It includes multiple *pools* (repositories) of educational material indexed with metadata and an open set of tools to produce, index, and reuse this material. Other well-known European projects driven by the same motivation are PROMETEUS (http://www.prometeus.org/) and GESTALT (Wade & Doherty, 2000). In the USA the reusability approach has been promoted by EOE Foundation (http://www.eoe.org/) and GEM Consortium (http://www.geminfo.org/).

Adaptive Web-based educational systems (Brusilovsky & Peylo, 2003) emerged as an alternative to the traditional "one size fits all" approach in the development of educational courseware. These systems build a model of the goals, preferences and knowledge of each individual student, and use this model throughout the interaction with the student in order to adapt to the needs of that student. The first pioneer adaptive Web-based educational systems were developed in 1995-1996 (Brusilovsky, Schwarz, & Weber, 1996a, 1996b; De Bra, 1996; Nakabayashi et al., 1995; Okazaki, Watanabe, & Kondo, 1996). Since that time, a number of systems have been created all around the world. The majority of adaptive Web-based educational systems are based on technologies developed in the areas of adaptive hypermedia

(AH) (Brusilovsky, 1996) and intelligent tutoring systems (ITS) (Polson & Richardson, 1988).

The methods and tools developed by both researchers of courseware reuse systems and adaptive Web-based educational systems can contribute to creating better Web-enhanced courses. We believe that a way to the future starts on the crossroads of courseware reuse and adaptive educational systems. This chapter attempts to bridge the gap between the information retrieval abilities of modern educational material repositories and the just-in-time delivery and personalization power of ITS and AH technologies. We start with a brief analysis of these approaches comparing their strong and weak points (illustrated later in Table 1).

The courseware reuse frameworks such as ARIADNE allow a course author to search for the relevant learning objects in repositories of educational material and "paste" them into their courses (Figure 1). This approach reduces course development time and improves the quality of courses by making high-quality educational material available for the learning community. At the same time, current implementations of this approach have at least two serious problems.

Firstly, courses developed with this reusability approach suffer from "one size fits all" problem. When identifying relevant material and organizing it within a course section, teachers have to think about the class in general. The students in any class have different interests, knowledge, backgrounds, and learning styles. Some material carefully selected by the teacher can be useless for some students and only distract them. Some material that is important for particular students might not even be selected. An organization of material that benefits one category of learners may create obstacles for other categories. This problem is becoming especially important in Web-based education where the variety of learners taking the same course is constantly increasing.

Secondly, modern reusability frameworks implicitly assume that a learning object is a moveable

Figure 1. Courseware reuse approach to course design and delivery. Authoring tools allow the teachers to find and include resources into their course material. The student accesses static course material.

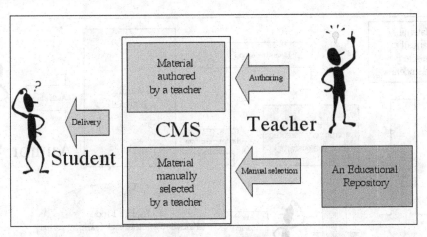

entity—usually a file that is stored in a repository and can be reused by *copying* the learning object into the course to be created. However, fragments of adaptive educational content in modern Web-based systems are often not files but services delivered by dedicated Web servers. These activities cannot be simply packaged, stored, and copied the same way as an image, a text file, or even an applet—they have to reside on a dedicated server and launched from it on demand. An inability of modern reusability frameworks to handle interactive services makes it impossible for their users to work with more highly interactive learning content that is highly interactive or adaptive by its nature. In turn, without this kind of advanced content, courses developed with existing frameworks are most often simple "page turners".

The situation in the world of adaptive Web-based systems is quite different. These systems offer a different set of benefits to their users. Adaptive e-learning systems solve the "one size fits all" problem by attempting to provide the best support for every student. Using individual student models and educational material enhanced with pedagogical metadata (such as required competencies, or relevancy to learning styles) adaptive hypermedia systems (AHS) and intelligent tutor-

ing systems (ITS) are able to dynamically select the most relevant learning material from their knowledge bases and present it at the right time and in the right way for every individual student, thus making the best use of every fragment of educational material (Figure 2). Many of these systems are able to offer advanced interactive and adaptive learning activities to their users. Observing students' work with these activities is the best way for these systems to keep their student models up-to-date.

The problems of existing adaptive e-learning systems are also quite different from the problems of existing reusability frameworks. The source of these problems is simple: Adaptive educational systems are not designed for the modern e-learning context, where a teacher or course provider is typically interested in developing a specifically targeted course by reusing existing educational content from multiple repositories. Currently, existing adaptive e-learning systems have to be used as a whole, not component by component. This creates a significant obstacle for their practical application. While adaptive technologies themselves can be applied to achieve any specified learning goals, in most existing systems, educational goals are pre-defined by the

Figure 2. An adaptive educational hypermedia system can adaptively serve relevant educational material to every student; however, it is not designed for the modern e-learning context

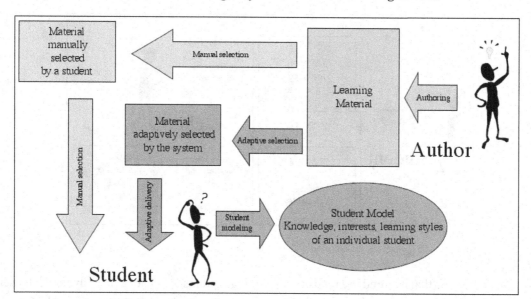

authors (of the adaptive content). The adaptivity in the course is frequently embedded across the content itself or is in the actual adaptive system, which executes the content. A teacher who is interested in reusing some adaptive content from an existing adaptive hypermedia system has only one choice—to accept the whole system with its goals and sacrifice his or her specific teaching goals. Naturally, except from the authors of existing adaptive systems themselves, such acceptance is difficult to achieve. Secondly, most known adaptive hypermedia systems are built around "closed corpus" learning material and are not able to take into account any external content. Those who adopt such adaptive systems have to accept the inability to benefit from any new content coming from existing repositories of learning material.

As we can see from the analysis above, both leading approaches have strengths and weaknesses (Table 1). While their strong points allow them to support a reasonable number of e-learning scenarios, their weaknesses prevent them from

supporting the most exciting and promising model of e-learning—allowing teachers to reuse adaptive and interactive learning activities in the context of their courses. Adaptive e-learning systems can include "hardwired" adaptive and interactive activities, but they provide little support for the teacher in reusing external activities organized along his or her preferred course structure. Reusability frameworks allow the teacher to develop a course reusing some external activities, but they cannot handle interactive and adaptive content.

A good illustration of this unfortunate situation is the case of ELM-ART LISP problems. ELM-ART is an adaptive LISP course (Brusilovsky, Schwarz, & Weber, 1996b) that includes many LISP programming problems. ELM-ART problems are more than just textual problem statements. These problems are fully interactive learning activities backed by ELM-ART's unique knowledge-based functionality. In response to student program solutions sent to an ELM-ART server, the system can check, diagnose, and correct them. The results of this diagnosis are used

Table 1. The features of the e-learning paradigms compared

	Reusability frameworks	Adaptive E-Learning systems	Adaptive Content Services
Support teacher in developing a custom E-Learning course	Yes	No	Yes
Allow the use of external repositories of learning material	Yes	No	Yes
Can adapt to individual students	No	Yes	Yes
Can include advanced learning activities	No	Yes	Yes
Allow reuse of external advanced learning activities	No	No	Yes

to update the student model that ELM-ART uses to adapt to that student. ELM-ART problems cannot be moved or copied—they have to be served directly from a dedicated ELM-ART server. At the moment, in order to work with ELM-ART problems a student has to login to ELM-ART and to navigate to the parts of the ELM-ART adaptive hypermedia course where these problems are located. Imagine that a computer science teacher wants to reuse ELM-ART problems to enrich her/his own LISP course that is different from the one supported by ELM-ART. This would greatly enrich the course allowing it to benefit from more than 10 years of research behind ELM-ART adaptive diagnosis technology. Currently, it is simply not possible—these problems cannot be extracted from ELM-ART and reused elsewhere. If a teacher wants to use these problems, s/he has to use the whole ELM-ART course giving up her "own" course structure. Alternatively, if a teacher insists on her/his own way to teach LISP, s/he will be unable to use the ELM-ART problems and settle for simpler "reusable" learning content such as static Web pages or pictures. ELM-ART problems are only some of the hundreds of advanced adaptive and interactive content items, which currently are available on the Web. They can be used in their original context (as long as the original system is running which is often not the case), but cannot be reused in the context of

new courses. Moreover, this situation prevents content developers from creating new advanced (and expensive) interactive content. Without clear prospects for broad reuse, the cost of developing advanced content is rarely justified.

To address this problem we argue that e-learning needs a new reusability framework that shifts the focus from reusable "static" learning objects to reusable "dynamic" adaptive content services. This new framework should allow course developers to develop their courses in their preferred way, while facilitating the reuse of powerful, adaptive and interactive content. It should also allow content developers to focus on developing more advanced content. An adaptive content services framework will combine strong features of the two analyzed approaches (Table 1). The authors of this chapter have been exploring the ideas of adaptive content services in their projects for several years and developed a new vision of a service-based distributed architecture for adaptive e-learning. In this chapter, we present our vision of this architecture, analyze several known problems, and describe our attempts to implement these architectures in our Adaptive Personalized E-Learning Service (APeLS) and KnowledgeTree frameworks. It is important to stress that both frameworks, while implementing innovative ideas, attempt to stay close to the needs of practical Web-based education. The authors integrate a vision of academic researchers with a solid practical experience in commercial e-learning. To prove our ideas we have used our frameworks in several real courses at the University of Pittsburgh and Trinity College, Dublin.

ADAPTIVE SERVICES FOR E-LEARNING

The research challenge discussed in this chapter was to develop a framework for e-learning that combines the attractive features of the modern reusability approach to e-learning with the power of adaptive Web-based systems. It means that the target framework should keep the winning features of the reusability approach allowing teachers to structure a course according to their specific needs while also helping them to reuse existing relevant learning content instead of creating everything from scratch. At the same time, the framework should allow teachers to create adaptive courses and reuse not just files, but any interactive learning activity. This challenge was addressed by several research groups, which suggested and explored a range of innovative ideas (see *Related Work* section).

This chapter presents and compares the frameworks developed by research groups in Pittsburgh and Dublin. Both groups attempted to address the problem as a whole and it resulted in two solutions, which are very similar in a number of critical features. The first key feature of our solutions was to separate the course management system (also referred to as a learning management system) from the content. In our vision, the course management system is a portal that provides structured access to educational content without storing it. The content itself comes directly from different content services that are independent from any portal and generally reside on different servers distributed over multiple locations. Portals are maintained by *course providers* while content services are maintained by *content providers*.

Many portals can use the same content service in different contexts.

The second key feature was to separate content specification from the real content. In the traditional (reuse) model the search for the relevant content starts with some kind of content specification in terms of duration, pedagogical type, topics covered, etc. The teachers then attempt to find the desired content in a repository by issuing a formal search query in terms of content metadata. Finally, the relevant content is manually selected, copied, and integrated into the course. In our model, the teacher is able to stop at the stage of specification of the desired material (a narrative in APeLS, a sequence of lectures with objectives in KnowledgeTree). The portal at runtime, resolves this specification by automatically finding or generating relevant content.

The key features of our frameworks listed above allow us to achieve the target functionality. The portal-service separation makes it easy for the system to reuse any interactive or adaptive content that cannot be just embedded into the traditional course management system. The separation of content specification and resolution in time opens the way to adaptivity. While staying within the objectives specified by a teacher in a content specification, the framework can take into account knowledge, goals, and other features of an individual student and adaptively select, generate, and arrange relevant learning content. In addition, this architecture solves the problem of outdated content. The resource repositories are being constantly updated. Some better resources could be added to the existing repositories, some completely new repositories could become available. When content specification is resolved dynamically the overall system can benefit from the best content available at the time of using the system.

It is important to note that the proposed architecture is not a radical replacement, but an extension of the existing reusability approach. The new architecture allows teachers to be flexible by specifying content requirements as well as allowing them to reuse customizable, distributed and dynamic services. At the same time new functionality does not replace the old one, but safely co-exists with it. A teacher who wants to use a specific piece of content (either a file or a service) can still use the existing approach based on manual selection of content and its static allocation to a specific location in the courseware. Figure 3 presents a combination of automatic runtime selection of material based on the concepts in the course structure specified by the teacher, as well as allowing teacher intervention in manually selecting material for the course. It indicates how the teacher can provide the overall course structure i.e. define the scope, concepts and kinds of learning activities to be included in the course, and indicate the kinds of adaptivity that the teacher would like to be offered to the student, for example, adaptivity-based on student's prior knowledge/competencies, goals, learning styles etc. The adaptive service then reconciles this structure (course requirements) with appropriate composed learning material (learning objects) and includes

appropriate adaptive techniques to support kinds of adaptivity indicated by the teacher. The teacher is also able to include manually selected content if she so wishes. The adaptive (personalized) course is then offered to the student. It should be noted that in better adaptive e-learning systems, the selection of actual content is made while the student is using the course, so that the very latest student and content information is used to satisfy the students learning needs. When first logging on to the adaptive course, the student is asked about various aspects to assist in populating that student's model. Instruments to illicit a student's model could include questionnaires, pre-tests, or monitoring instruments which augment the student model during the usage of the course. A more comprehensive description of the challenges and methodology for adaptive course composition and the tools that support it, are presented in Dagger, Wade, and Conlan (2004).

Since our groups were driven by similar goals, our solutions are very similar—they advocate the distributed architecture based on reusable and adaptive content services and runtime adaptive

Figure 3. The target system should combine the benefits of courseware reuse systems and adaptive Web-based educational systems

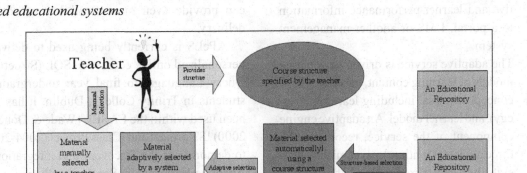

resolution of content specifications. At the same time, technically our solutions are quite different and demonstrate two possible approaches to the incremental move from the current approach based on courseware management systems and learning objects to the more powerful frameworks based on open portals and distributed adaptive content services. These solutions are presented in the two following sections.

ADAPTIVE PERSONALIZED E-LEARNING SERVICE

The Adaptive Personalized e-learning Service (APeLS) was developed as a service to deliver personalized educational courses based on a multi-model, metadata driven approach (ADLI, 2003). Two important features of the architecture address the twin goals of Adaptive Content Services:

- The adaptive courseware is NOT offered as content but rather as a service which can be delivered through a portal (or a conventional learning management system). APeLS offers a service interface via which the adaptive course can be delivered. The interface also offers a separate API to pass administrative and learner performance information to a portal, LMS or another management system.
- The adaptive service is driven by separate models of learning content, narrative (i.e. a concept traversal including learning strategy), and learner model. An adaptive engine component of the service, reconciles the three models at runtime to dynamically generate the personalized course for the learner. By allowing the learner access to the learner model, he/she is free to re-personalize and adapt of the course during runtime.

The Content Model contains metadata descriptions of the actual small size learning ob-

jects (we term the learning objects "pagelets" to indicate their typical size as occupying less than a screen area). The Narrative Model only refers to concepts which may be selected as part of a course. There is no direct reference between the narrative model and actual content. The mapping between narrative and content is performed at run-time by the adaptive engine, which reconciles the metadata imperatives of the narrative model with the metadata of the content model. Thus the narrative and content models are linked via a shared (or mapped) metadata vocabulary. The metadata used in APeLS is an extension of the IEEE LOM (IEEE LTCS WG12, 2002) and ADL SCORM (ADLI, 2003). The third model upon which APeLS provides adaptivity is the learner model. These models can be populated from the learning portal, Learning Management System (LMS), or (more typically) captured via a learner instrument under the control of the learner. The APeLS architecture is extensible in that other models can be developed by the content service provider and can be easily integrated into the service. One such model would be a 'terminal' or 'device' model. This allows adaptivity based on the presentation power of the learners access device (e.g., PDA, laptop, eBook etc.). In this way the Adaptive Personalized E-Learning Service can provide even more flexibility of content delivery.

APeLS is currently being used to deliver a personalized online courses in SQL (Structured Query Language) to final year undergraduate students in Trinity College, Dublin. It has also been used within the EASEL (Wade & Doherty, 2000) IST project and iClass Project (2004-2008) to demonstrate the discovery and integration of Adaptive Hypermedia Services with traditional (static) online learning content.

APeLS Models and Architecture

APeLS utilizes a number of metadata and information repositories (Figure 4):

- **Learner metadata repository:** This repository stores all of the metadata representing the individual learners in the system. This metadata conforms to the Learner Model (Owen Conlan, Wade, Bruen, & Gargan, 2002; O'Keeffe, Brady, Conlan, & Wade, 2006).
- **Content metadata repository:** Stored in this repository are the metadata records, conforming to the Content Model corresponding to each piece of learning content (or learning object metadata)
- **Narrative metadata repository:** Stored in this repository are the metadata records that describe the learning objectives and pedagogical approach for each narrative in the narrative repository (i.e. description of the available narratives).
- **Content repository:** All of the pagelets referred to by the Content Model Repository are contained in this repository
- **Narrative repository:** The narrative repository stores all of the narratives used to construct personalized courses.

There are also two candidate group repositories:

- **Candidate content groups:** The groups in this repository reference metadata in the Content Metadata Repository that fulfill the same learning goal. The content model metadata determines how the content differs, i.e. technically or in educational approach.
- **Candidate narrative groups:** This repository determines groups of narratives that encapsulate the same knowledge, but employ different pedagogical approaches to structuring the content.

At the core of APeLS is the adaptive engine (AE), which uses the Java Expert System Shell (JESS) with customized functions as the basis of its rules engine. The role of the rules engine is to produce a model for a personalized course based on a narrative and the learner model. The XML-based personalized course model encapsulates the structure of the learner's course and contains the candidate content groups that fulfill the learner's

Figure 4. Adaptive Hypermedia Service Architecture

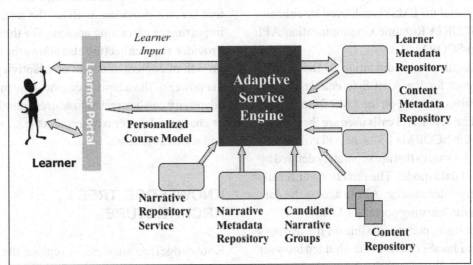

learning requirements in accordance with the narrative. The candidate content groups can be thought of as the abstraction layer between the narrative (which defines various dynamic courses in terms of concepts) and the actual content (fine grained learning objects).

The AE also utilizes a candidate selector for choosing the appropriate narrative by reconciling information in the learner model with the candidate narrative groups. The candidate selector is also used to choose the appropriate piece of content to deliver from a candidate content group when the personalized course content is being generated from the personalized course model.

The AE has a learner modeler component that enables input from the course to be translated into changes in the learner's information. This learner modeler component is used to populate the learner's model when the learner initially enters the adaptive hypermedia service. It can also be used directly during runtime to modify the learner's model—these modifications may either be initiated by the learner or by the engine itself and can be initiated directly from the JSP frontend.

The APeLS service is based on the notion that an adaptive content provider should be a service provider rather than a repository for extraction of content. Communication between APeLS and a learning portal (or LMS) is achieved by enhancing the SCORM Runtime Communication API as used in SCORM v1.3.

This requires a modification to the HTML frame layout for the APeLS to enable calls to API functions residing on the LMS from APeLS content. The actual API calls used are the same as those used in SCORM v1.3 as the API is designed to get and set values that are separately defined by an external data model. The remote APeLS calls the Content Interworking API to access the data model on the learning portal (or LMS).

The learning content (visible on the learners screen) and JavaScript API (via a hidden browser frame) are delivered to the learner's browser.

An API function, (which is in the hidden frame) is called from the content frame, for example, LMSGetValue ("cmi.core.lesson_status"). The hidden API frame then communicates the request to the learning portal (or LMS). The learning portal returns the value (in this case of cmi.core.leason_status) to the API Frame. The API function returns the value to content frame from which it may be passed back to the Adaptive Hypermedia Service (Figure 5).

Using these services, the deep complexity of the various metadata models (content, narrative, user) is simplified. The exported information model of the learner (and her performance) is made available via the API. The modified SCORM v1.3 interface facilitates integration with IMS and SCORM Compliant LMSs with only very minor adjustment of the information model passed between the learning portal (LMS) and the Adaptive Content Service. There is no change to the actual API function signatures (Conlan, Wade, Gargan, Hockemeyer, & Albert, 2002).

APeLS offers teachers the ability to scope the overall course (or part of a course) they wish to use from the Adaptive Service Provider, while still allowing a considerable degree of learner adaptivity within that scope. The service-oriented approach empowers the teacher to construct courseware or educational experiences from different content service providers without the necessity of importing or extracting content. For the Content Provider, the architecture also allows the graceful growth of content and axes of adaptivity. Using the power of the adaptive engine, new models of adaptivity can be created to address new markets or changing learner requirements (e.g., mobility and wireless access).

KNOWLEDGE TREE ARCHITECTURE

KnowledgeTree attempts to replace the current monolithic course management systems (CMS)

Figure 5. Learning portal and Adaptive Service Interface

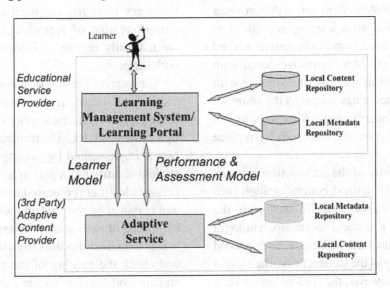

such as Blackboard (Blackboard Inc., 2002) or WebCT (WebCT, 2002) with a community of communicating servers. The architecture anticipates the presence of at least three kinds of servers: activity servers, learning portals, and student model servers (Figure 6). A *learning portal* plays a role similar to a modern CMS. It allows a teacher to design a course and manages the student interaction with the course. The difference between KnowledgeTree and a LMS/CMS is that the learning content (activities) in KnowledgeTree resides not in the portal, but in multiple distributed *activity servers*. An activity server plays a role similar to an educational repository in the sense that it hosts some (usually specialized) learning content. Unlike repositories that are essentially pools for storing learning materials that can be copied and inserted into courses, an activity server is responsible for both storing, and delivering *learning activities*. A portal has an ability to query activity servers for relevant activities and launch remote activities selected by students. An activity server is able to inform portals about available activities and provide complete support for a student working with one of its activities. The

student model server collects data about student performance from each portal and each activity server that work with a student. It also provides information about the student that can be used by adaptive activity servers to personalize their communication with the student. The presence of multiple adaptive activities requires a centralized student modeling architecture.

With the KnowledgeTree architecture, a teacher develops a course using one of the existing portals and many activity servers. A student works through the portal serving this course, but interacts with many learning activities served directly by various activity servers. The adaptivity is supported by a student model server that collects student performance data from the portal and the activity servers. A student model server can reside on the student's own computer and support just one user. It also can reside on a university computer and support the whole class of students.

The KnowledgeTree architecture is open and flexible. It allows the presence of multiple portals, activity servers, and student modeling servers. The open nature of it allows even small research groups or companies to be "players" in the new e-learning market. An activity server that provides some specific innovative learning activities can be immediately used in multiple courses served by different portals. An innovative portal with a good interface can successfully compete with other portals since it has access to the same set of resources as other portals. A more powerful student model server can successfully replace older servers.

The open nature of the architecture is based on several clearly defined communication protocols between components. To start with, the architecture has a protocol for transparent login and authentication. Each adaptive activity should know the identity of the student to use the correct student model, however, the student logs in only once. Second, it has a standard protocol for a portal to send a query to the activity servers and the standard protocol for the activity servers to respond. Third, it has a protocol for an activity server to send the information about the student progress to the student model server and a protocol to request information about the student from the student model. In addition to that, our architecture needs a resource discovery/exchange protocol. To benefit from rich distributed learning content, a portal should know about many servers and types

of activities they can offer. However, the resource discovery issue has not been addressed in the current version of KnowledgeTree. Currently, we manually register existing activity servers with the portal.

The current version of KnowledgeTree provides very simple implementation of the first three protocols. Every activity is called directly by a dedicated URL. The transparent authentication is implemented by passing a session and a student identifier as a part of activity URL. The session identifier is required for security reasons and is issued by the student model server at the beginning of each session. Every activity server is able to extract this data from the activity URL and check the validity of the request with the student model server. We use a simple http-based communication language between components that we have developed in our past research on distributed intelligent tutoring (Brusilovsky, Ritter, & Schwarz, 1997).

The KnowledgeTree architecture allows multiple portals that can support different educational paradigms and approaches. Moreover, while the APeLS architecture suggests adaptive services as the main source of adaptivity, in KnowledgeTree adaptive functionality can reside on several components including activity servers, value-adding services, and portals. At the moment, we have implemented two versions of the portal also called KnowledgeTree that is targeted to support a lecture-based educational process and is focused on dynamic and adaptive selection of learning activities. The KnowledgeTree model allows an author to develop a course as a tree of modules (Figure 7) and to specify educational material for each module. We distinguish primary material that comprises a minimal set of activities necessary for an average student to learn the module and additional material that enhances the learning experience and provides relevant activities for the students with different learning styles and levels of knowledge.

Figure 6. Main components of the KnowledgeTree distributed architecture

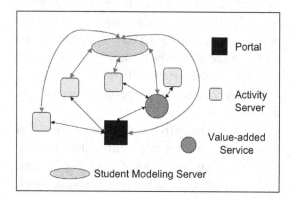

To select the material for each section an author specifies an educational goal for a section in terms of metadata associated with necessary learning activities. During the course design process, the educational goal is used by the system to select a subset of relevant educational activities from multiple learning repositories known to the system. From this pre-selected subset of activities an author can manually select the most relevant primary and additional learning activities. To complement the set of activities found in the repositories, some activities can be designed by the author. The learning goal specified by the author is retained and stored with the module. When a particular student accesses the module during the educational process, the portal uses this learning goal as well as the student model to select and present adaptively the most relevant additional material for the given student *at runtime*. Adaptive runtime selection and adaptive navigation support techniques allow the system to accommodate the volatile and expanding nature of learning repositories and student individual differences (Figure 7).

In addition to the overall architecture, a set of protocols, and the KnowledgeTree portal, the list of components developed so far includes several protocol-compliant activity servers, three value-adding services (Brusilovsky, Sosnovsky, & Yudelson, 2004), and two student modeling servers. All of the activity servers were developed for the area of teaching programming. The WebEx system (Brusilovsky, 2001) serves interactive annotated program examples, the QuizPACK (Brusilovsky & Sosnovsky, 2005) serves parameterized questions, and WADEIn II (Brusilovsky & Loboda,

Figure 7. KnowledgeTree portal enables a teacher to structure a course as a tree of modules; teaching material from multiple repositories can be statically or dynamically attached to any node of the course

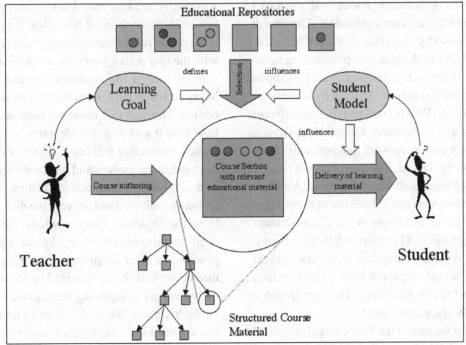

Figure 8: KnowledgeTree portal showing a range of interactive activities assembled for an introductory programming course. The left side shows the structure of the course. The right side shows an opened question delivered from QuizPACK activity server.

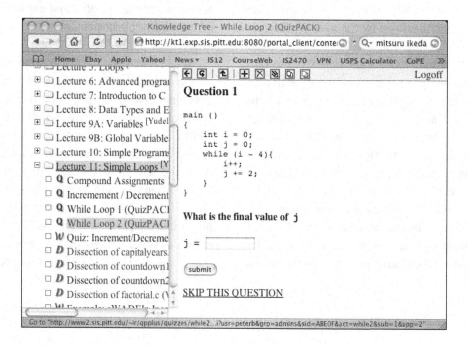

2006) delivers demonstrations and exercises related with expression evaluation. The fourth server Knowledge Sea (Brusilovsky, Chavan, & Farzan, 2004) is domain independent, and currently used to provide an interactive access to open corpus learning material. All activity servers are self-containing Web servers running on different platforms and completely independent from a portal. Each server can work independently from the KnowledgeTree architecture, but will require a student to login in this mode of work. All these servers implement our simple transparent login protocol, resource delivery protocol, and student modeling protocol. They can work (with transparent login) with any compliant portal and student modeling server. Figure 8 shows the interface of our most recent KnowledgeTree server with a QuizPACK question opened.

The first version of the KnowledgeTree portal together with WebEx and QuizPACK servers and a primitive student model server was piloted in fall 2001. Since then we have used progressively more powerful versions of the portal and all along with the four activity servers as a primary course support tool in the context of several courses. Many activities have been reused in more than one course. Through this reuse we have appreciated how easy it was to assemble a new course from reused interactive activities. The students have been using the system and its components on an everyday basis. All components of the system were formally evaluated and got very positive feedback from the students. The KnowledgeTree system itself was also highly praised by our students for providing a clear single-point interface to many interactive activities organized by lectures. Currently, we are completing the second version of the architecture. We have also just completed the second version of the student model server CU-MULATE that implements, in full, the centralized user modeling approach developed in our earlier research. (Brusilovsky, 1994).

RELATED WORK

The components of the distributed service-based architecture that we are proposing have been investigated in a number of past research and development efforts.

The problem of searching for relevant educational activities in learning repositories is well explored by courseware reuse movement (Wade & Doherty, 2000; Verhoeven, Cardinaels, Van Durm, Duval, & Olivié, 2001). Solutions developed within this field can be directly adopted by our framework. One of the European reuse oriented projects, MTS (Graf & Schnaider, 1997) has explored the issue of runtime resolution of content requests. More recently, learning object metadata groups (such as LTSC, http://ltsc.ieee.org) contributed to the development of metadata standards that can be used to develop a universal resource search mechanism. Unfortunately, the existing standard does not include several metadata elements that are essential for adaptive selection and generation of learning content. This problem is discussed in more detail in (Conlan, Wade, Gargan, Hockemeyer, & Albert, 2002).

Several consortia and organizations such as uPortal (http://www.uportal.org), AICC (http://www.aicc.org), and ADL (ADLI, 2003) explore the issues of distributed component-based architectures for e-learning as an alternative to monolithic courseware management systems. These groups have already produced some solutions for transparent authentication and communication standards between a portal and an "intelligent" learning activity. Unfortunately, the current solutions cannot be used "as is" to support distributed adaptive e-learning services. APeLS attempts to stay faithful to the SCORM and AICC approach by providing a necessary extension to the content API (Conlan, Hockemeyer, Lefrere, Wade, & Albert, 2001).

The problem of gathering and sharing metadata of distributed resources has been carefully investigated in the field of Web information retrieval. Some interesting centralized and decentralized architectures were suggested. In the context of e-learning EDUTELLA (http://edutella.jxta.org/) and LOMster (Ternier, Duval, & Vandepitte, 2002) projects develop frameworks or peer-to-peer metadata exchange.

A wide variety of powerful adaptation methods and techniques have been explored in the field of adaptive Web-based educational systems. This field is our primary source of ideas for developing both the portals and the adaptive content services. In particular, adaptive generation of educational content in response to educational objectives was explored in DCG (Vassileva & Deters, 1998) and ActiveMath (Melis et al., 2001) systems.

The issue of user and student modeling for multi-component adaptive systems has been well researched in the fields of ITS and user modeling. A number of user and student model servers have been already reported (Kobsa, 2001; Kay, Kummerfeld, & Lauder, 2002). These works can certainly contribute to the development of the user model component of KnowledgeTree framework.

DISCUSSION

This chapter advocates the benefits of a service-based architecture for distributed adaptive e-learning that integrates the most powerful features of courseware reuse frameworks and adaptive educational systems. This architecture was designed independently by two research groups at the University of Pittsburgh and Trinity College, Dublin in an attempt to overcome several problems of modern e-learning architectures. Both groups combine extensive expertise in e-learning research, e-learning standardization activities and industrial e-learning projects. It is certainly remarkable that our groups come with very similar solutions to the problems identified in this chapter. While the common parts of our approaches have been stressed in a previous section, here we would like to list a few key differences.

The main difference between KnowledgeTree and APeLS stems from their approach to using existing standards and frameworks for e-learning. The APeLS architecture facilitates the migration to service-based adaptivity by enhancing existing e-learning frameworks and standards, yet achieving a very flexible and low complexity solution. While critiquing current metadata and component-oriented standards, the APeLS team chooses to extend the standards whenever it is necessary instead of completely rejecting them. Thus, the APeLS approach provides a means by which service-oriented distributed paradigm can be leveraged to provide the necessary freedom and open adaptive e-learning service framework. In contrast, KnowledgeTree has started as a research project with a goal to develop a new architecture for e-learning that takes into account current standards, but does not commit to use them.

One outcome of this difference is that APeLS attempts to stay very close to and evolve current LMS paradigm initiated by AICC and supported by ADL SCORM that stresses a two-component model (LMS—content). KnowledgeTree project considers this model as not appropriate for adaptive distributed content and argues for a 3-4-component model: portal—(value-adding service)—content—student model server.

Similarly, APeLS is structured to work with (1) existing courseware management systems (CMS), (2) via a generic web portal or (3) in a 'chained' approach where one APeLS service uses other instances of APeLS services. In (1) or (2) APeLS does not require the CMS or the portal to be adaptive. It is envisaged that adaptive selection and structuring of content (from a particular adaptive service) is delivered via an adaptive service. The APeLS architecture is designed to be recursive if required, i.e. an adaptive service can invoke another adaptive service for a (subset) of the course it is trying to deliver. In comparing KnowledgeTree and APeLS, APeLS does not distinguish between an "adaptive portal" or an "adaptive service". In contrast, KnowledgeTree, supports the separate concepts of a portal, a value-adding service, and an activity. Thus, KnowledgeTree allows portals, services, and content to be adaptive i.e. portals are used to provide adaptivity across services. In this vision, an adaptive portal provides different adaptive support such as, for example, as adaptively selecting the best of existing static or adaptive content and adaptively arranging it for the student.

Analysis of existing differences between our approaches is very helpful to understand the spectrum of opportunities in implementing the new architecture. It is important to note, however, the differences between the approaches are not critical. In fact, both approaches can easily co-exist within the same distributed architecture. It is the current challenge for our research groups to develop a practical architecture where our approaches can co-exist and benefit from each other. We are attempting to gather a community of researchers who are also interested to work on service-based architectures for adaptive e-learning. Having such a community working together is an essential precondition to producing a solution that will be acceptable for stakeholders with different prospects. Some of the future development of APeLS is being conducted within the EU 6th Framework project, iClass, which is developing an open framework for adaptive and non adaptive e-learning targeted at secondary level education (http://www.iclass.info). The authors invite any research or development team interested to work in this direction to get in contact with them.

REFERENCES

ADLI. (2003). Sharable Content Object Reference Model (SCORM) (Version 1.3): Advanced Distributed Learning Initiative.

Blackboard Inc. (2002). Blackboard Course Management System (Version 5.1): Blackboard Inc.

Brusilovsky, P. (1994). Student model centered architecture for intelligent learning environment. In *Fourth International Conference on User Modeling* (pp. 31-36). Hyannis, MA: MITRE.

Brusilovsky, P. (1996). Methods and techniques of adaptive hypermedia. *User Modeling and User-Adapted Interaction, 6*(2-3), 87-129.

Brusilovsky, P. (2001). WebEx: Learning from examples in a programming course. In W. Fowler & J. Hasebrook (Eds.), *WebNet'2001, World Conference of the WWW and Internet* (pp. 124-129). Orlando, FL: AACE.

Brusilovsky, P., Chavan, G., & Farzan, R. (2004). Social adaptive navigation support for open corpus electronic textbooks. In P. De Bra & W. Nejdl (Eds.), *Third International Conference on Adaptive Hypermedia and Adaptive Web-Based Systems (AH'2004)* (LNCS 3137, pp. 24-33). Eindhoven, the Netherlands: Springer-Verlag.

Brusilovsky, P. & Loboda, T. D. (2006). WADEIn II: A case for adaptive explanatory visualization. In M. Goldweber & P. Salomoni (Eds.), *11th Annual Conference on Innovation and Technology in Computer Science Education, ITiCSE'2006* (pp. 48-52). Bologna, Italy: ACM Press.

Brusilovsky, P. & Peylo, C. (2003). Adaptive and intelligent Web-based educational systems. *International Journal of Artificial Intelligence in Education, 13*(2-4), 159-172.

Brusilovsky, P., Ritter, S., & Schwarz, E. (1997). Distributed intelligent tutoring on the Web. In B. du Boulay & R. Mizoguchi (Eds.), *AI-ED'97,* *8th World Conference on Artificial Intelligence in Education* (pp. 482-489). Amsterdam: IOS.

Brusilovsky, P., Schwarz, E., & Weber, G. (1996a). A tool for developing adaptive electronic textbooks on WWW. In H. Maurer (Ed.), *WebNet'96, World Conference of the Web Society* (pp. 64-69). San Francisco: AACE.

Brusilovsky, P., Schwarz, E., & Weber, G. (1996b). ELM-ART: An intelligent tutoring system on World Wide Web. In C. Frasson, G. Gauthier & A. Lesgold (Eds.), *Third International Conference on Intelligent Tutoring Systems, ITS-96* (LNCS 1086, pp. 261-269). Berlin: Springer Verlag.

Brusilovsky, P., & Sosnovsky, S. (2005). Individualized exercises for self-assessment of programming knowledge: An evaluation of QuizPACK. *ACM Journal on Educational Resources in Computing, 5*(3), Article No. 6.

Brusilovsky, P., Sosnovsky, S., & Yudelson, M. (2004). Adaptive hypermedia services for e-learning. On *Workshop on Applying Adaptive Hypermedia Techniques to Service Oriented Environments at the Third International Conference on Adaptive Hypermedia and Adaptive Web-Based Systems (AH'2004)*. Eindhoven, The Netherlands: Technische University Eindhoven.

Conlan, O., Hockemeyer, C., Lefrere, P., Wade, V., & Albert, D. (2001). Extending educational metadata schemas to describe adaptive learning resources. In *Twelfth ACM Conference on Hypertext and Hypermedia (Hypertext 2001)* (pp. 161-162). Aarhus, Denmark: ACM Press.

Conlan, O., Wade, V., Bruen, C., & Gargan, M. (2002). Multi-model, metadata-driven approach to adaptive hypermedia services for personalized eLearning. In P. De Bra, P. Brusilovsky & R. Conejo (Eds.), *Second International Conference on Adaptive Hypermedia and Adaptive Web-Based Systems (AH'2002)* (LNCS 2347, pp. 100-111). Málaga, Spain.

Conlan, O., Wade, V., Gargan, M., Hockemeyer, C., & Albert, D. (2002). An architecture for integrating adaptive hypermedia services with open learning environments. In P. Barker & S. Rebelsky (Eds.), *ED-MEDIA'2002—World Conference on Educational Multimedia, Hypermedia and Telecommunications* (pp. 344-350). Denver, CO: AACE.

Dagger, D., Wade, V., & Conlan, O. (2004). A framework for developing adaptive personalized eLearning. In J. Nall & R. Robson (Eds.), *World Conference on E-Learning, E-Learn 2004* (pp. 2579-2587). Washington, DC: AACE.

De Bra, P. M. E. (1996). Teaching hypertext and hypermedia through the Web. *Journal of Universal Computer Science, 2*(12), 797-804.

Forte, E., Forte, M. W., & Duval, E. (1996). ARIADNE: A supporting framework for technology-based open and distance lifelong education. In F. Maffioli, M. Horvat & F. Reichl (Eds.), *Educating the engineer for lofelong learning. SEFI Annual Conference '96* (pp. 137-142). Vienna, Austria.

Graf, F. & Schnaider, M. (1997). IDEALS MTS— EIN modulares Training System für die Zukunft. On *8. Arbeitstreffen der GI-Fachgruppe 1.1.5/7.0.1 "Intelligent Lehr-/Lernsysteme*. München: Technische Universität München.

IEEE LTCS WG12 (Artist). (2002). *IEEE Standard for Learning Object Metadata*.

Kay, J., Kummerfeld, B., & Lauder, P. (2002). Personis: A server for user modeling. In P. De Bra, P. Brusilovsky & R. Conejo (Eds.), *Second International Conference on Adaptive Hypermedia and Adaptive Web-Based Systems (AH'2002)* (LNCS 2347, pp. 203-212). Málaga, Spain.

Kobsa, A. (2001). Generic user modeling systems. *User Modeling and User Adapted Interaction, 11*(1-2), 49-63.

Melis, E., Andrès, E., Büdenbender, J., Frishauf, A., Goguadse, G., Libbrecht, P., et al. (2001). ActiveMath: A web-based learning environment. *International Journal of Artificial Intelligence in Education, 12*(4), 385-407.

Nakabayashi, K., Koike, Y., Maruyama, M., Touhei, H., Ishiuchi, S., & Fukuhara, Y. (1995). An intelligent tutoring system on World-Wide Web: Towards an integrated learning environment on a distributed hypermedia. In H. Maurer (Ed.), *ED-MEDIA'95—World conference on educational multimedia and hypermedia* (pp. 488-493). Graz, Austria: AACE.

Okazaki, Y., Watanabe, K., & Kondo, H. (1996). An Implementation of an intelligent tutoring system (ITS) on the World-Wide Web (WWW). *Educational Technology Research, 19*(1), 35-44.

O'Keeffe, I., Brady, A., Conlan, O., & Wade, V. (2006). Just-in-time generation of pedagogically sound, context sensitive personalized learning experiences. *International Journal on E-Learning, 5*(1), 113-127.

Olimpo, G., Persico, D., Sarti, L., & Tavella, M. (1990). On the concept of database of multimedia learning material. In *World Conference on Computers and Education* (pp. 431-436). Amsterdam: North Holland.

Polson, M. C. & Richardson, J. J. (Eds.). (1988). *Foundations of intelligent tutoring systems*. Hillsdale: Lawrence Erlbaum Associates.

Ternier, S., Duval, E., & Vandepitte, P. (2002). LOMster: Peer-to-peer learning object metadata. In P. Barker & S. Rebelsky (Eds.), *ED-MEDIA'2002—World Conference on Educational Multimedia, Hypermedia and Telecommunications* (pp. 1942-1943). Denver, CO: AACE.

Vassileva, J. & Deters, R. (1998). Dynamic courseware generation on the WWW. *British Journal of Educational Technology, 29*(1), 5-14.

Verhoeven, B., Cardinaels, K., Van Durm, R., Duval, E., & Olivié, H. (2001). Experiences with the ARIADNE pedagogical document repository. In *ED-MEDIA'2001—World Conference on Educational Multimedia, Hypermedia and Telecommunications* (pp. 1949-1954). Tampere, Finland: AACE.

Wade, V. P. & Doherty, P. (2000). A meta-data driven approach to searching for educational resources in a global context. In G. Davies & C. Owen (Eds.), *WebNet'2000, World Conference of the WWW and Internet* (pp. 136-145). San Antonio, TX: AACE.

WebCT. (2002). WebCT Course Management System (Version 3.8). Lynnfield, MA: WebCT, Inc.

Chapter XIV
An Adaptive E–Learning Platform for Personalized Course Generation

Enver Sangineto
University of Rome "La Sapienza," Italy

ABSTRACT

In this chapter we show the technical and methodological aspects of an e-learning platform for automatic course personalization built during the European funded project Diogene. The system we propose is composed of different knowledge modules and some inference tools. The knowledge modules represent the system's information about both the domain-specific didactic material and the student model. By exploiting such information, the system automatically builds courses whose didactic material is customized to meet the current student's degree of knowledge and her/his learning preferences. Concerning the latter, we have adopted the Felder and Silverman pedagogical approach in order to match the student's learning styles with the system learning objects' types. Finally, we take care to describe the system's didactic material by means of some present standards for e-learning in order to allow knowledge sharing with other e-learning platforms and knowledge searching by means of possible Semantic Web information retrieval facilities.

MOTIVATIONS AND GOALS

The aim of this chapter is to present the "intelligent" facilities of the *Diogene* platform, built during the European funded projects *Diogene* (IST-2001-33358) (Diogene, 2005). Diogene is a Learning Management System (LMS) able to automatically generate personalized courses by assembling learning material using both static and statistic knowledge.

Static knowledge includes information concerning the available learning material (which in turn is composed of a set of atomic learning objects, *LOs*), as well as an ontology-based description of the didactic relationships holding among the concepts of the specific domain (called domain concepts, *DCs,*). Statistic information is collected by the system during the learning sessions and represents both the student's knowledge about the DCs and the student's preferred learning modalities. The latter include preferences concerning the LOs' type (e.g., visual versus verbal, intuitive versus concrete, etc.). The way in which such preferences are taken into account in the course generation process follows the pedagogical theory proposed by Felder and Silverman in (Felder & Silverman, 1988) (see section "The Learning Preferences and the Felder and Silverman Pedagogical Theory").

The novelties of our approach with respect to other course generation/personalization systems can be summarized as follows.

- Didactic information concerning a specific domain (e.g., "Euclidean Geometry," "Object Oriented Programming Languages," etc.) is explicitly represented using an ontology. Such description is not dependent on the specific LOs currently available to the system but it is an *abstract* representation of the didactic relationships holding among the main concepts the domain is composed of. The possible relationships are: prerequisite, ordering and hierarchical relations. We will show how our proposed simple knowledge representation structure can be very efficiently exploited for course generation purposes as well as its ability to describe the most important didactic information. The knowledge representation framework we propose is domain independent.

- Statistic information is collected by the system by means of a continuous monitoring of the learner's successes and failures obtained during the interactive test activities (executed at the end of each learning session). Such information is used in order to

personalize the courses of the subsequent learning sessions.

- The Felder and Silverman pedagogical approach, based on the correspondence between teaching styles and learning styles, is concretely adopted by Diogene. This is done in three steps. First, when a given LO *l* is stored in the system's database we automatically classify *l* using Felder and Silverman's teaching styles and a mapping function based on the *l*'s resource type. Second, we use a test proposed in (Felder and Soloman) to classify the student's learning styles. Finally, for each learner's didactic query we select the most suitable LOs by matching the learning and the teaching styles.

RELATED WORKS

In this section of the chapter we provide an overview of the existing course generation platforms and adaptive LMS, comparing them with the Diogene characteristics.

We underline that Diogene is an intelligent and adaptive platform which *actively* participates in the learning process, as opposed to most of the common e-learning platforms which usually play only the *passive* role of LOs' containers. For instance, the well known Ariadne platform (Duval et al., 2001) is based on a digital library of LOs which are indexed using educational metadata standards. Nevertheless, the Ariadne platform only aims at building a library of reusable learning components for the sharing of such components among different (human) teachers. The library is then a *passive* repository and there is no automatic building of courses nor any adaptation on the user profile.

This situation is very common in the new generation of Web-based learning platforms, especially in the commercial systems (e.g., Blackboard, Docent, and Lotus). Indeed, they are born to support modern distance learning, for example, in long-distance university courses, and usually only work as passive content containers, in which teachers and students can exchange documents and information. In Seal and Przasnyski (2001), the authors propose a system able to collect the students' feedback during the whole duration of the course so as to enable the teacher to adapt the course to classroom needs. Nevertheless, no automatic adaptation is expected and the feedback is analyzed by hand.

In Adorni et al (2003), the authors propose a prototype system based on an intelligent agent approach. Each learner can *delegate* her/his learning processes to a population of agents. Indeed, each learner owns (and sometimes shares) a set of agents whose main tasks are: profiling, searching, indexing, retrieval, control and supplying of LOs to the learner.

In Ronchetti and Saini (2003), the authors show a complete system of knowledge management in an e-learning scenario. The system is composed of the following entities:

- A course database.
- Semantic metadata attached to each course.
- A *knowledge navigator* (KN).
- An *automatic link generator* (ALG).

Learning material (the LOs of the course database) are typically available courses or lectures archived in any LMS. Moreover, the authors use a metadata *catalogue* to store the associations between each LO and its (set of) topic(s). Topics are organized in an ontology expressing membership and subclass relations as well as other relations such as pre-requisite relation, conceptual similarity relation and so on. The authors have chosen to build their ontology on the basis of two givens: that an ontology needs to collect a large consensus in its community's specific area in order to be valid; and that their system is interested only in

computer science topics. For these reasons they have selected and extended the ACM "Computing Curricula 2001 for Computer Science" (ACM). Furthermore, an important platform instrument is the knowledge navigator. The KN allows browsing over ontological relations. For instance, the learner can find the topic which is related to a given LO and then find either similar topics or pre-requisite topics whose study can be important for the LO itself. Moreover, while the KN is a tool enabling "explicit navigation of the ontology," the ALG is a tool for "implicit navigation." The AGL has the responsibility of automating performing a limited exploration of the ontology, in the region near to the LO which the student is presently using. As a result, it produces a list of LOs that are related to what the student is presently studying. This list is made available to the student by means of a suitable button dynamically attached to the LO's Web pages.

In Trigano and Giacomini (2004), Trigano and Giacomini propose a system called CEPIAH for helping teachers to implement pedagogical Web sites and to produce online courses. Using CEPIAH the teacher can automatically generate educational Web site structures, adding the pedagogical contents in these structures, then visualize, manage and participate in the courses. The students can visualize and participate to the courses using the navigator integrated in the system. Both the Web sites and the courses are generated starting from answers given by the user (the teacher) to two interactive questionnaires: a pedagogical questionnaire and a GUI-related questionnaire. Within this conceptual framework, the authors take into account two major aspects, namely: the human computer interface (HCI) of the Web sites (the colors, the shapes of menus and buttons, etc.) and the modeling, by means of IMS learning design (IMS Learning Design, 2003; Koper & Tattersall, 2005), of teaching scenarios which are based on various pedagogical approaches. For instance, the courses structure automatically online generated by the system, is based on teaching scenarios which integrate, according to the case, the features of different pedagogical theories such as the behaviorism, the constructivism, the socio-constructivism, etc. The system's inference mechanism is based on a rule-based engine. The rules specify the way in which pedagogical models are assembled. The modules are IMS learning design components, which can be created either at generation time or conceived beforehand and recorded in XML files respecting the standard.

Benayache and Abel (Benayache & Abel, 2005) developed the eMEMORA system for automatic course generation. In the eMEMORA system, resources, information and other knowledge is organized in a "course memory." This memory can be accessed by teachers when they want to re-use resources, as in a thematic resource base, as well as learners who can directly use the memory for their learning necessities. eMEMORA is based on two ontologies, the first (*application ontology*) describes the specific didactic domain while the second (*domain ontology*) represents the teaching resources (persons, documents, etc.). The latter uses some concepts of the Learning Object Metadata standard (IEEE LOM, 2002). The system can also describe pedagogical relations (e.g., the "pre-requisite of" relation) using *topic maps*. Each learning resource is directly attached to one or more topics by an "occurrence link."

Weber et al. (2001) present an adaptive course generation system called NetCoach. Like our system, also the NetCoach knowledge base represents the concepts of the didactic domain the system is specialized on and, as it happens with Diogene, NetCoach is able to exploit prerequisite relations among the concepts in order to create a sequential ordering of the concepts needed to the student for her/his learning goals. Moreover, the system provides another type of relation: the "inference" relations. A concept A is linked to B by means of an inference relation when it holds that every time a learner knows A implies also that the learner knows B. In the student model of a given learner, those concepts whose student's knowledge about has not been directly tested by the system but it is only inferred via inference relations are specially marked. Anyway, it is not clear if it is always possible to assert the student's knowledge of a concept which is generically related to another concept successfully studied by the student. Moreover, the knowledge representation the authors propose does not contain neither hierarchical nor pedagogical ordering relations as in Diogene (see section "Didactic Knowledge Representation"), which our experience has shown us to be necessary components of a didactic description of a non-trivial domain. Indeed, the aim of NetCoach is to provide to the student possible warnings concerning the learning path she/he chooses inside a prefabricated curriculum (e.g., a digital book made of chapters and subchapters linked with the above mentioned relations), while the aim of Diogene, as it will be shown in the

Figure 1. A simple taxonomy for LMSs

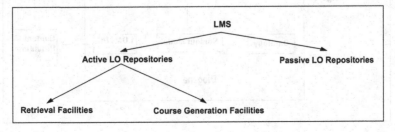

next sections, is to build a course by assembling heterogeneous learning material (e.g., LOs given by possibly different content providers) and, thus, it needs a deeper description of the didactic relationships among the DCs. Finally, even if the Student Model proposed in Weber et al. (2001) is very flexible and permits the learner to directly modify it (*adaptable* facilities (Weber et al., 2001)), it does not describe the student's learning preferences and there is not the possibility to customize the courses (*adaptive* facilities (Weber et al., 2001)) basing on a general pedagogical strategy which accounts for the learner peculiarities as in the case of the Diogene system.

WebCT (WebCT) is another example of online course generation system. The WebCT courses are composed of HTML pages linked in order to suggest to the student a learning path. The TopClass system (TopClass) builds courses by assembling units of learning material (ULMs) such as: pages, tests or hierarchically structured ULMs. TopClass assesses the student knowledge by tracking her/his results to the interactive tests.

Although it is out of the scope of this chapter to give a complete survey of existing LMSs, we propose in Figure 1 a simple taxonomy which includes most of the state-of-the-art systems.

Referring to Figure 1, we indicate with *passive LO repositories* such LMSs which are mainly aimed at being containers of shareable learning material. In these systems, discovering or exploiting possible pedagogical relations among LOs is a responsibility of the human teacher. Examples of such systems are: Blackboard, Docent, Duval et al. (2001); Lotus, Seal and Przasnyski, (2001). Vice versa, examples of LMSs with *Retrieval Facilities* are: Adorni et al. (2003); Ronchetti and Saini (2003). These systems exploit an explicit representation of the semantic relations holding among the system's LOs in order to provide to the user with facilities for LO retrieval/browsing which exploit such semantic links. Finally, those systems which are able to automatically suggest to the learner a possible assembly of learning material are categorized as LMSs with *Course Generation Facilities* (Benayache & Abel, 2005; TopClass; Trigano & Giacomini, 2004; WebCT, Weber et al., 2001). Diogene belongs to this category.

A PLATFORM OVERVIEW

In this section we present an overview of the Diogene architecture (Figure 2). The main idea

Figure 2. The main Diogene Structure

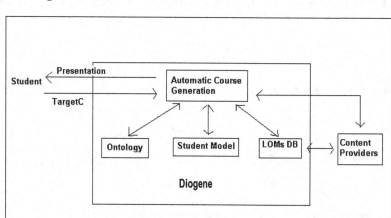

is that a student approaching the system can choose among a set of topics (DCs) she/he wants to learn. The student only has access to the ontology vocabulary (the set of DCs without any relation) in which each DC is associated with a brief textual explanation of its meaning. Once the student has chosen the DCs she/he is interested in, the system's planning mechanism builds a course (a *presentation*) which satisfies both the student's present knowledge (the *cognitive state*) and her/his preferred *learning preferences*. This is done as follows.

The student's chosen DCs are collected in the *target concepts* set (*TargetC*), which is input to the system. Both the student's *Cognitive State* and the *learning preferences* are stored in the *student model*. The planning mechanism matches the target concepts with both the didactic domain's description (the *ontology*) and the cognitive state. The result of this match is the set of DCs (called *learning path*) which is necessary to the student to learn all the target concepts.

In this way the system can cover student's possible lacunae by automatically adding necessary pre-requisite DCs to the set she/he has chosen, or it can decompose such a set into a more detailed one; or, finally, order it in the best didactic way. Once the Learning Path has been built and ordered, for each DC of the Learning Path the system chooses a suitable LO, i.e. a Web-deliverable resource explaining the related DC. A LO can be a lesson (an HTML page), a Simulation (a Java applet), a Test (an HTML page with an evaluating form) etc. The Diogene's LOs are indexed by means of the IMS Metadata 1.2.2 (LTCS) standard and stored in the learning object metadata (LOM) database (Figure 2). The LOs are chosen taking into account the student's learning preferences. The final set of selected LOs is the presentation. Once the presentation is ready it is delivered to the learner.

DIDACTIC KNOWLEDGE REPRESENTATION

We propose some knowledge representation rules in order to describe fundamental properties of the didactic domain. These rules have to be:

1. *Domain independent.* Indeed, Diogene is conceived for a general-purpose application.
2. They have to describe the *essential pedagogical relationships* among domain concepts (DCs) which need to be taken into account in the learning path generation process. The two most important relationships that need to be described are: *necessity* links and *ordering* links.
3. They are not intended to provide an exhaustive knowledge representation framework. Indeed *they are tailored to our planning purposes and needs*, while a universal treatment of ontology-based representations, valid also for non-didactic purposes, is beyond the scope of this work.

Below we show three syntactic relations among the ontology's domain concepts which constitute our proposed knowledge representation framework satisfying Points 1-3 above (Capuano et al., 2003).

- **HP (has part):** $HP(x, y_1, y_2, ..., y_n)$ means that the concept x is composed of the concepts $y_1, y_2, ..., y_n$, that is to say: to learn x is *equivalent* to learn the set of concepts y_1 and y_2 ... and y_n.
- **R (requires):** $R(x, y)$ means that to learn x it is necessary to have already learnt y. This relation establishes also a constraint on the domain concepts' order in a given learning path (y must precede x).

- **SO (suggested order):** *SO(x, y)* means that it is preferable to learn *x* and *y* in this order. Note also that this relation establishes a constraint on the DCs' order but in this case it is not necessary to learn *y* if we are interested only in *x*.

Furthermore, we have the following relation which links domain concepts and learning objects' metadata:

- **EB (explained by):** *EB(d, l)* means that the domain concept *d* can be explained by means of the learning object indexed by the Metadata *l* (*l* is sufficient to explain *d*).

Some Properties of the Ontologies

The *HP* relation is used to describe the decomposition of an abstract concept (e.g., math analysis) into a set of more specific sub-concepts (e.g., limits, derivatives, integrals and series: see Figure 3). It is worth underlining that the knowledge representation methodology chosen does not allow for disjunction representation. In other words, no alternative decompositions are allowed (e.g., "limits, derivatives, integrals and differential equations" versus "limits, derivatives, integrals and series"). Indeed, as a well-known knowledge representation result, each representation approach should reach a trade-off between expressiveness and computational costs. We have chosen to prevent disjunction representation both to avoid backtracking mechanisms in the planning phase and because it is not clear how the system can conceptually choose among different decompositions. For this reason, we demand to the ontology designer the responsibility to choose the most suitable decomposition of concepts in a given domain.

The relations *R* and *SO* are *inherited* through the relation *HP*. Formally we have that:

Property 1. *Order inheritance*:

1. If $HP(d, ..., d_1, ...)$ and $R(d, d_2)$ then $R(d_1, d_2)$.
2. If $HP(d, ..., d_1, ...)$ and $SO(d_2, d)$ then $SO(d_2, d_1)$.

Figure 3. A simple example of knowledge representation for the didactic domain "math." LO_1, LO_2, etc are the system's learning objects, respectively represented by the metadata MT_1, MT_2, ..., each of which is in turn associated with one or more atomic DCs. Note that "analysis" is not atomic.

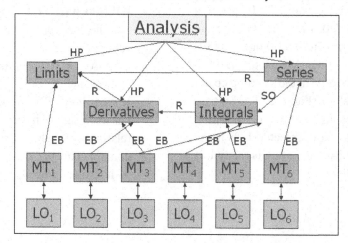

Definition 1. A *presentation P* is an ordered list of LOMs ($l_1, ..., l_n$) with the following properties:

1. The union of the (LOs related to the) LOMs of *P* is sufficient to explain to the student all the *target concepts* of the input list *TargetC* (see section "A Platform Overview").

2. For each $l_i, l_j \in P$, if: $EB(d_1, l_i)$ and $EB(d_2, l_j)$ and $d_1 \prec d_2$, then $i < j$. Where the partial order relation $\prec$ between domain concepts is recursively defined as follows:
   a. if $R(x, y)$ then $y \prec x$
   b. if $SO(x, y)$ then $x \prec y$
   c. if $HP(z, ..., x, ...)$ and $HP(w, ..., y, ...)$ and $z \prec w$ then: $x \prec y \wedge x \prec w \wedge z \prec y$.

3. *P* satisfies as much as possible the student's learning preferences.

While Points 1 and 3 of the above definition are self-explanatory, Point 2 needs some remarks. It is a consequence of both the transitivity property of the order relations *R* and *SO* and the above defined Property 1. It defines a partial order on the DCs. As a consequence of this, LOMs belonging to a same presentation have to respect this partial order. If, for instance, a presentation contains the LOMs l_i and l_j, which explain, respectively, the concepts "derivatives" and "limits," then l_j has to precede l_i. The same situation holds when l_i and l_j explain DCs not directly linked to each other by an order relation (requires or suggested order) but are components, by means of the "has part" relation, of DCs directly linked by an order relation (see Step 2.c above).

In Section "Automatic Course Generation and Tailoring," we will show the planning algorithms needed to generate a presentation satisfying points 1 and 3 above, together with the linearization procedure to totally order it according to point 2. Before concluding this section, we provide a final definition which will be useful in further sections and some remarks.

Definition 2. A concept *x* is named *atomic* if there is no concept *y* s.t. $HP(x, y)$.

We chose to link LOMs (by means of the relation *EB*) only with atomic DCs. Indeed, a non-atomic concept *x* is composed of sub-concepts (e.g., *y, z*) and the learning of *x* is equivalent to the learning of its components *y* and *z* (see the definition of *HP*). Only when no further decomposition is possible by means of *HP*, then we switch to the lower knowledge representation level, i.e. from the ontology to the metadata. This is not a limiting constraint because a LO *l* explaining *x* can be automatically attached to *both y* and *z* satisfying the constraint.

It is worth noticing that we have no subset relation. Indeed we do not represent sets at all. Furthermore, the didactic knowledge representation proposed in this section is domain-independent because no assumption on a particular domain is done. In fact, we only represent *pedagogical relations* among the domain's topics, such as prerequisite, ordering and hierarchical relationships which do not involve any representation of the topics' *content*. For instance, the two relations shown in Figure 3: *Requires (series, limits)* and *SuggestedOrder (integrals, series)* do not contain any domain-specific semantics on the math analysis domain. Two equivalent relations in the Statistics domain could be the following: *Requires (principal component analysis, covariance matrix)* and *SuggestedOrder (principal component analysis, linear discriminant analysis)*. These relations can then be used in order to construct a specific ontology on a specific domain: in this manner the system can be specialized to work on automatic course generation on that domain using that ontology. We will see in section "A Case Study" how, during the Diogene project, we have built an ontology on the computer science domain.

We can likely state that the proposed relations constitute a minimal set of necessary pedagogical relations for automatic course generation. In fact, it would be very hard to describe pedagogical learning material without hierarchical and prerequisite relations. Other ordering relations (e.g., our *SO* relation) could be not mandatory but our empirical experience suggested to us the necessity of an ordering link between different topics which not necessarily implies prerequisite relationship. On the other hand, further relations (e.g., similarity relations among concepts (Dicheva & Dichev, 2006)) are harder to give an operational meaning and seem to be more suitable for browsing-/retrieval-based system (see Figure 1) in which a human user can select and order the retrieved material. In section "Automatic Course Generation and Tailoring," we will show how our simple knowledge representation rules are operationally exploited by the system for course building. Finally, as abovementioned, we point out that this is a specialized ontology for automatic course generation purposes while a general-purpose knowledge representation is beyond the scope of this work. The ontology, as well as the links between DCs and LOMs have to be off-line manually set by a teacher (e.g., the "ontology designer").

THE STUDENT MODEL

The Diogene Student Model is composed of two modules: the cognitive state and the learning preferences. We use the former to describe the knowledge degree achieved by each student about every DC. This evaluation regards both previously acquired student knowledge and skills learned using the Diogene platform. Moreover, the learning preferences module contains information about the student perceptive capabilities, that is, the preferred types of resources and learning styles for the specific student.

The cognitive state and the learning preferences describe the current state of the student's profile by means of two different sets of atomic facts each of which is associated with fuzzy truth degrees. The next subsections show both the modules in more details.

The Cognitive State

The *cognitive state* is composed of a set of student's beliefs representing the system's knowledge about each student's knowledge. If the ontology is composed of n DCs $(d_1,...,d_n)$, then the cognitive state of a given student is represented by the set:

$Beliefs = \{B_1, B_2,..., B_n\}$,
each B_i being a belief so defined:
$B_i = <d_i, Evaluation_i>$,

where d_i is the i-th ontology DC, while $Evaluation_i$ is a fuzzy value ranging in [0, 1]. For instance, if a DC d is associated to a value of $Evaluation = 0.8$, this indicates that Diogene believes the student knows quite a lot about the related concept d.

The values of each $Evaluation$ are continuously and automatically updated by the system in the following manner. The automatic course generation algorithm (see the next section) attaches at the end of each presentation a set of interactive tests. An interactive test is a particular test-type LO linked to a set of DCs (those which are dealt with in the test). The student's answers to such tests allow the system to directly estimate and modify her/his student model. This is done by averaging on all the test results so far obtained on each specific DC.

The Learning Preferences and the Felder and Silverman Pedagogical Theory

In Felder and Silverman (1988), Felder and Silverman propose five couples of student's categories (which will later become four couples). These categories derive both from previous psychological studies (such as Jung's well-known theory of psychological types) and from some authors' empirical observations. The most important observation is that each person usually shows her/his preference for one or more modalities in the way she/he receives-elaborates information.

For example, one can prefer to receive information by means of either the visual sensory channel or the auditory sensory channel. In the former case, her/his learning process is better suited for visual material (e.g., pictures), in the latter for sounds or texts (which are composed of words, then strictly related to the auditory information processing).

For this reason, Felder and Silverman propose to categorize each learner in different *learning categories*, each of which is denominated using a pair of adjectives (e.g. "*visual* versus *verbal*") representing the range of possibilities for each category (a student can be more or less visual or verbal). Moreover, for each learning category, there is a corresponding *teaching category*, which indicates the type of teaching most suited for the corresponding preferred way to receive-process information during learning. The Felder-Silverman main four categories are the following:

- **Sensing vs. intuitive learner:** It represents the abstraction level of the learning material the student prefers. A *sensing* student likes learning facts and needs more practical case studies. An *intuitive* student usually prefers innovation and dislikes repetition.
- **Visual vs. verbal learner:** It indicates whether the student prefers auditory (textual) or visual documents.
- **Active versus reflective:** It indicates how the student prefers to process information: actively (through engagement in activities or discussions) or reflectively (through introspection).
- **Sequential vs. global:** It indicates how the student progresses toward understanding. Sequential students prefer sequential explanations while global students usually prefer an initial overview of the involved topics which possibly shows them the most important steps and relations they are going to study.

The first two categories regard the way in which we prefer to receive information during the learning process while the other two relations regard the way in which we prefer to elaborate it. It is worth noting that the four couples of categories are not mutually excluding. On the contrary, each learner can be classified using a combination of values, one for each of the four categories. For instance, a given learner can be very intuitive, quite visual, strongly reflexive and indifferent with respect to the sequential-global choice.

We have adopted Felder and Silverman's categories for two reasons. First of all, their approach is based on a sufficiently large experimentation which has validated the proposed classes on an engineering student population (Felder & Silverman, 1988). Second, although other approaches are likely based on a stronger cognitive model formalization, the Felder and Silverman theory provides some useful pragmatic instruments to customize teaching depending on the student's profile. Even if we cannot deal with all the aspects of this theory (e.g., the ones thought for human made frontal lessons), it gives us an effective way to select the most appropriate learning material for each given student. From an operational point of view, we have:

1. To classify every Diogene's learner in her/his learning categories. This is achieved by online proposing to each student the Felder and Soloman test (Felder & Soloman).
2. To associate (off-line) each LO of the system's repository with its most suitable teaching categories.

The second issue is achieved exploiting the values of the "learning resource type" attribute of the IMS metadata standard, which are strings ranging in the set:

{"*Exercise,*" "*Simulation,*" "*Questionnaire,*" "*Diagram,*" "*Figure,*" "*Graph,*" "*Index,*" "*Slide,*"

"Table," "Narrative Text," "Exam," "Experiment," "ProblemStatement," "SelfAssesment"}

With the help of a few pedagogic experts we have classified all these types of resources using Felder and Silverman's teaching styles, by associating to each resource type a quadruple of fuzzy values. For example:

Teaching Styles(Exercise) = <<"Sensing-Intuitive," 0>, <"Visual-Verba,l" 0.5>, <"Active-Reflective," 0>, <"Sequential-Global," 0.5>>

that is, an exercise is classified as very sensing and active and indifferent with respect to the dichotomy visual-verbal and sequential-global. Another example is:

Teaching Styles(Simulation) = <<"Sensing-Intuitive," 0.3>, <"Visual-Verbal," 0>, <"Active-Reflective," 0>, <"Sequential-Global," 0.5>>

When a given LO *l* is added to the system's repository, we use a look-up table indexed by the value of its "learning resource type" attribute in order to associate *l* with the corresponding fuzzy value quadruple.

On the other hand, the learning preferences component of the student module contains the corresponding representation of the specific student's learning styles obtained using the interactive test. For instance, the following is a learning preference representation for a hypothetic student:

Learning Preferences = <<"Sensing-Intuitive," 0.7>, <"Visual-Verbal," 0.3>, <"Active-Reflective," 0.6>, <"Sequential-Global," 0.9>>.

The above representation describes a learner who is more intuitive than sensing (0.7 against 0.3), more visual than verbal (0.3 against 0.7), a bit more reflective than active and very much oriented to a global processing of information rather than a sequential one. In the next section we will show how the student's learning preferences and the teaching styles associated with LOMs are matched by the system.

AUTOMATIC COURSE GENERATION AND TAILORING

Starting from the set of target concepts *TargetC* (see Figure 2), the automatic course generation algorithm follows all the *HP* and *R* relations of the ontology and iteratively includes new DCs in the learning path. Note that the *SO* relation is not taken into account in this phase. A DC *d* is added to the list *LearningPath* if and only if:

1. It can be reached by means of a sequence of *HP* and *R* relations starting from the DCs of *TargetC* (i.e., *LearningPath* is the transitive closure of *TargetC* with respect to *HP* and *R*) and:
2. *d* is not already known to the student. This fact is checked in the cognitive state: if *d* is associated with a value greater than 0.5 then *d* is assumed to be sufficiently known.

The *LearningPath* obtained is then pruned excluding the non-atomic DCs. As a final step, it is ordered with respect to Property 1. To this aim, we build (off-line) the *Augmented Graph*: a graph representation of the ontology which is explicitly augmented with relations *R* and *SO* recursively following property 1. For example, if: $HP(d, ..., d_1, ...)$ and $R(d, d_2)$ then we explicitly add to the augmented graph an edge linking the nodes corresponding to d_1 and d_2 and labeled with the relation $R(d_1, d_2)$. We are now able to order (online) the obtained *LearningPath*: starting from the nodes in the augmented graph corresponding to *TargetC* we only have to follow the edges in a depth-first visit of the graph. The result is a total ordering of the *LearningPath*, that is, an order in which, for every two DCs d_1 and d_2 ($d_1 \neq d_2$), either $d_1 \prec d_2$ or $d_2 \prec d_1$. This is the order in which the

Figure 4. A zoom on the ICT Ontology

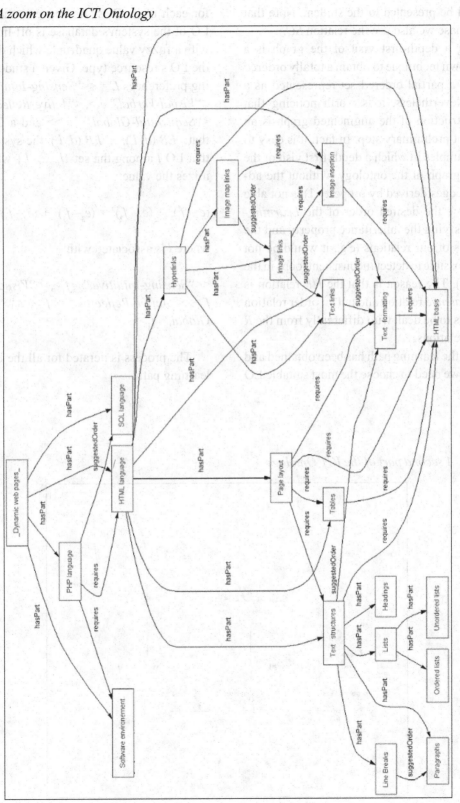

DCs will be presented to the student. Note that in this phase we also use the relation *SO*.

Using a depth-first visit of the graph is a well-known technique to obtain a totally ordered set from a partial ordered set represented as a graph. Nevertheless, it is worth noticing that the construction of the augmented graph is an important preliminary step. In fact, it is easy to show examples in which a depth-first visit of the original graph of the ontology (without the additional edges derived by property 1) is not able to produce the desired order of the *Learning-Path* satisfying the inheritance property and the semantics of our relations (e.g., it would be not always possible to detect inconsistent loops in the ontology). The reason is that the *HP* relation is an *equivalence* relation and not an order relation and needs to be dealt with differently from the *R* and *SO* relations.

Once the learning path has been obtained and ordered, we need to choose the most suitable LO

for each of its DCs. As abovementioned, each LO of the system's database is off-line indexed with a fuzzy value quadruple which depends on the LO's resource type. Given a student's learning preferences L = <<*"Sensing-Intuitive,"* e_1>, <*"Visual-Verbal,"* e_2>, <*"Active-Reflective,"* e_3>, <*"Sequential-Global,"* e_4>> and a DC d such that: $EB (d, l_1), ... EB (d, l_n)$, the system selects that LO l among the set $\{l_1, ..., l_n\}$ which minimizes the value:

$$(e_1 - f_1)^2 + (e_2 - f_2)^2 + (e_3 - f_3)^2 + (e_4 - f_4)^2,$$

where l is associated with:

<<*"Sensing-Intuitive,"* f_1>, <*"Visual-Verbal,"* f_2>, <*"Active-Reflective,"* f_3>, <*"Sequential-Global,"* f_4>>.

The process is iterated for all the DCs of the learning path.

Figure 5. A second part of the ICT Ontology

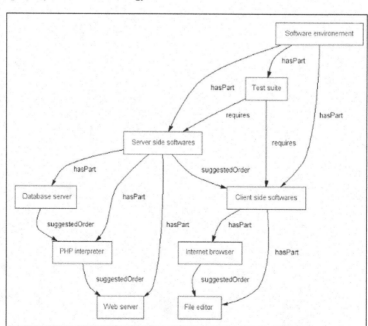

Figure 6. The editing of a LOM by means of the KMS

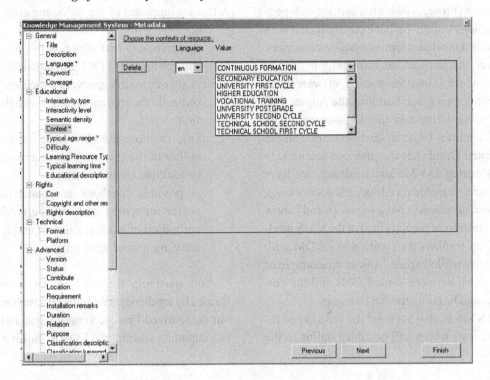

A CASE STUDY

In this section we show some functionalities of our platform in a specific domain: the information and communication technology (ICT) subjects. Indeed, although Diogene is a general-purpose platform, thought to be used as an automatic course generation/personalization in all didactic domains, it has been applied to ICT topics in the European-funded project Diogene (Diogene, 2005).

Concerning the ontology creation we have adopted choices similar to those suggested in Ronchetti and Saini (2003), selecting taxonomies approved by authoritative entities in the ICT area with the double objective of covering our target domain (ICT topics) in an exhaustive way and of collecting a large consensus in the specific didac-

tic community. For this reason our ontology has been built on the base of the ACM "Computing Classification System" (CCS) (ACM). This classification is mainly used by ACM for classification purposes, publications, etc. We began from this taxonomy and therefore:

1. We added topics (DCs) in the lowest levels of the taxonomic hierarchy (which is represented by our *has part* relations)
2. We linked the resulting DCs with the necessary *requires* and *suggested order* relations.

Figures 4 and 5 show a zoom on a small part of the ontology regarding the argument "dynamic Web pages creation" which has entirely been added to the original ACM classification.

For the ontology editing we have adopted the Protege tool (Protege) which is a domain-independent ontology editor. We have customized it with our specific knowledge representation constraints. Moreover, we have added some plug-ins to the Protege, which is an open-source software, such as the ontology's graph building, the Augmented Graph construction and the consistency check tool (which must be necessarily executed on the Augmented Graph; see the previous section).

Concerning LO Metadata editing, we have built a suitable metadata editor called *knowledge management system* (KMS). Figures 6 and 7 show some snapshots of the interface of the KMS module. Figure 6 shows the creation of a LOM with our system, while Figure 7 shows an example of link creation between some LOMs and the corresponding DCs (i.e., the *EB* relation).

The KMS is also used for the creation of interactive tests which will be added online to the learning path and used to update the student model. A test is composed of the following elements:

- A question (a text with possible associated images and/or HTML documents).
- A set of possible answers which are shown online to the student together with the question.
- One or more possible right answers (the author of the test can choose among single or multiple choice tests).
- A possible feedback associated to each correct or wrong answer. The feedback is composed of a text document and it is possibly associated with images.

Summarizing, the off-line operations performed by teacher(s) are: Ontology creation (using our customized Protege version), test authoring, LO metadata editing and LO-DC linking (using

Figure 7. The creation of links between the LOMs and the DCs by means of the KMS

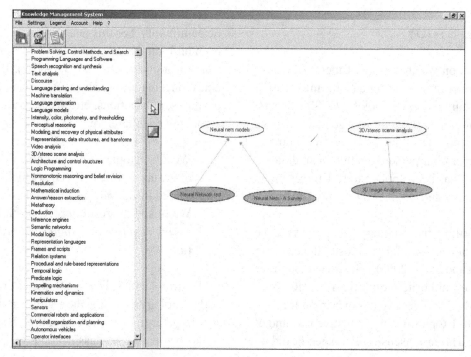

KMS). However, it is worth noticing that the ontology creation is usually separated by the other operations since it regards the structuring of a whole domain and it is usually done by the so called "ontology designer," using a common terminology in semantic Web-based e-learning systems.

Once the static knowledge of the system has been set as abovementioned, Diogene provides each learner with the possibility of initializing both her/his cognitive state and her/his learning preferences. By default, the cognitive state is initialized with all DCs associated to 0 (which makes it possible for a student to skip the cognitive state initialization), while skipping the Felder

and Soloman test for the learning preferences initialization will lead the system to choose LOs not caring of their resource type (since all the learning categories will be associated to the value 0.5). We remark that the cognitive state is not a static representation but a dynamic one, which is updated using the online test results. At the end of each learning session, the specific learner's student model is persistently stored in the system's database (see Figure 2).

Finally, when the student model has been initialized, the student can input a query containing the set of target concepts she/he is interested in. The system's output is computed building the learning path and the corresponding presentation.

Figure 8. An example of presentation built by the system. The full list of the names of the LOs is shown on the left side of the screen while the window on the centre is used to show each single LO once the student clicks on its name.

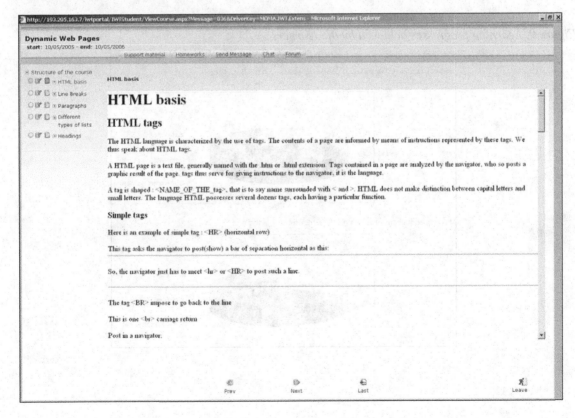

Figure 8 shows the presentation corresponding to the query: *Text Structures*. Given this target concept and the ontology of Figures 4-5, the system produces the following ordered Learning Path: *HTML basis, line breaks, paragraphs, ordered list, unordered list, headings*. In this execution example we have used a cognitive state with every concept associated with the value 0. Note that, despite the fact that *text formatting* is atomic, it is not included in the final learning path because the link with *text structure* is only a *SO* association. The learning path is not shown to the student, being a system's internal representation of the necessary arguments satisfying the student's query. What is instead shown to the student is the list of the names of the selected LOs corresponding to the Presentation. On the left side of Figure 8, *HTML basis, line breaks, paragraphs* and *headings* are the names of the LOs associated to the homonymous DCs, while *different types of lists* is a LO chosen for the DCs *ordered list* and the *unordered list*.

Suppose now a second student asking for a course about "page layout" is quite confident with arguments such as tables and text formatting but knows little about text structures and most of the related topics. The following is an example of possible cognitive state as a result of previous tests/initialization:

Beliefs = {<Page layout, 0.2>, <Tables, 0.7>, <Text formatting, 0.6>, <HTML basis, 0.6>, <Text structures, 0>, <Line breaks, 0>, <Paragraphs, 0>, <Lists, 0.8>, <Headings, 0>, ...}

The resulting ordered Learning Path is: *line breaks, paragraphs, headings, page layout*.

Figure 9. Learning progresses achieved by the learners

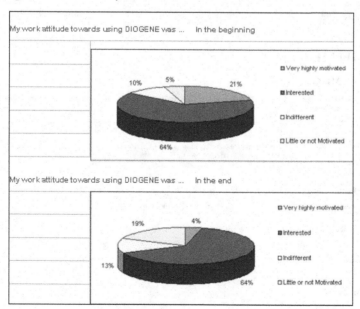

EXPERIMENTAL RESULTS

For lack of space we cannot provide full details on the final experimentation of the Diogene project, referring the interested reader to the project's Final report (Diogene, 2005).

The Diogene's evaluation has been based on a set of 137 learners, belonging to 6 of the 8 different companies and university departments, partners of the project. The evaluation method was based on performance recordings, online questionnaires, interviews of the involved learners and analysis of the system's reports and log information. The evaluation has been conducted between April and October 2004.

Figure 20 shows the overall learning progresses obtained by the learners (the question "work attitude" refers to the fact that all the courses used for the evaluation concern topics of interest of the learners' real life work).

CONCLUSION AND FUTURE TRENDS

In this chapter we have presented the Diogene platform, a learning management system with student-adaptable course generation functionalities. These functionalities include the automatic generation and personalization of (complex) courses starting from the system's knowledge on: (1) the student's current skills and preferences and (2) the didactic domain. This is possible because the system contains a representation of the student's knowledge and her/his learning preferences. Moreover, the platform is provided with both an abstract representation of the didactic domain (by means of an ontology) and the description of each single Learning Object (by means of an associated metadata). The system's LOs are indexed using modern e-learning standards to enable knowledge sharing among different platforms. Moreover, the system's didactic knowledge representation satisfies a new methodology described in this

chapter. This allows the system to efficiently perform inferences on student's query and to compute the best presentation of the topics she/he is interested to.

We believe that in the near future further emphasis should be given in research and developing of automatic tools able to exploit knowledge on the student knowledge and preferences in order to customize learning courses. As we have seen in section "Related Works," most of the existing LMSs are based either on the concept of (passive) learning material sharing or on offering more or less powerful browsing facilities to retrieve material from their database. Only few systems are able to propose to the learner a structuring of their material in a complete course which takes into account pedagogical relationships and prerequisites among the contained topics and/or exploit the student's feedback to previous tests in order to customize the learning offer. Nevertheless, we believe that a major difference between a common search engine such as Google and an intelligent learning platform should pass through the possibility of the latter to provide structured and personalized courses rather than simple unassembled material.

Some recent works seem to follow this direction in proposing either frameworks for a formal didactic knowledge representation or complete automatic course generation systems. Besides the already mentioned systems (e.g., CEPIAH, eMEMORA or NetCoach), the work performed at the Open University of the Netherlands (OUNL) by Koper and his staff in developing a Learning Design formal approach is noticeable. In Tattersall et al. (2005) Koper and colleagues propose the "educational modeling language (EML)," a UML-like approach to assembly LOs in a *unit of study*, each unit expressing the semantic relationships among the contained LOs. Although EML is conceived for a human designer and not for an automatic course generator, it is a valid basis for LO structuring. Hierarchical relationships among LOs similar to those proposed in this chapter are presented by Mizoguchi et al. in Kitamura and Mizoguchi (2003). In Sanrach and Grandbastien (2000), the authors propose an environment for automatic creation of Web-deliverable courses (ECSAIWeb). ECSAIWeb is based on a Student Model having the same principles of NetCoach. The ECSAIWeb engine is a *production-rule* based system (Russell & Norvig, 2003) in which LOs are described by means of *learning units*. A learning unit is composed of a "contents" part containing the references to a given LO, a "pre-conditions" part which defines the LO's prerequisites and a "post-actions" part specifying how the system must change the Student Model status after the student has passed the test corresponding to the unit's LO.

ACKNOWLEDGMENT

This research was supported by the Information Society Technologies project Diogene (IST-2001-33358). Further details can be found on the project Web site (Diogene, 2005).

REFERENCES

ACM Web Site. Retrieved from http://www.acm.org/class/

Adorni G., Sugliano A. M., & Vercelli G. (2003, September). AI embedded into LMS agents: The UniGe E_Learning portal experience and future scenario. In *Proceedings of the Workshop on Artificial Intelligence and e-learning, Eighth National Congress of Italian Association for Artificial Intelligence* (pp. 23-26). Pisa, Italy.

Benayache, A. & Abel, M.-H. (2005). Using knowledge management method for e-learning. In G. Chiazzese, M. Allegra, A. Chifari, & Ottaviano S. (Eds.), *Methods and technologies for learning*. Southampton, UK: WIT Press.

Blackboard Web Site. Retrieved from http://www.Blackboard.com/

Capuano, N., Gaeta, M., Micarelli, A., & Sangineto, E. (2003, June 28-July 1). An intelligent web teacher system for learning personalization and semantic web compatibility. In *Proceedings of the Eleventh International PEG Conference*. St. Petersburg, Russia.

Dicheva, D. & Dichev, C. (2006), Confronting some ontology-building problems in educational topic map authoring. In *Workshop on Applications of Semantic Web Technologies for e-Learning (SW-EL@AH'06)*, Ireland.

Diogene Web site. (2005). Retrieved from http://www.crmpa.it/diogene

Docent Web Site. Retrieved from http://www.docent.com

Duval E. et al. (2001). The Ariadne knowledge pool system. *Communication of the ACM, 44*(5), 73-78.

Felder, R. M. & Silverman, L.K. (1988). Learning and teaching styles in engineering education. *Engineer Education, 78*(7), 674-681.

Felder, R. M. &Soloman, B. A. The Felder and Soloman's *Learning Styles Questionnaire*. Retrieved from http://www.engr.ncsu.edu/learning-styles/ilsweb.html

IEEE LOM 2002. *IEEE Standard for Learning Object Metadata*.

IMS Learning Design Information Model, Version 1.0 (2003). IMS Global Learning Consortium Inc. Retrieved from http://www.imsglobal.org/learningdesign

Kitamura, Y. & Mizoguchi, R. (2003, March 12). An ontological schema for sharing conceptual engineering knowledge. In *Proceedings of the International Workshop on Semantic Web Foundations and Application Technologies* (pp. 25-28). Nara, Japan.

Koper, R. & Tattersall, C. (Eds.). (2005). *Learning design: A handbook on modelling and delivering networked education and training*. New York: Springer.

Lotus LearningSpace Web Site. Retrieved from http://www.pugh.co.uk/Products/lotus/learning-space.htm.

Learning Technology Standardization Committee (LTSC) Web Site. Retrieved from http://ltsc.ieee.org/wg12/index.html

Protege Web Site. Retrieved from http://protege.stanford.edu

Ronchetti, M. & Saini, P. (2003, September 23-26). The knowledge management problem in an e-learning system: A possible solution. In *Proceedings of the Workshop on Artificial Intelligence and e-learning, Eighth National Congress of Italian Association for Artificial Intelligence*. Pisa, Italy.

Russell, S. J. & Norvig, P. (2003). *Artificial intelligence* (2nd ed.). Upper Saddle River, NJ: Prentice Hall.

Sanrach, C. & Grandbastien, M. (2000). EC-SAIWeb: A Web-based authoring system to create adaptive learning systems. In P. Brusilovsky, O.

Stock, & C. Strapparava (Eds.), *AH 2000* (LNCS 1892, 214-226).

Seal, K. C. & Przasnyski, Z. H. (2001). Using the World Wide Web for teaching improvement. *Computers and Educations, 36*, 33-44.

Tattersall, C., Vogten, H., Brouns, F., Koper, R., van Rosmalen, P., Sloep, P., & van Bruggen, J. (2005). How to create flexible runtime delivery of distance learning courses. *Educational Technology and Society, 8*(3), 226-236.

TopClass Web Site. Retrieved from http://www.wbtsystems.com

Trigano, P. & Giacomini, E. (2004). Toward a Web based environment for evaluation and design of pedagogical hypermedia. *Journal of Educational Technology & Society, IEEE Learning Technology Task Force, 7*(3).

WebCT Web Site. Retrieved from http://www.webct.com

Weber, G., Kuhl H. C., & Weibelzahl S. (2001). Developing adaptive Internet based courses with the authoring system NetCoach. In *Proceedings of the Third Workshop on Adaptive Hypermedia (UM2001)*.

Section III.c
Education and Content Perspective

Chapter XV
Pedagogical Scenario Modeling, Deployment, Execution, and Evolution

Yvan Peter
TRIGONE Laboratory, France

Xavier Le Pallec
TRIGONE Laboratory, France

Thomas Vantroys
TRIGONE Laboratory, France

ABSTRACT

The rise of the pedagogical scenario approach supported by the standardization of IMS learning design is changing the focus from the pedagogical objects to the activities that support learning. With the standardization, comes the promise of the reuse of successful designs for the pedagogical scenarios. However, the uptake of this approach relies on a sound support of the users both at the design phase and at the execution phase and the level to which successful design can be adapted for reuse in both phases. This chapter covers the whole lifecycle of pedagogical scenarios and shows the current level of support one can find in existing learning management systems and tools. It presents, also, the way to enhance this support through the use of model-driven engineering for the design and deployment phase and implementation techniques to provide execution engines that allow flexible runtime execution.

INTRODUCTION

The management and reuse of learning objects has now reached a certain maturity thanks to the standards such as sharable content object reference model (SCORM) (ADL, 2006) that enables the reuse of learning objects across learning management systems (LMS) and learning object metadata

(LOM) (LTSC, 2002) that defines metadata for their description. Content object repository discovery and registration/resolution architecture (CORDRA) (CORDRA, 2006) completes this with the means to federate object repositories and to enable the retrieval of learning objects. Thanks to this set of standards, the cost of design is lessened because of the possible reuse and the better perenniality of the resources. This level of maturity has not been reached already when one considers the pedagogical scenarios design. Indeed, the focus is evolving from the resources to the activities. The emerging standard related to these scenarios is IMS learning design (IMS-LD) (IMS, 2003). However, designing pedagogical scenarios is still an expert job at least because there is still a lack of proper editors. Having however succeeded in the design of a pedagogical scenario, it is still common to re-engineer it or to make it evolve slightly because the context or the hosting learning management systems (LMS) changes or because the learners have difficulties with some activities. These modifications of the scenarios can happen between two executions (iterative design) or at runtime if the LMS can support it. In this chapter, we will present solutions to support the lifecycle of pedagogical scenarios from the design time to the deployment on a specific LMS and the execution and runtime evolution. These solutions aim at keeping the pedagogical design across different contexts which will lessen the cost of the design while permitting a continuous adaptation.

This chapter is divided into four parts. The first part gives some background on IMS-LD and provides an example scenario for the chapter. The second part presents the current level of support for IMS-LD considering both authoring tools and existing LMS. The third part presents a proposition based on model-driven engineering to support the implementation of an IMS-LD scenario into a LMS that does not provide support for IMS-LD. The fourth part presents an alternative approach that is to build an execution engine that can then

be integrated into existing LMS to provide direct support for the scenarios. In the conclusion we will show how these two approaches complement each other and contribute to the uptake of the pedagogical scenarios by supporting their whole lifecycle.

THE PEDAGOGICAL SCENARIO APPROACH

The pedagogical scenario approach is raising interest because it is seen as a mean to reintroduce pedagogical reflection based on the different existing theories into the planning of teaching and learning activities (Schneider et al., 2005; Earp & Pozzi, 2006). This holds primarily in the domain of e-learning where the focus has mostly been put on learning resources up to now. Indeed by the means of pedagogical planning, the learning objects are put into the context of learning activities with a specific pedagogy in mind. The main standard for the description of learning scenarios is IMS-LD (IMS, 2003). In the next sections, we will review the main elements of the language and provide an example scenario. We will also analyze the main features provided by the specification.

IMS-LD

The IMS-LD meta-model, that is, the set of modeling concepts, permits defining learning designs. A learning design corresponds to a pedagogical scenario. It is made up of learning objectives, prerequisites, components and a method. Components and Method are the main features of the IMS-LD:

- Components of a learning design refer to the list of activities, roles and environments that make it up (bricks of scenario):
  1. Activities are tasks in the learning process.

2. Roles consist in sub-roles of learner and staff members.

3. Environments are sets of services (mail, chat, forum…) and learning objects. Each environment is generally used at least by one activity.

- The method defines the behavior of a LD scenario: What is the first activity? The second one? When do they start? Who is concerned by the first activity? etc. The behavioral description starts with plays. They represent main activities and run in parallel. Each play defines a sequence of acts. Within an act, roles will perform activities. Only one activity is associated to one role (through the *role-part* concept). Referenced roles and activities are defined in previous components of the learning design. The behavioral description of a LD scenario essentially consists in this *play/act/role-part* structure.

The concepts of IMS-LD are grouped into three levels: A, B and C that correspond to the addition of specific functions. Level A corresponds to the basic specification of the scenario organization (activities, etc.). Level B adds the properties and conditions that enable conditional control flow. Level C provides notification mechanisms.

An Example Scenario

We will now present an example of a LD scenario to get an overview of its power and complexity. This example, illustrated in Figure 1, is taken from our experience in distance learning.

General description. This course involves a *tutor* and a set of *students* (two *roles*) in the study of a book chapter and personal project work. This is modeled by two plays that run in parallel. These plays are called *play one* and *play two*. *Play one* is made up of three acts which are therefore carried out sequentially. Act *theory 1* is dedicated to the study of the first book chapter. While

students are studying this document, they may ask questions on a forum (*asynchronous conference service*) and the tutor may provide answers as well as other students. When this act is over, there is a 2 hours—chat session in order to close the study definitively (act *discussion 1*). Students do exercises in the final act (*practice*) while the tutor may answer students' questions. This last act is very similar to the only act of *play two*. This act (*project 1*) is dedicated to a personal student project under the monitoring of the tutor.

Detailed description. So far, we have described the scenario in the scope of IMS-LD level A. Now we must use level B to go into the details of act *theory 1*. In this act, we want students to study the first chapter. But if some of them have difficulties, we would like them to shift to another activity where they will learn some prerequisites before coming back to the study. Since only one activity may be assigned to one role within an act, we use the *activity structure* concept to define a composite activity. Such activity is made up of several (sub-)activities and thus provides a way to assign several activities to one role in an act. While creating a composite activity, we have to specify if activities will be carried out sequentially ("sequence" value) or selected by the performer role as she/he wants ("select" value). We must also rely on properties and conditions within the composite activity so as to define if the student shall switch to the *study chapter 1 prerequisites* activity.

First, we define the *Chapter1_Prerequisites* property. It is a local property, that is to say, there will be one property instance for each student. Initially, the value of this property is set to "acquired" and each *prerequisites* activity is hidden (its *isvisible* property is set to "false"). During *study chapter 1 course* activity, the tutor may decide that some students have to study prerequisites. She/he can then set their *Chapter1_Prerequisites* property to "required" through the *monitor* service. For these students, the prerequisites activity will replace their current *course* activity (prerequisites.

Figure 1. Example of pedagogical scenario (LD-oriented UML activity diagram)

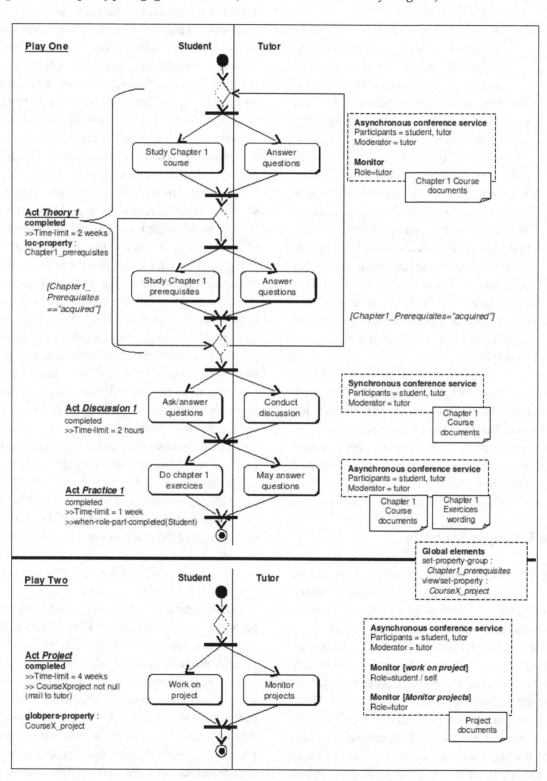

isvisible="true" and course.isvisible="false"). This automatic replacement relies on IMS-LD conditions mechanisms (particularly *if-then-else* and *change-value-property)*. When a student has finished her/his prerequisites activity, the previous property is set to "acquired" and a condition reacts in order to replace the prerequisites activity by the course one.

Main Features of IMS-LD

IMS-LD aims to standardize the description of pedagogical scenarios. Support of these scenarios by LMS implies the support of the IMS-LD concepts and features. Here, we examine five main features of IMS-LD for which a LMS has to provide corresponding mechanisms.

1. **Properties management:** This feature allows defining global/local and personal/group properties and consulting/changing their values. In our scenario, we define *Chapter1_prerequisites* and *CourseX_project* properties. The former is a local property: it is associated to one execution and there is one value for each user. The latter is a global and personal property. This one has its own life, that is to say it does not stop when the unit of learning is over, and there is one value for each participant. The underlying idea of this property is that each student may have her/his project in her/his e-portfolio. Properties values may be changed by LMS users (generally tutors) through the *monitor* service. This can be used to control activities execution as illustrated in the scenario.

2. **Trigger mechanism:** A trigger mechanism is available in LD to execute specific actions during the scenario. The related events are the following: when a property value changes, when all students end an activity, when all activities are terminated in an act and when the last act is over.

3. **Conditional flow control:** Properties management and trigger mechanism are really interesting thanks to the *conditional flow control* mechanism. The flow is controlled through *if <conditions> then <actions> else <actions>* and *when-property-value-is-set* statements. When a property value changes, all conditions of type *if-then-else* are evaluated. Conditions are expressed with logic operators and properties. An action may be *show/hide an element* (any type of element) or *change property value*. For example, when *Chapter1_prerequisites* is set to "required", the *study chapter 1 course* activity is hidden and the *study chapter 1 prerequisites* one is shown.

4. **Time management:** *Time-limit* concept is the basic mechanism to control activity sequencing. Activities may be terminated (and following ones may be launched) according to specific time limits.

5. **Group management:** One property of a LD role is related to the number of its performers (*min* and *max*). When the definition of a role specifies that it may be performed by more than one person, it means that it represents a group. Thus, it is possible to associate a group to one or more activities. Except for time management which is related to the activities, all other mechanisms take into account this group: it is possible to define a property for a group or for a person; to launch a notification when a group or a person ends an activity; conditions may be expressed through group or personal properties.

CURRENT TECHNOLOGICAL SUPPORT FOR IMS-LD

For IMS-LD to gain a wide acceptance there is a need for tools that help teachers and designers in the use of the language at both design time and when it comes to the implementation of the scenario. Greller (2005) states that the success of these tools is dependent on "how well they integrate into an existing e-learning architecture" and "how easy to use they are for academics." In the next section we will review existing authoring tools, for which the latter requirement is important. The former requirement is more directed towards existing LMS and their support of IMS-LD which we will examine in the following section.

Authoring Tools

The IMS-LD language is born in the specific context of the Open University NederLand (OUNL) and has been designed with an industrial production model in mind where many actors participate to the design of the pedagogical scenarios: subject experts, instructional designers, graphical designers, etc. With the standardization, the language has reached a greater scope and it is now a challenge to provide tools that can be used by teachers on an individual basis or in small organizations (Griffiths & Blat, 2005; Lundgren-Cayrol et al., 2006). The most advanced LD authoring tools are: Reload, MOT+, LAMS. Reload is the only one to propose a complete compliance with IMS-LD (levels A, B and C). It uses a form-based graphical user interface which is closely related to the XML grammar of the language and is thus not very easy to handle for novice users. MOT+ is limited to LD level A, but it proposes a graph-based GUI which seems to be more intuitive, but still it does not hide the complexity of LD concepts. Finally LAMS also proposes a graph-based GUI but it is really dedicated to educational concerns in opposition to MOT+ which is a meta-editor and not a dedicated one. Unfortunately LAMS is not really a LD editor. It only provides an IMS-LD export functionality and its ability to define complex environments is limited.

Other tools are appearing that try to enhance adoption by hiding the complexity or at least by permitting an adaptation to the users' vocabulary.

One such tool is the ASK learning designer Toolkit that enable the pedagogical designer to user their own notation (i.e., graphical representation) for the definition of learning scenarios (Sampson et al., 2006). Finally, the Collage prototype (Hernandez-Leo et al., 2006) proposes to build pedagogical scenarios by assembling pedagogical design patterns (e.g., jigsaw). For each pattern, the corresponding IMS-LD definition is known by the tool and taken in charge, so the complexity of IMS-LD is hidden from the author.

Authoring tools are still in their infancy, however, taking the stability of the older tools in one hand and the new alternative proposals on the other hand, we can bet that a new generation of tools will emerge that are both easier to use and providing a comprehensive support for IMS-LD.

IMS-LD and Current Learning Management Systems

In the first part of this chapter, we have presented the main features provided by the IMS-LD specification. Almost no LMS support the specification. However, in this part, we will analyze to what extent these features can be found in LMS. For this purpose, we have selected widely used platforms: Claroline (http://www.claroline.net/), Ganesha (http://www.anemalab.org/ganesha/) and Moodle (http://moodle.org/) for open-source LMS and Blackboard (http://www.blackboard.com/) and WebCT (http://www.webct.com/) for commercial LMS.

1. **Properties management:** All of studied platforms propose a real management for personal properties through the ability to mark or to comment an assignment whose name is given by a manager: a manager can create personal properties and monitor them. For example, this ability is used by the SCORM modules of each platform. But for all of them, there is no possibility to create group properties or to specify the lifetime

of a property as recommended in IMS-LD. Group properties, like the name of a group or its maximal capacity, exist but they are ad hoc properties. Managers cannot create new ones. This is the main reason why *global properties* feature of a SCORM learning object is very limited in these LMS.

2. **Trigger mechanism:** The five platforms provide essentially only one trigger point: when a personal activity is ended (we consider time limit as another mechanism). There is no fine-grained trigger mechanism with events like *when a property value changes* in the studied LMS.

3. **Conditional control flow:** All studied LMS (except Claroline) provide a conditional control flow mechanism in their SCORM module: *prerequisites* and *completionReq* permits starting and ending an activity through conditions written in AICC_Script (basic logic predicates). However, it is not possible to associate actions like change a property value, show/hide any type of element. In addition, the control is limited to the SCORM learning object and cannot refer to the whole course environment (set of learning objects and LMS services). This is the main weakness of studied LMS concerning IMS-LD support.

4. **Time management:** Moodle, Blackboard and WebCT provide an efficient support for this feature, yet without the ability to combine it with properties/event mechanisms.

5. **Group management:** This is the second main weakness of studied platforms concerning IMS-LD support. Every platform allows managing students groups (own document repositories, discussions, forums …). They also provide definition of rules and associated access rules to contents or tools. But properties trigger and conditional control flow mechanisms are not available when considering groups. For example, there is no way, in any platform, to specify

that activity B may be active when previous activity A has been completed by every students of the group.

DEPLOYMENT AND EXECUTION OF IMS-LD SCENARIOS

Support for IMS-LD within existing LMS is not easy since the concepts proposed by these systems are different from the concepts of IMS-LD. This is normal since one is targeted at providing learning objects and tools to the learners and tutors, while the other is dedicated to the organization of the activities and implies some sort of runtime support for its execution. In this part, we will present two approaches towards the implementation of pedagogical scenarios on LMS. The first one tries to organize the LMS resources based on the scenario while the second one seeks to provide support for the scenario execution within the LMS.

Deployment on Current LMS: The BRICOLES Project

The work we present consists in one of the BRICOLES project results (Caron et al., 2005, 2006) whose main objective is to suggest MDE[1]-based solutions to reintroduce teacher in e-learning courses design. The idea is to organize the LMS resources based on the IMS-LD scenario. The tool set currently supports Claroline, Ganesha and Moodle. Since the execution facility is missing within these LMS, there is a need to help the actors perform their activities in a pre-structured environment. One very simple solution may consist in giving the scenario to students in order to explain the primary pedagogical intentions which underlie the provided e-learning environment. A map must be attached to the scenario where students may find correspondences between the scenario and resources on the LMS. A more advanced solution consist in reflecting finely the scenario on the LMS resources by their name, their order, the presence of small textual help in each forum, document repositories, etc.

Examples of Scenario-Based Implementation

We illustrate such implementation (on the previous scenario) using Claroline with two different strategies. Claroline is a good example since it is very user-friendly but also very limited in terms of functionalities.

The first strategy may be named time-strategy because it relies on a time limit for each act through the use of the agenda (see Figure 2).

It consists in first creating in *documents and links* a directory for each play, a subdirectory for each act and a sub-subdirectory for each activity where documents will be placed. Secondly, if a forum is needed in one LD (learning-) activity, a forum is created in the Claroline course with the name *[ActName].[Activity_Name]*. This forum will be in the forum category created for owner

Figure 2. Example of Claroline implementation of a LD scenario with Time-Strategy

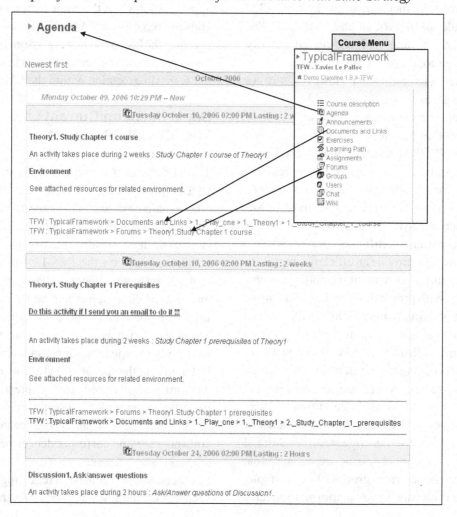

Figure 3. Example of Claroline implementation of a LD scenario with Wiki-Strategy

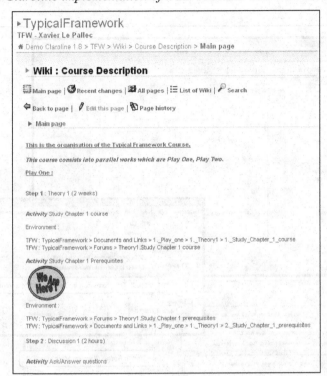

play. The final point is the main one: each LD activity is transformed into an entry in the course agenda (as illustrated in Figure 2). Each entry contains URLs of associated learning objects or services in order to present an environment which corresponds to the activity. Duration is also associated to each entry in the agenda.

When time is not pertinent, we may use a Wiki-strategy which uses Claroline Wiki.

This strategy starts with creating a wiki page which represents the organization of all the activities with links to related resources (learning objects and services) (see Figure 3). The benefit of this strategy is that the tutor has a structural description of her/his course and she/he has great expressive capabilities to exploit it thanks to Wiki.

We have seen that if most-used e-learning Web platforms have a lot of functionalities they do not provide a support to execute pedagogical scenarios. However, a designer may implement a scenario in such LMS by applying mapping rules according to her/his context (scenario complexity, her/his skills about the chosen LMS, etc). The resulting learning environment is far from being as powerful as with a scenario runtime engine but it remains correct, permits an opportunistic approach and has the benefit to provide a familiar environment to users (tutors and students).

Building Automatically an Environment from a LD Scenario

The model-driven engineering approach permits to build automatically a learning environment from LD scenarios. The designer (instructional designer or teacher) follows a four-step production cycle (see Figure 4):

Figure 4. Bricoles project: Four steps to automatically build a Claroline environment from a LD scenario

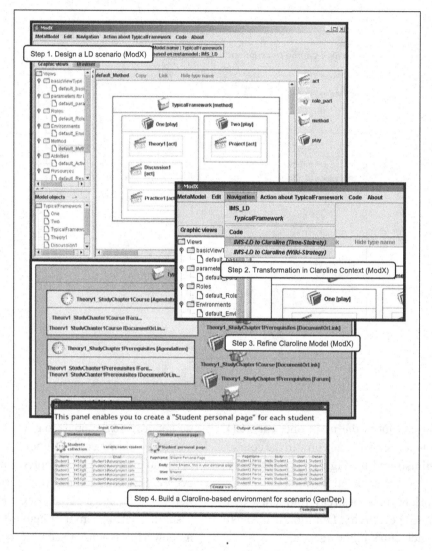

- She/he defines the LD scenario.
- She/he chooses the targeted LMS, the way to map her/his scenario and gets a model of her/his scenario which is expressed with the concepts of the platform. We called this model a *technological model* or a platform specific model (PSM).
- She/he refines the technological model because it was not possible to express some

subtleties related to the final realization in the LD scenario.
- She/he uses a deployment tool to implement the technological model on her/his LMS.

For the first step, the designer may use any LD authoring tool or our graphic modeling tool ModX (ModX, 2006). To model a pedagogical scenario, we have defined the metamodel for

IMS-LD and associated a graphical syntax to it. This is a LD dedicated version of ModX—with functions which are related to import/export of IMS-LD native documents—where we have also included the best-practices methodology in order to assist the designer when she/he defines a LD model (Le Pallec et al., 2006).

For the second step, the designer must use ModX in order to benefit from its model transformation abilities. The designer may transform her/his scenario into Claroline, Moodle or Ganesha technological model. For each LMS, there are one or more kinds of mappings proposed. The resulting model is expressed in a meta-model (i.e., the concepts) related to the selected LMS. For this, we have defined one meta-model for each LMS.

For the third step, the designer goes on using ModX because it allows editing, and so refining the previous technological model. Finally, the designer runs GenDep (GenDep, 2006) in order to implement the previous refined technological model on her/his LMS. GenDep will build a learning environment on an instance of Claroline, Ganesha or Moodle from the technological model. It will interact with the designer to know which students and tutor(s)—already present in the platform—have to be associated to the created learning environment. This process will result in a pre-structured environment based on the LMS resources built according to the pedagogical scenario.

EXECUTION AND RUNTIME EVOLUTION OF PEDAGOGICAL SCENARIOS

At the moment, there are very few solutions compatible with IMS-LD standard or at least targeted at pedagogical scenarios (Britain, 2004). This is particularly true when one considers the execution of these scenarios which is considered in this part. In a first step, we will consider the architecture of IMS-LD execution engines. Next, we will consider how flexibility can be provided by such engines so as to permit a continuous adaptation of the pedagogical scenario. Finally, we will see how execution engines can be integrated into learning management systems.

Execution of Pedagogical Scenarios

The execution of pedagogical scenarios requires two elements: *a learning design engine* that can interpret the IMS-LD scenario and keep track of the activities so as to provide the right activities with the related resources and services to the participants, and a client or *player* that will provide a learning environment for the learners and tutors. The learning design engines can be developed in two ways:

- **Embedded in a learning management System** as in .LRN (.LRN, 2006). This approach has the benefit of permitting a tight integration with the LMS services which enables a rich learning environment, in terms of services and user interface. However, this means an ad hoc development that can hardly be reused in another setting.
- **As a standalone service** with well defined interfaces that permit its integration into a LMS. This approach provides the advantage of a reuse of the execution service. However, since the service is generic, one has to take care of the integration issues both with the support services (e.g., chat, mail) and with the player.

In the following, we will concentrate more on the second type of approach based on examples such as the CopperCore engine (http://coppercore. org/) and its extensions as well as the Cooperative Open Workflow engine (http://cow.objectweb. org/). Based on these, we will delve into the technological basis and the means to provide flexibility. We will also cover the issues related to the integration into a LMS.

Developing a Learning Design Engine: Design and Technologies

The Design

Users of the pedagogical scenarios will interact with the player for different purposes: to get the activities they have to perform, to manage the scenarios, etc. The player then relies on the learning design engine to manage these tasks. Hence, the LD engine should provide the following services:

- **Runtime services** to provide the right activities, resources and pedagogical services to the actors. The main interaction mode between the player and the engine is pull mode, i.e., the player retrieves the information from the engine.
- **Administration services** to provide the means to administrate and instantiate the pedagogical scenarios. This means defining the students and support staff participating in a particular instance, creating groups, etc.
- **Monitoring services** to provide the means for a tutor to monitor the progress of the students/groups in a particular instance. This type of service is also interesting to be able to put in evidence problems related to the scenario itself, which would trigger a re-engineering of the scenario.

The engine must take care of the models but also of the instances (called *runs* in CopperCore). This corresponds to the actors and groups, the resources but also to keep track of the position of everybody in the scenario (current activities, etc). Since a pedagogical scenario can last for a long time (e.g., weeks or months), the engine should take care of the persistence of this information.

Technologies

Since the engine must be integrated into an existing learning environment, it should provide interfaces for this. Middleware technologies such as common object request broker architecture (CORBA), Java remote method invocation (RMI) and distributed component object model (DCOM) provide the basis for a remote integration and the means to define the interfaces (Raj, 2007). However, while solving the integration problem, these technologies do not support the developer in providing robust software since every service such as persistence or security has to be managed explicitly. Component standards have appeared to solve the problem by a declarative management of these non functional properties. The definition and configuration of the services to provide is then used by a component container to provide a suitable runtime environment. The Enterprise JavaBeans (EJB) specification is one of these component models (Burke & Monson-Haefel, 2006). It has been used to develop both CopperCore and COW, so we will provide a brief description for it. The EJB model defines three types of components:

- **Entity beans** provide an object-oriented view of the persistent information managed by the software. Each modification to an entity is persisted in a permanent storage, typically a relational database.
- **Session beans** are associated to a client and can be seen as the providers of the service. Sessions can be stateless or stateful. In the latter case, they can manage the interactions with the user/client. Sessions typically provide the business logic and manipulate the entities according to the business rules.
- **Message driven beans** (MDB) allow asynchronous communication based on the Java messaging service (JMS) standard. Upon receipt of a message, the MDB can interact with sessions or entities.

During the deployment, the container uses an XML descriptor provided with the beans to provide a suitable runtime environment. This deployment descriptor defines the configuration of the beans and non-functional services. After deployment the beans interfaces are available through Java RMI and eventually as Web Services for the session beans. Indeed, it is still difficult to integrate third party services which may not be developed with the same model. To cope with this heterogeneity problem, Web Services are the current solution (Walsh, 2002). The principle is to use existing standards like HTTP or XML to realize remote procedure call. Simple object access protocol (SOAP) allows an easy integration by using an XML language to realize the method invocation. The exposed interfaces are described with an XML language called WSDL (Web Service Description Language). Based on this, one can envision an enhanced reuse of existing services which can be combined to provide new services. This is the Service-Oriented Architecture (SOA) vision. One example in the domain of technology enhanced learning is the E-Learning Framework (Wilson et al., 2005). This framework intends to standardize all the useful services of a learning environment so as to allow for a greater reuse of existing implementations. Since the LD engine is an execution service, it should be provided as a Web Service to enhance integration. This is the case of both CopperCore and COW.

Existing Implementations

In this part, we will focus on CopperCore and SLeD implementation and the Cooperative Open Workflow engine which are the main examples of standalone execution services. Among the few implementations we can also mention works presented in (Chen et al., 2005) and (Hagen et al., 2006). The former follows the same architectural principles as the ones we will see hereafter. Based

on the implementation work they raise questions about the interpretation of some IMS-LD constructs. The latter is also a prototype to question the implementation of the standard.

The CopperCore Engine

The CopperCore engine is one of the results of the Active Learning for Adaptive Internet (aLFanet) IST project (Santos et al., 2004). The objective is to provide a reference implementation of IMS-LD. CopperCore handles the three levels of IMS-LD, that is static (level A) and dynamic scenarios based on properties and conditions (level B) as well as notifications (level C). Level B and C support are in fact a contribution from the SLeD project presented hereafter (McAndrew et al., 2005). CopperCore has been built as a proof of concept and demonstrator and for this reason it provides a command line and a Web-based client that should not be useful in an embedded setting (McAndrew et al., 2004). It is based on J2EE (Java 2 enterprise edition) technologies and provides three levels of interfaces for its integration into a LMS (cf. Figure 5):

- A set of java objects that shield the developer from the intricacies of J2EE development, in particular the access to the session beans' interfaces.
- The remote method invocation (RMI) interfaces provided by the Enterprise Java-Beans component framework which is also restricted to java environments.
- The Web service interfaces based on WSDL that can be used at a distance and in a heterogeneous setting.

For these three levels, we will find a learnflow interface corresponding to the runtime services describe beforehand and an administration interface.

Figure 5. CopperCore architecture and interfaces

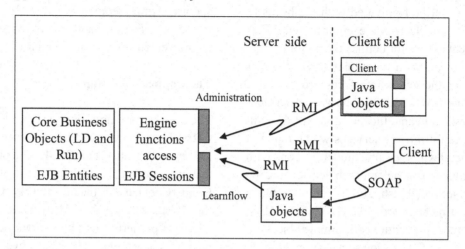

The SLED Project

The service-based learning design system (SLeD) project started in 2004 and had multiple follow-up to extend the work (SLeD 2) and to assess its use in real settings (SliDe project, Barret-Baxendale (2005)). In addition to contributing to CopperCore, the aim of the project was to provide another implementation that enables the integration of new services which can be used in the pedagogical scenarios (e.g., assessment engine, e-portfolio, etc.). This work is made in the spirit of the service-oriented architecture (SOA) and e-learning framework. The objective of the project was to explore the tension between generic service description as used in IMS-LD that facilitate reuse of the design and a rich service description which would provide a higher integration and functionality (Weller et al., 2006). Indeed, to fully take the benefit of SOA, it is necessary to have standardized services which truly enable to switch implementations transparently and permit to define a service with few information (identifier and configuration data). This has led to the proposition of the architecture presented in as an output of the SLeD 2 project (Vogten et al, 2006). The IMS content package provides the definition of the needed services within the IMS-LD scenario. This is used in the integration layer to manage the relevant services implementations. The integration layer is responsible for calling the right service and provides the input data based on the performed activities and user inputs as well as catching notifications from the services and forwarding to other services as necessary (e.g., to notify the end of an activity to the LD engine). Since there is scarcely a standard for the services, an adaptation layer is necessary to accommodate different implementations with different APIs. For each service type (e.g., forum, e-portfolio, etc.) it is necessary to define a common interface and for each service implementation, one has to develop a translator that will implement this interface and make the right calls on the actual service.

The adaptation layer is only necessary because of the low maturity of the field regarding standardization. In the long term, the situation should evolve driven by the work done by standardization bodies like the IMS consortium. An example of this is the IMS enterprise services specification (IMS, 2004).

Figure 6. SLeD architecture for a service oriented LD

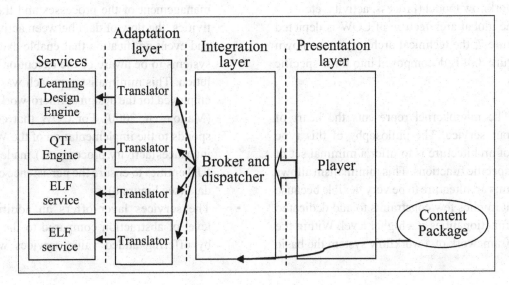

The COW Project

The Cooperative Open Workflow (Vantroys & Peter, 2005) developed by the TRIGONE laboratory since 2001 aims at providing a bridge between the concept of activity in the EMLs (Educational Modeling Language) and in workflows systems in order to execute learning scenarios. COW has been built using workflow technologies with the idea that learning scenarios are only a certain kind of processes. This workflow-based execution service has been designed around the following principles:

- To design a service centered on the user (Bourguin et al., 2001) which allows a continuous adaptation to provide the best learning experience.
- To recognize the importance of the scenario model and to make it constantly available and easy to handle.
- To provide flexibility mechanisms allowing the realization of the preceding principles.

To provide an easy integration of this execution service into a LMS and to foster reusability, the development is based on existing standards at both technical and pedagogical levels. As the project began before the rise of IMS-LD, the main concepts come from the workflow world but there are several links between classical workflow processes and learning scenarios. Based on a meta-modeling approach, we have designed a translator that can map IMS-LD concepts into workflow concepts (Vantroys & Peter, 2003), which shows the two approaches are compatible.

At the technical level, the development is based on J2EE standards in particular using EJB components and useful interfaces are also published as Web Services to enhance integration. The implementation of the service follows the workflow management facility (WMF) specification (WMF, 2000) of the Object Management Group (OMG, 2006) and the workflow reference model of the workflow management coalition (WfMC, 1995). The WMF describes the architecture of a workflow engine by defining the interfaces of the different objects. Each object represents a concept in a workflow model (process, activity, etc.).

The global architecture of COW is depicted in Figure 7; the technical architecture is shown in Figure 8. It is decomposed into three specific layers:

- The microkernel represents the heart of our service. The philosophy of this type of architecture is to offer a minimal set of specific functions. This minimalism allows this architecture to be very flexible because it implies few constraints to add dedicated functionalities at a higher level. Within the framework of a workflow system the basic

functionalities relate to the rudimentary management of the processes and the activities, the flow of data between activities and event notification that enable external systems to be aware of the execution evolution. This minimalist approach was also employed for the design of micro-workflow (Manolescu, 2000). For COW that corresponds to the implementation of the WMF interfaces (activity, process, etc.), made with EJB entities to ensure the persistence of the data (see Figure 8).

- The services layer offers an additional level of abstraction compared to the core by offering added value services which

Figure 7. COW global architecture

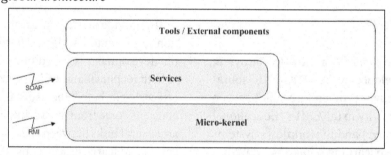

Figure 8. COW internal architecture

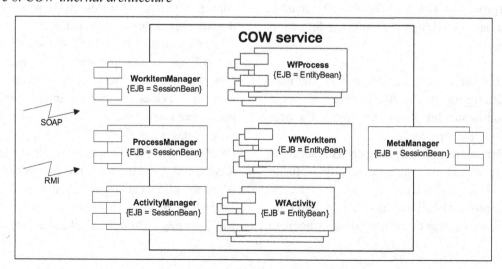

correspond to the runtime, administration and monitoring services. These interfaces abstract the complexity of the kernel based on the façade design pattern (Gamma et al., 1995). The basic services are implemented as EJB sessions.

- The external tools and components correspond to the clients of the services offered by the system. This level corresponds to the player and offers user interfaces to the monitoring tools, model management, and activities for the learners and staff.

Support for the Flexible Execution of Pedagogical Scenarios

Many adaptations to the pedagogical scenario will be done at design time when one reuses a scenario. The adaptations to the actual context may also be done during deployment (e.g., to link a service to a specific implementation). However, even with these late adaptations, one cannot envision all the events that can occur during the execution of the scenario nor the particular difficulties of the learners or differences in the way they approach the learning activities (e.g., learning styles, knowledge level, etc.). There are even some times when one does not know beforehand all the activities needed. Because of this it is necessary to support runtime modification of the scenario.

The aLFanet project which is at the origin of CopperCore has also developed an adaptation component for IMS-LD. The runtime adaptations provided are targeted at guiding the users to improve their learning experience according to a constructed user model (Boticario et al., 2004). This is based on machine learning to detect user categories and to keep the memory of the successful interactions related to the different categories. The learning part relies on a multi-agent system. The adaptation of the scenario relies on modifications to the properties in level B to change the course of the activities.

Another approach which is more related to the context of learning rather than the learners themselves is presented in (Zarraonandia et al., 2006). Design patterns and aspect-oriented programming are used to extend the CopperCore implementation with adaptation features. Adaptations are defined using a language that describes the manipulations of the scenario. To this end, they have defined the set of modifications that can be achieved for the elements in level A and B (e.g., change activity title, add an activity, change a property value, etc.). Modifications are expressed within an adaptation command file which may be accompanied with a manifest that provides IMS-LD fragments used in the modifications. Adaptations can then be defined for specific contexts which will be triggered based on the acquisition of contextual information. However, for this approach to work, the considered context should be limited otherwise the combination of values and corresponding adaptations could not be handled.

The flexibility brought by COW is found according to two axes: the first relates to the possibility to modify the model of the scenario in the course of execution, the second relates to the possibility to modify the interpretation of the scenario (i.e., the behavior of the engine). The first axis rests on mechanisms of introspection and intercession and the principle of open implementation (Kiczales et al., 1991) which make it possible to handle the model in order to add/withdraw/modify activities and to modify the sequencing of these activities. One can also modify the activity model (e.g., changing tools or learning objects, modifying activities assignment to roles). These changes can be realized for one learner or for a group of learners. The second axis of flexibility relates to the behavior of the engine itself. Indeed, it is impossible for the programmer to foresee all the use cases of the system. The modification of the behavior relies on the use of the strategy design pattern to be able to provide ad hoc behavior depending on the context. It is then necessary to identify the flexibility points within the engine and to use the strategy pattern at these points. The way of managing the time constraints is a typical example of behavior which one must be able to adapt. Indeed, the management of time is one of the other properties of COW. Two temporal concepts are provided: duration and deadlines. The first represents the minimal or maximum time to perform an activity. The second concept specifies the periods during which work must happen. In order to manage the calculation of the durations and the deadlines, it is possible to use various "strategies", such as for example taking into account the weekends or not. One can thus dynamically adapt calculation according to the context of use and the wishes of the users. The strategy pattern is also used to allow various behaviors when constraints are violated, for example, to send an e-mail to the learner or the tutor, or to validate in an automatic way the activity.

Integration of Learning Scenario Execution Services in LMS

As indicated previously, there are few LMS integrating support for learning scenarios. The solution is thus to integrate a third party execution service like CopperCore or COW into the LMS. From a technological point of view that does not seem to be a problem because these services have been designed to be integrated. They use in particular SOAP for the access to their API. By exploring this question a little, one notes that it is not so simple because integration requires necessarily modifications of the LMS and it is also necessary to determine the desired level of integration, from slightly coupled to strongly integrated into the LMS. This choice will also depend on non-technical parameters. It will be directed by the level of knowledge of the users and by their level of adoption of IMS-LD and the learning scenarios approach. If the users have little knowledge and where one simply wishes to add a new functionality to the LMS without changing

its architecture, a weak coupling can be selected. It is for example the case of (Berggren et al., 2005). They have integrated CopperCore player into Moodle in order to offer a new functionality to the users of Moodle. CopperCore player is regarded as a simple resource of the type "Web link". Thus the users are redirected on the Web interface of the player when necessary. This approach is simple but presents disadvantages. The first one relates to the user interface which does not correspond to the traditional ergonomics of the LMS. The second point relates to the communication. The engine can use learning resources provided by the LMS, but it has no possibility to return information to the LMS. Because of these limitations, the authors plan a stronger integration in order to have a bidirectional communication. It is to obtain a better integration that (Harrer et al., 2005) had an approach based on the development of a communication module called "remote control component", to integrate the CopperCore engine with Cool Mode (Pinkwart, 2003). They extended CopperCore to produce events related to the execution. These events are listened to by the LMS. Thus a bidirectional communication is possible. A third integration more strongly coupled is explained in (Vantroys & Peter, 2003). COW was integrated into a commercial LMS, the "Campus Virtuel" of the French enterprise Archimed (Archimed, 2006). The "Campus Virtuel" already contained a learning scenario service which did not fulfill all the requirements of the users, in particular in term of flexibility of the learning path. Here what was needed was a strong integration with bidirectional communication so as to maintain the existing modes of operation. There was also the additional constraint of not changing the user interfaces and to avoid to the maximum modifying the other existing functionalities.

Figure 9 summarizes the integration. For the existing components managing the learning scenarios, a large development was carried out to replace the old service based on COM components. In the new architecture, the services related to the

Figure 9. COW integration in the Campus Virtuel

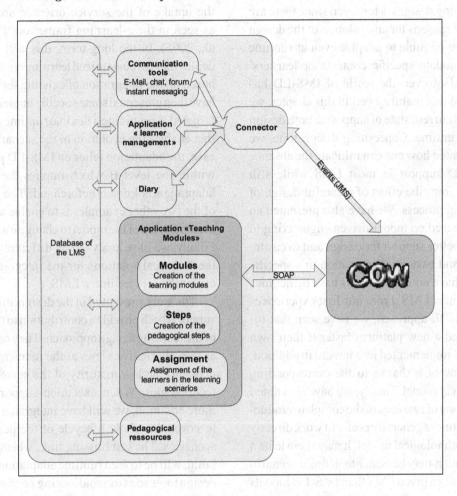

activities ("teaching modules") interact with the COW engine to retrieve information for a specific user (e.g., the available activities to perform). The integration was carried out by using SOAP. For the communication with the other services (chat, forum, etc.) which are not directly related to the execution of the scenario, an event-driven type of connector was developed in the same spirit as the approach described above. For instance, an event can be generated by the engine that will result in the publication of an entry in the diary.

CONCLUSION

Hummel et al. (2004) conclude that "...*staff and educational developers can already benefit from the philosophy of IMS-LD by focusing on learners' activities and objectives...*" (p. 125), and that the final objective is the emergence of educational best practices expressed as reusable learning designs which can then be adapted for use in particular contexts and executed in IMS-LD compliant environments. To achieve this vision, it is necessary to provide a suitable support to the designers of the learning activities and to have means to execute these learning designs. Moreover, since there are many good reasons for an evolution of the design it should be possible to adapt it even at runtime to accommodate specific contexts or learners' problems. However, the world of IMS-LD has not reached that maturity yet. In this chapter, we present the current state of support at both design time and runtime. Concerning design time, we have presented how one can mitigate the absence of IMS-LD support in most LMS while still benefiting from the effort of a careful design of the learning process. We have also presented an approach based on model-driven engineering to provide a better support for design and to ensure a faithful and easy implementation in a specific LMS. We have noted that tutors have difficulties to adopt a new LMS. From our first experiences with our MDE approach, we have seen that tutors grasped a new platform faster if their own course was implemented into it with, in addition, an overview of it thanks to the corresponding technological model. Finally, we have also noted that, after one or two uses of the complete production cycle, tutors generally prefer to work directly with the technological model. It may seem to be a problem, but it may be easier to define a scenario in the terms of a given LMS than IMS-LD models which are complex. Technological models may be more relevant than we planned at the beginning. We plan to study what may be the new practices brought by technological models.

Concerning runtime support for pedagogical scenarios, we have presented the design and technologies for an execution engine and the main existing services. It is important to note that the main implementations comply with existing standards from the technical perspective and from the pedagogical perspective: EJB components, Web Services, IMS Question and Test Interoperability (IMS, 2006), etc. This approach provides the opportunity to take the benefit of existing tools and services, a good basis for reuse of the developed services and facilitates the integration

with other services. This prepares the way for the uptake of the service-oriented architecture as seen in the e-learning framework (Wilson et al., 2005). In the long term, this will allow the deployment of customized learning environments based on the integration of existing services. We have then presented some specific implementation targeted at providing a flexible runtime execution that enables the evolution of the scenario. In one case, the adaptation relies on IMS-LD properties within the level B which implies the range of adaptation is known beforehand. The approach of the two other examples is to enable an explicit manipulation of the model to change it at runtime. Finally, we have analyzed on different examples the technical solutions for the integration of an execution service into a LMS.

The work presented in the design and runtime supports both provide a contribution to the uptake of the learning design approach. They can be seen as two alternative views at the moment, but this is due to the low maturity of the corresponding technologies. When execution support will be more common, we will have integrated solutions to cover the whole lifecycle of the pedagogical scenarios. The last missing link, which is still to build, will be to feed runtime adaptations into the design tools so as to avoid loosing good evolutions and their rationale. This will enable a continuous evolution of the scenarios.

REFERENCES

ADL. (2006). ADL Web site for SCORM related specifications. Retrieved June 2006 from http://www.adlnet.gov/scorm/

Archimed. (2006). Archimed Web site. Retrived October 2006 from http://www.archimed.fr

Barrett-Baxendale M., Hazelwood P., Oddie A., Anderson M., & Franklin T. (2005). *SLeD Integration Demonstrator—Final Report*. retrieved September, 2006, from http://www.hope.ac.uk/slide/

Berggren A., Burgos D., Fontan J.M., Hinkelman D., Hung V., Hursh A., & Tielemans G. (2005). Practical and pedagogical issues for teacher adoption of IMS learning design standards in Moodle LMS. *Journal of Interactive Media in Education, 2005*(02).

Boticario, J.G., Santos, O.C., Barrera, C., Gaudioso, E., Hernandez, F., Rodriguez, A., van Rosmalen, P., & Koper, R. (2004). *Defining adaptive learning design templates for combining design and runtime adaptation in aLFanet*. Retrieved June, 2006, from http://hdl.handle.net/1820/210

Bourguin, G., Derycke A., & Tarby J.C. (2001). Beyond the interface: Co-evolution inside interactive systems—A proposal founded on activity theory. In J. Vanderdonckt, A. Blandford, & P. Gray, (Eds.), *People and computers XV—Interaction without frontiers* (pp. 297-310). Lille, France.

Britain, S. (2004). *A review of learning design: concept, specifications and tools: Report for the JISC e-learning pedagogy programme*. Retrieved September, 2006, from http://www.jisc.ac.uk/uploaded_documents/ACF83C.doc

Burke, B. & Monson-Haefel, R. (2006). *Enterprise JavaBeans 3.0* (5th ed.). Sebastopol, CA: O'Reilly.

Caron, P.-A., Derycke, A., & Le Pallec, X. (2005). Bricolage and model driven approach to design distant course. *E learn 2005: World Conference on E-Learning in Corporate Government, Healthcare & Higher Education* (pp. 2856-2864). Vancouver: Association for the Advancement of Computing in Education (AACE).

Caron, P.-A., Le Pallec, X., & Sockeel, S. (2006). Configuring a Web-based tool through pedagogical scenarios. *IADIS Virtual Multi Conference on Computer Science and Information Systems (MCCSIS 2006)*.

Chen, M.C., Chen, C.T., Cheng, Y.C., & Hsieh, C.Y. (2005, July 5-8). On the development and implementation of a sequencing engine for IMS learning design specification, *5th IEEE International Conference on Advanced Learning Technologies* (pp. 636- 640). Kaohsiung, Taiwan: IEEE Computer Society.

CopperCore (2006). *CopperCore platform home page*. Retrieved June, 2006, from http://coppercore.org

CORDRA (2006). *What's "CORDRA"™*. Retrieved June, 2006, from http://cordra.net/docs/info/whatscordra/v1p00/info-whatscordra-v1p00.php

Earp, J. & Pozzi, F. (2006, December 6-8). Fostering reflection in ICT-based pedagogical planning. In R. Philip, A. Voerman & J. Daziel (Eds.), *Proceedings of the First International LAMS Conference 2006: Designing the Future of Learning* (pp. 35-44).

Gamma, E., Helm, R., Johnson, R., & Vlissides, J. (1995). *Design patterns: Elements of reusable object-oriented software*. Boston: Addison-Wesley.

GenDep. (2006), ModX and *GenDep Web site*. Retrieved September, 2006, from http://noce.univ-lille1.fr/projets/ModX/

Greller, W. (2005). Managing IMS learning design. *Journal of Interactive Media in Education, 2005*(12).

Griffiths, D. & Blat, J. (2005). The role of teachers in editing and authoring units of learning using IMS learning design. *International Journal on Advanced Technology for Learning, Special Session on "Designing Learning Activities: From Content-based to Context-based Learning Services," 2*(4).

Hagen, K., Hibbert, D., Kinshuk. (2006, July 5-7). Developing a Learning Management System based on the IMS learning design Specification,

Sixth International Conference on Advanced Learning Technologies (ICALT'06) (pp. 420-424).

Harrer, A., Malzahn, N., Hoeksema, K., & Hoppe, U. (2005). Learning design engines as remote control to learning support environments. *Journal of Interactive Media in Education (Advances in learning design. Special Issue), 2005*(05).

Hernández-Leo, D., Villasclaras-Fernández, E. D., Asensio-Pérez, J. I. , Dimitriadis Y., Jorrín-Abellán, I. M., Ruiz-Requies, I., & Rubia-Av, B. (2006). COLLAGE: A collaborative learning design editor based on patterns. *Journal of Educational Technology & Society, 9*(1), 58-71.

Hummel, H., Manderveld, J., Tattersal, C., & Koper, R. (2004). Educational modelling language and learning design: New opportunities for instructional reusability and personalised learning. *International Journal of Learning Technology, 1*(1), 111-126.

IMS. (2003). IMS learning design information model—version 1.0. *IMS Global Learning Consortium, Inc.* Retrieved September, 2006, from http://www.imsglobal.org/learningdesign/index.html

IMS. (2004). Enterprise services specification—version 1.0 final specification. *IMS Global Learning Consortium, Inc.*, Retrieved September, 2006, from http://www.imsglobal.org/es/index.html

Kiczales, G., des Rivières, J., & Bobrow, D. (1991). *The art of the Metaobject Protocol.* Cambridge, MA: The MIT Press.

Le Pallec, X., de Moura Filho, C., Marvie, R., Nebut, M., & Tarby, J.-C., (2006). Supporting generic methodologies to assist IMS-LD modeling. *The 6th IEEE International Conference on Advanced Learning Technologies (ICALT'2006)* (pp. 923-927).

.LRN. (2006) *.LRN platform web site.* Retrieved September, 2006, from http://www.dotlrn.org/

LTSC. (2002). IEEE LTSC, Draft Standard for Learning Object Metadata. *IEEE 1484*(12), 1-2002.

Lundgren-Cayrol, K., Marino, O., Paquette, G., Léonard, M., & de la Teja, I. (2006). Implementation and deployment process of IMS learning design: Findings from the Canadian IDLD research project. *Proceedings of the Sixth International Conference on Advanced Learning Technologies (ICALT 2006)* (pp. 581-585).

Manolescu, D. A. (2000). *Micro-Workflow: A Workflow Architecture Supporting Compositional Object-Oriented Software development.* Unpublished doctoral dissertation, University of Illinois.

McAndrew, P., Nadolski, R., & Little A. (2005). Developing an approach for learning design players. *Journal of Interactive Media in Education (Advances in learning design. Special Issue), 2005*(14).

McAndrew, P., Woods, W.I.S., Little, A., Weller, M.J., & Koper, R., & Vogten, H. (2004, July 3-7). Implementing learning design to support Web-based learning. *Tenth Australasian World Wide Web Conference (AusWeb 2004)*, Gold Coast.

ModX. (2006). *ModX Web site.* Retrieved September, 2006, from http://noce.univ-lille1.fr/projets/ModX/

OMG. (2006). *Object Management Group official web site.* Retrieved October 2006 from http://www.omg.org

Peter, Y. & Vantroys, T. (2005). Platform support for pedagogical scenarios. *Educational Technology and Society Journal, 8*(3), 122-137.

Pinkwart, N. (2003). A Plug-In Architecture for Graph Based Collaborative Modeling Systems. In U. Hoppe, F. Verdejo, & J. Kay (Eds.) *Proceedings Of Artificial Intelligence in Education: Shaping the Future of Learning through Intelligent Technologies* (pp. 535-536). Amsterdam: IOS Press.

Raj, G. S. (2007). *A Detailed Comparison of CORBA, DCOM and Java/RMI*. Retrieved February, 2007, from http://my.execpc.com/~gopalan/misc/compare.html

Sampson, D., Karampiperis, P., & Zervas, P., (2006). Authoring Web-based learning scenarios based on the IMS learning design: Preliminary evaluation of the ASK learning designer toolkit, *IEEE International Conference on Computer Systems and Applications* (pp. 1003-1010).

Santos, O. C., Barrera, C., & Boticario, J. G. (2004). An overview of aLFanet: An adaptive iLMS based on standards. *Adaptive Hypermedia and Adaptive Web-Based Systems* (LNCS 3137, pp. 429-432). New York: Springer.

Schneider, D., Synteta, P., Frété, C., Girardin, F., & Morand, S. (2003, December 7-13). Conception and implementation of rich pedagogical scenarios through collaborative portal sites: Clear focus and fuzzy edges. *ICOOL 2003—International Conference on Open and Online Learning*. University of Mauritius.

Vantroys, T. & Peter, Y. (2003). COW, a Flexible Platform for the Enactment of Learning Scenarios, *9th Conference Groupware (CRIWG 2003)*, France (LNCS 2806, pp. 168-182). Berlin: Springer-Verlag.

Vogten, H., Martens, H., Nadolski, R., Tattersall, C., van Rosmalen, P., & Koper, R., (2006, July 5-7). CopperCore service integration—Integrating IMS learning design and IMS question and test interoperability. *Sixth International Conference on Advanced Learning Technologies (ICALT 2006)* (pp. 378-382).

Walsh, A. E. (2002). *UDDI, SOAP, and WSDL: The Web Services Specification Reference Book*, Upper Saddle River, NJ: Pearson Education.

Weller, M., Little, A., McAndrew, P., & Woods, W. (2006). Learning design, generic service descriptions and universal acid. *Educational Technology & Society Journal, 9*(1), 138-145.

Wilson, S., Olivier, B., Jeyes, S., Powell, A., & Franklin, T. (2005). *A Technical Framework to Support e-Learning*. Retrieved September, 2006, from http://www.elearning.ac.uk/frameworks/resources

Workflow Management Coalition. (1995). The Workflow Reference Model. *WfMC-TC-1003, Version 1.1, 19 January 1995*. Retrieved October, 2006, from http://www.wfmc.org/

WMF. (2000). Object Management group. *Workflow Management Facility, Version 1.2*. Retrieved October, 2006, from http://www.omg.org/technology/documents/formal/workflow_management.htm

Zarraonandia, T., Dodero, R.M., & Fernandez, C. (2006). Crosscutting runtime adaptations of LD execution. *Educational Technology & Society Journal, 9*(1), 123-137.

ENDNOTE

[1] model driven engineering (MDE) is the subject of chapter "model-driven engineering (MDE) and model-driven architecture (MDA) applied to the modelling and deployment of technology enhanced learning (TEL) systems: Promises, challenges and issues"

Chapter XVI
Impact of Context–Awareness on the Architecture of Learning Support Systems

Andreas Schmidt
FZI Research Center for Information Technologies, Germany

ABSTRACT

Recently, the situatedness of learning has come to the center of attention in both research and practice, also a result of the insight that traditional learning methods in the form of large de-contextualized courses lead to inert knowledge; that is, knowledge that can be reproduced, but not applied to real-world problem solving. In order to avoid the inertness, pedagogy tries to set up authentic learning settings, an approach increasingly shared in e-learning domain. If we consider professional training, it is the immediacy of purpose and context that makes it largely different to learning in schools or academic education. This immediacy has the benefit that we actually have an authentic context that we need to preserve. The majority of current e-learning approaches, however, ignores this context and provides de-contextualized forms of learning as a multimedia copy of traditional presence seminars. We show how making learning solutions aware of the context actually affects their architecture and present a showcase solution in the form of the Learning in Process service-oriented architecture.

INTRODUCTION

In the wake of constructivism dominating pedagogy research during the last years, the situatedness of learning has come to the center of attention, also a result of the insight that traditional learning methods in the form of large de-contextualized courses lead to inert knowledge; that is, knowledge that can be reproduced, but not applied to real-world problem solving (Bereiter & Scardamalia 1985; Renkel et al., 1996). In order to avoid the inertness, pedagogy tries to set up authentic learning settings, an approach increasingly shared in the e-learning domain. If we consider professional training, it is the immediacy of purpose and context that makes it largely different to learning in schools or academic education. This immediacy has the benefit that we actually have an authentic context that we need to preserve. The majority of current e-learning approaches, however, ignores this context and provides de-contextualized forms of learning as a multimedia copy of traditional presence seminars.

Context-aware system behavior can foster learning processes in several areas:

- If we consider the delivery of appropriate learning content, we can support employees in embedding learning activities into their work processes. We can recommend fine-grained learning resources, and make the recommendations aware of derived learning needs *(what)*, but also aware of interruptibility and stress level *(when and how)*.

- Within learning objects, we can adapt the instructional strategy to the learner's current situation, such as modifying the difficulty level or the playfulness in response to (1) personal characteristics, but also (2) whether it is the end of a long and hard day of meetings, after a period of boring paperwork, or early in the morning.

- Finally, we can also foster informal learning activities by bringing together learners that are dealing with the same topic areas or the same business process activities as soon as we know what others were doing recently.

In this chapter, we want to present a systematic service-oriented approach of extending current learning support services (which comprise learning management systems, learning content management systems, communication and collaboration services) with context-aware functionality. This approach covers all aspects of dealing with context information, that is, context acquisition,

context management, context augmentation, and context-aware adaptation of system behavior.

BACKGROUND

What is Context?

Although it seems to have become common sense to acknowledge that "context" is important to consider for state-of-the-art system development in general and learning support in particular, there is no shared understanding of what "context" is. Bazire & Brézillon (2005) have analyzed the scientific literature of several fields in order to find out the commonalities and came up with a vague notion of a set of constraints that can influence the behavior of a system in a given task. The most generally accepted definition in the community of ubiquitous computing is given by Dey (2001):

Context is any information that can be used to characterize the situation of an entity. An entity is a person, place, or object that is considered relevant to the interaction between a user and an application, including the user and applications themselves.

This still does not define what is "the situation". In Schmidt (2006), the situation of a user is defined as a relevant subset of the state of the world at a given point in time (including the respective knowledge of history and expectations for the future at that point in time).

These definitions leave the most important question open: what is actually relevant? From a theoretical point of view, this question cannot be answered exhaustively. From a practical point of view, we can approach this problem by considering the two aspects of context-awareness (Schmidt, 2005a): (1) knowing about the user of the user and (2) adapting system behavior to this context. Context acquisition methods determine the supply side and context-aware (learning) support methods determine the demand side. Typical learning support methods (Schmidt, 2005) are about retrieving or recommending resources; an important guiding concept for adaptation of such system behavior is the notion of "subjective relevance" (Swanson, 1986). While traditional information retrieval assumes that relevance of a result with respect to a query can be objectively assessed (i.e., relevance is a function of the query and the resource), the notion of subjective relevance postulates that relevance also depends on the user (and her/his context).

Context and Learning Processes

Although the situatedness of learning has been investigated extensively, the notion of an operationalized context with distinct features has only rarely been approached. Prior work is rather scattered among various communities, each with its only limited notion of context A brief summary of the most important approaches shall be summarized in the following (cp. Schmidt & Braun, 2006):

- **Business-process-oriented knowledge management** (BPOKM, e.g., Abecker, 2004) has realized the importance of the process context for context-aware delivery and storage of knowledge assets. Recently, the approach was further developed towards informal learning techniques, for example, in Farmer (2003). While it is true that business processes are an important element of the work context, they definitely are too narrow, although there are some approaches extending it like Hädrich and Priebe (2005).
- **Macroadaptive e-learning approaches** like Woelk and Agarwal (2002) or Davis et al. (2005) mainly adapt to the learner in terms of delivery. They filter the learning content based on the learner's competencies and the knowledge requirements of the current

position or business process context. While this is an important step into the direction of context-aware learning support, they only consider rather static elements of the context, which does not allow for deeper integration of working and learning processes. Interesting developments are in the direction of context-aware recommendations like in Lemire et al. (2005), but they have still a notion of context too limited for holistic workplace learning support.

- **Microadaptive e-learning approaches** and adaptive hypermedia approaches are probably the area of research with the longest history and highest activity (Park & Lee, 2002). They focus primarily on the learning object behavior itself and how to adapt it to the learner and her characteristics. The main problem of current adaptive e-learning approaches is that they do not consider learning in a work context, but rather set up artificial contexts in learning labs. They allow for a deep contextualization on the personal level, but neglect the organizational context completely.

As one of the first approaches to bring together the views of the different communities into a holistic ontology of context in a workplace setting was the ontology developed with the Learning in Process project (Schmidt, 2005), which will be presented in the case study section.

Existing Architectural Approaches

Existing architectures for e-learning systems like the LTSA architecture (IEEE, 2003), or the Learning Services Stack (Blackmon & Rehak, 2003) do not consider context at all. It is not the case that these architectures do not allow for context awareness, but they do not provide clear separations (resulting later in clear interfaces) that are essential for manageable context aware behavior.

Although so far context awareness of learning solutions has not been approached from an architectural point of view, there are two areas where we can identify relevant architectural considerations: context-aware applications in general and adaptive educational hypermedia systems as a very specialized form of context-aware learning support system.

For the area of context-aware applications, one of the most recent and most comprehensive architectural approaches is that of Henricksen and Indulska (2006). They divide the functionality into six layers. The lower-most layer is the *context gathering layer* consisting of sensors and interpreters/aggregators for deriving more abstract context information from low-level sensor data. The next layer is the context reception layer that provides an interface between the gathering layer and the *context management layer*. This layer is responsible for storing context data in a context repository and keeping it consistent. The next layer adds the *query* functionality to the repository, providing expressive descriptive possibilities. Ontop of this layer is the *adaptation layer* for encapsulating the adaptation logic for the top-most layer *(application layer)*.

The reference architecture for adaptive educational hypermedia systems from Karampiperis, and Sampson (2005) divided the functionality into two layers: (1) the runtime layer and the (2) the storage layer. The storage layer divides the models needed into the user model, the adaptation model, the domain model and the media space. On the runtime layer, three components are identified: a presenter, an adaptation rule parser, and a behavior tracker (for updating the user model).

CHALLENGES OF CONTEXT AWARENESS AND ARCHITECTURAL PROBLEMS

At first sight, context awareness simply translates into making existing learning management systems taking into account the characteristics of the context of the user, for example, by showing only learning offers that are relevant to the current context. But this naïve view does not hold when investigating the problem more closely (and it does also show why commercial personalization falls short):

User context is hard to model. It seems so easy to speak about context as a kind of synonym for everything that was so far not considered, but modeling it (i.e., making it computationally accessible) is a challenge: How to identify features with which to describe it? How to distinguish features from irrelevant ones? How to find the right level of abstraction? Understanding context is by magnitudes harder than understanding a domain for which we model explicit interaction between a user and the system. Usually modeling context involves investigation of contextual influence factors to subjective relevance and other issues.

User context is hard to make use of. Even if we have a fair context schema, it remains still a challenge to actually operationalize context awareness. Between a statement like "this should be considered when interacting with the user" and an algorithm that answers how to adapt system behavior is a huge difference. It also involves a lot of trial and error so that flexibility to implement adaptivity is needed. But what is even more important is that context awareness changes the paradigm of learning support. If we want to respond to contextual needs of a user, it means embedding it into the work environment, and embedding is only possible if we break up monolithic learning management systems into individual, loosely coupled services and applications. The system does no longer pre-structure separate learning times, but rather provides functionality to initiate learning processes and to suggest learning opportunities: (reactive) learning management becomes (proactive) learning support.

User context is hard to acquire. Even if we know how to model and use context information, we still have to deal with the problem of acquiring it. For many contextual features there are no "sensors" and never will be. So we have to rely on heuristics and indirect methods that need to consider a wide range of sources like desktop activity, existing data in ERP systems, communication history, etc. And we need to realize that the heuristics yield imperfect results: incomplete, uncertain, outdated and contradictory information.

How do these challenges affect the design of an architecture of learning support systems:

- **Specialized context middleware:** The sheer complexity of dealing with context information demands for factoring it out of other functional components: it is not just an add-on, but a task of its own. Especially the integration and aggregation of various context sources and the imperfection of the context information itself should be hidden from services concerned with learning.

- **Service-oriented architecture:** The paradigm of learning support instead of learning management demands for a new type of flexibility. This can only be provided with a state-of-the-art service-oriented approach.

- **Shared context manager:** While at first sight, the services require different aspects of the context (often at different abstraction levels), a deeper investigation reveals that there is sufficient overlap so that they have synergies from a shared user context manager.

- **Separation of adaptation and context:** The naïve view may view a direct mapping of context features to adaptation parameters. But something like "preferred conciseness" (adaptation parameter) is not in the context (because it is way too application-specific), but rather a result of features like skill level, general learning characteristics, etc. So we need a clear separation and a calculation of adaptation parameters.

- **Separation of pedagogical strategies and enabling infrastructure:** On a fine-grained level, there is no sound body of knowledge about how contextual factors affect learning processes and especially the appropriateness of guiding interventions.

- **Background domain knowledge:** Both for the aggregation of low-level context information and for the translation of context features into adaptation parameters, domain-specific background "knowledge" is needed

- **Asynchronous interaction patterns:** Context-aware applications do not only respond to actions of user, but also to context changes, for example, for recommending proactively. But this means that we cannot solely rely on request-response interactions, but need a publish-subscribe pattern. But as we do not want every context change to be reflected at the user interface, we need a coordinating instance mediating context changes.

A REFERENCE ARCHITECTURE FOR CONTEXT-AWARE LEARNING SUPPORT

Based on the previous sections, a reference architecture for context-aware learning support systems can be derived, which is summarized in Figure 1.

The lower-most layer consists of **external information sources**. This could be sources for eliciting user context information, but also sources for providing learning material. These raw external sources are wrapped so that they provide context information in line with a system-wide context ontology and provide a well-defined behavior, either a push sources (data is materialized in the context manager) or as pull sources (queries on demand, need to support a declarative query language). On top of this layer is the **infrastructure layer** that provides the following basic services:

- A *user context management service* stores collected or inferred user context information and provides a consistent view (Schmidt, 2006) on it, abstracting from contradictions, uncertainty, and outdated information. This service needs to provide both a declarative query language for query-response interaction and a subscription facility for asynchronous notification.
- An *artifact repository* provides access to all types of artifacts that could play a role for learning processes. These artifacts could be learning objects, documents, or communication artifacts. In many cases, this artifact repository will store just the metadata and a link to a physical resource.
- An *ontology service* provides open and declarative access to (1) a shared conceptual model forming the basis of the services' interaction and (2) background knowledge needed for adaptive behavior. Via a centralized ontology service, a loosely-coupled architecture becomes possible without losing a high degree of semantic coherence.

On top of this infrastructure come the **learning support services**. These provide reusable functionality that is needed by applications that try to support learning processes. Typical services on this layer are: competency assessment, competence gap analysis, or on-demand learning program compilation.

These services are all reactive in the sense that they are invoked in the request-response paradigm. But context awareness usually requires also proactive behavior that responds to changes of the context. In order to encapsulate strategies for proactive learning support, a **learning coordination layer** is introduced. This layer subscribes to the user context management service, makes use of the learning support services and initiates activities in the two remaining layers. The strategies on this layer basically represent the pedagogical approaches which translate knowl-

edge of the context of the user into interventions into learning processes.

The **adaptation layer** is responsible for (1) translating interventions by the learning coordination layer into application-specific *actions* and (2) user context information into *adaptation parameters* that accompany the actions. The main task of this layer is to provide context-aware interfaces to end user applications that can be context-aware, but usually are not. From an architectural point of view, it is desirable that service types are defined (like LMS, instant messaging application, etc.).

The top-most (**end user applications**) layer is represented by those application end users (i.e., learners) actually interact with. This includes classical learning runtime environments (like they form part of learning management solutions), but also communication and collaboration services for more informal forms of learning. Some of these applications will explicitly know about the user's context, but many of them will not. These are supposed to provide interfaces for adaptation. These interfaces are used by the underlying adaptation layer.

The architecture provides a flexible framework for various pedagogical approaches that make use of knowledge of the context of the learner:

- Highly automated approaches can recommend learning opportunities to the learner, for example, suggesting learning objects designed to deliver certain competencies, or suggesting colleagues that can provide help in problem solving, based on organizational models of processes, tasks, roles and their respective competency requirements.
- On the micro-level, learning objects can adapt their presentation to context-dependent personal preferences, for example, affecting the conciseness or playfulness of learning objects.
- Learner-empowering approaches (e.g., based on personal learning environments) can

be less intervening and can provide more relevant navigational options and can take into account personal goals and how they fit into the situation.

Which of these approaches is actually taken depends on the strategies implemented in the learning coordination layer which can flexibly orchestrate both the learning services and the end user applications.

In the spirit of other e-learning standards, it is clear that the roll-out of context-aware systems in the large at least a small set of context ontologies in order to be able to reuse (1) wrappers for context sources, (2) learning coordination strategies responding to context changes, and (3) developing reusable context-aware learning content. But this does not affect the architecture as such, which assumes that within the system there is a shared ontology. Whether this shared ontology is achieved through individual adaptation at each installation or already in the production phase, is a different topic.

CASE STUDY: LEARNING IN PROCESS

This reference architecture has been implemented in two demonstrators within the EU project *Learning in Process* (Schmidt, 2005). Its primary goals have been the integration of working and learning on a process level and learning management, knowledge management, human capital management and collaboration solutions on a technical level. One of the early insights was that isolated and monolithic learning management systems are not suitable for integrating learning into personal and organizational activities. So the project concentrated on providing fine-grained learning on demand embedded into work processes based on a methodological framework (context-steered learning (Schmidt & Braun, 2006)).

Context-steered learning seems to be a natural transition from e-learning and knowledge management approaches. It is based on the assumption that there are small learning units that can be

Figure 1. Reference architecture for context-aware learning support systems

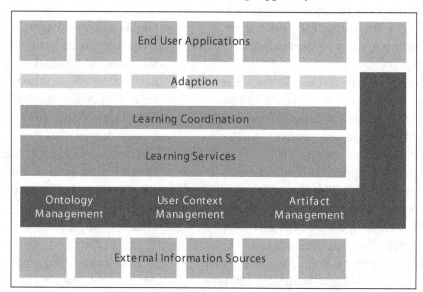

used on demand. Context-steered learning can be visualized as a process cycle, which appears as an on-demand 'detour' of the working processes and can be broken down into the following system primitives (see Figure 2):

- **Initiate:** In the first phase, the system detects based on observations of the work context and background knowledge (which competencies are required in which context) if there is a learning opportunity. This functionality refers to the timing (when) and modality (how) of interventions.

- **Select:** Appropriate learning resources that help to satisfy the learner's knowledge need and that fit to the learner requirements are selected. This could be learning objects, casual documents, but also colleagues or external "experts" for informal communication.

- **Deliver:** It may seem that recommending learning objects (or other documents) already implies that we have determined what to recommend. But this is only partially true.

Certain resources cannot be understood by the learner because she does not meet the prerequisites. So it is often necessary to compile longer learning programs that incorporate the prerequisites.

- **Adapt:** This is the domain of classical micro adaptivity in e-learning. This incorporates the adaptation of presentation (e.g., adapting the level of detail to be presented, or the difficulty of exercise) and behavior of (active) learning content (e.g., simulations that can reference cases from the current working environment).

- **Record:** One often neglected aspect in the business context of classical formal training is certificates that can be obtained after successfully attending training activities. As a replacement in more informal context where no certificates exist, electronic portfolios can take the role.

After completion of this micro learning process, the learner returns to his/her working process and has the possibility to apply the newly acquired

Figure 2. Context-steered learning (based on Schmidt & Braun, 2006)

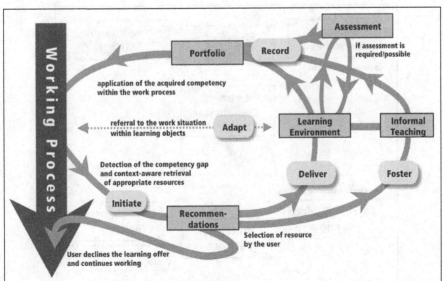

competencies—and to return to the learning process if it has turned out that learning was not as successful as expected. This could involve communicating to a recommended colleague.

The architecture of the developed system for supporting context-steered learning (see Figure 3) was basically organized into three layers: infrastructure, learning services and end-user applications, where the middle layer already had the separation into a proactive learning coordinator and reactive services. In the following section, we want to briefly present some of the key components.

User Context Manager

Identification of what context actually is one of the basic challenges. We need to operationalize the different situational factors that affect the appropriateness system behavior (like recommending learning opportunities, adapting presentation, etc.). Within LIP we have elaborated the following features (see also Figure 4):

- **Personal:** This encompasses previously acquired knowledge or competencies, goals (divided into short-term and long-term), preferred interactivity level and semantic density (for learning content), preferred communication channel (synchronous/asynchronous, voice/written), and current time capacity/time pressure.
- **Social:** This refers to qualified relationship information towards other users, which especially affects the informal learning part by communicating with other learners.
- **Organizational:** This encompasses organizational unit, role(s), current business process (or process step) and current task (as an activity that cannot be easily mapped to a business process).
- **Technical:** This encompasses user agent (operating system, browser, plugins, etc.), bandwidth, and available audio devices.

However, modeling (i.e., identifying the relevant context features) is not enough. The ac-

Figure 3. Architecture of LIP

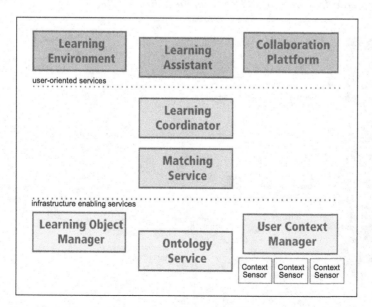

quisition is the much harder part. A key enabler for that was an appropriate context management infrastructure that is geared towards the special requirements of high-level context information, which are the aspects of imperfection and dynamics. As it is typically not possible to acquire context information on a high abstraction level directly, the system has to use indirect methods with limited certainty and precision of its results. The combination of different methods (sometimes even one method on its own) yields contradictory results. These problems are aggravated by the dynamic nature of user context information where different elements of the context change at a different pace. Here we have used a probabilistic representation, feature-specific aging mechanisms, and conflict resolution methods (described in more detail in Schmidt (2006)).

As context sensors, we have relied on a wide range of different sources: browser plugins for

Figure 4. LIP Context Ontology

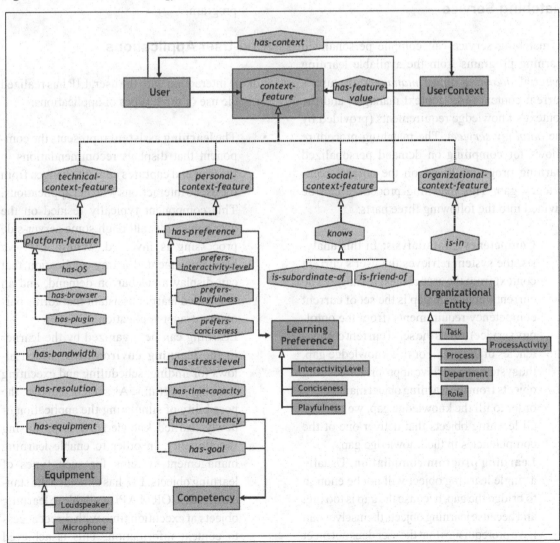

Internet Explorer and Mozilla for browsing activities (and Windows explorer actions on the file system), a Microsoft Office plugin for information about active documents, and Microsoft Outlook plugin for access to calendar and contacts. These low-level application events were aggregated into context changes using heuristics (which were often specific to the company environment), for example, using information about document templates (which are good indicators in administrative environments), the location on the network drive, the structure of intranet applications, or simple keyword extraction techniques.

Matching Service

A matching service can compile personalized learning programs from the available learning material (*learning object manager*), the user's current context (user context manager) and the context's knowledge requirements (provided by the *ontology service*). The matching procedure allows for compiling on demand personalized learning programs based on the current competency gap. This matching procedure can be divided into the following three parts:

- **Competency gap analysis:** In this analysis, the system retrieves the user's current context from the user context manager. The current knowledge gap is the set of current competency requirements (from the ontology service) minus the set of current competencies of the user. For this knowledge gap, the system can retrieve appropriate learning objects from the learning object manager. In order to fill the knowledge gap, we retrieve all learning objects that deliver one of the competencies in the knowledge gap.
- **Learning program compilation:** Usually a single learning object will not be enough to bridge the gap, because the gap is too big, and because learning objects themselves can have prerequisites that the user does not meet

yet. Therefore, we need to provide the user with a complete learning program. This is accomplished by recursively adding learning objects for unsatisfied prerequisites and other didactical dependencies (which are part of learning object metadata) and pruning based on features in the user's context.
- **Preference-based ranking:** After compiling several possible learning programs, the system ranks the alternatives according to the user or organizational preferences (soft criteria). As a result of this process, the user can be presented with the ranked list, from which he can select the desired learning program.

End-User Applications

For the interaction with the user, LIP has realized or made use of three types of applications:

- The **learning assistant** represents the component that displays recommendations to the user and captures context changes from the user's interactions with her applications. This component typically resided on the user's machine, although some server-side processing is involved. Within LIP, we have implemented a tray application that can display a sidebar on demand, and an embedded learner assistant that forms part of an intranet application.
- Learning can be organized by the learner in the **learning environment**, which allows for finding, scheduling and executing learning programs. As sketched above, the possibility of simulating the application of newly learned knowledge is a promising functionality. In order to enable learning management systems for such types of learning objects, LIP has extended the standardized SCORM API available to learning objects at execution time with direct access to context information. This is achieved

through mapping the context features to the CMI data model of SCORM. This technically enables the creation of truly adaptive learning objects.

- A **collaboration platform** was "contextualized" with the help of this service by providing contextualized expert finder functionality, group formation and interaction spaces, where learners can themselves create "knowledge assets" which can be made available (e.g., by recommendation or in self-steered learning processes) to other learners based on the context in which they were created.

Evaluation results

The Learning in Process system was developed with a high degree of end-user involvement through formative evaluation with instruments like scenario-based evaluation techniques (cp. Cook et al., 2004). Involved as end users were two medium-sized companies in the IT industry; their tasks ranged from administrative up to programmer and consultant. The summative evaluation was based on a set of around 100 learning objects (and less pedagogically designed documents), several of them from external sources like Microsoft training material. The evaluation was carried out on site of the companies with around 50 employees in total with the final prototype system as described above.

Results of both the formative and summative evaluation have shown a high degree of acceptance for the context-steered learning method, although usability issues with GUI-related components turned out to be very critical. During the evaluation procedure, the corporate culture was discovered to be crucial for the success of such a learning method. Learning of employees within working processes must be highly appreciated and must be understood as a shared responsibility of both the individual and the organization,

and the collected data must not be used for any other purpose than facilitating their learning. Otherwise, such a system will not be used in an appropriate way.

The architecture proved to be able to accommodate to different company IT environments, one of them mainly based on Microsoft technologies, the other one mainly on open source software. The service-oriented approach allowed for an easy adaptation.

FUTURE TRENDS

With the first experiences with context-awareness in learning support systems, it has become possible to develop architectural patterns embodying best practices in this area. Such a reference architecture should be complemented by shared reference ontology connecting the different actors and entities conceptually. Interfaces of services do not provide enough semantic glue to ensure smooth interoperation of different services in such a setting. Such a reference ontology must also provide the conceptual integration with other corporate systems like competence management, knowledge management, or business process management. A first step towards this has been presented in Schmidt and Kunzmann (2006).

Another issue to be considered is the implications of *e-learning 2.0*: the importance of content and learning material generated by learners themselves. Currently, the architecture reflects the separation of roles between content creators and learners, but if we move to more democratic system paradigms, we have to consider personal learning environments and semantic desktop environments as possible technical enablers. These bottom-up approaches will have a deep impact on the architecture of learning support systems. But as the notion of a personal learning environment is still emerging, it is too early to see a reference architecture for e-learning 2.0 developing.

CONCLUSION

Reference architectures are an important step towards rolling out new technologies on the market on a larger scale. With the described architecture, an important step has been made for context-aware learning support, but there is still a long way to go before context awareness (apart from very simple adaptive behavior) becomes a standard feature of learning environments. This can be traced back to the fact that dealing with context poses several hard challenges (Schmidt, 2005a): how to model, how to acquire and how to make reasonable use of it. This is not primarily a technical issue, but also a methodical issue. In pedagogy, we have no model for contextualized computer-based learning support. But as soon as we can roll out first products, training experts can experiment with the new possibilities.

REFERENCES

Abecker, A. (2004). Business-process oriented knowledge management: Concepts, methods and tools. Doctoral thesis, University of Karlsruhe, Germany. Retrieved from http://digbib.ubka.uni-karlsruhe.de/volltexte/1000003269

Bazire, M. & Brézillon, P. (2005, July 5-8). Understanding Context Before Using It. In *Modeling and Using Context: 5th International and Interdisciplinary Conference CONTEXT 2005*, Paris (pp. 35-54). New York: Springer.

Bereiter, C. & Scardamalia, M. (1985). Cognitive coping strategies and the problem of 'inert knowledge'. In S. Chipman, J. Seagal, R. Glaser (Eds.), *Thinking and learning skills. Volume 2.* Hillside, NJ: LEA.

Blackmon,W. & Rehak, D. (2003). Customized learning: A Web services approach. In *World Conference on Educational Multimedia, Hypermedia and Telecommunications (EDMEDIA 03).*

Cook, J., Bradley, C., & Franzolini, P. (2004, July 21-26). Gathering Users' Requirements Using the Artifact-Claims-Implication Technique. In *Proceedings of Ed-Media 2004*, Lugano, Switzerland.

Davis, J., Kay, J., Kummerfeld, B., Poon, J., Quigley, A., Saunders, G., & Yacef, K.(2005). Using workflow, user modeling and tutoring strategies for just-in-time document delivery. *Journal of Interactive Learning, 4,* 131-148

Dey, A.K. (2001). Understanding and using context. *Personal and Ubiquitous Computing Journal 1*(5), 4-7.

Farmer, J. (2003, September 1-5). Ad hoc coach system: Supporting task-oriented teaching and learning under time pressure. In M. Rauterberg, M. Menozzi, J. Wesson, (Eds.), *Human-Computer Interaction INTERACT '03: IFIP TC13 International Conference on Human-Computer Interaction*, Zurich, Switzerland.

Hädrich, T & Priebe, T. (2005). Supporting knowledge work with knowledge stance-oriented integrative portals. In *Proceedings of the Thirteenth European Conference on Information Systems.*

Henricksen, K. & Indulska, J. (2006). Developing context-aware pervasive computing applications: Models and approach. *Journal of Pervasive and Mobile Computing, 2*(1), 37-64.

IEEE (2003). IEEE 1484.1 IEEE Standard for Learning Technology Systems Architecture (LTSA).

Karampiperis, P. & Sampson, O. (2005). Adaptive learning resources sequencing in educational hypermedia systems. *Educational Technology & Society, 8*(4), 128-147.

Park, O.C. & Lee, J. (2004). Adaptive instructional systems. In D.H. Jonassen, (Ed.), *Handbook of research for educational communications and technology* (2nd ed.) (pp. 651-684). Mahwah, NJ: Lawrence Erlbaum.

Lemire, D., Boley, H., McGrath, S., & Ball, M. (2005). Collaborative filtering and inference rules for context-aware learning object recommendation. *International Journal of Interactive Technology and Smart Education, 2.*

Renkl, A., Mandl, H., & Gruber, H. (1996). Inert knowledge: Analyses and remedies. *Educational Psychologist, 31*(2), 115-121.

Schmidt, A. (2005, April). Bridging the gap between e-Learning and knowledge management with context-aware corporate learning solutions. In Althoff et al. (Eds.), *Professional Knowledge Management. Third Biennial Conference, WM 2005*, Kaiserlautern, Germany. Revised Selected Papers. (LNAI 3782, pp. 203-213). New York: Springer.

Schmidt A. (2005a, October). Potentials and challenges of context-awareness for learning solutions. In *Proceedings of the 13th Annual Workshop of the SIG Adaptivity and User Modeling in Interactive Systems*, Saarbrücken, Germany.

Schmidt, A. (2006). Ontology-based user context management: The challenges of dynamics and imperfection. In *Proceedings of the International Conference on Ontologies, Databases and Ap-plications of Semantics (ODBASE 2006)*, (LNCS 4275, pp. 995-1011). New York: Springer.

Schmidt, A. & Braun, S. (2006). Context-aware workplace learning support: Concepts, experiences and visions. In W. Nejdl, K. Tochtermann, (Eds.), *Innovative Approaches for Learning and Knowledge Sharing. Proceedings of the First European Conference on Technology-Enhanced Learning (EC-TEL 06),* Heraklion, Crete (LNCS 4227, pp. 518-524).

Schmidt. A. & Kunzmann, C. (2006). Towards a reference ontology for combining competence management and technology-enhanced workplace learning. In *Proceedings of OntoContent '06, On the Move Federated Conferences (OTM)* (LNCS 4278, pp. 1078-1087) New York: Springer.

Swanson, D.R. (1986). Subjective versus objective relevance in bibliographic retrieval systems. *Library Quarterly, 56*(4), 389-398.

Woelk, D. & Agarwal, S. (2002). Integration of e-learning and knowledge management. In *World Conference on E-Learning in Corporate, Government, Health Institutions, and Higher Eduction. Volume 1* (pp. 1035-1042).

Chapter XVII
Design and Evaluation of Web–Based Learning Environments using Information Foraging Models

Nikolaos Tselios
University of Patras, Greece

Christos Katsanos
University of Patras, Greece

Georgios Kahrimanis
University of Patras, Greece

Nikolaos Avouris
University of Patras, Greece

ABSTRACT

In this chapter, methods and tools for effective design and evaluation of Web-based learning environments are presented. The main aspect addressed by this proposal is that of increasing findability of information in large Web sites of learning information content by applying methods and tools based on the information foraging model. It is argued that through this approach, issues of learning content structure and usability may be also addressed. In particular, we propose four different ways to have information foraging theory informing the design. Directives, to ensure proper learning content structuring and cues with strong scent, tools based on LSA to automate the design and evaluation process, methods to construct archetypal learner's profiles from user data and added functions to realize collaborative information filtering and personal information patch creation, thus allowing learners to organize their reference materials in a meaningful and constructive way.

INTRODUCTION

During the last years, there has been a growing demand for adopting innovative approaches to the design and delivery of Web based education. The benefits of interactive hypermedia and the increasing popularity of the Web open a new paradigm for the authoring, design and delivery of learning material, and has carved the path for the so called **Web-based learning environments (WBLE)**. It has been widely accepted that the hyper-medial structure of the Web could promote learning. Some researchers characterize the Web as an active learning environment that supports creativity (Becker & Dwyer, 1994). According to Thuring, **Mannemann and Haake** (1995), the Web encourages exploration of knowledge and browsing behaviors that are strongly related to learning.

Theories of learning standing on theoretical bases of *objectivism* and *constructivism* (Jonassen, 1992; Vrasidas, 2000), can inspire the design and usage of WBLEs. The aspects that each theoretical standpoint puts more emphasis in, can transcribe the design and development of certain WBLEs and the associated learning activities that are followed. One of the most promising constructivism-based models, which emphasizes the role of social interactions and cultural artifacts in triggering cognitive elaboration and resulting in co-construction of knowledge among the members of communities of practice (Lave & Wenger, 1991), for designing WBLEs is the one proposed by Duffy and Kirkley (2004). The basic pedagogical goals of the model are to engage students in inquiry, provide structure, support collaborative inquiry, conduct performance-based assessment and promote reflection and transfer.

Apart from the pedagogical design aspects that have to be followed, the interaction design of the WBLE plays a significant role in how these principals come into real practice. According to Duffy and Kirkley (2004), effective design of such systems should encompass two basic entities. The learning content management system (LCMS), and a separate, although tightly interconnected by means of hyperlinks, learning management system (LMS). Despite the fact that in the second module exists an important body of design knowledge as well as good practices and plethora of useful tools (forum, calendars, assignments, etc.); this is rarely the case for the first one.

For example, concerning the links of learning content that lists the learning resources on a single screen lead to a linear reading strategy by the students. In a WBLE realized according to the aforementioned model, when the designers developed a new interface where the resources were linked to the task, the students found it more beneficial, and there were few students that reported that they read everything first (Gunawardena, 2004). In addition, from a psychological perspective, the learner needs to consult links with high-quality residues, in order to proceed seamlessly, establish a *flow state* and not get overly frustrated while she is involved in the task (Csikszentmihalyi, 1990). Therefore, apart from the disposition of links of learning content, the *proximal cues* of such links (i.e the hyperlinks' descriptions), that give the learner a sense of the access path of the desired information sources, are crucial for the success of the learning task.

As a result, the process of design and adaptation of appropriate learning content with respect to the needs and particularities of the medium, could serve efficiently even pedagogically neutral WBLEs, since the effective separation of learning content from learning tools greatly enhances its organization, reusability and maintainability. This is a critical point, since one of the most common pitfalls in WBLEs is the use of existing course materials without adapting them to the online delivery method. Thus, often learners are unable to find, evaluate, and use materials relevant to their studies, which renders learning activity problematic. Although the key requirement still remains the quality of the instructional design itself, this should not be treated as an excuse to overcome the aforementioned issues. Educators and developers should be concerned about determining their role and developing adequate techniques to diminish any negative influence of the tools' design on the educational process (Tselios, Avouris, Dimitracopoulou & Daskalaki, 2001). Towards this goal, we argue that concerns such as learning content design, findability, proper information structure, and overall usability issues should be properly encapsulated into the WBLE's course design lifecycle.

Findability is defined as the degree to which a particular object is easy to discover or locate and consequently the degree to which a system or environment supports navigation and retrieval (Morville, 2005). The concept of findability is of fundamental importance for the Web in general, and WBLEs in particular. The problem is that findability is a concept that lies between user-centered design, engineering, and proper learning content creation. This mutual responsibility is usually threatened by the chance that no stakeholder considers herself as accountable. Furthermore, the *usability* of an educational environment is related to its pedagogical value (Kirkpatrick, 1994) and evaluation of its usability should be part of the processes of establishing its quality. According to Hayes (2000), user-centered design of online course delivery systems should examine in particular the effort required by the user to take ownership of the system's functionality and should concentrate on ease of use. While there is a large corpus of theoretical and practical knowledge relating to software usability evaluation in general and educational software in particular, there are no well-established techniques relating to WBLEs usability evaluation (Heines, 2000).

The main underlying idea of our proposal is that the theoretical notion of information foraging could serve as a *unifying glue* to properly address the aforementioned issues. In our approach, we examine the notion of architecture for e-learning systems, from an *information architecture* perspective (i.e., structure of learning mate-

rial). Information architecture is the practice of structuring information (knowledge or data) for a purpose. We do not investigate the issues of infrastructure or component implementation, from a technical point of view, nor do we attempt to explain how e-learning systems are implemented and operated. In particular, we argue that efficient and effective learning content presentation and structuring is of central importance, for delivering a deep and constructive learning experience via WBLEs. Boland (1987) claims that the information is inward-forming, thus, a mediator between knowledge and the learning "process." Therefore, it is crucial to understand the way learners' interact and retrieve information within these systems using theoretical models of learners' behavior. This is not to argue that information design and architecture can cause learning. We perceive the issue of proper WBLE design as a means of *enabling* possibilities to learn. Learners themselves will seek and acquire needed elements of information. Independently of the pedagogical model adopted, this process requires knowledge acquisition, integration of usually heterogeneous knowledge "segments," evaluation of the information, goal reformulation and actions selection, leading to deeper understanding and knowledge construction. Designers should seek to improve the abilities of learners to manage and navigate knowledge resources and create environments that increase the capacity of learners to function and forage for their own knowledge. It is of paramount importance that the mediation of the WBLEs is transparent and intuitive and does not interfere with the learning "process."

In this chapter, we will present a set of tools for design and evaluation of WBLEs. For this reason, the basic aspects of information foraging theory are presented first. The presented accumulated knowledge will be unified and explained under the prism of the notion of information foraging theory and will be embedded into a set of conceptual design and evaluation tools aiming to lead the realization of WBLEs. Finally, tools to automate parts of the design and evaluation process will be presented as well as future directives to extend the proposed approach.

BACKGROUND

Models of Information Foraging

The core idea of *information foraging* theory (Pirolli & Card, 1995) is that information seeking and retrieval is analogous to the food foraging mechanisms developed by anthropologists and ecologists (Stephens & Krebs, 1986). The user adapts her/his behavior (or even the structure of the system interface) in order to maximize her/his information gain per specific effort (unit cost). The theory refers to cognitive activities associated with assessing, seeking, and handling information sources.

In exploring and searching for information on the Web, users become recipients of many and multiple "segments" of information. While navigating through different information clusters, users assess the appropriateness of following a particular path by considering a representation, usually a textual or graphic description, of the distant content. Furnas (1997) coined the term "residue" to describe the hint that a representational object holds (e.g., a hyperlink) of what lies behind it. Residue was recast and refined by Pirolli (1997) as information "scent" and defined as a user's "(imperfect) perception of the value, cost, or access path of information sources obtained from proximal cues, such as WWW links." Thus, in the context of WBLEs, information scent refers to the learner's use of *proximal cues*—snippets that exist in the environment s/he interacts with, such as text and graphic hyperlinks—in judging information sources and navigating through information spaces that will allow her/him to retrieve valuable information and acquire knowledge. If the scent of information is sufficiently pungent, learners will be generally more able to find, evaluate, and use materials relevant to their studies.

Comprehension-based linked model of deliberate search (*CoLiDeS*) is a similar comprehension-based cognitive model explaining users' information foraging in the WWW (Kitajima & Polson, 1997). According to CoLiDeS, the cognitive processes that mainly determine users' information foraging behavior are parsing, focusing, comprehension and selection and every low-level action of the user is a two-phase process (Blackmon, Polson, Kitajima & Lewis, 2002). During the *attention phase* the user creates a mental representation of the page by dividing it into a collection of sub-areas. Subsequently, the user is focusing on a sub-area that s/he believes is semantically closer to her/his goal. Following, during the *action-selection* phase, the user comprehends all the widgets in the sub-region s/he has focused and chooses to act on the one whose description is perceived to be closer to her/his goal.

We argue that study of these predictive models is of major importance in the frame of WBLEs. In an information-rich world, like a WBLE, the real design problem to be solved is not how to collect more information (e.g., learning content), but rather to increase the amount of relevant information encountered by a learner as a function of the amount of time that the learner invests in interacting with the system. The information architecture of the system determines the time costs (resource costs) and opportunity costs associated with exploring and finding information. Learners' attention affordances are limited and they have to be spread optimally throughout a learning task so that maximum learning gains can be achieved. If a learner can deploy effective search strategies within the WBLE ecology, the opportunities for knowledge building and learning are greatly enhanced.

For example, a learner often has to combine information from various patches of the site to extract personal meaning and understanding. Important information foraging decisions include reflections on how much time to spend on processing a collection of information or whether or not to pursue a particular type of information content (*information diet*). While exploring an information patch, there will be a point where the information scent goes below some threshold; it is the point where the learner realizes that the benefits (in terms of information gain) of staying at the specific information patch are significantly diminished. Thus, s/he decides to leave the specific area of the WBLE s/he was exploring in order to search for a more profitable hypertext area.

Understanding Courseware Offered in WBLEs

In an effort to model various approaches on learning, Mayes and Fowler (1999) developed a "framework for understanding courseware" that links a theory of learning to certain kinds of WBLEs and associated interaction and information design requirements for each category as illustrated in Figure 1. We argue that by combining the ascertainments of this model with the insight that the information foraging models gives, the problem of

effective design and evaluation of WBLEs could be handled and tackled more efficiently.

Mayes and Fowler describe the basic "unit of conceptual learning" as a cycle. The main stages of the learning cycle refer to conceptualization, construction and dialogue. *Conceptualization* refers to the learners' initial contact with other peoples' concepts. This involves an interaction between the learner's pre-existing framework of understanding and a new exposition. It is conceived as the basic mechanism of learning according to objectivist approaches. *Construction* refers to the process of building and combining concepts through their use in the performance of meaningful tasks like problem-solving, laboratory work, writing, etc. This stage constitutes the core of the learning opportunities according to constructivists. In education, however, as Laurillard (1993) has pointed out, the goal is testing of understanding, often of abstract concepts. This stage is best characterized in education as *dialogue*. The conceptualizations are tested and further developed during conversation with both tutors and fellow learners, and in the reflection on these (Mayes & Fowler, 1999).

Mayes and Fowler discriminate between three kinds of courseware appropriate to each stage of the learning cycle judging from a learner-centered perspective. *Primary courseware* is courseware that just conveys subject matter and is appropriate for conceptualization. The quality of primary courseware will be mainly determined by the match between material and learner on the dimensions of conceptual demands and requirements for prior understanding. The main requirement for such systems is to match the characteristics of a system to the expectations and knowledge of the user. Interaction between the learner's prior understanding and the primary exposition produces just an initial interpretation. What is crucial for this primary exposition is to orient the learner towards the subject matter. Primary courseware should also provide the learner with the appropriate structures on how to navigate and find appro-

Figure 1. Mayes and Fowler's (1999) taxonomy of courseware

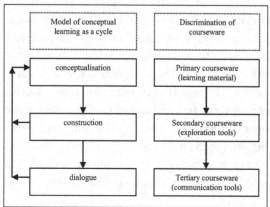

priate information. Learners using WBLEs seek information while looking for answers to their questions and achieving their goals.

Prior to this, the designer should organize learning content with respect to the learning goals, the pedagogical model adopted, and the particularities of the Web as a medium. Information should be well structured and organized at the Web site level, page level and paragraph or list level to reduce the chances of learners becoming bored, disinterested or frustrated. As a result, models to explain learner's behavior while searching for information such as *information foraging theory* could directly inform design in those aspects by providing abstract cognitive models of the learner's information search behavior.

Secondary courseware describes the environment and set of tools by which the learner performs learning tasks, and the tasks (and task materials) themselves (Mayes & Fowler, 1999). Careful task analysis and model-based evaluation, found to produce solid results and guide effectively design and evaluation of such systems (Tselios, Kordaki & Avouris, 2002). Proper information architecture, as derives from information foraging theories and established user research, is also crucial on the success of a learning scenario. Available exploratory tools should be efficiently interconnected with learning content. Possible approaches are tunnel (assumes optimal content ordering), hierarchical (top down decomposition) and matrix (relaxed hierarchy) structuring of Web pages (Danaher, McKay & Seeley, 2005). Hybrid designs are a mix of the aforementioned approaches, each of which can be described along the continuum from matrix and tunnel designs. The latter form allows the user to engage in discovery learning while still maintaining the focused forward movement of the tunnel program (Danaher, McKay & Seeley, 2005). However, the most crucial aspect is the basic suitability of the task imposed by the tutors for its educational purpose. To evaluate the wider usability of this kind of courseware will involve devising cognitive

measures of conceptual engagement (Garrison, Anderson & Archer, 2001).

Tertiary courseware is material which has been produced by previous learners, in the course of discussing or assessing their learning tasks. It may consist of dialogues between learners and tutors, or peer discussions, or outputs from assessment. Tertiary material can refer to the questions, answers and discussion that are typically posted to an asynchronous conferencing system. Other more sophisticated applications such as tools to provide *collaborative filtering* discussed in the next section, can be also used for mediating communication or collaboration between students and teachers.

In the following section, we present our approach for design and evaluation of WBLEs, using the deeper understanding provided by Mayes and Fowler's (1999) taxonomy as well as the models of information foraging. Specifically we argue that predictive models of human behavior can be used as a way to understand and interpret the behavior and searching strategies of learners during information foraging in a WBLE.

DESIGN AND EVALUATE WBLEs BASED ON INFORMATION FORAGING

Information foraging can provide much-needed coherence and insight and lead both the design and evaluation process of WBLEs. However, it should be stressed that, we do not underestimate the value of established research-based results and guidelines (Nielsen, 2000; Koyanl, Balley, & Nall, 2004). For example, we should highlight that studies report that *content* is more important than *navigation, visual design, functionality,* and *interactivity* (Nielsen, 2000). This is even more true in the case of WBLEs. On the contrary, we argue that results from user studies should be equally taken into account together with the notion of information foraging.

As a result, we propose an extension of the traditional design and evaluation models of WBLEs. We distinguish the mediating and aligning role of information foraging theories, as a tool to properly embed pedagogical models, take into account information architecture issues and encapsulate usability research towards formulation of our design and evaluation approach. By building on this notion, we propose four new tools that could inform the design and evaluation process:

1. First, specific directives that comply with information foraging theory, and provide design with strong information scent and rich information patches. In addition they are coupled with summarized, established, research-based knowledge related to Web design and information architecture.
2. Our list of directives is supported with a tool capable of automatically evaluating the semantic appropriateness of the hyperlinks' descriptions presented in a WBLE. In addition, we envisage a tool to automate the card sorting procedure which is described in the future trends section.
3. In addition, ways to provide valuable insight while in the process of interpreting user interaction data such as log files are possible through the notion of information foraging.
4. Finally, the ideas proposed do not tackle only issues mainly related to the LCM module of the WBLE. For instance, allowing learners to take advantage of the trails followed by others through collaborative information filtering (Wexelblat & Maes, 1999) gives them the opportunity to reflect upon other colleagues' learning strategies, thus giving richer collaboration and dialogue possibilities.

Therefore, by having the aforementioned models directly informing the design and evaluation process of WBLEs, we argue that two distinct types of impasses could be tackled. One type of problems can be detected at a Web page level due to inadequate scent emitted from the proximal cues in Web pages. Another type of impasses can be traced at a Web site level, and is caused by flaws in the information architecture of Web-based educational systems.

At a Web page level the categories of possible problems that could be identified and the solutions proposed are:

- **Weak scent cues:** When a correct link is not semantically similar to the learner's goal and there are no other correct links that have moderate or strong similarity, the learner is faced with a cognitive dead-end. Usually, learners encounter inadequate scent on Web pages that use short and/or ambiguous link labels. The above ascertainment well confronts with research-based results. Resnick and Sanchez (2004) conducted a controlled experiment to explore the relative value of a user-defined structure versus user-generated labels. Resnick and Sanchez's data shows that labels matter more than structure. Therefore, good labels and links are of utmost importance for a WBLE design. Feedback on learners' location should be provided, combined with descriptive tabs and menus. Despite careful labelling, cues as well as content delivery should be presented having in mind the observed behavior of learners while interacting with a Web page. Studies (Morkes & Nielsen, 1998; Nielsen, 2000) report that about 80% of users scan any new page and only 16% read word by word. Those findings well confront with the information foraging models presented in the previous section.
- **Competing cues:** A competing cues problem occurs when a page contains one or more links that are semantically similar to the learner's goal but do not lead to the targeted information resulting to cognitive overload,

frustration and in a loss of orientation. The cause of this problem can be either the choice of semantically improper proximal cues or the existence of highly general link labels. A solution to such cases is greater specificity and clarity that makes individual links distinct from each other. A single word may not emit sufficient scent, but on the other hand too many words can be difficult to read. Text links usually provide much better information about the target than graphics do (Nielsen, 2000). Also, items that are in the top center of the page or left and right panels have a high probability of being considered links. Research indicates that users tend to stop scanning a list as soon as they see something relevant with their goal. Thus, important items should be placed at the beginning of lists (Spyridakis, 2000). The aforementioned argument has been backed by research studies as well. If headings are too similar to one another, users may have to hesitate and re-read to decipher the difference (Morkes & Nielsen, 1998), a result which is fully compatible with the information foraging theory. Headings should provide strong cues that orient users and inform them about page organization and structure.

- **Unfamiliar cues:** This occurs when the WBLE users do not comprehend a link due to varying reading experiences, topic knowledge and culture backgrounds—a common phenomenon in Web environments. Possible reasons are technical terms or unusual words that are novel for a particular learners' segment and only learners who comprehend the meaning can actually perceive the scent and then click on it. To avoid confusing the user, the title for a page should be consistent with its heading in the content area. Familiar words should be used since words that are more frequently seen and heard are better and more quickly recognized (Leech, Ray-

son & Wilson, 2001). To ensure that links are effectively used, designers should use meaningful link labels, provide consistent clickability cues, and designate when links have been clicked (Miller & Remington, 2000).

Concerning the physical layout of a Web page, users generally look at the top center of a page first, therefore all critical content and navigation options should be toward the top of the page. Well-written headings are an important tool for helping learners scan quickly. Additionally, users prefer moderate amounts of white space; especially on content, they like white space to separate paragraphs. In a related study, use of white space between paragraphs and in the left and right margins increased comprehension by almost 20% (Lin, 2004).

In addition to this, to further optimize reading comprehension, the number of words in sentences and the number of sentences in paragraphs should be minimized so as the text can be more scannable (Nielsen, 2000). An optimal result seems to be obtained when a sentence does not contain more than 20 words and a paragraph does not contain more than six sentences. Further at the point, since in the frame of WBLEs reading speed is most important, research suggests using longer line lengths (75-100 characters per line (Dyson & Haselgrove, 2001)). Additionally, reading tasks seem to benefit from scrolling. Scrolling allows readers to advance in the text without losing the context as may occur when they are required to follow links. Paging allows learners to construct better mental representations of the text as a whole and to remember the location of the information they found. Research (Schwarz, Beldie & Pastoor, 1983) shows that inexperienced users prefer paging.

The main goal of a WBLE is to provide an environment that promotes learning and knowledge building, thus learners will rarely have extended knowledge of the topic covered. Although there might be some learners that have well-formulated goals and abundant relevant knowledge, usually this is not the case. Therefore, volume and proper structure of information and learner-system interaction greatly determine the efficiency of the learner to forage and acquire meaningful information. According to Rosenfeld and Morville (1998), identifying the right structure depends on how familiar the learners are with the taxonomy or classification of the content of the WBLE. *Exact schemes*, such as alphabetical order or organizational structure, are best used when it is certain that learners know the specific labels for the information they are seeking. *Ambiguous schemes*, such as organization by topic area, are preferred when the learners may not know keywords or specific content names, or when they may need to browse through the content to find what they need. Other issues that can be tackled referred to the overall learning content architecture with the proposed design solutions are:

- **Too abstract starting nodes:** The starting pages of the WBLE-learner interaction may be so general that none are more than weakly similar to a particular subject, thus reducing the probability that the learner will select the 'correct' path. This situation can be resolved by making less general the links during the first steps of the learner so that they can emit enough scent for his/her learning activity.
- **Misclassified nodes:** The designers of the WBLE may have misclassified either a page containing a concept description, so that picking links that seem closer to the learner's goal may not lead to the information s/he seeks. Different learners may try different ways to find information depending on their own interpretations of a problem and the layout of a page. Some learners find important links easily when they have a certain label, while others may recognize the link best with an alternative name. So, establishing

alternative ways to access the exact same information can help some learners find what they need (Ivory, Sinha, & Hearst, 2001).

- **Too long information paths:** Long information paths usually have the intrinsic problem of *too abstract starting pages* mentioned above. In a broad, shallow structure, a larger number of more specific headings appear on a Web page, raising the probability of a close semantic match to a learner's goal and thus a shorted information path. In a well-designed WBLE, scent should increase as the learner traverses an information path and gets closer to accomplishing her/his goal. A modest change in the probability of selecting the correct link at each step has a major impact on the overall success rate. Research has shown that the likelihood for a user getting frustrated and unsatisfied is significantly increased after three clicks (Huberman, Pirolli, Pitkow, & Lukose, 1998), therefore lengthier paths should be avoided.
- **Insufficiently specific end-points:** The end-points of an information path may not be sufficiently specific. In a situation like this, the page a learner visits in the end of his/her information seeking path retrieves an unreasonably large number of information objects. This can lead the learner to a cognitive overload and cause frustration and disappointment. As the learner traverses her/his information path s/he should be offered gradually more and more specific information in the domain s/he is studying.

The proposed tools address mainly the kind of primary courseware of the Mayes and Fowler's taxonomy, mainly learning content design issues in the LCMS module as described previously, but also touch aspects related to secondary and tertiary courseware. In particular, the proposed specific directives, automated tools and data log files analysis through the lens of information foraging can ensure a well-designed content structure that orients the learner and helps him/her navigate towards the most beneficial learning material. The goal is to provide a structure within which the learner is engaged in inquiry, critical thinking and problem solving relevant to the performance objectives and thus support their learning process. Indeed, the structure is meant to permit the learners to expend their energy focused on problem solving related to the core concepts rather than to the content structuring and findability issues.

Lack of adequate information structure cannot be tackled using a powerful search engine inside the WBLE. When clear labels and prominent, navigation options are established, users tend to browse rather than search. Searching is no faster than browsing in this context (Katz & Byrne, 2003). Even if search engines are used they are not a substitute for good content organization (Nielsen, 2000) and do not always improve learners' search performance.

Design of a WBLE should be not simply viewed as a means for proper content delivery but also as a key determinant of its trustworthiness and credibility. For motivated learners, ineffective design (busy layout, small print, too much text) has a significant negative impact on perceived credibility (more than the corresponding good effect of a good design (Sillence, Briggs, Fishwick, & Harris, 2004)). Even affective aspects of the user interface such as chromatic model combinations (Papachristos, Tselios, & Avouris, 2005) could significantly influence the learner's motivation and engagement with educational environments.

Another approach of understanding user behavior in a Web site is based on a *posteriori* monitoring of the behavior of many users by using machine learning and data mining techniques (Srivastava, Cooley, Deshpande, & Tan, 2000) in an effort to associate the observed actions of the user with her/his goal. Such methods have been also used in the context of e-learning systems to understand learners' behavior and extract valuable information for their design and evaluation (e.g., Pahl, 2006). Most of these methods are based on

the analysis of server log files and thus they have some intrinsic problems of missing data, mainly due to the nature of the medium and the stateless nature of the http protocol. Another implication of the information foraging theory is that it can allow the analysis of learners' paths from information in Web server logs.

Although there are many software tools for discovering usage patterns from Web server logs, none of them allows us to extrapolate user goals. Chi, Pirolli, Chen and Pitkow (2001) demonstrate a way—the algorithm *inferring user need by information scent* (IUNIS)—to take surfing patterns and infer the associated information need of a given user. IUNIS identifies the documents that a user accessed during a browsing session and the order they were accessed. Applying the longest repeating subsequence (LRS) paths that are repeated by multiple learners can be identified, and therefore more likely to be relevant to a specific learning task or goal. Each of these repeated paths helps to trace back and cluster the learners together when similar needs are identified. Designers of WBLEs can then construct learner types, or "learner profiles," for a particular system. By efficiently constructing learner profiles, developers can know their learners' information diet and increase the profitability of items in their diets by decreasing the amount of resources expended when foraging for desirable items. By generating learner profiles from analyzing the server logs of an existing WBLE, future iterations of the environment can better meet its learners' needs, leading to greater satisfaction and reducing the costs associated with foraging.

As discussed previously, another interesting idea that could substantially increase the learning effect of WBLEs is collaborative information filtering. Collaborative filtering allows learners to forage for information in groups, much like a group of humans collaborate to hunt for food within an environment. By tagging a history of use to a digital learning object, a single learner can benefit from the foraging of others. Interaction history of other foragers is described by Wexelblat and Maes (1999) as footprints which allow users to leave traces in the virtual environment. The interaction history of others, attached to an object can come from automated sources, such as access logs, or active sources, such as online papers that allow learners to leave commentary. Additionally, a learner could re-organize the virtual learning environment, having in hand functions such as wikis to organize personal representations of referenced material and information, thus creating (individually or collaboratively) novel and rich information patches. In this way, collaborative information filtering activities can increase the sense to which learners feel a part of a group. At the same time during such activities the learners are encouraged and motivated to persist in their inquiries by seeing other learners expending effort.

The proposed approach is compatible with the inspiring work of research reported by Guzdial, Rick and Kehoe (2001). They report the effectiveness of CoWeb—a collaborative Web site that facilitates open authoring where any student can edit or create pages. In real-life applications, this behavior is mainly attributed to the collaborative information gathering philosophy developed gradually by their tutors. For instance, they report cases of CoWeb being used as a collaborative bookmark, hotlist or glossary space where the entire class finds information, posts links into pages and extends the structure with new pages for new kinds of bookmarks. The result is a collaboratively produced information space that becomes a useful resource for anyone on the topic of the class and gets reused and expanded by future classes.

In another case, students collaboratively produced a project library by posting their assignments after grading. Other students used the high-scoring projects as sources for ideas and, in programming classes, as sources for code that could be re-used in new projects. Occasionally, students from the first term revisited the CoWeb during the second term, answering questions and sometimes changing and improving their cases. As the project case library grew larger, some students began creating indices or recommendations of their favorite cases. In another class CoWeb was used to implement a form of "close reading" where students identified sections to discuss by placing asterisks around the phrases of interest, examined other students' annotations and expanded on them on separate discussion spaces linked with each phrase. Thus, learners were able to reflect upon their arguments and strategies and engage in a constructive dialogue that strengthens their own 'sense making' and thus, according to social constructivism, the learning outcome.

By expanding our view of the computer as a tool for solving specific problems to the computer as a medium that facilitates communication and shared knowledge construction, we can fundamentally change the way we think and learn (Perrone, Repenning, Spencer, & Ambach, 1996), thus presenting a novel form of tertiary courseware according to Mayes and Fowler's (1995) vision. Collaborative authoring environments, such as wikis and highly interactive Web technologies like flash and AJAX framework offer the opportunity to embed personal information patches into next generation WBLEs, using visual notations such as concept maps to illustrate learning paths and correlate concepts with each other.

Automating Aspects of WBLEs Design and Evaluation Process

Research (Resnick & Sanchez, 2004) has shown that link labels matter more than content structure. Therefore, good link labels (i.e., emitting sufficient information scent) are necessary in a WBLE to properly guide learners to the information they seek for their studies. In the literature, there is an abundance of rules and guidelines on providing efficient and effective link labels (Miller & Remington, 2000; Spyridakis, 2000; Nielsen, 2000; Koyanl, Balley, & Nall, 2004). Among others these guidelines suggest that designers should support scanning of the page, use meaningful link labels that convey all the necessary information for their destinations, make sure that they are consistent with their targets, make sure that each link label clearly differentiates one link from another, provide consistent clickability cues, designate when links have been clicked, prefer using text for links rather than graphics and provide alt text and associated texts whenever graphical links are used.

Despite the abundance of guidelines concerning the appropriate ways to provide efficient and effective link labels, it is crucial—especially for practitioners—to offer an increased level of automation (Chi, Pirolli, & Pitkow, 2000) in the design and evaluation process of WBLEs and provide an objective measure of the appropriateness of the hyperlink descriptions. One such tool that we have implemented to increase the usefulness and applicability of our proposal, is one that automatically evaluates the semantic appropriateness of the hyperlinks' descriptions presented in a Web-based environment (Katsanos, Tselios, & Avouris, 2006). This tool, named InfoScent Evaluator (ISEtool), is capable of simulating learners' activity and interaction with a WBLE according to information foraging theory. The basic underlying assumption in our tool is that learners have some information goal and their surfing patterns through the WBLE are guided by information scent. The tool attempts to quantify the concept of information scent, using latent semantic analysis (LSA) (Landauer & Dumais, 1997).

LSA was developed to mimic human ability to detect deeper semantic associations among words, phrases or whole sentences. LSA builds a semantic space representing a given user population's understanding of words, sentences, and whole texts from documents that these users are likely to have read. The meaning of a word, sentence or any text is represented as a vector in a high dimensional space, typically with about 300 dimensions. LSA generates the space from a very large collection of documents that are assumed to be representative of a given user population's reading experiences. The degree of semantic relatedness or similarity between any pair of texts, such as the description of a learner's goal and a link label on a Web page, is measured by the cosine value between the corresponding two vectors. Each cosine value lies between +1 (identical) and –1 (opposite). Near-zero values represent two unrelated texts. Another important measure provided by LSA is term vector length, a measure that is correlated with word frequency and that estimates how much knowledge about a word or phrase is embedded in the designated LSA semantic space. Words with low frequency in the corpus have short vector lengths.

LSA also served as a computational model of information scent in ACWW, a conceptual artifact based on cognitive walkthrough evaluation (Blackmon, Kitajima, & Polson, 2005) method and the CoLiDES theory. However, despite the fact that the results presented seem to be very promising, lack of integration of useful functions— such as automatic grabbing of links, storage of results, automatic prediction and walkthrough of a user's path—inspired us to create a more complete and automated tool described briefly in the following.

The main components of the ISEtool architecture are diagrammatically represented in Figure 2. A typical usage scenario of ISEtool is the following: First, the designer defines the profile of the learners by choosing one of the available LSA semantic spaces (e.g., general reading up to first year college). Subsequently, the designer describes a typical learner's goal in a text box using free text. These typical goals should be acquired by representative users of the targeted learner profiles by means of exploratory methodologies (interviews, surveys, etc.).

Next, the ISEtool loads the page in its embedded internal browser and parses the page that the designer has defined as the entry point of the learners' interaction with the WBLE under examination. It collects all available links on the page, it finds and stores link types and type of the pointed file. It also finds and stores the "proximal cue" of each link by grabbing the textual description, if it is a text hyperlink or the alternative text (e.g., ALT tag), if it is a graphical hyperlink. At this point it should be mentioned that in cases of missing alt tags in graphical hyperlinks, the user of the tool is notified and asked to optionally enter his description of the image (alternatively he can ask for the learners' descriptions by means of exploratory methodologies).

Additionally to this, the tool also discriminates automatically the external and internal links. The calculation of information scent for all links is achieved by running in a transparent and automated way, one-to-many analysis of the LSA algorithm (http://lsa.colorado.edu/). LSA computes and returns the semantic similarity (LSA index) of the learner's goal against all the proximal cues of the links. The calculated information scent for each proximal cue can be also depicted in the internal browser of the tool next to each hyperlink. At a next step the evaluator can use the tool to automatically select the link found to "emit" the higher scent, thus the one with the higher probability to be followed by the simulated learner with the specified goal. Subsequently the tool "visits" the next page and repeats the same process until the designer decides that the user goal is met or that a dead-end has been reached.

The tool offers a number of options to the designer and can be used during the design and evaluation of a WBLE to identify all the aforementioned categories of Web page and Web site level problems that are caused due to inadequate scent

Figure 2. Architecture of the ISEtool

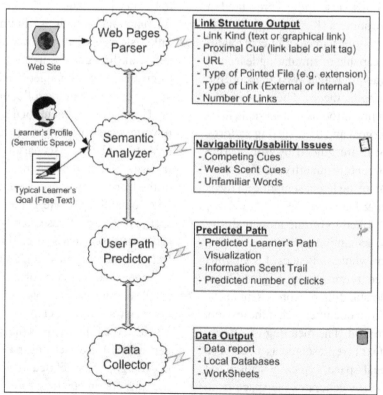

emitted from the proximal cues in the WBLE. The user of the tool can sort the spreadsheet-like link structure produced by the tool according to any column and change the default color coding (e.g., define intervals and color ranges of semantic similarity) adjusting the tool to her/his needs and preferences, in order to get a better insight of the output. At the same time s/he can inspect the annotated version of the page under examination in the internal browser so that s/he can also take into account the layout of the page. Moreover, the tool produces warnings of unfamiliar cues based on the LSA term vector length of each proximal cue, a measure that is correlated with word frequency. When some of the words used in the proximal cues of the links have short-term vector lengths (e.g., they have low frequency in the defined corpus), this is a good indication that the learners modeled by the semantic space selected will perceive them to be relatively meaningless and thus they will be incapable of relating them semantically to their goal. At a site level analysis, the tool provides at any step of the simulation a graphical visualization of the predicted learner's path and the scent trail followed. Thus, the designer can identify and investigate further cases of steps in the trail that have low scent (e.g., below a threshold that s/he defines) or lead the learner to the "wrong" path. Finally, it is worth mentioning that ISEtool also allows exporting the results of the simulation in different formats for further analysis.

In order to present to a greater extent the utility of ISEtool, we demonstrate its use by a detailed representative example, shown in Figure 3. In this example an evaluator of a WBLE (OpenCourse-Ware on critical thinking—http://philosophy. hku.hk/think/) firstly defines the main page of the WBLE as the entry point of interaction, a typical learner information goal and a typical learner profile. Subsequently, the tool automatically parses and analyzes the semantic similarity of all the proximal cues (i.e., links' descriptions) against the typical learners' goal and displays the results. At this point, the evaluator notices

a warning of the tool for unfamiliar words (e.g., "sentitial logic"). These warnings could be translated to strong indications that the learner of the specified profile will probably find these words meaningless and thus will be unable to relate them semantically with her/his goal. S/he decides to write down the issue and discuss with the designer for a more appropriate term after s/he finishes with the evaluation of the WBLE for all the identified learner profiles. Then, s/he sorts the links by their semantic appropriateness (LSA index) and inspects carefully the output of the tool. S/he observers that there are some cues that possibly compete for the learners' attention (e.g., "what is critical thinking?"—0.76, "argument analysis"—0.66, "a mini guide to critical thinking"—0.60). By taking advantage of the internal browser of the tool, s/he quickly realizes that the most beneficial cue is "argument analysis" and the others are possibly classified as competing cues.

At a next step, the evaluator uses the tool to "follow" the "correct" cue and repeat the parsing and semantic analysis. This time s/he also changes the default color coding (i.e., defines ranges and colors of semantic similarity) adjusting the tool better to her/his needs. Subsequently, s/he realizes that there are again some proximal cues with comparable LSA index but this time s/he concludes that they all contribute to the learners' goal and thus s/he decides not to classify them as competing cues. Next, s/he uses the tool to 'follow' the aforementioned cues and inspect the learners' predicted path and scent trail followed by taking advantage of the corresponding functionalities offered by the tool. S/he notices that the predicted learner's path is reasonable in terms of depth (i.e., two clicks) but suspects that there is a misclassified node problem at a Web site level, since the scent seems to drop, instead of increase, as the learner traverses the predicted path.

FUTURE TRENDS

Figure 3. A representative example of using ISEtool to analyze a WBLE against a typical learners'
goal

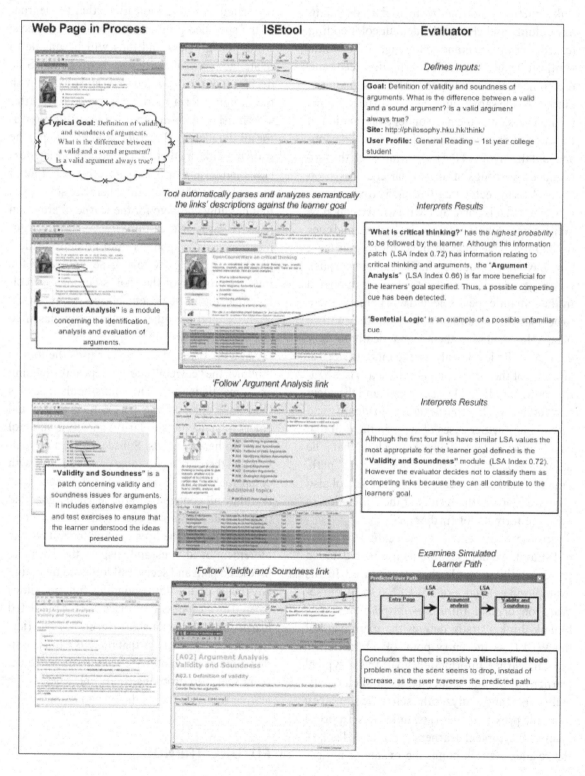

Despite the encouraging results obtained using ISEtool, there are still some issues to tackle. For instance, initially when a Web page of the WBLE is analyzed, the alternative text (e.g., the ALT Tag) of each graphical link is assumed to be the proximal cue of this link. Even if all the graphical links have alternative text, for a learner with a graphical browser the actual proximal cue is the graphic itself. Currently, the adopted solution is to notify the user of the tool for such instances and ask for her/his descriptions. Additionally to this, there are WBLEs where a set of links is presented in a nested menu-like approach. Thus, the learner primarily focuses on the general description, and spreads the rest of her/his attention to identify the desired menu sub-item, which is anticipated by taking into account the context communicated by the header. At the moment, our tool cannot mimic this behavior, thus often leading to "flat" or misleading results.

Future work contains conducting studies with real users (e.g., actual learners using various WBLEs), in order to further validate the accuracy of the developed tool. Additionally to this are studies of how goal reformulation occurs while learners explore a WBLE towards finding desired patches of information. Finally, to a broader context, are studies of possible extensions to the developed model such as data describing learners' profiles or specific particularities of the learning domain. Further research is needed on the effects of other aspects of the WBLEs, such as credibility and aesthetics and their influence in learner's motivation and engagement, as well.

Another tool that we envisage is one that automates the card sorting technique by calculating semantic similarity of each Web page and clustering accordingly the information space. This tool addresses the problem of reasonable content structuring and helps avoiding the aforementioned Web site level problems during the design of a WBLE. Although, card-sorting study results can be stable with 20 or even fewer participants

(Tullis & Wood, 2004), a model-based technique could further accelerate the design and evaluation lifecycle of a WBLE. A typical scenario of the tool we envisage is the following: First the designer inputs all the titles of the pages that the WBLE will contain. The tool then runs an automated analysis, using the LSA algorithm and machine learning techniques. LSA is used to calculate the semantic similarity among all the pages, while clustering algorithms are applied to group together semantically similar pages. The output of the tool is the recommended clustering of the pages comprising the learning sections of the WBLE. Specifically, the tool clusters the described information space, suggests how the pages should be distributed and which pages should have links to each other, according to their semantic similarity. A possible variation to the previous scenario could include the definition of the desired number and/or the labels of the learning sections to be created. This variation implements an automated process of a closed-card sorting technique where the designer specifies in advance the number and/or the names of the learning sections to be created and the tool places each page to a learning section according to their semantic similarity.

CONCLUSION

In this chapter we have described our proposal for design and evaluation of WBLEs that couples efficiently learning models, learning content design and usability requirements based on the notion of information foraging theory. Since the task of finding information related to a specific subject of study in an efficient and effective manner is of fundamental importance in the frame of WBLEs, we argue that information foraging can propel our understanding of the ways learners cope with a complex learning hyperspace. While the supporting value of a coherent learning content architecture scheme to learning activities designed under the influence of behavioristic pedagogical paradigms is rather straightforward, we argue that even approaches based on a socio-cultural view on learning could equally benefit from the application of information foraging theory. In particular we proposed four different ways to have information foraging theory informing the design and evaluation of WBLEs. Directives, to ensure proper learning content structuring and cues with strong scent, tools based on LSA to automate the design and evaluation process, ways to construct archetypal learner's profiles by combining information foraging theory and user data and learning tools to realize collaborative information filtering and personal information patch creation, thus allowing learners to organize their reference materials in a meaningful and constructive way. Those tools could be also treated as a way to examine learners' goals, their decision-making processes and adaptations to the information access system environment. This knowledge can then be extended and used to develop methodologies and tools that lead both the design and the evaluation process of WBLEs.

Such an example is the InfoScent Evaluator tool (ISEtool) which automatically evaluates semantic appropriateness of the hyperlinks' descriptions of a complex learning hyperspace. The utility of the tool is twofold: to explore alternative designs and solutions ("what-if" scenarios) and to support formative and summative usability evaluations, reducing the need to involve actual learners which is costly and time-consuming. Initial application of the tool showed promising results, thus further validating our argument that researchers can make use of this knowledge in assessing interaction design of WBLEs.

However, despite the fact that the notion of information foraging seems compatible to the principles of active learning, large scale, real-world application of our proposals will greatly serve our effort to better clarify other, possibly unforeseen at the moment, particularities of a WBLE's design and evaluation lifecycle. Additionally, findings and conclusions from studies of how learners form their goals, what strategies they follow, what criteria they use to evaluate information and how they adapt to the given learning environment, can update existing or form new design and evaluation techniques for Web-based educational systems.

ACKNOWLEDGMENT

We thank European Social Fund (ESF), Operational Program for Educational and Vocational Training II (EPEAEK II) and particularly the Program PYTHAGORAS, for funding the above work.

REFERENCES

Becker, D. & Dwyer, M. (1994). Using hypermedia to provide learner control. *Journal of Educational Multimedia and Hypermedia, 3*(2), 155-172.

Blackmon, M., Kitajima, M., & Polson, (2005). P. Tool for accurately predicting website navigation problems, non-problems, problem severity, and effectiveness of repairs. In *Human Factors in Computing Systems CHI '05 Conference Proceedings* (pp. 51-58). Portland, OR: ACM Press.

Blackmon, M., Polson, P., Kitajima, M., & Lewis, C. (2002). Cognitive Walkthrough for the Web. In *Human Factors in Computing Systems CHI '02 Conference Proceedings* (pp. 464-470). Mineapolis, MN: ACM Press.

Boland R. (1987). The in-formation of information systems. In R. J. Boland & R. A. Hirschheim (Eds.), *Critical issues in information systems research* (pp. 363-379). Hoboken, NJ: John Wiley & Sons.

Chi, E., Pirolli, P., & Pitkow, J. (2000). The scent of a site: A system for analyzing and predicting information scent, usage, and usability of a Website. In *Human Factors in Computing Systems CHI*

2000 Conference Proceedings (pp. 161-168). The Hague, Netherlands: ACM Press.

Chi, E. H., Pirolli, P., Chen, K., & Pitkow, J. (2001). Using information scent to model user information needs and actions on the Web. In *Human Factors in Computing Systems CHI '05 Conference Proceedings* (pp. 490-497). Seattle, WA: ACM Press.

Csikszentmihalyi, M. (1990). *Flow: The psychology of optimal experience.* New York: Harper and Row.

Danaher, B., McKay, H., & Seeley J. (2005). The information architecture of behavior change Websites. *Journal of Medical Internet Research.* 7(2), e12.

Duffy, T. & Kirkley J. (2004). Learning theory and pedagogy applied in distance learning: The case of Cardean University. In T.M. Duffy J.R. Kirkley (Eds.), *Learner-centered theory and practice in distance education: Cases from higher education* (pp. 107-141). Mahwah, NJ: Erlbaum.

Dyson, M.C. & Haselgrove, M. (2001). The influence on reading speed and line length on the effectiveness of reading from screens. *International Journal of Human-Computer Studies, 54,* 585-612.

Furnas, G. (1997). Effective view navigation. In *Human Factors in Computing Systems CHI '97 Conference Proceedings* (pp. 367-374). Atlanta, GA: ACM Press.

Garrison, D.R., Anderson, T. & Archer, W. (2001). Critical thinking, cognitive presence, and computer conferencing in distance education. *American Journal of Distance Education, 15*(1), 7-23.

Gunawardena, C. N. (2004). The Challenge of Designing Inquiry-based Online Learning Environments: Theory into Practice. In T. Duffy and J. Kirkley (Eds.), *Learner centered theory and practice in distance education: Cases from higher education* (pp. 143-158). Mahwah, NJ: Lawrence Erlbaum Associates.

Guzdial, M., Rick, J., & Kehoe, C. (2001). Beyond adoption to invention: Teacher-created collaborative activities in higher education. *Journal of the Learning Sciences, 10*(3), 265-279.

Hayes, R. (2000). Exploring Discount Usability Methods to Assess the Suitability of Online Course Delivery Products. *The Internet and Higher education, 2*(2-3), 119-134.

Heines J.M. (2000). Evaluating the effect of a course Web site on student performance. *The Journal of Computing in Higher Education, 12*(1), 57-83.

Huberman, B., Pirolli, P., Pitkow, J., & Lukose, R. (1998). Strong Regularities in World Wide Web Surfing. *Science, 280*(5360), 95-97.

Ivory, M.Y., Sinha, R.R., & Hearst, M.A. (2001). Empirically validated Web page design metrics. In *Human Factors in Computing Systems CHI '01* (pp. 53-60). Seattle, WA: ACM Press.

Katsanos, C., Tselios, N., & Avouris, N. (2006). *InfoScent Evaluator: A semi-automated tool to evaluate hyperlinks' semantic appropriateness of a Web site.* In J. Kjeldskov & J. Paay (Eds.), Proceedings of OZCHI 2006 (pp. 373-376). Sydney: ACM Press.

Katz, M. , & Byrne, M. (2003). Effects of Scent and Breadth on Use of Site Specific Search on E-commerce Websites. *ACM Transactions on Computer-Human Interaction, 10*(3), 198-220.

Kirkpatrick, D. (1994). *Evaluating Training Programs.* San Francisco: Berrett-Koehler.

Kitajima, M. & Polson, P. (1997). A comprehension-based model of exploration, *Human-Computer Interaction, 12,* 345-389.

Koyanl S., Balley R., & Nall J., (2004). *Research-Based Web Design & Usability Guidelines.* USA: Computer Psychology.

Landauer, T. & Dumais, S. (1997). A solution to Plato's problem: The Latent Semantic Analysis theory of acquisition, induction, and representation of knowledge. *Psychological Review, 104,* 211-240.

Laurillard, D. (1993). *Rethinking University Teaching. A framework for the effective use of educational technology.* London: Routledge.

Lave, J. & Wenger, E. (1991). Situated *learning: Legitimate peripheral participation.* Cambridge, MA: Cambridge University Press.

Leech, G., Rayson, P., & Wilson, A. (2001). *Word Frequencies in Written and Spoken English: Based on the British National Corpus.* Retrieved May 2003, from htpp://www.comp.lancs.ac.uk/ucrel/bncfreq.

Lin, D. (2004). Evaluating older adults' retention in hypertext perusal: Impacts of presentation media as a function of text topology. *Computers in Human Behavior, 20*(4), 491-503.

Mayes, J. & Fowler, C. (1999). Learning technology and usability: A framework for understanding courseware usability and educational software design. *Interacting with Computers, 11*(5), 485-497.

Miller, C.S. & Remington, R.W. (2000). A computational model of Web navigation: Exploring interactions between hierarchical depth and link ambiguity. In *Proceedings of the 6th Conference on Human Factors and the Web.*

Morkes, J. & Nielsen, J. (1998). *Applying writing guidelines to Web pages.* Retrieved May 2003, from http://www.useit.com/papers/Webwriting/rewriting.html

Morville, P. (2005). *Ambient findability: What we find changes who we become.* Sebastopol, CA: O'Reilly Publications.

Nielsen, J. (2000). *Designing Web usability.* Indianapolis, IN: New Riders.

Pahl. C. (2006). Data mining for the analysis of content interaction in Web-based learning and training systems. In S. Ventura and C. Romero (Eds.), *Data Mining in E-Learning* (pp. 41-56). Southampton, UK: WIT Press.

Papachristos, E., Tselios, N., & Avouris, N. (2005). Inferring relations between color and emotional dimensions of a Web site using Bayesian Networks. *Interact 2005* (pp. 1075-1078). Rome: Springer.

Perrone, C., Repenning, A., Spencer, S., & Ambach, J. (1996). Computers in the classroom: Moving from tool to medium. *Journal of Computer-Mediated Communication, 2*(3). Retrieved April 2, 2002, from http://www.ascusc.org/jcmc/

Pirolli, P. & Card, S. (1999). Information foraging. *Psychological Review, 106*(4), 643-675.

Pirolli, P. (1997). Computational models of information scentfollowing in a very large browsable text collection. In *Human Factors in Computing Systems CHI '97 Conference Proceedings* (pp. 3-10) Vienna: ACM Press.

Resnick, M. & Sanchez, J. (2004). Effects of organizational scheme and labeling on task performance in product-centered and user-centered retail Websites. *Human Factors, 46.*

Rosenfeld L. & Morville P. (1998). *Information Architecture for the World Wide Web.* Sebastopol, CA: O'Reilly Publications.

Schwarz, E., Beldie, I.P., & Pastoor, S. (1983). A comparison of paging and scrolling for changing screen contents by inexperienced users. *Human Factors, 24,* 279-282.

Sillence, E., Briggs, P., Fishwick, L., & Harris, P. (2004). Trust and mistrust of online health sites. In *Human Factors in Computing Systems CHI'04* (pp. 663-670). Vienna: ACM Press.

Spyridakis, J. (2000). Guidelines for authoring comprehensible Web pages and evaluating their success. *Technical Communication, 47*(3), 359-382.

Srivastava, J., Cooley, R., Deshpande, & M., Tan, P-N. (2000). Web usage mining: Discovery and applications of usage patterns from Web data. In *ACM KDD Explorations, 1*(2), 12-23.

Stephens, D. & Krebs, J. (1986). *Foraging theory.* Princeton, NJ: Princeton University Press.

Thuring, M., Mannemann, J., & Haake, J. (1995). Hypermedia and cognition: Designing for comprehension. *Communications of the ACM, 38*(8), 57-66.

Tselios, N., Avouris, N., Dimitracopoulou, A., & Daskalaki, S. (2001). Evaluation of distance-learning environments: Impact of usability on student performance. *International Journal of Educational Telecommunications, 7*(4), 355-378.

Tselios N., Avouris N. & Kordaki M., (2002). Student Task Modeling in design and evaluation of open problem-solving environments. *Journal of Education and Information Technologies, 7*(1), 19-42.

Tullis, T. & Wood, L. (2004). How many users are enough for a card-sorting study? In *Proceedings of UPA'2004*. Minneapolis, MN.

Vrasidas, C. (2000). Constructivism versus objectivism: Implications for interaction, course design, and evaluation in distance education. *International Journal of Educational Telecommunications, 6*(4), 339-346.

Wexelblat, A. & Maes, P. (1999). Footprints: History-rich tools for information foraging. In *Human Factors in Computing Systems CHI 99 Conference Proceedings* (pp. 270-277). Pittsburgh, PA: ACM Press.

Compilation of References

.LRN. (2006) .*LRN platform web site*. Retrieved September, 2006, from http://www.dotlrn.org/

Abecker, A. (2004). Business-process oriented knowledge management: Concepts, methods and tools. Doctoral thesis, University of Karlsruhe, Germany. Retrieved from http://digbib.ubka.uni-karlsruhe.de/volltexte/1000003269

ACM Web Site. Retrieved from http://www.acm.org/class/

ADL (2006). *SCORM*. Advanced Distributed Learning. Retrieved September 23, 2006, from http://www.adlnet.gov/scorm/index.cfm

ADL—Advanced Distributed Learning (2004), *Sharable Content Object Reference Model (SCORM)* (2nd ed.). Retrieved from http://www.adlnet.org

ADLI. (2003). Sharable Content Object Reference Model (SCORM) (Version 1.3): Advanced Distributed Learning Initiative.

Adorni G., Sugliano A. M., & Vercelli G. (2003, September). AI embedded into LMS agents: The UniGe E_Learning portal experience and future scenario. In *Proceedings of the Workshop on Artificial Intelligence and e-learning, Eighth National Congress of Italian Association for Artificial Intelligence* (pp. 23-26). Pisa, Italy.

Advanced Distributed Learning ADL (2004). SCORM Sharable Content Object Reference Model. Retrieved February 2, 2006, from http://www.adlnet.org/index.cfm?fuseaction= scormabt

AHA! (2006). Retrieved from http://aha.win.tue.nl

Albrecht F., Koch N., & Tiller T. (2000). SmexWeb: An adaptive Web-based hypermedia teaching system. *Journal of Interactive Learning Research, Special Issue on Intelligent Systems/Tools in Training and Lifelong Learning,* 367-388.

Alexander, B. (2006). A new wave of innovation for teaching and learning? *EDUCAUSE Review, 40*(March/April), 32-44.

Allen, P. & Frost, S. (1998). *Component-based development for enterprise systems: Applying the SELECT perspective*. New York: Cambridge University Press.

Allert, H. (2005). *Modeling Coherent Social Systems for Learning*. Thesis Dissertation. Hannover University, Germany.

Alonso, G., Casati, F., Kuno H. & Machiraju, V. (2004). *Web services: Concepts, architectures and applications*. Berlin, Germany: Springer Verlag.

Álvarez, J.-M., Evans, A., & Sammut, P. (2001, October 1-5). Mapping between levels in the metamodel architecture. In *The Proceedings of the 4th International Conference UML* (pp. 34-46). Toronto, Canada.

Ambjörn, N., Mikael, N., Matthias, P., & Fredrik, P. (2005). Contributions to a public e-learning platform: Infrastructure; architecture; frameworks; tools. *International Journal of Learning Technology, 1*(3), 352-381.

Amin, K., Nijsure, S., & von Laszevski, G. (2002). Open Collaborative Grid Services Architecture (OCGSA), In *Euroweb 2002 Conference, The Web and the GRID: From e-Science to e-Business* (pp. 101-107). Oxford, UK: The British Computer Society.

Anderson, J. R., Boyle, C. F., Corbett, A. T., & Lewis, M. W. (1990). Cognitive modeling and intelligent tutoring. *Artificial Intelligence, 42*, 7-49.

Anderson, J., Corbett, A., Koedinger, K., & Pelletier, R. (1995). Cognitive tutors: Lessons learned. *The Journal of Learning Sciences, 4*, 167-207.

Andrews, K., Guetl, C., Moser, J., Vedran Sabol, V., & Lackner, W. (2001). Search result visualization with xFIND. In E. Kapetanios & H. Hinterberger (Eds.), *Proceedings of the Second International Workshop on User Interfaces to Data Intensive Systems (UIDIS 2001)* (pp. 50-58). Zurich, Switzerland: IEEE Computer Society Press.

Andronico, A., Carbonaro, A., Casadei, G., Colazzo, L., Molinari, A., & Ronchetti, M. (2003). Integrating a multi-agent recommendation system into a Mobile Learning Management System. *Artificial Intelligence in Mobile System 2003.*

Anéma (2007).The Ganesha plateform website. Retrieved March, 2007, from http://www.anemalab.org/ganesha/

Anido, L., Llamas, M., Fernández, M.J., Caeiro, M., Santos, J., & Rodríguez, J. (2001). A component model for standardized web-based education. *ACM Journal of Educational Resources in Computing, 1(2)*, 1-21.

Ankolenkar, A., Burstein, M., Son, T.C., Hobbs, J., Lassila, O., Martin, D., McDermott, D., McIlraith, S., Narayanan, S., Paolucci, M., Payne, T., Sycara, K., & Zeng, H. (2001). *DAML-S: Semantic markup for Web services.* Retrieved October 14, 2006, from http://www.daml.org/services/daml-s/2001/05/daml-s.pdf

Apostolopoulos, T. K. & Kefala, A. (2003). A configurable middleware architecture for deploying e-learning services over diverse communication networks. *IASTED CATE International Conference.* Rhodes, Greece.

Archimed. (2006). Archimed Web site. Retrived October 2006 from http://www.archimed.fr

ASPF (2005). Contribution de l'AS "Conception d'une plateforme pour la recherche en EIAH" à "l'ingénierie des EIAH." *Special issue "Conceptions et usages des plates-formes de formation" de la revue STICEF (Sciences et Technologies de l'Information et de la Communication pour l'Education et la Formation), (12).*

Audio learning is back. (2005, March 12, 2005). from http://www.kineo.co.uk/kineo-press-releases/audio-learning-survey.html

Australian Flexible Learning Framework. (2005). *E-learning Benchmarking, Project—Report*, I & J Management Services, Australian Flexible Learning Framework (Framework), September 2005.

Avgeriou, P., Papasalouros, P., Retails, S., & Skordalakis, E. (2003). Towards a pattern language for learning management systems. *Educational Technology & Society, 6(2)*, 11-24. Retrieved from http://ifets.ieee.org/periodical/6-2/2.html

Avgeriou, P., Retalis, S., & Skordalakis, M. (2003). An architecture for open learning management systems. In Y. Manolopoulos et al. (Eds.), PCI 2001, Springer-Verlag, Berlin Heidelberg. (LNCS 2563, pp. 183-200).

Avgeriou, P., Retalis, S., & Skordalakis, M. (2003). An architecture for open learning management systems. In Y. Manolopoulos et al. (Eds.), *Advances in Informatics*, (LNCS 2563, pp. 183-200). Berlin Heidelberg: Springer-Verlag.

Bacelo P.T.A., & Becker, K. (2002). A component-based architecture tosupport collaborative application design, In Haake & J. Pino (Eds.), *Groupware: Design, implementation and use.* (LNCS 2440, pp. 134-143). London: Springer-Verlag.

Baird, D. E., & Fisher, M. (2005). Neomillennial user experience design strategies: Utilizing social networking media to support "Always on" Learning styles. *Journal of Educational Technology Systems, 34(1)*, 5-32.

Balachandran, A., Voelker, G., & Bahl, P. (2003). Wireless hotspots: Current challenges and future directions. In *Proceedings for WMASH'03.*

Balas, J. L. (2005). Blogging is so last year—now podcasting is hot. *Online treasures. Computers in Libraries, 25*(10), 29-32.

Barack, L. (2006). American library association sponsors tech boot camp. *School Library Journal, 52*(7), 20-20.

Barrett-Baxendale M., Hazelwood P., Oddie A., Anderson M., & Franklin T. (2005). *SLeD Integration Demonstrator—Final Report.* retrieved September, 2006, from http://www.hope.ac.uk/slide/

Barritt, C. & Lewis, D. (2000, April 22). Reusable learning object strategy—definition, creation process and guidelines for building. *Cisco Systems, Inc.* Retrieved October 14, 2006, from http://www.reusablelearning.org/Docs/Cisco_rlo_roi_v3-1.pdf

Baruque, L., Porto, F. A. M., & Melo, R. N. (2003). Towards an instructional design methodology based on learning objects. In *Proceedings of the IASTED International Conference on Computers and Technology in Education (CATE 2003),* (pp. 259-264), Anaheim, Calgary, and Zurich: ACTA Press.

Bazire, M. & Brézillon, P. (2005, July 5-8). Understanding Context Before Using It. In *Modeling and Using Context: 5th International and Interdisciplinary Conference CONTEXT 2005,* Paris (pp. 35-54). New York: Springer.

Beaumont, I. (1994). User modeling in the Interactive Anatomy Tutoring System ANATOM-TUTOR. *User Models and User Adapted Interaction Journal, 4*(1), 21-45.

Becker, D. & Dwyer, M. (1994). Using hypermedia to provide learner control. *Journal of Educational Multimedia and Hypermedia, 3*(2), 155-172.

Benayache, A. & Abel, M.-H. (2005). Using knowledge management method for e-learning. In G. Chiazzese, M. Allegra, A. Chifari, & Ottaviano S. (Eds.), *Methods and technologies for learning.* Southampton, UK: WIT Press.

Bentley, R., Horstmann, T., & Trevor, J. (1997). The World Wide Web as enabling technology for CSCW: The case

of BSCW. *Computer-Supported Cooperative Work: The Journal of Collaborative Computing, 6(2),* 111-134.

Bereiter, C. & Scardamalia, M. (1985). Cognitive coping strategies and the problem of 'inert knowledge'. In S. Chipman, J. Seagal, R. Glaser (Eds.), *Thinking and learning skills. Volume 2.* Hillside, NJ: LEA.

Berggren A., Burgos D., Fontan J.M., Hinkelman D., Hung V., Hursh A., & Tielemans G. (2005). Practical and pedagogical issues for teacher adoption of IMS learning design standards in Moodle LMS. *Journal of Interactive Media in Education, 2005*(02).

Beuschel, W. (2003). Ubiquitous e-learning: Are we there yet? In P. Walsh & J. Meade (Eds.), *Proceedings of the 3rd IEEE International Conference on Advanced Learning Technologies (ICALT'03)* (pp. 414-415). Los Alamitos, USA: IEEE Computer Society.

Bézivin, J., & Gerbe, O. (2001). Towards a precise definition of the OMG/MDA framework. In *Proceedings of Automated Software Engineering.* USA.

Bhatti, N., Bouch, A., & Kuchinsky, A. (2000). Integrating user–perceived quality into Web server design. *Computer Networks Journal, 33*(1-6), 1-16.

Bieber, G., & Carpenter, J. *Introduction to service-oriented programming (Rev 2.1).* Retrieved February 6, 2007, from http://www.openwings.org/download/specs/ServiceOrientedIntroduction.pdf

Biström, J. (2005). *Peer-to-peer networks as collaborative learning environments.* Paper presented at HUT T-110.551 Seminar on Internetworking. Retrieved October 13, 2006 from http://www.sit.fi/~johnny/collp2p.pdf

Blackboard Web Site. Retrieved from http://www.Blackboard.com/

Blackboard Inc. (2002). Blackboard Course Management System (Version 5.1): Blackboard Inc.

Blackmon, M., Kitajima, M., & Polson, (2005). P. Tool for accurately predicting website navigation problems, non-problems, problem severity, and effectiveness of repairs. In *Human Factors in Computing Systems CHI*

'05 Conference Proceedings (pp. 51-58). Portland, OR: ACM Press.

Blackmon, M., Polson, P., Kitajima, M., & Lewis, C. (2002). Cognitive Walkthrough for the Web. In *Human Factors in Computing Systems CHI'02 Conference Proceedings* (pp. 464-470). Mineapolis, MN: ACM Press.

Blackmon, W. & Rehak, D. (2003). Customized learning: A Web services approach. In *World Conference on Educational Multimedia, Hypermedia and Telecommunications (EDMEDIA 03)*.

Boland R. (1987). The in-formation of information systems. In R. J. Boland & R. A. Hirschheim (Eds.), *Critical issues in information systems research* (pp. 363-379). Hoboken, NJ: John Wiley & Sons.

Booth, D., Haas, H., McCabe, F., Newcomer, E., Champion, M., Ferris , C., & Orchard, D. (Eds.). (2004). Web services architecture. *W3C Working Group Note 11 February 2004*. Retrieved October 14, 2006, from http://www.w3.org/TR/ws-arch/

Borja, R. R. (2005). Podcasting craze comes to k-12 schools. *Education Week, 25*(14), 8.

Bote-Lorenzo, M. L., Dimitriadis, Y. A., & Gómez-Sánchez, E. (2003). Grid characteristics and uses: A grid definition. In F. Fernández et al. (Eds.), *European Across Grids Conference* (LNCS 2970, pp. 291-298). Berlin: Springer-Verlag.

Bote-Lorenzo, M.L., Hernández-Leo, D., Dimitriadis, Y. A., Asensio-Pérez, J. I., Gómez-Sánchez, E., Vega-Gorgojo, G. & Vaquero-González, L.M. (2002). Towards reusability and tailorability in collaborative learning systems using IMS-LD and grid services. *International Journal on Advanced Technology for Learning, 1*(3), 129-138.

Boticario, J., & Gaudioso, E. (2000). A multi-agent architecture for a Web-based adaptive educational system. *Tech. Rep. TR SS-00-01*. Retrieved October 10, 2006 from http://citeseer.ist.psu.edu/390570.html

Boticario, J.G., Santos, O.C., Barrera, C., Gaudioso, E., Hernandez, F., Rodriguez, A., van Rosmalen, P.,

& Koper, R. (2004). *Defining adaptive learning design templates for combining design and runtime adaptation in aLFanet*. Retrieved June, 2006, from http://hdl.handle.net/1820/210

Botturi, L., Cantoni, L., Lepori, B., & Tardini, S. (2007). Fast Prototyping as a Communication Catalyst for E-Learing Design. In M. Bullen & D. Janes (Eds.) *Making the transition to e-learning: strategies and issues* (pp. 266-283). Hershey, PA: Information Science Publishing.

Botturi, L., Derntl, M., Boot, E., & Gigl, K. (2006). A Classification Framework for Educational Modeling Languages in Instructional Design. In *Proceedings of the 6ᵗʰ IEEE International Conference on Advanced Learning Technologies (ICALT 2006)*. Kerkrade, The Netherlands.

Bouch, A., Kuchinsky, A., & Bhatti, N. (2000). Quality is in the eye of the beholder: meeting users' requirements for Internet quality of service. *ACM Conference on Human Factors in Computing Systems* (pp. 297-304). Hague, The Netherlands.

Bouras, C. & Tsiatsos, T. (2005). Educational virtual environments: Design rationale and architecture. *Multimedia Tools and Applications Journal*. New York: Kluwer Academic Publishers.

Bourguin, G., Derycke A., & Tarby J.C. (2001). Beyond the interface: Co-evolution inside interactive systems—A proposal founded on activity theory. In J. Vanderdonckt, A. Blandford, & P. Gray, (Eds.), *People and computers XV—Interaction without frontiers* (pp. 297-310). Lille, France.

Boyle, C. & Encarnacion, A. O. (1994). MetaDoc: An adaptive hypertext reading system. *User Models and User Adapted Interaction Journal, 4*(1), 1-19.

Brady, A., Conlan, O., & Wade V. (2004). Dynamic composition and personalization of pda-based e-learning—personalized mlearning. *E-Learn'04 Conference* (pp. 234-242). Washington, USA.

Bransford, J.D., Brown, A.L., & Cocking; R.R. (Eds.). (2000). *How people learn: Brain, mind, experience, and school. Expanded Edition*. Washington, DC: National Academies Press.

Brar, A., & Kay, J. (2005). Privacy and security in ubiquitous personalized applications. In *Proceedings of the UM 2005 Workshop on Privacy-Enhanced Personalization* (pp 47-54). Retrieved October 6, 2006 from http://www.isr.uci.edu/pep05/papers/w9-proceedings.pdf

Briggs, L. L. (2006). Born-again technologies. *T H E Journal, 33*(9), 18-19.

Britain, S. (2004). *A review of learning design: concept, specifications and tools: Report for the JISC e-learning pedagogy programme*. Retrieved September, 2006, from http://www.jisc.ac.uk/uploaded_documents/ACF83C.doc

Brown, J. S., & Burton, R. R. (1978). Diagnostic models for procedural bugs in basic mathematical dkills. *Cognitive Science, 2*, 155-192.

Brusilovsky, P. & Loboda, T. D. (2006). WADEIn II: A case for adaptive explanatory visualization. In M. Goldweber & P. Salomoni (Eds.), *11ᵗʰ Annual Conference on Innovation and Technology in Computer Science Education, ITiCSE'2006* (pp. 48-52). Bologna, Italy: ACM Press.

Brusilovsky, P. & Peylo, C. (2003). Adaptive and intelligent Web-based educational systems. *International Journal of Artificial Intelligence in Education, 13*(2-4), 159-172.

Brusilovsky, P. (1994). Student model centered architecture for intelligent learning environment. In *Fourth International Conference on User Modeling* (pp. 31-36). Hyannis, MA: MITRE.

Brusilovsky, P. (1995). Intelligent learning environments for programming: The case for integration and adaptation. In *Proceedings of the International Conference on Artificial Intelligence in Education, AIED* (pp. 1-7). Washington, US.

Brusilovsky, P. (1996). Methods and techniques of adaptive hypermedia. *User Modeling And User-adapted Interaction Journal, Special Issue: Adaptive Hypertext & Hypermedia, 6*(2-3), 87-129.

Brusilovsky, P. (2000). Adaptive hypermedia: From intelligent tutoring systems to Web-based education (LNCS 1839, pp. 1-7). Berlin/Heidelberg: Springer.

Brusilovsky, P. (2001). Adaptive hypermedia. In A. Kobsa (Ed.) *User Modeling and User Adapted Interaction, Ten Year Anniversary Issue, 11*(1/2), 87-110.

Brusilovsky, P. (2001). WebEx: Learning from examples in a programming course. In W. Fowler & J. Hasebrook (Eds.), *WebNet'2001, World Conference of the WWW and Internet* (pp. 124-129). Orlando, FL: AACE.

Brusilovsky, P. (2004). Knowledge Tree: A Distributed Architecture for Adaptive E-Learning. *Proceedings of the 13ᵗʰ International World Wide Web Conference* (pp. 104-113). New York.

Brusilovsky, P., & Peylo, C. (2003). Adaptive and intelligent Web-based educational systems. In P. Brusilovsky & C. Peylo (Eds.), *International Journal of Artificial Intelligence in Education 13* (2-4), 159-172.

Brusilovsky, P., & Sosnovsky, S. (2005). Individualized exercises for self-assessment of programming knowledge: An evaluation of QuizPACK. *ACM Journal on Educational Resources in Computing, 5*(3), Article No. 6.

Brusilovsky, P., (2001). Adaptive hypermedia. *User Modeling and User-Adapted Interaction Journal, 11*(1-2), 87-110.

Brusilovsky, P., Chavan, G., & Farzan, R. (2004). Social adaptive navigation support for open corpus electronic textbooks. In P. De Bra & W. Nejdl (Eds.), *Third International Conference on Adaptive Hypermedia and Adaptive Web-Based Systems (AH'2004)* (LNCS 3137, pp. 24-33). Eindhoven, the Netherlands: Springer-Verlag.

Brusilovsky, P., Karagiannidis, C., & Sampson, D. (2001). The benefits of layered evaluation of adaptive applications and services. *International Conference on User Modeling, Workshop on Empirical Evaluations of Adaptive Systems* (pp. 1-8). Sonthofen, Germany.

Brusilovsky, P., Ritter, S., & Schwarz, E. (1997). Distributed intelligent tutoring on the Web. In B. du Boulay

& R. Mizoguchi (Eds.), *AI-ED'97, 8ᵗʰ World Conference on Artificial Intelligence in Education* (pp. 482-489). Amsterdam: IOS.

Brusilovsky, P., Schwarz, E., & Weber, G. (1996). *ELM-ART: An intelligent tutoring system on World Wide Web.* Intelligent tutoring systems, Berlin, Springer-Verlag, (LNCS 1086, pp. 261-269).

Brusilovsky, P., Schwarz, E., & Weber, G. (1996). A tool for developing adaptive electronic textbooks on WWW. In H. Maurer (Ed.), *WebNet'96, World Conference of the Web Society* (pp. 64-69). San Francisco: AACE.

Brusilovsky, P., Schwarz, E., & Weber, G. (1996). ELM-ART: An intelligent tutoring system on World Wide Web. In C. Frasson, G. Gauthier & A. Lesgold (Eds.), *Third International Conference on Intelligent Tutoring Systems, ITS-96* (LNCS 1086, pp. 261-269). Berlin: Springer Verlag.

Brusilovsky, P., Sosnovsky, S., & Yudelson, M. (2004). Adaptive hypermedia services for e-learning. On *Workshop on Applying Adaptive Hypermedia Techniques to Service Oriented Environments at the Third International Conference on Adaptive Hypermedia and Adaptive Web-Based Systems (AH'2004)*. Eindhoven, The Netherlands: Technische University Eindhoven.

Bull, G. (2005). Podcasting and the long tail. *Learning and Leading with Technology, 33*(3), 24-25.

Burke, B. & Monson-Haefel, R. (2006). *Enterprise JavaBeans 3.0* (5ᵗʰ ed.). Sebastopol, CA: O'Reilly.

Buschmann, F., Meunier, R., Rohnert, H., Sommerlad, P., & Stahl, M. (1996). *A system of patterns.* Chichester, UK: John Wiley & Sons.

Bussler, C., Fensel, D., & Maedche, A. (2002, December). A conceptual architecture for semantic Web enabled Web services. *SIGMOD Record, 31*(4), 24-49.

Caballé, S., & Xhafa, F. (2003). A study into the feasibility of generic programming for the construction of complex software. In *Proceedings of the 5ᵗʰ Generative Programming and Component Engineering/Net. Objectsdays 2003* (pp. 441-446). Retrieved March 10,

2007, from http://www.old.netobjectdays.org/pdf/03/papers/ws-yrw/441.pdf

Caballé, S., Paniagua, C., Xhafa, F., & Daradoumis, Th. (2005). A grid-aware implementation for providing effective feedback to on-line learning groups. In R. Meersman et al. (Eds.), *On the Move to Meaningful Internet Systems 2005* (LNCS 3762, pp. 274-285). Berlin: Springer-Verlag.

Caballé, S., Xhafa, F., Daradoumis, T., & Marquès, J.M. (2004). Towards a generic platform for developing CSCL applications using grid infrastructure. In *Proceedings of the First International Workshop on Collaborative Learning Applications of Grid Technology.* Chicago: IEEE Computer Society

Cambell, G. (2005). There's something in the air: Podcasting in education. *EDUCAUSE Review, 40*(6), 32-47.

Capuano, N., Carrolagi, P., Combas, J., Crestani, F., Gaeta, M., Herber, E., Sangineto, E., Stefanov, K., & Vergara, M. (2005). Learning design and run-time resource binding in a distributed e-learning environment. In *Proceedings of 1ˢᵗ International Kaleidoscope Learning GRID Special Interest Group Workshop on Distributed e-Learning Environments.*

Capuano, N., Gaeta, M., & Pappacena, L. (2003). An e-Learning platform for SME manager upgrade and its evolution toward a distributed training environment. In *2ⁿᵈ International LeGE-WG Workshop on e-Learning and Grid Technologies: A Fundamental Challenge for Europe.* Paris.

Capuano, N., Gaeta, M., Micarelli, A., & Sangineto, E. (2003, June 28-July 1). An intelligent web teacher system for learning personalization and semantic web compatibility. In *Proceedings of the Eleventh International PEG Conference.* St. Petersburg, Russia.

Carlson, S. (2004). Duke university will give ipod music players to all freshmen (Duke university). *Chronicle of Higher Education, 50*(47), 1.

Carnevale, D. (2005). To size up colleges, students now shop online. *The Chronicle of Higher Education, 51*(40), A25-26.

Caron, P.-A., Le Pallec, X., & Sockeel, S. (2006). Configuring a Web-based tool through pedagogical scenarios. *IADIS Virtual Multi Conference on Computer Science and Information Systems (MCCSIS 2006).*

Caron, P.-A., Derycke, A., & Le Pallec, X. (2005). Bricolage and model driven approach to design distant course. *E learn 2005: World Conference on E-Learning in Corporate Government, Healthcare & Higher Education* (pp. 2856- 2864). Vancouver: Association for the Advancement of Computing in Education (AACE).

Caron, P.-A., Derycke, A., & Le Pallec, X. (2005). The Bricoles project: Support socially informed design of learning environment. In *The Proceedings of the International Conference on Artificial Intelligence in Education (AIED 2005)* (pp. 759-761). Amsterdam: IOS Press.

Caron, P.-A., Le Pallec, X., & Sockeel, S. (2006). Configuring a web-based tool through pedagogical scenarios. In *IADIS Virtual Multi Conference on Computer Science and Information Systems* (MCCSIS 2006).

Carpenter, J., & Bieber, G. (2003). *Openwings component service specification Ver 1.0 Final, 2003.* Retrieved September 19, 2006, from http://www.openwings.org/download/specs/Openwings_Component_Services.pdf

Carr, N. (2006). Keys to effective communications. *American School Board Journal, 193*(8), 40-41.

Cebeci, Z. & Tekdal, M. (2006). Using podcasts as audio learning objects. *Interdisciplinary Journal of Knowledge and Learning Objects, 2,* 47-57.

Celentano, A., & Gaggi, O. (2006). Context-aware design of adaptable multimodal documents. *Multimedia Tools and Applications, 29*(1), 7-28.

Cesarini, M., Monga, M., & Tedesco; R. (2004). Carrying on the e-learning process with a workflow management engine. In *Proceedings of the 2004 ACM Symposium on Applied Computing* (pp. 940-945). New York: ACM Press.

Chan, A., & Lee, M. J. W. (2005). *An mp3 a day keeps the worries away: Exploring the used of podcasting to address preconceptions and alleviate pre-class anxiety amongst undergraduate information technology students.* Paper presented at the Good practice in practice: Proceedings of the Student Experience Conference, Charles Stuart University.

Chan, T. et al. (1997). *Global Education ON the Net.* Berlin: Springer-Verlag.

Chao-Tung, Y. & Hsin-Chuan, H. (2005). An e-Learning platform based on grid architecture. *Journal of Information Science and Engineering, 21*(5), 911-928.

Chen, M.C., Chen, C.T., Cheng, Y.C., & Hsieh, C.Y. (2005, July 5-8). On the development and implementation of a sequencing engine for IMS learning design specification, *5th IEEE International Conference on Advanced Learning Technologies* (pp. 636- 640). Kaohsiung, Taiwan: IEEE Computer Society.

Chen, N. & Shin, Y. (2001). Stream-based lecturing system and its instructional design. In *Proceedings of International Conference of Advanced Learning Technologies* (pp. 94-95).

Chi, E. H., Pirolli, P., Chen, K., & Pitkow, J. (2001). Using information scent to model user information needs and actions on the Web. In *Human Factors in Computing Systems CHI '05 Conference Proceedings* (pp. 490-497). Seattle, WA: ACM Press.

Chi, E., Pirolli, P., & Pitkow, J. (2000). The scent of a site: A system for analyzing and predicting information scent, usage, and usability of a Website. In *Human Factors in Computing Systems CHI 2000 Conference Proceedings* (pp. 161-168). The Hague, Netherlands: ACM Press.

Chikofsky, E. J. & Cross, II J. H. (1990). Reverse engineering and design recovery: A taxonomy. *IEEE Software, 7*(1), 13-17.

Chiku, M. et al. (2001). A dialog visualization tool Gijiroku, *Proceedings of the 62nd Annual Conference of the Information Processing Society of Japan* (pp. 241-244).

Choquet, C. & Iksal, S. (2007). Modeling tracks for the model-driven re-engineering of a TEL system. *Journal of Interactive Learning Research (JILR), 18*(2), 161-184.

Chou, L. D. Wu, C. H., & Lee, S. P. (2004). Position-aware multimedia mobile learning systems in museums. *Web-Based Education Conference* (pp. 416-229). Innsbruck, Austria.

Clancey, W. J. (1984). Methodology for building an intelligent tutoring system. In W. Kintsch, J. R. Miller, & P. G. Polson (Eds.), *Methods and Tactics in Cognitive Science* (pp. 51-84). Hillsdale, NJ: Lawrence Erlbaum Associates.

Clark, J., & DeRose, S. (Eds.). (1999). XML path language (XPath)—version 1.0. *W3C Recommendation 16 November 1999*. Retrieved October 14, 2006, from http://www.w3.org/TR/xpath

Claroline (2007). *The Claroline official website*. Retrieved March, 2007, from http://www.claroline.net/en

Clyde, L. (2005). Some new internet applications coming now to a computer near you. *Teacher Librarian, 33*(1), 54-55.

Collier, G. (2002). E-*Learning Application Infrastructure*. Sun Microsystems White Paper.

Conati, C., Gertner, A., VanLehn, K., & Druzdzel, M. (1997). On-line student modeling for coached problem solving using Bayesian networks. *International Conference on User Modeling (UM97)* (pp. 231-242). Chia Laguna, Italy.

Conlan, O. & Wade, V. (2004). Evaluation of APeLS—an adaptive e-learning service based on the multi-model, metadata-driven approach. *International Conference on Adaptive Hypermedia & Adaptive Web-based Systems (AH2004)* (pp. 291-295). Eindhoven, Netherlands.

Conlan, O. (2005). *The multi-model, metadata driven approach to personalized e-Learning services*. Unpublished doctoral dissertation University of Dublin, Trinity College, Dublin. Retrieved October 10, 2006 from https://www.cs.tcd.ie/Owen.Conlan/publications/Conlan_Thesis.pdf

Conlan, O., Lewis, D., Higel, S., O'Sullivan, D., & Wade, V. (2003). Applying adaptive hypermedia techniques to semantic Web service composition. In *Proceedings of the International Workshop on Adaptive Hypermedia and Adaptive Web-Based Systems (AH 2003)*. Retrieved October 13, 2006 from http://wwwis.win.tue.nl/ah2003/proceedings/paper5.pdf

Conlan, O., Hockemeyer, C., Lefrere, P., Wade, V., & Albert, D. (2001). Extending educational metadata schemas to describe adaptive learning resources. In *Twelfth ACM Conference on Hypertext and Hypermedia (Hypertext 2001)* (pp. 161-162). Aarhus, Denmark: ACM Press.

Conlan, O., Wade, V., Bruen, C., & Gargan, M. (2002). Multi-model, metadata-driven approach to adaptive hypermedia services for personalized eLearning. In P. De Bra, P. Brusilovsky & R. Conejo (Eds.), *Second International Conference on Adaptive Hypermedia and Adaptive Web-Based Systems (AH'2002)* (LNCS 2347, pp. 100-111). Málaga, Spain.

Conlan, O., Wade, V., Gargan, M., Hockemeyer, C., & Albert, D. (2002). An architecture for integrating adaptive hypermedia services with open learning environments. In P. Barker & S. Rebelsky (Eds.), *ED-MEDIA'2002—World Conference on Educational Multimedia, Hypermedia and Telecommunications* (pp. 344-350). Denver, CO: AACE.

Cook, J., Bradley, C., & Franzolini, P. (2004, July 21-26). Gathering Users' Requirements Using the Artifact-Claims-Implication Technique. In *Proceedings of Ed-Media 2004*, Lugano, Switzerland.

CopperCore (2006). *CopperCore platform home page*. Retrieved June, 2006, from http://coppercore.org

Corbiere, A. & Choquet, C. (2004). A model-driven analysis approach for the re-engineering of e-learning systems. In *ICICTE'04* (pp. 242-247). Samos, Greece.

Corbière, A. & Choquet, C. (2004). Designer integration in training cycles: IEEE LTSA model adaptation. *International Conference on Computer Aided Learning in Engineering Education (CALIE 2004)*, Grenoble (pp. 51-62).

CORDRA (2006). *What's "CORDRA"™*. Retrieved June, 2006, from http://cordra.net/docs/info/whatscordra-v1p00/info-whatscordra-v1p00.php

CORDRA: technical introduction and overview. (2004, May 2). *Learning Systems Architecture Lab at Carnegie Mellon University.* Retrieved October 14, 2006, from http://lsal.org/lsal/expertise/projects/cordra/intro/intro-v1p00.html

Crawford, C., Smith, R. A., & Smith, M. S. (2006). *Podcasting in the learning environment: From podcasts for the learning community, towards the integration of podcasts within the elementary learning environment.* Paper presented at the Society for Information Technology and Teacher Education International Conference 2006, Orlando, Florida, USA.

Cristea, A. I. & de Mooij, A. (2003). LAOS: Layered WWW AHS authoring model and their corresponding algebraic operators. *International World Wide Web Conference (WWW'03),* Alternate Track on Education, Budapest, Hungary.

Csikszentmihalyi, M. (1990). *Flow: The psychology of optimal experience.* New York: Harper and Row.

Cumming, G., Okamoto T. & Gomes, L. (1998). *Advanced research in computers in education.* Amsterdam: IOS Press.

Curtis, M., Luchini, K., Bobrowsky, W., Quintana, C., & Soloway, E. (2002). Handheld use in K-12: A descriptive account. In *Proceedings IEEE International Workshop WMTE.*

Czajkowski , K., Ferguson, D.F., Foster, I., Frey, J., Graham, S., Sedukhin, I., Snelling, D., Tuecke, S. & Vambenepe, W. (2005). *The Web services resource framework (WSRF).*

Czarnecki, K. & Helsen, S. (2003). Classification of Model Transformation Approaches. In *Proceedings of the OOPSLA'03 Workshop on the Generative Techniques in the Context Of Model- Driven Architecture.* Anaheim, CA.

Czarnecki, K. (2005). Overview of Generative Software Development, In J.-P. Banâtre et al. (Ed.), *Unconventional Programming Paradigms (UPP) 2004* (LNCS 3566, pp. 313-328). Berlin: Springer-Verlag.

Czarnecki, K., & Eisenecker, U.W. (2000). *Generative programming: Methods, techniques, and applications.* Boston: Addison-Wesley.

Dagger, D., Wade, V., & Conlan, O. (2004). A framework for developing adaptive personalized eLearning. In J. Nall & R. Robson (Eds.), *World Conference on E-Learning, E-Learn 2004* (pp. 2579-2587). Washington, DC: AACE.

Dalziel, J. (2003). *Implementing learning design: The learning activity management system (LAMS).* Retrieved October 27, 2005, from http://www.lamsinternational.com/documents/ASCILITE2003.Dalziel.Final.pdf

Danaher, B., McKay, H., & Seeley J. (2005). The information architecture of behavior change Websites. *Journal of Medical Internet Research. 7*(2), e12.

Daradoumis, T., Martínez, A. & Xhafa, F. (2006). A layered framework for evaluating online collaborative learning interactions. *International Journal of Human-Computer Studies. Special Issue on "Theoretical and Empirical Advances in Groupware Research," 64*(7), 622-635.

Daradoumis, T., Xhafa, F., & Juan Pérez, A. (2005). A framework for assessing self peer and group performance in e-learning. In T.S. Roberts (Ed.), *Self, peer, and group assessment in e-learning* (pp. 279-294). Hershey, PA: Idea Group.

Davenport, T. (1997). *Working knowledge.* Boston: Harvard Business School Press.

David, B.T., & Chalon, R., & Delotte, O. (2005). Model-driven engineering of cooperative systems. In *The Proceedings of the 11th International Conference on Human-Computer Interaction (HCII 2005).* Las Vegas, NV.

Davis, A. (2004). Developing an infrastructure for online learning. In T. Anderson and F. Elloumi (Eds.), *Theory and Practice of Online Learning.* Athabasca University, Athabasca, AB.

Davis, J., Kay, J., Kummerfeld, B., Poon, J., Quigley, A., Saunders, G., & Yacef, K.(2005). Using workflow, user modeling and tutoring strategies for just-in-time document delivery. *Journal of Interactive Learning, 4*, 131-148

DCMI. (2002). *Dublin Core Metadata Initiative.* http://dublincore.org.

De Bra, P. & Calvi, L. (1998). AHA: A generic adaptive hypermedia system. *ACM HYPERTEXT'98 Conference, Workshop on Adaptive Hypertext and Hypermedia* (pp. 5-12). Pittsburgh, USA.

De Bra, P. M. E. (1996). Teaching hypertext and hypermedia through the Web. *Journal of Universal Computer Science, 2*(12), 797-804.

De Bra, P., & Calvi, L. (1998). AHA! An open adaptive hypermedia architecture. *The New Review of Hypertext and Multimedia, 4*, 115-139.

De Bra, P., Brusilovsky, P. & Houben, G.J. (1999). Adaptive hypermedia: From systems to framework. *ACM Computing Surveys, 31*(4).

De Bra, P., Houben, G., & Wu, H. (1999). AHAM: A Dexter-based reference model for adaptive hypermedia. *ACM HYPERTEXT'99 Conference* (pp. 147-156). Germany.

De Bra, P., Houben, G.-J., & Wu, H. (1999). AHAM: A Dexter-based reference model for adaptive hypermedia. In J. Westbomke, U.K. Wiil, J.J. Leggett, K. Tochtermann, & J.M. Haake (Eds.), *Proceedings of the Tenth ACM Conference on Hypertext and Hypermedia* (pp. 147-156). New York, USA: ACM Press.

De Bra, P., Smits, D., & Stash, N. (2006). The Design of AHA! In U.K. Wiil, P.J. Nürnberg, & J. Rubart (Eds.), *HYPERTEXT 2006, Proceedings of the 17th ACM Conference on Hypertext and Hypermedia* (pp. 171-195). Retrieved October 11, 2006 from http://portal.acm.org/citation.cfm?id=1149941.1149942

De Jonge, M. (2005). Build level components. *IEEE Transactions on Software Engineering, 31*(7).

Derntl, M. (in press). coUML: A visual language for modeling cooperative environments. In L. Botturi & T. Stubbs (Eds.), *Handbook of visual languages.*

Derntl, M., & Motschnig-Pitrik, R. (2003). *Patterns for Blended, Person Centred Learning: Strategy, Concepts, Experiences, and Evaluation* (Tech. Rep.). University of Vienna.

Descy, D. (2005). Podcasting: Online media delivery—with a twist. *TechTrends, 49*(5), 4-6.

Devedzic, V. (1999). Using design patterns in ITS development. In S. Lajoie & M. Vivet (Eds.), *Proceedings of the International Conference on Artificial Intelligence in Education, AIED* (pp. 657-659). Amsterdam, Netherlands.

Devedzic, V. (2001). A pattern language for architectures of intelligent tutors. In J. Moore, C. Redfield, & W. Johnson (Eds.), *Proceedings of the International Conference on Artificial Intelligence in Education AIED* (pp. 542-544). San Antonio, TX.

Devedzic, V., & Harrer, A. (2002). Architecural patterns in pedagogical agents. In S. Cerri, G. Gouarderes, & F. Paraguacu (Eds.), *Proceedings of the 6th International. Conference on IntelligentTtutoring Systems ITS* (pp. 81-90). Biarritz, France: Springer.

Devedzic, V., & Harrer, A. (2005). Software patterns in ITS architectures. *International Journal of Artificial Intelligence in Education, 15*(2), 63-94.

Devedzic, V., & Harrer, A. (2005). Software patterns in ITS architecture. *International Journal of Artificial Intelligence in Education, 15*(2), 63-94.

Dewanto, B.-L. (2005). Model-driven architecture (MDA): Integration and model reuse for open source e-learning platforms. *Eleed Journal (E-learning and Education), 1.*

Dewey, J. (1897). My pedagogic creed. *The School Journal, LIV*(3), 77-80.

Dey, A.K. (2001). Understanding and using context. *Personal and Ubiquitous Computing Journal 1*(5), 4-7.

Dicheva, D. & Dichev, C. (2006), Confronting some ontology-building problems in educational topic map authoring. In *Workshop on Applications of Semantic Web Technologies for e-Learning (SW-EL@AH'06)*, Ireland.

Dillenboug, P. (1999). *Collaborative learning, cognitive and computational approaches.* Amsterdam: Pergamon Press.

Dillenbourg, P. (1999). Introduction; What do you mean by "Collaborative Learning?" In P. Dillenbourg (Ed.), *Collaborative learning. Cognitive and computational approaches* (pp. 1-19). Oxford: Elsevier Science.

Dimitrakos, T., Mac Randal, D., Wesner, S., Serhan, B., Ritrovato, P. & Laria, G. (2004). Overview of an architecture enabling grid-based application service provision. In *Proceedings of European Across Grids Conference AxGrid 2004.* Berlin: Springer Verlag (LNCS 3165).

Diogene Web site. (2005). Retrieved from http://www.crmpa.it/diogene

Docent Web Site. Retrieved from http://www.docent.com

Dodero, J.M. & Diaz D. (2006). Model-driven instructional engineering to generate adaptable learning materials. *In IEEE International Conference on Advanced Learning Technologies (ICALT'2006)* (pp. 1188-1189). Kerkrade, The Netherlands.

Dolog, P., Henze, N., Nejdl, W., & Sintek, M. (2004). Personalization in distributed e-learning environments. In *Proceedings of the 13ᵗʰ International World Wide Web Conference* (pp. 170-179).

Dolog, P., Henze, N., Nejdl, W., & Sintek, M. (2004). The personal reader: Personalizing and enriching learning resources using semantic Web technologies. *Lecture Notes in Computer Science, Adaptive Hypermedia and Adaptive Web-Based Systems, Volume 3137/2004* (pp. 85-94). Berlin / Heidelberg: Springer.

Dolonen, J., Chen, W., & Morch, A. (2003). Integrating software agents with FLE3. In B. Wasson, S. Ludvigsen, & U. Hoppe (Eds.), *Proceeding of the International Conference on Computer Supported Collaborative Learning CSCL* (pp. 157-161). New York: Kluwer Academic Publishers.

Draft standard for learning object metadata. (2002, July 15). *Learning technology standards committee of the IEEE.* Retrieved October 14, 2006, from http://ltsc.ieee.org/wg12/files/LOM_1484_12_1_v1_Final_Draft.pdf

Draft standard for learning technology—learning technology systems architecture (LTSA). (2001, November 30). *Learning Technology standards committee of the IEEE.* Retrieved October 14, 2006, from http://ltsc.ieee.org/wg1/files/IEEE_1484_01_D09_LTSA.pdf

Dryden, G. & Vos, J. (2001). *The learning revolution.* London: Network Educational Press Ltd.

Dublin Core Metadata Initiative. (2004, December 20). *Dublin core metadata element set, version 1.1: reference description.* Retrieved October 14, 2006, from http://dublincore.org/documents/dces/

Duffy, T. & Kirkley J. (2004). Learning theory and pedagogy applied in distance learning: The case of Cardean University. In T.M. Duffy J.R. Kirkley (Eds.), *Learner-centered theory and practice in distance education: Cases from higher education* (pp. 107-141). Mahwah, NJ: Erlbaum.

Dusa, A., Deconinck, G., & Belmans, R. (2005). On dependable embedded services and Openwings. In *Proceedings of the International Conference on Next Generation Web Services Practices (NWeSP 2005).* Retrieved February 6, 2007, from http://ieeexplore.ieee.org/iel5/10610/33519/01592440.pdf?arnumber=1592440

Duval E. et al. (2001). The Ariadne knowledge pool system. *Communication of the ACM, 44*(5), 73-78.

Dyson, M.C. & Haselgrove, M. (2001). The influence on reading speed and line length on the effectiveness of reading from screens. *International Journal of Human-Computer Studies, 54,* 585-612.

Earp, J. & Pozzi, F. (2006, December 6-8). Fostering reflection in ICT-based pedagogical planning. In R. Philip, A. Voerman & J. Daziel (Eds.), *Proceedings of the First International LAMS Conference 2006: Designing the Future of Learning* (pp. 35-44).

Eash, E. K. (2006). Podcasting 101. *Computers in Libraries, 26*(4), 16-20.

EduTechWiki. (2007). *Socio-Constructivism*. Retrieved October 20, 2006, from http://edutechwiki.unige.ch/en/Socio-constructivism

Edutools. (2007). Retrieved March, 2007, from http://www.edutools.info/index.jsp?pj=1

ELeGI (2006). *European Learning Grid Infrastructure*. EU IST Research Project. Retrieved from http://www.elegi.org/

Elissavet, G. & Economides, A. A., (2003). An evaluation instrument for hypermedia courseware. *Journal of International Forum of Educational Technology & Society and IEEE Learning Technology Task Force*, 6(2), 31-44.

Elliott, J. (1993). What have we learned from action research in school-based evaluation. *Educational Action Research*, 1(1), 175-186.

Empirix (2003). *Assuring QoE on next generation networks*. White Paper, Retrieved from http://www.empirix.com/Empirix/Corporate/resources/resources+white+papers.html

Endrei, M., Ang, J., Arsanjani, A., Chua, S., Comte, P., Krogdahl, P., et al. (2004). Patterns: Service-oriented architecture and Web services. *IBM Redbook*. Retrieved February 9, 2007, from http://www.redbooks.ibm.com/redbooks/SG246303/

Entwistle, N. (2000). Promoting deep learning through teaching and assessment: conceptual frameworks and educational contexts. In *Proceeding of the TLRP Conference*, Leicester. Retrieved October 14, 2006, from: http://www8.caret.cam.ac.uk/pub/ acadpub/Entwistle2000.pdf

Farance, F., & Tonkel, J. (2001). *LTSA Specification—Learning Technology Systems Architecture, Draft 8*. Retrieved from http://www.edutool.com/ltsa

Farmer, J. (2003, September 1-5). Ad hoc coach system: Supporting task-oriented teaching and learning under time pressure. In M. Rauterberg, M. Menozzi, J. Wesson, (Eds.), *Human-Computer Interaction INTERACT*

'03: IFIP TC13 International Conference on Human-Computer Interaction, Zurich, Switzerland.

Favre, J.M. (2004). Towards a basic theory to model driven engineering. In *3rd Workshop in Software Model Engineering (WiSME 2004)*.

Felder, R. (1993). Reaching the second tier: Learning and teaching styles in college science education. *Journal of College Science Teaching, 23*(5), 286-290.

Felder, R. M. & Silverman, L.K. (1988). Learning and teaching styles in engineering education. *Engineer Education, 78*(7), 674-681.

Felder, R. M. & Soloman, B. A. The Felder and Soloman's *Learning Styles Questionnaire*. Retrieved from http://www.engr.ncsu.edu/learningstyles/ilsweb.html

Feldstein, M., & Masson, P. (2006). Unbolting the chairs: Making learning management systems more flexible. *eLearn Magazine, 1*(2).

Flanagan, B., & Calandra, B. (2005). Podcasting in the classroom. *Learning and Leading with Technology, 33*(3), 20-22, 25.

Forte, E., Forte, M. W., & Duval, E. (1996). ARIADNE: A supporting framework for technology-based open and distance lifelong education. In F. Maffioli, M. Horvat & F. Reichl (Eds.), *Educating the engineer for lofelong learning. SEFI Annual Conference '96* (pp. 137-142). Vienna, Austria.

Fosster, I., Kesselman, C., Nick, J.M. & Tuecke, S. (2002). The Physiology of the Grid: An Open Grid Services Architecture for Distributed Systems Integration. In *Proceedings of 4th Global Grid Forum Workshop*.

Foster, I. (2002). What is the Grid? A Three Point Checklist. *GRID Today*, July.

Foster, I., & Kesselman, C. (1998). *The Grid: Blueprint for a future computing infrastructure*. San Francisco: Morgan Kaufmann.

Foster, I., Kesselman, C. & Tuecke, S. (2001). The anatomy of the grid: Enabling scalable virtual organizations.

International Journal of Supercomputer Applications and High Performance Computing, 200-222.

Fowler, M., Beck, K., Brant, J., Opdyke, W., & Roberts, D. (1999). *Refactoring: Improving the design of existing code*. Boston: Addison-Wesley.

Fröschl, C. (2005). *User modeling and user profiling in adaptive e-learning systems*. Unpublished master's thesis, Graz University of Technology, Graz, Austria. Retrieved September 19, 2006, from http://www.iicm. tu-graz.ac.at/thesis/cfroeschl.pdf

Fryer, W. A. (2005). *Digital definers of the new teacher education*. Texas Tech University.

Furnas, G. (1997). Effective view navigation. In *Human Factors in Computing Systems CHI '97 Conference Proceedings* (pp. 367-374). Atlanta, GA: ACM Press.

Gamma, E., Helm, R., Johnson, R., & Vlissides, J. (1995). *Design patterns: Elements of reusable object-oriented software*. Boston: Addison-Wesley.

García-Barrios, V. M. (2006). Real-time learner modeling: Using gaze-tracking in distributed adaptive e-Learning environments. In M. Cicin-Sain, I.T. Prstacic & I. Sluganovic (Eds.), *Proceedings of the international Convention MIPRO 2006 (CE)* (pp. 185-190).

García-Barrios, V. M. (2006). Adaptive e-Learning systems: Retrospection, opportunities and challenges. In *Proceedings of the International Conference on Information Technology Interfaces (ITI 2006)*.

García-Barrios, V. M., Gütl, C., & Mödritscher, F. (2004). EHELP—Enhanced E-Learning Repository: The use of a dynamic background library for a better knowledge transfer process. In M. Auer & U. Auer (Eds.), *Proceedings of the International Conference on Interactive Computer Aided Learning (ICL 2004)*.

Garrison, D.R., Anderson, T. & Archer, W. (2001). Critical thinking, cognitive presence, and computer conferencing in distance education. *American Journal of Distance Education, 15*(1), 7-23.

Gašević, D., Djurić, D., & Devedžić, V. (2006). *Model-driven architecture and ontology development*. New York: Springer.

GenDep. (2006), ModX and *GenDep Web site*. Retrieved September, 2006, from http://noce.univ-lille1. fr/projets/ModX/

Georgiev, T., Georgieva, E., & Smrikarov, A. (2004). M-learning—A new stage of e-learning. In *Proceedings CompSysTech 2004*.

Ghelman, R., Siqueira, S. W. M., & Melo, R. N. (2006). Providing accessibility to distributed and heterogeneous learning objects. In E. C. Zambrano & R. P. C. Nascimento (Eds.), *Euro-American Conference on Telematics and Information Systems (EATIS 2006)*. Accessibility and internationalization of Web-based information systems (pp. 150-156).

Gleeson, G. (2006). *The Investigation of Grid Architectures in the Context of E-Learning*. Project Report.

Globus (2006). *Globus Toolkit GT4*. Retrieved from http://www.globus.org/toolkit/

Globus (2006). *Information Services (MDS): Key Concepts*. Retrieved from http://www-unix.globus.org/toolkit/docs/4.0/info/keyindex.html

Goldstein, I. P. (1970). *Overlays: A theory of modelling for computer aided instruction* (Tech. Rep. No. AI Memo 406). Cambridge, MA: MIT.

Gomes, G. R. R., Siqueira, S. W. M., Braz, M. H. L. B., & Melo, R. N. (2005). LORDiLIS: integrating learning objects repositories and digital libraries. In *PGL Conference: Vol. 3. Consolidating eLearning Experiences*. Sao Paulo: Getulio Vargas Foundation.

Gomes, G. R. R., Siqueira, S. W. M., Braz, M. H. L. B., & Melo, R. N. (2006). Integrated searches over digital libraries and e-learning systems. *In WCCSETE 2006 Congresso Mundial de Educação em Engenharia, Tecnologia e Ciência da Computação*. Itanhaém / Santos.

Gomes, G. R. R., Siqueira, S. W. M., Braz, M. H. L. B., & Melo, R. N. (2006). Integrated access to learning objects repositories and digital libraries. In *IRMA International Conference: Vol. 17. Emerging Trends and Challenges in Information Technology Management* (pp. 736-739). Hershey, PA: IRM Press.

Gordon-Murnane, L. (2005). Saying "I do" To podcasting. *Searcher, 13*(6), 44-51.

Gowthaman, K., Mustafa, K., & Khan, R. A. (2005). Re-engineering legacy source code to model-driven architecture. In *Proceedings of the 4th Annual ACIS International Conference on Computer and Information Science (ICIS)*.

Graf, F. & Schnaider, M. (1997). IDEALS MTS—EIN modulares Training System für die Zukunft. On *8. Arbeitstreffen der GI-Fachgruppe 1.1.5/7.0.1 "Intelligent Lehr-/Lernsysteme*. München: Technische Universität München.

Graff, M. (2003). Cognitive style and attitudes towards using online learning and assessment methods. *Electronic Journal of e-Learning, 1*(1), 21-28.

Grandbastien, M., Oubahssi, L., & Claës, G. (2003). A process-oriented approach for modelling online learning environments. In *Intelligent Management Systems, AIED2003 supplemental proceedings, volume 4* (pp. 140-152). University of Sydney pub., Retrieved March, 2007, from http://www.cs.usyd.edu.au/~aied/vol4/vol4_oubahssi.pdf

Greller, W. (2005). Managing IMS learning design. *Journal of Interactive Media in Education, 2005*(12).

Grew, P., & E. Pagani, E. (2005). Towards a wireless architecture for mobile ubiquitous e-Learning. In *Proceedings of the International Workshop on Learning Communities in the Era of Ubiquitous Computing* (pp. 20-29).

Grew, P., & Pagani, E. (2006). Channeling the bricks-and-mortar lesson onto students' devices. In *Proceedings of the IASTED International Conference on Web-Based Education*.

Grew, P., Giudici, F., & Pagani, E. (2006). Specification of a functional architecture for e-Learning supported by wireless technologies. In *Proceedings of the 2nd IEEE International Workshop on Pervasive Learning*.

Grew, P., Longhi, I., & Pagani, E. (2005). Functional architecture of a Web-based distributed system for University Curricula Support. In *Proceedings of the IASTED International Conference on Web-Based Education* (pp. 332-337).

Grew, P., Longhi, I., Pagani, E., De Cindio, F., & Ripamonti, L. (2004). An open-source LMS evolves as learning/teaching/testing environment. In *Proceedings of the International Conference on Technology-Enhanced Learning (TEL'04)*.

Griffiths, D. & Blat, J. (2005). The role of teachers in editing and authoring units of learning using IMS learning design. *International Journal on Advanced Technology for Learning, Special Session on "Designing Learning Activities: From Content-based to Context-based Learning Services," 2*(4).

Grigoriadou, M., Papanikolaou, K., Kornilakis, H., & Magoulas, G. (2001). INSPIRE: An intelligent system for personalized instruction in a remote environment. *Adaptive Hypertext and Hypermedia Workshop*. Sonthofen, Germany.

Griswold, W., Boyer, R., & Brown, S. et al. (2002). *ActiveCampus—Sustaining educational communities through mobile technology*. UCSD CSE Technical Report #CS2002-0714, University of California, San Diego.

Grob, H L., Bensberg, F., & Dewanto, B L. (2003). Model-driven architecture (MDA): Integration and model reuse for open source e-learning platforms. *E-learning and education (eleed) Journal*. Retrieved from http://eleed.campussource.de/

Grob, H. L., Bensberg, F, & Lofi Dewanto, B. (2006). Model-driven architecture (MDA): Integration and model reuse for open source e-learning platforms. *Eleed. Digital peer publishing*. Retrieved from http://eleed.campussource.de/archive/1/81/

Grob, H. L., Bensberg, F., & Dewanto, B. L. (2004). Developing, deploying, using and evaluating an open source learning management system. *Journal of Computing and Information Technology 12*(2), 127-134.

Growth in virtual learning, data management, blogging and podcasting expected in 2006. (2006). *Electronic Education Report* Retrieved 2, 13.

Gruber, T.R. (2001, September 8). What is an ontology? *Knowledge systems, AI laboratory, Stanford University.* Retrieved October 14, 2006, from http://www-ksl.stanford.edu/kst/what-is-an-ontology.html

Gudgin, M., Hadley, M., Mendelsohn, N., Moreau, J. J., & Nielsen, H, F. (Eds.). (2003). SOAP version 1.2 part 1: messaging framework. *W3C recommendation 24 June 2003.* Retrieved October 14, 2006, from http://www.w3.org/TR/soap12-part1/

Gudgin, M., Hadley, M., Mendelsohn, N., Moreau, J. J., & Nielsen, H, F. (Eds.). (2003). SOAP version 1.2 part 2: adjuncts. *W3C Recommendation 24 June 2003.* Retrieved October 14, 2006, from http://www.w3.org/TR/soap12-part2/

Gunawardena, C. N. (2004). The Challenge of Designing Inquiry-based Online Learning Environments: Theory into Practice. In T. Duffy and J. Kirkley (Eds.), *Learner centered theory and practice in distance education: Cases from higher education* (pp. 143-158). Mahwah, NJ: Lawrence Erlbaum Associates.

Gütl, C., & García-Barrios, V.M. (2005). The application of concepts for learning and teaching. In M. Auer & U. Auer (Eds.), *Proceedings of the International Conference on Interactive Computer Aided Learning (ICL 2005).*

Gütl, C., & García-Barrios, V.M. (2005). Towards an advanced modeling system applying a service-based approach. In P. Goodyear, D. Sampson, D.J. Yang, Kinshuk, T. Okamoto, R. Hartley, & N. Chen (Eds.), *Proceedings of the IEEE International Conference on Advanced Learning Technologies (ICALT 2005)* (pp. 860-862). IEEE Computer Society Press.

Gütl, C., & Mödritscher, F. (2005). Towards a generic adaptive system applicable for Web-based learning management environments. In A. Jedlitschka & B. Brandherm (Eds.), *Proceedings of the Annual Workshop of the SIG*

Adaptivity and User Modeling Interactive Systems (ABIS 2005) (pp. 26-31).

Gütl, C., García-Barrios, V. M., & Mödritscher, F. (2004). Adaptation in e-Learning environments through the service-based framework and its application for AdeLE. In J. Nall & R. Robson (Eds.), *Proceedings of the World Conference on E-Learning in Corporate, Government, Healthcare, and Higher Education (E-Learn 2004)* (pp. 1891-1898).

Gütl, C., Pivec, M., Trummer, C., García-Barrios. V. M., Mödritscher, M., Pripfl, J., et al. (2005). AdeLE (Adaptive e-Learning with Eye-Tracking): Theoretical background, system architecture and application scenarios. *European Journal of Open, Distance and E-Learning (EURODL), 2005, 2.* Retrieved October 13, 2006, from http://www.eurodl.org/materials/briefs/2005/Christian_Gutl_GBA.htm

Gutwin, C., Stark, G., & Greenberg, S. (1995). Support for workspace awareness in educational groupware. In J. L. Schnase & E. L. Cunnius (Eds.) *ACM Conference on Computer Supported Collaborative Learning* (pp. 147-156). Mahwah, NJ: Lawrence Erlbaum Associates.

Guzdial, M., Rick, J., & Kehoe, C. (2001). Beyond adoption to invention: Teacher-created collaborative activities in higher education. *Journal of the Learning Sciences, 10*(3), 265-279.

Hädrich, T & Priebe, T. (2005). Supporting knowledge work with knowledge stance-oriented integrative portals. In *Proceedings of the Thirteenth European Conference on Information Systems.*

Hagen, K., Hibbert, D., Kinshuk. (2006, July 5-7). Developing a Learning Management System based on the IMS learning design Specification, *Sixth International Conference on Advanced Learning Technologies (ICALT'06)* (pp. 420-424).

Hargis, J., & Wilson, D. Fishing for learning with a podcast net.

Harrer A., McLaren, B.M., Walker, E., Bollen, L., Sewall, J. (2006) Creating cognitive tutors for collaborative learning: Steps toward realization. User modeling and user-adapted interaction. *The Journal of Personalization Research, 16,* 175-209.

Harrer, A. (1997). Both sides of the coin—Blending cognitive and motivational aspects into a tutoring strategy. In T. Ottmann, Z. Halim, & Z. Razak (Eds.), *Proceedings of the International Conference on Computers in Education, ICCE* (pp. 188-195). Kuching, Malaysia.

Harrer, A. (2000). *Unterstützung von Lerngemeinschaften in verteilten intelligenten Lernsystemen.* Doctoral dissertation, Universität München, München, Germany.

Harrer, A. (2003). Software engineering methods for re-use of components and eesign in educational systems. *International Journal on Computers and Applications, Special Issue on Intelligence and Technology in Educational Applications, 25*(1).

Harrer, A., Malzahn, N., & Roth, B. (2006). The Remote Control Approach—How to Apply Scaffolds to Existing Collaborative Learning Environments. In Y. Dimitriadis, I. Zigurs, & E. Gomez-Sanchez (Eds.), *Proceeding of CRIWG* (Vol. LNCS 4154, pp. 118-131). Berlin: Springer.

Harrer, A., Malzahn, N., Hoeksema, K., & Hoppe, U. (2005). Learning design engines as remote control to learning support environments. *Journal of Interactive Media in Education (Advances in learning design. Special Issue), 2005*(05).

Harrer, A., McLaren, B., Walker, E., Bollen, L., & Sewell, J. (2005). Collaboration and cognitive tutoring: Integration, empirical results, and future directions. In C.-K. Looi, G. McCalla, B. Bredeweg, & J. Breuker (Eds.), *Proceedings of the International Conference on Artificial Intelligence in Education AIED* (Vol. 125, pp. 266-273). Amsterdam: IOS Press.

Harris, J. (2002). *An Introduction to Authoring Tools.* ASTD's Learning Circuits online magazine, Retrieved October 20, 2006, from http://www.learningcircuits. org/2002/mar2002/harris

Hayes, R. (2000). Exploring Discount Usability Methods to Assess the Suitability of Online Course Delivery Products. *The Internet and Higher education, 2*(2-3), 119-134.

Heines, J. M. (2000). Evaluating the effect of a course Web site on student performance. *Journal of Computing in Higher Education, 12*(1), 57-83.

Helic, D. (2006). Technology-supported management of collaborative learning processes. *International Journal of Learning and Change, 1*(3), 285-298.

Henricksen, K. & Indulska, J. (2006). Developing context-aware pervasive computing applications: Models and approach. *Journal of Pervasive and Mobile Computing, 2*(1), 37-64.

Heppell, S. (2006). Pushing podcasts. *The Times Educational Supplement,* 82.

Hernández-Leo, D., Villasclaras-Fernández, E. D., Asensio-Pérez, J. I. , Dimitriadis Y., Jorrín-Abellán, I. M., Ruiz-Requies, I., & Rubia-Av, B. (2006). COLLAGE: A collaborative learning design editor based on patterns. *Journal of Educational Technology & Society, 9*(1), 58-71.

Herremans, A. (1995). *Studies #02 New Training Technologies.* UNESCO Paris, ILO International Training Centre.

Herrmann, K., Hoppe, U., & Pinkwart, N. (2003). A checking mechanism for visual language environments. In U. Hoppe, F. Verdejo, & J. Kay (Eds.), *Proceedings of the 11th International Conference on Artificial Intelligence in Education, AIED* (pp. 97-104). Amsterdam: IOS Press.

Huberman, B., Pirolli, P., Pitkow, J., & Lukose, R. (1998). Strong Regularities in World Wide Web Surfing. *Science, 280*(5360), 95-97.

Hui, S. (2000). *Video-On-Demand in Education.* Retrieved from http://www.cityu.edu.hk/~ccncom/net14/vod2. htm

Hummel, H., Manderveld, J., Tattersal, C., & Koper, R. (2004). Educational modelling language and learning design: New opportunities for instructional reusability and personalised learning. *International Journal of Learning Technology*, *1*(1), 111-126.

Hyperwave. (2006). E-Learning Suite (eLS). Learning Management System (LMS). Retrieved February 6, 2007, from http://www.hyperwave.com/e/products/elearning_suite

I.P.O.C. ('ipods on campus'). (2006). *BizEd*, *5*(2), 46, 48.

Ibrahim, H. (2001). *Examining the impact of the guided constructivist teaching method on students' misconceptions about concepts of Newtonian physics*. University of Central Florida, Orlando, Florida.

IEEE (2003). IEEE 1484.1 IEEE Standard for Learning Technology Systems Architecture (LTSA).

IEEE 802.11 (1999). Part 11: Wireless LAN Medium Access Control (MAC) & Physical Layer (PHY) Specifications, IEEE standard 802.11.

IEEE 802.16 (2004). Part 16: Air Interface for Fixed Broadband Wireless Access Systems, IEEE standard 802.16.

IEEE LOM 2002. *IEEE Standard for Learning Object Metadata*.

IEEE LTCS WG12 (Artist). (2002). *IEEE Standard for Learning Object Metadata*.

IEEE, (2000). Draft Standard for Learning Technology—Public and Private Information (PAPI) for Learner. *IEEE P1484.2/D6*. Retrieved from http://ltsc.ieee.org/

IEEE-LTSA draft 9. (2001). *Draft Standard for Learning Technology—Learning Technology System Architecture*. IEEE LTSC pub.

IEEE-LTSC. (2007). Retrieved March, 2007, from http://ieeeltsc.org

Ikeda, M., & Mizoguchi, R. (1994). FITS—A framework for an ITS—A computational model of tutoring. *Journal of Artificial Intelligence in Education, 5*(3), 319-348.

Illmann, T., Martens, A., Seitz, A., & Weber, M. (2000). A pattern-oriented design of a Web-based and case-oriented multimedia training system in medicine. *In Proceedings of the 4th World Conference on Integrated Design & Process Technology*. Dallas, USA.

Illmann, T., Martens, A., Seitz, A., & Weber, M. (2001). Structure of training cases in Web-based case-oriented training systems. In K. Okamoto T. Hartley R. & K. J. (Eds.), *ICALT 2001—IEEE International Conference on Advanced Learning Technologies*. IEEE Computer Society.

IMS (2003). *IMS learning design information model—version 1.0*. IMS Global Learning Consortium, Inc. Retrieved from http://www.imsglobal.org/learningdesign/index.html

IMS (2003). *IMS learning design version 1.0 final specification*. Technical report.

IMS AccessForAll Meta-data Overview. (2004, July 12). *IMS Global Learning Consortium, Inc.* Retrieved October 14, 2006, from http://www.imsglobal.org/accessibility/accmdv1p0/imsaccmd_oviewv1p0.html

IMS Global Learning Consortium (2001). *IMS Content Packaging Best Practice Guide Version 1.1.2*. IMS.

IMS Learner Information Package Summary of Changes; (2005, January 4). *IMS Global Learning Consortium, Inc.* Retrieved October 14, 2006, from http://www.imsglobal.org/profiles/lipv1p0p1/imslip_sumcv1p0p1.html

IMS Learning Design Information Model, Version 1.0 (2003). IMS Global Learning Consortium Inc. Retrieved from http://www.imsglobal.org/learningdesign

IMS Learning Resource Meta-Data Information Model—Version 1.2.1 Final Specification; (2001, September 28). *IMS Global Learning Consortium*. Retrieved October 14, 2006, from http://www.imsglobal.org/metadata/imsmdv1p2p1/imsmd_infov1p2p1.html

IMS Question and Test Interoperability Overview. (2005, January 24). *IMS Global Learning Consortium, Inc.* Retrieved October 14, 2006, from http://www.imsglobal.org/question/qti_v2p0/imsqti_oviewv2p0.html

IMS. (2003). IMS learning design information model—version 1.0. *IMS Global Learning Consortium, Inc.*

Retrieved September, 2006, from http://www.imsglobal. org/learningdesign/index.html

IMS. (2003). *IMS—Instructional Management Systems—Global Learning Consortium—Version 1.0*, Final Specification, Draft 2003. Retrieved from http://www. imsproject.org/profiles/index.html

IMS. (2004). Enterprise services specification—version 1.0 final specification. *IMS Global Learning Consortium, Inc.*, Retrieved September, 2006, from http://www.ims-global.org/es/index.html

Inaba, A. & Okamoto, T. (1997). Negotiation process model for intelligent discussion coordinating system on CSCL environment. In *Proceedings of the AIED 97* (pp. 175-182).

Inaba, A., Ikeda, M., & Mizoguchi, R. (2003). What learning patterns are effective for a learner's growth?—An ontological support for designing collaborative learning. In *Proceedings of the International Conference on Artificial Intelligence in Education* (pp. 219-226). Sydney, Australia.

Inaba, A., Ohkubo, R., Ikeda, M., Mizoguchi, R. & Toyoda, J. (2001). An instructional design support environment for CSCL, artificial intelligence in education—AI-ED in the wired and wireless future. In J.D. Moore, C. Redfield & W.L. Johnson (Eds.), *Frontiers in Artificial Intelligence and Applications*, 68 (pp. 130-141).

Isakson, C. (2006). Podcasts in education. *The Education Digest, 71*(8), 79-80.

Ishizuka, K. (2005). Tell me a story. *School Library Journal, 51*(9), 24-25.

ISO-IEC JTC1 SC36. (2004). *SC36 HomePage*. Retrieved from http://jtc1sc36.org/

Ivory, M.Y., Sinha, R.R., & Hearst, M.A. (2001). Empirically validated Web page design metrics. In *Human Factors in Computing Systems CHI'01* (pp. 53-60). Seatle, WA: ACM Press.

Jacobs, L. C. & Chase, C. I., (Eds.). (1992). *Developing and using tests effectively: A guide for faculty.* San Francisco: Jossey-Bass.

Jansen, M. (2003). Matchmaker—A framework to support collaborative Java applications. In U. Hoppe, F. Verdejo, & J. Kay (Eds.), *Proceedings of the 11th International Conference on Artificial Intelligence in Education AIED* (pp. 529-530). Amsterdam: IOS Press.

JLI! Development Group (2005). *JLI!—Just Learn It! Home Page.* Retrieved from http://jli.retecivica.milano. it/index.php

JLI! Development Group (2005). JLI!—Just Learn It! *SourceForge Project.* Retrieved from http://sourceforge. net/projects/jli/

Johnson, W. L., Rickel, J., & Lester, J. (2000). Animated pedagogical agents: Face-to-face interaction in interactive learning environments. *International Journal of Artificial Intelligence in Education, 11.*

Kadel, R. (2006). Coursecasting: The wave of the future? *Learning and Leading with Technology, 33*(5), 48-49.

Kaleidoscope (2006). *Kaleidoscope.* EU IST Research Project. Retrieved from http://www.noe-kaleidoscope. org/

Kaplan, E. (2006). Trend: Podcasting in academic and corporate learning. *Learning Circuits.*

Kaplan-Leiserson, E. (2002). Glossary. American society for training & development (ASTD) *Online Magazine All About E-Learning.* Retrieved from http://www. learningcircuits.org/glossary.html

Kapur, G. (2004). *Project management for information, technology, business and certification.* Upper Saddle River, NJ: Prentice Hall.

Karagiannidis, C., Sampson, D., & Brusilovsky, P. (2001). Layered evaluation of adaptive and personalized educational applications and services. *International Conference on Artificial Intelligence in Education, Workshop on Assessment Methods in Web-based Learning Environments and Adaptive Hypermedia* (pp. 21-29). San Antonio, TX.

Karampiperis, P. & Sampson, O. (2005). Adaptive learning resources sequencing in educational hypermedia systems. *Educational Technology & Society, 8*(4), 128-147.

Katsanos, C., Tselios, N., & Avouris, N. (2006). *InfoScent Evaluator: A semi-automated tool to evaluate hyperlinks' semantic appropriateness of a Web site.* In J. Kjeldskov & J. Paay (Eds.), Proceedings of OZCHI 2006 (pp. 373-376). Sydney: ACM Press.

Katz, M. , & Byrne, M. (2003). Effects of Scent and Breadth on Use of Site Specific Search on E-commerce Websites. *ACM Transactions on Computer-Human Interaction, 10*(3), 198-220.

Kay, J & Kummerfeld, R. J. (1994). An Individualised course for the C programming language. *International World Wide Web Conference.* Chicago.

Kay, J. (2000). Stereotypes, student models and scrutability. *Lecture Notes in Computer Science, Intelligent Tutoring Systems, Volume 1839/2000* (pp. 19-30). Berlin / Heidelberg: Springer.

Kay, J., Kummerfeld, B., & Lauder, P. (2002). Personis: A server for user modeling. In P. De Bra, P. Brusilovsky & R. Conejo (Eds.), *Second International Conference on Adaptive Hypermedia and Adaptive Web-Based Systems (AH'2002)* (LNCS 2347, pp. 203-212). Málaga, Spain.

Kaye, R. (1994). Computer supported collaborative learning in a multi-media distance education environment. In C.E. O'Malley (Ed.), *Computer Supported Collaborative Learning* (pp. 125-143). Berlin: Springer-Verlag.

Kent, S. (2002). Model-Driven Engineering. *In Proceedings of IFM 2002* (LNCS 2335, pp. 286-298). Berlin Heidelberg: Springer-Verlag.

Kiczales, G., des Rivières, J., & Bobrow, D. (1991). *The art of the Metaobject Protocol.* Cambridge, MA: The MIT Press.

Kinshuk, Sampson, D.G., Patel, A., & Oppermann, R. (Eds). (2006). Special issue: Current research in learning design. *Journal of Educational Technology & Society, 9*(1).

Kirkpatrick, D. (1994). *Evaluating Training Programs.* San Francisco: Berrett-Koehler.

Kitajima, M. & Polson, P. (1997). A comprehension-based model of exploration, *Human-Computer Interaction, 12*, 345-389.

Kitamura, Y. & Mizoguchi, R. (2003, March 12). An ontological schema for sharing conceptual engineering knowledge. In *Proceedings of the International Workshop on Semantic Web Foundations and Application Technologies* (pp. 25-28). Nara, Japan.

Kleppe, A., Warmer, J., & Bast, W. (2003). *MDA explained.* Boston: Addison-Wesley.

Kobsa, A. (2001). Generic user modeling systems. *Journal of User Modeling and User-Adapted Interaction, 11*(1-2), 49-63.

Koch, N., & Rossi, G. (2002). Patterns for adaptive Web applications. In *Proceedings of the Seventh European Conference on Pattern Languages of Programs* (pp. 179-194). Universitätsverlag Konstanz.

Kolbitsch, J., & Maurer, H. (2006). The transformation of the Web: How emerging communities shape the information we consume. *Journal of Universal Computer Science, 12*(2), 187-213.

Koper, R. & Oliver, B. (2004). Representing learning design of units of learning. *Educational Technology & Society, 7*(3), 97-111.

Koper, R. & Tattersall, C. (Eds.). (2005). *Learning design: A handbook on modelling and delivering networked education and training.* New York: Springer.

Koper, R. (2003). Combining re-usable learning, resources and services to pedagogical purposeful units of learning. In A. Littlejohn (Ed.), *Reusing online resources: A sustainable approach to eLearning* (pp. 46-59). London: Kogan Page.

Koper, R., & Tattersall, C. (2005). *Learning design: A handbook on modelling and delivering networked education and training.* Berlin: Springer-Verlag.

Koschmann, T. (1996). Paradigm shifts and instructional technology: An introduction. In T. Koschmann (Ed.), *CSCL: Theory and practice of an emerging paradigm* (pp. 1-23). Mahwah, NJ: Lawrence Erlbaum Associates.

Koyanl S., Balley R., & Nall J., (2004). *Research-Based Web Design & Usability Guidelines*. USA: Computer Psychology.

Kreger, H.: Web Services—Conceptual Architecture (WSCA 1.0) (2001, May). *IBM Software Group*. Retrieved October 14, 2006, from http://www.ibm.com/software/solutions/webservices/pdf/WSCA.pdf

Kuhn, T. (1962). *The structure of scientific revolutions*. University of Chicago Press.

Kurtev, I. (2005). *Adaptability of model transformations*. PhD Thesis. University of Twente, The Netherlands.

Kurtev, I., Bézivin, J., & Aksit, M. (2002). Technological spaces: An initial appraisal. *CoopIS, DOA'2002 Federated Conferences*. Irvine, CA: Industrial track.

Laforcade, P. (2005). Towards a UML-based educational modeling language. In *Proceedings of the IEEE International Conference on Advanced Learning Technologies ICALT'05* (pp. 855-859). Kaohsiung, Taiwan.

Laforcade, P. (2007). Graphical representation of abstract learning scenarios: The UML4LD experimentation. In *Proceedings of the IEEE International Conference on Advanced Learning Technologies ICALT'07*, Niigata, Japan.

Laforcade, P., Barbier, F., Nodenot, T., & Sallaberry, C. (2003). Profiling co-operative problem-based learning situations. In *Proceedings of the 2nd IEEE International Conference on Cognitive Informatics (ICCI'2003)*. London: IEEE Computer Society Press.

Landauer, T. & Dumais, S. (1997). A solution to Plato's problem: The Latent Semantic Analysis theory of acquisition, induction, and representation of knowledge. *Psychological Review, 104*, 211-240.

Landers, P. (2002). *Leonardo da Vinci Project—Home Page*. Retrieved from http://learning.ericsson.net/mlearning2/project_one/index.html

Landers, P. (2002). *M-learning Initiatives in 2001*. Retrieved from http://learning.ericsson.net/mlearning2/project_one/thebook/chapter4.html

Laria, G. (2005). Learning GRID Scenarios. *Kaleidoscope Learning GRID newsletter, 3*. Kaleidoscope.

Laurillard, D. (1993). *Rethinking University Teaching. A framework for the effective use of educational technology*. London: Routledge.

Lave, J. & Wenger, E. (1991). Situated *learning: Legitimate peripheral participation*. Cambridge, MA: Cambridge University Press.

Lavrin, A., & Zelko, M. (2005). Knowledge sharing in digital ecosystems for small and medium enterprises. In *Proceedings of the 13th Interdisciplinary Information Management Talks (IDIMT-2005)*. Retrieved October 7, 2006, from http://www.sea.uni-linz.ac.at/conferences/idimt2005/session_f.pdf

Le Pallec, X., de Moura Filho, C., Marvie, R., Nebut, M., & Tarby, J.-C., (2006). Supporting generic methodologies to assist IMS-LD modeling. *The 6th IEEE International Conference on Advanced Learning Technologies (ICALT'2006)* (pp. 923-927).

Le Pallec, X., Renaux, E., & Moura, C. O. (2005). ModX. In *Tools Exhibition in European Conference on Model Driven Architecture—Foundations and Applications*. Nuremberg, Germany.

Learning Technology Standardization Committee (LTSC) Web Site. Retrieved from http://ltsc.ieee.org/wg12/index.html

Leech, G., Rayson, P., & Wilson, A. (2001). *Word Frequencies in Written and Spoken English: Based on the British National Corpus*. Retrieved May 2003, from htpp://www.comp.lancs.ac.uk/ucrel/bncfreq.

Lelouche, R. (1999). Intelligent tutoring systems from birth to now. *KI -Künstliche Intelligenz, 4*, 5-11.

Lemire, D., Boley, H., McGrath, S., & Ball, M. (2005). Collaborative filtering and inference rules for context-aware learning object recommendation. *International Journal of Interactive Technology and Smart Education, 2*.

Levesque, K., Lauen, D., Teitelbaum, P., Alt, M., Librera, S., & Nelson, D. (2000). *Vocational education in the United States: Toward the Year 2000*. Washington, DC:

U.S. Department of Education, Office of Educational Research and Improvement.

Library of Congress. (2000). Network Development and MARC Standards Office. MARC21 format for bibliographic data: including guidelines for content designation. 2000 ed.

Licklider, J.C.R. (1968). The computer as a communication device. *Science and Technology*.

Lim, K. Y. T. (2005). *Now hear this—exploring podcasting as a tool in geography education*.

Lin, D. (2004). Evaluating older adults' retention in hypertext perusal: Impacts of presentation media as a function of text topology. *Computers in Human Behavior, 20*(4), 491-503.

Lingnau, A., Kuhn, M., Harrer, A., Hofmann, D., Fendrich, M., & Hoppe, U. (2003). Enriching traditional classroom scenarios by seamless integration of interactive media. In V. Devedzic, J. Spector, D. Sampson, & Kinshuk (Eds.), *Proceedings of the International Conference on Advanced Learning Technologies ICALT* (pp. 135-139). Los Alamitos, CA.

Loh, M.-P., Wong, Y.-P., & Wong, C.-O. (2005). Facial expression analysis in e-Learning systems—The problems and feasibility. In P. Goodyear, D. Sampson, D.J. Yang, Kinshuk, T. Okamoto, R. Hartley, & N. Chen (Eds.), *Proceedings of the IEEE International Conference on Advanced Learning Technologies (ICALT 2005)* (pp. 442-446). IEEE Computer Society Press.

Loidl, S. (2006). Towards pervasive learning: WeLearn. Mobile. A CPS package viewer for handhelds. *Journal of Network and Computer Applications archive, 29*(4), 277 -293.

Lotus LearningSpace Web Site. Retrieved from http://www.pugh.co.uk/Products/lotus/learningspace.htm.

LTSC. (2002). IEEE LTSC, Draft Standard for Learning Object Metadata. *IEEE 1484*(12), 1-2002.

LTSC—Learning technology standards committee (2002). *IEEE standard for learning object metadata specification*.

Lum, L. (2006). The power of podcasting. *Diverse Issues in Higher Education, 23*(2), 32-35.

Lundgren-Cayrol, K., Marino, O., Paquette, G., Léonard, M., & de la Teja, I. (2006). Implementation and deployment process of IMS learning design: Findings from the Canadian IDLD research project. *Proceedings of the Sixth International Conference on Advanced Learning Technologies (ICALT 2006)* (pp. 581-585).

Lyardet, F., Rossi, G., & Schwabe, D. (1998). Using design patterns in educational multimedia applications. In *Proceeding of ED-MEDIA'98*, Friburg, Germany. Retrieved October 14, 2006, from http://www.inf.puc-rio.br/~schwabe/papers/edmedia98.pdf

Malkin, G. (1998). Routing Information Protocol (RIP)—Version 2. *RFC 2453*. Work in progress.

Manes, A.T. (2001, March 12). Enabling open, interoperable, and smart Web services—the need for shared context. *World Wide Web Consortium*. Retrieved October 14, 2006, from http://www.w3.org/2001/03/WSWS-popa/paper29

Manninen, J., Nevgi, A., Matikainen, J., Luukannel, S. & Porevuo, M. (2000). *Ohjelman tuottamat pedagogiset ja teknologiset innovaatiot*. Leonardo da Vinci Report.

Manolescu, D. A. (2000). *Micro-Workflow: A Workflow Architecture Supporting Compositional Object-Oriented Software development*. Unpublished doctoral dissertation, University of Illinois.

Marinilli, M. (2005). *Model-driven user adapted systems and applications*. PhD Thesis.

Martel, C., Vignollet, L., Ferraris, C., David, J.-P., & Lejeune, A. (2006). Modelling collaborative learning activities in e-learning platforms. In Kinshuk, R. Koper, P. Kommers, P. Kirschner, D. Sampson, & W. Didderen (Eds.), *Proceedings of the International Conference. on Advanced Learning Technologies ICALT* (pp. 707-709). Los Alamitos, CA: IEEE Computer Society.

Martens, A. (2003). Centralize the tutoring process in intelligent tutoring systems. In Ch. Jutz, F. Flückiger, K. Waefler (Ed.), *Proceedings of the 5th International*

Confernece on New Educational Environments ICNEE (pp. 209-214). Lucerne, Switzerland: net4net.

Martens, A. (2004). *Ein Tutoring Prozess Modell für fallbasierte Intelligente Tutoring Systeme.* AKA Verlag infix.

Martens, A. (2005). Modeling of Adaptive Tutoring Processes. In Z. Ma (Ed.), *Web-based intelligent e-learning systems: Technologies and applications* (pp. 193-215). Hershey, PA: Information Science Publishing, Idea Group Inc.

Martens, A. (2006). Time in the adaptive tutoring process model. In T.-W. C. Mitsuru Ikeda Kevin D. Ashley (Ed.), *Proceedings of the 8ᵗʰ InternationalConference on Intelligent Tutoring Systems ITS* (pp. 134-143). New York: Springer.

Martens, A., & Himmelspach, J. (2005). Combining intelligent tutoring and simulation systems. *In Proceedings of the International Conference on Simulation in Human Computer Interfaces, SIMCHI, Part of the Western Multi Conference WMC* (pp. 65-70), New Orleans, USA.

Martens, A., Bernauer, J., Illmann, T., & Seitz, A. (2001). "Docs 'n drugs—the virtual polyclinic" An intelligent tutoring system for Web-based and case-oriented training in medicine. In *Proeedings of the American Medical Informatics Conference AMIA* (pp. 433-437). Washington, US.

Martínez, A., de la Fuente, P., & Dimitriadis, Y. (2003). Towards an XML-based representation of collaborative interaction. In B. Watson et al. (Eds.), *Proceedings of the International Conference on Computer Support for Collaborative Learning 2003*, Bergen (pp. 379-384). Dordrecht: Kluwer Academic Publishers.

Mayes, J. & Fowler, C. (1999). Learning technology and usability: A framework for understanding courseware usability and educational software design. *Interacting with Computers, 11*(5), 485-497.

McAndrew, P., Nadolski, R., & Little A. (2005). Developing an approach for learning design players. *Journal of Interactive Media in Education (Advances in learning design. Special Issue), 2005*(14).

McAndrew, P., Woods, W.I.S., Little, A., Weller, M.J., & Koper, R., & Vogten, H. (2004, July 3-7). Implementing learning design to support Web-based learning. *Tenth Australasian World Wide Web Conference (AusWeb 2004)*, Gold Coast.

McGrath, J.E. (1991). Time, interaction and performance: A theory of groups. *Small Group Research, 22*(2), 147-174.

McGuinness, D. L., & van Harmelen, F. (Eds.). (2004). OWL Web ontology language—overview. *W3C Recommendation 10 February 2004.* Retrieved October 14, 2006, from http://www.w3.org/TR/owl-features/

McNeil, S., Price, J.D., Boger-Mehall, S., Robin, B. & Willis, J. (Eds.), *Technology and Teacher Education Annual 1998.* Charlottesville, VA: Association for the Advancement of Computing in Education.

Melis, E., Andrès, E., Büdenbender, J., Frishauf, A., Goguadse, G., Libbrecht, P., et al. (2001). ActiveMath: A web-based learning environment. *International Journal of Artificial Intelligence in Education, 12*(4), 385-407.

Mellow, P. (2005). The media generation: Maximize learning by getting mobile. *Proceedings for ASCILITE 2005: Balance, Fidelity, Mobility: Maintaining the momentum?* (pp. 469-476).

Mens, T. & Van Gorp, P. (2005). A taxonomy of model transformation. In *Proceedings of the International Workshop on Graph and Model Transformation (GraMoT).* Tallinn, Estonia.

Miller, C.S. & Remington, R.W. (2000). A computational model of Web navigation: Exploring interactions between hierarchical depth and link ambiguity. In *Proceedings of the 6th Conference on Human Factors and the Web.*

Mizoguchi, R., Ikeda, M., & Sinitsa, K. (1997). Roles of Shared Ontology in AI-ED Research. In B. du Boulay & R. Mizoguchi (Eds.), *Proceedings of the International Conference on Artificial Intelligence in Education, AIED.*

Mödritscher, F., García-Barrios, V. M., & Gütl, C. (2004). Enhancement of SCORM to support adaptive e-Learning within the Scope of the Research Project AdeLE. In

J. Nall and R. Robson (Eds.), *Proceedings of the World Conference on E-Learning in Corporate, Government, Healthcare, and Higher Education (E-Learn 2004)* (pp. 2499-2505).

Mödritscher, F., García-Barrios, V. M., & Gütl, C. (2004). The past, the present and the future of adaptive e-Learning: An approach within the scope of the research project AdeLE. In M. Auer & U. Auer (Eds.), *Proceedings of the International Conference on Interactive Computer Aided Learning (ICL 2004)*.

Mödritscher, F., García-Barrios, V.M., Gütl, C., & Helic, D. (2006). The first AdeLE Prototype at a Glance. In E. Pearson & P. Bohman (Eds.), *Proceedings of the World Conference on Educational Multimedia, Hypermedia and Telecommunications (ED-MEDIA 2006)* (pp. 791-798).

ModX. (2006). *ModX Web site*. Retrieved September, 2006, from http://noce.univ-lille1.fr/projets/ModX/

Molter, G. (1998). *The notion of Software Architecture*. Retrieved October 20, 2006, from http://wwwagss.informatik.uni-kl.de/Projekte/GeneSys/

Moodle (2006). *About Moodle*. Retrieved February 8, 2007, from http://docs.moodle.org/en/About_Moodle

Morkes, J. & Nielsen, J. (1998). *Applying writing guidelines to Web pages*. Retrieved May 2003, from http://www.useit.com/papers/Webwriting/rewriting.html

Morville, P. (2005). *Ambient findability: What we find changes who we become*. Sebastopol, CA: O'Reilly Publications.

Moura, S. L., Coutinho, F., Siqueira, S. W. M., & Melo, R. N (2005). *Integrating repositories of learning objects using Web-services to implement mediators and wrappers*. Paper presented at The International Conference on Next Generation Web Services Practices 2005 (NWeSP'05), Seoul, South Korea.

Moura, S. L., Coutinho, F., Siqueira, S. W. M., & Melo, R.N (2005). Integrating repositories of learning objects using Web-services and ontologies. *International Journal Of Web Services Practices, Seoul, 1*(1-2), 57-72.

Moura, S. L., Coutinho, F., Siqueira, S. W. M., & Melo, R.N (2005). *LORIS: integrating distributed and heterogeneous metadata repositories of learning objects*. Paper presented at the 3rd PGL Conference: Consolidating eLearning Experiences, São Paulo, Brazil.

Mühlenbrock, M., Tewissen, F., & Hoppe, U. (1998). A framework system for intelligent support in open distributed learning environments. *Journal of Artificial Intelligence in Education, 9*, 256-274.

Muller, T. (1998). *A sound study of conceptual understanding during constructivist teaching*. University of North Dokota, Grand Forks.

Muntean, C. H. & McManis, J. (2006). Fine grained content-based adaptation mechanism for providing high end-user quality of experience with adaptive hypermedia systems. *W3C International World Wide Web Conference (WWW'06), Hypermedia and Multimedia Track* (pp. 53-62). Edinburgh, UK. New York: ACM Press.

Muntean, C. H. & McManis, J. (2006). *The value of QoE-based adaptation approach in educational hypermedia: Empirical evaluation*. Springer-Verlag, Berlin (LNCS 4018, pp.121-130).

Muntean, C. H. & McManis, J. (2006). End-user quality of experience oriented adaptive e-learning system. *Journal of Digital Information, Special Issue on Adaptive Hypermedia, 7*(1). Retrieved from http://journals.tdl.org/jodi/issue/view/29

Muntean, C. H., McManis, J., & Muntean, G.-M. (2006). Improving the performance of content delivery in Web-based information systems. *China-Ireland International Conference on Information and Communications Technology* (pp. 430-435). Hangzhou, China.

Murphy, M. & McTear, M. (1997). Learner modeling for intelligent CALL. In Jameson A., Paris C. & Tasso C. (Eds.) *International Conference on User Modeling (UM97)* (pp. 301-312). Wien Austria: Springer-Verlag.

Murray, S., Ryan, J., & Pahl, C. (2003). A tool-mediated cognitive apprenticeship approach for a computer engineering course. In *Proceedings of International Con-*

ference on Advanced Learning Technologies ICALT'03 (pp. 2-6). IEEE.

Murray, T. (1999). Authoring intelligent tutoring systems. *International Journal of Artificial Intelligence in Education, 10*(3/4), 98-129.

Murray, W. (2005). Breaking the ITS monolith: A hybrid simulation and tutoring architecture for ITS. In C.-K. Looi, G. McCalla, B. Bredeweg, & J. Breuker (Eds.), *Proceedings of the International Conference on Artificial intelligence in education AIED* (Vol. 125, pp. 890-892). Amsterdam: IOS Press.

Muukkonen, H., Hakkarainen, K., & Lakkala, M. (1999). Collaborative technology for facilitating progressive inquiry: Future learning environment tools. In C. Hoadly & J. Roschelle (Eds.), *Proceedings of the International Conference on Computer Supported Collaborative Learning CSCL.*

Nagaoka K. (2005). A response analyzer system utilizing mobile phones. In *Proceedings of the IASTED International Conference on Web-Based Education* (pp. 579-584).

Naj. (2005). Ask naj. *Distance Education Report, 9*(19), 3-4.

Najjar, J., Duval, E., Ternier, S., & Neven, F. (2003). Towards Interoperable Learning Object Repositories: the ARIADNE Experience. In *IADIS International Conference WWW/Internet 2003* (pp. 219-226). Algarve, Portugal.

Nakabayashi, K., Koike, Y., Maruyama, M., Touhei, H., Ishiuchi, S., & Fukuhara, Y. (1995). An intelligent tutoring system on World-Wide Web: Towards an integrated learning environment on a distributed hypermedia. In H. Maurer (Ed.), *ED-MEDIA'95—World conference on educational multimedia and hypermedia* (pp. 488-493). Graz, Austria: AACE.

Neely, S., Lowe, H., Eyers, D., Bacon, J., Newman, J., & Gong, X. (2004). An architecture for supporting vicarious learning in a distributed environment. In *Proceedings of the 2004 ACM symposium on applied computing* (pp. 963-970). ACM Press.

Nejdl, W. & Wolpers, M. (1999). KBS hyperbook—a data-driven information system on the Web. *W3C International World Wide Web Conference (WWW99).* Canada.

Nejdl, W., Wolf, B., Qu, C., Decker, S., Sintek, M., Naeve, A., Nilsson, M., Palmer, M. & Risch, T. (2002). EDUTELLA: A P2P Networking Infrastructure Based on RDF. In *Proceedings of World-Wide Web Conference WWW'2002.* ACM.

Newell, A. (1982). *The knowledge level.* Artificial intelligence, *18*(1).

Ng, M. H., Hall, W., Maier, P., & Armstrong, R. (2002). The application and evaluation of adaptive hypermedia techniques in Web-based medical education. *Association for Learning Technology Journal, 10*(3), 19-40.

Nickull, D. (2005). Service-oriented architecture. White-paper. *Adobe Systems, Inc.* 2005, Retrieved February 9, 2007, from http://www.adobe.com/enterprise/pdfs/Services_Oriented_Architecture_from_Adobe.pdf

Nielsen J. (Ed.). (1994). *Heuristic evaluation. Usability inspection methods.* New York: Wiley.

Nielsen, J. (2000). *Designing Web usability.* Indianapolis, IN: New Riders.

Nieminen, P. (2001). Video lecturing for international students. In *Proceedings of International PEG Conference* (pp. 162-168).

Nodenot, T., Laforcade, P., Marquesuzaà, C., & Sallaberry, C. (2003). Knowledge modeling of co-operative learning situations: Towards a UML profile. In *Proceedings of the 11th International Conference on Artificial Intelligence in Education (AIED'2003).* Sydney, Australia. International AI-ED Society.

Nonoka, I. (1995). *The knowledge-creating company.* Oxford University Press.

O'Droma M.S., Ganchev, I., & McDonnell, F. (2003). Architectural and functional design and evaluation of e-learning VUIS based on the proposed IEEE LTSA reference model. *The Internet and Higher Education, 6*(3), 263-276.

O'Keeffe, I., Brady, A., Conlan, O., & Wade, V. (2006). Just-in-time generation of pedagogically sound, context sensitive personalized learning experiences. *International Journal on E-Learning (IJeL), Special Issue: Learning Objects in Context, 5*(1), 113-127.

O'Malley, C. (Ed.). (1994). Computer supported collaborative learning. *NATO ASI series.* F-128. Berlin: Springer-Verlag.

OASIS (2006). *Web Services Notification 1.3.* Retrieved from http://docs.oasis-open.org/wsn/wsn-ws_base_notification-1.3-speccs-01.pdf

Oblinger, D.G. (2006). *Learning Spaces.* Washington, D.C.: EDUCAUSE. Retrieved October 6, 2006, from http://www.educause.edu/books/learningspaces/10569

Oblinger, D.G., & Oblinger, J.L. (Eds.). (2005). *Educating the Net Generation.* Washington, D.C.: EDUCAUSE. Retrieved October 8, 2006, from http://www.educause.edu/ir/library/pdf/pub7101.pdf

OECD. (2003). *Beyond rhetoric: Adult learning policies and practice*s. Paris: OECD Publications, 2003.

Okamoto, T. (2000). A distance ecological model to support self/collaborative-learning via Internet. In *Proceedings of the International Conference of Computer on Education 2000* (pp. 795-799).

Okamoto, T., Cristea, A.I. & Kayama, M. (2000). Towards intelligent media-oriented distance learning and education environments. *Proceedings of the International Conference of Computer on Education 2000* (pp. 61-72).

Okazaki, Y., Watanabe, K., & Kondo, H. (1996). An Implementation of an intelligent tutoring system (ITS) on the World-Wide Web (WWW). *Educational Technology Research, 19*(1), 35-44.

Olimpo, G., Persico, D., Sarti, L., & Tavella, M. (1990). On the concept of database of multimedia learning material. In *World Conference on Computers and Education* (pp. 431-436). Amsterdam: North Holland.

Oliver, B. (2005). *Mobile blogging, 'skyping' and podcasting: Targetting undergraduates' communication skills in transnational learning contexts.*

Oliver, C. (2005, September 13). College's course material soon to be all in hand. *Sydney Morning Herald*, p. 38.

OMG (2001). *UML 1.4 specification formal/01-09-67.*

OMG (2005). *MOF 2.0/XMI Mapping Specification—v2.1, formal/03-05-01.*

OMG (2005). *Meta Object Facility (MOF) 2.0 Query/View/Transformation Specification Final Adopted Specification ptc/05-11-01.*

OMG (2006). *MDA specification guide.* Version 1.0.1. Report—omg/03-06-01.

OMG (2006). *Object Constraint Language Specification version 2.0.* formal/2006-05-01 (full specification).

OMG (2006c). Meta Object Facility (MOF) Specification version 2.0. OMG document formal/06-01-01.

OMG. (2006). *Object Management Group official web site.* Retrieved October 2006 from http://www.omg.org

OpenUSS (2007). Open Source University Support System. Retrieved March, 2007, from http://openuss.sourceforge.net/openuss/

Oubahssi, L. & Grandbastien, M. (2006). From learner information packages to student models: Which continuum?. In M. Ikeda, K. Ashley & T.-W. Chan (Eds.), *The 8th International Conference on Intelligent Tutoring Systems Proceedings.* (LNCS 4053, pp. 604-614).

Oubahssi, L. (2005). *Conception de plates-formes logicielles pour la formation à distance, présentant des propriétés d'adaptabilité à différentes catégories d'usagers et d'interopérabilité avec d'autres environnements logiciels,* PhD dissertation, University Paris5, René Descartes, France.

Oubahssi, L., Grandbastien, M., Ngomo, M., & Claës, G. (2005). The activity at the center of the global open and distance learning process. In *Proceedings of AIED (Artificial Intelligence in Education)* (pp. 386-394). Amsterdam: IOS Press.

OVAE. (2006). *Technology and Distance Learning.* Office of Vocational and Adult Education, U.S Department of Education, Adult Education and Literacy. Retrieved

October 20, 2006, from http://www.ed.gov/about/offices/list/ovae/pi/AdultEd/tdlearn.html

Pagani, E., & Rossi, G.P. (2001). A framework for the admission control of QoS multicast traffic in mobile ad hoc networks. In *Proceedings of the ACM International Workshop WoWMoM* (pp. 3-12).

Pagani, E., Tebaldi, S., & Rossi, G.P. (2004). A service discovery infrastructure for heterogeneous wired/bluetooth networks. In *Proceedings of the International Workshop on Ubiquitous Computing (IWUC 2004).*

Pahl. C. (2006). Data mining for the analysis of content interaction in Web-based learning and training systems. In S. Ventura and C. Romero (Eds.), *Data Mining in E-Learning* (pp. 41-56). Southampton, UK: WIT Press.

Pankratius, V. & Vossen, G. (2003). Towards e-Learning grids: Using grid computing in electronic learning. In *Proceedings of IEEE Workshop on Knowledge Grid and Grid Intelligence* (pp. 4-15). IEEE.

Pankratius, V. & Vossen, G. (2003). Towards e-learning resource infrastructures: Using grid computing in electronic learning. *Technical Report* 98. Dept. of Information Systems, University of Muenster.

Pankratius, V. & Vossen, G. (2003). Towards the utilization of grid computing in e-learning. In J. C. Cunha & O. F. Rana (Eds.), *Grid computing: Software environments and Tools.* Springer Verlag.

Papachristos, E., Tselios, N., & Avouris, N. (2005). Inferring relations between color and emotional dimensions of a Web site using Bayesian Networks. *Interact 2005* (pp. 1075-1078). Rome: Springer.

Papanikolaou K. A., Grigoriadou M., Kornilakis H., & Magoulas G. D. (2003). Personalizing the interaction in a Web-based educational hypermedia system: The case of INSPIRE. *User Modeling and User-Adapted Interaction Journal, 13*(3), 213-267.

Papazoglou, M.P. (2003). Service-oriented computing: Concepts, characteristics and directions. *Proceedings of the Fourth International Conference on Web Information Systems Engineering (WISE'03).* Retrieved February

9, 2007, from http://csdl.computer.org/dl/proceedings/wise/2003/1999/00/19990003.pdf

PAPI Learner, Draft 8 Specification. (2002, February 1). Retrieved October 14, 2006, from http://edutool.com/papi/

Paquette, G. (2004). *Instructional engineering in networked environments.* San Francisco: Pfeiffer & Company, J. Wiley.

Paquette, G., Aubin, C., & Crevier, F. (1999). MISA: A knowledge-based method for the engineering of learning systems. *Journal of Courseware Engineering, 2.*

Paquette, G., Rosca, I., Mihaila, S., & Masmoudi, A. (2006). TELOS, a service-oriented framework to support learning and knowledge management. In S. Pierre (Ed.), *E-learning networked environments and architectures: A knowledge processing perspective.* Berlin: Springer-Verlag.

Paramythis, A., & Loidl-Reisinger, S. (2004). Adaptive learning environments and e-Learning standards. *Electronic Journal on E-Learning, 2*(1), 181-194.

Park, O., & Lee, J. (2003). Adaptive instructional systems. *Educational Technology Research and Development, 2003*(25), 651-684.

Park, O.C. & Lee, J. (2004). Adaptive instructional systems. In D.H. Jonassen, (Ed.), *Handbook of research for educational communications and technology* (2nd ed.) (pp. 651-684). Mahwah, NJ: Lawrence Erlbaum.

Pawlowski, J. & Bick, M. (2006). Managing and re-using didactical expertise: The didactical object model. *Educational technology and society, 9*(1), 84-96.

Pawlowski, J. M. (2000). The Essen Learning Model—A multi-level development model. In *Proceedings of the International Conference. on Educational Multimedia, Hypermedia & Telecommunications ED-MEDIA.* Montreal, Quebec, Canada.

Peltoniemi, M., & Vuori, E. (2004). Business ecosystem as the new approach to complex adaptive business environments. In *Proceedings of eBusiness Research Forum (eBRF 2004).* Retrieved October 7, 2006, from http://www.tut.fi/units/tuta/tita/tip/Peltoniemi_Vuori_eBRF2004.pdf

Perkins, C., & Royer, E. (1999). Ad hoc on-demand distance vector routing. In *Proceedings of the 2nd IEEE Workshop Mobile Computing Systems and Applications.*

Perrone, C., Repenning, A., Spencer, S., & Ambach, J. (1996). Computers in the classroom: Moving from tool to medium. *Journal of Computer-Mediated Communication, 2*(3). Retrieved April 2, 2002, from http://www.ascusc.org/jcmc/

Peter, Y. & Vantroys, T. (2005). Platform support for pedagogical scenarios. *Educational Technology and Society Journal, 8*(3), 122-137.

Pethokoukis, J. M. (2005). Podcasting: Grab your mike and go. *U.S. News & World Report, 139*(11), 58-58.

Petrova, K. (2005). Mobile Learning Using SMS: A Mobile Business Application. In *Proceedings for the 18th Annual Conference of the National Advisory Committee on Computing Qualifications* (pp. 412-417).

Pilar da Silva, D., Van Durm, R., Duval, E., & Olivié, H. (1998). Concepts and Documents for Adaptive Educational Hypermedia: A Model and a Prototype. *ACM HYPERTEXT'98 Conference, Workshop on Adaptive Hypertext and Hypermedia* (pp. 35-43). Pittsburgh, USA.

Pinkwart, N. (2003). A Plug-In Architecture for Graph Based Collaborative Modeling Systems. In U. Hoppe, F. Verdejo, & J. Kay (Eds.) *Proceedings Of Artificial Intelligence in Education: Shaping the Future of Learning through Intelligent Technologies* (pp. 535-536). Amsterdam: IOS Press.

Pinkwart, N. (2005). *Collaborative Modelling in Graph Based Environments.* Unpublished doctoral dissertation, Gerhard-Mercator-Universität Duisburg.

Pinkwart, N., Harrer, A., Lohmann, S. & Vetter, S. (2005). Integrating portal based support tools to foster learning communities in university courses. In V. Uskov, (Ed.), *Proceedings of International Conference*

on *Web-Based Education WBE* (pp. 201-206). Anaheim, CA: ACTA Press.

Pirolli, P. & Card, S. (1999). Information foraging. *Psychological Review, 106*(4), 643-675.

Pirolli, P. (1997). Computational models of information scentfollowing in a very large browsable text collection. In *Human Factors in Computing Systems CHI '97 Conference Proceedings* (pp. 3-10) Vienna: ACM Press.

Pitner, T.; Drasil, P. (2006). An e-Learning 2.0 Environment—Principle, technology and prototype. In K. Tochtermann, & H. Maurer (Eds.), *Proceedings of I-KNOW '06, 6th International Conference on Knowledge Management* (pp. 543-550).

Pivec, M., Pripfl, J. & Trummer, C. (2005). Adaptable e-learning by means of real-time eye-tracking. In P. Kommers & G. Richards (Eds.), *Proceedings of World Conference on Educational Multimedia, Hypermedia and Telecommunications 2005* (pp. 4037-4041). Chesapeake, VA: AACE.

PlanetMDE (2006). *Planet MDE model driven engineering: Official website.* Retrieved March, 2007, from http://planetmde.org/

Polson, M. C. & Richardson, J. J. (Eds.). (1988). *Foundations of intelligent tutoring systems.* Hillsdale: Lawrence Erlbaum Associates.

Preece, J. (Ed.). (2000). *Online communities: Designing usability, supporting sociability.* Chichester, UK: John Willey & Sons.

Prendinger, H., & Ishizuka, M. (2005). Human physiology as a basis for designing and evaluating affective communication with life-like characters. *IEICE Transactions on Information and Systems, Special Section on Life-like Agent and its communication, E88-D*(11), 2453-2460.

Pressman, R. S., (2005). *Software engineering—A practitioner's approach.* New York: McGraw-Hill Professional.

Production, R. E. C. a. (2006). *Exploiting the educational potential of podcasting.* Retrieved from http://recap.ltd.uk/articles/podguide4.html

Protege Web Site. Retrieved from http://protege.stanford.edu

Ractham, P., & Zhang, X. (2006). Podcasting in academia: A new knowledge managementparadigm within academic settings. *SIGMIS-CPR*, 314-317.

Rainie, L., & Madden, M. (2005). Online *activities and pursuits: Podcasting catches on*. Pew Internet and American Life Project, April 3, 2005, pp. 1-5.

Raj, G. S. (2007). *A Detailed Comparison of CORBA, DCOM and Java/RMI*. Retrieved February, 2007, from http://my.execpc.com/~gopalan/misc/compare.html

Ramboll Management. (2005). *The use of ICT for learning and teaching in initial vocational education and training*. Final Report to the EU Commission, DG Education & Culture, November.

Ramsay, J., Barbasi, A., & Preece, J. (1998). A psychological investigation of long retrieval times on the World Wide Web. *Interacting with Computers Journal*. Elsevier Publishing House.

Ramsay, W. & Ransley, W. (1986). A method of analysis for determining dimensions of teaching style. *Teaching and Teacher Education, 2*(1), 69-79.

Ramsden, P. (1992). *Learning to teach in higher education*. New York: Routledge.

Rawlings, A., Van Rosmalen, P., Koper, R., Rodriguez-Artacho, M., & Lefrere, P. (2002). *Survey of Educational Modelling Languages (EMLs)*, Version 1, CEN/ISSS WS/LT.

Read, B. (2005). Abandoning cassette tapes, Purdue University will podcast lectures in almost 50 courses. *The Chronicle of Higher Education, 52*(3), A32.

Read, B. (2005). Lectures on the go. The *Chronicle of Higher Education, 52*(10), A39-42.

Read, B. (2006). Berkeley offers free podcasts of courses through iTunes. *The Chronicle of Higher Education, 52*(35), A44.

Read, B. (2006). Turning campus radio on its head. *The Chronicle of Higher Education, 52*(30), A35-37.

Rehak, D., Dodds, P. & Lannom, L. (2005). *A model and infrastructure for federated learning content repositories*. Paper presented at the 14th International World Wide Web Conference—WWW 2005, Chiba, Japan.

Renkl, A., Mandl, H., & Gruber, H. (1996). Inert knowledge: Analyses and remedies. *Educational Psychologist, 31*(2), 115-121.

Resnick, M. & Sanchez, J. (2004). Effects of organizational scheme and labeling on task performance in product-centered and user-centered retail Websites. *Human Factors, 46.*

Rheingold, H. (2002). *Smart mobs*. New York: Perseus Books.

Riding, R.J. (1997). On the Nature of Cognitive Style. *Educational Psychology, 17*(1-2), 29-49.

Ritrovato, P., Allison, C., Cerri, S.A., Dimitrakos, T., Gaeta, M. & Salerno, S. (2005). *Towards the Learning Grid*. Amsterdam: IOS Press.

Ritter, S. (1997). Communication, cooperation and competition among multiple tutor agents. In B. du Boulay & R. Mizoguchi (Eds.), *Proceedings of the International Conference on Artificial Intelligence in Education AIED* (pp. 31-38). Kobe.

Ritter, S., & Koedinger, K. (1996). An architecture for plug-in tutor agents. *International Journal of Artificial Intelligence in Education, 7*(3/4), 315-347.

Rohmer, J. (2004). *Yesterday, Today, and Tomorrow of AI Applications*. Invited Talk at IFIP World Congress.

Ronchetti, M. & Saini, P. (2003, September 23-26). The knowledge management problem in an e-learning system: A possible solution. In *Proceedings of the Workshop on Artificial Intelligence and e-learning, Eighth National Congress of Italian Association for Artificial Intelligence*. Pisa, Italy.

Roschelle, J. & Teasley, S.D. (1995). The construction of shared knowledge in collaborative problem solving, In C.E. O'Malley (Ed.), *Computer-Supported Collaborative Learning* (pp. 69-97). Berlin: Springer-Verlag.

Rosenfeld L. & Morville P. (1998). *Information Architecture for the World Wide Web*. Sebastopol, CA: O'Reilly Publications.

Russell, S. J. & Norvig, P. (2003). *Artificial intelligence* (2ⁿᵈ ed.). Upper Saddle River, NJ: Prentice Hall.

Sadat, H., & Ghorbani, A.A. (2004). On the evaluation of adaptive Web systems. In *Proceedings of Workshop on Web-based Support Systems 2004* (pp. 127-136).

Safran, C. (2006). *A concept-based information retrieval approach for user-oriented knowledge transfer*. Unpublished master's thesis, Graz University of Technology, Graz, Austria. Retrieved October 7, 2006, from http://www2.iicm.edu/cguetl/education/thesis/csafran

Safran, C., García-Barrios, V. M., & Gütl, C. (2006). A Concept-based context modelling system for the support of teaching and learning activities. In C. M. Crawford, R. Carlsen, K. McFerrin, J. Price, R. Weber, & D. A. Willis (Eds.), *Proceedings of the International Conference on Society for Information Technology and Teacher Education (SITE 2006)* (pp. 2395-2402). Chesapeake, VA: AACE.

SAIL project (2005). *Scalable Architecture for Interactive Learning*. Retrieved from http://docs.telcenter.org/display/SAIL/Home

Sampson, D., Karampiperis, P., & Zervas, P., (2006). Authoring Web-based learning scenarios based on the IMS learning design: Preliminary evaluation of the ASK learning designer toolkit, *IEEE International Conference on Computer Systems and Applications* (pp. 1003-1010).

Sanrach, C. & Grandbastien, M. (2000). ECSAIWeb: A Web-based authoring system to create adaptive learning systems. In P. Brusilovsky, O. Stock, & C. Strapparava (Eds.), *AH 2000* (LNCS 1892, 214-226).

Santos, O. C., Barrera, C., & Boticario, J. G. (2004). An overview of aLFanet: An adaptive iLMS based on standards. *Adaptive Hypermedia and Adaptive Web-Based Systems* (LNCS 3137, pp. 429-432). New York: Springer.

Santos, O. C., Boticario, J. G. & Barrera, C. (2005). aLFanet: An adaptive and standard-based learning environment built upon dotLRN and other open source developments. In *The 2005 dotLRN conference*. Madrid, Spain.

Schmidt A. (2005a, October). Potentials and challenges of context-awareness for learning solutions. In *Proceedings of the 13ᵗʰ Annual Workshop of the SIG Adaptivity and User Modeling in Interactive Systems*, Saarbrücken, Germany.

Schmidt, A. & Braun, S. (2006). Context-aware workplace learning support: Concepts, experiences and visions. In W. Nejdl, K. Tochtermann, (Eds.), *Innovative Approaches for Learning and Knowledge Sharing. Proceedings of the First European Conference on Technology-Enhanced Learning (EC-TEL 06)*, Heraklion, Crete (LNCS 4227, pp. 518-524).

Schmidt, A. & Winterhalter, C. (2004). User context aware delivery of e-learning material: Approach and architecture. *Journal of Universal Computer Science (JUCS), 10*, 28-36.

Schmidt, A. (2005, April). Bridging the gap between e-Learning and knowledge management with context-aware corporate learning solutions. In Althoff et al. (Eds.), *Professional Knowledge Management. Third Biennial Conference, WM 2005*, Kaiserlautern, Germany. Revised Selected Papers. (LNAI 3782, pp. 203-213). New York: Springer.

Schmidt, A. (2006). Ontology-based user context management: The challenges of dynamics and imperfection. In *Proceedings of the International Conference on Ontologies, Databases and Applications of Semantics (ODBASE 2006)*, (LNCS 4275, pp. 995-1011). New York: Springer.

Schmidt, D. C. (2006). Model-driven engineering. *IEEE Computer, 39*(2).

Schmidt, S., Stal, M., Rohnert, H., & Buschmann, F. (2000). *Pattern-oriented software architecture-patterns for concurrent and networked objects*. Chichester, UK: John Wiley & Sons.

Schmidt. A. & Kunzmann, C. (2006). Towards a reference ontology for combining competence management and technology-enhanced workplace learning. In *Proceedings of OntoContent '06, On the Move Federated Conferences (OTM)* (LNCS 4278, pp. 1078-1087) New York: Springer.

Schneider, D., Synteta, P., Frété, C., Girardin, F., & Morand, S. (2003, December 7-13). Conception and implementation of rich pedagogical scenarios through collaborative portal sites: Clear focus and fuzzy edges. *ICOOL 2003—International Conference on Open and Online Learning.* University of Mauritius.

Schulzrinne, H., Casner, S., Frederick, R., & Jacobson, V. (1996). RTP: A transport protocol for real-time applications. *RFC 1889.* Work in progress.

Schulzrinne, H., Rao, A., & Lanphier, R. (1998). Real time streaming protocol. *RFC 2326.* Work in progress.

Schwarz, E., Beldie, I.P., & Pastoor, S. (1983). A comparison of paging and scrolling for changing screen contents by inexperienced users. *Human Factors, 24,* 279-282.

SCORM 2004 3rd Edition, Sharable Content Object Reference Model overview. (2006, August 18). *Advanced Distributed Learning Initiative.* Retrieved October 14, 2006, from http://www.adlnet.gov/downloads/290.cfm

Scouller, K. (1998) The influence of assessment method on students' learning approaches: Multiple choice question examination versus assignment essay. *Higher Education, 35,* 453-462.

Seal, K. C. & Przasnyski, Z. H. (2001). Using the World Wide Web for teaching improvement. *Computers and Educations, 36,* 33-44.

Seale, J. (2003). *E-learning accessibility practices within higher education: A review.* Paper presented at the British Educational Research Association Annual Conference, Heriot-Watt University, Edinburgh, 11-13 September 2003. Retrieved October 20, 2006, from http://www.leeds.ac.uk/educol/documents/00003152.htm

Sermersheim, J. (2006). Lightweight directory access protocol. *RFC 4511.* Work in progress.

Servidge, P. (1999). How long is too long to wait for a Web site to load? *Usability News.*

Sevcik, P. J. (2002). Understanding how users view application performance. *Business Communications Review, 32*(7), 8-9.

Sharma, S. & Kitchens, F. (2004). Web services architecture for m-Learning. *Electronic Journal on e-learning, 2*(1), 203-216.

Sillence, E., Briggs, P., Fishwick, L., & Harris, P. (2004). Trust and mistrust of online health sites. In *Human Factors in Computing Systems CHI'04* (pp. 663-670). Vienna: ACM Press.

Siqueira, S. W. M., Braz, M. H. L. B., & Melo, R. N. (2003c). E-Learning environment based on framework composition. In *Proceedings of the 3rd IEEE International Conference on Advanced Learning Technologies (ICALT 2003)* (pp. 468-468). Athens, Piscataway: IEEE Computer Society.

Siqueira, S. W. M., Braz, M. H. L. B., & Melo, R.N. (2004). Composing frameworks to achieve an e-learning framework. In *Proceedings of the IASTED International Conference on Computers and Technology in Education (CATE 2004)* (pp. 118-123). Anaheim, Calgary, and Zurich: ACTA Press.

Siqueira, S.W.M., Braz, M.H.L.B. & Melo, R.N. (2003). From scenarios to a generic architecture for education and training systems. In *Proceedings of the IASTED International Conference on Computers and Technology in Education (CATE 2003)* (pp. 103-108). Anaheim, Calgary, and Zurich: ACTA Press.

Siqueira, S.W.M., Braz, M.H.L.B. & Melo, R.N. (2003). Web technology for education and training. In *4th International Workshop on Management of Information on the Web—Web-Based Teaching and Learning (MIW'2003)* (pp. 337-341). Prague, DEXA Workshops, IEEE Computer Society.

Sloan, S. (2005). Podcasting: *An exciting new technology for higher education.* Paper presented at the Emerging Technology in Education, San Jose State University.

Small, T. & Haas, Z. (2003). The shared wireless infostation model—A new ad hoc networking paradigm (or Where there is a Whale, there is a Way). In *Proceedings of the ACM International Symposium MobiHoc* (pp. 233-44).

Smith, M. K., Welty, C., & McGuinness, D. L. (Eds.). (2004). OWL Web ontology language-guide. *W3C Recommendation 10 February 2004*. Retrieved October 14, 2006, from http://www.w3.org/TR/owl-guide/

Smyth, B. & Cotter, P. (2002). Personalized adaptive navigation for mobile portals. *European Conference on Artificial Intelligence* (pp. 608-612). Lyon, France.

Sommerville, I. (2006). *Software Engineering* (8th ed.). Upper Saddle River, NJ: Pearson Education.

Sotomayor, B. (2006). *The Globus Toolkit 4 Programmer's Tutorial*. University of Chicago Department of Computer Science.

Specht, M., Kravcik, M., Klemke, R., Pesin, L., & Huttenhain, R. (2002). Adaptive learning environment in WINDS. *ED-MEDIA'02* (pp. 1846-1851), Denver, CO: AACE Press.

Sprankle, B. (2006). Podcasting with purpose. *Principal, 85*(4), 62-63.

Spyridakis, J. (2000). Guidelines for authoring comprehensible Web pages and evaluating their success. *Technical Communication, 47*(3), 359-382.

Srivastava, J., Cooley, R., Deshpande, & M., Tan, P-N. (2000). Web usage mining: Discovery and applications of usage patterns from Web data. In *ACM KDD Explorations, 1*(2), 12-23.

Stephens, D. & Krebs, J. (1986). *Foraging theory*. Princeton, NJ: Princeton University Press.

Swain, H. (2006). Let them tune in to the degree dj. *The Times Higher Education Supplement(1728),* 58-59.

Swanson, D.R. (1986). Subjective versus objective relevance in bibliographic retrieval systems. *Library Quarterly, 56*(4), 389-398.

Synnes, K., Parnes, P., Widen, J. & Schefstroem, D. (1999). Student 2000: Net-based learning for the next millennium. In *Proceedings of the World Conference on the WWW and Internet 1999* (pp. 1031-1036).

Szyperski, C. (2002). *Component Software*. 2nd edition. Component Software Series. ACM Press, New York: Addison Wesley.

Tannenbaum, A. & van Steen, M. (2006). *Distributed systems: Principles and paradigms* (2nd ed). Upper Saddle River, NJ: Pearson Prentice-Hall.

Tattersall, C., Vogten, H., Brouns, F., Koper, R., van Rosmalen, P., Sloep, P., & van Bruggen, J. (2005). How to create flexible runtime delivery of distance learning courses. *Educational Technology and Society, 8*(3), 226-236.

TeamDev (2006). JExplorer Features. *TeamDev Ltd.* Retrieved September 20, 2006, from http://www.jniwrapper.com/pages/jexplorer/overview

Teevan, J., Jones, W., & Bederson, B.B. (2006). Personal information management. *Communications of the ACM, SPECIAL ISSUE: Personal information management, 49*(1), 40-43.

Ternier, S., Duval, E., & Vandepitte, P. (2002). LOMster: Peer-to-peer learning object metadata. In P. Barker & S. Rebelsky (Eds.), *ED-MEDIA'2002—World Conference on Educational Multimedia, Hypermedia and Telecommunications* (pp. 1942-1943). Denver, CO: AACE.

The United Kingdom Government (1993). *Connecting the learning society*. The United Kingdom Government's consultation paper.

Thuring, M., Mannemann, J., & Haake, J. (1995). Hypermedia and cognition: Designing for comprehension. *Communications of the ACM, 38*(8), 57-66.

TopClass Web Site. Retrieved from http://www.wbt-systems.com

TRAILS (2004). *Personalised and collaborative trails of digital and non-digital learning objects*. Retrieved May, 2006, from http://www.noe-kaleidoscope.org

Training, C. (2005). *Podcasting in academic and corporate learning.* eCornell Research Blog, www.ecornell. com

Triantafillou, E., Pomportsis. A, & Georgiadou, E. (2002). AESCS: adaptive educational system base on cognitive styles. *International Conference on Adaptive Hypermedia and Adaptive Web Based Systems (AH'2002), Workshop on Adaptive Systems for Web-Based Education* (pp. 10-20). Malaga, Spain.

Trigano, P. & Giacomini, E. (2004). Toward a Web based environment for evaluation and design of pedagogical hypermedia. *Journal of Educational Technology & Society, IEEE Learning Technology Task Force, 7*(3).

Trigone (2007). *ModX, the Trigone MOF modelling tool.* Retrieved March, 2007, from http://noce.univ-lille1. fr/projets/ModX/

Tselios N., Avouris N. & Kordaki M., (2002). Student Task Modeling in design and evaluation of open problem-solving environments. *Journal of Education and Information Technologies, 7*(1), 19-42.

Tselios, N., Avouris, N., Dimitracopoulou, A., & Daskalaki, S. (2001). Evaluation of distance-learning environments: Impact of usability on student performance. *International Journal of Educational Telecommunications, 7*(4), 355-378.

Tullis, T. & Wood, L. (2004). How many users are enough for a card-sorting study? In *Proceedings of UPA'2004.* Minneapolis, MN.

Türker, A., Görgün, I., & Conlan, O. (2006). The challenge of content creation to facilitate personalized e-Learning experiences. *International Journal on E-Learning, 5*(1), 11-17.

Turner, M., Budgen, D., & Brereton, P. (2003). Turning software into a service. *Computer, 36*(10), 38-44.

van Joolingen, W., Lazonder, A., de Jong, T., Savelsbergh, E., & Manlove, S. (2005). Co-lab: Research and development of an online learning environment for collaborative scientific discovery learning. *Computers in Human Behavior, 21*, 671-688.

Vantroys, T. & Peter, Y. (2003). COW, a Flexible Platform for the Enactment of Learning Scenarios, *9th Conference Groupware (CRIWG 2003),* France (LNCS 2806, pp. 168-182). Berlin: Springer-Verlag.

Vassileva, J. & Deters, R. (1998). Dynamic courseware generation on the WWW. *British Journal of Educational Technology, 29*(1), 5-14.

Verhoeven, B., Cardinaels, K., Van Durm, R., Duval, E., & Olivié, H. (2001). Experiences with the ARIADNE pedagogical document repository. In *ED-MEDIA'2001— World Conference on Educational Multimedia, Hypermedia and Telecommunications* (pp. 1949-1954). Tampere, Finland: AACE.

Viteli, J. (2000). Finnish future: From e-learning to m-Learning? In *Proceedings for the ASCILITE Conference.*

Vogten, H., Martens, H., Nadolski, R., Tattersall, C., van Rosmalen, P., & Koper, R., (2006, July 5-7). CopperCore service integration—Integrating IMS learning design and IMS question and test interoperability. *Sixth International Conference on Advanced Learning Technologies (ICALT 2006)* (pp. 378-382).

Vossen, G. & Westerkamp, P. (2003). E-Learning as a Web service, in *Proceedings of the Seventh International Database Engineering and Applications Symposium (IDEAS'03).*

Vossen, G. & Westerkamp, P. (2004). Maintenance and exchange of learning objects in a web services based e-Learning System. *Electronic Journal of E-Learning, 2*(2), 292-304.

Vrasidas, C. (2000). Constructivism versus objectivism: Implications for interaction, course design, and evaluation in distance education. *International Journal of Educational Telecommunications, 6*(4), 339-346.

W3C (2006). *Web Services Addressing 1.0.* Retrieved from http://www.w3.org/Submission/ws-addressing/

W3C (2006). Document Object Model (DOM). *World Wide Web Consortium.* Retrieved September 18, 2006, from http://www.w3.org/DOM/

W3C (2006). Device Independence. Access to a Unified Web from Any Device in Any Context by Anyone. World Wide Web Consortium. Retrieved October 5, 2006, from http://www.w3.org/2001/di/

W3C. (1999). *Web Content Accessibility Guidelines 1.0.* W3C Recommendation. Retrieved October 20, 2006, from http://www.w3.org/TR/1999/WAI-WEBWEB-CONTENT-19990505/

W3C—World Wide Web Consortium. (2006). *Composite Capabilities/Preferences Profile Public Home Page.* Retrieved from http://www.w3.oorg/Mobile/CCPP/

Wade, V. P. & Doherty, P. (2000). A meta-data driven approach to searching for educational resources in a global context. In G. Davies & C. Owen (Eds.), *WebNet'2000, World Conference of the WWW and Internet* (pp. 136-145). San Antonio, TX: AACE.

Walsh, A. E. (2002). *UDDI, SOAP, and WSDL: The Web Services Specification Reference Book*, Upper Saddle River, NJ: Pearson Education.

Wang, G., & Fung, C.K. (2004). Architecture paradigms and their influences and impacts on component-based software systems. In *Proceedings of the 37th Annual Hawaii International Conference on System Sciences.* Retrieved February 9, 2007, from http://csdl.computer.org/comp/proceedings/hicss/2004/2056/09/205690272a.pdf

Wang, H. & Zhang, D. (2003). MDA-based development of e-learning system. In *Proceedings of the 27th Annual International Computer Software and Applications Conference (COMPSAC'03).*

Wang, H., Chignell, M., & Ishizuka, M. (2006). Empathic tutoring software agents using real-time eye tracking. *Proceedings of the 2006 Symposium on Eye Tracking Research & Applications* (pp. 73-78).

Wang, Y., & Kopsa, A. (2005). A software product line approach for handling privacy constraints in Web personalization. In *Proceedings of the UM 2005 Workshop on Privacy-Enhanced Personalization* (pp. 35-46).

Warlick, D. (2005). Podcasting. *Technology & Learning, 26*(2), 70.

Watson, P. (2003). Databases and the grid. In F. Berman et al. (Eds.), *Grid computing: Making the global infrastructure a reality* (pp. 363-384). Chichester, UK: John Wiley & Sons, Inc.

WebCT Web Site. Retrieved from http://www.webct.com

WebCT. (2002). WebCT Course Management System (Version 3.8). Lynnfield, MA: WebCT, Inc.

Weber, G. & Möllenberg, A. (1995). ELM-Programming-Environment: A tutoring system for LISP beginners, cognition and computer programming. In Wender, K. F., Schmalhofer F. & Böcker, H. D. (Eds.) *Cognition and Computer Programming* (pp. 373-408). Toronto: Ablex Publishing Corporation.

Weber, G. (1999). Adaptive learning systems in the World Wide Web. *International Conference on User Modeling (UM'99)* (pp. 371-378). Banff, Canada.

Weber, G., Kuhl H. C., & Weibelzahl S. (2001). Developing adaptive Internet based courses with the authoring system NetCoach. In *Proceedings of the Third Workshop on Adaptive Hypermedia (UM2001).*
Weber, G., Kuhl, H. C., & Weibelzahl, S. (2001). Developing adaptive internet based courses with the authoring system NetCoach. *Workshop on Adaptive Hypertext and Hypermedia* (pp. 35-48). Sonthofen, Germany.

Weber, G., Specht, M. (1997). User modelling and adaptive navigation supporting WWW-based tutoring systems. *International Conference on User Modeling (UM'97)* (pp. 289-300). Sardinia, Italy.

Weibelzahl, S. & Weber, G. (2002). Advantages, opportunities, and limits of empirical evaluations: Evaluating adaptive systems. *Künstliche Intelligenz Journal, 3*, 17-20.

Weiser, M. (1998). The future of ubiquitous computing on campus. *Communications of the ACM, 41*(1), 41-42.

Weiss, A. (2005). The power of collective intelligence. *netWorker, 9*(3), 16-23.

Weller, M., Little, A., McAndrew, P., & Woods, W. (2006). Learning design, generic service descriptions and universal acid. *Educational Technology & Society Journal, 9*(1), 138-145.

Wexelblat, A. & Maes, P. (1999). Footprints: History-rich tools for information foraging. In *Human Factors in Computing Systems CHI 99 Conference Proceedings* (pp. 270-277). Pittsburgh, PA: ACM Press.

Who's involved in standards? (2005, March 09). *CE-TIS—Centre for Educational Technology Interoperability Standards.* Retrieved October 14, 2006 from http://www.cetis.ac.uk/static/whos-involved.html

Wiederhold, G. (1992). Mediators in the architecture of future information systems. *IEEE Computer, 25*(3), pp. 38-49.

Wikipedia. (2006). *Vocational Education.* Retrieved October 20, 2006, from http://en.wikipedia.org/wiki/Vocational_education

Wile, D. S. (1997). Abstract Syntax from Concrete Syntax. In *Proceedings of the 19th International Conference on Software Engineering* (pp. 472-480). Boston.

Wile, D. S. (2001). Supporting the DSL spectrum. *Journal of computing and information technology, 9*(4), 263-287.

Wiley, D. L. (2006). Secrets of podcasting: Audio blogging for the masses. *Online, 30*(1), 62-62.

Williams, P. E., & Nsw, O. *Tools of the trade: Learning technologies for distance learners.*

Wilson, S., Olivier, B., Jeyes, S., Powell, A., & Franklin, T. (2005). *A Technical Framework to Support e-Learning.* Retrieved September, 2006, from http://www.elearning.ac.uk/frameworks/resources

WMF. (2000). Object Management group. *Workflow Management Facility, Version 1.2.* Retrieved October, 2006, from http://www.omg.org/technology/documents/formal/workflow_management.htm

Woelk, D. & Agarwal, S. (2002). Integration of e-learning and knowledge management. In *World Conference on E-Learning in Corporate, Government, Health Institutions, and Higher Eduction. Volume 1* (pp. 1035-1042).

Workflow Management Coalition. (1995). The Workflow Reference Model. *WfMC-TC-1003, Version 1.1, 19 January 1995.* Retrieved October, 2006, from http://www.wfmc.org/

Wright, R. (2005). Tafe gets the e-learning formula right. *Business Strategy Australasia*, (4).

Xhafa, F., Caballé, S., Daradoumis, Th., & Zhou, N. (2004). A grid-based approach for processing group activity log files. In R. Meersman et al. (Eds.), *On the Move to Meaningful Internet Systems 2004* (LNCS 2392, pp. 175-186). Berlin: Springer.

Yang, C.-T. & Ho, H.-C. (2005). A sharable e-Learning platform using data Grid technology. In *Proceedings of IEEE International Conference on e-Technology, e-Commerce and e-Service EEE'2005* (pp. 592- 595). New York: IEEE.

Yatani, K., Onuma, M., Sugimoto, M., & Kusunoki, F. (2004). Musex: A system for supporting children's collaborative learning in a museum with PDAs. *Journal of Systems and Computers in Japan, 35*(14), 54-63.

Young, J. R. (2005). New princeton web service offers recordings of public-policy lectures. *The Chronicle of Higher Education, 51*(49), A34.

Young, J. R. (2005). Stanford university makes podcasts of lectures available through Apple's iTunes. *The Chronicle of Higher Education, 52*(11), A44.

Zarraonandia, T., Dodero, R.M., & Fernandez, C. (2006). Crosscutting runtime adaptations of LD execution. *Educational Technology & Society Journal, 9*(1), 123-137.

Zhang, G., Jin, Q., & Lin, M. (2005). A framework of social interaction support for ubiquitous learning. In *Proceedings of the 19th IEEE International Conference AINA.*

Zumbach, J., Hillers, A., & Reimann, P. (2003). Supporting distributed problem-based learning: The use of feedback in online learning. In T. Roberts (Ed.), *Online collaborative learning: theory and practice* (pp. 86-103), Hershey, PA: Idea Group.

About the Contributors

Claus Pahl is a senior lecturer and the leader of the Web and Software Engineering research group at Dublin City University, which focuses on Web technologies and e-learning applications in particular. Pahl has published more than 125 papers including a wide range of journal articles, book chapters, and conference contributions on e-learning. He is on the editorial board of the *International Journal on E-Learning* and the *International Journal of Technology-Enhanced Learning* and is a regular reviewer for journals and conferences in the area of software, Web, and learning technologies and their applications. He has extensive experience in educational technologies, both as an instructor using technology-supported teaching and learning at undergraduate and postgraduate level and as a researcher in Web-based learning technology. The IDLE environment, developed by him and his students, has been in use in undergraduate teaching since 1999.

* * *

Nikolaos Avouris (hci.ece.upatras.gr/avouris) was born in Zakynthos, Greece (1956). He has a degree in electrical engineering from NTUA Greece (1979) and MS (1981), and a PhD (1983) from the University of Manchester UMIST, UK. He served in various research positions in the UK, Italy, and Greece and then joined the University of Patras, as associate professor (1994-2001) and full professor of software engineering and human-computer interaction (2001- today). He is the founder and head of the Human-Computer Interaction Group. His main interests are related to design and evaluation of interactive systems, usability engineering, collaboration technology, context-aware computing systems and analysis and evaluation of collaborative activities.

Christos Bouras obtained his diploma and PhD from the Department Of Computer Engineering and Informatics of Patras University (Greece). He is currently an associate professor in the above department. Bouras is also a scientific advisor of Research Unit 6 in Research Academic Computer Technology Institute (CTI), Patras, Greece. His research interests include analysis of performance of networking and computer systems, computer networks and protocols, telematics and new services, QoS and pricing for networks and services, e-learning networked virtual environments and WWW issues. He has published 200 papers in various well-known refereed conferences and journals. He is a co-author of seven books in Greek. He has been a PC member and referee in various international journals and conferences. He has participated in R&D projects and he is member of experts in the Greek Research and Technology Network (GRNET), advisory committee member to the W3C, member of WG3.3 and WG6.4 of IFIP, Task Force for Broadband Access in Greece, ACM, IEEE, EDEN, AACE and New York Academy of Sciences.

Maria Helena L.B. Braz is an assistant professor at IST, Technical University of Lisbon (TULisbon), in Portugal, where she teaches courses in programming, databases, technical drawing and computer graphics. She holds a BSc in electronics and telecommunications engineering (1978), a MS in operational research and systems engineering (1984), both from IST, TULisbon, and a PhD in computer science (1990) from the Pontifical Catholic University of Rio de Janeiro, Brazil. Her research interests are now focused on e-learning. She has participated in several international research projects and has written more than 20 papers for conferences, journals, and books.

Peter Brusilovsky has been working in the area of adaptive systems and e-learning for many years. He participated in the development of several adaptive Web-based educational systems including ELM-ART, a winner of 1998 European Academic Software Award. He was involved in developing practical e-learning courses and systems as a director of computer managed instruction at Carnegie Technology Education, one of the first e-learning companies in the USA. Currently he continues his research on adaptive e-learning as a professor at the School of Information Sciences, University of Pittsburgh. Brusilovsky has published numerous research papers and several books on adaptive systems and e-learning. He is the editor of *Technology, Instruction, Cognition, and Learning* and a board member of several other journals.

Santi Caballé (scaballe@uoc.edu) has a master's degree and bachelor's degree in computer science from the Open University of Catalonia. Since 2003, he has been an assistant professor at the Open University of Catalonia teaching a variety of courses in computer science in the areas of information systems, software engineering and collaborative learning. Since 2006, he has been working as an associate professor of the Department of Computer Science, Multimedia and Telecommunication at the Open University of Catalonia where he coordinates several online courses in the area of software engineering. He is a member of the distributed, parallel and collaborative systems research group at the Open University of Catalonia, where he is currently working toward his PhD His research focuses on e-learning, software engineering, network technologies, distributed learning, computer-supported collaborative learning, interaction analysis, grid technologies.

Pierre-André Caron is a PhD student in computer science at the University of Lille 1. His thesis "Model driven engineering to construct pedagogical devices on LMS and Web 2.0 application" shows that it is possible to define with MDE an infrastructure allowing "dispositives" modeling and building on LMS and Web 2.0 application. This infrastructure is particularly suited for the specific case of a small team of teachers using pedagogical "bricolage."

Jason Caudill (www.jasoncaudill.com) currently works as a graduate assistant for technical documentation and training at the University of Tennessee in Knoxville, TN, where he is pursuing his PhD in instructional technology. Caudill also teaches extensively as an adjunct professor of business, with several years of experience in both on-ground and online environments. Caudill's research interests include technical management, mobile technology, and open source software applications. Caudill's most recent publication is titled "The Growth of m-Learning and the Growth of Mobile Computing—Parallel Developments" and will be appearing in an upcoming issue of the *International Review of Research in Open and Distance Learning.*

Stephen R. Chastain (www.stephenchastain.info) is currently a technology trainer with the University of Tennessee in Knoxville, TN. He is completing his PhD in instructional technology; researching podcasting's effects on learning in higher education. His research interests are podcasting and learning, the integration of multimedia and technology, and open-source alternatives for education. He presents regularly at technology conferences on the topics of social software, podcasting, and Web development. His latest publication is in *Learning and Leading Technology,* February 2006, "Gimp: Open Source Photo Editing." In addition to technology, Stephen is a professional photographer who enjoys spending time with his family.

Christophe Choquet has a special interest in defining how to collect, represent and analyze students' activity data in order to provide significant feedback to pedagogical designers on the uses of their learning systems. The main purpose is to increase the awareness and the integration of designers into the educational software lifecycle by allowing the comparison between designers' intentions and observed uses and by supporting the pedagogical reengineering process. He has authored around 40 peer-reviewed articles and is involved in several international program committees. He is a member of the Computer Laboratory of the University of Maine (LIUM, France) and was the leader of the project called "Design Patterns for Recording and Analyzing Usage of Learning Systems" in the European Network of Excellence KALEIDOSCOPE (http://www.noe-kaleidoscope.org/pub/).

Owen Conlan is a research lecturer at Trinity College Dublin, where he is a member of the Knowledge and Data Engineering Group. He has received a PhD from the University of Dublin, based on work on personalized e-learning. He has participated in national and EU-level project on adaptive hypermedia systems. His research areas are adaptive systems, personalized e-learning, adaptive hypermedia, strategies for adaptation, and using adaptive hypermedia techniques for the customized delivery of educational material. Owen has published extensively in journals and conferences in this context.

Thanasis Daradoumis (adaradoumis@uoc.edu) has a PhD in information sciences from the Polytechnic University of Catalonia—Spain, a master's degree in computer science from the University of Illinois, and a bachelor's degree in mathematics from the University of Thessaloniki—Greece. Since 1984, he has been an assistant professor at several universities in the USA, Greece and Spain, teaching a variety of courses in mathematics and computer science. Since 1998, he has been working as a professor in the department of computer science, multimedia and telecommunication at the Open University of Catalonia where he coordinates several online courses as well as the development of teaching materials appropriate for virtual learning. His research focuses on e-learning and learning technologies, ontologies and semantic Web, distributed learning, CSCL, CSCW, interaction analysis, grid technologies.

Eleftheria Giannaka obtained her diploma from the Informatics Department of the Aristotelian University of Thessaloniki (Greece) and her master's degree from the Computer Engineering and Informatics Department of Patras University. She is currently a PhD candidate of the Department of Computer Engineer and Informatics of Patras University. Additionally, Giannaka is working as an R&D computer engineer at the Research Unit 6 of the Computer Technology Institute in Patra (Greece). Her interests include computer networks, system architecture, internet applications, electronic commerce, database implementation and administration, virtual reality applications, performance evaluation, programming and distributed virtual environments.

Francesco Giudici received his graduate degree in computer science from the Università degli Studi di Milano, Italy, in 2005. From March 2005 to October 2005 he worked as research assistant at the department of information science and communication of the University of Milan. Since November 2005 he has been a PhD student at the information science and communication department of the Università degli Studi di Milano. His main research interests concern mobile ad hoc networks (MANETs), vehicular ad hoc networks (VANETs), network architectures, network security, wireless technologies, and performance evaluation.

Gerard Gleeson has recently finished his postgraduate studies at Dublin City University. Gleeson has recently completed his MS in software engineering. He has focused in particular on component- and service-based software architectures. His central project has investigated service- and grid-based technologies for learning technology infrastructures.

Monique Grandbastien has been a professor in computer science at University Henri Poincare Nancy1, France, since 1989. She has been the head of a research team on computers and education and supervised many graduate and PhD students. She authored many papers, book chapters, and edited books and proceedings in the domain of computers and education and more recently e-learning. She is the founding president of the French Association for ICT in Education and she is currently involved in conference committees as well as in several journal editorial boards. Her research interests range from knowledge models for technology enhanced learning systems to interoperability and standards issues for e-learning platforms.

Philip Grew studied linguistics at the University of Chicago and classics at the Università degli Studi di Milano, where he now teaches English for computer science and digital communication. He has pursued projects in technology for teaching and online learning since1988, including implementing a learning management system for on-screen assessment at the Dipartimento di Informatica e Comunicazione. Since 1995 he has played a role in several community-networking initiatives for the City of Milan, the university, and a private-sector innovation institute.

Christian Gütl is assistant professor at the Institute for Information Systems and Computer Media (IICM), Graz University of Technology, Austria. He holds a PhD in computer science and a master's degree in communication engineering and economics. He is also head of Gütl IT Research & Consulting, co-founder and CFO of Infodelio Information Systems, member of IEEE and ACM, and active member of the MPEG-7 community. Gütl has managed numerous commercial and research projects, and he worked as an expert for international institutions in Europe. His academic contributions include a large number of publications in reputable journals and international conferences.

Andreas Harrer is research and teaching assistant at the Department of Computer Science at the University of Duisburg-Essen. He holds a diploma and PhD title both from Technische Universität München. His main research interests are the computer support of collaborative learning utilizing intelligent analysis and feedback mechanisms. This work is also influenced by the utilization of methods from software engineering, such as pattern approaches and re-factoring to systematically develop these learning support applications. He is the leader of the subproject "Artificial Intelligence in Education" within the Network of Excellence "Kaleidoscope" funded by EC/TEL.

Cristina Hava Muntean is a lecturer with the School of Informatics, National College of Ireland, Dublin. She graduated "Politehnica" University of Timisoara, Romania in 2000 with a bachelor's degree from the Computer Science Department and was awarded a PhD degree from Dublin City University, Ireland in 2005 for research on end-user quality of experience aware adaptive hypermedia systems. Her research interests include end-user quality of experience, adaptive hypermedia systems and personalized e-learning over wired and wireless networks using various devices. In these areas she has written a book and over 25 peer-reviewed publications in prestigious international conferences and journals. Muntean is a reviewer for international journals and conferences in the area of Web-based e-learning.

Giorgos Kahrimanis (hci.ece.upatras.gr/kachrimanis), was born in Athens, Greece (1979). He has a degree in electrical and computer engineering from University of Patras, Greece. He is currently a PhD candidate at the same university pursuing doctoral research that spans from human computer interaction with emphasis on computer supported collaborative work (CSCW) to computer supported collaborative learning (CSCL). His special research interests are methods for evaluation of collaborative activities and the design of suitable tools for interaction analysis.

Christos Katsanos (hci.ece.upatras.gr/Katsanos), was born in Kozani, Greece (1982). He has a degree in electrical and computer engineering from University of Patras, Greece (2004). Currently, he is PhD candidate at the same university pursuing doctoral research in the area of Web usability. His main research interests include design and evaluation of interactive systems (with an emphasis on Web-based applications), methodologies and tools for evaluating Web usability, design and evaluation of Web-based learning environments, information retrieval in the Web, artificial intelligence techniques focused on human computer interaction and user modeling. He is a member of the research team of Human-Computer Interaction (HCI-Group) since September 2004.

Mize Kayama obtained her PhD in information systems from the University of Electro-Communications in Japan. She is currently an associate professor of information engineering at Shinshu University in Japan. Her research interests include learning technologies, especially for collaborative technologies.

Pierre Laforcade received a PhD in computer science from the UPPA University at Pau (France) in 2004. He is currently an associate professor at the Laval University Institute of Technology and a researcher fellow at the Computer Science Laboratory of Le Mans (LIUM). His research interests include instructional design, model-driven-engineering, and visual educational modeling languages.

Miltiadis Lytras holds a PhD in information systems from the Department of Management Science and Technology, AUEB (2004), an MBA from the AUEB (1998) and a BS in informatics from AUEB (1995). Miltiadis is the editor-in-chief of the *International Journal of Knowledge and Learning* as well as the editor-in-chief of *International Journal of Teaching and Case Studies*. He serves also as the co-editor-in-chief of the *International Journal on Semantic Web and Information Systems*. Lytras is currently an assistant professor in the Computer Engineering and Informatics Department—CEID (University of Patras), and in the Department of Library Science and Information Systems (ATEI Athens). His research focuses on Semantic Web, knowledge management and e-learning, with more than 80 publications in these areas. He has co-edited and co-edits 25 special issues in international journals and has authored/edited 12 books. He is the founder and officer of the Semantic Web and Information Systems Special

Interest Group in the Association for Information Systems as well as the co-founder of AIS SIG on Reusable Learning Objects and Learning Design. He serves as the editor-in-chief of nine international journals while he is associate editor or editorial board member in seven more. Currently, he serves as member of the scientific advisory board of ELEGI Project. Finally, Lytras is the president of the OPEN RESEARCH SOCIETY, aiming to promote the vision of the Knowledge Society worldwide.

Alke Martens is a research and teaching assistant at the Department of Computer Science at the University of Rostock in the research group Modeling and Simulation. She received her degree from the University of Hildesheim, has been part of the artificial intelligence research group at the University of Ulm, and received her PhD from the University of Rostock, Germany, in the area of formal methods for intelligent tutoring systems. Her current research interests are formal methods, software engineering, modeling and simulation, teaching and training systems, and a combination thereof. Current application domains of her research are medicine and education of computer scientists.

Rubens Nascimento Melo is a senior professor and researcher in the field of databases at the Computer Science Department of the Pontifical Catholic University of Rio de Janeiro, PUC-Rio. He holds a BS in electronic engineering (1968), a MS (1971) and a PhD (1976) degree in computer science from the Air Force Institute of Technology (ITA) in Sao Paulo. Currently, he is associate professor at PUC-Rio where he leads the Database Research Lab (TecBD). One of his current interests is the application of database technology to distance learning. In this field he has also served as director of the Center of Distance Education under the vice-rectory for Academic Affairs of PUC-Rio.

Gabriel-Miro Muntean is a lecturer in the School of Electronic Engineering, Dublin City University, Ireland, which awarded him a PhD in 2003 for research in quality-oriented adaptive multimedia streaming over wired networks. He was awarded the bachelor's and master's degrees in software engineering from the Computer Science Department, "Politehnica" University of Timisoara, Romania in 1996 and 1997 respectively. Muntean's research interests include quality of service and performance issues of adaptive multimedia streaming, and personalized e-learning over wired and wireless networks and with various devices. Muntean has published over 50 papers in prestigious international conferences and journals, as well as a book and a book chapter. Muntean served as member of technical program committees of important international conferences, and acted as reviewer for well-known journals, conferences and funding agencies. He is a member of IEEE.

Naomi Nagata received the BA in business administration from Senshu University, Japan in 2004 and a MA in business administration from Senshu University, Japan in 2006. She is now a PhD student at Electro-Communications University. Her research interests are knowledge spaces map, collaborative learning support, and artificial intelligence. She is a member of Japanese Society for Information and System in Education (JSISE) and Japan Society for Education Technology (JSET), Information System Society of Japan (ISSJ).

Toshie Ninomiya graduated from the Department of Science and Technology, Keio University, in 1993, and worked in Toyota Motor Corporation as an engineer of industrial technology. She has experience in education. She is currently a research associate at the University of Electro-Communications,

Graduate School of Information Systems. Her research interests are in personalized adaptability of e-learning environment including mentoring and monitoring system.

Thierry Nodenot, a former primary school teacher received his PhD from Toulouse University (France) in 1992 and the research supervisor degree from Pau University (France) in 2005, all in computer science. He is currently an associate professor at the Institute of Technology of Bayonne (France) and does his research at the LIUPPA laboratory in the domain of educational technology. His research interests particularly concern the design of technology-enhanced learning systems (TEL): visual languages for instructional design; knowledge engineering for TEL systems; model-driven engineering techniques and tools applied to the design of TEL systems.

Toshio Okamoto obtained his PhD from Tokyo Institute of Technology in 1988. He is currently a professor at the University of Electro-Communications (UEC), Graduate School of Information Systems, and a director of the Center for E-Learning Research and Promotion in UEC. His research interests include theoretical and application studies/design of artificial intelligence, e-learning, computer-supported collaborative learning systems and curriculum development in information education. He is a convener of WG2 (collaborative technology) of LTSC/ISO SC36 (Learning Technologies Standards Committee).

Lahcen Oubahssi is an associate professor in computer science at the University du Maine (Institute of Technology of Laval) in Laval, France. He received his PhD in December 2005 from the University Paris 5 (France). His PhD dissertation is entitled "Design of a software platform for formation, presenting properties of adaptability to various categories of users and of interoperability with other software environments." His main research interests are technology enhanced learning, engineering issues, teaching scenarios, e-learning platforms architecture, and e-learning platforms re-engineering.

Elena Pagani received her graduate degree in computer science from the Università degli Studi di Milano, Italy, in 1992. From 1992 to 1993, she had a grant of the National Research Council (CNR) for the Telecommunication Research Project (Progetto Finalizzato Telecomunicazioni). In 1999, she received her PhD in computer science from the Università degli Studi di Milano. In October 1999, she became an assistant professor, and since March 2006 she has been as associate professor at the Information Science and Communication Department of the Università degli Studi di Milano. Her research interests concern networks protocols and architectures, wireless technologies, and performance evaluation.

Xavier Le Pallec is associate professor in Computer Science at the University of Lille 1. He obtained his PhD in 2002 from the same university in the field of meta-groupware and meta-modeling. He is interested in application of model driven engineering to construct learning environment on LMS. He is responsible for a distance learning master's in computer science (called e-services).

Yvan Peter is associate professor in computer science at the University of Lille 1. He obtained his PhD in 1998 from the University of Franche-Comté, France in the field of middleware engineering. He is interested in the development of flexible software to support learning and collaboration. He is member of the core group of the European Network of Excellence Kaleidoscope in the field of technology enhanced learning and responsible for the national project p-LearNet about pervasive learning environments.

Enver Sangineto received his degree in computer science at the University of Pisa in 1995. In 2001 he received a PhD in computer engineering at the University of Rome "La Sapienza. He has been working from 2001 to 2006 at the Artificial Intelligence Laboratory of the University of Rome "Roma Tre" and with the CRMPA (a research center of the University of Salerno, Italy). In this period he has been interested mainly in e-learning and applications of artificial intelligence to e-learning. He has participated to various European e-learning projects and he was the technical and scientific responsible of the Diogene European project (IST-2001-33358). His scientific interests include also computer vision and pattern recognition. In 2006 he joined the Department of Computer Science of the University "La Sapienza" of Rome with a post-doctorate position. He has published various papers in important national and international scientific conferences, journals and books.

Andreas Schmidt is department manager within the Research Division Information Process Engineering at the FZI Research Center for Information Technologies in Karlsruhe, Germany. He received his degree in computer science from the University of Karlsruhe and was working in several national and European research projects. Within the project "Learning in Process," where he was leading the scientific activities, he has developed a competency-oriented methodology for supporting work-integrated learning on demand. His research interests include workplace learning support, competence management, context-aware services, ontology-based techniques, and information and service integration. He is an assistant lecturer at the University of Karlsruhe with a lecture on Information Integration and Web Portals.

Sean Wolfgand Matsui Siqueira is an assistant professor at the Department of Applied Informatics, Federal University of the State of Rio de Janeiro (UNIRIO), Brazil. He holds a PhD in computer science from the Pontifical Catholic University of Rio de Janeiro (PUC-Rio), Brazil. From 1997 to 2005, he was a member of the PUC-Rio's Database Research Lab (TecBD). From December 2005 to August 2006 he was an assistant professor at the Informatics Institute, Federal University of Goias, Brazil. His research interests include information integration, knowledge management, Web-services and ontologies, data warehousing, customer relationship management, database marketing, e-learning, semantic models, user models, frameworks, adaptable systems and e-health.

Thrasyvoulos Tsiatsos obtained his bachelor's degree, his master's degree and his PhD from the Computer Engineering and Informatics Department of Patras University (Greece). He is currently lecturer in the Department of Informatics of Aristotle University of Thessaloniki as well as research member at the Research Unit 6 of Research Academic Computer Technology Institute. His research interests include computer networks, telematics, networked virtual environments, multimedia and hypermedia. More particular, he is engaged in distant education with the use of computer networks, real time protocols and networked virtual environments. He has published more than 40 papers in journals and in well-known refereed conferences and he is co-author in two books. He has participated in R&D projects such as OSYDD, RTS-GUNET, ODL-UP, VES, ODL-OTE, INVITE, EdComNet and VirRAD and he is currently involved in the projects SAPSAT (vocational education and training program) and promotion of broadband in western region of Greece.

Nikolaos Tselios (hci.ece.upatras.gr/Tselios), was born in Athens, Greece (1973). He has his PhD (2002) and degree (1997) in electrical and computer engineering from University of Patras, Greece. Currently;,he is an adjunct lecturer and postgraduate fellow at the University of Patras, Greece. His main interests are related to design and evaluation of software interaction systems (with an emphasis on educational systems), design and evaluation of Web-based learning environments, cognitive models, context-aware computing systems and artificial intelligence techniques for human computer interaction.

Thomas Vantroys is associate professor in computer science at the University of Lille 1. He obtained his PhD in 2003 from the University of Lille 1 in the field of flexible workflow engine for e-learning. He is interested in the SOA and more particularly in service orchestration in the context of pervasive-learning.

Vincent P. Wade is a senior lecturer in the Department of Computer Science, Trinity College Dublin and research director for the Knowledge and Data Engineering Group. Vincent is also director of the Center for Academic Practice and Student Learning. The Center is responsible for the supporting Trinity College's academic staff in the areas of teaching learning, research and learning technologies. Having graduated from University College Dublin with a BS (Hons) in computer science in 1988, he completed his postgraduate studies in Trinity College Dublin before taking the position of lecturer in the Computer Science Department in 1991. The Knowledge and Data Engineering Group focuses on knowledge and data management research and has established an international reputation in three related research areas, namely telecommunications & network management, e-learning and e-business services and health telematics.

Fatos Xhafa (fatos@lsi.upc.edu) received his PhD in computer science from the Polytechnic University of Catalonia (Barcelona, Spain) in 1998. He joined the Department of Languages and Informatics Systems of the Polytechnic University of Catalonia as an assistant professor in 1996 and is currently associate professor of this department. He is member of the ALBCOM Research Group of this department and also is external member of the Distributed, Parallel and Collaborative Research Group of the Open University of Catalonia. His research is supported by several research projects from Spain, European Union and NSF/USA. He has published in leading international journals and conferences. He serves in the editorial board of the *International Journal of Computer Supported Collaborative Learning* and has served as co-chair/PC member for many conferences and workshops.

Index

A

AccessForAll-LORIS 148, 150
adaptation layer 296, 309, 311
adaptation system (AS) 5–24
adaptive e-learning systems (AeLS) 155–165, 167, 169
adaptive hypermedia systems (AHS) 155–158, 245
adaptive personalized e-learning service (APeLS) x, 243, 247–248, 250–252, 257–258
AdeLE architecture 4–16
ad hoc networks 64–66, 71, 74–77
administrative services 213, 215
AHA! 3, 20, 157, 163–171
ambient intelligence 76–77
ARIADNE 244
ARISTOTLE architecture 73–77
asynchronous communication 201, 210–212
authentication layer 68
automatic course generation 272–274
automatic link generator (ALG) 264

B

Blackboard 66, 83, 253, 263, 266, 288, 289
BRICOLES project 289
business-process-oriented knowledge management (BPOKM) 308

C

career and technical education (CTE) 199. *See also* vocational education and training (VET)
Claroline 289–294
cognitive state 267, 270, 272, 277–278
collaboration services 209, 211
Collaborative Learning Purpose Library (CLPL) 221, 223–227, 235
collaborative workplace 40–41
collaborative workplace data model 40–41

common object request broker architecture (CORBA) 119, 294
communication object instance (COI) 7
comprehension-based linked model of deliberate search (CoLiDeS) 323
computation independent model (CIM) 119–124
computer-mediated communication 64–65
computer aided instruction (CAI) 3
computer supported collaborative learning (CSCL) x–xii, 30, 103–104, 106, 109, 111–112, 219–242
content-related services 213
content-tracking system (CTS) 5, 15
content object repository discovery and registration/resolution architecture (CORDRA) 284
content object repository discovery and registration/resolution architecture (CORDRA) project 141
context-awareness 306–319
Cooperative Open Workflow (COW) 294–295, 297–301
CopperCore 293–296, 299–300
course management systems (CMS) 252, 258
CSCL activity management
subsystem 227–232
CSCL awareness subsystem 233–234
CSCL feedback subsystem 234
CSCL functionality component 232–233
CSCL knowledge management component 227, 234, 235
CSCL knowledge processing subsystem 232

D

didactic goals 2, 5, 7, 9–10
didactic knowledge representation 267–270
Diogene 58
Diogene Student Model 270–272
Docs 'n Drugs 107–109

domain ontology 265
dynamic e-learning repository 6, 12–14, 16

E

e-learning framework (ELF) project 141–142, 145
e-pedagogy 25–43
educational modeling languages (EML) 119, 123
educational virtual environments (EVE) 88
ELM-ART 156, 246–247
eMEMORA 265
entity beans 294
European Learning Grid Initiative (ELeGI) 58
evaluation strategy 158–159
expert module 99, 103, 107–111
eye-tracking system (ETS) 4–5

F

Felder and Silverman pedagogical theory 270–272

G

Ganesha 288, 289, 293
Globus Toolkit 51–52
grid architecture vii–xii, 44–61

I

IMS-LD 284–287
IMS learning design 139, 143
information and communication technology (ICT)
        x–xii, 197–200, 206, 216, 220, 273–275
information system (IS) 18
INSPIRE 157–158
intelligent tutoring system (ITS) viii–xii, 98–115,
        244–245, 257
InterBook 157
interoperability 189–191
ISO production process model 179–180

J

JLI!—Just Learn It! 66–68
JointZone 158

K

Kaleidoscope 58
knowledge market 33–34
knowledge navigator (KN) 264
KnowledgeTree 247–248, 252–257, 258

L

layered-based evaluation 158–159
learner achievement evaluation 160–161
learner module 99, 103, 106–107, 109, 111
learner to learner interaction 40–41
learning content management system (LCMS) 28,
        46, 57, 321, 328
Learning in Process (LIP) project xii, 306, 308,
        312–317
learning management system (LMS) 28, 40, 46,
        51, 53, 56–57, 59, 65–67, 83, 148, 183, 186,
        189–191, 252–253, 258, 283–295, 300–301,
        321
learning object metadata (LOM) 284
learning objects (LOs) 46
learning objects repositories' integration system
        (LORIS) 138, 145–149
learning objects repositories and digital libraries
        integration system (LORDiLIS) 148, 150
learning resource infrastructure 34–38
learning support services 307, 311
Learning Technology Standards Committee (LTSC)
        257
learning technology system architecture (LTSA)
        176, 178–179
local communication services 70–71, 77
LORIS architecture 145–149
Lotus Virtual Classroom 66–67

M

m-learning 64–69, 72–77
macroadaptive e-learning approaches 308
matching service 316
message driven beans (MDB) 294
meta-object facility (MOF) 120
microadaptive e-learning approaches 308
MISA method 177–178
model-driven architecture (MDA) 116–136
model-driven engineering (MDE) 116–136
modeling system (MS) 17
Moodle 66, 117–118, 126–128, 288, 289, 293, 300

O

Object Management Group (OMG) 224–225
ODL 181–182, 186–187
ontologies 53, 55, 88, 101, 117, 121, 134, 144,
        148–149, 152–153, 220, 239, 262–282,
        268–270, 308, 310–312, 316–317

ontology creation 275–277
open grid services architecture (OGSA) 49–50
OWL—Web Ontology Language 149

P

pattern language viii–x, 98–100, 102–103, 107, 109–112
pedagogical framework 28–29
pedagogical scenarios 293–301
platform independent model (PIM) 117, 120–124, 224–225
platform specific model (PSM) 117, 120–124, 224–225, 291
podcasting vii–xii, 80–97
presentation-abstraction-control (PAC) pattern 106–109
primary courseware 324
process regulation module 103–104, 107, 110–111
proposed life-cycle view 180–182
proposed process-oriented view 180
publisher-subscriber design pattern 109

Q

QoE adaptation layer 155, 171
QoEAHA 163–171
quality of experience (QoE) ix–xii, 154–174
quality of experience-aware adaptive e-learning system (QoE-AeLS) 161–162

R

RAPSODY-EX 28, 31–42
resource description framework (RDF) 139, 142

S

secondary courseware 325
sensory system (SS) 17, 19
service-oriented architecture (SOA) 295–296
session beans 294

sharable content object reference model (SCORM) 2, 9–11, 15, 19, 22, 26, 41, 46, 57, 59, 102, 138, 139, 143, 144, 190, 252, 257, 258, 283, 288–289, 302, 316
simple object access protocol (SOAP) 46, 48–49, 127, 129, 141, 147, 189, 190, 295, 300, 301
SLeD 295–297
software engineering 4, 113, 116–136, 176
synchronous communication 200–201, 209–210

T

technology enhanced learning (TEL) systems 116–136
tertiary courseware 325, 328, 330

U

ubiquitous communication services 70–71, 77
unified modeling language (UML) 120–121, 124–125
usage tracking language (UTL) 129–130
user client system (UCS) 17
user context manager 314–316
user interface module 99, 103, 106–107, 109
user modeling system 6–9

V

virtual private network (VPN) 71
visual quality assessment 169
vocational education and training (VET) x–xii, 197–218
vodcasts 85

W

Web-based learning environments (WBLE) xii, 320–339
WebCT 253, 288, 289
Web services resource framework (WSRF) 50–52
WiFi Protected Access (WPA) 71